Resources for Teaching

FIFTH EDITION

POETRY

An Introduction

Michael Meyer
University of Connecticut, Storrs

Stefanie Wortman
University of Missouri, Columbia

Ellen Kuhl
University of Massachusetts, Boston

Jill McDonough
Boston University

John Repp
Edinboro University of Pennsylvania

Christine Francis
Central Connecticut State University

Kathleen Morgan Drowne
University of North Carolina, Chapel Hill

Quentin Miller
Gustavus Adolphus College

BEDFORD/ST. MARTIN'S   BOSTON ♦ NEW YORK

1   0   9   8   7   6
f   e   d   c   b   a

For information, write: Bedford/St. Martin's, 75 Arlington Street, Boston, MA 02116
(617-399-4000)

ISBN-10: 0-312-45062-1
ISBN-13: 978-0-312-45062-5

Instructors who have adopted *Poetry: An Introduction*, Fifth Edition, as a textbook for a course are authorized to duplicate portions of this manual for their students.

Preface

This instructor's manual is designed to be a resource of commentaries, interpretations, and suggestions for teaching the works included in *Poetry: An Introduction, Fifth Edition*. The entries offer advice about how to approach individual selections and suggest possible answers to questions raised in the text. No attempt has been made to generate definitive readings of the works; the text selections are rich enough to accommodate multiple approaches and interpretations. Our hope is that instructors will take what they find useful and leave the rest behind. Inevitably, instructors will disagree with some of the commentaries, but perhaps such disagreements will provide starting points for class discussion.

In addition to offering approaches to selections, many of the entries suggest topics for discussion and writing. The format of the entries varies from itemized responses to specific questions to essays that present overviews of individual works. This flexibility allows each entry to be more responsive to the nature of a particular work and the questions asked about it in the text. Any time "Connections to Other Selections" questions are posed in the text at least one is answered in the manual for each selection, and all the entries include suggestions for further connections. The manual includes selected bibliographies for authors treated in depth, and critical readings are mentioned throughout the manual when they are felt to be particularly useful resources for teaching a work.

The manual also provides instructors with additional resources for teaching the selections in Chapter 23, "An Album of World Literature," and Chapter 22, "An Album of Contemporary Poems." There is a preface to each of the albums that includes suggestions for teaching this potentially unfamiliar material, and most of the connections questions posed in the text for these selections, with the exception of questions that explicitly ask students to write an essay, are answered in the manual.

Introductions in this manual offer suggestions for approaching *Poetry: An Introduction*'s editorial discussions in class and a number of "Tips from the Field" — class-tested teaching suggestions from instructors who have taught from previous editions. If you have a teaching tip that you would like to submit for the next edition of this instructor's manual, please send it to the attention of Christina Gerogiannis, Associate Editor, Bedford/St. Martin's, 75 Arlington Street, Boston, MA 02116. Your teaching suggestion should be approximately fifty words long and suggest ways of teaching a particular author or selection that have been especially effective in your classroom experience. If we use your teaching suggestion, we will be happy to acknowledge you in the manual and pay you an honorarium.

To provide additional options for teaching *Poetry: An Introduction*, this manual suggests thematic groupings of the poems into the following categories: Home and Family, Love and Its Complications, The Natural World, Other Cultures, and Work and Business. For more thematic groupings, see the new Thematic Contents on page xlii in the main text.

Other resources include a list of Bedford/St. Martin's literary reprint titles available to adopters of the anthology; a table of contents for *LiterActive*, the new multimedia CD-ROM that accompanies *Poetry: An Introduction* (free with student copies of the book: package ISBN: 0–312–46110–0); a table of contents for Literature Aloud, the audio CD featuring recordings of works from the text, available to instructors who have adopted the anthology (ISBN: 0–312–46140–2); and an appendix of film, video, and audio resources for teaching the selections in the book.

Throughout this edition of the manual are icons that highlight selections available on

 LiterActive

 Literature Aloud

 the companion Web site to *Poetry: An Introduction*, Fifth Edition at **bedfordstmartins.com/meyerpoetry**

This manual is conveniently arranged to follow the organization of the text. Page references corresponding to the text are included at the top of each right page of the manual and after the title of each entry.

Contents

v

Introduction:
Reading Imaginative Literature

ENCOUNTERING POETRY:
IMAGES OF POETRY IN POPULAR CULTURE

Students often come into an introductory poetry course intimidated and frightened. Despite their familiarity with song lyrics, they're often convinced that lyric poetry is "beyond" them. Others bring with them the assumption that writing and reading poetry is an elite undertaking that has no application in their daily lives.

The "Encountering Poetry" section should help to dispel some of your students' preconceptions. As the images of poetry in popular culture that open the book demonstrate, poetry is all around us. We run across it on public transportation, in advertisements, on product packaging, online, even on our friends' refrigerators. You might be tempted to use the poems in this section as a way to get students comfortable with interpreting poetry, but it's best to resist the urge. Spend your first class, or your first couple of classes, simply getting your students to appreciate poetry as a source of pleasure that they'll find in unexpected places. You might even want to ask your students to bring in their own examples of poetry from their personal environments. By getting them to think of poetry as something fun and accessible, you'll have gone a long way toward teaching them how to dig deeper into its pleasures.

THE ELEMENTS OF POETRY

Brief biographical notes for several major poets are included in the first entry for each poet. In addition, available resources relating to specific poets and their work are included in the first entry for each poet under the heading "Audiovisual Resources." Resources for each of the four poets treated in depth in Chapters 12–15 appear after the final perspective entry for that poet.

1

Reading Poetry

Perhaps the most difficult part of any introductory literature course is convincing the students that they can, in fact, read poetry. Students are often intimidated by previous experiences, either in high school or other college courses; they have often accepted that they "just don't get it." Thus it is important to develop students' confidence in themselves as readers. One way to do this is to get students to articulate what they see actually happening in the poem, to read what is "on the page."

This chapter contains several poems that lend themselves to such an application. Robert Hayden's "Those Winter Sundays," John Updike's "Dog's Death," and Elizabeth Bishop's "The Fish," among others, are poems that have a clear scene or situation that grounds them: they mean what they say in a concrete way. Other meanings and issues can be raised, of course, but Bishop's poem, for instance, is first and foremost about catching a fish. Students will often "get" this level of the poem but distrust their reading, figuring that it isn't what the poem is "really about." A good reading, however, is grounded in such particulars. You might want to have students offer a one- or two-sentence summary of the action of such poems: "The speaker in Bishop's poem catches an old fish, looks into his eyes, and lets him go." Students can then be encouraged to build on these readings once their "fear of poetry" has been deflated somewhat.

Even such poems as Robert Morgan's "Mountain Graveyard" can become more accessible; what may seem to some as mere wordplay will be more powerful if students slow down and picture the scene evoked by the title.

In some cases, you may be confronted by students who already have all the answers. Such students can easily intimidate a class. A useful exercise can be done with Robert Frost's "The Road Not Taken" (Chapter 13, text p. 354). Many students have encountered this poem in high school; most have "learned" that it is a poem about making a brave choice that leads the speaker to a life of independence or a poem of regret at lost possibilities. As the text points out, however, close attention to the verb tenses in the final stanza reveals a more ambiguous reading. You may want to distribute a copy of this poem (without commentary) to the class, and ask, "How old is the speaker in the poem?" Focusing attention on the last two stanzas can prove instructive even to experienced readers and can emphasize the importance of careful attention and multiple readings.

There are two strategies you may find effective in working with students' resistance to poetry and helping them understand the poems they are faced with: reading aloud and short writings. On the surface, this sounds obvious, but having to understand a poem well enough to read it or hearing it spoken can make a difference in students' appreciation of poetry. Tips on encouraging reading aloud can be found in this manual in the introduction to Chapter 7.

Similarly, you might want to assign students short, informal writing to help them think through some of the issues you want to cover in class. These writings can be based on questions in the text, questions of your own, or even student-generated questions based on issues that seem to interest them in discussion. Preparing them before class discussion can help students frame ideas to share. You may want to grade these assignments only on a pass/fail basis to give students the chance to do experimental thinking in a low-stakes environment. Chapter 25 of the text has a number of questions and strategies you might find useful in these assignments.

Web Ask students to research the poets in this chapter at **bedfordstmartins.com/ meyerpoetry**.

MARGE PIERCY, *The Secretary Chant* (p. 22)

This poem provides an opportunity to discuss point of view in poetry. The secretary's view of herself mirrors the way she is treated. She has become a variety of objects, a list of useful items because she is looked at as an object by people outside her. Her attitude toward herself is framed by other people's perceptions of her, although we must assume that she is aware of her ability to write satire. We get an inkling of her "real" self in the last three lines; the misspelled "wonce" mocks misperceptions of her intellect, while "woman" indicates that there is much more to be learned about the speaker.

In most companies, the job title "secretary" has been replaced by "administrative assistant." Many of your students may not fully understand exactly what a secretary is; you may want to explain what would have been expected of an entry-level female office worker in 1973. In discussion, consider asking your students whether the new title reflects any real changes in the job as Piercy describes it.

In a writing assignment, you might ask students to discuss the metaphors in this poem. What assumptions about women and secretaries do the metaphors satirize? How do sound patterns such as "Zing. Tinkle" (line 14) affect the satire?

POSSIBLE CONNECTIONS TO OTHER SELECTIONS

E. E. Cummings, "she being Brand" (text p. 73)

Katharyn Howd Machan, "Hazel Tells LaVerne" (text p. 77)

AUDIOVISUAL RESOURCES (manual p. 379)

ROBERT HAYDEN, *Those Winter Sundays* (p. 23)

Useful comparisons can be made between any of the poems in this text that speak of love's transcendence or amplitude and any others, like this one and Theodore Roethke's "My Papa's Waltz" (text p. 233), that speak of its difficulty — the time it sometimes takes to recognize love. Hayden's speaker looks back at his father's unappreciated Sunday labor, at last knowing it for what it was and knowing, too, that the chance for gratitude has long since passed. The poem gives a strong sense, especially in its final two lines, that the speaker has tended to "love's austere and lonely offices" (line 14). The repetition of "What did I know?" seems to be a cry into the silence not only of the past but of the poet's present situation as well. The poem plays the music of the father's furnace work, the hard consonant sounds "splintering, breaking" (6) as the poem unfolds and disappearing entirely by the poem's end.

You might begin discussion by asking students to describe the speaker's father in as much detail as possible based on the speaker's spare description. From the poem's second word, *too,* the poem reaches beyond itself to suggest something about the man without naming it. What other details contribute to our impression of him? Following that discussion, you could also ask for a description of the speaker. What does his language reveal about his character? And how does this character contrast with his father's character?

POSSIBLE CONNECTIONS TO OTHER SELECTIONS

Margaret Atwood, "Bored" (text p. 86)

Andrew Hudgins, "Elegy for My Father, Who Is Not Dead" (text p. 256)

Theodore Roethke, "My Papa's Waltz" (text p. 233)

JOHN UPDIKE, *Dog's Death* (p. 24)

This narrative poem subtly traces a family's emotional response to the illness and death of their pet dog. Ask students to find the events that lead to the dog's death. How does the speaker relate these events? He tells us the dog's age when he talks about her toilet training and immediately establishes the family's relationship to her by repeating their words: "Good dog! Good dog!" (line 4). Alliteration and assonance soften the story; after they have identified these sound patterns, ask students why the repeated sounds are appropriate to the subject matter. Direct their attention to the enjambment in lines 12–13. Why does the sentence span two stanzas? Might the speaker be reluctant to tell us the dog died?

> Ask students to explore contexts for John Updike on *LiterActive.*

When he relates his wife's reaction to the death, the speaker describes her voice as "imperious with tears" (14). After they have established a definition of the word *imperious,* ask students to determine why it might be used here. The ambiguous "her" and "she" in the final two lines of the stanza make us puzzle out for a moment the pronouns' referent. Is the speaker talking about his wife or the dog? Are both implied? How does this distortion of identity work in a discussion of death?

The final stanza reads as a eulogy; the consonants become harder — "drawing" (18), "dissolution" (18), "diarrhoea" (19), "dragged" (19) — perhaps because the speaker is working at closing off the experience. In a writing assignment, you might ask students to discuss the three uses of "Good dog." How does the last one differ from the first two? How does the poem prepare us for the change?

POSSIBLE CONNECTIONS TO OTHER SELECTIONS

Jane Kenyon, "The Blue Bowl" (text p. 125)

Ronald Wallace, "Dogs" (text p. 235)

WILLIAM HATHAWAY, *Oh, Oh* (p. 26)

The reader's delight in the surprise ending of this poem hinges on the mood set up by the language of the first fifteen lines. Which words create this idyllic mood? What happens to the poem if you replace these words with others? For example, what words could replace "amble" (line 1)? How might one wave besides "gaily" (10)? How could the caboose pass other than with a "chuckle" (15)? How does the poem read with your revisions?

Does the poet give any clues as to what lies ahead? What about the "black window" in line 9, the exact center of the poem? A writing activity dealing with denotation and connotation could develop from a study of this poem. Have students consider a picture (one of an old house works well) and describe it first as though it might be used as a setting for *Nightmare on Elm Street*, then for an episode of *The Brady Bunch*. Discuss the word choices that set the different moods.

POSSIBLE CONNECTIONS TO OTHER SELECTIONS

Mark Doty, "The Embrace" (text p. 497)

Robert Frost, "Design" (text p. 372)

AUDIOVISUAL RESOURCES (manual p. 376)

ROBERT FRANCIS, *Catch* (p. 28)

This poem casts metaphor-making as a game of catch between two boys. If you are using the poem to examine metaphor, you might ask students what is missing from the central metaphor that Francis creates: that is, when two boys are playing catch, they are tossing a ball to each other. If we interpret the two players of this game as the poet and the reader, does the game of catch seem one-sided, as though one player is firing a number of balls at the other? Once you catch the ball in a game of catch, you throw it back. Does the relationship between reader and poet work the same way?

Encourage students to enjoy listening to this poem. Like a good pitcher, Francis finds various ways of throwing strikes. Consider, for example, line 3, with its "attitudes, latitudes, interludes, altitudes," or "prosy" and "posy" later in the poem.

POSSIBLE CONNECTIONS TO OTHER SELECTIONS

Emily Dickinson, "Portraits are to daily faces" (text p. 315)

Robert Francis, "The Pitcher" (text p. 208)

ELIZABETH BISHOP, *The Fish* (p. 32)

Born in Worcester, Massachusetts, Elizabeth Bishop knew displacement early: her father died when she was an infant, and her mother was committed to an asylum when she was five. Bishop lived with relatives during her childhood and adolescence in Nova Scotia and New England; after completing a degree at Vassar College, she lived in New York City, Key West, and, for sixteen years, Brazil. Travel and exile, as well as the insistent yet alien presence of the "things of the world," figure prominently in her work.

 Ask students to explore contexts for Elizabeth Bishop and this poem — as well as a sample close reading — on *LiterActive* and at **bedfordstmartins.com/ meyerpoetry**.

The most arresting feature of "The Fish" is its imagery. Consider, for example, the brown skin that "hung in strips / like ancient wall-paper" (lines 10–11), the ornamentation of "fine rosettes of lime" (17), or the pause to mention and comment again on "the frightening gills" (24). Not only does Bishop have an eye for the particular, even the minute, but in this poem she exhibits an ability to dissect imaginatively flesh, bones, bladder, and the interior of the fish's eyes.

Play a recording of Randall Jarrell reading "The Fish" on *Literature Aloud*.

After you review the appearance of the fish, it might be a good idea to glance back at the poem's syntax. Note, for example, the syntactic simplicity and parallelism of lines 5–7, conveying with their flat factuality the fish's implacable "thereness." The syntax becomes a little more complex later on, as Bishop's vision penetrates into the interior of the fish's anatomy and, eventually, into its being. The fish is no longer a mere member of its species but a kind of military hero and a survivor that has escaped at least five attempts on its life.

Bishop's skill transforms the fish into a thing of beauty and an object of admiration, almost without our realizing it. At this point in the discussion, though, it would be a good idea to step back and see what she is looking at. The scene is simply an old fish, brown and battle-scarred, with sullen jaw, staring back at the speaker (Bishop, we assume). Not an ideal setting for the epiphanic moment.

But that is, of course, what occurs — signaled to us by the repetition of the word *rainbow*. In a sense, both fish and poet have transcended themselves — the one by surviving, the other by seeing beyond the ugliness. Victory, indeed, fills up the boat.

POSSIBLE CONNECTIONS TO OTHER SELECTIONS

Lisa Parker, "Snapping Beans" (text p. 51)
David Solway, "Windsurfing" (text p. 112)

AUDIOVISUAL RESOURCES (manual p. 387)

PHILIP LARKIN, *A Study of Reading Habits* (p. 34)

This poem about a speaker's developing disillusionment with reading is a clever satire of the speaker's attitude. Note the poem's intricate rhyme pattern. The poet's use of a complex poetic form while having the poem's speaker use slang and trite phrases provides an excellent opportunity to make students aware of the difference between the poet and the speaker of a poem. Does the slang used in Larkin's poem help to identify the speaker with a particular time period? With what current words would your students replace such words as "cool" (line 4), "lark" (8), "dude" (13)? Is any of the slang used in this poem still current?

After your students have read Larkin's poem, you might ask them to discuss their previous (and present) reading habits or have them write a short essay on this subject. What do they expect to gain from reading? Escape? Pleasure? Knowledge?

POSSIBLE CONNECTIONS TO OTHER SELECTIONS

Anne Bradstreet, "The Author to Her Book" (text p. 137)
Billy Collins, "Introduction to Poetry" (text p. 42)

ROBERT MORGAN, *Mountain Graveyard* (p. 36)

Ask students if they agree with the assertion that "Mountain Graveyard" is "unmistakably poetry." If they think it is poetry, is it a good poem? Meyer's strong argument in the text may be intimidating, but students should be encouraged to develop their own sense of what poetry is as they work through these chapters. Further, this poem and the next afford opportunities (because of their highly unorthodox forms) to lead students into a discussion of the authority of the printed word: Is a piece of literature good because "the book says so"? Is a story "art" because it is anthologized? It might be useful to return to these questions when your class finishes its consideration of poetry.

As a writing activity, have students choose another setting (college campus, supermarket, playground) and develop a set of anagrams for the new locale. Do different arrangements of the anagrams change the overall meaning of the set? Are any of the arrangements poetry?

POSSIBLE CONNECTIONS TO OTHER SELECTIONS

Helen Chasin, "The Word *Plum*" (text p. 209)
E. E. Cummings "l(a" (text p. 37; following)

E. E. CUMMINGS, *l(a* (p. 37)

E. E. Cummings was born in Cambridge, Massachusetts, the son of a Congregationalist minister. He earned a degree from Harvard University and began writing his iconoclastic poems after coming upon the work of Ezra Pound. His experimentation with syntax and punctuation reflects a seriously playful attitude toward language and meaning and a skepticism about institutional authority.

> Ask students to explore contexts for E. E. Cummings on *LiterActive*.

At first glance, "l(a" seems to be a poem spewed out by a closemouthed computer held in solitary confinement. As with Morgan's "Mountain Graveyard," however, the poem comes into its own as the reader not only deciphers but brings meaning to the text. Implied here is a simile between a falling leaf and loneliness. The use of a natural image to suggest an emotion recalls Japanese haiku (see Chapter 9 of this manual).

The vertical quality of the poem illustrates the motion of a single leaf falling. Students might also point out the repetition of the digit *one* (indistinguishable in some texts from the letter *l*), along with other "aloneness" words, such as *a* and *one*. If ever a poem's medium enhanced its message, this one surely does.

POSSIBLE CONNECTION TO ANOTHER SELECTION

Robert Morgan, "Mountain Graveyard" (text p. 36; preceding)

AUDIOVISUAL RESOURCES (manual p. 374)

ANONYMOUS, *Western Wind* (p. 38)

Students should be aware that, in England, the coming of the west wind signifies the arrival of spring. How is the longing for spring in this lyric connected to the overall sense of longing or to sexual longing? These brief four lines contain examples of several poetic devices worth noting. Ask students to consider the effects of the apostrophe and the alliteration in the first line. Many modern poets would consider these techniques artificial and overdone, but this poet seems to be interested in making a strong statement in just a few words. Does it work? Also, consider the use of the expletive "Christ" (line 3). This word makes the reader feel the intensity of emotion being conveyed and turns the poem into a kind of prayer — it is both sacred and profane.

For purposes of comparison, consider this poem in conjunction with another lyric that uses the same apostrophe, Percy Bysshe Shelley's "Ode to the West Wind" (text p. 257). Students should note that "Western Wind" is much more personal and less formal in diction than Shelley's poem.

POSSIBLE CONNECTIONS TO OTHER SELECTIONS

Robert Herrick, "Delight in Disorder" (text p. 226)
Percy Bysshe Shelley, "Ode to the West Wind" (text p. 257)

REGINA BARRECA, *Nighttime Fires* (p. 39)

This narrative poem has a recurrent theme, indicated by the repetitions of the word *smoke*. Smoke is the end of the father's quest, but what, exactly, is he looking for? His daughter, the speaker, provides a clue when she tells us that her father lost his job, so he had time to pursue fires. Smoke is the father's assurance that there is justice in the world because fires destroy rich and poor people alike. Ask students to look at the images the speaker uses to describe her father: What kind of man is he? How

> Play a recording of Regina Barreca reading "Nighttime Fires" on *Literature Aloud*.

would they characterize the daughter's relationship to him? Does the mother also think of these drives as "festival, carnival" (line 15)? In some respect, the carnival is the father's performance before his family, in which the "wolf whine of the siren" (9) is matched by his "mad" (8) expression.

In a writing assignment, you might ask students to examine the metaphors describing the father. What do these figures tell us about his life? For example, in the final image of the father, his eyes are compared to "hallways filled with smoke" (31). Why is he likened to a house? What might this image tell us about his life?

POSSIBLE CONNECTION TO ANOTHER SELECTION

Robert Hayden, "Those Winter Sundays" (text p. 23)

BILLY COLLINS, *Introduction to Poetry* (p. 42)

Using a series of colorful metaphors, the speaker of this poem — a poetry instructor — describes his (or her) frustration with student expectations in an introductory poetry class. Depending on the reader's point of view, the speaker's attitude might be amusing or insulting. As a teacher you probably find yourself nodding with recognition of the instructor's foiled attempts to get students to appreciate poetry for what it is, but your students might see things differently.

"Introduction to Poetry" offers you an excellent opportunity to gauge your own students' expectations of your role in the course. Ask them if they think the speaker is being fair. Do they believe the instructor uses the poem's metaphors literally in classroom assignments, or are they simply meant to describe the instructor's wishes? Do the metaphors make sense to your students?

Ask your students, also, whether they see a little bit of themselves or their peers in the poem's students. As new readers of poetry, it's likely that they do, indeed, want to know what a poem "means." Do they see humor in the speaker's confession metaphor, or do they cling to the notion that they must discover what Meyer calls the "definitive reading" of a poem?

For a writing exercise, consider having your students respond to the speaker. How would they characterize the instructor's expectations?

POSSIBLE CONNECTIONS TO OTHER SELECTIONS

Mark Halliday, "Graded Paper" (text p. 507)
Richard Wakefield, "In a Poetry Workshop" (text p. 509)

HELEN FARRIES, *Magic of Love* (p. 44)

Note the ways in which this poem fulfills the greeting-card formula, especially with its "lilting" anapests, internal rhymes, and tried-and-true (and terribly trite) metaphors, all designed to lift the reader's spirits.

You might begin discussion by asking why this poem has withstood the test of time (as greeting-card verse). The pleasure of this specific poem comes not as much from its theme, which is nothing particularly new, as from its elements of sound, especially its internal, and full, end-stopped rhyme. Because poetry evolved, at least partly, from an oral tradition — using rhymes as mnemonic devices — you may even use this poem as a vehicle for discussing the very basic history of poetry. You may ask, for example, *why* strict rhyme and meter serve as such an effective mnemonic device. Does this poem use its devices pleasurably?

JOHN FREDERICK NIMS, *Love Poem* (p. 44)

Greeting cards must speak to the anonymous masses. Nims's poem, while maintaining a simplicity of diction and a directness of sentiment, is far stronger than the greeting-card verse, in part because it is addressing a specific person.

The poem is obviously not a piece to be carved on the pedestal of some faceless ideal; students will probably have at least some curiosity about a poem that begins "My clumsiest dear." After they have become accustomed to this violating of poetic convention, ask them to review the poem for other refreshing and surprising uses of language. They might mention, for example, the use of "shipwreck" as a verb in line 1, the play on "bull in a china shop" (line 3), or the projective quality of "undulant" in line 8 to describe the floor as it appears to the drunk. Again, unlike conventional verse, this poem concludes with an almost paradoxical twist to the most salient feature of this woman who breaks things: Her absence would cause "all the toys of the world [to] break."

In a writing assignment, you might ask students to compare this poem with Shakespeare's sonnet "My mistress' eyes . . ." (text p. 243).

BRUCE SPRINGSTEEN, *You're Missing* (p. 46)

Many of your students may be familiar with this song from Springsteen's double-platinum album, *The Rising,* which won the 2002 Grammy for Best Rock Album. Most of the album's songs — including this one — commemorate the September 11th attack on the World Trade Center and have been praised by reviewers for avoiding sentimentality and blind anger. Ask your students whether knowing that this song is about a World Trade Center victim influences their reading of the lyrics.

Listening to a recording of the song will undoubtedly provide students with a richer understanding of the tone. (If you can't obtain a copy of the CD to play in class, note that a portion of the song can be heard for free at **brucespringsteen.net**.) It may be helpful to ask students whether their interpretations of the lyrics change when the music is added. You might ask your students to consider how the words and notes interact in this particular song and whether one seems stronger or weaker than the other. To further class discussion comparing the recording of "You're Missing" to the printed version, read the work aloud to your students, being careful to pause only for line breaks. Then ask students to consider whether the music contributes more to their understanding of the song.

AUDIOVISUAL RESOURCES (manual p. 359)

S. PEARL SHARP, *It's the Law: A Rap Poem* (p. 47)

In a meter and vernacular that will likely be familiar to your students, this poem provides an analysis of what our nation's laws reveal about our collective behavior. This analysis is followed by disgust for the behavior that made the laws necessary. The poem ends with an optimistic response, rendering the laws impotent by presenting "rules." These rules focus on producing positive, creative behavior rather than forbidding negative, destructive behavior.

Sharp states more than once her analysis of what our laws reveal about our cultural behavior: "The rules we break are the laws we make / the things that we fear, we legislate" (lines 3–4); "The laws that we make are what we do to each other / There is no law to make brother love brother" (18–19). This absence of a law enforcing love is the impetus for Sharp's creation of the more positive "rules": the distinction between "rules" and "laws" provides an alternative to the despair of legislation. This is an insistent poem, attacking its point from several angles. The solution Sharp provides for the distressing lessons our laws teach us about ourselves is present in the importance of the rules she presents, beginning with her directive in line 25, "Listen up!" The rules emphasizing education, kindness, and sobriety underscore the need for personal responsibility and self-respect.

You might want to compare other features of rap with more traditional poetic conventions: end rhyme, allusion, alliteration, meter, and clever turns of phrase. Ask students to describe these conventions and to give examples of them from this poem. If you have worked with other twentieth-century poetry, contrast the types of conventions apparent in rap and in other modern poems.

POSSIBLE CONNECTION TO ANOTHER SELECTION

Gwendolyn Brooks, "We Real Cool" (text p. 98)

PERSPECTIVE

ROBERT FRANCIS, *On "Hard" Poetry* (p. 48)

Discussing hard poetry through its opposite, soft poetry, may be the best way into a discussion of this piece. Hard poetry does not use excess words, does not lapse into sentimentality, does not have an undefined or loose form. The hard poem sustains tension between poet and speaker, reader and text. You may want to put Francis's ideas to the test by asking students to find specific lines from "You're Missing" that support an argument about whether the lyrics can be characterized as "hard" poetry. Are the speaker's tone and the images used in the song sentimental — or "soft"? Students should be able to point to a number of lines that allow for multiple interpretations — that challenge the reader and create some "resistance." For example, you might ask them to discuss Springsteen's repeated use of the phrase "Everything Is Everything" in lines 3, 4, 8, 9, 22, and 23. What does the word *everything* signify in each of these lines? Does its meaning remain constant or does it change by the end of the song? You might also ask students whether they feel the lyrics are tightly organized. How effective is Springsteen's use of rhyme and repetition?

POSSIBLE CONNECTIONS TO OTHER SELECTIONS

Helen Farries, "Magic of Love" (text p. 44)
Langston Hughes, "Cross" (text p. 403)
Bruce Springsteen, "You're Missing" (text p. 46)

RUDYARD KIPLING, *If—* (p. 49)

This poem offers advice from an older man to a younger man; if we take the speaker's use of "son" literally, they are father and son. The meter and rhyme are easy to identify; the advice provided makes for familiar content. The reminder that such advice is dated, by the presence of the final line and its address to a male reader, may provide for more interesting class discussion than the poem itself. Points for discussion could include an examination of the world presented through the advice offered here: Do students think this is a realistic or pessimistic world vision? To keep discussion focused, write a list on the board of some of the disasters presented in the poem: examples include getting blamed for something that's not your fault (line 2), being doubted (3), and being lied about (6). The poem refers to being a man; do your students think this refers to masculinity or universality?

In your efforts to encourage student readings, you may want to try a close examination of the last stanza with your class. What do your students make of the "unforgiving minute" (29) and the "sixty seconds' worth of distance run" (30)? A simple rewording might be that one should try to do one's best even when circumstances are against you and time is tight. What are some circumstances in which this analogy might seem fit? What are some unforgiving minutes your students are familiar with? Test taking? Paying the rent? Cramming lunch in between classes? Juggling school and job?

POSSIBLE CONNECTIONS TO OTHER SELECTIONS

Robert Herrick, "To the Virgins, to Make Much of Time" (text p. 79)

Marge Piercy, "The Secretary Chant" (text p. 22; question 1, following)

Dylan Thomas, "The Hand That Signed the Paper" (text p. 140)

CONNECTION QUESTION IN TEXT (p. 50) WITH ANSWER

1. Discuss Kipling's treatment of what a man is in contrast to Marge Piercy's description of what a woman is in "The Secretary Chant" (p. 22). What significant differences do you find in their definitions?

   Kipling's poem depends on a tradition of advice given to the young and the triumph of will in the face of adversity. Piercy's poem, on the other hand, provides an ironic metaphor for womanhood. Whereas Kipling's poem describes the *behavior* of an adult, Piercy's poem describes the *inner* being and the dehumanizing effects of adult working life. Kipling assumes a reader's awareness of the difficulties of dealing in the world: the poorly placed trust and bad decisions, the disappointments in other people, the trying times. With these examples, he emphasizes the need to accept that disappointment and misfortune are a part of adulthood. Piercy assumes that the reader is familiar with the idea of a person being defined by her job and the notion that secretarial work is dominated by the use of machines and is therefore relatively trivial. Whereas Kipling's poem is optimistic, Piercy's is pessimistic. The secretary's defeated resignation to her fate, her lament that she "wonce / was / a woman" (lines 22–24), lies in stark contrast to Kipling's speaker's joyous proclamation that overcoming life's inevitable obstacles will make his hearer "a Man" (line 32).

MARY OLIVER, *Mindful* (p. 50)

As a "good scholar" (line 26) of the world, Oliver rejoices in observations of the ordinary. You might have your students look closely at how she contrasts the grand with the mundane in the sixth stanza, seeming to suggest that the two are completely separate. Does Oliver maintain this distinction in the poem? Do her descriptions of the natural world — of grass and the ocean — suggest that they are in fact "very extravagant" (22)?

While the speaker clearly delights in her work of looking and listening, she does not present it as unambiguously pleasant. The line breaks in the second and third stanzas turn colloquialisms into potential dangers. By separating "kills me" (5) from "with delight" (6) and "like a needle" (8) from "in the haystack" (9), Oliver suggests an element of fear in the state of mindfulness. The sixth stanza underscores this feeling, aligning "the fearful, the dreadful" (21) with "the exceptional" (20). In what ways might the speaker's attention to the world put her at risk?

POSSIBLE CONNECTIONS TO OTHER SELECTIONS

John Keats, "Ode on a Grecian Urn" (text p. 96)

Galway Kinnell, "Blackberry Eating" (text p. 189)

CONNECTION QUESTION IN TEXT (p. 51) WITH ANSWER

1. Explain why you think this poem and John Frederick Nims's "Love Poem" (p. 44) are sentimental or not.

    Although both poems reveal deeply held *sentiments*, they cannot accurately be described as *sentimental*. Meyer defines *sentimentality* as a device that "exploits the reader by inducing responses that exceed what the situation warrants" and describes it as "momentarily sweet but wholly insubstantial" (text p. 45). Neither applies to Nims's and Oliver's poems. Although Nims's poem deals with a subject — love — that is very prone to sentimental treatment, he takes a surprising and fresh look at what makes a person lovable in the eyes of another. Nims's speaker revels in his lover's clumsiness, lack of cunning, unpredictability, awkwardness, and forget-fulness; Oliver's poem celebrates the glories of life, but she focuses on quotidian events and scenes rather than "the exceptional" (line 20). Her ambiguous choice of words — moving between the celebratory and the menacing — also undercuts any possibly sentimental moments. The complex emotion of "Mindful" is at odds with the pure emotions of sentimental literature. Though both Nims and Oliver display some of the exuberance that can appear in a sentimental poem, their original takes on the subjects they choose avoid sentimentality.

LISA PARKER, *Snapping Beans* (p. 51)

This poem, in the voice of a college student returning home to Grandma's, con-trasts the familiarity of family with new knowledge of the outside world. "Snapping Beans" is a kind of shorthand for the tenuous middle ground the speaker and grand-mother share, with Grandma's home still comforting and beautiful to the speaker. Students will probably be able to relax with Parker's straightforward narrative, simple vocabulary, accessible imagery, and earnest tone. The sudden violent dispatch of the leaf from the tree and Grandma's observation of it provide a parallel to the speaker's sepa-ration from the grandmother's world.

Students are likely to be familiar with the distance between loved ones and the shifts that occur when we grow up and move away from our families. Consider asking them to spend ten or fifteen minutes engaged in a journal-writing exercise that examines how their own relationships with family members have changed since they left for college. Asking them to read aloud selections from their writing could establish a sense of com-munity in the classroom.

POSSIBLE CONNECTIONS TO OTHER SELECTIONS

Margaret Atwood, "Bored" (text p. 86)

Robert Frost, "Birches" (text p. 365)

Gary Soto, "Behind Grandma's House" (text p. 181; question 1, following page)

1. Discuss the treatment of the grandmother in this poem and in "Behind Grandma's House" by Gary Soto (p. 181).

    The tough wisdom of Soto's grandmother stands in possible contrast to the uncertain level of self-awareness of Parker's: Soto's grandmother is certainly aware of the connection between her words and her action. Parker's grandmother may or may not be aware of the comparison her observation of the "hickory leaf, still summer green" (41) provides, illuminating the speaker's predicament.

ALBERTO RÍOS, *Seniors* (p. 53)

You might begin your discussion of this poem by asking students to talk about its use of slang, particularly in the first stanza. The slang establishes the speaker's environment as well as his conversational tone. As the poem progresses, it focuses on the speaker, and the tone becomes more meditative. Although they modify his relationship to other people, the images of cavities, flat walls, and water (particularly in stanza 3) distance the speaker from the social realm, until he is left "on the desert" in the last stanza.

Students might write an essay on these images. How does their evocation of sexual experience prepare us for the poem's last line? What is the speaker trying to say about sex? About life? How does the language of the final stanza compare with that of the first stanza? What might this changed diction indicate in the speaker's attitude toward himself and the world?

POSSIBLE CONNECTIONS TO OTHER SELECTIONS

T. S. Eliot, "The Love Song of J. Alfred Prufrock" (text p. 456; question 2, following)
Sharon Olds, "Sex without Love" (text p. 93; question 1, following)

CONNECTIONS QUESTIONS IN TEXT (p. 54) WITH ANSWERS

1. Compare the treatment of sex in this poem with that in Sharon Olds's "Sex without Love" (p. 93).

    Olds talks about sex as a sport, noting how lovers who have sex without love treat their bodies as separate from "truth." The images Olds uses to make her point are unlike Ríos's imagery. Ríos talks about bodies as continually fading away. His speaker calls the body of the woman he first kissed almost "nonexistent" (line 18), comparing all sexual experiences to a "flagstone wall" (22), vacationing in Bermuda, swimming ("all water," 27). For Ríos's speaker, sex provides a vehicle for capturing the past; for Olds's speaker, sex is the subject for a lesson about love.

2. Think about "Seniors" as a kind of love poem and compare the speaker's voice with the one in T. S. Eliot's "The Love Song of J. Alfred Prufrock" (p. 456). How are these two voices used to evoke different cultures? Of what value is love in these cultures?

    J. Alfred Prufrock's voice bespeaks an empty culture, characterized by "sawdust restaurants" and "yellow smoke" as well as by empty conversations and rituals. "Prufrock" is a love poem that never comes to be because the speaker is too fearful to act: "Do I dare / Disturb the universe?" Ríos's speaker also describes a lost culture, particularly in his use of slang and his references to materialism in the first two stanzas. In fact, many of the images in "Seniors" are complemented by similar, though starker, images in "Prufrock." In each poem, love symbolizes the speaker's individual feelings of loss and the collective emptiness of the culture.

AUDIOVISUAL RESOURCES (manual p. 380)

PHILLIS LEVIN, *End of April* (p. 54)

In Levin's poem, the found object, a broken robin's egg, becomes a figure for the speaker's relationship. You might begin by having students discuss how "thinking of you" (line 4) conditions the speaker's description of the egg. Does the speaker's view of the "you" cause her to dwell on the egg as insubstantial and hollow? If the egg stands in for the damaged relationship, what do students make of "broken, but not shattered" in the third line? Does it suggest hope of a repair, or does it refer to the speaker?

At the end of the poem, Levin goes beyond the physical scene to imagine the creature that once lived in the shell. Though she mentions its wings (23), Levin does not directly identify "What had been there" (19) as a bird. This omission retains some of the wildness of the newly hatched robin and leaves some mystery to occasional stirring that tears the speaker's heart. Levin underscores this action with the only full end rhyme of the poem: "heart" (21) and "apart" (24).

POSSIBLE CONNECTIONS TO OTHER SELECTIONS

John Donne, "A Valediction Forbidding Mourning" (text p. 150)

Robert Hass, "A Story about the Body" (text p. 278; question 1, following)

CONNECTION QUESTION IN TEXT (p. 55) WITH ANSWER

1. Explain how the descriptive details in "End of April" and in Robert Hass's "A Story about the Body" (p. 278) reveal the emotions of each speaker.

    Both Levin and Hass use images of breakage and death in the natural world to stand in for emotional injuries. After finding a broken egg, Levin internalizes the escape of the robin from its shell and imagines the bird breaking painfully out of her own body. In Hass's poem it is not the speaker but another artist who uses bees to convey her grief at being desexualized in the eyes of the speaker. Both poets choose flying creatures as figures, but use them to very different ends. In "End of April," the bird is not only alive but also absent, having flown away from its confinement. The emotional core of Levin's poem is the feeling of being left behind by a lover. The artist in Hass's poem, on the other hand, is primarily hurt by a sense of having lived past her youth. The bowl of dead bees suggests that she has left her sexual appeal behind with the speaker.

ALFRED, LORD TENNYSON, *Crossing the Bar* (p. 55)

Tennyson wrote "Crossing the Bar" near the end of his life, and though he went on to write other poems, he requested that this be the last poem published in any collection of his work. The speaker expresses a calm acceptance of death but is aware of its contradictions. Tennyson's use of nautical imagery conveys some of this ambiguity, the voyage standing both for entering a frightening unknown and embarking on an exciting journey. The speaker's trip takes him both away from and toward home. Ask students what it means to identify God as a "Pilot" (15) if the speaker has been separated from him up to this point?

The figure of the sandbar in this poem functions as a boundary line. Separating the safe waters near land and the rougher sea beyond, the bar also separates life from death or from the afterlife. It interrupts the continuous flow of the tide as the "clear call" (2) and the "evening bell" (9) interrupt the passage of time. The horizontal is bisected by a vertical axis. You might discuss with students the religious significance of these images. The Christian idea of resurrection depends on a vertical movement out of "Time and

Place" (13). Call students' attention to the fact that these two words, in addition to *Pilot*, are capitalized in the last stanza.

POSSIBLE CONNECTIONS TO OTHER SELECTIONS

John Donne, "A Valediction Forbidding Mourning" (text p. 150)

Randall Jarrell, "The Death of the Ball Turret Gunner" (text p. 71)

Dylan Thomas, "Do Not Go Gentle into That Good Night" (text p. 247; question 1, following)

CONNECTION QUESTION IN TEXT (p. 56) WITH ANSWER

1. Compare the speaker's mood in "Crossing the Bar" with that in Dylan Thomas's "Do Not Go Gentle into that Good Night" (p. 247).

   Both Tennyson and Thomas confront death bravely, but their views of what death will bring are very different. Tennyson approaches death as if it were a wise and trustworthy captain. Not only does he not fear his fate, but he also looks forward to a peaceful journey. Thomas, on the other hand, wants to defy death. Rather than accepting fate gracefully like Tennyson does, Thomas urges his dying father to fight as long and as hard as he can. Thomas's tone is angry and rebellious. While Tennyson takes a filial stance toward death, acting dutifully and respectfully, Thomas's loyalty is to his human father. He challenges the traditional view of the supernatural father figure in subverting the natural order of birth and death.

LI HO, *A Beautiful Girl Combs Her Hair* (p. 56)

Like his predecessor Li Po, Li Ho did not serve as a civil servant, an unusual choice for poets of the T'ang Dynasty in China. He wrote poems while riding on a donkey and revised them at the end of each day.

Juxtaposition, one of the most important techniques in Chinese poetry, is amply evident in this poem, as is one of Li Ho's characteristic touches: supernatural mystery appearing alongside unvarnished description ("singing jade"; "her mirror / two phoenixes / a pool of autumn light"). The poet deftly brings the senses into play; the girl's "spilling hair" has a precise fragrance; it is not simply black but the "color of raven feathers / shining blue-black stuff"; and it defeats her "jade comb," which in the middle of the poem falls without sound.

You might ask students to think about where the speaker is in relation to this scene and what significance his location might have for his exasperation. Reading the poem without the speaker's outburst in lines 23–26 might lead to a productive discussion of the effects of metaphor and connotation. What sort of girl is this "wild goose" with blackest hair so carefully attended? How much does the speaker know of her? How much does he wish to know?

POSSIBLE CONNECTIONS TO OTHER SELECTIONS

Sylvia Plath, "Mirror" (text p. 145)

David Solway, "Windsurfing" (text p. 112)

Cathy Song, "The White Porch" (text p. 129; question 1, following)

CONNECTION QUESTION IN TEXT (p. 57) WITH ANSWER

1. Compare the description of hair in this poem with that in Cathy Song's "The White Porch" (p. 129). What significant similarities do you find?

Song's "The White Porch" has a tone similar to that of this poem, with alluring, almost seductive images of a woman's hair. Both women's hair is thick and unmanageable. Each woman gathers vegetation from the garden, again pointing to her ripe sexuality. In both poems hair serves as a way of knowing the women, a means of access to their restlessness and self-consciousness. You might ask students to comment on differences in the poems resulting from the difference in speakers. Li Ho's speaker watches the woman dress her hair and is upset by her "slovenly beauty" (line 24). The speaker in Song's poem is the possessor of the hair and of the erotic power it symbolizes and releases.

LUISA LOPEZ, *Junior Year Abroad* (p. 57)

In this deceptively casual narrative poem, Lopez explores the confused thoughts of a young woman. The narrator, a junior in college, ponders what happened when an old boyfriend visited her for Christmas, not knowing that she had fallen for a new beau. The details of the poem betray her conflicted understanding of her relationships with her "old lover" (line 27), her "new boy" (22), and herself. Most important, she considers herself alone.

This poem offers an excellent opportunity to help students understand the importance of details in narrative poetry. They're likely to empathize with the woman's dilemma: by college, most people have experienced the excitement, guilt, and confusion of casting off an old love for a new one. Have them paraphrase the poem, and ask what is lost when it is reduced to the story line. It may also be useful to explore each of the poem's metaphors and similes in class: What secrets do the phrases and words "shelf life" (line 4), "muslin" (6), "cocoon" (9), "circus pony" (16), "snake" (18), "two old friends" (31), "traffic" (36), and "currency" (36) reveal about the speaker's perceptions of the visit and of her "betrayal" (18)? Who exactly is she betraying?

"Junior Year Abroad" is also tantalizing in its ambiguity. The final stanzas are unclear: Did the speaker's old boyfriend rape her, or did she guiltily consent to "one last time"? As a writing assignment, pose this question to students and ask them to examine the poem's details to determine what happened.

POSSIBLE CONNECTIONS TO OTHER SELECTIONS

A. E. Housman, "When I was one-and-twenty" (text p. 223)
Edna St. Vincent Millay, "I, Being Born a Woman and Distressed" (text p. 614)
Sharon Olds, "Sex without Love" (text p. 93)

THOMAS LUX, *The Voice You Hear When You Read Silently* (p. 58)

Repetitions are key to reading Lux's poem. As he questions how speaking is related to voice and to memory, each new instance of the word takes on a new inflection, demonstrating how the context of speech continually changes its meaning. The speaker's experiences fill the word with connotations, which may be inaccessible to the person hearing or reading them. Lux's description of the minute details in the barn shows how a single word can bring up a wealth of associations for each individual.

Once students have thought about how Lux suggests language works, have them discuss the implications of this belief on his work as a poet. Does the poem have to work around the fact that words mean different things to different people?

The last sentence of Lux's poem begins in the same way as the title, enacting on a larger scale the single word repetitions throughout the poem. What is the effect of having the first line of the poem continue the syntax of the title? When we come to the last line, have we come full circle or has Lux achieved a new understanding of voice?

POSSIBLE CONNECTIONS TO OTHER SELECTIONS

Barbara Hamby, "Ode to American English" (text p. 87)
Thomas Lux, "Onomatopoeia" (text p. 196)
Henry Reed, "Naming of Parts" (text p. 176)

2

Writing about Poetry

Comments often overheard in introductory literature classes suggest that many students believe that they are simply incapable of understanding poetry. Thus their attempts to find meaning in poems are often hindered by their feelings of intimidation and ineptness. The Questions for Responsive Reading and Writing in Chapter 2 may prove to be particularly useful to these insecure students because they break down general poetry analysis into smaller components, which students may feel better able to manage. These questions, however, can also aid more confident and capable students in their analysis and interpretation of poetry by offering specific places for them to begin their literary investigations.

You might also use these questions in class to teach your students how to approach writing about poetry. Have your students work individually or in small groups, exploring possible answers to these questions using assigned poems. Brief written responses to these questions might lead to longer, more detailed interpretations at a later time. Of course, not every question will relate meaningfully to every poem. To help students learn to apply a certain type of question in their analysis, you might devise an exercise in which your students decide which questions are best suited to which particular poems in a set. You might also remind them that these questions about poetry are open-ended and often require more than a one-word or one-sentence response. Ask your students to provide evidence for their answers by quoting directly from the poems they have chosen to analyze. Also, it is important for students to feel comfortable using the terminology that describes particular elements of poetry; be sure to refer them to the Glossary of Literary Terms included in the anthology (text p. 741) if they are having trouble understanding any of these terms.

Chapter 2 includes a brief sample student paper analyzing Elizabeth Bishop's poem "Manners" (text p. 62). Ask your students to read the poem and then discuss how they might approach the assignment that was given to this student writer. What specific aspects of the poem might they choose to explore? What would they do differently from the writer of the sample? You may consider assigning your class a writing task similar to the one described in this chapter, using any poem your students have studied. The sample paper, while not necessarily a blueprint for effective poetry analysis, may offer your students a useful model of strong student writing that they may try to emulate. At the same time, you might ask your students to treat the sample student paper as an unfinished draft of an essay and have them suggest revisions that would make the paper even more effective.

Ask students to explore contexts for Elizabeth Bishop on *LiterActive*.

3

Word Choice, Word Order, and Tone

Because poetry depends for its effects on the concentrated use of language, word choice can play a pivotal role in determining the meaning of a poem. For instance, in Martín Espada's "Latin Night at the Pawnshop," the choice of the word *appari-tion* as the first noun in the poem echoes Ezra Pound's "In a Station of the Metro." One word sets up an allusion to a key imagist poem and thus puts Espada's poem in the context of that tradition. Still, students may remain unconvinced that word choice is all that important to a poem.

 Ask students to explore the poetic elements in this chapter on *LiterActive* or at **bedfordstmartins.com/ meyerpoetry**.

As an exercise to emphasize the importance of word choice, you might have students type a short poem or section of a poem on a word processor. Most word processors now come with a thesaurus function that allows the user to replace a word with a synonym provided from a list. Have students replace either a couple of key words in the poem or a word in each line with the synonyms offered, and then read their new poems to the class. After a few examples, it should become clear how important word choice is to the overall effect of the poem.

You might try a similar exercise for word order with some of the selections. Having students think hypothetically about other options for a poem can help them develop an appreciation for the reasons a poem is the way it is. In general, counterfactuals help sharpen critical thinking skills.

The reasons a poem conveys a certain tone are sometimes hard to pin down and can initially prove frustrating for students. You might find it helpful to encourage students to look at not only word choice but also other features of the poem in their discussions of tone.

The pairing of Thomas Hardy's and David Slavitt's poems about the *Titanic* can very effectively show students the workings of diction. The popularity of the James Cameron movie *Titanic* will ensure that students know something about the event itself. A similar pairing that can prove interesting is John Keats's "Ode on a Grecian Urn" and Sharon Olds's "Sex without Love." Both poems describe a beautiful aesthetic object but differ greatly in their ultimate conclusions — a difference that has much to do with tone. It may be a challenge, but having students articulate this difference in class discussion or a short writing assignment can prove useful to their understanding of how tone and theme are related.

RANDALL JARRELL, *The Death of the Ball Turret Gunner* (p. 71)

Randall Jarrell attended Vanderbilt University and so became influenced by the Agrarian literary movement, an anti-industrial movement that sought to reinstate the values of an agricultural society. Jarrell's poem probably reflects on personal experience, as he was an air force pilot from 1942 until the end of World War II. Like most of his poems, however, this one evokes universal human pain and anguish, regardless of its specific circumstances.

Play a recording of Randall Jarrell reading "The Death of the Ball Turret Gunner" on *Literature Aloud*.

The textual discussion of this poem calls attention to Jarrell's intentional use of ambiguity in some of his word choices, but is the overall tone of the poem ambiguous? How would you describe the speaker's attitude toward his subject? Have students look at Alfred, Lord Tennyson's "The Charge of the Light Brigade" (text p. 231) for another depiction of death in war. What are the word choices Tennyson makes in order to create the tone he wants? How does the tone of Tennyson's poem compare to that of Jarrell's?

The scene depicted in Jarrell's poem might almost be a synopsis of one of the major story lines in Joseph Heller's novel *Catch-22*. Compare Jarrell's word choices and the mood created by them with Heller's depiction of the gunner in Chapter 5 of *Catch-22*:

> That was where he wanted to be [atop the escape hatch, ready to parachute to safety] if he had to be there at all, instead of hung out there in front like some goddam cantilevered goldfish in some goddam cantilevered goldfish bowl while the goddam foul black tiers of flak were bursting and billowing and booming all around and above and below him in a climbing, cracking, staggered, banging, phantasmagorical, cosmological wickedness that jarred and tossed and shivered, clattered and pierced, and threatened to annihilate them all in one splinter of a second in one vast flash of fire. (New York: Dell, 1974, p. 50)

POSSIBLE CONNECTIONS TO OTHER SELECTIONS

Wilfred Owen, "Dulce et Decorum Est" (text p. 122)

Alfred, Lord Tennyson, "The Charge of the Light Brigade" (text p. 231)

AUDIOVISUAL RESOURCES (manual p. 377)

E. E. CUMMINGS, *she being Brand* (p. 73)

This poem is a naughtily playful allegory of a young man's attempt to initiate a sexual experience with his girlfriend. Language accommodates the situation of the poem nicely, since some men seem to respond to cars and women with equal measures of affection and caretaking and refer to both cars and women as "she." Cummings drops innuendos of his witty double entendres early on. Listen, for example, to the opening eight lines, in which the poet seems to pause over words like "stiff" (line 4), "universal" (6), and even "springs" (8), which could suggest springs of affection. Knowing the "secret" of the poem, the class should enjoy lines such as "next / minute i was back in neutral tried and / again slo-wly;bare,ly nudg. ing (my" (13–15). This work also offers good opportunities to discuss the function of punctuation in poetry.

Ask students to explore contexts for E. E. Cummings on *LiterActive*.

POSSIBLE CONNECTIONS TO OTHER SELECTIONS

Sharon Olds, "Sex without Love" (text p. 93)

Marge Piercy, "The Secretary Chant" (text p. 22)

JUDITH ORTIZ COFER, *Common Ground* (p. 75)

This poem examines a shared heritage through the genetic legacy that is the body. The broad homily of the first stanza becomes more pointed and personal in the second, as the speaker confides in the reader about her awareness of her own aging face and hands. She uses the changes in her body to examine the ways in which her consciousness is evolving to contain the perspectives of her family members, lives shared and "pain and deprivation / I have never known" (lines 12–13). Students might benefit from a discussion of what Cofer might mean by "the stuff of your origin" (7) rising up through your pores. To help focus discussion, it might be helpful to assign five minutes of freewriting on students' individual family traits. In the poem, the arrows that point downward also point inward at the common ground of the title, the new understanding of a shared heritage. Through a shared appearance, the speaker discovers other things she has in common with her family members. How do shared physical traits help your students identify with family members? Do they imagine these connections might become more pronounced with age?

POSSIBLE CONNECTIONS TO OTHER SELECTIONS

Elizabeth Bishop, "Manners" (text p. 62)

Theodore Roethke, "My Papa's Waltz" (text p. 233)

AUDIOVISUAL RESOURCES (manual p. 373)

COLETTE INEZ, *Back When All Was Continuous Chuckles* (p. 76)

Much of the surprise in this poem comes from the juxtaposition of humor and death. Some words fall obviously on one side or the other: "cemetery" (line 6), "hilarious" (7), "ghost" (8), "Silly billies" (12). What are the connotations of more ambiguous words, such as "helpless" (1) or "grinding" (5)? Do they foreshadow the pretending in the last stanza?

You might ask students about the forms jokes take. What kind of expectations do they set up, and do the jokes in this poem meet those expectations? The disconnection between joke and punch line, which produces an "'I don't get it'" (10), is a figure for the way the child's expectations of life are overturned. The author of the poem was an orphan herself, living first in an orphanage in Belgium and then with several foster families in the United States. The jokes she writes into this narrative work as a line of defense against painful realities, both personal (Doris's mother's cancer) and public (the war).

POSSIBLE CONNECTIONS TO OTHER SELECTIONS

Gwendolyn Brooks, "We Real Cool" (text p. 98; question 1, following)

Theodore Roethke, "My Papa's Waltz" (text p. 233)

CONNECTION QUESTION IN TEXT (p. 77) WITH ANSWER

1. Discuss the tone of this poem and that of Gwendolyn Brooks's "We Real Cool" (p. 98).

    Both Inez and Brooks use light tones that conflict with their grave subject matter. Inez's tone is playful as it attempts to re-create the joking of the two young girls. Brooks's tone is as cool as her characters. Her reticence mimics their fatalistic pose. For both poets, the tone is a barrier between the self and the trauma at the center of the poem. At the same time, their use of the colloquial brings death down from grand abstraction and places it squarely among the elements of everyday life.

KATHARYN HOWD MACHAN, *Hazel Tells LaVerne* (p. 77)

You might begin discussing this poem by talking about names and how they, too, have connotative value. Would our expectations be the same if the poem were titled "Sybil Speaks with Jacqueline"? By and large this poem does a good job at getting across its meaning through denotative language. But the fact that Hazel does use language almost exclusively in denotative terms is in itself a sign of her personality. As in a dramatic monologue by Robert Browning, Hazel tells more about herself, her social class, and her impenetrably matter-of-fact outlook on life than she does about her encounter with the frog. We as readers then fill in the gaps of the speaker's perceptions as well as piece together her outlook and attitude.

You might ask students to respond to Hazel's personality. She is likable; her matter-of-factness cuts through any of the fairy tales the world might try to sell her, and she's funny. Students can probably provide examples of characters from TV shows who are like Hazel and whose humor derives from their plainspoken concreteness. We all admire the survivor who cannot be duped.

Play a recording of Katharyn Howd Machan reading "Hazel Tells LaVerne" on **Literature Aloud**.

POSSIBLE CONNECTIONS TO OTHER SELECTIONS

Robert Browning, "My Last Duchess" (text p. 177; question 1, following)

Marge Piercy, "The Secretary Chant" (text p. 22)

CONNECTION QUESTION IN TEXT (p. 78) WITH ANSWER

1. Although Robert Browning's "My Last Duchess" (p. 177) is a more complex poem than Machan's, both use dramatic monologues to reveal character. How are the strategies in each poem similar?

    The speakers of each poem reveal something about themselves as they try to narrate a story. The speaker of this poem repeats the line "me a princess," indicating that her bravado is just a front for her dreams. The speaker of Browning's poem uses more sophisticated language, and he believes that he is in control of the narrative situation, but the more he talks the more he reveals about his true desires and motives. His asides are what give him away; as he pauses to consider how he should express something, he gives us the opportunity to analyze not only the content of his speech but his expression of it as well.

MARTÍN ESPADA, *Latin Night at the Pawnshop* (p. 78)

This imagist poem describes a scene of a man looking into the window of a pawnshop. In the instruments suspended there, he sees the apparition of a salsa band. The poet compares the instruments to a dead man with a toe tag.

There is nothing apparently "difficult" about this poem, so students may be quick to dismiss it, feeling that they "get the point" instantly. The challenge for discussion then becomes to fill in the considerable space around the poem. The liveliness of a salsa band coupled with the fact that the poem takes place on Christmas, a day of celebration, contribute to the poem's blunt emotional overtones. What does the speaker's presence at a pawnshop on Christmas suggest? The speaker is implicitly mourning the passage of something vital. Unlike the Christmas ghosts of a character students are familiar with, Dickens's Scrooge, this apparition does not seem to provide any comfort or hope for the future. The apparition is the *absence* of the band, with its instruments apparently sold cheaply. As a way of pointing out what exactly has been lost, emphasize all of the economic allusions in the poem (pawnshop, Liberty Loan, golden, silver, price tags). Does the poem seek to make a broad point about class and culture in contemporary America? Consider the title as a follow-up to this question. Students may think of other examples of the various ways in which immigrants in America must "sell out" their culture for more fundamental survival needs (i.e., money).

POSSIBLE CONNECTIONS TO OTHER SELECTIONS

Ruth Fainlight, "The Clarinettist" (text p. 154)

Louis Simpson, "In the Suburbs" (text p. 100)

PAUL LAURENCE DUNBAR, *To a Captious Critic* (p. 79)

The vocabulary of this poem may pose a challenge for your students, so remind them to look up words they don't know, like "captious," "deplores" (line 1), and "abdicate" (4). Otherwise, they will miss Dunbar's witty insult to his critic. Depending on their preconceived ideas about poetry, students may be surprised to find it serving such a function. If they are surprised, ask them if "To a Captious Critic" reminds them of something else they've seen or heard, maybe on TV or the Internet. How would a twenty-first-century critic be likely to respond?

In opening up this small poem, it might help your students to know that Dunbar, one of the first African American poets to achieve wider recognition, wrote both in standard English poetic language and in black folk dialect. Why does he choose the former in writing this response? What does that choice say about the critic? Some of the formality in the poem, such as the "dear" in the first line, is ironic, but does it also give Dunbar greater authority in answering his detractor?

POSSIBLE CONNECTIONS TO OTHER SELECTIONS

Anne Bradstreet, "The Author to Her Book" (text p. 137)

David McCord, "Epitaph on a Waiter" (text p. 252)

ROBERT HERRICK, *To the Virgins, to Make Much of Time* (p. 79)

Robert Herrick, son of a well-to-do London goldsmith, rather halfheartedly became an Anglican clergyman assigned to Dean Prior in Devonshire, in the west of England. He wrote poems secretly, making up for many of them alluring, exotic, phantom mistresses. After losing his position when the Puritans rose to power, Herrick published his only book, containing some 1,200 poems, in 1648.

This is one of the better-known poems of the carpe diem (seize the day) tradition. Here Herrick is advising young women in a tone of straightforward urging to make the most of their opportunities for pleasure while they are in the prime of youth and beauty. These "virgins," Herrick implies, are like the sun at its zenith or a flower in full bloom; they will soon begin to decline and may never have the same opportunities for marriage again. The word *virgins,* rather than *women,* accommodates the advice in the last stanza to "go marry" and carries with it as well the connotation of sought-for sexual fulfillment. Some of your students might point out how a young woman's situation is much more complex today than it apparently was in Herrick's time, as "seizing the day" can and often does mean pursuing opportunities for career over those for marriage.

One possible way to enter a discussion of the poem is to consider the arrangement of the argument. The speaker has a definite intent: to communicate bits of wisdom to the "virgins" of the title. What effect does the order of his points of argument have on the way the poem reads? What would happen if we were to rearrange the first three stanzas: Would the message of the poem remain exactly the same?

POSSIBLE CONNECTIONS TO OTHER SELECTIONS

Robert Frost, "Nothing Gold Can Stay" (text p. 371)

Richard Wilbur, "A Late Aubade" (text p. 84)

AUDIOVISUAL RESOURCES (manual p. 384)

ANDREW MARVELL, *To His Coy Mistress* (p. 81)

After graduating from Cambridge University in 1639, Andrew Marvell left England to travel in Europe. Almost nothing is known of his life from this time until he became the tutor of the daughter of a powerful Yorkshire nobleman in 1650. Most of his poems seem to have been written during the next seven years. He served for a short time as John

Milton's assistant when Milton was Latin secretary for the Commonwealth, and he represented Hull, his hometown, in Parliament from 1659 until he died.

This seduction poem is structured with a flawless logic. Marvell begins with a hypothetical conjecture, "Had we but world enough, and time," which he then disproves with hyperbole, promising his "mistress" that he would devote "an age at least" to praising her every part. Time is, of course, far more limited, and the poem's second section makes clear time's ravages on beauty. The third section expounds the carpe diem theme: if time is limited, then seize the day and triumph over life's difficulties with love.

 Ask students to explore contexts for Andrew Marvell and this poem — as well as a sample close reading — on *LiterActive* and at **bedfordstmartins.com/ meyerpoetry**.

From his initial tone of teasing hyperbole, the poet modulates to a much more somber tone, employing the metaphysically startling imagery of the grave to underscore human mortality. Lines 31–32 are an example of understatement, calculated to make the listener react and acknowledge this world as the time and place for embracing.

Play a recording of Paul Muldoon reading "To His Coy Mistress" on *Literature Aloud*.

Some classes may need help in recognizing that the verbs in the first part of the poem are in the subjunctive mood, while those in the last are often in the imperative. At any rate, students should easily recognize that the last section contains verbs that all imply a physical vigor that would seize time, mold it to the lovers' uses, and thus "make [time] run" (46) according to the clock of their own desires.

The poem seems far more than a simple celebration of the flesh. It confronts human mortality and suggests a psychological stance that would seize life (and face death) so that fulfilling of one's time would be a strategy of confronting time's passing.

As a writing topic you might ask students to explain the radical and somewhat abrupt change in tone between the opening twenty lines and the rest of the poem. Marvell offers more than one reason to temper his initial levity.

Refer students to Bernard Duyfhuizen's " 'To His Coy Mistress': On How a Female Might Respond" (text p. 82) for a contemporary perspective on the poem.

TIP FROM THE FIELD

I use point-of-view writing assignments that ask students to assume a persona in a poem or story and respond to the other characters or situations in the selection accordingly. For example, I have students read Andrew Marvell's "To His Coy Mistress" and then write an essay from the point of view of the wooer or the wooee.

— SANDRA ADICKES, *Winona State University*

POSSIBLE CONNECTIONS TO OTHER SELECTIONS

John Keats, "Ode on a Grecian Urn" (text p. 96)
Richard Wilbur, "A Late Aubade" (text p. 84)

AUDIOVISUAL RESOURCES (manual p. 378)

P E R S P E C T I V E

BERNARD DUYFHUIZEN, *"To His Coy Mistress": On How a Female Might Respond* (p. 82)

You might ask your students in a writing assignment to use Duyfhuizen's analysis as a model in writing their own description of a female's response to a male poet's address. They could use the poems in this section (Robert Herrick's "To the Virgins, to Make Much of Time" [text p. 79] and Richard Wilbur's "A Late Aubade" [text p. 84]), or they might choose a poem like Shakespeare's "Shall I compare thee to a summer's day?" (text p. 243). Students could also choose an address by a female poet to a male — Margaret Atwood's "you fit into me" (text p. 135), for example — or a poem by a woman about a relationship with a man — Jane Kenyon's "The Shirt" (text p. 496) — and analyze the male's response.

RICHARD WILBUR, *A Late Aubade* (p. 84)

A prolific poet, critic, translator, and editor, Richard Wilbur (b. 1921) studied at Amherst and Harvard and was awarded the Pulitzer Prize and the National Book Award in 1957 for *Things of This World.* Influenced by the works of the metaphysical poets and Wallace Stevens, Wilbur's poetry has been described by poet and critic John Ciardi as often concerned with "the central driving intention of finding that artifice which will most include the most of life."

It is difficult to translate the forms of Renaissance charm and wit into the more hurried, less mannered tones of the twentieth century. So Wilbur seems to find as he writes his "late" aubade ("late," one supposes, as in "late Corinthian," as well as late in the day), in which going means staying and seizing the day dictates staying in bed. Despite the turnabout in manners and customs, this poem achieves its own special charm. You might begin discussion, though, by asking the class to evaluate the speaker here as rhetorician or persuader. Does he keep to the rules of logic, or does he beg some questions and employ loaded language in other instances? Obviously, he has no admiration for women who spend hours in either libraries or shopping malls, and with dead-pan doggerel he sets up a rhyme in stanza 1 between "carrel" (line 1) and "Ladies' Apparel" (4) that devalues both activities. Likewise, he colors the attitude of the person being addressed by talking of planting a "raucous" (5) bed of salvia (which yield bright blue or red flowers) or lunching through a "screed" (7) (the archaism is deliberate here) of someone's loves.

The poem is an appeal to the assumed and presumed sensuality of both the speaker and the woman he addresses. Thus the Matisselike still life of chilled white wine, blue cheese, and ruddy-skinned pears with which Wilbur concludes the poem is a fitting tricolor tribute to the senses, even though the woman here is still the one who serves and waits.

A writing assignment could be organized around a comparison of Herrick's "To the Virgins, to Make Much of Time" (text p. 79), Marvell's "To His Coy Mistress" (text p. 81), and this poem. Wilbur's poem is more conversational and relaxed, reflecting a commonality of spirit between the lovers. The speaker here dwells more on the prolonged moment than on the bleak foreknowledge of death.

POSSIBLE CONNECTIONS TO OTHER SELECTIONS

Robert Herrick, "To the Virgins, to Make Much of Time" (text p. 79; questions 1 and 2, following)

Andrew Marvell, "To His Coy Mistress" (text p. 81; questions 1 and 2, following)

Sharon Olds, "Sex without Love" (text p. 93)

CONNECTIONS QUESTIONS IN TEXT (p. 85) WITH ANSWERS

1. How does the man's argument in "A Late Aubade" differ from the speakers' in Herrick's and Marvell's poems? Which of the three arguments do you find most convincing?

Unlike the other two writers, Wilbur's speaker is not immediately concerned with the passing of his youth. Herrick's and Marvell's poems try to convince their listeners to seize the moment because they feel the pressure of old age and mortality. Consequently, their rhetoric is loftier than Wilbur's, encompassing history and popular mythology. Wilbur's speaker tries to convince his lover in relatively simple language — "Isn't this better?" (line 12) — that the morning is more pleasantly spent in bed with him than elsewhere. Students are likely to find Wilbur's speaker the most convincing; his rhetoric is influenced by the "give the people what they want" philosophy of the twentieth century, whereas the other two poets are influenced by models of classical rhetoric of the English Renaissance. If the consensus tends this way, you might want to consider how rhetoric changes over time.

2. Explain how the tone of each poem is suited to its theme.

Herrick's speaker argues from a position of wisdom, even condescension, which is fitting because the theme urges young women to live the moment of their youth. Marvell's poem seems more desperate; the speaker feels the pressure of "Time's wingéd chariot" (line 22) because he, along with his lover, senses his own passing youth. Wilbur's speaker is not as young — this is a *late* aubade — so his tone, his language, and his argument are all more leisurely, as though he is not worried about losing the moment of his youth as much as he would simply like his lover to remain in bed with him.

AUDIOVISUAL RESOURCES (manual p. 383)

SHARON OLDS, *Last Night* (p. 85)

Olds's aubade is more internal than any of the other poems in this group. She doesn't directly address the "you" of the poem until almost halfway through (line 12), and even then she focuses mainly on the experience of the speaker. Rather than trying to seduce, as Marvell and Wilbur do, Olds explores the meaning of sex. The image of the chrysalis (7) and the phrase "without language" (8) provide keys to understanding the tone of this poem. Feelings during sex are indescribable, enclosing the speaker inside of her own senses; they exist outside of regular human interaction.

While Herrick urges young people to marry while they are vital and full of life, Olds describes sex in terms of death; it is not tender but "like killing, death-grip / holding to life, genitals / like violent hands clasped tight" (13–15). The brutality of this section helps readers to understand "I am almost afraid" in the first line. You may wish to mention to your students the tradition that equates orgasm with a kind of death. The French, in particular, use the euphemism "*le petit mort,*" suggesting that a lover is emptied or negated in some way at climax. This view of sex sets the stage for the end of Olds's poem, in which the couple reemerges "clasped, fragrant, buoyant" (28). The awakening the next morning becomes a resurrection. Though the middle section of the poem uses the language of death, Olds ends up affirming the resilience of life.

Since Olds presents a female perspective on the love poem, you might have students look at "Last Night" in conjunction with Duyfhuizen's comments (text p. 82) on "To His Coy Mistress." Does Olds's poem share any features with Duyfhuizen's imagined response? Does the speaker's relation to her partner, who "secured" (26) and kept her "sealed" (24), bear any resemblance to the relationship Marvell implies?

POSSIBLE CONNECTIONS TO OTHER SELECTIONS

H. D. [Hilda Doolittle], "Heat" (text p. 118)

Robert Herrick, "To the Virgins, to Make Much of Time" (text p. 79; question 1, following)

Andrew Marvell, "To His Coy Mistress" (text p. 81; questions 1 and 2, following)

CONNECTIONS QUESTIONS IN TEXT (p. 86) WITH ANSWERS

1. How does the speaker's description of intimacy compare with Herrick's and Marvell's?

    In their *carpe diem* poems, both Herrick and Marvell glorify youth as the natural time for intimate relationships. Herrick characterizes youth as warm and sunny while the prospects for old age are dreary. Marvell, too, understands love in terms of the passing day and argues the urgency of loving while the day is, or while the lovers are, young. Marvell suggests that death is naturally solitary, that a couple cannot exist beyond the grave. Therefore, the young should rush to embrace life rather than wait patiently while death approaches. Olds, on the other hand, does not see sex and death as mutually exclusive. While Herrick and Marvell use the sun to symbolize youthful intimacy, the action of Olds's poem takes place at night and is only reflected upon in the light of morning. Intimacy is warm for Herrick, but unpleasantly hot for Olds, who imagines herself and her partner as "dragonflies / in the sun" (lines 2–3). In "Last Night," *eros* is mixed up with *thanatos*, the death drive. Rather than holding death at bay, intimacy allows Olds's speaker to die and be reborn.

2. Compare the speaker's voice in Olds's poem with the voice you imagine for the coy mistress in Marvell's poem (p. 81).

    Given Marvell's counterarguments in "To His Coy Mistress," we expect that the mistress has appealed to patience and reason in rebuffing the speaker. Her function in this relationship is to maintain propriety. The speaker tries to convince her to give up caution and allow herself to be ruled by passion. The speaker in Olds's poem is also concerned with control over the situation, but in this case she has already released it. She loses herself in the sexual act, and the next day she has to consider its meaning. Both the coy mistress and the speaker of Olds's poem have anxieties about intimacy that contrast with the purely positive views put forward by Marvell.

MARGARET ATWOOD, *Bored* (p. 86)

This adult speaker reflects on her boredom as a young girl spending time with her father. She recounts their activities together, and ultimately realizes that her mature perceptions differ greatly from her childhood perceptions. She ends with the wistful realization, "Now I would know." Careful readers will notice that the relationship between the speaker and the "he" of the poem is likely that of a daughter and father; she sits in the back seat, helps him to build a garden, and learns about nature from him. It might be interesting to discuss why no one else exists in the poem. Is it primarily about him or about her? If the daughter is sitting in the back seat, it is likely that her mother is sitting in the front seat; why is her mother never mentioned?

The poem's single stanza doesn't help to identify points at which the speaker's attitude, point of view, or definition of boredom shift. It may be productive to have students identify and discuss these points: when boredom transmutes into "looking hard and up close at the small / details" (lines 13–14), or when her activity merges with "what / the animals spend most of their time at" (24–25). How does the meaning of the word *bored* change from the title through line 37? Students might be more likely to recognize the pun with "board" (4) — an object that almost seems an extension of the speaker in the early lines. However, the more elusive pun on boring as digging or burrowing represents a crucial turn in the speaker's perspective, as it allows the speaker to connect her activities with those of the animals her father "pointed . . . out" (27–28). "Boring" — a negative word to any child — becomes a positive word from the speaker's adult perspective because it connotes digging deeper in order to find meaning, resulting in a mature appreciation of her father.

Possible Connections to Other Selections

Robert Hayden, "Those Winter Sundays" (text p. 23; question 1, following)

A. E. Housman, "When I was one-and-twenty" (text p. 223)

Connection Question in Text (p. 87) with Answer

1. Write an essay on the speaker's attitude toward the father in this poem and in Robert Hayden's "Those Winter Sundays" (p. 23).

   The two poems end with strikingly similar sentiments: The penultimate line of Hayden's poem is, "What did I know, what did I know," and the final line of Atwood's is "Now I would know." Both speakers look back on their youthful relationship with their fathers from the point of view of a relatively wise and experienced adult. Yet a much greater gulf exists between the speaker of "Those Winter Sundays" and his father, who is associated with "the chronic angers of that house" (line 9). Atwood's speaker has a more intimate relationship with her father, who whistles, boats, and drives a car. Hayden's speaker's father works too hard and is alienated from his family. The bond of love between them is apparent, but it is an intense kind of "tough love."

Audiovisual Resources (manual pp. 371–72)

BARBARA HAMBY, *Ode to American English* (p. 87)

In many ways, Hamby's poem reenacts the qualities she loves in American English. The pace and length of her sentences mimics its raciness, bordering on mania. She describes American language as "pill-popping" (line 2) and later compares nouns to "Corvettes on dexedrine" (42). Differing from British English, which Hamby implies is stolid and backward looking, American English changes constantly to accommodate new phenomena. Its beauty is "quotidian" (27), rooted in the minutiae of life, in consumerism, TV culture, and pop religion.

The piling up of examples like "hotrod, hotdog, hot flash" (9) and "Cheetoes, Cheerios, chili-dog" (39) demonstrate "the mongrel / plenitude of American English" (21–22). In this poem, Hamby's use of alliteration does more than just enhance the sounds of the language; it refers back to the dictionary as a catalog of language. Hamby creates her own catalogs of words that might not appear in a formal dictionary, recording a more casual but lively American lexicon.

The wide differences in American language also indicate the social fragmentation of the country. Thinking of linguistic variety brings to mind not just "Ebonics, Spanglish" (14), but "the battle cry of the Bible Belt" (17), the "low-rider, boom-box cruise" (24), and "the bomb of it all" (23). However, language also unites us all, or almost all. Playing on the literal meaning of the grammatical term, Hamby cites "the inability of 90% of the population / to get the past perfect" (15–16).

Possible Connections to Other Selections

Florence Cassen Mayers, "All-American Sestina" (text p. 250; question 1, following)

Lydia Huntley Sigourney, "Indian Names" (text p. 622; question 2, following)

Walt Whitman, From *Song of Myself* (text p. 180)

CONNECTIONS QUESTIONS FROM TEXT (p. 89) WITH ANSWERS

1. Discuss the strategic use of American phrasing in this poem and in Florence Cassen Mayers's "All-American Sestina" (p. 250), and compare the tone of each poem.

    Hamby uses American slang to celebrate the casualness of American language, which is a consequence of the ideal of a classless society. She compares it with British English, which she finds "too cultured by half" (line 6), preferring the constantly renewing, if vulgar, American idiom. In contrast, Mayers uses standard turns of phrase to reveal the static nature of American language. Her variation on the sestina form reveals the interchangeability of many clichés and suggests an emptiness behind the dreams they encapsulate. Both writers employ many hyphenated words. For Hamby, they show the melting-pot quality of American speech while for Mayers they bind words together in units that are emptied of meaning.

2. Write an essay comparing the themes of Hamby's poem and Lydia Huntley Sigourney's "Indian Names" (p. 622). Compare how the diction of each controls its tone.

    Hamby views American English as a young and vibrant language that is constantly evolving. The diction of her poem is drawn largely from speech and even from commercial language, which suggests that what characterizes American English is the most of-the-moment, popular phrase. By contrast, Sigourney writes in traditional English poetic language; the words she uses to describe the landscape draw on the British and American romantic traditions. However, the frequent interspersing of geographical names mimics how the Indian legacy lives on within a predominating European aesthetic. Sigourney reminds us how much of the language we use to talk about America comes not from European ancestors but rather from the Native Americans who lived here before those settlers arrived. The presence of Indian names on the American map resists the kind of romanticizing that sees the Native Americans as a "noble race and brave," but one entirely of the past (line 2). In spite of the violent removal of Native Americans from the landscape, "their name is on your waters, / Ye may not wash it out" (7–8).

THOMAS HARDY, *The Convergence of the Twain* (p. 89)

Between the ages of fifteen and twenty-one, Thomas Hardy was apprenticed to an architect in his native Dorchester, an area in southwest England that he was to transform into the "Wessex" of his novels. He went to London in 1862 to practice as an architect and pursue a growing interest in writing. Though he enjoyed a successful career as a novelist, Hardy stopped writing fiction after publishing *Jude the Obscure* in 1895, concentrating instead on the poetry that ranks him among the major English poets.

This poem ushers in an event that some consider to be the beginning of the modern era: the sinking of the *Titanic*. The final two stanzas support this idea. What is the true significance of the event, according to the speaker? What are the implications of a God who is described as both "The Immanent Will that stirs and urges everything" (line 18) and "the Spinner of the Years" (31)? On a superficial level, the "twain" of the title signifies the ship and the iceberg; what are some of the word's connotative meanings?

The *Titanic* as described in this poem is "gaily great" (20) in its luxurious opulence, but Hardy also stresses the ship's "vaingloriousness" (15), planned by the "Pride of Life" (3). It is as though in this dramatic gesture of invention and design humanity became the tragic overreacher. In a writing assignment, you might ask the class to compare the tones of the speakers in this poem and in Percy Bysshe Shelley's "Ozymandias" (text p. 621).

The "marriage" between ship and iceberg is suggested through the use of several words and phrases, such as "sinister mate" (19), "intimate welding," as in "wedding" (27), and "consummation" in the final line.

Hardy, the master celebrator of "Hap" (see text p. 599), assigns the disaster to Fate, or as he allegorizes it, the "Immanent Will" (18) that directs all things and the "Spinner of the Years" (31), who decides when time has run out.

POSSIBLE CONNECTIONS TO OTHER SELECTIONS

Stephen Crane, "A Man Said to the Universe" (text p. 164)

David R. Slavitt, "Titanic" (text p. 91)

Wallace Stevens, "The Emperor of Ice-Cream" (text p. 624)

AUDIOVISUAL RESOURCES (manual p. 375)

DAVID R. SLAVITT, *Titanic* (p. 91)

Although Slavitt's poem acknowledges the power of fate, it focuses on human attitudes rather than cosmic forces. The first stanza, for example, calls attention to our gullibility; its weary yet affectionate tone originating in the "this is how we are" shrug of the two *who* clauses. The speaker ponders death, deciding that because "we all go down" (line 4) it would be better to do so with some company and some notice from the rest of the world. But the speaker's gentle urging that it wouldn't be "so bad, after all" (11) to go "first-class" (14) includes some simple, unambiguous descriptions of what such a mass loss of life would actually be like: "The cold water" (11–12), which would be "anesthetic and very quick" (12); the "cries on all sides" (13). Death always wins, "we all go down, mostly / alone" (4–5), so wouldn't it be fine to die "with crowds of people, friends, servants, / well fed, with music" (4–5)?

You might ask students to compare in a short paper the attitudes toward fate in "Titanic" and Hardy's "The Convergence of the Twain" (text p. 89) and how each poem's diction and tone contribute to the communication of these attitudes.

POSSIBLE CONNECTION TO ANOTHER SELECTION

Thomas Hardy, "The Convergence of the Twain" (text p. 89; questions 1 and 3, following)

CONNECTIONS QUESTIONS IN TEXT (p. 91) WITH ANSWERS

1. How does "Titanic" differ in its attitude toward opulence from "The Convergence of the Twain" (p. 89)?

   In Hardy's poem the opulence of the passengers aboard the *Titanic* is emblematic of their lack of humility, and it seems partially responsible for the crash. Slavitt's poem, at least on the surface, celebrates the style with which the same passengers exited the world, arguing that, as long as we have to die, we might as well be having fun while we do it.

3. Compare the speakers' tones in "Titanic" and "The Convergence of the Twain."

   Hardy's poem is serious, formal in its use of language, form, and rhyme. "Titanic" is much more colloquial, less brooding in its tone and its language. Both poems could be described as philosophical, but Slavitt's brand of philosophy is more home-spun and optimistic.

PETER MEINKE, *(Untitled)* (p. 91)

This poem takes the form of a father's apology to his son for more than ten years of abuse. We can infer from the details that the abuse was not physical but verbal; the son's limp body is always described in response to emotional rather than corporal pain. The poem begins in media res with an uncapitalized first word, seeming to pick up in the middle of the characters' lives together; the father's perspective — and the poem's tone — shifts at the end of the first sentence. Whereas the poem's first half describes the son's fear and hurt, its second half describes the father's grief over his behavior as well as an oblique promise of reform.

Some students are likely to take this poem personally, recalling their own difficult relationships with their fathers; others may immediately rail in anger at the speaker. Should classroom discussion get off track, have students examine the structure of the poem's lines, looking for clues to the father's attitude about his behavior. Point out, if necessary, that examples of the son's pain are described ahead of the actions that caused it (implying the father's lack of appreciation of cause and effect), whereas the word order of the poem's second half emphasizes the father's active responsibility for his son's mental state. How does the poem's tone change if the word order of the lines is reversed? Ask students to consider, also, how the boy is described in the poem's two separate parts: Do they notice that he is at first portrayed as "vulnerable" (line 3), "thin" (5), "boneless" (6), "pale" (6), and "bent" (7), but then as "beautiful and fair" (14) and "bright" (16)? As a possible writing assignment, have students examine how the father's judgment of his son's appearance correlates with his judgment of himself.

POSSIBLE CONNECTIONS TO OTHER SELECTIONS

Ben Jonson, "On My First Son" (text p. 607)
Theodore Roethke, "My Papa's Waltz" (text p. 233)

JOANNE DIAZ, *On My Father's Loss of Hearing* (p. 92)

The epigram Diaz chooses for this poem underscores the benefit she sees to her father's hearing loss. Rather than focusing on the heightening of other senses that we sometimes associate with deafness or blindness, she believes his blessing is in the reduction of sensory information. Her question, "What else / is there but loss?" (lines 7–8), sounds despairing, but by the end of the poem, she suggests that this loss is merciful. Her father is "Abled differently" (1) in an emotional sense; he becomes less susceptible to the exhausting demands of his children and the surface patter of "sarcastic jokes, the snarky dialogue / of British films" (9–10). Hearing loss also disconnects him from the natural world, as he can't hear the "crack of thawing ice" (16) or "the scrape of his / dull rake in spring" (17–18). It creates a distance between him and the world that allows him to free his desires, "released like saffron pistils in the wind" (20), and to free his love, which "hurts much less" (28) when its demands are less immediate.

Though the poem praises the loss of senses, Diaz's careful description of the impressions her father no longer receives seems to celebrate them as well. You might have your students discuss in what ways this poem contradicts itself. Would the poet be content to lose her hearing? How does she use imagery as a way of imagining her father's experience?

POSSIBLE CONNECTIONS TO OTHER SELECTIONS

Margaret Atwood, "Bored" (text p. 86; question 2, following)
Peter Meinke, "(Untitled)" (text p. 91; question 1, following)

Mary Jo Salter, "Home Movies: A Sort of Ode" (text p. 260)
William Carlos Williams, "To Waken an Old Lady" (text p. 144)

CONNECTIONS QUESTIONS IN TEXT (p. 93) WITH ANSWERS

1. Discuss the relationship between love and pain in "On My Father's Loss of Hearing" and in the Meinke poem that precedes it.

   Though the points of view and the conclusions these poems reach are very different, they both see love as a devotion to others that leaves us open to hurt. In Meinke's poem, the speaker realizes that his son has been looking to him for affirmation and that, in not providing it, he has caused profound pain. Though he loves the son, he has taken for granted that "you knew / you were beautiful and fair" (lines 14–15). Diaz writes from the child's point of view, but in the beginning her speaker is similarly callous or unconscious about her effects on the father. The desires of his children, to which parents are supposed to attend, weigh him down. Through the course of both poems, the speakers realize the burden that parent-child love puts on others. Diaz recognizes it only as her father manages a partial escape from those demands, but Meinke's epiphany spurs him to apologize and to celebrate his son.

2. Compare the speakers' attitudes toward the fathers in Diaz's poem and in Margaret Atwood's "Bored" (text p. 86).

   In both Diaz's and Atwood's poems, the adult child achieves more sympathy for her father than she previously had. In Atwood's poem, this occurs through reflection on childhood memories. The times the speaker spent with her father were mundane and repetitive, and as a child, she would have characterized them as boring. As she grows up, though, she realizes that it "wasn't even boredom" (line 12) she was experiencing but a close attention to the details of life. Any frustration she had with her father and his boring occupations gives way to her understanding of the value of routine and observation. When she writes, "Now I would know" (39), she suggests not only that she would have a greater tolerance for the seemingly boring activities but also that she has a greater appreciation for the father who engaged her in them.

   The catalyst for Diaz's poem is not the memory of childhood experience, but a change in later life. The father's hearing loss makes the speaker reflect on the changing nature of their relationship and how her desires have affected him in the past. She seems not only to understand the father better but to recriminate herself and her siblings for pushing their "sorrows and complaints" (line 5) on him. While Atwood's attitude is sympathetic, Diaz's has a stronger element of pathos.

SHARON OLDS, *Sex without Love* (p. 93)

The word *beautiful,* which begins the second sentence of this poem, may puzzle students at first. Coupled with the ambiguity of the initial question (which may indicate either the speaker's envy or her disdain), the appeal of the lovers as performing artists may signal a positive view of them. But students will soon recognize that the beautiful images of the poem are surface images only; they are also empty and somewhat violent. The textural imagery — "ice" (line 3), "hooked" (4), and even "red as steak" (6) — suggests an undertone of danger in this act. As an artist, the poet must show the lovers as beautiful forms, but as an artist with a social consciousness, she must also explore the vacuum beneath the forms.

A discussion of the poem's imagery may begin with an exploration of all the possible meanings of its initial question. The speaker examines not only the moral implications of this self-centered experience but also the mechanics of the physical act:

how as well as *why* they do it. Discuss the shift in tone from the portrayal of the lovers as ice skaters and dancers in the initial lines to their likeness to great runners. This last metaphor solidifies the coldness of the speaker's assessment. Like great runners, the lovers concentrate only on the movement of their bodies, surrendering their mental and emotional health to the physical act. Students will see that the energy and concentration of runners are essential to a track event but not to an act of mutual communication. It is essential for the couple to think of themselves as athletes in order to escape the negative moral and potentially painful emotional implications of their act.

The poem's religious images contrast with its athletic metaphors. Beginning with "God" (line 9) and moving into "light / rising slowly as steam off their joined / skin" (11–13), the speaker subtly distinguishes between the false, body-bound vision of the lovers and the "true religion" that is implied through their negation. Ask students to identify the speaker's tone in these lines: Is she really talking about a religious experience, or is she pointing out the lovers' self-absorption? The mathematical language with which the speaker imagines her subjects talking about themselves, "just factors" (21), is undercut by her derogatory tone. Although *they* may act as if they are God, if we are searching for truth, we know that we can never really be single bodies alone in the universe. The implied "truth" here is a communal one, just the opposite of what is described.

In a writing assignment, you might ask students to explore what is not said in the poem. What is the alternative? Why would the speaker not state her idea of truth directly?

POSSIBLE CONNECTIONS TO OTHER SELECTIONS

E. E. Cummings, "she being Brand" (text p. 73; question 1, following)

Alberto Ríos, "Seniors" (text p. 53)

Richard Wilbur, "A Late Aubade" (text p. 84; question 2, following)

CONNECTIONS QUESTIONS IN TEXT (p. 94) WITH ANSWERS

1. How does the treatment of sex and love in Olds's poem compare with that in Cummings's "she being Brand" (p. 73)?

   Cummings and Olds do not share a similar notion of sex in these poems. Cummings's speaker is flippant, implying in his language that having sex is like driving a new car. Olds also talks about sex as mechanistic, but her disdain for that attitude is obvious. Cummings's speaker is less interested in the "truth" of the sexual relationship than he is in making the experience live on the page. Olds's speaker implies with regret that "truth" and love are ignored by those who have sex without love. One of the ways to reveal the different attitudes of these speakers is to compare their poems' very different images and sounds.

2. Just as Olds describes sex without love, she implies a definition of love in this poem. Consider whether the lovers in Wilbur's "A Late Aubade" (p. 84) fall within Olds's definition.

   The lovers in Wilbur's poem may well fall under Olds's definition of sex without love. The speaker in "A Late Aubade" clearly cares for their physical relationship, urging his beloved to forget worldly business and get them some wine and cheese. However, Wilbur's speaker's deliberate persuasive appeal to his lover establishes verbal communication, which is not even present in Olds's poem.

AUDIOVISUAL RESOURCES (manual p. 379)

CATHY SONG, *The Youngest Daughter* (p. 96)

This poem describes the experience of a grown woman who has stayed at home to take care of her aging parents. The speaker is bound by duty to stay in the family home until her parents die. The long-standing nature of her situation is presented early on in images: "the sky has been dark / for many years" (lines 1–2). The escape planned at the end of the poem is symbolized by the thousand paper cranes in the window, flying up in a sudden breeze. The speaker suggests ambivalence about the mother through the "sour taste" in her mouth in line 26 and the "almost tender" (30) way the speaker soaps the blue bruises of her mother's body. The toast to the mother's health following an acknowledgment that the speaker is not to be trusted demonstrates the ambivalence further: Once the mother dies, the youngest daughter can leave home; the sour taste and tenderness for her circumstances, the familiar silence and the migraines, will all change for both better and worse.

Asking students to analyze their own ambivalence about their parents in journal entries could help them establish a connection with Song's narrative. Spend a little time before the writing period suggesting circumstances that could provide context for their writing. Their departures for college may provide illustration of their changing relationships with their parents.

POSSIBLE CONNECTION TO ANOTHER SELECTION

Lisa Parker, "Snapping Beans" (text p. 51)

JOHN KEATS, *Ode on a Grecian Urn* (p. 96)

The speaker's attitude toward this object of beauty is a rapt expression of awe at its evocative and truth-bearing power and presence. Life portrayed on the urn is forever in suspended animation: no one gets old; the "wild ecstasy" goes undiminished; the love, never consummated, is yet never consumed and wearied of. Keats seems to admire this portrait of the sensuous ideal, which exists unmarred by mortality or the vagrancy of human passion.

Ask students to explore contexts for John Keats on *LiterActive*.

The significant question about this ode (beyond the meaning of the closing two lines and whether the speaker or the urn pronounces all or a part of them) appears to rest with "Cold Pastoral!" (line 45) and the ambivalence these words imply. Earlier, in stanza 3, Keats had admired the love "for ever warm and still to be enjoyed" (26) that was portrayed on the urn. Has the temperature of the urn changed by stanza 5? Has the speaker discovered, in essence, that even though the urn portrays a sensuous ideal of courtship and pursuit, it is still merely a cold form that, because it is deathless, can never feel the warmth of human life?

Still one of the best studies on this ode is the essay (bearing the same title as the ode) by Earl R. Wasserman in *The Finer Tone: Keats's Major Poems* (Baltimore: Johns Hopkins UP, 1953, 1967, 11–63). For the record, Wasserman argues that the closing lines are spoken by the poet to the reader; as Wasserman explains, the ode is *on* a Grecian Urn, not *to* the urn. Hence "it is Keats who must make the commentary on the drama" (59).

POSSIBLE CONNECTIONS TO OTHER SELECTIONS

Emily Dickinson, "Success is counted sweetest" (text p. 312)

John Keats, "To Autumn" (text p. 127; question 3, following)

Andrew Marvell, "To His Coy Mistress" (text p. 81; question 1, following)

Richard Wilbur, "Love Calls Us to the Things of This World" (text p. 630; question 2, following)

1.   Write an essay comparing the view of time in this ode with that in Marvell's "To His Coy Mistress" (p. 81). Pay particular attention to the connotative language in each poem.

     In Keats's ode, time wastes human beings but does not affect art. Art provides hope, friendliness, and beauty to human beings, making their misery more understandable in its "truth." In Marvell's poem, which dwells much more in the physicality of human experience, the speaker urges his listener to "make [the sun] run" (line 46), because time will destroy her anyway. The difference in the poems' treatments of time results from their different subjects. Whereas Keats's ode discusses art *vs.* human existence, Marvell's work claims that human existence is all we have.

2.   Discuss the treatment and meaning of love in this ode and in Richard Wilbur's "Love Calls Us to the Things of This World" (p. 630).

     Keats presents the moment before the kiss as the peak of a relationship because this moment is full of anticipation and ripeness, but Wilbur makes the very earthly lovers into heavenly angels. The value of anticipation over experience in Keats's mind is ambiguous, however. After all, he describes his vision as a "Cold Pastoral" in stanza 5. Perhaps he thinks that loving is more important than art, but it is hard to tell. Unlike Keats's speaker, the speaker in Wilbur's poem traces the moment after the epiphany, when souls descend from fresh laundry into the living bodies of lovers waking to ordinary day.

3.   Compare the tone and attitude toward life in this ode with those in John Keats's "To Autumn" (p. 127).

     In "To Autumn" Keats celebrates a moment at the end of fall, asking us to appreciate the passage of time in his timeless work of art. In a sense the Grecian urn, a celebration of timeless beauty in art, competes with the ephemeral season of autumn. The poems are perfectly juxtaposed; one celebrates finitude, the other immortality. "To Autumn" appeals directly to the senses, whereas in "Ode on a Grecian Urn" the urn stands between the speaker and his audience, and between the audience and the ephemeral experience frozen forever on the urn. "Ode on a Grecian Urn" creates a sense of aesthetic distance and self-consciously questions the meaning and value of art in a way that "To Autumn" does not.

AUDIOVISUAL RESOURCES (manual p. 377)

GWENDOLYN BROOKS, *We Real Cool* (p. 98)

Gwendolyn Brooks, who grew up in Chicago and who won the Pulitzer Prize in 1950, has been a deeply respected and influential poet for more than forty years.

In this poem, Brooks sets forth a tableau in a montage of street language. The poetic conventions she uses include alliteration, assonance, and internal rhyme. Students may be so taken with the sounds of the poem that they will be surprised that it has a decidedly somber focal point. How does the rest of the poem prepare us for the final line? Is there a "message" implicit in the poem? If so, how is the message affected by the poem's spare yet stunning language?

Ask students to explore contexts for Gwendolyn Brooks on *LiterActive.*

Play a recording of Gwendolyn Brooks reading "We Real Cool" on *Literature Aloud.*

The repeated "we" sounds the menacing note of the communal pack, its members secure perhaps only when they are together. The truncated syntax reflects both a lack of and a disdain for education, yet the poem celebrates the music of its vernacular, a quality that would be mostly lost were the pronouns to appear at the beginnings of lines.

Brooks's attitude toward this chorus that finds strength in numbers is a measured anger against its self-destructiveness. The absence of "we" in the final line is a silent prophecy of their future, moving us toward an understanding of the poem's theme: death (burial/shovel) at an early age and the corruption of a golden opportunity to spend youth more wisely. The "Golden Shovel" also bespeaks an ironic promise that the events of the last line sadly belie.

POSSIBLE CONNECTION TO ANOTHER SELECTION

Langston Hughes, "Jazzonia" (text p. 400)

AUDIOVISUAL RESOURCES (manual pp. 372–73)

ERIC ORMSBY, *Nose* (p. 98)

This curious poem, stiff and formal in tone, provides a scholarly examination of a part of the body rendered silly by comics like Jimmy Durante and Groucho Marx. The complex nature of the nose is present in Ormsby's assertion that the nose both "snuffles" (line 2), a decidedly ignoble activity, and "recoils / in Roman nobility" (2–3). The poem moves from the role the nose has played in classical sculpture to an exploration of its bulbous qualities in comparing the nose to corms and rhizomes. In the third stanza the poem touches on how the nose divides the face, creates the symmetry we have agreed is beautiful, and plays with the idea of exulting, rising up from the horizontal surfaces of the sleeping face.

Exult comes from the Latin *ex-*, "out," and *salire*, "to leap." Its original meaning in English is to spring or leap up for joy; this definition is now obsolete. The current meaning of *exult* is to rejoice exceedingly, to be elated or glad. You might find it helpful to make two lists of words on the board: words that Ormsby uses to evoke the noble lines of the nose and words he uses to stress its earthy function.

POSSIBLE CONNECTIONS TO OTHER SELECTIONS

Alice Jones, "The Larynx" (text p. 99; question 1, following)
Theodore Roethke, "Root Cellar" (text p. 114)

CONNECTION QUESTION IN TEXT (p. 99) WITH ANSWER

1. Compare the central idea of "Nose" with "The Larynx," the next poem by Alice Jones. Which poem do you prefer? Why?

   Although both Jones and Ormsby examine a familiar part of our anatomy with vivid vocabulary and imagery, Jones focuses more on medical language. Students may take pleasure in the numerous contrasts in Ormsby's poem or prefer the pleasure of phrases like "puzzle box / of gristle" (lines 14–15) in Jones's lines.

ALICE JONES, *The Larynx* (p. 99)

The long breathy sentence of this poem focuses attention on the reader's own larynx when the poem is read aloud. Having a student read the poem to the class could help students see the function the long sentence structure serves. The complex mechanisms involved in creating a single tone are described in both scientific terms and poetic phrases. The scientific language, like "transparent sacs knit / with small vessels into a mesh" (lines 7–8), progresses into the more poetic phrases of the final third of the poem: "they flutter, / bend like birds' wings finding just the right angle to stay / airborne" (23–26).

Ask students how their understanding of the poem would be different if Jones had left out the explicit mention of song. The explication of how the voice works comes to a clear culmination; without it, students might have got lost in reading the poem. Asking which lines provide hints that the poem is leading toward song could help direct discussion.

POSSIBLE CONNECTIONS TO OTHER SELECTIONS

Helen Chasin, "The Word *Plum*" (text p. 209)
Alice Jones, "The Foot" (text p. 222; question 1, following)
Eric Ormsby, "Nose" (text p. 98)

CONNECTION QUESTION IN TEXT (p. 100) WITH ANSWER

1. Compare the diction and the ending in "The Larynx" with those of "The Foot" (p. 222), another poem by Jones.

   Jones takes advantage of rich anatomical vocabulary in both poems. "The Larynx" uses phrases such as "epiglottic flap" (line 1) and "bronchial / fork" (3–4) to introduce an instructive tone before departing for more figurative language. "The Foot" makes a litany of "calcaneus, talus, cuboid, / navicular, cuneiforms, metatarsals, / phalanges" (3–5) to introduce the oblique evolution that produced this miraculous support. While "The Larynx" examines the process by which the larynx produces sounds, "The Foot" takes a journey of discovery through the anatomy of the foot to arrive at "the distal nail" (22), the reminder of our cave-dwelling ancestors and their claws.

LOUIS SIMPSON, *In the Suburbs* (p. 100)

Students may resist this spare poem's desolate presentation of the fate of the American suburbanite. The suburban phenomenon began a dozen years before Simpson published his poem, but the poem is as relevant as ever because Americans continue to move to the suburbs. At least some of your students are likely to be from suburban households. A discussion of the American Dream may be a productive place to begin, perhaps even before students have read the poem. It might also be useful to have them define "middle class," in terms of both yearly income and life-style choices. Once you have established (and perhaps complicated) their sense of the middle class in America, you can work your way into the poem: Where does the speaker of this poem get off equating a middle-class existence with a "waste" (line 2) of life? Does "middleclass" (3) necessarily mean suburban or vice versa? Is the situation as fatalistic as the poet suggests it is? (Half of the poem's six lines contain the phrase "were born to" [lines 2, 3, 5], and the first line is "There's no way out.")

This apparently simple poem is complicated considerably by the final two lines. The poet connects a suburban life-style with one of religious devotion. Because of the negative diction ("no way out" in line 1, "waste" in line 2, for example), the comparison invites a discussion not only of the worst aspects of middle-class existence but of religion, too. But what alternatives are there? Consider, too, the positive aspects of suburbia and religion. What connotations does the poem's last word, "singing," carry? At the end of the discussion you might point out how powerful word choice can be for generating ideas in a simple, spare poem like this one.

Comparisons of this poem to John Ciardi's "Suburban" (text p. 518) are likely to yield observations of a stark difference in tone. Ciardi's poem is funny; Simpson's is quite serious. Yet do the poems share a similar attitude about what is important in life? Does the speaker of "Suburban" lead a typical middle-class life? Does the speaker in "In the Suburbs"? How do the differences in speaker and point of view affect the reader's reception of each poem?

POSSIBLE CONNECTIONS TO OTHER SELECTIONS

John Ciardi, "Suburban" (text p. 518; question 1, following)

Florence Cassen Mayers, "All-American Sestina" (text p. 250)

CONNECTION QUESTION IN TEXT (p. 101) WITH ANSWER

1. Write an essay on suburban life based on this poem and John Ciardi's "Suburban" (p. 518).

   Based on the speakers' attitudes in these two poems, the suburbs are, ostensibly, devoid of life, or repressed. Mrs. Friar, the neighbor in Ciardi's poem, fails, out of an overdeveloped sense of propriety, to value the "organic gold" (line 11) of the dog's "repulsive object" (5). The speaker in Simpson's poem regards suburban, middle-class life as a "waste [of] life" (2). Yet each poem concludes on a hopeful note, stressing the life that is beneath an otherwise sterile-seeming appearance: Simpson's poem concludes with the hopeful last word, "singing" (6), and Ciardi's hints at the "resurrection" (20) into plant life of even the foul "repulsive object."

AUDIOVISUAL RESOURCES (manual p. 381)

JANE YOLEN, *Fat Is Not a Fairy Tale* (p. 101)

In this poem, Yolen challenges the cultural assumption that all heroines should be thin. Her clever reimagining of fairy-tale titles shows how deeply ingrained our ideas are about female bodies. Yolen's tone is mostly humorous, but there is also a note of despair in the poem. The image of the princess "flinging herself down the stairs" in line 7 implies the self-destructive nature of obsessive thinness. Plumpness, on the other hand, is associated with all things good: "the sun, wheels, cookies" (line 21).

Yolen sees the fairy tale she desires as existing far off in the future, "for a teller not yet born, / for a listener not yet conceived, / for a world not yet won" (17–19). Yet she herself writes books for children, often with fairy-tale elements. Your students might be interested to know that she wrote one called *Sleeping Ugly*, a feminist reading of the Sleeping Beauty story. How do your students read the last stanza in light of Yolen's other writing? Why does she defer the writing of these new fairy tales to a future storyteller?

POSSIBLE CONNECTIONS TO OTHER SELECTIONS

Sylvia Plath, "Mirror" (text p. 145)

William Shakespeare, "My mistress' eyes are nothing like the sun" (text p. 243)

A NOTE ON READING TRANSLATIONS

SAPPHO, *Hymn to Aphrodite* with four translations by HENRY T. WHARTON, THOMAS WENTWORTH HIGGINSON, MARY BARNARD, and JIM POWELL (pp. 103–105)

In this appeal to Aphrodite, Sappho asks that the lover who has spurned her be afflicted with yearning and filled with desire for Sappho. All but one of these versions of this poem, Sappho's most famous, try to conform to the original's stanzaic form — a form that has come to be known as the sapphic. A sapphic is three eleven-syllable lines followed by one five-syllable line, or two eleven-syllable lines followed by one sixteen-syllable line. The Greeks used a metrical system based on syllable length rather than stress: Thus a Greek metric foot would consist of a combination of short and long syllables rather than unstressed and stressed syllables. This metric system, called quantitative, is difficult in English, where it is usually replaced — as in these versions — with a more familiar accentual-syllabic approximation.

Despite their common formal aims and their dedication to accurately rendering the original, each of these poems is unique. Both Wharton's and Higginson's versions sound high-flown and a bit archaic — almost biblical — to our ears, and they wouldn't have sounded like ordinary speech to nineteenth-century readers, either. Compare, for instance, Higginson's elaborate cry "weigh me not down with weariness and anguish / O Thou most holy!" (lines 3–4) with Barnard's "Don't, I beg you, / cow my heart with grief!" (3–4). Where Higginson's version is grandiose, full of ornate phrasing, Barnard's is colloquial and sisterly. Barnard stresses the ties between the speaker and the goddess in her closing, where Aphrodite acts as a confidante, whereas in other versions she is cast in a less consoling role: as military ally (in Wharton and Powell), as venerated deity, "Sacred protector" (34) in Higginson. Though Mary Barnard's diction is the most accessible, Jim Powell's version is most faithful to the meter of the classical Greek, and his diction is the most up-to-date: his use of contractions and of italics to add emphasis makes his version sound almost casual.

Studying this poem makes clear how much of translation is interpretation, how much a translator is limited or informed by the context in which he or she is writing. You might want to discuss Higginson's editorial decision to change the pronoun for Sappho's lover from "she" to "he" in the sixth stanza, though the lover was certainly a woman in the original (25–30). The practice of editing poems in such a way was not uncommon in previous centuries — even Shakespeare was not immune. Although students may find this sort of obvious editing troubling, it is interesting to note the extent to which these translators' choice of a style or a level of diction change the poem in equally — or more — profound ways.

PABLO NERUDA, *Verbo* with three translations by BEN BELITT, KRISTIN LINKLATER, and ILAN STAVANS (pp. 106–108)

Since Neruda's poem is in free verse, these translators are concerned primarily with how to replicate Neruda's diction and how to use his line breaks to emphasize the sense of the sentences. Belitt's translation reveals how compact Neruda's writing is — in the first stanza, it takes him several more words than Neruda used to convey the images of the dog and the river. In the second stanza, he uses compounds like "gap-toothed" (line 11) and "blood-letting" (13) to help him convey Neruda's economy of phrase. In focusing on the imagery of the poem, Belitt translates a few specific words in more concrete ways than the other translators. For example, he translates "aspereza" or "asperas" as both "gravel" (8) and "acrid" (21). Both Linklater and Stavans translate these words as "roughness" and "rough." These two translations are quite similar in diction, but they differ significantly in how the translators break the lines in the last stanza. While Linklater follows Neruda's original line breaks, Stavans recuts the lines to reinforce the phrases. The effect is that Stavans emphasizes the effect of the words while Linklater emphasizes the act of wanting itself.

4

Images

Students are already very familiar with imagery through advertising. You may find it an interesting exercise to have students compare ads and poems dealing with similar subject matter: a recruitment commercial and Owen's "Dulce et Decorum Est," for instance. This may prove to be a controversial exercise — be prepared for students' resistance. You may instead (or additionally) want to have students focus on several advertisements or television shows and write a short response to the imagery they find there. This exercise can be beneficial because it will show students they already know how to read imagery, and it will also help sharpen their critical thinking skills by applying analysis in an area they are unused to.

 Ask students to explore *imagery* on *LiterActive* and at **bedfordstmartins.com/ meyerpoetry**.

Still, students can sometimes have trouble with very imagistic poems: such poems may require more effort on the part of students than they suspect. It often may help to ask students to consider why it is that a poet focuses so closely on a given scene or object. Walt Whitman's "Cavalry Crossing a Ford" can seem like just a pretty scene unless one puts it in the context of the Civil War and realizes the possible fate in store for these men — a fate of which Whitman was all too aware from his work in a hospital. If students can be helped to see that poets often use images to emphasize significance or preserve a fleeting moment, they may appreciate the poems more.

Another important point in this chapter is that images need not be exclusively visual. Sally Croft's "Home-Baked Bread" and Cathy Song's "The White Porch" both use a variety of imagery to enhance the sensual themes of the poems. William Blake's "London" is full of auditory images, while Theodore Roethke's "Root Cellar" and Jimmy Santiago Baca's "Green Chile" use smell and taste, respectively. Baca's poem raises an interesting point about the cultural specificity of imagery, particularly when compared with a poem such as Richard Wilbur's "A Late Aubade." Some students may, in fact, be more familiar with the taste of green chile con carne than bleu cheese and wine.

Ask students to research the poets in this chapter at **bedfordstmartins.com/ meyerpoetry**.

You may find that it helps to have students experiment with their own writing in this chapter: they could be asked to write a descriptive paragraph or poem concretely rendering an object, a scene, or an activity. This can serve to emphasize ideas raised in class about the significance of detail.

The paragraph from T. E. Hulme at the end of the chapter can also be useful in this regard, as it highlights some of these ideas. It can also provide a good starting place for discussions either now or later in the class about the distinction between poetry and prose.

WILLIAM CARLOS WILLIAMS, *Poem* (p. 110)

William Carlos Williams was born and lived most of his life in Rutherford, New Jersey, a town near Paterson, the city that provided the title and much of the subject mat-

41

ter of his "modern epic" poem *Paterson*. He had a thriving medical practice for fifty years, delivering more than 2,000 babies and writing his poems, novels, short stories, and essays at night and in the moments he could snatch between patient visits during the day.

This poem is an imaged motion, but the verse has a certain slant music, too. Notice the *t*-sounds that align themselves in the second tercet, the consonance in "hind" (line 8) and "down" (9), the repetitions in "pit of" (10), "empty" (11), and "flowerpot" (12). Sound also helps convey the poem's sense of agility and smoothness.

Students may initially resist this poem because, being apparently simple, it may not conform to their expectations. If this situation arises, or perhaps even if it doesn't, you can use this opportunity to ask the question "What should poetry do or be?" In all likelihood, you can convince skeptics that Williams's poem does what they don't think it does. In any case, it is an opportunity to refine a definition of poetry while exploring its power to appeal to our imagination.

POSSIBLE CONNECTIONS TO OTHER SELECTIONS

Matsuo Bashō, "Under cherry trees" (text p. 254)
Ezra Pound, "In a Station of the Metro" (text p. 129)

AUDIOVISUAL RESOURCES (manual p. 383)

JEANNETTE BARNES, *Battle-Piece* (p. 111)

This poem provides an attentive examination of a battlefield that is now used for picnic grounds. Few who visit, according to the speaker, recognize the tragic history of the war monument. Barnes contrasts the fleeting engagement of picnickers at the peaceful site with the "sharp surprise" (lines 30–31) of the soldiers who died there, using vivid images to reconstruct the past. Barnes's tone could be construed as judgment passed on those who frequent the area without taking the time, as she does, to reconstruct the events that made it monumental. The picnickers "get gone" (2), and the "prize of plastic daisies" (13) is belittled with the acknowledgment that "nobody calls this lazy" (14).

You might ask your students to assign a chronology to the poem; what kinds of transitions does Barnes provide between her discussion of current events and her imagining of the events of 1864 at this site? In the first stanza, the "sting, snap, / grit in clenched teeth" convey a sense of immediacy. Barnes suggests that these horrible images of war are still available for understanding even though the public is indifferent.

Through her use of the words "shock" and "surprise," Barnes also compares the "shock" (18) of her own vision of this battle with the "sharp / surprise" (30–31) of death's scythe arriving, until the fallen soldiers are "astonished by the sky" (33). The past overshadows the present in this poem, and the shock of the soldiers' deaths is more genuine than the plastic daisies used to honor their sacrifices. You might want to ask students how Barnes conveys this primacy of past over present: her techniques include the picknickers' lack of names, while the soldiers are identified as "Clem, Eustace, Willy" (9). Further, the soldiers filch apples and chew spruce gum, while the picnic baskets remain unimagined in this poem.

POSSIBLE CONNECTIONS TO OTHER SELECTIONS

Wilfred Owen, "Dulce et Decorum Est" (text p. 122)
Henry Reed, "Naming of Parts" (text p. 176)

WALT WHITMAN, *Cavalry Crossing a Ford* (p. 112)

Walt Whitman is, with Emily Dickinson, one of the two poetic giants of the American nineteenth century. Born in Huntington, Long Island, he grew up in Brooklyn, leaving school at age eleven for a job as an office boy in a law firm. His poetry grew out of his experiences as a reporter, teacher, laborer, and Civil War nurse. He self-published the first edition of his book — his life's work, really — *Leaves of Grass* in 1855.

Ask students to explore contexts for Walt Whitman on *LiterActive*.

Whitman's descriptive words lend a colorful, paradelike quality to this scene. The flashing arms with their musical clank along with the guidon flags fluttering gaily create an image that suggests liveliness and energy. Yet "Behold" in lines 3 and 4, with its biblical overtones and its arresting sense of absorbing the sight ("be-hold"), is more stately than *look* or *see* and, with its long vowels, is almost ministerial. How does Whitman manage these two apparently contrasting tones?

The speaker in this poem (we can assume Whitman himself) seems to be fairly distant from the scene and possibly slightly elevated to see the entire picture. He scans the troops with a panning gaze that is, nonetheless, able to come in for some close-ups as he looks at the brown-faced men, "each group, each person, a picture" (4).

A productive discussion of this poem might take into account Whitman's lines and how their rhythm contributes to the description in the poem. Does the momentum of the lines have anything to do with the movement of the troops? To what degree is the description "arranged," and to what degree does it mirror the speaker's perception of the scene as it impresses itself on him?

POSSIBLE CONNECTIONS TO OTHER SELECTIONS

Walt Whitman, From *Song of Myself* (text p. 180)

William Carlos Williams, "Poem" (text p. 110)

AUDIOVISUAL RESOURCES (manual pp. 382–83)

DAVID SOLWAY, *Windsurfing* (p. 112)

"Windsurfing" is a poem full of action and motion. The poem begins with "It"; the poet does not pause long enough to even explain exactly what "it" is, but instead allows the motion of the poem to mirror the motion of the windsurfer. The man who is windsurfing is referred to directly only twice; the man and the windsurfer move so forcefully together that the two share a single identity. The intensity of the motion of the windsurfer as it careens across the water is suggested through the carefully chosen verbs ("plunge" [line 20], "snapping" [37], "lashing" [38], "shearing" [39], "lunging" [27], etc.), which reveal the violence, grace, and beauty of the scene.

Because "Windsurfing" conveys one particular scene vividly, you may wish to ask students to compare the water imagery, the fluidity of motion between the man and his windsurfer, and the sensual imagery to those of other poems with similar settings (such as Matthew Arnold's "Dover Beach" [text p. 115]).

POSSIBLE CONNECTIONS TO OTHER SELECTIONS

Elizabeth Bishop, "The Fish" (text p. 32; question 2, following)

Li Ho, "A Beautiful Girl Combs Her Hair" (text p. 56; question 1, following)

CONNECTIONS QUESTIONS IN TEXT (p. 114) WITH ANSWERS

1. Consider the effects of the images in "Windsurfing" and Li Ho's "A Beautiful Girl

Combs Her Hair" (p. 56). In an essay explain how these images elicit the emotional responses they do.

Solway's imagery moves fluidly, one metaphor leading into another with active verbs. Li Ho's imagery is somewhat more startling, juxtaposing images that seem to have less to do with one another but that create an overall impression that ultimately coheres.

2. Compare the descriptions in "Windsurfing" and Elizabeth Bishop's "The Fish" (p. 32). How does each poet appeal to your senses to describe windsurfing and fishing?

The fish in Bishop's poem is not in motion the way the windsurfer is. Bishop's speaker regards the fish, then looks more closely and more closely still, describing details as they impress themselves on her and relying on simile and details to convey an impression of the fish as though she is slowly zooming in with a camera. Solway's windsurfer is moving much more quickly, and he provides us with metaphors that change at rapid-fire pace, mimicking the movement of his subject.

THEODORE ROETHKE, *Root Cellar* (p. 114)

The theme of this brief lyric with its powerful images is stated in the penultimate line: "Nothing would give up life." In the darkness of the root cellar, dank with a perpetual humidity, nothing sleeps; the atmosphere is ideal for engendering life. Normally we associate the underground with death and decay, but here decay is shown to be a source of life.

Ask students to explore contexts for Theodore Roethke on *LiterActive*.

Some of the imagery in this poem is aimed at the olfactory sense, particularly when Roethke summons up the "congress of stinks" (line 6). "Congress" is an especially appropriate word choice here, for it can mean not only a political body but sexual intercourse as well. Coming together, as all these odoriferous bodies do, brings forth life out of putrefaction, mold, slime, and bulbous decay.

The sense of sight, however, also operates in the poem, and we are asked to use our imaginative powers to see shoots "lolling obscenely" (4) or hanging down "like tropical snakes" (5). Even our sense of touch is called on to apprehend the "leaf-mold, manure, lime, piled against slippery planks" (9). Note, too, the consonance of *m*s and *p*s in this carefully constructed line. As ugly and odoriferous as some of these images are, the poem ends on a small cry of victory — "Even the dirt kept breathing a small breath" (11) — and this closing line recapitulates the tone of admiration, even wonder, that Roethke seems to feel as he enters the root cellar.

POSSIBLE CONNECTION TO ANOTHER SELECTION

John Keats, "To Autumn" (text p. 127)

AUDIOVISUAL RESOURCES (manual p. 380)

MATTHEW ARNOLD, *Dover Beach* (p. 115)

Matthew Arnold was born in the English village of Laleham, in the Thames valley. His father was a clergyman and a reformist educator, a powerful personality against whom the young Arnold rebelled in a number of ways, including nearly flunking out of Oxford. After several years as private secretary to a nobleman, in 1851 Arnold became an inspector of schools, a post he held for thirty-five years. For the characteristic jauntiness of his prose style, Walt Whitman once referred to him as "one of the dudes of literature."

Many of us have had the experience of looking out on a landscape and registering its beauty (and possibly its tranquility) and its undercurrent of something lost or awry.

Such is the case for the speaker of "Dover Beach" as he looks out at the shore awash in moonlight. The private moment has its wholeness, for he stands in the "sweetness" of the night air with his beloved. But all the security and peace he could expect to feel are shaken by his concerns beyond the moment and his awareness of the ravages that history brings to bear on the present. We are not fragments of our time alone, the poem seems to say; we are caught in the "turbid ebb and flow / Of human misery" (lines 17–18) that Sophocles heard so long ago.

In the third stanza Arnold goes beyond commenting on the sadness that seems an inevitable part of the human condition, as his thoughts turn to the malaise of his own time. Faith, which once encircled humanity, is now only the overheard roar of its waters withdrawing to the rock-strewn edges of the world. In short, for whatever happens there is no solace, no consolation or reason to hope for any restoration, justice, or change. Humankind is beyond the tragic condition of Sophocles, and in this poem Arnold seems to be tipping the balance toward a modernist existential worldview. The tone of the poem barely improves by the final stanza, for the image Arnold leaves us with is that of "ignorant armies" clashing in the night — the sound and fury once again signifying nothing.

The images of Dover Beach or some other imagined seascape work well to evoke the tone that Arnold is trying to convey. In discussion, or perhaps as a writing topic, you might ask the class to review the poem for natural details and images (in lines 9–14 or most of the third stanza, for example) that suggest the dreary, stark, and ominous portrait Arnold is painting here.

General essays on this poem appear in A. Dwight Culler's *Imaginative Reason: The Poetry of Matthew Arnold* (New Haven: Yale UP, 1966) and James Dickey's *Babel to Byzantium* (New York: Farrar, 1968).

POSSIBLE CONNECTIONS TO OTHER SELECTIONS

Anthony Hecht, "The Dover Bitch" (text p. 529; question 2, following)
Wilfred Owen, "Dulce et Decorum Est" (text p. 122; question 1, following)

CONNECTIONS QUESTIONS IN TEXT (p. 116) WITH ANSWERS

1. Explain how the images in Wilfred Owen's "Dulce et Decorum Est" (p. 122) develop further the ideas and sentiments suggested by Arnold's final line concerning "ignorant armies clash[ing] by night."

   The crippled soldiers in Owen's poem illustrate the final line of Arnold's, their decrepitude confirming what Arnold only hinted at. The gruesome images — "coughing like hags" (line 2), "blood-shod" (6), "choking, drowning" (16) — graphically demonstrate the consequences of those "ignorant armies clash[ing] by night."

2. Contrast Arnold's images with those of Anthony Hecht in his parody "The Dover Bitch" (p. 529). How do Hecht's images create a very different mood from that of "Dover Beach"?

   In a conversational style and lighthearted tone, Hecht's speaker refers to the immediate pleasures of a more bawdy reality while defending the implied listener in Arnold's poem. Hecht's images evoke the daily life of the woman, contrasting sharply with Arnold's interest in the more philosophical issues of his day. Although we cannot assume much about the listener in Arnold's poem (is she even real?), we might presume that she would be far more respectful toward the speaker than Hecht's images imply. Indeed, Hecht intimates that the listener is a "loose woman": "I give her a good time" (26).

AUDIOVISUAL RESOURCES (manual p. 349)

JIMMY SANTIAGO BACA, *Green Chile* (p. 117)

You might begin a discussion of this poem by focusing on the way the differences between the red and green chiles reflect the differences between the speaker and his grandmother. Students may note that in the poem the red chiles function as decoration while the green chiles symbolize passion and tradition. For example, the speaker likes to have "red chile" (line 1) with his "eggs and potatoes for breakfast" (1, 2) and also uses them as decoration throughout his house (3, 4).

The speaker's use of red peppers could be seen as signs of the speaker's assimilation into mainstream United States culture, for the speaker eats a traditional breakfast of "eggs and potatoes" (1–2), whereas the grandmother prepares "green chile con carne / between soft warm leaves of corn tortillas / with beans and rice" (32–34). In contrast to the speaker, who uses red chile peppers as decoration, the grandmother views the green chile peppers as a "gentleman" (19) — more than a decoration, green chile peppers represent "passion" (31) and "ritual" (45). Considering the contrast in the function of the red and green chile peppers, ask your students to discuss what the speaker could be implying about the differences between his generation and his grandmother's generation. Is it possible that the speaker finds himself separated from the passion and intensity of the Hispanic community in which his grandmother lives? How does the image of the chile peppers work to reconcile the life-style of the speaker with the life-style of the grandmother? What could the speaker hope to convey in the sexual description of his grandmother's relationship with the green chile?

Because of the implicit and explicit connections between food and sexuality, you might ask students to further explore those links through other poems in which food and eating are framed in sexual terms — the vegetables in Roethke's "Root Cellar" (text p. 114), for example, or the food metaphors in Sally Croft's "Home-Baked Bread" (text p. 126), and Elaine Magarrell's "The Joy of Cooking" (text p. 153).

POSSIBLE CONNECTIONS TO OTHER SELECTIONS

Elaine Magarrell, "The Joy of Cooking" (text p. 153)
Lisa Parker, "Snapping Beans" (text p. 51)
Theodore Roethke, "Root Cellar" (text p. 114)

AMY LOWELL, *The Pond* (p. 118)

The first three lines of Lowell's poem consist of direct description of the natural world: the leaves, the water, and the sound of the frogs. Following the dash at the end of the third line, she moves into metaphor, comparing the frogs' croaking to "Cracked bell-notes" (line 4). At the end of the poem the man-made object intrudes on the natural scene. However, the human creation is broken, and this brokenness is the reason it is able to mimic the animal sound. You might ask your students why Lowell introduces the metaphor in the last line. Do they read it as a comment on the act of writing poems?

POSSIBLE CONNECTIONS TO OTHER SELECTIONS

Ezra Pound, "In a Station of the Metro" (text p. 129)
William Carlos Williams, "The Red Wheelbarrow" (text p. 273)

H. D. [HILDA DOOLITTLE], *Heat* (p. 118)

Hilda Doolittle was born in Bethlehem, Pennsylvania, and educated at private schools in Philadelphia. In 1911 she moved to London, where she married English poet Richard Aldington. Although an American poet and novelist, H. D. was involved with the Bloomsbury group for a time and was an important figure in the imagist movement as well. Ezra Pound, who encouraged her poetic aspirations and submitted her work to *Poetry* magazine under the name "H. D., Imagiste," was probably the most influential of a group of friends that included T. S. Eliot, William Carlos Williams, and D. H. Lawrence. At the request of the poet, Sigmund Freud agreed to accept her as a subject of study in 1933, and H. D.'s later poems, such as "The Walls Do Not Fall" (1944), are markedly influenced by her own and her mentor's interests in psychoanalysis, religion, and mythology.

One way to open up discussion is to examine the nature of the heat, the wind, and the fruit as they are described in the poem. In what sense are these things abstract? What qualities are associated with each? Do students all have the same impression of the type of heat the speaker is describing? Heat becomes a living force in these lines, capable of occupying space and offering resistance to seemingly denser objects: "Fruit cannot drop / through this thick air —" (lines 4–5). The ripeness and fullness implied in the images of the fruit in the second stanza are somewhat threatened by the relentless heat. We can almost feel the fruit shriveling in response, deprived of oxygen, unable to participate in the natural cycle that will make them fall to the ground. A heat that is able to blunt the points of pears and round grapes (8–9) acquires the power of an elemental force.

The image of the cutting plow in lines 10 through 13 builds on the personification of the wind in the first line. The wind becomes a creative agent, a matching elemental force called up to cut through the heat and restore order in the natural world. However, the plow is also a domestic tool at the service of human beings. The poet's words conjure and direct the wind. By framing the poem as an invocation, the poet calls attention to her own ability to control this natural scene.

POSSIBLE CONNECTIONS TO OTHER SELECTIONS

Ezra Pound, "In a Station of the Metro" (text p. 129)
William Carlos Williams, "Poem" (text p. 110)

AUDIOVISUAL RESOURCES (manual p. 374)

SHEILA WINGFIELD, *A Bird* (p. 119)

Much of the mystery in this poem resides in the ambiguous "its" of the last line. The speaker comes upon a dead bird and observes that "The wind / Was fluttering its wings" (lines 3–4). Does the wind reanimate the bird, giving it the movement that it can no longer generate? Or does the wind, itself moving, take up the bird's flight? What are the consequences of these two readings?

You might ask your students why they think Wingfield begins the poem with "Unexplained" (1). Who does she expect to do the explaining? Is it a human task to make sense of nature, or is it necessary for some higher power to comprehend the purpose of beings in the world?

POSSIBLE CONNECTIONS TO OTHER SELECTIONS

Elizabeth Bishop, "The Fish" (text p. 32)
Phillis Levin, "End of April" (text p. 54)

MARY ROBINSON, *London's Summer Morning* (p. 119)

This poem, set in eighteenth-century London, refers to the act of listening to "the busy sounds / of summer's morning" (lines 1–2). Aural details convey the sounds of the street: shouting "chimney-boy" (4), rattling "milk-pail," "tinkling bell" (7), and "the din of hackney-coaches" (10). Robinson moves on to visual details, listing the "neat girl" (19) walking with a hat box, the sunlight "on the glitt'ring pane" (21), and "pastry dainties" (27). The sounds have roused the speaker, who now watches the street. The opening line invites the reader to acknowledge the familiarity of these sights and sounds, then pulls the focus from the street to the bedroom, where "the poor poet wakes from busy dreams" (41) to write the poem, and concludes with an image of the poet in the act of writing.

When your students try to work on their own listings of the morning's events, draw their attention to the use of aural and visual detail; Robinson's poem does not get tangled in narrative but focuses on sight and sound. What are some of the ways in which other senses could enter this litany? As a preparatory writing exercise, you might want to ask your students to move through the poem, expanding it to include other details such as the taste of the vegetables the vendors offer, the smells of the horses pulling the hackney coaches, and the weight of the "busy mop" (18) in the hands of the housemaid.

POSSIBLE CONNECTIONS TO OTHER SELECTIONS

William Blake, "London" (text p. 121; question 1, following)
Ezra Pound, "In a Station of the Metro" (text p. 129)
William Wordsworth, "London, 1802" (text p. 148)

CONNECTION QUESTION IN TEXT (p. 120) WITH ANSWER

1. How does Robinson's description of London differ from William Blake's "London," the next poem? What would you say is the essential difference in purpose between the two poems?

   Blake opens his vision of London with "I wander" (1); Robinson constructs her poem around the sounds and visions available through a bedroom window. Robinson's poem is a cheerful list of images accompanied by the music of a busy street on a summer morning, while Blake sets his poem in "midnight streets" (13). Blake's vision of London is essentially a negative view of a corrupt city; Robinson's vision is positive and innocent of Blake's bleak account.

WILLIAM BLAKE, *London* (p. 121)

William Blake's only formal schooling was in art, and he learned engraving as an apprentice to a prominent London engraver. After his seven years' service, Blake made his living as a printer and engraver, writing poetry on the side. The private mythology that came to dominate his poems was worked out in almost total obscurity: at the time of his death Blake had acquired some notice for his art but almost none for his writing. Ask students to explore contexts for William Blake on *LiterActive*.

This poem may seem pessimistic, but is it entirely so? If students would go so far as to call it "apocalyptic," does their knowledge of history help them to discern where the speaker's attitude comes from? The use of "chartered" (line 1) to describe streets and the River Thames makes all of the boundaries in the poem seem unnatural and rigid; the cries heard are cries of pain and sadness. Like the rigidities of the chartered streets, the legislation of the "mind-forged manacles" (8) does nothing to promote civil liberty and happiness. Blake implies here that the "manacles" of religion and government that should protect individuals fail miserably to ensure good lives. Children are sold into near slavery as chimney sweeps, their own dark and stunted faces casting a pall (appall) on the benevolent state and the Christian tradition. Soldiers sent off to war die or kill other soldiers. Sexual restrictions invite prostitution and thus promote disease, which may, in turn, afflict marriages and resulting births. Social regulations ("manacles") thus induce societal ills.

The image of the soldier dying for the state, for example (11–12), is described in a condensed and effective manner that suggests not only his lucklessness (or helplessness) but also the indifference of a government removed from the individual by class ("Palace" [12]), its insularity ("walls" [12]), and the imperturbable security of law.

Comparison of the two versions of the final stanza provides an excellent writing topic. Notice, though, how much more endemic the societal failings and wrongdoings appear in the second (revised) version. Instead of "midnight harlot's curse," the phrase becomes the "midnight streets" (13) (evil as pervasive) and "the youthful Harlot's curse" (14) (a blighting of innocence at an early age). By reversing "marriage hearse" and "infant's tear," Blake suggests not a mere (and societally sanctioned) cause-effect relation between marriage and the birth of afflicted infants but the presence of syphilis in even the youngest members of society and the conditions that would sustain its presence.

How do the urban ills of contemporary society compare with those of Blake's time? It might be an interesting exercise to ask students to write a poem about contemporary social ills, either urban or rural, in Blake's style. What has changed?

POSSIBLE CONNECTIONS TO OTHER SELECTIONS

Claribel Alegría, "I Am Mirror" (text p. 571)
George Eliot, "In a London Drawingroom" (text p. 598)

AUDIOVISUAL RESOURCES (manual p. 372)

WILFRED OWEN, *Dulce et Decorum Est* (p. 122)

This poem is an argument against war, not against a country. So often war is an act surrounded by image-making words of glory and honor and flanked by the "nobility" of slogan sentiments. Here Owen has presented the actuality of battle and death by a particularly dehumanizing and agonizing weapon: poison gas. He wants his audience to know a little more exactly what war entails.

The famous indictment of war centers on the experiences and emotions of a disillusioned World War I soldier. It might be necessary to provide a little background about the nature of warfare during "the war to end all wars." The ground war was fought mostly in trenches, where not only did close and relentless combat last much longer than anyone initially expected, but the threat of illness from decomposing bodies and diseases that bred in the mud of the trenches was very real. You are likely to push some buttons by doing so, but you may want to try to discuss the final lines first.

Ask students to explore contexts for Wilfred Owen on *LiterActive*.

Owen seems to want to collar and talk to each reader directly. After the vividness of his description, some of which is in the present tense, Owen's attitude toward the "lie" (line 28) that his "friend" (26) might tell is disdainful, and understandably so.

You may want to ask students where the notion that it is noble to fight for one's country comes from. Under what circumstances does such a notion break down? Is war still glamorized by way of songs, films, and poetry?

Matthew Arnold, "Dover Beach" (text p. 115)

Sharon Olds, "Rite of Passage" (text p. 279)

AUDIOVISUAL RESOURCES (manual p. 379)

PATRICIA SMITH, *What It's Like to Be a Black Girl (for Those of You Who Aren't)* (p. 123)

Using vernacular with a matter-of-fact tone, this poem defines race and gender in very personal terms, examining, simultaneously, how the speaker's race shapes her sexuality and how her gender and sexuality affect her understanding of her race. The poem uses a second-person perspective to establish an immediate connection with the reader; it conveys a sense that "you're not finished" (line 2). There are forces that make "something, / everything, wrong" (3–4), your own physical appearance is insufficient, and blue food coloring and "a bleached / white mophead" (6–7) would be preferable to your own eyes and hair. This is also a coming-of-age poem, moving from "being 9 years old" (1) to "finally having a man reach out for you" (18). Sexuality, physicality, athleticism, and profanity are all present and fiercely accounted for. The final image, caving in around a man's fingers, presents a good opportunity for discussion: Is the speaker responding to the man's touch in relief or in defeat? Ask students to defend their opinion with reference to other lines in the poem.

You might want to ask students to attempt a freewriting exercise that defines them in terms of their gender and ethnicity. What's it like being a White Boy? An Asian Girl? How do gender and ethnicity work to define us all?

POSSIBLE CONNECTIONS TO OTHER SELECTIONS

Margaret Atwood, "you fit into me" (text p. 135)

Gwendolyn Brooks, "We Real Cool" (text p. 98)

CHARLES SIMIC, *To the One Upstairs* (p. 123)

You might begin by having your students compare the opening of this poem with the beginning of a traditional prayer. Simic's address is not reverent as a prayer would be but rather mocks a reverence for authority, especially in the workplace. In this poem, the maker of the world has the tools of the modern office to assist with his task. Ask your class whether the images of the ink and staples trivialize creation. How much does placing the "One Upstairs" in this context diminish his power? What do they make of the speaker's apparent contempt for the "Boss of all bosses of the universe" (line 1)?

The speaker is careful to distance himself from the supplicants, whom he characterizes as "begging" (16) and "Sputtering" (17). By contrast, his appeal to the higher power doesn't plead but demand. He even chastises the listener for his indifference to prayers: "Stop pretending you're too busy to notice" (20). Yet in the final stanza he changes his approach and focuses on his own creative act. Since the "One Upstairs" is ignorant of his own name, the speaker invents some for him. The power to make things up is solely in the speaker's hands and the addressee can only choose to accept or to reject the names offered. The last line belies the defiant tone of the beginning of the poem. In spite of any misgivings, the speaker has an urgent need to "scribble" (25) a message to the "One Upstairs." That he does so "in the dark" (25) reveals his ultimate powerlessness.

Stephen Crane, "A Man Said to the Universe" (text p. 164)

Emily Dickinson, "I know that He exists" (text p. 344; question 1, following)

John Donne, "Death Be Not Proud" (text p. 290)

Mark Jarman, "Unholy Sonnet" (text p. 246)

CONNECTION QUESTION IN TEXT (p. 124) WITH ANSWER

1. Discuss the themes in Simic's poem and in Emily Dickinson's "I know that He exists" (p. 344).

   Simic's poem is cynical about the function of God. Like some workplace supervisors, he's there and he's in charge, but he doesn't seem to be actually doing much. This perceived inefficacy leads to Simic's moral question to God: "Doesn't it give you the creeps" (line 15) to hear people's fervent but unanswered prayers? In spite of his concerns, Simic's last lines reaffirm his faith in the existence, at least, of a God, whose presence he keeps attempting to grasp by naming it.

   Dickinson's poem also mixes belief in God with uncertainty about his attributes. Like Simic, she comments on his silence and invisibility, but instead of imagining that absence covers powerlessness, she sees God's hiding as necessary to salvation. It separates him from our "gross eyes" (line 4) so that he can surprise us in the "fond Ambush" (6) of grace. However, Dickinson retains some doubt about the remove at which God stands. The stakes of this game, she notes, are high, and the nearness of death can make it "Look too expensive!" (14).

RAINER MARIA RILKE, *The Panther* (p. 124)

Born in Austria-Hungary (now the Czech Republic), Rainer Maria Rilke was educated in Catholic schools but later rebelled against his faith. He migrated to Munich after studying philosophy at Prague. In 1909 he went to Paris, a gathering place for many artists at the time. Rilke's images have been described as having classical plasticity: precise, chiseled, and visual. His mixture of squalor and art may have come from the time he spent in Paris.

The form and content of "The Panther" unite to indicate increasing confinement. In each of the stanzas, Rilke moves from exterior to interior and from action to inaction, leaving the reader with something more finite to consider each time — paralleling the confinement experienced by the panther. The first line of the first stanza refers to the world beyond the bars: by the end of the stanza, there are only "a thousand bars; and behind the bars, no world" (line 4). In the first line of the second stanza, the panther is moving in "cramped circles, over and over" (5); at the end of the stanza, we find "a mighty will [which] stands paralyzed" (8). The third stanza traces the path of an image as it penetrates "the curtain of the pupils" (9) until it "plunges into the heart and is gone" (12). This final image is so far within the panther that it remains unidentifiable. As a result, like the panther, we are forced by the form of the poem into a stillness and a recognition of our inability to control the situation. In a sense, Rilke is dropping the curtain over our own pupils.

POSSIBLE CONNECTION TO ANOTHER SELECTION

Emily Dickinson, "A Bird came down the Walk —" (text p. 187; question 1, following)

CONNECTION QUESTION IN TEXT (p. 125) WITH ANSWER

1. Write an essay explaining how a sense of movement is achieved by the images and rhythms in this poem and in Dickinson's "A Bird came down the Walk —" (p. 187).

Dickinson's bird moves with jerky movements, reflected in her brief, restless lines, until the end of the poem when the bird's movements are compared to rowing. Rilke's panther is at once more graceful and more cramped. His "ritual dance around a center / in which a mighty will stands paralyzed" (lines 7–8) is almost hypnotic so that we are especially surprised by the unexplained rushing image in the final stanza.

AUDIOVISUAL RESOURCES (manual p. 380)

JANE KENYON, *The Blue Bowl* (p. 125)

The speaker of this poem recounts how she and someone else (presumably a husband or lover) buried their dead cat the day before the poem is written. The burial is ritualistic; the speaker compares herself and her fellow undertaker to "primitives." Though they go about the burial rather methodically, the event has affected them deeply. They are "silent" (line 12) the rest of the day and seemingly empty: "we worked, / ate, stared, and slept" (12–13).

Play a recording of Donald Hall reading "The Blue Bowl" on *Literature Aloud.*

The title of this poem provides its most challenging point of interpretation. In addition to asking about the blueness of the bowl, ask students why the title focuses on the seemingly inconsequential bowl at all; why not entitle the poem "The Burial"? The bowl's blueness calls attention to other colors in the poem that may have otherwise been overlooked: the cat's "long red fur" (7) and the incongruous "white feathers / between his toes" (7–8). There is something *off*, something unsettling about the entire poem. Note how the first line, read alone, raises fundamental questions about meaning: Do primitives bury cats with bowls? The speaker has difficulty communicating; she interrupts her description ("long, not to say aquiline, nose" [9]) in the same way that the robin or the neighbor of the final simile say "the wrong thing" (17).

Burial is meant to be a neat, finalizing procedure, but death is a messy business, both physically and emotionally. Nothing about it can be satisfying. In discussing the psychological implications of burial and comparing this poem to John Updike's "Dog's Death" (text p. 24), students may be reluctant to leap over the next level of taboo into a comparison of human burial to pet burial. How might the nature of "The Blue Bowl" have changed if the speaker were burying a person rather than a pet? How might it have remained the same?

POSSIBLE CONNECTIONS TO OTHER SELECTIONS

Rachel Hadas, "The Red Hat" (text p. 225)
John Updike, "Dog's Death" (text p. 24; question 1, following)

CONNECTION QUESTION IN TEXT (p. 126) WITH ANSWER

1. Write an essay comparing the death of this cat with the death of the dog in Updike's "Dog's Death" (p. 24). Which poem draws a more powerful response from you? Explain why.

   One difference is that the cat of Kenyon's poem is never described as it was when it was alive. We do not see it die, whereas we witness the death of the dog in Updike's poem firsthand. Kenyon's speaker states that "There are sorrows keener than these" (line 11) as she buries the cat, but Updike's speaker shows us the grief of the family. It is likely that students will find Kenyon's poem unsettling and will find Updike's poem viscerally upsetting or pathetic.

AUDIOVISUAL RESOURCES (manual p. 377)

SALLY CROFT, *Home-Baked Bread* (p. 126)

This poem describes a seduction by way of cooking, cleverly departing from the title of the source of the epigraph, *The Joy of Cooking*, into another popular text from the 1970s, *The Joy of Sex*. The great-aunt of the second stanza is an interesting inroad. Great-aunts are generally associated more with cooking than with seduction; is this one figured into the poem as a contrast to the amorous speaker, or does she reinforce the idea that all women have their "cunning triumphs" (line 2), which are sometimes hidden or only suggested?

"Cunning triumphs," appearing amid the measured dryness of a cookbook text, certainly has the potential to arrest someone's poetic sensibilities. *Cunning* seems more appropriately applied to the feats of Odysseus than to the food in *The Joy of Cooking*. At any rate, "cunning triumphs" rises, as it were, beyond the limits of technical discourse. It shines, it sparkles, it almost titillates the kitchen soul.

"Insinuation" (3), too, is a pivotal word in the poem. It looks back on the questioning attitude of the opening lines and points toward the wily, winding seductiveness of what will follow.

At first we hear the speaker reading and questioning the cookbook. Then we hear the speaker transformed into a new identity — of Lady Who Works Cunning Triumphs. She is addressing someone she would charm and seduce.

The poem achieves a unity through the repetition of certain images, such as the room that recalls the great-aunt's bedroom as well as the other reiterated images, of honey, sweet seductiveness, warmth, and open air.

Possible Connections to Other Selections

Elaine Magarrell, "The Joy of Cooking" (text p. 153)
Cathy Song, "The White Porch" (text p. 129)

JOHN KEATS, *To Autumn* (p. 127)

"To Autumn" was the last major lyric Keats wrote. But despite its tone and imagery, particularly in the last stanza, there is no indication that Keats had an exact foreknowledge of his impending death.

Personification is a major device in this poem. In stanza 1, which suggests the early part of the day, autumn is the "bosom-friend" (line 2) of the sun and a ripener of growing things. In stanza 2, which has a midday cast, autumn is a storekeeper and a harvester or gleaner. In the final stanza, which reflects "the soft-dying day" (25), the image of autumn is less directly named, but the idea of the contemplative is suggested. One sees things ripening in the opening stanza; in stanza 2, autumn feels the wind and drowses in the "fume" (17) of poppies; in the final stanza, autumn and the reader both are invited to listen to the special music of the close of the day and of the year.

Ask students to explore contexts for John Keats on *LiterActive*.

In his brief poetic career, Keats seems to have grown into a more serene acceptance of death, preferring the organic ebb and flow of life over the cool, unchanging fixity of the artifact.

Possible Connections to Other Selections

Robert Frost, "After Apple-Picking" (text p. 364; question 1, following)
John Keats, "Ode on a Grecian Urn" (text p. 96)
Theodore Roethke, "Root Cellar" (text p. 114; question 2, following)

1. Compare this poem's tone and its perspective on death with those of Robert Frost's "After Apple-Picking" (p. 364).

   More metaphoric, perhaps, than literal, the apple picker's description of the recent harvest in "After Apple-Picking" could be a summary of his life. Already drowsy, he allows the time of day and the season to ease him into a reverie. The harvest he contemplates is a personal one — the apples he picked or let fall. This musing might occasion more brooding than is found in "To Autumn," in which the poet surveys more impersonally the season's reign and the year's end. "To Autumn" captures the last moments before winter, preserving them in all their ripeness and sensuality. Although both poems imply that death is near, Keats's speaker is far less willing to yield to it before appreciating the last moments of life as fully as he can.

2. Write an essay comparing the significance of this poem's images of "mellow fruit-fulness" (line 1) with that of the images of ripeness in Theodore Roethke's "Root Cellar" (text p. 114). Explain how the images in each poem lead to very different feelings about the same phenomenon.

   The images in "To Autumn" provide a sharp contrast to those in "Root Cellar." The root cellar is "a congress of stinks" (line 6), a place where ripeness is dank and almost obscene. Keats's images of fruitfulness are, in his word, "mellow" (1). One reason for the difference could be that Keats describes the end of a harvest, the cessation of growth, whereas Roethke traces the undying process that will begin growth all over again.

KATE CLANCHY, *Spell* (p. 128)

Though Clanchy's poem does not have a regular rhyme pattern, the frequent internal rhymes and slant rhymes contribute to the incantatory nature of the poem. Her spell collapses several distinctions: between lovers, between seer and seen, between reader and writer, and between the particular "you" (line 1) reading and the "wayward mass" (8) of readers who will find the poem. If this undifferentiation is the magic that the poem works, then what is its outcome? What kind of creation does Clanchy achieve by confusing her own role in its making?

In "Spell," Clanchy also identifies the body with a book. The lover's chest muscles "arch as great books part" (5); the speaker's own hair is like "silk-thread bookmarks" (9); and the skin on her face is like "tissue leaves" (11). You might have your students discuss clichés that compare people with books: being able to read someone like a book or having a life like an open book. How do Clanchy's figures move away from these standard ways of formulating the comparison? The clichés assume that being like a book means being entirely knowable. Would Clanchy agree?

POSSIBLE CONNECTION TO ANOTHER SELECTION

Emily Dickinson, "There is no Frigate like a Book" (text p. 330; question 1, following)

CONNECTION QUESTION IN TEXT (p. 129) WITH ANSWER

1. Compare "Spell" and Dickinson's "There is no Frigate like a Book" (p. 330) on the act of reading. Which poem do you think is more demanding on the reader? Explain why.

   Clanchy uses the figure of the book to collapse the distance between two people, making the addressed lover both reader and writer and making herself both writer and subject. Moreover, the figures in the poem begin to merge with the book itself, their bodies imitating its physical features. Dickinson sees the book as a means not to turn inward but rather to travel outward in the world. The comparison of a book to a ship and to a horse reveals its purpose in crossing geographical distances and encountering people and ideas one would never meet in everyday life. Moreover, Dickinson believes that books are democratizing. No matter how poor, people can travel in this "Chariot / That bears the Human soul" (lines 7–8). Both poems suggest the way that reading takes people beyond narrow subjectivity, either by identifying completely with another person or by surpassing the limits of individual experience. Clanchy's poem requires the reader to make sense of these confusions of consciousness while Dickinson's poem issues an ethical challenge to expand the soul through reading.

EZRA POUND, *In a Station of the Metro* (p. 129)

Ezra Pound was born in Idaho and grew up in Philadelphia, eventually attending the University of Pennsylvania. There he befriended William Carlos Williams and H. D. (Hilda Doolittle) and concentrated on his image as a poet (affecting capes, canes, and rakish hats) as well as on his studies. He later attended Hamilton College and returned to UPenn for graduate work in languages, completing a master of arts in 1906. Two years later he moved to London, beginning a lifelong voluntary exile during which he worked as secretary to William Butler Yeats; began and abandoned numerous literary movements; started his "epic including history," *The Cantos*; lived in Paris, Venice, and Rapallo (Italy); furthered the literary careers of Ernest Hemingway, James Joyce, T. S. Eliot, Robert Frost, and Marianne Moore, among others; broadcast for Benito Mussolini and ended up under arrest for treason. Declared insane at his trial, Pound spent twelve years in a Washington, D.C., hospital. Freed through the efforts of his writer friends, Pound spent the rest of his life in Italy. Despite his glaring shortcomings, Pound is seen by many as the most technically accomplished poet and one of the most gifted critics of his generation.

Pound helped articulate the ideas of imagism, one of his early efforts to "make it new." Although the halves of this poem work as if the second half were describing the first, each of the two lines possesses its own integrity as well as a capacity to make us see those faces.

POSSIBLE CONNECTION TO ANOTHER SELECTION

Matsuo Bashō, "Under cherry trees" (text p. 254)

AUDIOVISUAL RESOURCES (manual p. 380)

CATHY SONG, *The White Porch* (p. 129)

The speaker in this poem establishes a conversation with her listener in the first stanza: "your" (line 10), "think" (12). She projects her listener into the future even as she captures the present moment through the description of her newly washed hair. The second stanza moves the conversation toward sexual innuendo, comparing the speaker's arousal to a flower, a flock of birds, and a sponge cake with peaches. Ask students to determine how these images give us a sense of what the speaker is like. What is her relationship to the listener? The final stanza returns us to the initial image of hair, but whereas the first stanza moves toward the future, the third plunges us back into the past. Students will enjoy comparing the images describing the mother to those describing the lover in the final lines. Like the rope ladder (an allusion to Rapunzel?), the poem is column-shaped, inviting its listener into the experience of reading it as it talks about a sexual relationship.

In a writing assignment, ask students to examine the concrete nouns and participial verbs in the poem. How do they evoke the speaker's message? How do images of domestic life summon the speaker's more "philosophical" side?

POSSIBLE CONNECTIONS TO OTHER SELECTIONS

Sally Croft, "Home-Baked Bread" (text p. 126; question 1, following)
Li Ho, "A Beautiful Girl Combs Her Hair" (text p. 56)

CONNECTION QUESTION IN TEXT (p. 131) WITH ANSWER

1. Compare the images used to describe the speaker's "slow arousal" (line 22) in this poem with Sally Croft's images in "Home-Baked Bread" (p. 126). What similarities do you see? What makes each description so effective?

    Croft also uses domestic images to talk about sexual intimacy and poetry writing. Both "Home-Baked Bread" and "The White Porch" invite the listener into the experience, promising food and warmth; each poem, for example, uses peaches to seduce its listener. The imagery is full of anticipation and ripeness. There is an element of danger, too, in each poem, enticing the audiences into delicious but forbidden experiences.

PERSPECTIVE

T. E. HULME, *On the Differences between Poetry and Prose* (p. 131)

As a class exercise, you might ask students to bring in examples of prose that contradict Hulme's claims. Students might want to bring in examples of prose they read elsewhere. In another writing assignment, you might ask students to flesh out Hulme's theory with especially vivid examples of poems that "hand over sensations bodily."

5

Figures of Speech

The material in this chapter can build on issues raised in the previous two: Considerations of word choice, tone, and images both influence and reflect choices in figurative speech. You might have your students draw these connections explicitly by having them select a poem from this chapter and analyze it both in terms of its figurative language and also in terms of concepts discussed earlier. Doing so will help them understand how various elements make up the poem's total effect.

Ask students to explore the poetic elements in this chapter on *LiterActive* and at **bedfordstmartins.com/meyerpoetry**.

Another possible exercise for this chapter would be to have students think about and list instances of figurative language used in their everyday speech, working either alone or in small groups. You might have them do this at the beginning of the chapter (after a brief discussion of figurative language) and again at the end: The difference in the number of instances they derive should be encouraging.

It is likely that students are already aware of the difference between simile and metaphor; the distinction will become important to them only if they can understand that it has some significance. Similes tend to call attention to the comparison itself, as in Margaret Atwood's "you fit into me" or William Wordsworth's "London, 1802": The comparison becomes an important feature of the poems, foregrounding the "you and me" in Atwood's case, or John Milton in Wordsworth's. Conversely, metaphors tend to focus on the *content* of the comparison, shifting the focus from the separate entities being compared to the nature of those entities, as in Dickinson's "Presentiment — is that long Shadow — on the lawn — ."

Ask students to research the poets in this chapter at **bedfordstmartins.com/meyerpoetry**.

Metonymy and synecdoche can be difficult for students to grasp; for some reason, they find it more difficult to remember "metonymy" than "metaphor." You might find it useful to point out (or to have students point out) uses of metonymy in everyday language: "The White House confirms" or "University A beat University B" or "The Chancellor's office responded." This can help students get a grasp of the concepts involved and defuse their anticipation of being unable to understand these terms.

Paradox and oxymoron can be useful tools to encourage students' critical thinking skills. Puzzling out paradoxes and explaining oxymorons often require students to think in unusual ways. Poems that lend themselves to this are Donne's "Batter My Heart" and "Death Be Not Proud," as well as nearly any poem by Emily Dickinson.

WILLIAM SHAKESPEARE, *From* Macbeth *(Act V, Scene v)* (p. 134)

After asking students to identify each of the things to which Shakespeare's Macbeth compares life, and to consider how life is like each of them, have them decide which of these figures of speech is the most effective. Does one overpower the others, or does the overall effect depend on the conjunction of all of them?

Ask students to explore contexts for William Shakespeare on *LiterActive*.

Have students recall other things to which they have heard life compared. Are these common images examples of strong figurative language or merely clichés? For example, "Life is a bed of roses" conveys the idea that life is easy and beautiful, but it is such a well-worn phrase that it now lacks the impact it might once have had. As a writing assignment, have students come up with their own similes and metaphors and explain how life is like the image they have created.

See Robert Frost's " 'Out, Out —' " (text p. 368) for one example of how a modern poet has made use of Shakespeare's famous passage. Students familiar with William Faulkner's *The Sound and the Fury* might be able to comment on how another twentieth-century writer has used the reprinted passage from *Macbeth*.

POSSIBLE CONNECTION TO ANOTHER SELECTION

Robert Frost, " 'Out, Out —' " (text p. 368)

AUDIOVISUAL RESOURCES (manual p. 380–81)

MARGARET ATWOOD, *you fit into me* (p. 135)

Students may need help with the allusions called up by the first two lines of this poem: the hook and eye that fasten a door shut; the buttonhook used to fasten women's shoes in the early twentieth century. You might ask students to compose a poem in which a figure of speech produces first pleasant associations and later unpleasant or, as in Atwood's poem, lurid ones. You might also ask the class in a brief writing assignment to determine how the simile and its expansion work. Would the poem be as successful, for example, if "eye" were not a part of the human anatomy?

POSSIBLE CONNECTION TO ANOTHER SELECTION

Emily Dickinson, "Wild Nights — Wild Nights!" (text p. 318)

AUDIOVISUAL RESOURCES (manual p. 371–72)

EMILY DICKINSON, *Presentiment — is that long Shadow — on the lawn —* (p. 136)

As noted in the text, Dickinson uses richly connotative words such as *shadow* and *darkness* to express in a few words the sense of fear and danger inherent in her "Presentiment." You might explore with your students other connotations of the word *presentiment*. Are all premonitions warnings about negative occurrences? Have any of your students had premonitions about good things? What kinds of words might one want to use in order to express — economically — the possibility of pleasant surprise? You could have students, individually or in groups, try to identify specific words and then a controlling metaphor that would be appropriate to express this alternative kind of surprise.

Ask students to explore contexts for Emily Dickinson on *LiterActive*.

POSSIBLE CONNECTION TO ANOTHER SELECTION

Emily Dickinson, "Success is counted sweetest" (text p. 312)

ANNE BRADSTREET, *The Author to Her Book* (p. 137)

This speaker regards her collection of poetry as though it were her child, considering both its penchant for brattiness and her mother's affection for it. Ask students to trace the extended metaphor in this poem, pointing out the way that diction influences tone. What, for example, do the words *ill-formed* and *feeble* (line 1) tell us about the speaker's attitude toward her work? Does this attitude change at all as the poem progresses? Although her initial attitude toward the book is disdain, the speaker's reluctance to part with her creation in the final lines could be the result of both modesty and affection.

Sound patterns and meter are also good topics for discussion of this poem. The meter is iambic pentameter, but there are variations in rhythm that are linked to meaning. Line 15 presents the problem of metrical arrangement, providing an example in line 16: "Yet still thou run'st more hobbling than is meet."

In a writing assignment, you might ask students to discuss the way this poem talks about the writing process. How does Bradstreet suggest a book is written?

POSSIBLE CONNECTIONS TO OTHER SELECTIONS

William Shakespeare, "Not marble, nor the gilded monuments" (text p. 491)
Ronald Wallace, "Building an Outhouse" (text p. 152)

ROSARIO CASTELLANOS, *Chess* (p. 138)

You might begin by asking students what associations they have with the game of chess. Traditionally, chess is thought of as an intellectual game — a game that relies on intricate moves and countermoves, with players anticipating one another's strategies as they plan their own. Considering the emphasis on strategy, chess could be called a "mind game" that two people agree to play. Thus, in lines 2 and 3, the reader learns that in adding chess as "one more tie / to the many that already bound . . ." the players have very deliberately set up and engaged in the "mind game" of chess. Encourage students to notice the confrontational terms the poet uses to describe the competition — the board was "between" the players, they "divided" the pieces, they "swore to respect" the rules, and the "match" began (lines 5–9).

Ask students to discuss why two people might choose to add another "tie" (2) to a relationship, for although there are hints in the first stanza that what's been set up is more than a simple chess game, the final stanza leaves little doubt about the metaphoric scope of the contest. By using the hyperbolic "centuries" in line 10, the poet intensifies the sense that the players have reached a stalemate. That they are meditating "ferociously" (11) for a way to deal "the one last blow" (12) that will "annihilate the other one forever" (13) underscores the hostile nature of the contest.

While the features of the competition revealed in the second and third stanza will probably provide students with much to discuss, perhaps the most interesting feature of this poem occurs in the first stanza, where the speaker characterizes the relationship between the players with these words: "Because we were friends and sometimes loved each other" (1). There are no clues in the poem as to the gender of either player or to the nature of the "love" referred to in the opening line. Obviously, there is already some relationship between the players, since they decided to "add one more tie / to the many that already bound [them]" (2-3). Likewise, the plural word "games" implies that other interactions have taken place or exist as possibilities. While it may prove interesting for students to debate their own perceptions of the gender of the players in this poem, it may be helpful at some point to acknowledge that the real key is not the gender of the players but the nature of the relationship — are these lovers in the romantic and sexual sense, or are they friends who love? Students' understanding of the last two lines may vary depending on their understanding of the "love" relationship. Is the last blow a competitive personal rivalry, a way of ending the relationship, or something even stronger and more violent?

POSSIBLE CONNECTION TO ANOTHER SELECTION

Rita Dove, "Fox Trot Fridays" (text p. 224)

EDMUND CONTI, *Pragmatist* (p. 139)

As a writing assignment, you might ask the class to discuss whether the mixed tone of this poem is successful. Is, for example, "coming our way" (line 2) too liltingly conversational for the idea of apocalypse?

POSSIBLE CONNECTIONS TO OTHER SELECTIONS

Samuel Taylor Coleridge, "What Is an Epigram?" (text p. 252)
William Hathaway, "Oh, Oh" (text p. 26)

DYLAN THOMAS, *The Hand That Signed the Paper* (p. 140)

Dylan Thomas's *Eighteen Poems,* published in 1934, when he was twenty, began his career as a poet with a flourish: Here, it seemed, was an answer to T. S. Eliot, a return to rhapsody and unembarrassed music. Thomas's poems became more craftsmanlike as he matured, but they never lost their ambition for the grand gesture, the all-embracing, bittersweet melancholy for which the Romantics strove. Thomas lived the role of the poet to the hilt: he was an alcoholic, a philanderer, a wonderful storyteller, a boor, and a justly celebrated reader of his own poems and those of others. Although he never learned to speak Welsh (he was born and grew up in Swansea, Wales), it is said that his poems carry the sounds of that language over into English. He died of alcohol poisoning during his third reading tour of the United States.

Ask students to explore contexts for Dylan Thomas on LiterActive.

Although Thomas seems to be referring to no specific incident in this poem, the date (1936) indicates a possible concern with the political machinations leading up to the outbreak of World War II. The "five kings [who] did a king to death" (line 4) may even recall the five major powers who signed the Treaty of Versailles to end World War I but in their severe dismantling of Germany set the stage for another war. Some critics suggest that the poem, especially in the last two stanzas, refers to a wrathful God. Which words or phrases would lend credence to this reading? Students may suggest other situations in which a person in power can, by performing a seemingly simple act, adversely affect people at long range.

Discuss the title's allusion to the saying "The hand that rocks the cradle rules the world." Both phrases make observations about the power inherent in the acts of a single person. How are the acts to which they refer alike and different? How does the allusion to motherhood create irony in the poem? (Students familiar with the 1992 horror film *The Hand That Rocks the Cradle,* which deals with a deranged babysitter, may have their own associations with this poem.)

POSSIBLE CONNECTIONS TO OTHER SELECTIONS

Alice Jones, "The Foot" (text p. 222)
Carl Sandburg, "Buttons" (text p. 168)

AUDIOVISUAL RESOURCES (manual pp. 381–82)

JANICE TOWNLEY MOORE, *To a Wasp* (p. 141)

Discuss with students how an awareness of the intensity and seriousness of purpose that usually accompany the use of apostrophe affect their reading of this poem, which is, after all, about a common insect. In what way is the fist in the last line being waved at both the speaker and the wasp? Whose fist is it? How does the word *chortled* in the first line help us understand the speaker's view of the wasp? Discuss the paradox inherent in the notion of "delicious death" (line 11).

John Donne, "The Flea" (text p. 597)
David McCord, "Epitaph on a Waiter" (text p. 252)

J. PATRICK LEWIS, *The Unkindest Cut* (p. 142)

Students will enjoy this humorous quatrain that is a play on the saying "the pen is mightier than the sword." To open discussion, ask students to point out the paradox inherent in this simple poem. Discuss also the title of the poem, pointing out that the title is an allusion to Shakespeare's *Julius Caesar* (3.2.188).

POSSIBLE CONNECTION TO ANOTHER SELECTION

Paul Laurence Dunbar, "To a Captious Critic" (text p. 79)

GARY SNYDER, *How Poetry Comes to Me* (p. 143)

Snyder's characterization of poetry departs from the traditional view of inspiration. Rather than coming in a flash of insight, poetry is "blundering" (line 1) and "Frightened" (3). Instead of being overtaken by poetry, the author retains control of the situation and has to "go to meet it" (5). The poem also calls upon the scene of a camper being encroached on by dangerous animals, but the meekness of poetry in Snyder's view makes this a very different story. Poetry is not an animal from which we need protection, but rather a cowering thing likely to be scared away.

You might have your students consider the images of light and dark in this poem. Poetry belongs to the realm of the dark. If the speaker wants to find it he has to venture out to the "Edge of the light" (6). The meeting must take place in the border area between light and darkness. What does the campfire, the light that holds poetry at a distance, symbolize? What does it provide for the speaker and what does it prevent?

POSSIBLE CONNECTIONS TO OTHER SELECTIONS

Wallace Stevens, "Anecdote of the Jar" (text p. 169)
Richard Wakefield, "In a Poetry Workshop" (text p. 509)

MARGARET ATWOOD, *February* (p. 143)

"February," on the surface, comprises the ruminations of a speaker whose cat wakes her up in the morning. The feeling it evokes is familiar to everyone, particularly those who live in northern climes: "time to get this depressing season over with." The speaker initially rejects sex (suggesting that people should spay and neuter not only their animals but themselves!) and embraces the human version of hibernation ("Time to eat fat / and watch hockey" [lines 1–2]). The cat seems to be responsible for her attitude, and by the end, she entreats it to "get going / on a little optimism around here" (32–33).

Though the speaker's tone is generally humorous, it might be productive to begin by encouraging students to locate all of the death imagery in the poem, obvious or otherwise. The cat's breath is "of burped-up meat and musty sofas" (10) for instance, and "famine / crouches in the bedsheets" (20–21) along with the speaker. Our efforts to propagate life seem to lead to death in the speaker's mind: "love . . . does us in" (19), heating our bodies produces pollution, etc. How does the speaker's humorous tone interact with the apparently serious subject matter and imagery? Ask students to try to figure out why she suddenly rejects this "month of despair / with a skewered heart in the centre" in lines 26 and 27, how the cat is converted into "the life principle, / more or less" (31–32). Is she shaking off the despair of the season by rejecting the cat? Is the cat somehow an emblem of winter, or is it an envoy of nature in general?

POSSIBLE CONNECTIONS TO OTHER SELECTIONS

Stephen Crane, "A Man Said to the Universe" (text p. 164)

Richard Wilbur, "A Late Aubade" (text p. 84)

WILLIAM CARLOS WILLIAMS, *To Waken an Old Lady* (p. 144)

The image of the birds in winter at first suggests a bleak meaning for old age. The "bare trees" (line 5) and "snow glaze" (6) don't seem to offer much refuge. However, Williams observes that winter provides the birds with rest and with seeds to eat. The barren elements of the landscape, including the "harsh weedstalks" (11) and "dark wind" (9), are made bearable, "tempered / by a shrill / piping of plenty" (16–18). Williams seems to suggest that old age, though it may seem harsh, has its share of comforts.

POSSIBLE CONNECTIONS TO OTHER SELECTIONS

Kelly Cherry, "Alzheimer's" (text p. 272)

Colette Inez, "Back When All Was Continuous Chuckles" (text p. 76; question 1, following)

Gary Soto, "Behind Grandma's House" (text p. 181)

CONNECTION QUESTION IN TEXT (p. 145) WITH ANSWER

1. Discuss the shift in tone in "To Waken an Old Lady" and in Colette Inez's "Back When All Was Continuous Chuckles" (p. 76).

    In Williams's poem, the shift in tone occurs partly through the change in verb tenses. The first half is marked by anxious present tense verbs — "cheeping" (line 3), "skimming" (4), "Gaining and failing" (7). After the turn, Williams uses past tense verbs to create a calmer mood — "rested" (12), "covered" (14), and "tempered" (16). This switch to the past tense suggests an acceptance of old age as largely backward looking. However, Williams returns to the -ing ending in the last line, this time in the form of a noun rather than a verb. The actions of the first half have now become a static element, one that contributes to the comforts of the winter scene.

    "Back When All Was Continuous Chuckles" begins in the voice of the young narrator. Her reflections are interspersed with examples of the jokes she told with her friend, and the diction draws from her vocabulary, with words like "moron" (line 2), "Freaky" (7), and "crabby" (14). As the poem progresses, the quoted jokes stop, and the language becomes less tied to the words of the young girl. Here the adult poet takes over to express feelings that her younger self did not know how to deal with. Though the friends go back to "flipping through joke books" (23), it is no longer important that we hear the jokes. Instead, we are left with the mature knowledge that the names on the cemetery headstones would soon become familiar.

ERNEST SLYMAN, *Lightning Bugs* (p. 145)

This three-line poem casts lightning bugs (also called "fireflies") as spies who invade the speaker's backyard. It might be difficult to sustain a discussion about such a short poem, but you could begin by asking students to describe the speaker, the conditions under which he might make this observation, and the sights and sounds that surround him. Does his paranoia come from his sense that he is alone or from his sense that he is all too crowded?

Without the title, we would think this poem is about people. The title frames the experience by identifying the image to be captured in the lines that follow. Then, the image of the "peepholes" (line 2), coming as it does before the "snapshots" (3), makes us first imagine the bugs as human beings who require peepholes to see who is outside. When mention of snapshots is added to this image, the bugs become like tourists, waiting for someone to come out of the house so they can take a picture. This is ironic, for it is really the bugs who are the celebrities, fascinating the speaker, who watches them.

POSSIBLE CONNECTION TO ANOTHER SELECTION

Ezra Pound, "In a Station of the Metro" (text p. 129)

SYLVIA PLATH, *Mirror* (p. 145)

Sylvia Plath grew up with an invalid father (he refused to seek treatment for what he thought was cancer but was actually diabetes) who died when she was eight. Her mother was a teacher, who by example and instruction encouraged her daughter's precocious literary ambitions (Plath published her first poem before she was nine). Plath attended Smith College on scholarship, won a Fulbright to study in England, received a number of awards for her writing, and eventually married the English poet Ted Hughes. In the last few harrowing months of her life (which she spent alone because Hughes was having an affair), she wrote most of her finest poems, sometimes at the rate of two or three a day. She killed herself on February 11, 1963.

Ask students to explore contexts for Sylvia Plath on LiterActive.

This poem speaks from the point of view of a mirror reflecting an aging woman. The poem's brilliant use of personification may mask some other concerns in the poem; you might begin discussion by asking students to consider why the poet chooses this device. Is it possible to speak from an inhuman point of view? This speaker claims to "have no preconceptions" (line 1) and to be "unmisted by love or dislike" (3). These are decidedly inhuman characteristics, yet the speaker has a human voice and a human consciousness. Does the use of personification express some desire, in this case, to shed what can be painful human emotions? How does that desire in the poet reflect the persona of the aging woman who is the subject (or object) of the second stanza?

Without the use of personification, the poem would simply be another flat statement on a woman watching herself grow old. But that action of watching is enlivened by the mirror taking on some organic attributes. The pink wall it reflects becomes part of its heart, for example, and despite the truth it gives back to the woman, it feels important and necessary. Without the responsive quality of the mirror, it is unlikely that the last images would be quite so startling. But the personified mirror literally acquires a depth it probably would not have otherwise, and it figures in the poem as a lake, a drowning pool, and the source of the "terrible fish" (18). In the final simile, the image is no longer a mere reflection but a figure of assault coming up out of the depths of self to frighten her.

POSSIBLE CONNECTION TO ANOTHER SELECTION

Li Ho, "A Beautiful Girl Combs Her Hair" (text p. 56)

AUDIOVISUAL RESOURCES (manual pp. 379–80)

CATHY SONG, *Sunworshippers* (p. 146)

In "Sunworshippers," Song combines elements of the sacred and the profane to describe complex feelings about the body. The speaker's reflection is sparked by seeing the "sunworshippers" in their position of devotion, laid out as if for a sacrifice. Yet there is "irreverence" (line 7) to their attitude, and their "dirty feet" (8) suggest unworthiness. These people are going about their worship in the wrong way, especially according to the speaker's mother who comments, " 'Look how they love themselves' " (1). She, on the other hand, is not "allowed to love [herself] too much" (29). She treats the body as a "temple" (15) which is shrouded in the "traveling revivalist tent" (16) of her clothes. Yet its health is gauged by the profane measure of "Caramel-colored stools" (21). As a means of subverting this dichotomy, she develops anorexia, which is described as a kind of puri- fying heat, lighting the "coal fire" (39) in her eyes. She eats only "radiance, / essential as chlorophyll, / the apple's heated core" (42–44). At the end she achieves a way, of "shin- ing / out of this world" (51–52), yet it is an ambiguous triumph, predicated as it is on her "impending disappearance" (41).

POSSIBLE CONNECTIONS TO OTHER SELECTIONS

Robert Hass, "A Story about the Body" (text p. 278)

Sharon Olds, "Sex without Love" (text p. 93)

Jane Yolen, "Fat Is Not a Fairy Tale" (text p. 101; question 1, following)

CONNECTION QUESTION IN TEXT (p. 147) WITH ANSWER

1. Write an essay comparing the themes in "Sunworshippers" and in Jane Yolen's "Fat Is Not a Fairy Tale" (p. 101).

    Song is preoccupied with religious or spiritual themes. She takes the colloquial term *sunworshippers* and interrogates its relation to actual worship. The young narrator is concerned with proper reverence to the gods, with the sacrifices required of her and others, and with the way self-love contrasts spiritual love. "Sunworshippers" takes an ambiguous stance toward the holiness of the body because it is still trying to work out the unclear relationship between body and soul. Yolen is more interested in the mythologies that humans create and the qualities that we enshrine in those stories. She believes that fairy tales perpetuate false ideas about the human body and, through her humorous renaming of familiar fairy-tale figures, suggests how chang- ing our stories would result in changes to our ways of thinking.

WILLIAM WORDSWORTH, *London, 1802* (p. 148)

William Wordsworth was born in the English Lake District, in Cockermouth, West Cumberland, and grew up roaming the countryside. He completed his undergraduate degree at Cambridge University in 1791 and spent a year in revolutionary France. By the age of twenty-seven, he had settled in Somersetshire to be near Samuel Taylor Coleridge, with whom, in 1798, he published one of the most influential volumes in the history of English poetry, *Lyrical Ballads.* Wordsworth enjoyed increasing public reward as a poet (becoming poet laureate in 1843) even as his private life suffered from frequent tragedy and disappointment.

The metonymic nouns following the colon in line 3 of "London, 1802" all point to areas within British culture and civilization that Wordsworth thinks have declined since John Milton's day. All things have suffered loss — from the strength of the church, the army, or the accomplishment of writers to the more immediate and individual quality of home life — in particular an "inward happiness," along with a sense of strength and security.

Milton seems to have represented for Wordsworth an epitome of the heroic, a kind of guiding star apart from other human beings, with a voice that was expansive, at one with the sublime in nature, and morally incorruptible.

POSSIBLE CONNECTIONS TO OTHER SELECTIONS

William Blake, "London" (text p. 121)

George Eliot, "In a London Drawingroom" (text p. 598)

AUDIOVISUAL RESOURCES (manual p. 383)

JIM STEVENS, *Schizophrenia* (p. 148)

The ways in which personification, stanzaic form, and title combine to create meaning in this poem can be a fruitful approach to discussion. Stevens personifies the house as a victim suffering from the turmoil of its inhabitants. You might ask students to find examples of ways in which the house is physically "hurt" by their activities (see especially lines 2–5 and 17–20). The sequencing and relative lengths of the stanzas draw the reader to important statements of meaning in the poem. The poem is framed by two identical statements that "it was the house that suffered most." Moving toward the center from these identical lines, 2–5 and 17–20 deal specifically with physical things happening to the house. The next two stanzas toward the center, lines 6–9 and 13–16, depict the people doing things to the house, using it as a means of carrying out their aggressions toward one another. The very center of the poem, set off by a three-line stanza when the ones surrounding it have contained four lines, specifies what has been going on between the people themselves.

It is the title, however, that brings the poem together as a whole and allows us to relate the suffering *of* the house to the suffering *in* the house. *Schizophrenia* literally means a split mind; it is a psychosis characterized by radical changes in behavior. Have the students notice the change in behavior and its effects on the house between the beginning and end of the poem. In the first nine lines, the house is being violently abused: Doors and dishes are slammed around, the carpets are intentionally scuffed, and grease, much harder to deal with than plain dirt, is ground into the tablecloth. In lines 5–9, the pattern moderates slightly: the slammed doors get locked, the dishes remain dirty instead of being slammed around, the feet stand still instead of scuffing. The third long stanza provides a transition into a mode of behavior radically opposite to what has come before. It casts the turmoil in terms of the inhabitants' violence toward one another but also indicates that this violence is no longer occurring. Instead, what we see in lines 12–16 is the people dividing the house between them, splitting it between them to stay out of one another's way and put an end to the fighting. Note the ominous tone of line 15, an allusion to the biblical warning that "a house divided against itself cannot stand." Indeed, the effects on the house of this new kind of warfare are all seen in terms of things splitting apart — the paint coming away from the wood, the windows breaking into pieces, the front door coming loose from its hinges, and the roof tiles coming off the roof. The last word (*madhouse*) of the poem proper, before the refrain of the last line, brings the reader back to the title. You might discuss with your students whether the word refers to the house itself, which the speaker contends is suffering, or whether it means a house that contains mad people, or both. Is the idea of "home," the combination of house and people, the real victim of the madness? Would "Madhouse" have been a better title than "Schizophrenia"?

POSSIBLE CONNECTIONS TO OTHER SELECTIONS

Emily Dickinson, "One need not be a Chamber — to be Haunted —" (text p. 325)
Langston Hughes, "doorknobs" (text p. 414)
Edgar Allan Poe, "The Haunted Palace" (text p. 159)

WALT WHITMAN, *A Noiseless Patient Spider* (p. 149)

In this poem, Whitman participates in a fairly long and distinguished tradition, starting with the homely tropes of Edward Taylor or Anne Bradstreet, that explores analogies between lower forms of natural life and the human condition. In this instance the analogy is effective because both soul and spider are isolated — and are trying to reach across vast space to forge connections between themselves and the rest of the world. The emphasis within the soul seems to be a reflective activity (musing, venturing, throw-

Ask students to explore contexts for Walt Whitman on *LiterActive*.

ing, seeking), while the activity of the spider seems more a physical compulsion, especially with the repetition of "filament."

POSSIBLE CONNECTION TO ANOTHER SELECTION

Emily Dickinson, "I heard a Fly buzz — when I died —" (text p. 324)

JOHN DONNE, *A Valediction: Forbidding Mourning* (p. 150)

The questions in the text show how richly metaphorical this metaphysical poem in fact is. Virtually every statement here is made through a comparison. The lovers should tolerate their separation with the same grace with which "virtuous men" leave this earth. They are not like the "Dull sublunary" lovers who need physical presence to sustain each other; they represent something finer. This sense of refinement is picked up and developed further in the simile in line 24, when the strength of the love between Donne and his wife is compared to gold, which does not shatter when beaten but expands to delicate, fine plate. Donne concludes his poem with the well-known compass metaphor. You might have to explain at this point what sort of compass Donne is describing, since we live in an age of computer graphics, not drafting skills. Because the compass here is used to draw circles, it is a most appropriate simile to describe unity and perfection.

POSSIBLE CONNECTIONS TO OTHER SELECTIONS

Anne Bradstreet, "To My Dear and Loving Husband" (text p. 492)
John Donne, "The Flea" (text p. 597)
William Shakespeare, "Shall I compare thee to a summer's day?" (text p. 243)

AUDIOVISUAL RESOURCES (manual p. 374)

LINDA PASTAN, *Marks* (p. 151)

In teaching this poem, it would probably be a good idea to discuss the social expectations of motherhood and those of being a student. The latter relationship, in which the person is constantly being judged and is answerable to an authority figure, is not always ego enhancing, a point that Eugène Ionesco carried to absurd limits in *The Lesson*. The situation of the mother in Pastan's poem seems not much better; although anyone in any job or academic setting is frequently under review, is not a mother's "job" more an act of ongoing generosity than a fulfilling of job or course requirements? Class discussion could challenge the appropriateness of the metaphor here.

Play a recording of Linda Pastan reading "Marks" on LiterActive.

The speaker's increasingly bitter, ironic tone serves (as irony often does) as a weapon against the "marks" (the hurt and disillusionment) inflicted on her by her family. Can she easily leave school, leave her responsibilities?

As a writing assignment, ask students to analyze how this poem challenges and mocks its central metaphor.

POSSIBLE CONNECTION TO ANOTHER SELECTION

Linda Pastan, "Pass/Fail" (text p. 504)

AUDIOVISUAL RESOURCES (manual p. 379)

THYLIAS MOSS, *Interpretation of a Poem by Frost* (p. 151)

Moss reimagines the scene of Frost's "Stopping by Woods on a Snowy Evening" to create an allegory for race relations in the United States. The absent owner in the original becomes, in this version, the separate-but-equal laws. The snow that blankets the ground symbolizes the power of whiteness to cover over all variations until "black and white are the only options" (line 13). The interloper in this scene, a young black girl in Moss's interpretation, obeys the boundaries set by Jim Crow "even in the absence of a fence" (5), signifying her acquiescence to the unfair laws. However, at the end of the poem, her promise presents a challenge to Jim Crow. She will "bear Jim no bastards" (21). While Frost's poem ends with a sleep that portends death, Moss ends with a sleep that suggests reproduction. The girl's promise, for now, prevents her from creating offspring of the harmful segregation.

POSSIBLE CONNECTIONS TO OTHER SELECTIONS

Langston Hughes, "Formula" (text p. 403)

Julio Marzán, "Ethnic Poetry" (text p. 173)

RONALD WALLACE, *Building an Outhouse* (p. 152)

Students will likely enjoy the scatological humor of this poem, which compares poetry to a toilet and, to a degree, to excrement. The last line, with its repetition of "sit on it" and its unmistakable reference to shit, is almost guaranteed to provoke laughter in class. You should have no trouble, either, in getting students to find the poem's many sophomoric puns and comparisons, such as "sweet smell" (line 4), "fly" (8), "load" (8), and the "nub" of a "pencil" (10).

If you'd rather avoid an extended classroom discussion of bodily functions, try to focus your students on the date of the poem (1991). At the writing of this sonnet (itself a form considered by many to be outdated), outhouses were obsolete in all but the poorest of American communities. Knowing that, what is Wallace implying about "building a poem" (1)?

POSSIBLE CONNECTIONS TO OTHER SELECTIONS

Anne Bradstreet, "The Author to Her Book" (text p. 137)

Katharyn Howd Machan, "Hazel Tells LaVerne" (text p. 77)

ELAINE MAGARRELL, *The Joy of Cooking* (p. 153)

This grisly poem is from the point of view of a disgruntled sibling who has, on a literal level, cooked parts of her sister and brother. On a metaphorical level, she is attacking their attributes which have injured her. Ask students whether they think the poem is humorous or horrifying. They are bound to recall some news story or horror movie featuring cannibalism, even of one's family members. Is the speaker's fantasy tempered by these incidents, or does her tone and her reliance on the discourse of cookbooks make it impossible to accept the poem as anything but a metaphor with humorous intent?

The tongue and heart are extended metaphors for the siblings. The sister is described as needing spices to make her more interesting. We can imagine that hers is not an effervescent personality. The brother, characterized as a heart, seems heartless. Whereas most hearts feed six, his "barely feeds two" (line 16). He is "rather dry" (10), requiring stuffing to make him palatable. Neither sibling is complete enough when left alone to warrant the speaker's unadorning description; she must "doctor them up" to make them palatable to her audience and herself.

POSSIBLE CONNECTIONS TO OTHER SELECTIONS

Sally Croft, "Home-Baked Bread" (text p. 126; question 1, following)

Maxine Hong Kingston, "Restaurant" (text p. 206)

1. Write an essay that explains how cooking becomes a way of talking about something else in this poem and in Sally Croft's "Home-Baked Bread" (p. 126).

   Croft at first questions *The Joy of Cooking*, wondering why it should treat its subject as one would a human mystery. Carried away by the language, she moves into the role of seductress, luring her listener into the erotic sensuality of her poem. Magarrell's adaptation from the same book takes an entirely different form. Her tone is bitter. Rather than seducing her listeners, she startles and perhaps alienates them through her arresting images.

RUTH FAINLIGHT, *The Clarinettist* (p. 154)

Alternating between artistic and athletic similes, this poem describes an orchestral musician on the verge of performing a solo. Probably the most effective way to begin class discussion is to have your students analyze each image and consider how it captures the tension of the clarinettist's role.

Students without a musical background, as well as those who have not attended a performance in a formal music hall, may have difficulty with some of the poem's allusions; you might want to bring in (or assign your students to find) photographs of a local or grand theater to help them visualize the images of the cherub of line 10 and the dancer of line 15. Some excellent images are available at the Web site for the Wang Theater in Boston (*wangcenter.org*), which recently underwent a major renovation of its interior. Students may also need help understanding that the "quattrocento chorus" of line 7 refers to early Italian Renaissance painting — *quattrocento* literally means fifteenth century in Italian — which usually had religious subjects; here again you may want to bring some pictures to class, perhaps Botticelli's *Adoration of the Kings* or Botticini's *Assumption of the Virgin*.

Note, too, that "The Clarinettist" has a definite gender tension going on. If students seem unable to overcome their difficulty with the poem's artistic and historical references, try focusing them on the conflict between the female clarinettist and the male conductor, examining how the poem's images contribute to a gendered reading.

POSSIBLE CONNECTIONS TO OTHER SELECTIONS

Martín Espada, "Latin Night at the Pawnshop" (text p. 78)
John Keats, "Ode on a Grecian Urn" (text p. 96)

PERSPECTIVE

JOHN R. SEARLE, *Figuring Out Metaphors* (p. 155)

In a writing assignment, ask students to find two poems in which the metaphors work and two in which they don't. Students should explain their choices in these essays — that is, define the metaphors in the poems and explain why they work (or why they don't). If possible, students should speculate about the characteristics of a successful metaphor based on the evidence of the poems they have chosen.

A class exercise or another writing assignment might involve students finding metaphors in sources other than poems — in the newspaper, for example, or in popular songs or television programs. Once found, these examples could also be analyzed as successful or unsuccessful metaphors.

6

Symbol, Allegory, and Irony

The discussion on symbol and allegory can follow naturally from the discussion of figurative language. In a sense, symbols are metaphors with one term left open, and it is up to the reader to complete them. Many of the poems in the previous chapter lend themselves well to symbolic readings — a good transition between the chapters might have students select a previously covered poem and examine its symbols.

Ask students to explore the poetic elements in this chapter on **LiterActive** *and at* **bedfordstmartins.com/ meyerpoetry**.

Another exercise that can be useful is to have students brainstorm a list of symbols found in popular culture and articulate the connotations that surround them: what the American flag means, for instance. (This exercise can also illustrate how symbols can have different meanings for different groups.) This can help give students a sense of how symbols work, and how they can be simultaneously specific and general.

Students often seem to believe that every poem is immediately symbolic, which can be simultaneously encouraging and frustrating in their zeal to leap to the "real" meaning of the poem. Alternately, they may be committed to a kind of relativism, in which they believe that some poems can be symbolic of anything. While it is true that some symbols are more loosely focused than others, one of the challenges of discussion in this chapter is to encourage students to offer well-thought-out readings. It is a difficult line to walk between putting pressure on students to read critically and shutting down all discussion because the students come to believe that the teacher has "the right answer," and unless they can provide this they are better off keeping quiet. In fact, students may use silence as a tactic to bring out "the right answer" from the teacher. In this chapter it is perhaps better to err on the side of caution and try to draw out students' own interpretations, even if these interpretations are initially somewhat off track. You may find it useful to avoid giving your own interpretations at all, relying instead on student input shaped by questions from you and from other students. Students may find this frustrating at first, particularly when they are used to being given answers by authorities, but ultimately it will sharpen their abilities as readers.

Irony can be difficult to explain directly — in this case, examples are a great help. Irony often depends on an understanding of the context, as Kenneth Fearing's "AD" illustrates. Without some understanding of want ads, the irony in this poem will not be evident. It may be useful to compare some kinds of irony to an inside joke in that they depend on a shared bit of information before the audience can "get it." Students may in fact be quite familiar with situational irony, as in Jane Kenyon's "Surprise." They may

Ask students to research the poets in this chapter at **bedfordstmartins.com/ meyerpoetry**.

be able to readily call incidents to mind in which all was not as it initially seemed. For an interesting take on irony, you might look at Linda Hutcheon's book *Irony's Edge: The Theory and Politics of Irony* (1994, Routledge, New York), which is an occasionally dense but well-supported argument about the place of irony in contemporary society.

ROBERT FROST, *Acquainted with the Night* (p. 157)

This poem investigates the mind of a speaker who has seen a part of humanity and of nature that he cannot overlook. His experience has led him to see things that other people have not necessarily seen. The poem invites us to read it on more than one level, as is the case with many of Frost's poems. You might ask students to discuss in a two-page essay how the clock functions in this poem. How does its presence modify the poem's tone? Do we read it literally, symbolically, or as a mixture of both?

> Ask students to explore contexts for Robert Frost on *LiterActive*.

> Play a recording of Robert Frost reading "Acquainted with the Night" on *Literature Aloud*.

POSSIBLE CONNECTIONS TO OTHER SELECTIONS

T. S. Eliot, "The Love Song of J. Alfred Prufrock" (text p. 456)

Robert Frost, "Stopping by Woods on a Snowy Evening" (text p. 370)

Octavio Paz, "The Street" (text p. 579)

EDGAR ALLAN POE, *The Haunted Palace* (p. 159)

Edgar Allan Poe was born in Boston, the son of itinerant actors. He lived an often harrowing life marked by alcoholism, disease, and misfortune, managing to eke out a rather precarious existence primarily as an editor for a number of newspapers and periodicals in Philadelphia, New York, and Baltimore. Although he was renowned in his lifetime as the author of "The Raven," his most abiding ambition was to be a respected critic. He died after collapsing in a Baltimore street.

> Ask students to explore contexts for Edgar Allan Poe on *LiterActive*.

Students may have had little exposure to allegory, since it is not frequently used by modern writers. Thus it might be useful to explicate at least one stanza of the poem, discussing how a particular part of the palace corresponds to a particular part of the human body or mind. Notice the two "characters" actually personified by Poe in the poem: Thought (line 5) and Echoes (29). Does there seem to be a particular reason for singling out these two?

What is the purpose of using such archaic expressions as "Porphyrogene" (22) and "red-litten" (42)? What other words in the poem seem especially well chosen for their connotative meanings?

As a short writing assignment or subject for further class discussion, ask your students to contrast the depictions of the "windows" and the "door" of the palace when they first appear in the poem (stanzas 3 and 4) with their portrayal in the last stanza, after the coming of the "evil things" (33). How do the windows and door seem to change?

POSSIBLE CONNECTIONS TO OTHER SELECTIONS

Emily Dickinson, "One need not be a Chamber — to be Haunted —" (text p. 325)

Jim Stevens, "Schizophrenia" (text p. 148)

AUDIOVISUAL RESOURCES (manual p. 385)

EDWIN ARLINGTON ROBINSON, *Richard Cory* (p. 161)

Edwin Arlington Robinson became a professional poet in the grimmest of circumstances: his father's businesses went bankrupt in 1893, one brother became a drug addict and another an alcoholic, and Robinson could afford to attend Harvard University for just two years. He eked out a livelihood from the contributions of friends and patrons, finally moving to New York City, where his work received more critical attention and public acceptance. He won three Pulitzer Prizes for his gloomy, musical verse narratives.

As a writing assignment, you might ask students to analyze how Robinson achieves the power of the final line of "Richard Cory," paying special attention to the regal language that describes Cory as well as the strong contrasts in the couplets of the final stanza.

POSSIBLE CONNECTIONS TO OTHER SELECTIONS

M. Carl Holman, "Mr. Z" (text p. 524)

Percy Bysshe Shelley, "Ozymandias" (text p. 621)

KENNETH FEARING, *AD* (p. 162)

How does the double meaning inherent in the title of the poem — "AD" is an abbreviation for "advertisement" as well as for "in the year of the Lord" — prepare the reader for the satire that follows? Notice how even the type used for this poem contributes to its meaning. The italicized words and phrases might occur in any high-powered advertising campaign. How is the effect of the advertising words undercut by the words in standard type? What is the effect of the reversal of type patterns in the last line?

Students should be aware that the poem alludes, in part, to the Uncle Sam "I want you" army recruiting posters. Discuss whether the purpose of the satire in "AD" is to expose a situation that exists, to correct it, or both. Is the situation to which the poem refers — the attempt to draw people into a horrifying occupation by making the work sound exciting and rewarding — confined to the pre–World War II era?

POSSIBLE CONNECTIONS TO OTHER SELECTIONS

Julia Ward Howe, "Battle-Hymn of the Republic," (text p. 607)

Janice Mirikitani, "Recipe" (text p. 547)

E. E. CUMMINGS, *next to of course god america i* (p. 163)

The speaker of this poem is trapped by jingoistic clichés that render his speech almost meaningless. His intent is to manipulate his audience, convincing them that the men who have sacrificed their lives in war are "heroic" and "happy" (line 10). As a writing assignment, you might ask students to analyze how Cummings portrays character without using direct description.

 Ask students to explore contexts for E. E. Cummings on *LiterActive*.

 Play a recording of E. E. Cummings reading "next to of course god america i" on *Literature Aloud*.

POSSIBLE CONNECTIONS TO OTHER SELECTIONS

Langston Hughes, "Un-American Investigators" (text p. 412)

Florence Cassen Mayers, "All-American Sestina" (text p. 250)

STEPHEN CRANE, *A Man Said to the Universe* (p. 164)

What sort of answer does the man in the poem expect to get from the universe? What does that say about the man? What other emotions, besides amusement, does this poem evoke? How does a reader's own perception of how the universe operates affect his or her response to the poem? Students are likely to concur that the more distance they feel between themselves and the man, the more amusing they find the poem.

POSSIBLE CONNECTIONS TO OTHER SELECTIONS

Robert Frost, "'Out, Out —'" (text p. 368)

Langston Hughes, "Lenox Avenue: Midnight" (text p. 404)

BOB HICOK, *Making it in poetry* (p. 165)

You might begin by asking your students why Hicok chooses such short lines in this poem. How do the frequent stops contribute to the humor of the poem and the attitude toward its subject? Because of these short lines, the repeated answer "Because I write poems" is broken differently each time the speaker gives it. The first time, "I write" carries the primary meaning of the sentence: it is the reason the poet has those checks. The second time, it is necessary to have "I write poetry" together as a unit. The addition of the final word explains the speaker's obscurity.

You might also discuss what effect the poem's inclusion in this anthology has on its meaning. What would Hicok say about having his work reprinted here?

POSSIBLE CONNECTIONS TO OTHER SELECTIONS

Alexander Pope, From *An Essay on Criticism* (text p. 204)

Richard Wakefield, "In a Poetry Workshop" (text p. 509, question 1, following)

Marilyn Nelson Waniek, "Emily Dickinson's Defunct" (text p. 276)

COMPARISON QUESTION IN TEXT (p. 165) WITH ANSWER

1. Compare the life of the poet in Hicok's poem and in Richard Wakefield's "In a Poetry Workshop" (p. 509).

   Poetry is a small part of the public life of the speaker in Hicok's poem, as evidenced by the small sums of money he receives from the journals that publish his work. He knows that writing poems is not the kind of public act that would make the bank teller recognize him. Wakefield's narrator has a very different experience because poetry is part of his public persona — he has to teach it. While Hicok worries that poetry is unknown to most people, Wakefield thinks it is overrun with useless rules. Both poems take an ironic stance toward poetry. The fact that we, as the audience, are reading Hicok's poem undercuts the idea that no one cares about his work, and Wakefield contradicts his own advice by creating a pattern of rhyme and rhythm.

JANE KENYON, *Surprise* (p. 165)

From the perspective of the woman "surprised," this poem encompasses many of the conflicting emotions of a surprise party in spare, deliberate imagery. Distracted by the unnamed male, and oblivious to the gathering elsewhere, the speaker notes all of the changes around her as a result of the onset of spring. The last three lines of the poem reverse the mood, suggesting that the speaker's surprise comes at the ease with which her husband/lover has deceived her, opening up the possibility that there is something wrong with their relationship.

It might be useful to begin by asking students if they have ever been involved in a surprise party — either as the victim or as the scheming organizer. A discussion of what a surprise party intends to do leads naturally into a discussion of what it often actually does. Similarly, the poem leads us from the mundane — "pancakes at the local diner" (line 1), "casseroles" (4) — to the surprising renewal of nature in springtime, to the woman's astounding realization that the man has had such an easy time lying to her. The word "astound," with its connotations of bewilderment, directs our attention away from the surprise party and into speculation about the relationship between them. The irony centers on the renewal of the spring birthday juxtaposed against some almost funereal undertones (consider "spectral" in line 8 and "ash" in line 9, for example). The tension between images enables us to interpret their relationship in a novel, surprising way.

POSSIBLE CONNECTIONS TO OTHER SELECTIONS

William Hathaway, "Oh, Oh" (text p. 26; question 1, following)

Sharon Olds, "Rite of Passage" (text p. 279; question 2, following)

CONNECTIONS QUESTIONS IN TEXT (p. 166) WITH ANSWERS

1. Write an essay on the nature of the surprises in Kenyon's poem and in Hathaway's "Oh, Oh" (p. 26). Include in your discussion a comparison of the tone and irony in each poem.

    "Oh, Oh" is much more humorous than this poem, but the effects are similar. In both cases the final line tells us something that we didn't know, something that causes us to rethink the rest of the poem, especially the title. In Hathaway's poem we know that something is coming, though, because the title clues us in. In this poem we may at first take the "surprise" to be simply the surprise party, so we are especially surprised to learn that there is something amiss between this couple who seem to have enjoyed their breakfast and spring walk.

2. Compare and contrast in an essay the irony associated with the birthday parties in this poem and Sharon Olds's "Rite of Passage" (p. 279).

    The irony in Olds's poem comes partially from the speaker's sense that her son and his friends are treating life so lightly at a birthday party. He is transformed from a frail, innocent thing to a general plotting the death of a weaker being. The young partygoers are not any more aware of this irony than the guests at the party in Kenyon's poem are. In both cases the irony is something shared only between the poet and the reader, although any adult at Olds's party would be likely to notice something vaguely disturbing in the boys' comments.

MARTÍN ESPADA, *Bully* (p. 166)

Espada's bitter poem builds on the irony that an elementary school named for Theodore Roosevelt — who before becoming the twenty-sixth president of the United States led his "Rough Riders" to victory in Cuba during the Spanish-American War (1896–98) — is now dominated by Latino children. Although your students will be able to formulate a basic understanding of the irony from the details provided by the poet, a more thorough understanding of the Spanish-American War and the Boston school system in 1987 will help them gain a much more nuanced appreciation of the poem. It would be well worthwhile to assign them the Critical Strategies question (#3) in the text as a brief writing or oral report assignment before tackling the poem in class; you may want to divide responsibilities so that some students look up the Spanish-American War, some research Roosevelt's role in it, and some try to find information on the Boston Public School system of the late 1980s, rather than overwhelming them with a major research project.

Students should be able to find a serviceable overview of the Spanish-American War and Roosevelt's role in it in a good encyclopedia (even online) or an American history survey textbook. The context of the Boston public schools in the late 1980s is likely to prove more elusive, especially because Espada has taken some liberties with fact for the purpose of his poem (the Roosevelt Elementary School in Hyde Park, a predominantly white working-class neighborhood on the edge of Boston, is actually named after Franklin Delano Roosevelt). The Boston public school system was found guilty of running racially segregated schools and forced by court order to desegregate in the 1970s: the busing program that ensued sparked riots and severe racial tensions that continue to linger. By the late 1980s schools in disadvantaged communities were still suffering from lack of funds (especially compared with schools in wealthier areas), and the city struggled to find a solution to the public school system's reputation for poor levels of education. Yet in September 1987, thirteen years after the controversial busing order was put into effect, a federal appeals court concluded that the city had shown a good effort to desegregate and decided that Boston no longer needed to follow racial guidelines in school assignments — essentially ending the era of court-ordered busing.

POSSIBLE CONNECTIONS TO OTHER SELECTIONS

E. E. Cummings, "Buffalo Bill 's" (text p. 595)

Langston Hughes, "Theme for English B" (text p. 502)

Janice Mirikitani, "Recipe" (text p. 547)

RENNIE MCQUILKIN, *The Lighters* (p. 167)

This poem examines the possible importance of what we choose to keep in later life. The voice is not that of the eighty-nine-year-old woman who is the poem's subject, but of an imaginative observer. The initials of the best man on one of the lighters indicates that they were favors distributed at the unnamed woman's wedding; while she is casting aside most of her other sentimental possessions, these remain valuable. The speaker suggests that they provide a symbolic entrance to the world of memory and nostalgia. Like the lighters, the "antique gap-toothed keys" (line 9) are also seen as possible connections to the world of the dead and a means by which she can remember those who left behind the cherished objects.

While the physical appearance of the woman is not directly mentioned, attributes of the things she keeps include "square-shouldered" (4), "gap-toothed" (9), and "high-backed" (11). The poem's mood is mildly mournful but conscious of the many ways in which this woman has been loved: children are present, and the word "boudoir" (3) conveys echoes of a nostalgic sensuality. The poem uses other resonant words as keys to its almost supernatural concluding image: The lighters are lined up "gravely" (8), the keys are thought to open a sunken chamber. This conclusion indicates the separation between the living and the dead; in this poem it is the dead who gather to remember the living, while the living remember the dead by accumulating their goods.

Consider asking students to write for a few minutes imagining the importance of a family treasure or personal memento. Why has the object been kept? What role could it play in connecting the keeper to another time or place?

POSSIBLE CONNECTIONS TO OTHER SELECTIONS

Andrew Hudgins, "Seventeen" (text p. 170)

William Carlos Williams, "To Waken an Old Lady" (text p. 144; question 1, following)

CONNECTION QUESTION IN TEXT (p. 168) WITH ANSWER

1. Compare the treatment of this elderly woman with that of William Carlos Williams's "To Waken an Old Lady" (p. 144). How is aging depicted in each poem?

    Both "The Lighters" and "To Waken an Old Lady" treat an ascetic impulse that comes with age. In the latter, the images of winter indicate that the end of life is a period of stillness and introspection. In McQuilkin's poem, the dividing of possessions and discarding of "mementos" (line 2) is a way of coming to terms with the fact of aging. For this woman, the "half a dozen square-shouldered Zippos" (4) serve both as a reminder of her past and as a kind of charm that resurrects the voices from her past. The rest of her things are peripheral to the remembrance of her husband and friends.

CARL SANDBURG, *Buttons* (p. 168)

This poem examines a topic that continues to be present whenever the media examine the costs of war; televised coverage of the wars in Vietnam and the Persian Gulf instigated similar commentary since this poem was written in 1915. Sandburg's poem hinges on the "laughing young man, sunny with freckles" (line 5), seemingly unaware of the meaning of his actions as he marks the day's casualties on the map "slammed up for advertising" (1) in a newspaper office. The map itself is a symbol for the war losses; the absence of gravity in the actions of the man who works to update that symbol is the inconsistency that drives the poem. The parenthetical examination of the "buttons" of the poem's title demonstrates the distance between the thoughtlessness of the young man and the tragic events played out on the actual battlefield.

Students are likely to be familiar with other media and their relationship to tragedy: How do television and radio announcers convey the gravity of the deaths they report? How do doctors and police officers on television series vary their emotional responses to crime and death depending on context?

POSSIBLE CONNECTIONS TO OTHER SELECTIONS

Jeannette Barnes, "Battle-Piece" (text p. 111)
Kenneth Fearing, "AD" (text p. 162; question 1, following)
Henry Reed, "Naming of Parts" (text p. 176; question 1, following)

CONNECTION QUESTION IN TEXT (p. 168) WITH ANSWER

1. Discuss the symbolic treatment of war in this poem, Kenneth Fearing's "AD" (p. 162), and Henry Reed's "Naming of Parts" (p. 176).

    Sandburg's poem establishes the symbol of buttons for the losses of wartime, with a parenthetical examination that imagines the actual deaths and wounds beyond the map and its markers of victory and loss. Fearing's poem symbolizes the burgeoning Nazi movement by imagining the absurdity of a help-wanted ad detailing the attributes required of would-be Nazis. Reed's poem focuses on a small task, part of a soldier's training; this task is explicitly nonviolent, an exercise in vocabulary and mechanics, not related to death and wounds. All three authors focus on some small detail of wartime, real or imagined, that allows the reader to grasp the actual horror of war.

WALLACE STEVENS, *Anecdote of the Jar* (p. 169)

Stevens's study in contrasts begins and ends with its setting, Tennessee. Discuss with your students why Stevens might have chosen this place. The jar on the hill is clearly different from its surroundings. It is round and purposeful, while the natural world is wild and disorderly. However, these contrasting elements are privileged differently as the poem develops. At the beginning, the "slovenly wilderness" (line 3) has a negative connotation. In the middle stanza, the elements appear to be in balance: the wilderness is "no longer wild" (6) and the jar rests firmly "upon the ground" (7), connected with nature. However, in the last stanza, we notice the jar's negative attributes, seeing that it is "gray and bare" (10).

Stevens's poem critiques Romantic ideas about the way human sensibility orders nature. At the end, the jar does not just order the wilderness around itself, it "[takes] dominion everywhere" (9). The rhymes around that phrase serve to reinforce the jar's dominance. The strong end-rhymes of "air," "everywhere," and "bare" call attention to the power that the jar embodies as it rules over nature.

POSSIBLE CONNECTIONS TO OTHER SELECTIONS

John Keats, "Ode on a Grecian Urn" (text p. 96; question 1, following)

Jane Kenyon, "The Blue Bowl" (text p. 125)

William Carlos Williams, "The Red Wheelbarrow" (text p. 273)

CONNECTION QUESTION IN TEXT (p. 169) WITH ANSWER

1. Compare the thematic function of the jar in Stevens's poem with that of John Keats's "Ode on a Grecian Urn" (p. 96). What important similarities and differences do you see in the meanings of each? Discuss why you think Stevens and Keats share similar or different ideas about art.

    Keats's urn is an art object. It bears the marks of human production and it represents familiar scenes from human life. Stevens's jar, on the other hand, is nearly invisible as art. It bears no representative intentions. It is meaningless, except for its placement on the hill. Stevens and Keats both see perception as ordering observations of the world into a coherent whole, but Stevens is ambiguous about how the artist controls this ordering. By taking his jar from the world of consumer products instead of from the museum, Stevens undermines the importance of art as a mirror for nature.

WILLIAM STAFFORD, *Traveling through the Dark* (p. 169)

This poem is a gut-wrenching narrative of a man who finds by the side of the road a deer that has been struck dead but whose unborn fawn is still alive. After hesitating a moment, he decides to pursue his original course of action and throw her over the edge of the road. Students might be taken aback by the speaker's reaction to this incident, especially the language he uses to describe the occurrence: "It is usually best to roll them into the canyon" (line 3). Do we believe that he is emotionless or simply that he must suspend his emotions in order to accomplish his task? What is the effect of the truncated final stanza?

One of the surprising qualities about this poem is just how much time Stafford takes to describe his car. Given this description, with its glowing light, its "warm exhaust," the "steady" engine that "purred," the car acquires a stronger lifelike sense than anything else in this poem, which laments the death of something beautiful in the natural world. The car, "aimed ahead," seems symbolically to foreshadow a darker, more inhuman future, in which mechanization replaces old-fashioned Fate.

Providing every physical detail of his encounter with the deer, the speaker sounds like a news reporter, calmly telling his story to his listeners. But the final stanza suggests that he is meditative and brooding, that this incident means much more to him than its details imply, that his thinking involves the fate of the deer as well as that of the human race.

The short final stanza emphasizes its contemplative tone, setting it against the previous stanzas, moving the focus away from the deer, toward the speaker and his fellow human beings. It also suggests the finality of his decision.

POSSIBLE CONNECTIONS TO OTHER SELECTIONS

Andrew Hudgins, "Seventeen" (text p. 170; following)

Langston Hughes, "Dream Variations" (text p. 401)

Alden Nowlan, "The Bull Moose" (text p. 171)

John Updike, "Dog's Death" (text p. 24)

A<small>UDIOVISUAL</small> R<small>ESOURCES</small> (manual p. 381)

ANDREW HUDGINS, *Seventeen* (p. 170)

This brutal poem describes the experience of a teenaged speaker who watches a dog nearly die as it spills out of a pick-up truck ahead of him. After a brief confrontation with the truck driver, it is up to the speaker to put the dog out of its misery. He does so, methodically, and indicates that some time has passed between the event and the present, during which he has been able to contemplate the meaning of it.

Seventeen is not that long ago for many college students, and it may be productive to begin by asking them to describe any defining moments or events that they experienced at or around that age. The speaker cusses at an adult for the first time in his life and expects "a beating" (line 18) in return, which is the punishment a child would have received. What he undergoes is much more painful; you might want to ask students to describe the psychological or social differences between being beaten up and having to do away with a suffering animal.

The poem relies on verbs to communicate the scene; you might want to isolate some of these verbs and discuss why the speaker chose them to paint the picture. It is interesting to note how the speaker begins to rely on adjectives — consider "blue" (33), "loose" (35), and "orange and purple" (36) — in the final six lines of the poem. Does this event somehow change the way he thinks about the world? How does the preponderance of adjectives versus verbs reflect the speaker's emotional or mental state? Why is it significant that he didn't know the words for "butterfly weed and vetch" at the time, but now, when he writes about the scene, he both uses these words and emphasizes that he didn't know the words before?

P<small>OSSIBLE</small> C<small>ONNECTIONS TO</small> O<small>THER</small> S<small>ELECTIONS</small>

Jane Kenyon, "The Blue Bowl" (text p. 125)
William Stafford, "Traveling through the Dark" (text p. 169; question 1, following)

C<small>ONNECTION</small> Q<small>UESTION IN</small> T<small>EXT</small> (p. 171) <small>WITH</small> A<small>NSWER</small>

1. Write an essay that compares the speakers and themes of "Seventeen" and "Traveling through the Dark" (p. 169).

   In both "Seventeen" and "Traveling through the Dark" the speakers come across animals in the road. Each speaker is presented with a moral dilemma: whether and how to kill the animal. Yet William Stafford's speaker seems more detached and ruminative — less emotional — and his moral dilemma is more complex. Hudgins's speaker, though it is clear that he must kill the dog, is also undergoing a certain rite of passage that we can assume has already happened to Stafford's. "Traveling through the Dark" is, perhaps, about complicated choices, "Seventeen" is about growing up.

ALDEN NOWLAN, *The Bull Moose* (p. 171)

This poem describes a conflict between man and nature, one in which man, through his actions, futilely attempts to make nature (that is, the moose) look ridiculous but is rewarded only by appearing cowardly and cruel. The speaker, observing the interactions of a lost bull moose and the townspeople, succeeds in making the townspeople and not the moose look ridiculous. The people demonstrate a complete misunderstanding of the moose; they lack respect for creatures of the wild in general and this trapped moose in particular. They condescend to the moose, treating it like a sideshow freak by feeding it beer, opening its mouth, planting "a little purple cap / of thistles on his head." Their affection for the animal is utterly skewed; they don't realize the moral problems inherent in so amiably agreeing that "it was a shame / to shoot anything so shaggy and cuddlesome." The moose's last act was one of power, strength, and dignity — it refused to die with bottles in its mouth or thistles on its head. As "the bull moose gathered his strength / like a scaffolded king, straightened and lifted its horns," it terrified the onlookers, even the wardens. But the final act of the young men, the honking of the car horns as the moose is executed, serves as both a way to mask their guilt by drowning out the sounds of the screaming moose, and as a sort of victory cry upon winning a cruel, unfair, and dishonorable battle.

POSSIBLE CONNECTION TO ANOTHER SELECTION

William Stafford, "Traveling through the Dark" (text p. 169; question 1, following)

CONNECTION QUESTION IN TEXT (p. 172) WITH ANSWER

1. In an essay compare and contrast how the animals portrayed in "The Bull Moose" and in Stafford's "Traveling through the Dark" (p. 169) are used as symbols.

    In both poems there is a violent clash between humanity and the animal world. In Nowlan's poem, the bull moose symbolizes the reluctant power of nature, which man has abused but which continues to be fearsome. Stafford's speaker thinks deeply and quickly about his ability to influence nature, and though his action is painful, he is ultimately humane in letting the unborn fawn expire.

JULIO MARZÁN, *Ethnic Poetry* (p. 173)

The phrase "The ethnic poet said" begins each of the poem's five stanzas, followed by a quotation and the response of the ethnic audience. In each case the poet speaks in language or imagery that isn't "conventional" — it seems to disrupt conventions of typical Western poetry or thought. In each case the audience responds by eating ethnic food or playing on ethnic instruments. In the final stanza, though, the poet quotes from Robert Frost's "Mending Wall," and the audience's response is to "deeply [understand] humanity" (line 20).

The poem invites us to consider the "proper" response to poetry as it satirizes the notion that poetry is a philosophical venture, that it is supposed to evoke in its listeners a deep understanding of human nature. The irony (and subtle humor) is made thicker by the fact that Frost's poem is about divisions between neighbors and that this poem begins with the assumption that there are differences between ethnic and other poetry. It might be interesting to apply the notion that poetry is meant to evoke a deep understanding about human nature to the poems excerpted within each stanza of "Ethnic Poetry." Is it possible to do so? Why does the "ethnic audience" choose to respond differently? What assumptions are made about the ethnicity of the poet and the audience in each stanza?

This poem may tend to touch off discussions of the "proper" response to poetry and the proper way to construct a poem. Langston Hughes's poem "Formula" (text p. 403) can deepen this discussion because it suggests that poetry is frequently elitist. Is it implicitly so? Has our perception of poetry made it an elitist form as much as the poet's conception that, as Hughes says, it "should treat / Of lofty things"? This is a good opportunity to get students to consider the nature of the barriers between "high" and "low" culture: Where do they experience poetry in their lives besides in college courses? And what is their response to it? Do they ever *read* poetry "for fun," or do they know anyone who does? Have they ever been to a poetry reading? Is the emphasis in contemporary music on lyrics or on melody, instrumentation, and so forth? Would students' responses to the lyrics of their favorite band be altered if those lyrics were presented in a classroom? (The general question: Does our understanding of poetry depend more on the context in which we read it or on the nature of the poetry itself?)

Robert Frost, "Mending Wall" (text p. 359)

Langston Hughes, "Formula" (text p. 403; question 1, following)

CONNECTION QUESTION IN TEXT (p. 173) WITH ANSWER

1. Write an essay that discusses the speaker's ideas about what poetry should be in "Ethnic Poetry" and in Langston Hughes's "Formula" (p. 000).

    Both poems ironically consider the notion that poetry "should treat / Of lofty things." In Hughes's poem, lofty poetry is not separated from poetry about every-day occurrences specifically by ethnicity; his concern is that poetry overlooks the pain of human existence. Marzán's concern is that listeners might tend to privilege poetry that seems deeply philosophical rather than culturally resonant.

SHERMAN ALEXIE, *On the Amtrak from Boston to New York City* (p. 174)

Alexie's poem depends on a dramatic irony — the white woman seated next to the poet on the train marvels at the monuments of "American history" (line 6) while Alexie is conscious of the culture that predated European colonization. Alexie's time "back East" (7) has made him confront a different part of American history than he sees in Washington, but he has learned little. However, Alexie chooses not to confront the woman with the knowledge that white achievements were not the first on the continent because "she smiled so much and seemed delighted" (27). He decides against exposing her cheerful, and probably unwitting, hypocrisy.

What does it mean for Alexie to refer to Spokane as "the city I pretend to call my home" (17)? Note that he also refers to the woman talking about "her country's history" (33). The poet's moves to distance himself from America foreshadow the surprise of the last line, in which he identifies the woman with "the enemy" who "thought I was one of their own" (37). This line is the only one in the poem that stands on its own, apart from the other stanzas. The break from the quatrain form suggests Alexie's break with the polite acquiescence to the white view of history. The rupture is an imagined one — his respect for elders prevents him from contradicting the woman — but in the poem it results in a revelation.

Diane Burns, "Sure You Can Ask Me a Personal Question" (text p. 227)

William Heyen, "The Trains" (text p. 201)

Lydia Huntley Sigourney, "Indian Names" (text p. 622)

JAMES MERRILL, *Casual Wear* (p. 175)

Merrill has been called a conversational poet. His familiarity with the lives of American aristocrats may result from his wealthy background, which especially influenced his earlier poetry.

Jeans, of course, are "casual wear," and by implication, this act of random terrorism appears to be a casual flourish of some unseen hand. That relation in sum seems to be the import of this poem. Because of the enjambment of lines between stanzas, students may not at first observe that the stanzas rhyme with an *abba* pattern — except the middle two lines of the first stanza. But then, what would rhyme with "Ferdi Plinthbower"? Rhyme, however — along with odd, lengthy names; precise statistics; and descriptions of human beings as proper demographic models — detracts from our ability to feel the weight of this crime against humankind and our intuitive understanding of the moral workings of the universe. The inverse parallels between "tourist" and "terrorist" seem just too chillingly neat.

So what might Merrill actually be saying in this poem? Perhaps he is not so much speaking out against terrorist activity as talking about the media, with its formulaic scenarios, and the number-plotting social scientists, who surround such an event with their own dehumanizing mist of facts and figures. In the final irony of the poem, we know the name of the clothing designer but not that of the terrorist's victim.

Comments on Merrill's poetry include *James Merrill: Essays in Criticism,* edited by David Lehman and Charles Berger (Ithaca: Cornell UP, 1983), and Judith Moffet's *James Merrill: An Introduction to the Poetry* (New York: Columbia UP, 1984).

POSSIBLE CONNECTION TO ANOTHER SELECTION

Peter Meinke, "The ABC of Aerobics" (text p. 285; question 1, following)

CONNECTION QUESTION IN TEXT (p. 175) **WITH ANSWER**

1. Compare the satire in this poem with that in Peter Meinke's "The ABC of Aerobics" (p. 285). What is satirized in each poem? Which satire do you think is more pointed?

    Meinke's satire directs itself at the frantic health-conscious exercising that has become a part of our culture. Merrill's addresses a different aspect of the same culture, the materialism and media hype that eradicate the individual, leaving us with facts, figures, and wardrobe reports. Merrill's poem has a sobering life-and-death message, whereas Meinke's seems to have more hope for immediate change. Merrill's speaker is bitter; Meinke's satire is comical.

AUDIOVISUAL RESOURCES (manual p. 378)

HENRY REED, *Naming of Parts* (p. 176)

The irony of this poem is situational. The instructor (no doubt an army sergeant addressing a group of raw recruits) is filled with self-importance as he drones on about naming the rifle parts, wholly oblivious to the silent beauty of the spring day. The season, though, arouses in the young recruit's thoughts reminders of a world far more vibrant than that of weaponry. Students should be able to distinguish between sergeant and recruit in the exchange of voices. The recruit's musings begin in the second half of the fourth line of each stanza, and the final line works to deflect the authoritative tone of the earlier part of the stanza. Discussion of rifle parts summons up with ironic aptness physical allusions, which the young recruit inevitably thinks of as he looks at the beautiful gardens in spring, assaulted by the vigorous bees.

POSSIBLE CONNECTIONS TO OTHER SELECTIONS

E. E. Cummings, "she being Brand" (text p. 73)
Linda Pastan, "Marks" (text p. 151)

RACHEL HADAS, *The Compact* (p. 177)

In the first stanza, Hadas emphasizes the change that is occurring in these girls' lives and the swiftness with which it is happening. The distance from the girls' to the boys' school is "short" and "steep" (line 1), and Hadas's repetition of "uphill" (1, 7) suggests that struggle is an important aspect of the journey. Whatever change is happening, it's too quick to be comprehensible to the girls — "We didn't know" (6) — but they seem to have made a "pact" to adhere to the rules of young womanhood in getting out their makeup. Hadas's poem turns on the various meanings of the word *compact*. You might have your students list as many contexts as they can for *compact*. It not only suggests the physical object of the makeup case, and an agreement between parties, but may also be used as an adjective to describe things packed tightly together or as a verb to indicate the action of bringing parts together.

The second stanza plays on the well-known formulation of love in Plato's *Symposium*. (Your students may be more familiar with this idea through the movie *Hedwig and the Angry Inch*.) In the dialogue, Aristophanes suggests that humans were once androgynous beings with four arms and legs and two heads. As a punishment for pride, Zeus split them in two with a lightning bolt, condemning them to spend their lives longing and searching for their lost halves. Hadas's powder compact is an understated refiguring of this myth. She personifies the object, suggesting that, while the two sides are separated, they are "longing to be closed" (14).

Finally, you might ask your students how this poem works as a sonnet. It does not follow either of the basic stanza patterns of the sonnet, but it does include a strong turn and, like the original sonnets, takes love as its subject.

POSSIBLE CONNECTIONS TO OTHER SELECTIONS

Marge Piercy, "The Secretary Chant" (text p. 22)
Sylvia Plath, "Mirror" (text p. 145)

ROBERT BROWNING, *My Last Duchess* (p. 177)

Robert Browning lived with his parents in a London suburb until he married Elizabeth Barrett at age thirty-four; he had previously left home only to attend boarding school and for short trips abroad. He and his wife lived in Italy for fifteen years, a period in which he produced some of his first memorable poems. *Men and Women,* published in 1855, gained Browning the initial intimations of his later fame. The poet returned to England after his wife died in 1861. His work continued to elicit increasing public (if not always critical) acclaim.

Ask students to explore contexts for Robert Browning on *LiterActive*.

Ironically, the speaker is talking about the portrait of his last duchess (how many went before?) to the marriage broker, who is handling the current arrangement between the duke and the broker's "master," the father of the bride-to-be.

Play a recording of Richard Howard reading "My Last Duchess" on *Literature Aloud*.

The last wife's principal fault was that she was too democratic in her smiles; she did not reserve them for the duke alone. The duke holds no regard for kindness and thoughtfulness; he thinks only of money, rank, and name. He treats women as objects and possessions.

The visitor seems to want to leave early, perhaps to warn his master of the unfeeling tyrant who would marry the master's daughter at a cut rate (cf. lines 47–54).

Students may have already read this dramatic monologue in high school. The second time around they should appreciate the irony even more as the duke reveals so much of his own character while ostensibly controlling the situation.

POSSIBLE CONNECTIONS TO OTHER SELECTIONS

Mark Halliday, "Graded Paper" (text p. 507)
Katharyn Howd Machan, "Hazel Tells LaVerne" (text p. 77; question 1, following)

1. Write an essay describing the ways in which the speakers of "My Last Duchess" and Katharyn Howd Machan's "Hazel Tells LaVerne" (p. 77) inadvertently reveal themselves.

    In both cases the speaker has a story to tell, and both speakers are trying to paint a favorable picture of themselves as they do so. The speaker of Browning's poem gets himself in trouble as he continues to talk, indicating the fate of his last duchess through unsuppressed expressions of his own unfulfilled desire. As he describes the portrait, he eventually gets away from art and into the character of the duchess, wondering all the while how he should express himself. The speaker of "Hazel Tells LaVerne" reveals her unconscious desire to be taken away from her situation as she repeats the line "me a princess," focusing (without meaning to do so) on herself rather than on the frog whose story she is narrating. Students with a background in psychology might be able to flesh out the motivations behind these speakers' tales even more.

AUDIOVISUAL RESOURCES (manual p. 373)

WILLIAM BLAKE, *The Chimney Sweeper* (p. 179)

There is an ironic distance in this poem between the speaker, who seems to be too young to make judgments, and Blake, who through his ironic perspective underscores the harm that comes from too meekly doing one's duty, not to mention the evil of a society indifferent to the plight of "thousands of sweepers" whose only pleasure is in dreams. Needless to say, sacrificing one's hair for the sake of on-the-job cleanliness is not a principle Blake would endorse.

Ask students to explore contexts for William Blake on *LiterActive*.

On the surface the poem could be interpreted as a dream of desire for some beneficent angel to release the boys from their "coffins of black" (the chimneys). More likely, the dream expresses a desire for release through death from the tortuous and life-threatening trials of sweeping soot from chimneys. Here again, irony operates, in that a dream of death makes it easier for the boy to face his life the next morning.

POSSIBLE CONNECTION TO ANOTHER SELECTION

Langston Hughes, "Negro" (text p. 398)

WALT WHITMAN, *From* Song of Myself (p. 180)

Whitman's *Leaves of Grass* was a radical departure from existing poetic norms. The form, the language, and the subject matter of the poems in the book challenged Victorian styles and mores. Whitman never found a wide audience during his lifetime, but his work changed the course of American poetry. In this excerpt from "Song of Myself," students will see Whitman's optimism and his democratic sensibility. He found the figure of grass important enough to feature it in the title of his book; this selection suggests why. Have your students discuss why grass is a perfect metaphor for Whitman's vision of America. What does he mean by saying that grass is the "flag of [his] disposition" (line 3)?

The long lines of "Song of Myself" signal that this poem is not shaped in traditional stanza patterns. In order to call your students' attention to how Whitman does structure his poem, have them analyze the first words of each line. What kind of shifts happen among the "I guess," "It may be" and "I perceive" sections? The changes in these repeated phrases advance the developing ideas of the poem.

POSSIBLE CONNECTIONS TO OTHER SELECTIONS

Emily Dickinson, "I heard a Fly buzz — when I died —" (text p. 324; question 1, following)

John Donne, "Death Be Not Proud" (text p. 290)

CONNECTION QUESTION IN TEXT (p. 181) WITH ANSWER

1. Compare attitudes toward death in Whitman's poem and in Emily Dickinson's "I heard a Fly buzz — when I died — " (p. 324).

    Whitman uses images of death that could be grotesque in another poet's hands — grass sprouting from the heads and mouths of dead bodies. Yet his tone is tender toward the dead and reverent. The grass that grows wildly from the graves is "beautiful" (line 12) and as the poet thinks about the people buried in them, he thinks "It may be if I had known them I would have loved them" (15). Yet the meaning of their deaths remains a mystery to him. He can't figure out what it is they are trying to say or what has become of them.

    In Dickinson's meditation on death, she adopts the persona of a dying person and imagines that the moment of death is one of intense stillness, so that the smallest sensation would be magnified to great significance. In this heightened state of awareness, the speaker is able to describe the sound of the fly metaphorically as "Blue — uncertain stumbling" (13). Then, finally, her senses fail and she can no longer "see to see" (16). While Whitman considers the impossibility of making the mental leap to understanding the dead, Dickinson attempts to imagine the moment at which the dying person becomes detached from his or her body.

GARY SOTO, *Behind Grandma's House* (p. 181)

In this poem Soto captures a moment that almost every individual experiences in growing up — the trying on of different identities to discover one that "fits." Ultimately, the grandma in the poem helps the speaker along in the process by showing him how the identity he is trying cannot work. Students may connect the episode described in this poem to times in their own lives when they've searched for an identity or tried too hard to prove something to themselves or others.

Ask students to explore contexts for Gary Soto on LiterActive.

You might begin the class discussion by suggesting that the real "happening" of the poem is the arrival of the grandma, who, with total nonchalance, sets the speaker straight on what it means to be tough. Ask students why Soto limited his description of the grandma to simply "her apron flapping in a breeze, / her hair mussed" (lines 19–20). She seems a fairly "typical" grandma in appearance — clearly she's not looking for a fight — yet her simple "Let me help you" (20) followed by a well-aimed punch teaches the speaker more about toughness than he learned through an entire alley's worth of vandalism.

POSSIBLE CONNECTION TO ANOTHER SELECTION

Sharon Olds, "Rite of Passage" (text p. 279; question 1, following)

CONNECTION QUESTION IN TEXT (p. 182) WITH ANSWER

1. Write an essay comparing the themes of "Behind Grandma's House" and Sharon Olds's "Rite of Passage" (p. 279).

    Both poems suggest that boys will be boys; in this poem we get the sense that some boys, like this speaker who "wanted fame" (line 1), will cross the boundaries of acceptable behavior to be accepted. In Olds's poem it seems that all boys are capable of doing so, but for them the notion of acceptable behavior changes with context. The boy in Soto's poem is not going to achieve fame by behaving this way in front of his grandmother, or even behind her house. The boys at the birthday party in Olds's poem will only achieve fame if they conform because they are at a party. The speaker in Olds's poem is unlike the grandmother in Soto's poem because she is outnumbered; her son is bound to go through his rite of passage with his peers. Soto's speaker also grows and learns something, but it is through the discipline of an elder rather than through the coaxing of friends.

AUDIOVISUAL RESOURCES (manual p. 381)

PERSPECTIVE

EZRA POUND, *On Symbols* (p. 182)

Consider Pound's use of the word *natural* in the first line of the passage. Does he mean that a symbol should be drawn from an object in nature or that a symbol should have a natural, easy relationship to the idea it is meant to symbolize? Students might suggest other interpretations. Does Pound's example of the hawk at the end of the passage help to clarify his meaning? Ask students what a hawk might symbolize. Using other Pound poems in this anthology, identify the symbols the poet uses and discuss whether they are "natural" in either sense of the word. Look at Edgar Allan Poe's "The Haunted Palace" (text p. 159), wherein the human mind and head are compared to a house, or Edna St. Vincent Millay's "I will put Chaos into fourteen lines" (text p. 244), in which writing poetry is compared to rape, as examples to discuss which method of using symbols they think conveys meaning most effectively.

7

Sounds

Encouraging students to read aloud is vital for this chapter. Although initially you may have to lead by example, you will probably want to shift the focus onto student readers at some point. In some cases you may find yourself confronting a considerable degree of resistance, particularly if there has not been much reading aloud previously. Much of this resistance stems from fear of embarrassment, and dealing with it requires either the creation of a "safe space" in which students can read without fear of others snickering or a slightly raucous classroom environment in which students don't feel as much pressure to be "cool."  Ask students to explore *sound* on *LiterActive* and at **bedfordstmartins .com/meyerpoetry**.

If you have a group of particularly shy students, you might find it helpful to assign students poems in advance, so that they have a chance to read the poem through a couple of times before being called on to speak out before the class. If you have a mix of extraverts and introverts, you might schedule the class so that the extraverts read "cold" and announce at the end of class the poems the introverts will read in the next session, to give them fair warning.

In most cases the addition of student voices to the classroom will help increase involvement and raise the energy level. If you have not featured much student reading in the class so far, this chapter would be an appropriate time to do so.

In addition to including student voices in the classroom, this chapter affords an opportunity to include the voices of the poets as well: the poems of Galway Kinnell, Hopkins, Carroll, Pope, and Kingston are available on audio recordings (Kinnell and Kingston read their own poems). Many of these recordings are available on the *Literature Aloud* CD-ROM that accompanies *Poetry*. It is perhaps a judgment call as to whether you should introduce these readings before students have done much reading on their own, in order to provide models of reading for them, or to wait [Web] Ask students to research the poets in this chapter at **bedfordstmartins.com/ meyerpoetry**. until after students have some experience, to keep from intimidating them into silence. If you have included recordings in previous chapters, this may not be an issue here. In any event, recordings can be very useful in giving students a sense of the reality of the people "behind the page." You may find it appropriate to do readings or bring in recordings of poems that have been popular with students earlier in the class and evaluate the poets' use of sound in relation to the students' own preference of these poems.

Thematically, there are some interesting poems in this chapter. If you do not want the focus on reading to overwhelm a discussion of these poems, you could use the reading as a springboard to raise the class's interest and energy, and to give them specific features to discuss when they make connections between the sound of a poem and its "message."

ANONYMOUS, *Scarborough Fair* (p. 184)

Your students may or may not be acquainted with the Simon and Garfunkel version of this ballad that was used in the 1960s as an antiwar song, and the use of this traditional ballad in that context may lead to some interesting discussion about the difference between the oral and written tradition.

As a ballad, "Scarborough Fair" follows a clear pattern: four feet to a line with an *abab* rhyme scheme and repeated second and fourth lines. In addition, in all but the first stanza, the first words of the stanza are "Tell her to" followed by the introduction of an impossible task that, if performed, will reconcile the speaker of the poem to the "bonny lass" who was once his true lover. The impossible nature of these tasks is perhaps a clue as to how much hope the speaker in the poem has of reconciliation.

The effect of the refrain is soothing — readers and listeners come to expect the repeated lines, and the rhythm of these lines is peaceful. The herbs that are mentioned in the refrain are associated with female power (parsley was used to decorate tombs, sage represents wisdom, rosemary is for memory, and thyme is thought to enhance courage). In addition, both sage and rosemary had the connotation of growing in gardens where women ruled the households. Why might the poet have chosen these herbs as repeated symbols in this ballad? What message might the poet have been trying to convey?

POSSIBLE CONNECTIONS TO OTHER SELECTIONS

Anonymous, "Bonny Barbara Allan" (text p. 585)

John Donne, "A Valediction: Forbidding Mourning" (text p. 150)

JOHN UPDIKE, *Player Piano* (p. 185)

This poem is a listening exercise in how to translate the sounds poetry can produce to musical analogues we have already heard. From light ditties through more somber 1920s chase-scene music, perhaps, to a medley of chords and light cadences, this poem explores a player piano's repertoire. In doing so, does the poem do anything *besides* impress us with its sounds? Does reading the poem allow us anything beyond the sheer joy of the sounds of words and the way they can be manipulated?

Ask students to explore contexts for John Updike on *LiterActive*.

POSSIBLE CONNECTION TO ANOTHER SELECTION

Lenard D. Moore, "Black Girl Tap Dancing" (text p. 234)

MAY SWENSON, *A Nosty Fright* (p. 186)

Because "A Nosty Fright" is much more about sound than sense, be sure to read it, or have students read it, aloud (this may be more difficult than one might anticipate, for the transposed consonants often have the effect of creating tongue-twisters). Does the fractured diction have any purpose other than humor? Remind students that people who are upset or frightened often find it difficult to speak clearly.

Notice that sometimes the poetic technique used here results in transpositions that are actual words. Do any of these seem appropriate in this poem, for instance, "Bat" in line 24 or "fright" in line 25? Do any of them seem out of place, like "mitten" (20)? Have students suggest definitions for some of the nonsense words and phrases, based on their sounds. Compare the poem with Lewis Carroll's "Jabberwocky" (text p. 200). Are the techniques for creating new words the same in both poems?

POSSIBLE CONNECTION TO ANOTHER SELECTION

Lewis Carroll [Charles Lutwidge Dodgson], "Jabberwocky" (text p. 200)

AUDIOVISUAL RESOURCES (manual p. 381)

EMILY DICKINSON, *A Bird came down the Walk* — (p. 187)

Silent reading of this poem, followed by reading it aloud, will reinforce the connection between sound and sense. In particular, students should hear the difference between the irregular movement of the first three stanzas and the smoothness of the last six lines, a difference created visually by punctuation but even more obvious when the poem is heard.

> Ask students to explore contexts for Emily Dickinson on *LiterActive*.

One of the poetic techniques that characterizes Emily Dickinson's poetry is her use of unexpected words and images. Consider her depiction of the bird's eyes and of his flight. How can eyes be "rapid" (line 9)? How can they hurry (10)? How can feathers "unroll" (15)? How is flight like rowing (16)? What is the effect created by the use of unusual language to describe an ordinary creature?

Compare the way the sounds of poetry are used to create a sense of an animal's movement in this poem and in Rilke's "The Panther" (text p. 124). Are the panther's movements in any way like the bird's?

POSSIBLE CONNECTIONS TO OTHER SELECTIONS

Gerard Manley Hopkins, "The Windhover" (text p. 605)

Rainer Maria Rilke, "The Panther" (text p. 124)

GALWAY KINNELL, *Blackberry Eating* (p. 189)

Some poems are memorable for their themes, while others are enjoyed not for what they say but for how they say it. This poem seems to fall into this second category, as Kinnell tries in lieu of the blackberries themselves to offer us a blackberry language. It would probably be a good idea to read this poem aloud in class. Kinnell plays with the kinesthesia of the sound in words such as *strengths* or *squinched*, which by their compacted consonance physically suggest to him the pressure of the tongue bursting open the berry's mysterious ("black art") icy sweetness. What other words are there (you might ask) that seem to touch the inside of the body before they are spoken? Look at some of the heavily consonantal words in lines 12 and 13, mark-

> Play a recording of Galway Kinnell reading "Blackberry Eating" on *Literature Aloud*.

ing especially words like *splurge* and *language*. Lines 4–6, besides containing good examples of consonance patterns, also express a pathetic fallacy, with Kinnell's imaginative supposition that blackberry bushes are punished with nettles for knowing the art of blackberry making. You might ask what, if anything, this image adds to the poem. Probably it underscores Kinnell's whimsical sense of the black artistry of blackberry making.

The sound then moves from the hard *b* of *blackberry* to the softer *s*'s of the final lines. Many assonant *o*'s occur in the first lines, *e*'s and *a*'s in the middle of the poem. The sounds attempt to capture the delectable berries, making the experience of reading the poem as sensuous as eating a berry.

More than providing a message of "truth" for its reader, this poem invites us into an experience of sound and image. The poem is about language in that it considers the difficulty of capturing an idea in words and communicating it effectively. Attempting to write a poem can be as much a learning experience about poetry as attempting to write about a poem. Perhaps some members of the class would like to try writing their own lyric beginning with the words *I love to*.

POSSIBLE CONNECTIONS TO OTHER SELECTIONS

Helen Chasin, "The Word *Plum*" (text p. 209)
Pablo Neruda, "The United Fruit Co." (text p. 577)

AUDIOVISUAL RESOURCES (manual pp. 377–78)

RICHARD ARMOUR, *Going to Extremes* (p. 190)

What are the "extremes" to which this poem goes? How does the poet connect the two words that describe the extremes?

Even if students are unfamiliar with scansion, they should be able to detect a difference in the way words are emphasized in lines 1 and 3 as opposed to lines 2 and 4. Ask them to describe how the sound shifts coincide with the action of the poem. In speaking lines 1 and 3 aloud, one can almost feel the sharp movements of the bottle. In lines 2 and 4, it is as though the bottle is at rest, with the person who has been shaking it now waiting to see whether or not the catsup will come. Having students actually "shake" an imaginary catsup bottle as they recite the poem might be an effective way to connect sound to sense.

POSSIBLE CONNECTION TO ANOTHER SELECTION

Margaret Atwood, "you fit into me" (text p. 135)

ROBERT SOUTHEY, *From "The Cataract of Lodore"* (p. 191)

Although Robert Southey is now known chiefly for his association with some of the great poets of the Romantic period, such as Wordsworth and Coleridge, he was very popular in his own time and became the poet laureate of England in 1813. He is also credited with the first published version of the children's story *The Three Bears*.

In a twenty-three-line introductory stanza that is not excerpted here, the poet reveals that his son and daughter had requested him to tell them — in verse — about the water at Lodore. He also introduces himself as the poet laureate. Does having this information in any way change your students' response to the poem that follows?

Are any lines in the poem especially memorable? Why is it appropriate that line 69, with its thirteen syllables, is metrically the longest line of the poem?

TIP FROM THE FIELD

One tip I've found helpful in teaching sound in poetry is to have students stand in a tight circle and recite the excerpt from "The Cataract of Lodore" in round-robin fashion, one after another. Each student reads a line in the order of the poem, repeating the poem several times, faster each time. The results, in terms of student response, are remarkable.

— NANCY VEIGA, *Modesto Junior College*

POSSIBLE CONNECTION TO ANOTHER SELECTION

A. E. Housman, "Loveliest of trees, the cherry now" (text p. 238)

PERSPECTIVE

DAVID LENSON, *On the Contemporary Use of Rhyme* (p. 194)

You might ask students to find contemporary poems that make subtle use of rhyme. Philip Larkin's poems are good examples of the effective use of slant rhyme and enjambment to camouflage the rhymes in a poem. Conversely, you might ask students to look for songs that don't use rhyme.

Students might be interested in speculating on why writers are returning to rhyme. Is more formal poetry appropriate for our time and culture? Or is it simply a question of rebelling against the norm (in our time, unrhymed poetry)?

GERARD MANLEY HOPKINS, *God's Grandeur* (p. 194)

Gerard Manley Hopkins was a deeply religious man, a Jesuit ordained in 1877. He had previously graduated from Oxford University and joined the Roman Catholic Church in 1866. He served a number of parishes before being appointed a professor of classics at University College, Dublin. Although he tried to keep his poetic vocation from interfering with his spiritual one, he wasn't successful, and he suffered greatly because of this conflict, once burning all his finished work and another time forsaking poetry for seven years.

Although this poem follows sonnet form and an exact rhyme scheme, the first eight lines still read very roughly. How does the poet achieve this effect? Note the disruptions in rhythm as well as the use of cacophonic sounds. Have students try reading line 4 aloud to better appreciate its difficulty. Is there any change in the level of disruption or the level of cacophony in the last six lines? What is the effect of the inserted "ah!" in the last line?

Compare the halting beginning and smooth ending of this poem to the similar transition that occurs in Emily Dickinson's "A Bird came down the Walk —" (text p. 187). How does Dickinson's bird compare with the bird image Hopkins evokes in the last two lines?

POSSIBLE CONNECTIONS TO OTHER SELECTIONS

William Wordsworth, "It Is a Beauteous Evening, Calm and Free" (text p. 633)
———, "The World Is Too Much with Us" (text p. 242)

AUDIOVISUAL RESOURCES (manual p. 376)

THOMAS LUX, *Onomatopoeia* (p. 196)

Lux's poem works as an extended redefinition of onomatopoeia, and he brings in as examples words and phrases we wouldn't normally classify that way. You might first have your class discuss what they know about onomatopoeia and give some of their own examples. Then ask them if "cerulean blue" or "dewlap" fit into their definitions. Lux wants to give onomatopoeia a broader significance; he thinks that many words, beyond the obvious ones like "plop" or "glug," mean the way they sound. Ultimately, the identification of the written word (or the "painting, the dance, the play") with the emotion goes beyond the immediate sensory experience: "the deaf can hear it, / the blind see it" (lines 28–29). Lux locates this knowledge in a number of places: the cells, the belly, the tongue, the heart, and finally, "beneath the breastbone" (30) — anywhere but in the mind. How do your students react to what seems like anti-intellectualism in "Onomatopoeia"? Do they respond to poems primarily with their brains or with their bodies?

POSSIBLE CONNECTIONS TO OTHER SELECTIONS

Louis Jenkins, "The Prose Poem" (text p. 271)
Thomas Lux, "The Voice You Hear When You Read Silently" (text p. 58)

1.   Choose a poem from this chapter and write an essay that explains how its "sound, the noise of the sound, is / the thing."

This question will produce a variety of responses. Some of the poems in this chapter use words purely for their musical qualities. Edgar Allan Poe's "Bells" (p. 197) uses the repeated syllable to mimic the sound that is its subject. In "The Trains" (p. 201), William Heyen hears in the name "Treblinka" the sound of a locomotive. The repetitions in Henry Wadsworth Longfellow's "The Tide Rises, the Tide Falls" (p. 202), on the other hand, suggest the eternal repetitions of that cycle. Other poets use sounds to convey tone, and sometimes the sounds of the poem cut across its meaning, as do the lilting rhymes of Eliza Griswold's grave "Occupation" (p. 202). Finally, some poems are so invested in sound that they eschew literal meaning. In "Jabberwocky" (p. 200), Lewis Carroll uses pure sound by inventing new words to convey his tone.

EDGAR ALLAN POE, *The Bells* (p. 197)

Divided into four sections, each corresponding to a type of bell (sleigh bells, wedding bells, alarm bells, and death-knells), this poem relies heavily on onomatopoeia. As the poem's stanzas grow increasingly longer and the subject becomes increasingly heavier, the reader moves through a series of psychological adjustments, exploited by the sonorous qualities of language.

The sound of the bells also becomes increasingly heavy as the poem progresses, from tinkling to tolling. Any discussion of this poem will depend largely on the way it is read aloud in class. You might have to coax students to read the poem as it calls to be read. Take, for example, the repetition of the word *bells* at the end of each stanza. How do we know how long to pause between each utterance of this word based on the rest of the words in that stanza? You may want to ask your students to try to quantify the pauses in the poem. Is it productive to treat each pause the same in a reading? Poe's poem can be thought of as an argument for why poetry should always be read aloud; much of its effect comes from the ways its sounds fall on the ear.

In addition to the effect of repetition and onomatopoeia, "The Bells" serves as a model for other poetic conventions, notably alliteration and assonance, and end-stopped rhyme. Students may become so caught up in Poe's sound-play that they overlook the meaning of the words or the effect of the poem's structure. You can prompt them to elucidate the theme by having them compare parts of speech in each of the four stanzas; what does the progression of the adjectives in the four stanzas tell us (from crystalline to liquid to mad to melancholy)? The same effect can be achieved with nouns, verbs, or adverbs. Would the poem's theme change if the order of the stanzas were mixed up? Have students compare the phrases "keeping time, time, time" and "Runic rhyme" in the first and last stanzas; has the rest of the poem changed the import of these phrases? Is it ironic that the "Runic rhyme" as described in the final stanza is "happy" when the mood seems to have changed from happy to melancholic? The poem's trajectory seems to be important to its theme. A comparison to Southey's "The Cataract of Lodore" (p. 191) might highlight this difference, as Southey's poem seems more driven by momentum than by a thematic focal point.

POSSIBLE CONNECTIONS TO OTHER SELECTIONS

Anonymous, "Bonny Barbara Allan" (text p. 585)
Robert Southey, From "The Cataract of Lodore" (text p. 191; question 1, following)

1. Compare Poe's sound effects with Robert Southey's in "The Cataract of Lodore" (p. 191). Which poem do you find more effective in its use of sound? Explain why.

    The poets use different methods to create their sound effects. Poe relies more on repetition than Southey does. "The Cataract of Lodore" strings together words that rhyme — "And rushing and flushing and brushing and gushing" (line 63) — rarely returning to a word that has already been used. Poe also combines rhyming words in quick succession — "By the twanging / And the clanging" (58–59) — but the refrain always returns to bells. Southey's poem thus conveys the sense of something rushing endlessly onward, whereas Poe's poem conveys the sense of something that resounds. Each is appropriate to its subject.

LEWIS CARROLL [CHARLES LUTWIDGE DODGSON], *Jabberwocky* (p. 200)

" 'Jabberwocky' is no mere piece of sound experimentation but a serious short narrative poem describing a young man's coming of age as he seeks out and kills the tribal terror." Test that description on your students, and they will, one hopes, turn around and tell you that the fun of this poem and the justification for its being reside in its sound and word creations.

Carroll kept his own glossary for some of the words in this poem, which Alice read through her looking glass. The glossary entries and copious notes about the poem are provided by Martin Gardner in *The Annotated Alice* (New York: Bramhall House, 1960, pp. 191–97). The notes are too extensive to include here, but as a sampling, here is the first stanza "translated":

'Twas time for making dinner (bryllyg — to broil),
    and the "smooth and active" (slimy + lithe) badgers

Did scratch like a dog (gyre — giaour)
    and drill holes (gimble) in the side of the hill:

All unhappy were the Parrots (now extinct; they lived on veal and
    under sundials),

And the grave turtles (who lived on swallows and oysters) squeaked.

Reality bores its head through the hills and holes of "Jabberwocky," and certain words in the poem have their place in the *OED*. These include *rath*, an Irish word for a circular earthen wall; *Manx*, a Celtic name for the Isle of Man; *whiffling*, smoking, drinking, or blowing short puffs; *Caloo*, the sound and name of an arctic duck; *beamish*, old form of *beaming*; *chortled*, Carroll's own coinage, meaning "laughed"; and *gallumphing*, another of Carroll's creations, which according to him is a cross between *gallop* and *triumphant* and means "to march on exultantly with irregular bounding movements."

POSSIBLE CONNECTION TO ANOTHER SELECTION

May Swenson, "A Nosty Fright" (text p. 186; question 1, following)

CONNECTION QUESTION IN TEXT (p. 201) WITH ANSWER

1. Compare Carroll's strategies for creating sound and meaning with those used by Swenson in "A Nosty Fright" (p. 186).

    Whereas Swenson transposes letters to create amusing sound patterns and effects, Carroll combines and alters words to invent a new language for his speaker.

Carroll's technique is harder to translate word for word; it requires more of his audience's imaginative effort.

WILLIAM HEYEN, *The Trains* (p. 201)

For students who don't know, explain that Treblinka is the name of a Nazi concentration camp located near Warsaw, Poland. To illustrate Heyen's use of sound, you may want to open discussion by reading the poem aloud to your class. By repeating the word *Treblinka*, and by relying on choppy words with sharp, hard consonant sounds, Heyen creates the sound and rhythm of the wheels of a train — a rhythm that is intensified with the repetition of *Treblinka* until it resonates within the reader. In this way the poet uses sound and rhythm to affect the reader. Ask students to provide specific examples from the poem of how sound is used to intensify the horror of Treblinka.

At first, Heyen tells the facts of the story, listing with detachment and distance the statistics of what was removed from Treblinka on freight trains. As the poem continues, however, the statistics gain strength and the reader's horror mounts with each new revelation: Clothing became paper (line 7), watches were saved and kept (8), and women's hair was used for mattresses and dolls (9).

In the fourth stanza, Heyen implies that many people are indirectly linked to the atrocities of Treblinka through the legacy of the material goods culled from the Holocaust. He suggests that the words of his poem might "like to use some of that same paper" (10); "One of those watches may pulse in your own wrist" (11), much like the rhythm of breathing or a pulse; and that someone the reader *knows* may "collect dolls, or sleep on human hair" (12). Ask students to consider the effect of this stanza. Is the poet implying a collective guilt for the Holocaust? Or is he implying that the horror of Treblinka lives on through the material legacy of the dead? In the end, no one escapes Heyen's indictment, and although Commandant Stangl of Treblinka may be dead at last, his legacy lives on in word and sound within anyone who hears the story.

POSSIBLE CONNECTION TO ANOTHER SELECTION

Sherman Alexie, "On the Amtrak from Boston to New York City" (text p. 174)

ELIZA GRISWOLD, *Occupation* (p. 202)

The women in Griswold's poem practice what's euphemistically called the oldest occupation, but they are also living in a country occupied by a foreign power. Occupation in the latter sense has forced them to make a living by the former. Much of the sentiment of "Occupation" is conveyed through objects. Your students will probably notice that the items lost are humble — "chickens, pots, carpets" (line 6). Now the women struggle even to scrape together some "bread or fifteen cents" (3).

The poem starts off on a relatively light note, almost suggesting a dance with the tapping of feet, but it ends with the heartbreaking suggestion of deaths by stoning. You might discuss with your class how Griswold makes such a shift in only a few lines. They probably associate rhymed couplets with light subjects or perhaps with epic poetry. How does this poet's use of couplets complicate her subject matter? Why does she include one unrhymed line? And why is it "weight in tin" that finds no match in Griswold's scheme?

POSSIBLE CONNECTION TO ANOTHER SELECTION

Taslima Nasrin, "At the Back of Progress . . ." (text p. 576)

HENRY WADSWORTH LONGFELLOW, *The Tide Rises, the Tide Falls* (p. 202)

The son of a prominent New England family, Longfellow was an enormously popular poet during his lifetime. Many of his poems, including "The Courtship of Miles Standish" and "Paul Revere's Ride," narrate events from American history. His work was known throughout Europe and translated into many languages, which made Longfellow one of the most famous Americans of his time.

In this short lyric, Longfellow uses the repeated line as a pattern against which the minimal actions of the poem stand out. The rising and falling of the tide is a continuous recurrence. Into this cycle comes the traveler, whose haste suggests he is an outsider in this tidal scene. Even his marks on the landscape will be quickly erased, as "The little waves, with their soft, white hands, / Efface the footprints in the sands" (lines 8-9). The final stanza reinforces his removal from the scene: "nevermore / Returns the traveler to the shore" (13-14). The repeated line comes in again to assert the supremacy of the gentle but endless movement of the ocean. How do your students read the figure of the traveler and his attempt to cut a straight path across the circular movement of time? Does he pose a threat to the scene? Or is he a tragic hero?

POSSIBLE CONNECTIONS TO OTHER SELECTIONS

Percy Bysshe Shelley, "Ozymandias" (text p. 621)
Alfred, Lord Tennyson, "Crossing the Bar" (text p. 55)

JOHN DONNE, *Song* (p. 203)

This poem explores a number of supposed impossibilities, ending with "a woman true, and fair" (line 18). The poem is at once bawdy and cynical; women are promiscuous, but the speaker also feels that they cannot be otherwise. Once students have discerned the speaker's attitude and his tone, take some time to investigate the way the speaker builds his argument. What types of mysteries does he use for comparison in the first stanza?

Donne manages to mix cynicism and lightheartedness here as he verbally throws up his hands at the possibility of finding an honest mind or a woman who is both true and fair. You might spend some time in class discussion exploring how he holds at bay the darker tones of his cynicism. Can we identify with Donne's dilemma today, or have attitudes toward women changed too much? What does the humor in the poem tell us about his fundamental attitude toward women? Students will probably appreciate the hyperbole in the poem. It is as though Donne were saying, "You might as well get with child a mandrake root, as find an honest mind."

The last stanza is especially humorous. Donne claims he would not even go next door to see this reputedly loyal woman. Her reputation for loyalty might hold long enough for his friend to write a letter describing her, but by the time the speaker arrived, she would have been false to two or three other lovers.

As a writing assignment, you might ask students to discuss the humor in this song, humor that would definitely include Donne's use of hyperbole. Students should then try to anticipate a listener's reaction to the speaker and decide whether the speaker is perfectly "straight" in his observations.

POSSIBLE CONNECTIONS TO OTHER SELECTIONS

Anonymous, "Scarborough Fair" (text p. 184)
John Donne, "The Flea" (text p. 597)

ALEXANDER POPE, From *An Essay on Criticism* (p. 204)

Alexander Pope was born in London and, after age twelve, grew up in Windsor Forest. Because his family was Catholic and because he had been afflicted with tuberculosis of the spine, most of his education was completed at home. Catholics couldn't attend university or hold office – chief routes to patronage in those days – so Pope became by necessity as well as by desire and talent the first writer to show that literature could be one's sole support. His work, beginning with translations of the *Iliad* and the *Odyssey,* was both critically approved and financially profitable.

You might begin discussion of this selection by reminding students that the debate over which should take precedence, sound or sense, has been of greater concern to poets than many of us realize or recall.

Pope enjoys a little self-reflective mockery in these lines, like the bumper sticker that reads "Eschew Obfuscation." What he says, he does: the iambs march with strict, tuneful regularity in line 4. The word *do* in line 10 is an expletive, or meter filler. Line 11 presents a parade of monosyllables. "Chimes" in line 12 sets up the anticipated "rhymes" in line 13, and line 21 exceeds its bounds, albeit slowly, with the long alexandrine. Line 20 ("A needless Alexandrine") is also a clever play on Pope's name and on himself.

Line 23 uses assonance and some alliteration to suggest what it means; line 24 is a fine example of "easy vigor," straightforward and brief enough; lines 32 and 33 imitate the thought through the manipulation of sounds, particularly the sibilance of the *s*-sound, the growling of the *r*'s, and the forcefulness of the blocks of heavy-stressed words, as in "when loud surges lash."

In line 34 the sounds get stuck in one's throat ("rock's vast weight") and reflect this resisting struggle. Accents in line 35 on "líne tóo lábors" and on "wórds móve slów" create an almost plodding rhythm that imitates the sense of the words. These lines contrast with lines 36 and 37, which contain far more light-stressed words and use a much more direct and smooth syntax.

Careful reading of much contemporary poetry will reveal the continuing validity of Pope's observations. In any case, the power of words fashioned into lines with close attention to sound can be amply demonstrated by observing the structure of popular songs and advertisements.

POSSIBLE CONNECTION TO ANOTHER SELECTION

Langston Hughes, "Formula" (text p. 403)

AUDIOVISUAL RESOURCES (manual p. 380)

HAKI R. MADHUBUTI, *The B Network* (p. 205)

Because Madhubuti's poem does not follow conventional capitalization and punctuation rules, the instances where he does use capitals or punctuation are more emphatic. You might discuss why he chooses to capitalize the words he does: *West, Black, Comprehend, While.* What are the important forces at work in this poem, and how do they interrelate?

It might help to give your class a little background on the Black Arts movement, in which Madhubuti was a prominent figure. In the 1960s, the Black Arts movement was closely connected to the political aims of Black Power. Its proponents wanted to forge a new aesthetic, separate from any ideas about art brought down from European models. "The B Network" argues for this kind of new cultural identity. Like many other works from the Black Arts period, it also draws on African American speech patterns for its musical qualities. Your students will certainly notice the alliteration in the poem, which Madhubuti hints at with his title, and will probably hear the many internal rhymes and assonance. They may also recognize this style of poetry, with its affinity to performance, as a predecessor to rap music. The last line of the poem, however, departs from the style of the rest of the poem: "write the exam" (line 34) sounds more prosaic than anything that has come before, and Madhubuti emphasizes the shift by setting the single line on its own. However, he continues the play of sounds by slant-rhyming "exam" with "brotherman." How significant a change in tone is this last line? What does the poet accomplish there?

POSSIBLE CONNECTIONS TO OTHER SELECTIONS

Langston Hughes, "Dream Boogie" (text p. 410; question 1, following)
Lenard D. Moore, "Black Girl Tap Dancing" (text p. 234)

CONNECTION QUESTION FROM TEXT (p. 206) WITH ANSWER

1. Compare the style and themes of "The B Network" with Langston Hughes's "Dream Boogie" (p. 410).

    Both "The B Network" and "Dream Boogie" draw parallels between African American music and racial uplift. They see bopping or boogieing as a form of defiance. Hughes's poem is more confrontational in that it seems to speak to a white audience that misinterprets the actions of the dancer. Madhubuti's is characteristic of the Black Arts movement because it does not assume a white audience, but rather speaks directly to African Americans.

MAXINE HONG KINGSTON, *Restaurant* (p. 206)

You may wish to begin a discussion of this poem by noting the way Kingston has structured the lines — they are rhymed couplets (though often the rhymes are slant), and they have no regular rhythm or meter. Because there is no particular meter, the rhymes are subtle and unpredictable, and the line breaks take the reader by surprise. This irregular rhythm lends a sense of breathlessness to the poem — readers rarely get to relax as they move from one line to the next, because many of the lines are heavily enjambed as they adhere to the poem's rhyme scheme. To demonstrate this breathless pacing, you might ask students to read aloud the first eight lines, where only lines five and eight are end-stopped and where all the rest of the lines create a strong sense of tension and resolution in the reader. The poem's breathless quality captures the breathlessness of the scene the speaker is describing — the frantic pace of a restaurant kitchen.

Have your students consider lines 15–16, when the speaker admits, "In this basement / I lose my size." Students may have different interpretations of these lines. One possible interpretation is that the speaker loses her individual identity in the basement as she slaves away. Other students might interpret these lines to mean that the speaker had imagined herself to be "too big" for this job — above it somehow — and as a result is diminished by the reality of her situation. Although the speaker may lose size, she still demonstrates a remarkable strength, lifting "a pot as big as a tub with both hands" (18).

The final lines of the poem contain a powerful image — one that students are not likely to miss for its unavoidable irony. After the exhausting ordeal in which so many workers expend so much energy to create a meal, the "clean diners" dine in luxury — "behind glass in candlelight" (25), blissfully unaware of the effort it took to create the meal they are enjoying. This is the first moment in the poem where the speaker moves from description into something more reflective, as the frantic pace of the kitchen slows to allow the workers to observe the fruits of their labor.

Student readings of this poem may be enriched by some understanding of Marxist literary theory (text p. 207), as Kingston presents a startling picture of difference based on privilege and wealth.

POSSIBLE CONNECTIONS TO OTHER SELECTIONS

Langston Hughes, "Dinner Guest: Me" (text p. 415)

Elaine Magarrell, "The Joy of Cooking" (text p. 153; question 1, following)

CONNECTION QUESTION IN TEXT (p. 207) WITH ANSWER

1. Write an essay analyzing how the kitchen activities described in this poem and in Elaine Magarrell's "The Joy of Cooking" (p. 153) are used to convey the themes of these poems.

    The kitchen in "Restaurant" is a metaphorical site in which working people must ultimately work together, and their frenetic activity stands in stark contrast to the diners who are gently illuminated in candlelight. The other poem applies the discourse of cooking to the culinary preparation of people, which acts as a metaphor for revenge. In both cases the preparation of food represents a fundamental human interaction, whether it divides or unites people. Both also cast the preparation of food as a cruel yet tender activity; you might ask students how dining can be considered both a cruel and tender experience.

AUDIOVISUAL RESOURCES (manual p. 377)

PAUL HUMPHREY, *Blow* (p. 207)

The class may not be familiar with the term *luffed,* which is a nautical word meaning "to turn the head of the ship into the wind." The woman here is metaphorically transformed into a sailing ship — appropriately enough as both would be spoken of as "she." The marvelous final line gives a blow to the gesture of the speaker trying to quell the woman's wind-filled skirt. Here the alliteration creates a kind of humor, and the quick end-stopped monosyllables with their *t* sounds emphasize the deftness that marks the woman's movements. Point out to the class how these short, light sounds are used, almost as a verbal photograph, to capture the moment.

POSSIBLE CONNECTION TO ANOTHER SELECTION

Robert Herrick, "Upon Julia's Clothes" (text p. 239)

ROBERT FRANCIS, *The Pitcher* (p. 208)

This poem ostensibly describes a baseball pitcher's art, but the poet seems also to be describing the art of poetry. When poems discuss poetry, it is always important to consider whether their claims are meant to be universal or whether they are meant to apply only to a specific type of poetry, usually the poetry that the poet favors. You might also consider how the poem functions on a literal level: Does the metaphor ever break down? In what sense is a reader analogous to a batter?

If a pitcher is too obvious, the batter will easily figure out how to hit the balls he throws. The pitcher and batter play a cat-and-mouse game in which the pitcher must stay within the boundaries but not pitch directly to the hitter. While the other players throw directly to one another, he must seem to throw a fast ball only to throw a curve and vice versa. But he cannot throw wildly, or he has failed to do his job. In a similar way, the poet's play with language must "avoid the obvious" and "vary the avoidance." Line 4, almost (but not quite) a repetition of line 3, does what it says by avoiding the repetition.

Like the pitcher's task of avoidance within bounds, the rhymes in the poem are not quite but almost there. We have the sense of a potential never actualized. The final lines illustrate the perfect rhyme that is avoided in the previous lines, indicating the completed pitch and the finished poem.

The poet, like the pitcher, chooses his words and delivers them as he feels he must, making the reader wait patiently. Ironically, the pitcher is on the defensive side, although he appears to be on the offensive as he aims at his target. This fact may lead us to question the real relationship between poet and audience suggested in this analogy.

POSSIBLE CONNECTION TO ANOTHER SELECTION

Robert Francis, "Catch" (text p. 28; question 1, following)

CONNECTION QUESTION IN TEXT (p. 208) WITH ANSWER

1. Write an essay comparing "The Pitcher" with another work by Francis, "Catch" (p. 28). One poem defines poetry implicitly, the other defines it explicitly. Which poem do you prefer? Why?

   "Catch," which explicitly compares baseball to poetry, takes a playful approach and uses sound to emphasize the fun of the boys' game. "The Pitcher" is implicit; as you read the poem it slowly becomes apparent that it's not just about baseball. "The Pitcher" is less overtly playful, but Francis obviously takes delight in using near-rhymes and couplets to mirror the interaction between a pitcher and batter. The goal of the poet/pitcher in the two poems is different as well. In "Catch" the game is played between two equals who share the same goals of throwing and catching. The relationship in "The Pitcher," on the other hand, is more adversarial: The protagonist (the poet) tries to prevent the batter (the reader) from hitting the ball.

HELEN CHASIN, *The Word* Plum (p. 209)

The title of this poem suggests that it is about words. The relationship of the word *plum* to the object plum will generate an interesting discussion of the nature of language. Do words correspond to objects? Does poetry do more than point dimly to the sensuous realm?

The alliteration and assonance make our lips move the way they might when we are eating a plum. They also call attention to the sound of the poem, so that it is also about writing poetry.

POSSIBLE CONNECTIONS TO OTHER SELECTIONS

Galway Kinnell, "Blackberry Eating" (text p. 189; question 1, following)
William Carlos Williams, "This Is Just to Say" (text p. 632)

CONNECTION QUESTION IN TEXT (p. 209) WITH ANSWER

1. How is Galway Kinnell's "Blackberry Eating" (p. 189) similar in technique to Chasin's poem? Try writing such a poem yourself: choose a food to describe that allows you to evoke its sensuousness in sounds.

   Both poets draw a direct comparison between the sound of the words associated with eating fruit and the experience of eating the fruit itself. It is perhaps no accident that they both use such sensuous language to describe fruits, the sexual organs of plants. Both poets anthropomorphize the fruit, to a degree; Chasin emphasizes the skin and flesh of plums, and Kinnell's blackberries, who know "the black art / of blackberry-making" (lines 5–6), fairly lower themselves into his mouth. If students choose foods besides fruit to write about, do those foods share any of the sensual qualities of fruit? (If you have covered T. S. Eliot's "The Love Song of J. Alfred Prufrock" [text p. 456], you might use these poems to make sense of Prufrock's deliberation over whether to "eat a peach.")

JOHN KEATS, *Ode to a Nightingale* (p. 209)

Earl R. Wasserman in *The Finer Tone: Keats's Major Poems* (Baltimore: Johns Hopkins UP, 1953, 1967) discusses this ode at length and places it in context with other Keats poems, including "Ode on a Grecian Urn" and "La Belle Dame sans Merci." He finds here a set of impossible contradictions, for it appears that happiness or ecstasy can be achieved only by an annihilation of self. As Wasserman writes, "By attempting to gain 'happiness,' one is brought beyond his proper bound, and yet, being mortal, he is still confined to the earthly; and thus he is left with no standards to which to refer, or rather, with two conflicting sets of standards" (183).

Ask students to explore contexts for John Keats on LiterActive.

As a result of his complete empathic entrance into the bird's state, the poet finds himself "too happy in thine happiness." The poet has exceeded his own mortal bounds. In stanza 2 he longs for escape from this world — through an inebriation from the waters of poetic inspiration. Such a fading or leave-taking would be a means of fleeing from the strain of mortality (stanza 3). The bird, which at first had signified beauty and oneness with nature, is now becoming identified with immortality and the ability to transcend the mortal state. The speaker admits his fascination with "easeful Death," but at the close of stanza 4, he realizes the ultimate dilemma: If he did die, the bird would go on singing but the speaker would be as responsive as "sod."

The introduction of Ruth is interesting, because she symbolizes life, family, and generational continuity. Having lost her husband, she stayed with her mother-in-law in an alien land, remarried, and bore a son.

The word *forlorn* recalls the speaker to his senses in stanza 8, for he realizes that in this world of death, spirit, and the imagination — this ethereal world of transcendent essences — he is as nothing, and the word *forlorn*, like a bell, not only recalls him to himself but could also serve as his death summons. Note how many of the poem's attractive sensuous details exalt physical, mortal life. At the close of stanza 5, for example, Keats rescues even the flies for our poetic appreciation.

POSSIBLE CONNECTIONS TO OTHER SELECTIONS

Jane Hirshfield, "August Day" (text p. 560)
Percy Bysshe Shelley, "Ode to the West Wind" (text p. 257)

HOWARD NEMEROV, *Because You Asked about the Line between Prose and Poetry* (p. 212)

The title of Nemerov's poem indicates that this is an address to another person. Who does Nemerov mean by "you" and is this the same person he addresses in the second line? What questions would readers have about the difference between the genres? The poem is oblique in its answer to these questions, so you might have your students talk about how individual words or phrases characterize this difference. For one thing, Nemerov revises the question posed to him by introducing the idea of a "gradient" (line 3). The genres are not separated by a line but rather exist on a continuum as does the precipitation as it changes from rain to snow, "From silver aslant to random, white, and slow" (4). That the gradient is "invisible" (3) suggests the difficulty of distinguishing poetry from prose, and Nemerov dramatizes this problem in the fifth line: "There came a moment that you couldn't tell." However, in the next moment one can "clearly" (6) tell. We know that the snowflakes that "flew instead of fell" represent poetry, but why would Nemerov choose this metaphor? In what way is prose earthbound and poetry flighted?

POSSIBLE CONNECTIONS TO OTHER SELECTIONS

Billy Collins, "Introduction to Poetry" (text p. 42)
Louis Jenkins, "The Prose Poem" (text p. 271)

PERSPECTIVE

DYLAN THOMAS, *On the Words in Poetry* (p. 213)

As Thomas emphasizes, the power of words often lies in their sound. Encourage students to read poetry aloud; in performance, the rhyme, rhythm, and character of a poem become more apparent. Thomas's own words on the subject of language and poetry are filled with character: "Out of them came the gusts and grunts and hiccups and heehaws of the common fun of the earth" (paragraph 2). Ask students to assess the effect of such words, identifying their denotations and connotations. Words, according to Thomas, clearly convey emotions. Thomas personifies words at the end of this excerpt, when he writes about their "forms and moods, their ups and downs, their chops and changes, their needs and demands" (2). Ask students to create a list of words that have obvious "moods" or "demands." They might also be interested in hearing some of Thomas's own poetry in connection with this perspective.

8

Patterns of Rhythm

As in Chapter 7, reading aloud can be of great benefit here. Abstract discussions of prosody will almost certainly turn students off. However, if students can understand how rhythm contributes to the overall impression a poem makes, they will be more likely to show interest in questions of meter. One way to emphasize this impression is to have students read these poems aloud.

Ask students to explore the poetic elements in this chapter on **LiterActive** *and at* **bedfordstmartins.com/meyerpoetry***.*

These readings will also show that even the strictest metrical forms are not absolute — no one really reads iambic meter da-dum da-dum da-dum, and students will find attempts to do so unnatural (and perhaps humorous). There are variations in rhythm built into the language, and often into the meter of the poems themselves. Once students understand this, they can approach prosody as a descriptive rather than prescriptive activity and can see scansion as a way of understanding effects rather than as an end in itself.

You may want to encourage this perception in the kinds of writing you have students do in this chapter. Critics almost never use exclusively prosody-based arguments about poems; students would be well advised to do the same. You might craft the writing assignments to have students talk about prosody among other features of a poem that contribute to its overall effect or meaning. This kind of assignment has the added advantage of keeping skills students have developed in previous chapters alive by continued use.

This chapter also lends itself well to the inclusion of popular culture — rap music, for instance, can be very sophisticated metrically. Students will probably immediately understand the difference in feeling between songs with a heavy beat (for instance, L. L. Cool J's "Momma Said Knock You Out") and ones where the rhythms are lighter and more trippingly phrased (the Fresh Prince's "Summertime"). Depending on the tastes of your class, the students themselves may be able to provide better and more current examples.

Ask students to research the poets in this chapter at **bedfordstmartins.com/meyerpoetry***.*

Another exercise you might try would be to have students look for patterns of rhythm in other kinds of language — Martin Luther King Jr.'s "I Have a Dream" speech lends itself particularly well to this application and can be compared in structure to the selection from Walt Whitman's "Song of the Open Road."

WALT WHITMAN, *From "Song of the Open Road"* (p. 216)

Walt Whitman's poem proclaims the glorious freedom of the open road, but its form is not completely "free." The stanzas are nontraditional, rather than totally anarchic. Ask students to look for links within and between the two stanzas, for patterns that hold them together. The first stanza, after beginning with the foreign word *allons*, uses sever-

Ask students to expore contexts for Walt Whitman on **LiterActive***.*

al exclamatory phrases, many of which begin with the word *let*. The second stanza also begins with a foreign word — *camerado* — and after one transitional exclamation proceeds with three phrases that repeat the word *give*. In addition, the second stanza mentions several items that are supposedly left behind in the first and replaces these old values with new ones: "my love" is offered as a replacement for money (lines 4 and 8), "myself" for preaching and law (6 and 9).

Ask students to recall other places where they have seen repetition used as a rhetorical device. They might mention speech making, legal documents, or the Bible. Discuss the implications of Whitman's use of a technique that characterizes the very things he wishes to abandon.

Ask students whether they find the narrator's attitude attractive or repulsive. Does he seem naive or insightful? Are they drawn to the idea of leaving books, laws, and religion behind for the "Open Road"?

POSSIBLE CONNECTIONS TO OTHER SELECTIONS

Alfred, Lord Tennyson, "The Charge of the Light Brigade" (text p. 231)

Walt Whitman, From "I Sing the Body Electric" (text p. 268)

WILLIAM WORDSWORTH, *My Heart Leaps Up* (p. 219)

The text discusses the enjambment in lines 8–9. What is the effect of the enjambment in the first two lines? Note that all of the lines between are end-stopped. Is there a thematic connection between the pairs of enjambed lines? Between the end-stopped lines?

Ask students to discuss what they think Wordsworth means by "the child is father of the Man" (line 7). Do any current songs or other elements of popular culture reflect this same sentiment, or is it dismissable as a nineteenth-century Romantic impulse?

POSSIBLE CONNECTIONS TO OTHER SELECTIONS

William Blake, "The Lamb" (text p. 228)

William Wordsworth, "It Is a Beauteous Evening, Calm and Free" (text p. 633)

TIMOTHY STEELE, *Waiting for the Storm* (p. 221)

The text thoroughly discusses the poem's metrics and how they contribute to its meaning. In addition, you may wish to discuss word choices in the poem. How can darkness be "wrinkling," as stated in line 1? Why do you suppose Steele uses such a prosaic title for a poem so full of poetic images? You might have students examine the individual images and discuss the senses to which they appeal. Is the poem mostly auditory, visual, tactile, or does it touch all of the senses? Why does Steele start and end with the images he does? Can your students suggest other prestorm sensations the poet might have included? Would their inclusion alter the poem's mood? You might have students decide on a topic for description and brainstorm to produce images that draw on each of the senses. Are some senses harder to utilize than others?

POSSIBLE CONNECTION TO ANOTHER SELECTION

Ezra Pound, "In a Station of the Metro" (text p. 129)

WILLIAM BUTLER YEATS, *That the Night Come* (p. 221)

William Butler Yeats was born in Dublin and spent his youth in Dublin, London, and Sligo (his mother's family's home) in the west of Ireland. After graduating from high school, Yeats decided to

Ask students to research contexts for William Butler Yeats on *LiterActive*.

attend art school (his father, J. B. Yeats, was a painter) and made poetry an avocation. He dropped out soon after and at age twenty published his first poems in the *Dublin University Review*. His poetic influences include Spenser, Shelley, Blake, and the pre-Raphaelite poets of 1890s London, but a perhaps equally important shaping force was his religious temperament. Never satisfied with Christian doctrine, he invented, piecemeal, a mythology that informs his poetry in often obscure ways. For range and power, no twentieth-century poet equals Yeats.

Play a recording of Samantha Egger reading "That the Night Come" on *Literature Aloud*.

Discuss the central metaphor of the poem: that the woman's longing for death is like a king's longing for the consummation of his marriage. Note especially the word *desire* (line 2). How can the desire for death possibly be equated with the desire for sex? Compare this poem to one of the *carpe diem* poems students have read. In the carpe diem tradition sexuality is opposed to death; in this poem is sexuality equated with death? Why does the speaker call death "proud" (3)? Does the speaker see death as a proud bridegroom awaiting his bride? Is this an allusion to Donne's "Death Be Not Proud" (text p. 290)?

POSSIBLE CONNECTION TO ANOTHER SELECTION

John Donne, "Death Be Not Proud" (text p. 290)

AUDIOVISUAL RESOURCES (manual p. 383)

ALICE JONES, *The Foot* (p. 222)

The anatomical terms make "The Foot" scholarly and intellectually precise. The speaker of the poem clearly knows a great deal about the foot — the scientific terminology communicates much more than most people know about their feet. Given that poems are scanned in metrical feet, you might suggest to your students that this poem can be read as a pun; the metrical feet of a poem, such as iambs, support the poem just as human feet support people. The scholarly and foreign terms used to describe the subject of the poem obscure the function of the foot, just as overly scholarly terminology about scansion can obscure the function (and enjoyment) of a poem.

Certainly, the poem can be read not only as a pun. The first line does reveal the speaker's surprise about the human foot — that it is our "improbable" support — and the ending returns to this sense of mystery when it alludes to our connection to "an ancestor" (line 23) with a "wild / and necessary claw" (24–25). It might be interesting to have students explore one or more of the following questions in writing: What effect does the poet achieve by using language the common reader does not understand? Likewise, why would a poet write about a familiar object and make it seem foreign? Does the poet intend to humble readers by suggesting that despite all our learning we still are rooted in a past that contains ancestors with claws rather than feet?

POSSIBLE CONNECTIONS TO OTHER SELECTIONS

Alice Jones, "The Larynx" (text p. 99)
Eric Ormsby, "Nose" (text p. 98)

A. E. HOUSMAN, *When I was one-and-twenty* (p. 223)

The basic metrical pattern here is iambic trimeter. The first stanza is tightly rhymed, with only two rhyming sounds. The second stanza picks up on the first rhyming word of stanza 1 (*twenty*), but Housman in this stanza uses more rhyming words (four sounds in the eight lines), as though he were opening up to experience.

Appropriately, given his unhappy romance, "rue," "two," and "true" echo one another in rhyme. Love in both stanzas is metaphorically treated with marketplace terminology. In the first stanza the wise man advises the speaker to keep his fancy free. In the second stanza the wise man observes that the heart "was never given in vain," and moreover the cost of buying or selling this seat of affection is immeasurable. The repetition of " 'tis true" is like a shaking of the head, of one in a state of endless "rue."

You might enter a discussion of this poem by asking students about their reactions to advice from elders. They will probably have stories about how they had to learn through experience, not advice. If that is the case, what is our relationship to the speaker of the poem? Are we meant to reject his advice, too, in favor of learning on our own? Is the speaker somewhat foppish, because he believes he has aged so much in just one year?

POSSIBLE CONNECTIONS TO OTHER SELECTIONS

Margaret Atwood, "Bored" (text p. 86)
Robert Frost, "Birches" (text p. 365)

RITA DOVE, *Fox Trot Fridays* (p. 224)

This is the first of a series of poems inspired by ballroom dance lessons Dove took with her husband. As an art form, dance has some rhythmic parallels with poetry. However, Dove's poem is not strictly metrical. Instead she alternates between three-beat units — "stride brush stride" (line 4), "heel-ball-toe" (6), and "slow satin smile" (7) — and two-beat units — "quick-quick" (5), "easy as taking" (9), and "rib to rib" (13). With these variations, she captures a dance-like pattern as well as a rhythm of interaction between partners. She also frequently ends lines on a conjunction or preposition, which draws the reader through the poem, across the usual places to pause.

The rhythmic life of dancing, and of poetry, is key to the relief that Dove seeks in "Fox Trot Fridays." Her suggestion that the dance is "easy as taking / one day at a time" (9–10) is ironic; readers know from the "grief" in the third line that it isn't really that easy. However, just as a practiced dancer makes even a hard dance look effortless, Dove learns through this hobby how to achieve a kind of ease. The rhythm of the fox trot is almost hypnotic; it allows the dancers to "count all the wonders in it" (17).

POSSIBLE CONNECTIONS TO OTHER SELECTIONS

Lenard D. Moore, "Black Girl Tap Dancing" (text p. 234)
Theodore Roethke, "My Papa's Waltz" (text p. 233)

RACHEL HADAS, *The Red Hat* (p. 225)

The child of the speaker of this poem has recently begun to walk to school alone. The speaker and her husband take turns secretly following the boy most of the way toward school. She finds this change toward maturity unsettling; rather than feeling joy at her child's newfound independence, she and her husband feel "empty, unanchored, perilously light" (line 21). The title of the poem, and its post-Christmas setting, emphasize the youth of the boy and the irrevocable loss of childlike innocence that is the basis for the poem's core emotion.

The poem is written in heroic couplets, but the poet prevents the rhythm from sounding singsongy with enjambment, punctuating the lines unevenly, ending a sentence midline, or often by altering the meter with a semicolon or colon. Ask students how this rhythm affects the poem's tone: Would it have been as poignant if the poet hadn't interrupted the rhythm with punctuation? if the rhymes had been end-stopped and full? Does the uneven meter have something to do with the poem's theme? This theme is obviously related to the sometimes painful passage from childhood into adulthood, the "pull / of something more powerful than school" (lines 15–16), less commonly presented from the parents' point of view than from a child's. With whom do students sympathize? Do they better understand the child's need to be independent or the parents' need to follow him at a distance?

POSSIBLE CONNECTIONS TO OTHER SELECTIONS

Peter Meinke, "(Untitled)" (text p. 91)
Sharon Olds, "Rite of Passage" (text p. 279)

ROBERT HERRICK, *Delight in Disorder* (p. 226)

The speaker of this poem prefers in women a slightly disheveled appearance to one that presents the wearer as though she is perfect. Not coincidentally, the poem's strength is not only in its artfulness, its reliance on poetic conventions like end-rhyme and alliteration, but also on the slight disorderliness of his rhythm. Vague impressions of court life in seventeenth-century England may be sufficient to initiate a discussion of the importance of dress at the time. If you are also discussing Ben Jonson's "Still to Be Neat," the next poem in this section, you might be able to get some mileage out of a discussion of the relationship between the two arts of fashion and poetry and the way they interact.

You might begin discussion of this poem by asking students what connotations the word *neat* holds for them. Then explore Herrick's use of *disorder,* as contrasted with our word *disorderly,* along with *wantonness.* Clearly, disorder and wantonness arouse in the speaker here a "fine distraction" and exercise a certain appeal that would not be present if the person addressed were prim and proper.

The speaker is bewitched but not bothered by his lady's "sweet disorder." Words are chosen to indicate a tantalizing of the passions by "erring" lace, "tempestuous" petticoats, and shoestrings tied with a "wild civility."

Herrick subtly illustrates his theme by working changes in the basic iambic tetrameter rhythm. Iambs change to trochees (cf. lines 2 and 4, for example), and in line 10 dactyls appear.

Ask students to turn back to the second question in the text and in a writing assignment analyze how patterns of rhyme and consonance work to create a subtle and pleasing artistic order.

POSSIBLE CONNECTIONS TO OTHER SELECTIONS

Ben Jonson, "Still to Be Neat" (text p. 226)
John Frederick Nims, "Love Poem" (text p. 44)

BEN JONSON, *Still to Be Neat* (p. 226)

Stepson of a bricklayer, Jonson was one of the first English writers to make his living by his pen. Admired for his lyrical poetry and literary criticism, Jonson is perhaps best known for his satiric comedies — including *Volpone* (1605), *The Alchemist* (1610), and *Bartholomew Fair* (1614) — and for the elaborate masques he created with designer Inigo Jones for the court of James I.

It may seem odd then that Jonson would choose to reject the elaborate fashions of the time, yet that is what he is doing in this poem. The speaker dislikes the artful manners and dress of the woman. "Sweet" refers both to her smell, which is sweet, and their relationship, which presumably has some difficulties, perhaps because of her preoccupation with her appearance. The speaker is suspicious about the reason for this preoccupation.

He asks the woman to be more sincere in her attentions to him, to pay less attention to her appearance. Neglecting herself is "sweet" to him because it is more natural, less deceptive. Words such as *adulteries* (line 11) and *face* play with the relationship between art and nature, intimating that the woman's efforts to make herself into a beautiful object only mar her natural beauty.

The disruptions in the rhythms reinforce Jonson's point until the final line. In line 6 the rhythm and the caesura in the middle of the line force the reader to slow down, emphasizing the speaker's insistence that the woman stop her artful motion and remove the mask. In the final line the iambic tetrameter brings the speaker's point home in a succinct statement of his case.

POSSIBLE CONNECTION TO ANOTHER SELECTION

Robert Herrick, "Delight in Disorder" (text p. 226; questions 1 and 2, following)

CONNECTIONS QUESTIONS IN TEXT (p. 227) WITH ANSWERS

1. Write an essay comparing the themes of "Still to Be Neat" and Herrick's preceding poem, "Delight in Disorder." How do the speakers make similar points but from different perspectives?

   Herrick's speaker asks for a similar absence of artistry and emphasis on irregularity. But the poems seem to treat the art–nature dichotomy differently. For Herrick, a "sweet disorder" may be part of the art, whereas for Jonson the relationship between art and nature is more troubled. Jonson's speaker does not want his beloved to be artful; Herrick's simply asks that the art not be "too precise in every part."

2. How does the rhythm of "Still to Be Neat" compare with that of "Delight in Disorder"? Which do you find more effective? Explain why.

   With trochees interrupting the iambic rhythm throughout, Jonson's poem is more insistent than Herrick's. The speaker in "Still to Be Neat" is calling for an end to false art. Herrick's smoother rhythm and more easily flowing syllables suggest the speaker's delight in observing the disorder of his lady's dress. The differences in meter are in keeping with the different relationship between art and nature in the two poems.

DIANE BURNS, *Sure You Can Ask Me a Personal Question* (p. 227)

Using one side of a well-worn conversation, this poem uses repetition to demonstrate the exasperation that comes from enduring the same questions again and again. The speaker is addressing a well-intentioned person, possibly an amalgam of all the people who have acted out the unheard portion of similar conversations. We know that the other participant in this conversation claims to have an "Indian Princess" great-grandmother (line 14), claims to have Indian friends, lovers, or servants, apologizes for the treatment of Native Americans by the U.S. government, and talks at length about Native American "Spirituality" (32). The serious theme beneath the numerous repetitions and the absence of the easy-to-imagine other participant provide a quick gloss of the stereotypes many people have of Native Americans. Burns's speaker addresses these images with humor, but it is humor that bites, is frustrated, and finally refuses to go along; the conversation about spirituality is a nodding, absentminded one with lots of "Uh-huh"s; the last three lines give away the speaker's frustration and annoyance and provide a terse ending for anyone who thought she was just kidding around. You may want to ask your students if they were surprised by this last line. What does she mean by this short declaration?

POSSIBLE CONNECTIONS TO OTHER SELECTIONS

Robert Browning, "My Last Duchess" (text p. 177)

Patricia Smith, "What It's Like to Be a Black Girl (for Those of You Who Aren't)" (text p. 123)

WILLIAM BLAKE, *The Lamb* (p. 288) and *The Tyger* (p. 229)

These two poems when paired make excellent examples of diction, rhythm, and sound and how these elements enhance tone. Ostensibly, each poem uses a four-stress pattern of trochaic feet, but the gliding *l* sounds of the opening of "The Lamb" make the first stress on "Little" seem much lighter than the emphasis "Tyger" receives. The rhyme in the opening two lines of "The Lamb" is feminine, again unlike the stressed rhyme in "The Tyger." Only one question ("Who made Thee?") is asked of the lamb, and that question is repeated several times, giving the poem a sense of childlike simplicity and innocence. In this poem, moreover, there is a figural pattern of exchangeable identities between Lamb and Creator (Lamb of God), and speaker as child and Christ as God's child. Unlike the fearful symmetry of "The Tyger," this poem reflects a wholeness and innocence by the cohesiveness of these identities.

Ask students to explore contexts for William Blake on LiterActive.

"The Tyger" poses far more questions about the creation of this powerful, regal beast, including the question in line 20: "Did he who made the Lamb make thee?" Ways of reading that question include the debate over the presence of evil in a God-created universe and the possibility of a second creator from whom darkness, evil, and fierce energy emanate. Could not the tiger stand for positive expressions of power? By and large, though, the questions in "The Tyger" go unanswered. Notice, for example, the substitution of *dare* in the final line for *could* in line 4.

Play recordings of Brian Murray reading "The Lamb" and "The Tyger" on Literature Aloud.

As a writing assignment, you might ask students to examine several elements in each poem, including rhythm, patterns of consonance and assonance, pace, tone, and even levels of ambiguity so that they are able on a fairly sophisticated level to articulate the differences between the two lyrics.

POSSIBLE CONNECTIONS TO OTHER SELECTIONS

William Blake, "Infant Sorrow" (text p. 587)

William Wordsworth, "I Wandered Lonely as a Cloud" (text p. 633)

CARL SANDBURG, *Chicago* (p. 230)

You might begin by introducing your class to the idea of the invocation. Traditionally, a poet would invoke the muse at the beginning of the work, asking for help with the task at hand. The root of invocation is *vocare*, to call. Here the higher power being called upon is also the subject of the poem, the city of Chicago. How does the power of the city differ from that of a muse or god? How does Sandburg characterize the city in these first lines? Some of his epithets reappear in the last lines of the poem. Here they take on a new character as the city itself takes possession of the names, "proud" to answer to them (line 23).

Sandburg's poem contains both short, heavily accented lines, as in the invocation, and long lines with a prose cadence. Like Whitman, he structures the prose sections with the rhetorical device of anaphora, beginning sentences with repeated words or phrases. These repetitions enhance the rhythm of the long lines. As an exercise, you might have your students reline the poem, breaking the long sentences into four- or five-beat lines. Then have them discuss how these changes alter the tone of the poem. What is gained or lost from the original?

POSSIBLE CONNECTIONS TO OTHER SELECTIONS

William Blake, "London" (text p. 121; question 1, following)
Dylan Thomas, "Fern Hill" (text p. 627)

CONNECTION QUESTION IN TEXT (p. 231) WITH ANSWER

1. Compare "Chicago" with William Blake's "London" (p. 121) in style and theme.

    Both "Chicago" and "London" are concerned with the darker side of city life. Sandburg sees Chicago as "wicked" (line 6), "crooked" (7), and "brutal" (8), and Blake hears in London a chorus of crying, sighs, and curses. However, the poems take different turns. In spite of the ugliness it contains, Chicago is "proud to be alive and coarse and strong and cunning" (10). Sandburg's looser structure and long lines seem to convey some of the reckless exuberance he admires in the city. Blake, on the other hand, uses a stricter form as a way of maintaining order in the face of chaos. His poem does not find anything to praise in the city. Its images grow increasingly grim until he ends on the sad oxymoron, the "Marriage hearse" (line 16).

ALFRED, LORD TENNYSON, *The Charge of the Light Brigade* (p. 231)

This poem praises and honors the light brigade, those "noble six hundred" men who charge "into the valley of Death" even though they know that they will die. The poem raises questions about the nature of bravery during wartime; the soldiers are praised for their glory, their honor, their nobility, but there is a nagging sense that their deaths could have been avoided. They knew that "some one had blundered" (line 12), but this logic is tempered by the sentiment behind the famous lines "Their's not to make reply, / Their's not to reason why, / Their's but to do and die" (13–15).

The rhyme and meter make the poem sound like a typical poem celebrating the heroes of war. The phrase "six hundred" is rhymed repeatedly, with "thundered" (21), "wondered" (31), and "sundered" (36); the word "blundered," which sounds a discordant note in the second stanza, is nearly buried by what appears to be the poem's laudatory tone. Students may debate about whether the poem focuses on praising the brigade for its courage or on criticizing the brigade for its blind obedience, which leads many of them to death. The effect would certainly be different if the sentiment of the second stanza were to come at the end of the poem. Because it doesn't, questions about the poem's tone and the speaker's attitude must take into consideration both the poem as a whole and the second stanza in particular. The "honor" that is proposed for the "noble six hundred" in the final stanza is altered not only by the second stanza but by the fact that the six hundred are less than six hundred in the stanzas 4 and 5.

POSSIBLE CONNECTIONS TO OTHER SELECTIONS

Wilfred Owen, "Dulce et Decorum Est" (text p. 122; question 1, following)
Walt Whitman, "Cavalry Crossing a Ford" (text p. 112)

CONNECTION QUESTION IN TEXT (p. 233) WITH ANSWER

1. Compare the theme of "The Charge of the Light Brigade" with Wilfred Owen's "Dulce et Decorum Est" (p. 122).

The tone of "Dulce et Decorum Est" makes its theme much more obvious; would students go so far as to say that the speakers of the two poems share the same attitude but that they simply differ in their degrees of subtlety? Is there a certain nobility associated with the warfare Tennyson describes, with its charges on horseback and sabers, as opposed to Owen's description of World War I with its invisible enemy, its lethal gas, and the horrors of trench warfare?

AUDIOVISUAL RESOURCES (manual p. 381)

THEODORE ROETHKE, *My Papa's Waltz* (p. 233)

From the perspective of a man looking back at his childhood, the speaker recollects the drunken lurchings of his working-class father as he waltzed around the room. The remembrance is one of those strong early memories that, years later, one sifts through. The rhythm of the poem reflects well those moments the speaker recalls with some pain. Notice the spondees, for example, in "My right ear scraped a buckle" (line 12) or in "You beat time on my head / With a palm caked hard by dirt" (13–14). The title, with its use of *Papa,* seems to indicate a memory from early childhood — as does line 12. It also connotes a certain gentle affection for "Papa," despite all the other memories.

Ask students to explore contexts for Theodore Roethke and this poem — as well as a sample close reading — on *LiterActive* and at **bedfordstmartins.com/ meyerpoetry**.

Play a recording of Theodore Roethke reading "My Papa's Waltz" on *Literature Aloud*.

POSSIBLE CONNECTIONS TO OTHER SELECTIONS

Regina Barreca, "Nighttime Fires" (text p. 39)

Dylan Thomas, "Do Not Go Gentle into That Good Night" (text p. 247)

NORMAN STOCK, *What I Said* (p. 234)

This powerful poem about one person's immediate reaction to the September 11th attack on the World Trade Center will bring goose bumps to just about every reader. Written in a breathless stream of consciousness, it reveals the honest, raw emotions of an American responding to the terror and loss. The shock of the final words, "let's kill them" (line 13), seems at first discordant with the tone of the poem, but this has, in fact, been the reaction of many Americans, as the ongoing hunt for Osama Bin Laden has proven. In this way the speaker serves as a synecdoche for the United States as a whole. At the same time, the poem highlights the irony of national hatreds: devastated and distraught by the terrorist attack, the speaker quickly reverts to the same blind hatred and murderous rage that inspired the attackers.

What's most notable about the use of rhythm and meter in this poem is that it follows no set pattern. The whole poem is one big run-on (not even a sentence, as it has no punctuation): it records the unstudied gut reactions of one New Yorker. But note how the stresses are spaced apart between dactyls and anapests. The unevenness of the poem's rising and falling meter suggests the speaker's confused alternation between despair and anger. Note, also, how the number of feet increases as the poem progresses, emphasizing the speaker's increasing panic. The lack of a pattern is what gives the poem its power. Ask your students whether "What I Said" would have been as effective if it were written in a more formal style, and they'll likely understand how a poet's careful attention to form affects a work's emotional impact.

POSSIBLE CONNECTIONS TO OTHER SELECTIONS

James Merrill, "Casual Wear" (text p. 175; question 1, following)

Bruce Springsteen, "You're Missing" (text p. 46)

1. Discuss the treatment of terrorism in "What I Said" and in James Merrill's "Casual Wear" (p. 175).

   The chief difference in how Stock and Merrill approach the subject of terrorism is emotion. Stock's poem is profoundly emotional, exposing raw feelings and the kind of despair and blind anger that in itself can lead to terrorist acts. Merrill, on the other hand, shows the media's cold, heartless, and fact-focused depiction of a terrorist act. The audience of each act of terrorism is inverted in the poems as well: Whereas Stock offers a searing insight into the nature of humanity by dwelling on one man's personal response to the death of thousands of New Yorkers; Merrill highlights how the act of broadcasting one woman's terrorist-related death to millions of emotionally unaffected people reduces her humanity.

LENARD D. MOORE, *Black Girl Tap Dancing* (p. 234)

The onomatopoeia in this poem, as well as the words that describe the dancer's action, makes for a heavily accented line. In some cases, every syllable on the line seems to be stressed, as in "arms whirl, whirl" (line 3) and "legs stamp, swing" (20). Have your students read the poem aloud and then discuss how the sounds relate to the subject of the poem. The emphatic stress patterns suggest the percussive sound of the taps. Moore achieves this effect through a compression of language. The constant action of the poem eliminates much of the need for conjunctions, prepositions, and pronouns. This is a great opportunity to draw students' attention to the wide range of descriptive verbs. Moore's "spiral" (7), "scissor" (12), and "propel" (27) describe the dancer's movements with great economy. What do your students make of his coinage "smokebeat" (21)? Do they have a picture of this movement? How many words would it take for them to describe it?

POSSIBLE CONNECTIONS TO OTHER SELECTIONS

Barbara Hamby, "Ode to American English" (text p. 87)
Langston Hughes, "Rent-Party Shout: For a Lady Dancer" (text p. 406)

RONALD WALLACE, *Dogs* (p. 235)

Discussing dogs, this speaker investigates his long-lasting guilt over accidentally hitting and subsequently killing a dog. He begins with the childhood memory of "hit[ting] one with / a baseball bat. An accident" (lines 1–2). The dog is put to sleep. From there he moves to a series of the most ignoble acts that dogs have inflicted on him, to the one act that gives him the most pain: those dogs "whose slow eyes gazed at me, in love" (14).

The basic form of the Petrarchan sonnet calls attention to the way in which emotion is presented in the poem. At what points does the poem's tone shift, and what is our emotional response when it does? For a speaker who's "been barked at, bitten, nipped, knocked flat, slobbered over, humped, sprayed, beshat" (9–10), it might seem unusual for the most painful act to have been being the recipient of love. But the speaker (presumably an adult looking back) has endured years of "the lasting wrath / of memory's flagellation" (5–6), which the couplet recalls from the octave. He feels guilty.

POSSIBLE CONNECTIONS TO OTHER SELECTIONS

Andrew Hudgins, "Seventeen" (text p. 170)
Jane Kenyon, "The Blue Bowl" (text p. 125)
William Shakespeare, "My mistress' eyes are nothing like the sun" (text p. 243; question 2, following)
John Updike, "Dog's Death" (text p. 24; question 1, following)

1. Compare this poem's theme to that of John Updike's "Dog's Death" (p. 24).

    Both speakers try to act as if the death of a dog is simply accidental, but their lives (or deaths) resonate anyway, causing pain in the lives of the speakers. Dogs seem helpless in both poems, as though waiting expectantly for humans to do something that will end their lives. But the speaker of Updike's poem doesn't seem to suffer the same "flagellation" of memory that Wallace's speaker suffers. The speaker of "Dogs" suffers guilt; the speaker of "Dog's Death" suffers pity. What do we suffer as we read each poem?

2. In an essay, discuss the strategies used in this sonnet and William Shakespeare's "My mistress' eyes are nothing like the sun" (p. 243) to create emotion in the reader.

    In both poems, the speaker relies on humor before expressing tenderness in the final two lines, but the effect is different. Shakespeare's sonnet is humorous throughout; there is no disturbing undercurrent like the one that taints the beginning of Wallace's poem. "Dogs," in a sense, manipulates our emotions more than Shakespeare's sonnet does because it drags us back and forth throughout the poem between deep, affecting pain and a light treatment of its subject.

PERSPECTIVE

LOUISE BOGAN, *On Formal Poetry* (p. 236)

You might ask students to compare Bogan's questions about form as repression with Whitman's assertion that "[t]he rhyme and uniformity of perfect poems show the free growth of metrical laws and bud from them as unerringly and loosely as lilacs or roses on a bush, and take shapes as compact as the shapes of chestnuts and oranges and melons and pears, and shed the perfume impalpable to form" (p. 270). Students could write an essay about these perspectives on "form" in poetry, using two or three examples from Chapter 24, "A Collection of Poems."

9

Poetic Forms

There is some degree of controversy over the role of form in poetry. The movement calling itself New Formalism advocates a widespread return to form and criticizes what it calls the status quo of open form. (A possible introduction to this position is in Dana Gioia's "Notes on the New Formalism" in the Autumn 1987 *Hudson Review*, reprinted in *Can Poetry Matter?* Also, see Timothy Steele's *Missing Measures* [1990, University of Arkansas Press, Fayetteville, AR].) There are also, however, several defenses of open form (perhaps the best of which is Stanley Plumly's "Chapter and Verse" in the January–February and May–June issues of *American Poetry Review*). You might find it interesting to introduce your students to this controversy and have them find their own positions on the matter. This exercise can help students understand that there are reasons for the choice to write in or out of traditional forms, and that traditional forms are not always or necessarily conservative. In addition, it emphasizes the idea that poetry is a dynamic genre, full of conflict and contradiction.

As in previous chapters, this material will likely be most appealing to students in terms of its relation to the overall impact of a poem — form only takes on meaning when married to content and presented in context. Quizzes that ask students to give the structure of a Petrarchan sonnet tend not to work as well as those that ask students to explain how the form of a particular sonnet contributes to its overall effect. (Some historical notes might be useful in this chapter, as the importance of traditional forms has as much to do with the history of those forms as with each current instance of the form.)

Web Ask students to research the poets in this chapter at **bedfordstmartins.com/ meyerpoetry**.

The section on sonnets is particularly good at emphasizing the different uses to which the form was put; each use, however, draws on the structure of the sonnet to help create meaning and coherence in the poem. Mark Jarman's "Unholy Sonnet," in conjunction with the sonnets from Donne found in Chapter 24, make good test cases. Students can see how the sonnet form allows Jarman to engage in a cross-century and cross-faith debate with Donne; the sonnet ensures that despite the historical and religious differences, the discussion takes place on the same terrain.

Another example that can help students understand the union of form and content can be found in the section on the villanelle — the kinds of repetition this form requires can be used for emphatic statement, as both Dylan Thomas's and Wendy Cope's poems demonstrate.

A. E. HOUSMAN, *Loveliest of trees, the cherry now* (p. 238)

The speaker in this poem greets life with a warmhearted joie de vivre. Although he is young, he already has a sense of life's limits. He means to enjoy the beauty of life every minute he is alive. Even then, he claims, he could not absorb all of the beauties of life. The connotations of rebirth and spring are reinforced by the mention of Eastertide in line 4.

Yet behind the gaiety and cheerful resolve is an awareness of the imminence of death. You might explore, either in class discussion or as a writing assignment, the question of whether this could be considered a carpe diem poem.

POSSIBLE CONNECTIONS TO OTHER SELECTIONS

Robert Frost, "The Road Not Taken" (text p. 354)

Robert Herrick, "To the Virgins, to Make Much of Time" (text p. 79)

AUDIOVISUAL RESOURCES (manual p. 376)

ROBERT HERRICK, *Upon Julia's Clothes* (p. 239)

Herrick uses so many of the elements of poetry — rhyme, rhythm, the sound and choice of words — so well in this brief lyric that it is worth taking some class time to analyze. The first tercet of iambic tetrameter is absolutely regular and thus suggests the sweetly flowing liquefaction of Julia's clothes. In the second tercet, trochees interrupt the established pattern to capture in rhythmic terms "that brave vibration." *Brave* is used here in the sense of "making a fine show or display," as in a banner waving.

POSSIBLE CONNECTION TO ANOTHER SELECTION

Paul Humphrey, "Blow" (text p. 207; question 1, following)

CONNECTION QUESTION IN TEXT (p. 240) WITH ANSWER

1. Compare the tone of this poem with that of Paul Humphrey's "Blow" (p. 207). Are the situations and speakers similar? Is there any difference in tone between these two poems?

   The situations are dissimilar in that Herrick's subject is "my Julia" (line 1) but the speaker of Humphrey's poem has no relationship with his subject. He is more self-deprecating than Herrick's speaker is; when the woman laughs and leaves in the final lines, we sense that she is laughing at him rather than at her situation. His gallantry becomes buffoonery. Herrick's emphasis is on the speaker's reverie; he is ecstatic rather than ridiculous.

SONNET

JOHN KEATS, *On First Looking into Chapman's Homer* (p. 241)

The principal theme of Keats's sonnet is discovery; he uses the sudden and unexpected discovery of the Pacific Ocean by early explorers of the Americas as a metaphor for those moments in life when we feel that a previously held view has been radically shaken.

You might ask students whether they have experienced a moment of discovery similar to that which Keats describes. After they have read Keats's poem, give them a few minutes to write about a moment when they felt a sense of revelation similar to that felt by "stout Cortez" and his men, and then discuss the results.

Ask students to explore contexts for John Keats on LiterActive.

A comparison of Keats's sonnets provides ample evidence of the poet's continual experimentation with form during his brief career. In "Chapman's Homer," Keats utilizes the characteristic division of the Italian sonnet into octave and sestet, with the opening eight lines setting up a situation or argument and the remaining six resolving it. You may wish to compare Keats's use of the sonnet form in "Chapman's Homer" with his use of the form in other poems in the chapter. In some sonnets Keats favors the Italian or Petrarchan form, but in "When I have fears" (text p. 610) he uses the English or Shakespearean rhyme scheme (three quatrains and a couplet).

WILLIAM WORDSWORTH, *The World Is Too Much with Us* (p. 242)

Like Hopkins in "God's Grandeur" (text p. 194), Wordsworth is protesting here the preoccupation with worldliness — banking, buying, getting, spending — that makes it increasingly difficult to feel the mystery and power in the natural world. Proteus (a god of the sea) and Triton (another sea god, who stirred up storms) lie dormant, their power to kindle in the human soul a spirit of awe suppressed in the commercialized world, where people have bartered their hearts away. "Great God!" is the speaker's spontaneous and ironic response to the decline of spirituality, for it appears that the pagan world possessed a stronger sense of godliness.

POSSIBLE CONNECTIONS TO OTHER SELECTIONS

Matthew Arnold, "Dover Beach" (text p. 115)
Gerard Manley Hopkins, "God's Grandeur" (text p. 194; question 1, following)

CONNECTION QUESTION IN TEXT (p. 242) WITH ANSWER

1. Compare the theme of this sonnet with that of Gerard Manley Hopkins's "God's Grandeur" (p. 194).

   Both Wordsworth's sonnet and "God's Grandeur" draw from the social and industrial worlds to discuss the greatness of creation and the human threat to that greatness. The speaker in Hopkins's sonnet places his faith in the creator, who can overcome the destructive actions of human beings. Wordsworth's sonnet returns to pagan myths for comfort, although the speaker has little hope of overcoming the bleakness of the world that is "too much with us." Hopkins dwells on bleak images of all "seared with trade," but he is convinced that nature is still available to us and that even humanity can be redeemed.

WILLIAM SHAKESPEARE, *Shall I compare thee to a summer's day?* (p. 243)

The speaker in this sonnet praises his beloved not only for her loveliness but also for her temperateness of manner. Unlike nature, which is forever changing, she shows a steady devotion. Moreover, the speaker tells us that this love will extend well into the future, even beyond the grave. Such love, like the art that celebrates it, confers a measure of immortality on the lovers and, self-reflexively, on the sonnet. Notice, for example, how the stressed words in the couplet reinforce this idea. *Long* is stressed in both lines of the couplet, along with other significant words that link continued "life" with "this," the sonnet that confers immortality, and "thee," the object the sonnet addresses.

Ask students to explore contexts for William Shakespeare on *LiterActive*.

Play a recording of Sir John Gielgud reading "Shall I compare thee to a summer's day?" on *Literature Aloud*.

POSSIBLE CONNECTIONS TO OTHER SELECTIONS

John Frederick Nims, "Love Poem" (text p. 44)
William Shakespeare, "My mistress' eyes are nothing like the sun" (text p. 243)

AUDIOVISUAL RESOURCES (manual p. 380)

WILLIAM SHAKESPEARE, *My mistress' eyes are nothing like the sun* (p. 243)

Students may have read this sonnet in high school, and you might begin by asking them what they think the mistress looks like. Some clarification of Shakespeare's use of the term *mistress* (beloved or chosen one) may be in order. This sonnet plays with the conventions and clichés of the Petrarchan sonnet, which elaborated on the extraordinary qualities of the maiden's eyes as compared to the splendor of the sun. But Shakespeare refuses to do this and thus argues for a poetry that avoids cliché and the excess metaphor that tries to outdo reality. He is, in fact, asserting the beauty of his beloved in the last line. She is as attractive as any other woman who has been "belied" (made to seem more beautiful) by false comparison.

🔊 Play a recording of Sir John Gielgud reading "My mistress' eyes are nothing like the sun" on *Literature Aloud*.

POSSIBLE CONNECTION TO ANOTHER SELECTION

William Shakespeare, "Shall I compare thee to a summer's day?" (text p. 243)

EDNA ST. VINCENT MILLAY, *I will put Chaos into fourteen lines* (p. 244)

In structure, Millay's list of paradoxes and resolutions adheres strictly to the verse form of the Italian, or Petrarchan, sonnet: It consists of fourteen lines of iambic pentameter with a rhyme scheme based upon an octave and a sestet. The octave is a single sentence describing the poet's efforts to force Chaos to unite with Order; the sestet recounts the happy results of such a union.

The poem accomplishes the apparently impossible feat of "containing" both Chaos "himself" and his various manifestations. The poet literally "puts Chaos into" the poem through personification, by portraying the abstract idea of Chaos as a character in a sonnet. The highly ordered verse form controls the disorderly, negative power of Chaos — "Flood, fire, and demon" (line 4) — by the physical act of shaping the words into the iambic pentameter line. One might expect that such restrictions would humble, even emasculate such a powerful figure, but according to the poet, the "sweet" sonnet form does not deprive Chaos of his energy; it concentrates the energy in a pattern of beauty and harmony — it "make[s] him good" (14).

The poet's use of figurative language reinforces the paradox inherent in the poem's structure. The image of "pious rape" in line 6 may seem irresolvably paradoxical in the 1990s, when a rape is such a highly charged negative issue. However, this is an excellent opportunity to encourage students to go beyond themselves in order to examine the poem on its own terms. The "rape" here is rape in a mythic sense; the dramatic situation in lines 3–8 recalls the creation myths of Hesiod or Genesis, with the poet herself as the agent who brings Order to Chaos and calls it "good." The poet insists that the forcible control exercised does not hurt Chaos but actually benefits him by adding sweetness and goodness to his formidable power.

The personification of Chaos as a male entity produces another paradox in addition to the contradiction created by juxtaposing the orderly sonnet form with a disorderly central character. Because we know that the poet is female, we have a highly unusual role reversal here — the male is raped by the female in the poem. The female poet forces Chaos into the "strict confines" (5) of the sonnet until he "mingles and combines" (8) with Order.

POSSIBLE CONNECTIONS TO OTHER SELECTIONS

Kate Clanchy, "Spell" (text p. 128)

Robert Frost, "Design" (text p. 373; question 1, following)

1. Compare the theme of this poem with that of Robert Frost's "Design" (p. 373).

    Frost's "Design," like "I will put Chaos," is structured as an Italian sonnet, but in contrast to Millay's poem, which begins with an abstract concept and uses imagery to make it more concrete, "Design" begins with a small, concrete image and extrapolates it to a larger, more abstract one. In general, Frost tends to affirm the power of poetic form to harness the chaos of life, to create a momentary stay against confusion, much as Millay does in "I will put Chaos." However, Frost's images of death and terror in "Design" suggest that if there is a controlling order in the universe, it is largely a force of evil. In contrast to Millay's theme, Frost suggests that Chaos can force Order to become a channel for his negative energy.

SEAMUS HEANEY, *The Forge* (p. 245)

Your students may have become accustomed to reading any poem about craft as an *ars poetica* or you may have to prod them a little. Either way, they should be able to make some parallels between what Heaney observes of the forge and how he conceives of his work as a poet. It is "unpredictable" (line 4), sacred, and requires some exertion. The blacksmith is an anachronism in that in the place of cars on the street, he remembers horse traffic. If this is a poem about poetry, what does that displacement in time say about the poet in society? It seems to suggest that poetry is a dying art (an idea that is partly belied by Heaney's great popularity).

In the first line, Heaney mediates his own authority by circumscribing his view of the scene: "All I know . . ." Instead of taking an omniscient point of view, he perceives only what he can from an outsider's perspective. As observers-readers of this poem, do your students relate to this viewpoint? Do they sometimes feel that the workings of poetry are obscure or inscrutable? For Heaney, that ambiguity contributes to the sacredness of the work. Hidden in that darkness, somewhere, is "an altar / Where [the blacksmith] expends himself in shape and music" (8–9).

The ringing of the hammer on the anvil in "The Forge" brings to mind Elizabeth Bishop's short story "In the Village," in which the young narrator has a moment of frightening self-revelation sparked by that sound. If you are interested in introducing fiction to your class, this might make a productive pairing.

POSSIBLE CONNECTIONS TO OTHER SELECTIONS

William Blake, "The Chimney Sweeper" (text p. 179)
Bob Hicok, "Making it in poetry" (text p. 165)

MOLLY PEACOCK, *Desire* (p. 245)

This somewhat complex treatment of desire reads almost like a riddle, and students may productively spend time trying to figure out exactly what the speaker is describing. The answer to the riddle is contained both in the title and in the final phrase: "Desire . . . the drive to feel" (line 14). But the metaphors and similes throughout the body of the poem present its chief interpretive problem: What exactly is the poet's point about desire, and why is it useful to define it the way she does?

The best way to reorganize the poem initially may be to list all of the metaphors for desire and to consider them individually; for instance, in what sense is desire "blunt" (10), "like a paw" (9)? Once you have done so, consider the metaphors together. Do they have anything in common? Students should notice that these metaphors often have to do with something animal and youthful, something wild and unsophisticated. The intimation is that socialization and civilization bring us farther away from our instinctive "drive to feel" (14), which is why desire is "what babies bring to kings" (5) as opposed to the material gifts that the three wise men brought to the infant Jesus.

POSSIBLE CONNECTIONS TO OTHER SELECTIONS

Sharon Olds, "Last Night" (text p. 85; question 1, following)
Walt Whitman, From "I Sing the Body Electric" (text p. 268)

CONNECTION QUESTION IN TEXT (p. 246) WITH ANSWER

1. Compare the treatment of desire in this poem with that of Sharon Olds's "Last Night" (p. 85). In an essay, identify the theme of each poem and compare their conceptions of desire. How alike are these two poems?

   Both Peacock and Olds see desire as a connection to more animal impulses, a blind grasping. However, Olds is much more fearful, suspecting that to give in to desire is to become subhuman. She equates fierce passion with death. Peacock, however, relates desire to birth and to babies' instinctual needs. The rhyme in her final couplet reveals her more positive take on the subject: the "drive to feel" (line 14) is more "real" (13) than later, learned yearnings.

MARK JARMAN, *Unholy Sonnet* (p. 246)

This poem is an example of an Italian, or Petrarchan, sonnet. You may wish to begin discussion by having students read the poem aloud, since the lines are so heavily enjambed that the rhythm and rhyme occur subtly. In dealing with this piece as a sonnet, you might point out that Italian sonnets are characterized by the usual fourteen lines of iambic pentameter, but unlike other sonnet forms, this type usually contains a shift in content between the octave and the sestet — a movement from suggestion to resolution.

🔊 Play a recording of Mark Jarman reading "Unholy Sonnet" on *Literature Aloud*.

This shift occurs in terms of both style and content in this poem. In the opening octave, many of the lines begin with a dactylic rather than an iambic foot (lines 1–4 each begin this way), and all of the lines in the octave have feminine endings. By contrast, the sestet lines each begin with a standard iambic foot and conclude with a masculine ending. In content, the repeated use of the word *after* — which occurs five times in the octave — sets up a sense of suspense in the first part of the poem that is then resolved through the repeated "there is" in the concluding sestet. In addition, the octave uses the pronouns *us* and *our*, while the answering sestet uses the pronouns *you* and *your*. Ask students to consider whether this shift in pronouns affects the reading of the poem. Does it strengthen or detract from the sense of resolution contained in the poem's concluding sestet?

POSSIBLE CONNECTIONS TO OTHER SELECTIONS

John Donne, "Batter My Heart" (text p. 596; question 1, following)
——, "Death Be Not Proud" (text p. 290; question 1, following)

CONNECTION QUESTION IN TEXT (p. 246) WITH ANSWER

1. Jarman has said that his "Unholy Sonnets" (there are about twenty of them) are modeled after John Donne's *Holy Sonnets* but that he does not share the same Christian assumptions about faith and mercy that inform Donne's sonnets. Instead, Jarman says, he "work[s] against any assumption or shared expression of faith, to write a devotional poetry against the grain." Keeping this statement in

mind, write an essay comparing and contrasting the tone and theme of Jarman's sonnet with Donne's "Batter My Heart" (p. 596) or "Death Be Not Proud" (p. 290).

Jarman's sonnet considers the disparity between what we are trying to do through practicing religion and what we actually do. He believes that the rituals of church-going do nothing to eradicate our basic (and base) human nature. The two sonnets by Donne describe a much more personal faith on the part of the speaker. Human activity does not interfere with his relationship with God or with his belief in eternal life through faith. The subject in Jarman's poem is collective first person and second person; in Donne's poems, the subject is first-person singular. In writing "a devotional poetry against the grain," Jarman is responding not only to Donne but also to modern views of religion. Yet in terms of form, Jarman's sonnet does work as a kind of inversion of Donne's logic; all three poems end with a bold sentiment in the final couplet.

VILLANELLE

DYLAN THOMAS, *Do Not Go Gentle into That Good Night* (p. 247)

This poem is a villanelle, a French verse form ordinarily treating light topics, whose five tercets and concluding quatrain use only two end rhymes. The first and third lines of the poem must alternatively conclude the tercets and form a couplet for the quatrain. Despite these formal restrictions, Thomas's poem sounds remarkably unforced and reflects quite adequately the feeling of a man who does not want his father to die.

Ask students to explore contexts for Dylan Thomas on *LiterActive*.

Just as remarkable is the poem's rich figurative language; this villanelle could be used as a summary example of almost all the points outlined in this chapter. Variety is achieved through the metonymies for death, such as "close of day" (line 2), "dark" (4), "dying of the light" (9). The overall effect is to describe death metaphorically as the end of a day and thus, in some sense, to familiarize death and lessen its threat. Even to describe death as "that good night" (1) reduces it to a gesture of good-bye. Other figures of speech include a pun on "grave" men (13) (both solemn and mortal); an oxymoron in "who see with blinding sight" (13); various similes, such as "blaze like meteors" (14); and the overall form of the apostrophe.

Play a recording of Dylan Thomas reading "Do not go gentle into that good night" on *Literature Aloud*.

Thomas introduces several examples of people who might be expected to acquiesce to death gently but who, nonetheless, resist it. "Wise men" (philosophers perhaps) want more time because so far their wisdom has not created any radical change ("forked no lightning"). Men who do good works (theologians possibly) look back and realize that the sum total of their efforts was "frail" and if they had devoted more time to a fertile field ("green bay"), their deeds might have been more effective. "Wild men" (inspired artists, writers) know their words have caught and held time, but they know, too, how in various ways — with their relations with others or perhaps with alcohol and drugs — they have "grieved" the sun. Grave men at the end of their lives realize too late that joy is one means of transcending time. All these groups experience some form of knowledge that makes them wish they could prolong life and live it according to their new insights.

As a writing assignment you might ask students to analyze a character or group of people that they have read about in a short story who seem to fit into one of the categories Thomas describes. What advice would he give them? How otherwise could they lead their lives?

John Donne, "A Valediction: Forbidding Mourning" (text p. 150)

Christina Georgina Rossetti, "In Progress" (text p. 618)

WENDY COPE, *Lonely Hearts* (p. 248)

Cope's villanelle, in its mimicry of the language of personal ads, has the flavor of a found poem. She incorporates a wide variety of "types" in the course of the poem: the "biker" (line 2), the "Gay vegetarian" (4), the "Executive" (7), the "lady with a son" (11). The repeated lines serve to unite them all in their shared desire, as well as in their geographical location. You might have your students discuss Cope's attitude toward the people who take out the personal ads. Does the line "Who knows where it may lead once we've begun?" (17) suggest an optimistic outlook?

POSSIBLE CONNECTIONS TO OTHER SELECTIONS

T. S. Eliot, "The Love Song of J. Alfred Prufrock" (text p. 456)

Janice Mirikitani, "Recipe" (text p. 547)

SESTINA

ALGERNON CHARLES SWINBURNE, *Sestina* (p. 249)

The speaker of this poem finds his pleasure in sleep and dreams; the harsh realities of waking life disappoint and fail to sustain his soul. Swinburne's "Sestina" is an unusual example of the form, in that the end words rhyme (the pattern is *ababab, bababa*). The rhymes connect the repeated words thematically: *day, way,* and *may* are contrasted to *night, light,* and *delight.*

"Sestina" has strong religious overtones, introduced by the poem's focus on the soul and reinforced by references to "wings" (4), "lordship" (9), and "heaven" (24). But religion, in this poem, is not necessarily a positive force. The speaker's soul thrives only in a dream state, and he chooses, as a result, to reject the *day,* possibly a metaphor for religious teaching and certainly a metaphor for reality. The envoy cements the speaker's dejection and loss of faith, asserting that "man hath no long delight" (line 39) regardless of what pleasures he may find singing under moonlight.

A little cultural history may help your students understand this poem. Swinburne was a London poet of the Victorian era, which was marked by sexual repression and religious emphasis on purity and restraint. But Swinburne was actively homosexual and given to scandalously masochistic behaviors, particularly self-flagellation. Rather than hide his predilections, he flaunted them — often inventing or exaggerating stories about his exploits — and earned a reputation as a decadent poet. His *Poems and Ballads* (1866), were reviled by critics for their overt celebration of things like sadomasochism, homosexuality, and necrophilia, as well as for their decidedly anti-Christian bent. In this context "Sestina" can be read as a celebration of illicit pleasures possible only out of sight of the respectable (daytime) public and forbidden by Victorian religion.

POSSIBLE CONNECTIONS TO OTHER SELECTIONS

Mark Jarman, "Unholy Sonnet" (text p. 246)

Walt Whitman, From "I Sing the Body Electric" (text p. 268)

FLORENCE CASSEN MAYERS, *All-American Sestina* (p. 250)

This poem is in a sense an inverted sestina because the first words of each line (rather than the end words) conform to the conventions of a sestina. The poem runs through a series of American clichés involving the numbers one through six and fits them into this difficult poetic form. Mayers departs from her own scheme a few times, though: What should be "six" in the third stanza is "sixty-" (line 14), and it wraps around to the next line, "four-dollar question"; and "hole in one" (27) in stanza 5 and "high five" (34) in stanza 6 break the pattern of having the number begin the line.

Students might debate about whether this poem raises important themes or whether it's just a clever exercise. You may want to gear discussion toward a consideration of what is particularly "all-American" about the clichés in the poem. (Is the fact that they are clichés all-American?) It might help to try to classify the images; the categories may vary, but most seem to have something to do with a kind of consumer hucksterism, as in "one-day sale" (8), "five-year warranty" (9), and "sixty-four-dollar question" (14–15); or with nostalgia, as in "five-cent cigar" (5), or "one-room schoolhouse" (36); or with excess, as in "six-pack Bud" (7), "two-pound lobster" (17), or "four-wheel drive" (25). Students may come up with entirely different categories. Encourage them to be flexible when creating these categories. Do they see an emerging pattern that might help to define "all-American"? Do any of the phrases not fit neatly into any category? A comparison to Cummings's "next to of course god america i" (text p. 163) may highlight these themes. But does Mayers critique America in the same way that Cummings does? Is it possible to read the poem as a celebration rather than a critique? Or is it simply a neutral portrait? In any case, why does she choose this form to represent it?

POSSIBLE CONNECTIONS TO OTHER SELECTIONS

E. E. Cummings, "next to of course god america i" (text p. 163; question 1, following)
Tato Laviera, "AmeRícan" (text p. 284)

CONNECTION QUESTION IN TEXT (p. 251) **WITH ANSWER**

1. Describe and compare the strategy used to create meaning in "All-American Sestina" with that used by Cummings in "next to of course god america i" (p. 163).

    Both poems rely on the distance between relatively meaningless American cultural clichés and real ideas to create meaning, but the speaker of Cummings's poem builds toward a definite point. In Mayers's sestina there is little progress. The poem's meaning wouldn't change much if the stanzas were rearranged; meaning comes primarily from the building panorama of clichés. Cummings's speaker begins with hollow phrases and departs from there to try to convince his audience that the war dead performed their duties cheerfully.

EPIGRAM

SAMUEL TAYLOR COLERIDGE, *What Is an Epigram?* (p. 252)

A. R. AMMONS, *Coward* (p. 252)

DAVID McCORD, *Epitaph on a Waiter* (p. 252)

PAUL LAURENCE DUNBAR, *Theology* (p. 252)

Note how crucial the technique of word selection becomes in poems that use as few words as these. Have students write in prose the ideas conveyed in each of the first three epigrams. These summaries will probably be considerably more verbose and less witty than the poems from which they stem. Which specific words in each epigram are used to condense meanings that might normally be expressed by means of longer words or phrases?

Also consider how important titles become in the epigrams by Ammons, McCord, and Dunbar. Have students discuss how each epigram would be different if it were presented without its title. Ammons's could be a statement of family pride. McCord's title informs the reader of his subject's occupation and his decease, whereas the poem might refer to anyone who had gone through life exceedingly preoccupied. What does McCord's poem imply about the waiter without saying it specifically? For how much of Dunbar's poem does the title "Theology" seem appropriate? Which words contribute to the serious tone implied by the title? Where does the meaning seem to shift?

Note: For a list of audiovisual resources for teaching Coleridge, see manual page 373.

LIMERICK

ANONYMOUS, *There was a young lady named Bright* (p. 253)

LAURENCE PERRINE, *The limerick's never averse* (p. 253)

KEITH CASTO, *She Don't Bop* (p. 254)

The name *limerick* derives from a form of extemporaneous nonsense verse that always ends with the refrain, "Will you come up to Limerick?" The five-line anapestic verses we now call limericks evolved during the nineteenth century at the hands of humorous versifiers like Edward Lear (1812–1888) and many anonymous writers.

The extemporaneous nature of limericks is an indication of the ease with which they can be composed. After reviewing the examples in the book, ask the students to compose some limericks, either individually or in small groups.

In addition to overtly bawdy situations, the limerick often relies on puns and other wordplay for its humor. "There was a young lady named Bright" plays on the term *relative* to draw attention to the possibility, implicit in certain theories of modern physics, that you can arrive in a place before you leave it. "She Don't Bop" plays on our familiarity with the phrase "rooty toot," related to "rootin' tootin'" as an onomatopoetic term indicating the sound of a trumpet and used to mean something noisy or riotous. The joke of Perrine's "The limerick's never averse" depends on a simple pun. You might draw students' attention to Perrine's departures from pure anapestic meter in the poem's first, fourth, and fifth lines. Do these variations in meter contribute anything to the poem?

You may wish to use a discussion of limericks to reinforce the point that anapestic meter — like the dactylic meter of "Hickory, dickory, dock" (text p. 217) — is used almost exclusively in light, humorous, or children's verse.

HAIKU

MATSUO BASHŌ, *Under cherry trees* (p. 254)

Bashō is usually considered the greatest of the haiku poets. He was born near Kyoto, growing up as the companion of a local nobleman's son. He moved to Edo (now called Tokyo) when he was twenty-three and eventually became a recluse, living outside the city in a hut. He made several long journeys, always relying for food and shelter on the generosity of local Buddhist temples and on other poets. *The Narrow Road to the Deep North,* a collection of interlocked prose and haiku chronicling one of these journeys, is perhaps his best-known work in the West.

CAROLYN KIZER, *After Bashō* (p. 254)

This poem demonstrates the importance Bashō still has, in many languages, for poets who write haiku. The reference to the "famous" (3) moon indicates the writer's familiarity with the moon as a constant trope in nature poetry in general and haiku in particular. Some Bashō poems that examine the moon include these:

> Felling a tree
> and seeing the cut end —
> tonight's moon.

> Harvest moon —
> walking around the pond
> all night long.

Bashō himself, writing more than a thousand years before Kizer, indicated his awareness of the familiarity of the moon as trope:

> It's not like anything
> they compare it to —
> the summer moon.

AUDIOVISUAL RESOURCES (manual p. 378)

SONIA SANCHEZ, *c'mon man hold me* (p. 255)

Although haikus usually *describe* a serene natural scene or intense emotion, this one is unusual in its imperative form: The speaker urges her lover to hold her. But in only three short lines, Sanchez manages to portray the speaker's deep longing for emotional as well as physical connection.

E L E G Y

THEODORE ROETHKE, *Elegy for Jane* (p. 255)

The last line of "Elegy for Jane" — "Neither father nor lover" — points out how Roethke's poem differs from many others written in this mode. Elegies for lovers and for family members are common, but Roethke expresses some uncertainty about how to mourn for a student. He foreshadows this ending with the line, "Even a father could not find her" (line 11). The girl's sadness is impenetrable, even more so to the poet, who does not have as close a relationship with her as a father would. Nevertheless, Roethke wants to "speak the words of [his] love" (20) over her, in spite of having "no rights in this matter" (21). His grief is deftly suggested with the repetition of "damp" from the first line, in which he describes her curls of hair, in the later vision of the grave.

Roethke compares Jane to several different birds, first a "wren, happy, tail into the wind" (5), then a "sparrow" (14), and finally a "skittery pigeon" (19). How do these figures contribute to the reader's picture of the student? What qualities does she have? The flitting action of the bird in the first strophe of the poem becomes a figure for her swift departure from life.

POSSIBLE CONNECTIONS TO OTHER SELECTIONS

A. E. Housman, "To an Athlete Dying Young" (text p. 606; question 1, following)
Ben Jonson, "On My First Son" (text p. 607)

1. Compare "Elegy for Jane" with A. E. Housman's "To an Athlete Dying Young" (p. 606). How does each poem avoid sentimentality in its description of a young person who has died?

   Roethke's focus on the complicated nature of his relationship with the girl keeps "Elegy for Jane" from being sentimental, as do the poet's minute observations of Jane's mannerisms. Housman's poem works very differently. Rather than establishing a personal tie to a particular individual, he deliberately does not name the young athlete, making him a figure of myth. He also subsumes his point of view in the "we." The triumphant athlete belonged to the town for a while. Housman avoids sentimentality by offering reasons why an early death might be positive.

ANDREW HUDGINS, *Elegy for My Father, Who Is Not Dead* (p. 256)

The speaker of this poem, unlike his father who is "ready" (line 2) to die, is not convinced "about the world beyond this world" (4). His father seems ready to die, happy "in the sureness of his faith" (3) that his journey into the afterlife will be like a vacation to a place where he will wait for his son to join him. The speaker is skeptical; he "can't / just say good-bye as cheerfully / as if he were embarking on a trip" (14–16). The difference in their attitudes is represented in terms of a ship; the speaker is convinced only that his father's "ship's gone down" (19), while the father is convinced that he will eventually wave and shout "welcome back" (21) to his son when his son's time comes.

The poem raises a crucial question: Will the son adopt his father's attitude when he himself is closer to death, or is he simply more skeptical than his father? Both options are raised; the speaker acknowledges, "He's ready. I am not" (14), but he also says "I do not think he's right" (13). Does our attitude toward death change as we get older because we have accepted our mortality, or is belief in the afterlife a defense mechanism? This question is central to the poem's interpretation, as is the speaker's focus: Is he more concerned about his father's death or his own? The poem is rather self-involved for an "elegy." Is the poet playing with two senses of the term, *elegy* — a poem of mourning and a meditation on death?

POSSIBLE CONNECTIONS TO OTHER SELECTIONS

Dylan Thomas, "Do Not Go Gentle into That Good Night" (text p. 247; question 1, following)
William Carlos Williams, "To Waken an Old Lady" (text p. 144)

CONNECTION QUESTION IN TEXT (p. 257) WITH ANSWER

1. Write an essay comparing attitudes toward death in this poem and in Dylan Thomas's "Do Not Go Gentle into That Good Night" (p. 247). Both speakers invoke their fathers, nearer death than they are; what impact does this have?

   Thomas's "Do Not Go Gentle into That Good Night" brings the speaker and his father into direct contact, which is a good starting point for contrasting these two poems. Would the speaker of Hudgins's poem express his sentiments differently if he were speaking to his father? Is there any trace of doubt or cynicism apparent in Thomas's speaker?

ODE

PERCY BYSSHE SHELLEY, *Ode to the West Wind* (p. 257)

Percy Bysshe Shelley was born to wealth in Horsham, Sussex. Educated in conventional privileges, he was taunted by his schoolmates for his unconventionality and lack of physical prowess. His rebellion against this environment helped make him both a nonconformist and a democrat. He was expelled from Oxford in 1811 for coauthoring a pamphlet called *The Necessity of Atheism.* He eventually married Mary Wollstonecraft Godwin and in 1818 settled in Italy, where he wrote his most highly regarded works, including "Prometheus Unbound" and "Ode to the West Wind." Shelley drowned while sailing with a friend, and his ashes were buried in a cemetery in Rome near the graves of his son, William Shelley, and John Keats.

The west wind in England is hailed as the harbinger of spring. As an introduction to this ode, you might have students read the anonymous "Western Wind" (text p. 38).

The tercets and couplets that form each section of this ode should pose no problems; basically, the tercets interweave (*aba, bcb, cdc, ded, ee*). Because Shelley is describing wind, the ethereal element, it is appropriate that the sounds of the couplet (*ee*), which appear at the end of every twelfth line in the first three sections, should have an airy, wind-rushed quality, as in "hear," "atmosphere," "fear."

The first three sections describe the powers the wind has in nature — on land in autumn, in the clouds in "the dying year" (winter), and on the bay (a mixture of land and sea) in the summer. When Shelley turns to his own problems, including his sense of despair and his need for inspiration (sections 4 and 5), the rhyme of the couplet (*ee*) is changed, and a more mournful, weighted sound ("bowed," "proud") is substituted. The rhyme scheme almost makes the poem generalize in the final section, when "Wind" and the promises of spring are bestowed on "mankind."

For a close reading of this ode, see S. C. Wilcox's, "Imagery, Ideas, and Design in Shelley's 'Ode to the West Wind,' " *Studies in Philosophy* 47 (October 1950): 634–49.

As a three-page writing assignment, ask students to analyze the symbolic meaning of the west wind.

POSSIBLE CONNECTIONS TO OTHER SELECTIONS

Robert Frost, "Storm Fear" (text p. 359)
Henry Wadsworth Longfellow, "Snow-Flakes" (text p. 613)

AUDIOVISUAL RESOURCES (manual p. 381)

MARY JO SALTER, *Home Movies: A Sort of Ode* (p. 260)

Salter names this a "Sort of" ode because it is not all praise or celebration. First, she catalogs the typical subjects of home movies: the family events and gatherings. In the next stanza, she describes the different scenes her father filmed because the other subjects "hadn't seemed enough" (line 1). The speaker reads these images as artistic statements that reveal her father's feeling of being "caged" (21). Notice that the "artistic or universal" subjects are scenes without people — studies of animals and plants and weather. Whose idea of art is this? Salter's poem does not aspire to the kind of pure natural imagery that her father's videography displays. Rather, she finds those sections of the home movies "generic." The images she recalls from that time period, preceding her parents' divorce, have a direct connection to the life of her family: "the pair of elephant bookends / I'd forgotten" (40–41), a bowl "handed down so many years / ago to my own kitchen" (47–48). The mother is happy among these everyday items, and the speaker's younger self "[smiles] because she does" (54). The two opposing ideas of art in this poem suggest some of the problems with the parents' relationship. The father's purely aesthetic images help him to escape from a quotidian reality in which he feels constricted. Yet to the mother's vision, those flowers and sunsets are sterile next to the objects of her daily life.

POSSIBLE CONNECTIONS TO OTHER SELECTIONS

Robert Hayden, "Those Winter Sundays" (text p. 23)
John Keats, "Ode on a Grecian Urn" (text p. 96; question 1, following)

CONNECTION QUESTION IN TEXT (p. 261) WITH ANSWER

1. Lines 51–52 allude to John Keats's "Ode on a Grecian Urn" (p. 96). Read Keats's poem and discuss the purpose of the allusion in Salter's ode.

    Keats's ode, with its famous line "Beauty is truth, truth beauty" (49), is one of the most recognized statements about the nature of art. He envies the permanence of the urn's artistic form, which will survive while people grow old and die. When Salter calls the mixing bowl "a Grecian / urn of sorts" (51–52), she emphasizes the passage of time that has relegated those events on the videotapes to memory.

PARODY

PETER DE VRIES, *To His Importunate Mistress* (p. 261)

Money is at the root of the distress in this work. In contrast, Marvell's main complaint was lack of time (text p. 81). "Picaresque" (line 7) is used in the sense of "our roguish affair." De Vries imitates Marvell's idiom quite closely. He picks up on the middle to high level of diction, the long sentences with verbs separated from their objects, and Marvell's rather Latinate style with the verbs coming at the ends of the sentences.

POSSIBLE CONNECTIONS TO OTHER SELECTIONS

Anthony Hecht, "The Dover Bitch" (text p. 529; question 1, following)
Andrew Marvell, "To His Coy Mistress" (text p. 81)

CONNECTION QUESTION IN TEXT (p. 262) WITH ANSWER

1. Read Anthony Hecht's "The Dover Bitch" (p. 529), a parody of Arnold's "Dover Beach" (p. 115). Write an essay comparing the effectiveness of Hecht's parody with that of De Vries's "To His Importunate Mistress." Which parody do you prefer? Explain why.

    The parodies have different aims: Hecht's parody goes at Arnold's poem directly, faulting the speaker for his effete lack of attunement to his lover's sexual desires, whereas De Vries's parody satirizes our culture, which seems to demand that we spend our time making money, not making love. De Vries's parody is also closer to the original in terms of its tone. Hecht's parody is more colloquial than the original, countering Arnold's measured lines with phrases like "etc. etc." (line 5) and "Anyway" (20). Students should articulate what makes a parody effective rather than simply state their preference for one or the other poem.

X. J. KENNEDY, *A Visit from St. Sigmund* (p. 263)

You might begin a discussion of "A Visit from St. Sigmund" by brainstorming in class about what students already know about Freud. Many students will undoubtedly have some prior knowledge of psychoanalytic theory, and because Freudian psychology has become part of our cultural literacy, even students with minimal knowledge of Freud's theories can enjoy this parody of Moore's "A Visit from St. Nicholas." Kennedy's tone in this poem is humorously satirical; at every opportunity he gives psychoanalysis a jab as he plays with the central tenets of Freud's theories. Mead's opening quotation provides Kennedy with a springboard into the poem. Her comparison between Santa and Freud is appropriate as both have become cultural icons — paternal figures concerned with the behavior (both good and bad) of girls and boys.

You might have students identify specific passages from the poem where the poet uses humor to gently poke fun at psychoanalytic humor. Responses might include the substitution of Freud's "baggage" (hangups, psychoses, a couch, symbols, subliminal meanings, the unconscious, phallic jokes) for the "baggage" of St. Nicholas in the original poem (stockings, reindeer, a sack, a sleigh, a jolly laugh, and so on). Play a recording of X. J. Kennedy reading "A Visit from St. Sigmund" on *Literature Aloud*.

You may want to read the original poem in conjunction with the parody to show how the poet manipulates Moore's famous poem. Students will see that Kennedy uses the original poem as merely the scaffold for "A Visit from St. Sigmund." The real joke here is on Freud, and the Christmas references simply add depth and richness to Kennedy's humor.

POSSIBLE CONNECTION TO ANOTHER SELECTION

Blanche Farley, "The Lover Not Taken" (text p. 382)

PICTURE POEM

MICHAEL McFEE, *In Medias Res* (p. 265)

Students will probably have fun identifying the puns in this portly poem. A handful for consideration: "His waist / like the plot / thickens" (lines 1–3) — just as in a murder mystery, his increasing girth is out to get him, as the darker tone of the second half of this poem implies. "Wedding / pants" (3–4) — do we read this as the pants from the suit he wore at his wedding, no doubt a smaller size, or as the waist "wedding," or uniting, with the waistband of the pants? "Breathtaking" (4) no longer means spellbinding but rather a kind of choking. The "cinch" (5) can be read either as a girth or belt, or a snap, an easy thing to do.

PERSPECTIVES

ROBERT MORGAN, *On the Shape of a Poem* (p. 265)

Students might enjoy analyzing Morgan's own "Mountain Graveyard" (text p. 36) in light of his idea that "all language is both mental and sacramental, is not 'real' but is the working of lip and tongue to subvert the 'real.'" How does his anagrammatic, spare prose "subvert the 'real'"?

Dylan Thomas's villanelle "Do Not Go Gentle into That Good Night" (text p. 247) is a good example to use when discussing Morgan's statement that "poems empearl irritating facts until they become opalescent spheres of moment, not so much résumés of history as of human faculties working with pain."

Ask students to think about form in other aspects of their lives — the formal behavior at a funeral, for example, as a way of dealing with painful emotion.

ELAINE MITCHELL, *Form* (p. 266)

By comparing form to a corset, Mitchell develops the idea that there is a time and a place to use form in poetry and a time and a place not to use it. Ask students to identify in the poem the various moments when the poet suggests that form can be helpful. Responses might include that it can "shape and deceive" (line 5), "It / 's an ace up your sleeve" (7–8), and "it / might be a resource" (12–13) or "your grateful slave" (14). Then ask students to identify places where the poet warns that form can prove too confining, such as "Don't try to force it" (3), "Ouch, too tight a corset" (6), "No need to force it" (9), and "sometimes divorce it" (16). Ultimately, Mitchell seems to be suggesting that poets need to recognize when form works to their advantage and when it is forced. When form is forced, poets need to be willing to abandon it rather than continue to impose form where it doesn't work.

By adhering to poetic form herself (three-line stanzas — except the final stanza — constructed with an *aba* rhyme scheme throughout), the poet forces her poem to conform to the restrictions of form she's set up. Indeed, she creates a very controlled rhythm (dactylic dimeter) and rhyme scheme to provide the poem with structure. Some students may recognize that, ironically, Mitchell forces words together and pulls them apart in totally outrageous ways in order to maintain the form she's established. Ask students to consider whether this effect is intentional.

10

Open Form

Whereas traditional forms depend on the interplay of the poet's current speech and an established form, open form hinges on the poet's (and the reader's) ability to discover a form that works toward the overall effect the poet wishes to produce. Just as in the previous chapter, each of the poems here can form the basis of a rewarding discussion about how form relates to content. With open form, the poet theoretically has absolute control over the form chosen, although some may choose a fairly constraining pattern to guide the poem — witness Peter Meinke's "The ABC of Aerobics." As a result of this freedom, the poem must actually withstand closer and more critical reading, as each formal choice takes on greater significance.

Poems like E. E. Cummings's "in Just-" obviously foreground the layout of the poem on the page as a formal technique. In fact, some of Cummings's poems cannot to be read aloud because of their formal experimentation. Cummings's poems, like those of William Carlos Williams, tend toward spareness and intense focus on the medium of language. By contrast, a poet like Walt Whitman uses repetition, catalog, and long rhythmic units to create a sense of plenitude and richness, a spilling over of language onto the page.

For some students, a poem like Galway Kinnell's "After Making Love We Hear Footsteps" may seem to be formless. This results from Kinnell's "plain speech" style and the seeming randomness of the line breaks. You may find it productive to push students to examine the breaks and rhythms in the poem more closely. The breaks serve to create units of meaning and to insert very slight pauses in the reading, which help create rhythms that add to the poem's overall mood. You might ask students why Kinnell chooses to put a stanza break between lines 18 and 19. Why not run the whole poem together? In both traditional and open forms, stanza breaks create a pause in which ideas can shift, focuses can change, or previous statements can be reassessed. Line breaks can do this on a much smaller scale. In either event, the white space on the page can be as telling as what is said in words.

Similarly, the absence of regular metrics or stanzas does not mean the absence of structure. Tato Laviera's "AmeRícan" demonstrates a use of repetition that is reminiscent of Whitman and serves to create a similar sense of flow and plenitude.

Web Ask students to explore the poets in this chapter at **bedfordstmartins.com/ meyerpoetry**.

As an exercise, you might have your students experiment with line breaks by taking a poem from the book and redoing the breaks. They might then give that poem to another student and have that student evaluate the new poem, asking themselves "Has the meaning of the poem (or parts of the poem) changed?" This exercise may help to emphasize felicitous or infelicitous choices in poetic structure. A related exercise might have students create found poems by taking a piece of prose and inserting line breaks. Students could again evaluate the results, looking for meanings that have been altered or significances that have been added by the change in form.

E. E. CUMMINGS, *in Just-* (p. 267)

Exactly how poems operate as a graphic medium on our visual sense is not well understood by critics. The open-endedness of the question provides a good occasion for students to make their own guesses. Notice, for example, that the most important thematic word in this poem, *spring*, either is set off from the line (as in line 2) or appears by itself, as in lines 9 and 18. In fact, the placement of *spring* at approximately the beginning, middle, and end of the poem is almost an organizational motif. Another repeated phrase, "whistles far and wee," also is placed first on one line (5) with "whistles" later receiving separational emphasis, over two lines (12 and 13), with "far and wee" receiving space — like long pulses on the whistle — and, at the close of the poem, on separate lines, as though the sound of the whistle were still present but moving away.

Ask sudents to explore contexts for E. E. Cummings on LiterActive.

The whistle is, of course, united with spring as a modern rendition of Pan's pipes drawing Persephone from the underworld and awakening the calls of birds and the sounds of wildlife. In response to the "goat-footed" (Pan) balloon man's pipes, "bettyandisbel" come running — the elision of their names mimicking the pronunciation, the swift movement, even the perception patterns of children.

Many other word patterns offer themselves for discussion in this poem. These comments are only a beginning, and an enthusiastic class can discover much more.

POSSIBLE CONNECTION TO ANOTHER SELECTION

Robert Frost, "The Pasture" (text p. 356)

WALT WHITMAN, *From "I Sing the Body Electric"* (p. 268)

Whitman's outpouring is an homage to the body, the soul, and poetry all at once. Whitman offers here an anatomy of wonder.

The rhythm of this portion of the poem is striking. Notice how many of the lines begin with a trochee or a spondee. The initial heavy stresses lend a kind of relentless thoroughness to Whitman's catalog of the human body. You might have the class scan a portion of the poem, say from line 25 to line 30. The lines change from heavily accented to a lighter, roughly iambic rhythm that suggests "the continual changes of the flex of the mouth."

Ask students to explore contexts for Walt Whitman on LiterActive.

The chief difficulty is, of course, discerning the exact relationship between these things. We tend to think of them as separate from each other. Does Whitman's poem help us to unify them in our minds? The poem lists a number of body parts: Do any of them tend to stand out or to form any sort of unexpected patterns?

Play a recording of Brian Murray reading "I Sing the Body Electric" on Literature Aloud.

POSSIBLE CONNECTIONS TO OTHER SELECTIONS

Algernon Charles Swinburne, "Sestina" (text p. 249)
Wisława Szymborska, "Nothing's a Gift" (text p. 583)

PERSPECTIVE

WALT WHITMAN, *On Rhyme and Meter* (p. 270)

In addition to assigning Consideration 3 as a writing topic, you might ask students to write a few paragraphs about Whitman's use of catalogs or lists as an element of the organic form he espouses. The excerpt from "I Sing the Body Electric" (text p. 268) is especially useful for this exercise. Why is Whitman's tactic of listing appropriate to his subject?

LOUIS JENKINS, *The Prose Poem* (p. 271)

Jenkins begins his response to misconceptions about prose poems with the rhetorical move of conceding a point: "The prose poem is not a real poem, of course." However, he ends with a jab at poetic traditionalists, in the figure of the boring teacher who won't stop lecturing. Tennyson is a convenient scapegoat for Jenkins: though widely popular in its time, his poetry has largely gone out of fashion. Jenkins is not alone, however, in complaining about the ridigity of the poetry canon, whose acolytes are sometimes hesitant to admit "a certain skill" in any writing that does not match its ideals.

In an interview with the *RipSaw* news, Jenkins recalled Frost's well-known statement, "A poem begins in delight and ends in wisdom," and bemoaned the fact that "[a] whole lot of poets try to jump right into wisdom and forget the delight." (You can read the whole interview at http://www.newsfromnowhere.com/louisjenkins2.html.) In this poem, his complaint against the teacher is funny, but he also maintains a sense of humor about his own poetry. As he characterizes the writers of prose poems as "too lazy or too stupid to break the poem into lines," he's poking fun at himself. How does this balance of humor contribute to the delight of the poem, and what wisdom does it lead the reader to in the end?

POSSIBLE CONNECTIONS TO OTHER SELECTIONS

Richard Hague, "Directions for Resisting the SAT" (text p. 505)
Philip Larkin, "A Study of Reading Habits" (text p. 34)

GALWAY KINNELL, *After Making Love We Hear Footsteps* (p. 271)

Kinnell's poetry is known for its directness, precision, and carefully controlled idiom. In his *Book of Nightmares,* from which this poem is taken, he explores the difficult project of explaining human mortality to our children. Love is his answer in many of the poems, but it requires confronting physical as well as emotional issues.

Play a recording of Galway Kinnell reading "After Making Love We Hear Footsteps" on **Literature Aloud**.

This is a popular poem with students because it vividly presents a scene that is familiar to many of them. Ask them to describe the speaker. What does his language tell us about his character?

You might ask students to explore in an essay the poem's auditory appeal. How do the various sounds create a mood for the speaker's discussion of his relationship to his child and his wife?

POSSIBLE CONNECTIONS TO OTHER SELECTIONS

Robert Frost, "Home Burial" (text p. 361; question 1, following)
Peter Meinke, "The ABC of Aerobics" (text p. 285)

CONNECTION QUESTION IN TEXT (p. 272) WITH ANSWER

1. Discuss how this poem helps to bring into focus the sense of loss Robert Frost evokes in "Home Burial" (p. 361).

   In concrete images such as the baseball pajamas and the expression "loving and snuggling," Kinnell's speaker establishes a sense of what his child is like. The boy's presence fills the poem as it fills the space between the speaker and his wife. Frost's poem explores what it would be like to have this space suddenly emptied, how he would talk to his wife about their loss, how it would affect their relationship. Frost's speaker's relationship to his wife is painfully awkward, just the opposite of

Kinnell's. As Kinnell's poem overflows with affection and love, Frost's echoes in emptiness, silence, grief, and loss.

KELLY CHERRY, *Alzheimer's* (p. 272)

This narrative poem illustrates the personal and emotional resonance within the clinical name of the title. The story centers on the moment at which the "crazy old man" (line 1) returns from the hospital and stands at his doorstep. What he remembers, from the far past, and what he doesn't recall, including the identity of his wife, establishes the scattered reality he is able to construct. Seeing the house triggers memories, but he is uncertain who the "white-haired woman" (27) is who greets him.

The man is characterized through careful examinations of everything he touches: the contents of his suitcase and the vision of the house he remembers "as his" (15) both paint a portrait of this nameless man's identity. The flowers around the house "slug it out for space, claw the mortar" (7), presenting a violent desperation not usually associated with "Roses and columbine" (7). The sun doesn't simply shine on the house; it "hardens the house, reifies it" (10): the scrappy verbs used to shape the reader's perception reflect on the "crazy old man" (1) as well. This dismissive label, a stereotype of someone with Alzheimer's, is undermined by the rich details associated with the house, the suitcase, and his memories of being younger. This detail, and the obsessive repetition and confusion surrounding the man's inability to recognize the "white-haired woman" (27), develop a character far richer than "Alzheimer's" or "crazy old man" indicates.

Play a recording of Kelly Cherry reading "Alzheimer's" on Literature Aloud.

Your students may benefit from some discussion of the different ways in which this man is characterized: How could they use a detailed description of a thing to describe a person? Ask students to write descriptions of a grandmother's purse, a sister's toolbox, a father's car, a friend's bookshelf: How do details of these objects help construct three-dimensional portraits of their owners?

POSSIBLE CONNECTIONS TO OTHER SELECTIONS

Anne Bradstreet, "The Author to Her Book" (p. 137)
Christina Georgina Rossetti, "In Progress" (text p. 618)

WILLIAM CARLOS WILLIAMS, *The Red Wheelbarrow* (p. 273)

This poem has a syllabically structured form, like a haiku, of four and two, three and two, three and two, and four and two syllables in each couplet. Also like a haiku, this poem is imagistic and suggestive rather than directly representational. Each couplet contains two stresses in its first line and one in its second.

Play a recording of William Carlos Williams reading "The Red Wheelbarrow" on Literature Aloud.

According to poet X. J. Kennedy, Williams was "gazing from the window of the house where one of his patients, a small girl, lay suspended between life and death." This information does enrich the first phrase, "so much depends," which seems to speak of a sympathetic vitality exchanged between ourselves and the objects of our landscape. Without this biographical detail, the poem is usually described as an example of imagism, in which the image is made to speak for itself.

Does the poem "improve" with our knowledge of Williams's situation while composing it? This question might be taken up in a writing assignment.

TIP FROM THE FIELD

To help students see the value in pure imagery, try connecting and comparing the importance of images in poetry to those in visual art. Students are often biased by their expectation that poems must have deep meanings. Conversely, they expect art to simply present them with something pleasing to look at and are intimidated if visual art expresses deep meaning. You might discuss the imagism movement, in which poets embraced the use of imagery alone to convey a poem's emotion and message, and then show slides of modern art in which the image is everything (i.e., Charles Demuth's *I Saw the Figure 5 in Gold* or anything by Andy Warhol). Then have your students write their own version of a poem like William Carlos Williams's "The Red Wheelbarrow" purely for the enjoyment of their own images.

— ROBIN CALITRI, *Merced College*

POSSIBLE CONNECTION TO ANOTHER SELECTION

William Carlos Williams, "Poem" (text p. 110)

NATASHA TRETHEWEY, *Domestic Work, 1937* (p. 274)

The theme of this poem lies in the irony that on the domestic's day off she has more domestic labor to do. Though the work she does in her own home is similar to her work on the job, the tone is drastically different. You might have your students list the words that contribute to the tonal shift. In the first strophe, the woman "[stares] down" (line 3) her reflection in the pot, suggesting a confrontation between the two selves. At home, she cranks up the stereo and sets the house "dancing" (13). The atmosphere is airy, open, and light as she "beats time on the rugs" (23). While cleaning at work is drudgery, cleaning at home is a sacred, and therefore joyful, act.

Most of the poem is told from an omniscient point of view, but as readers we are able to hear the woman's voice directly in the italicized lines. The first of these, *"Let's make a change, girl"* signals the turning point of the poem. The other two are lines that echo first a proverb and then a hymn. Why does Trethewey choose to emphasize her subject's faith? How does this particular character understand the relationship between faith and work?

POSSIBLE CONNECTIONS TO OTHER SELECTIONS

Sally Croft, "Home-Baked Bread" (text p. 126)
Katharyn Howd Machan, "Hazel Tells LaVerne" (text p. 77; question 1, following)

CONNECTION QUESTION IN TEXT (p. 274) WITH ANSWER

1. Compare the tone of Trethewey's poem with that of Katharyn Howd Machan's "Hazel Tells LaVerne" (p. 77).

   Trethewey writes from the third-person point of view, but her consciousness is close to her subject's, and therefore her tone is reverent and hopeful. Many of the verbs she uses, like "two-stepping" (line 18), "clapping" (21), and "beats time" (23), have musical connotations, which contribute to the liveliness of the poem. By mixing the secular and the sacred, she captures the joyful feeling of the domestic worker's day of rest. Machan, on the other hand, uses the first person in her narrative, and her character speaks in dialect, which gives the poem a more earthy feeling than Trethewey's. The voice is key in this rewriting of the frog-prince story and is essential to understanding Hazel as a no-nonsense character to whom high poetic diction would be foreign and possibly ridiculous.

GARY GILDNER, *First Practice* (p. 275)

In this poem Gildner examines a football coach's misuse of the power he holds over a group of young boys. The speaker does not respect this coach; he is afraid of him. But Gildner offers subtle hints that the coach is not worthy of the boys' respect at all. He has a "short cigar" (line 3), suggesting a Freudian lack of manliness; his derisive reference to "girls" (11) reinforces the notion that masculinity is an issue for him. Notice, too, that he refers to himself in the past tense: "he *was* Clifford Hill, he *was* / a man" (7–8), and "he *had once* killed" (9). This man's self is all in the past; the poem implies that he is trying to relive his glory through the young boys.

Although "First Practice" is open form, Gildner uses spacing to great effect in the middle of the poem. The long white space between the coach's statement that anybody who can't handle his methods should leave and the observation that "no one / left" (14–15) suggests the pregnant pause and tension that must have been palpable while the boys and the man waited to see if anybody would dare to go. Point out to your students that the poem's rhythm is irregular and there are no rhymes until the last three lines, which suddenly take on a rising anapestic dimeter in lines 25 and 26, followed by iambic dimeter and a decidedly masculine end syllable in line 27 that provides the poem's only rhyme (with *how* of line 24). The unique rhythmic quality of these lines draws attention to them and the poem's central irony: although the coach pressures the boys to be men and to fight hard, he's afraid of being identified as the cause of any injuries that may result.

POSSIBLE CONNECTIONS TO OTHER SELECTIONS

Judy Page Heitzman, "The Schoolroom on the Second Floor of the Knitting Mill" (text p. 508; question 1, following)
A. E. Housman, "To an Athlete Dying Young" (text p. 606)

CONNECTION QUESTION IN TEXT (p. 275) WITH ANSWER

1. Write an essay comparing the coach in this poem and the teacher in Judy Page Heitzman's "The Schoolroom on the Second Floor of the Knitting Mill" (p. 508).

    Both Gildner and Heitzman recall these authority figures years later because of the hurt they caused. Both the coach and the teacher seem to take the position that learning requires some pain. However, Gildner's Clifford Hill is overt in his methods. He makes the young men face one another directly and declares them enemies. Heitzman's Mrs. Lawrence is more subtle. Her class forms a single line that indicates unity, but when the narrator breaks a rule, the teacher punishes her by telling all of her classmates. Though her voice is quiet, the humiliated schoolgirl is sure that "everybody hears" (line 21).

MARILYN NELSON WANIEK, *Emily Dickinson's Defunct* (p. 276)

You might begin discussion of this poem by asking what associations students have with Emily Dickinson. For some background information, it might be interesting to read the text's introduction to Dickinson on page 301 and the Perspectives by Dickinson, Higginson, Todd, Wilbur, Gilbert and Gubar, Wolff, Bennett, Smith, and Wallace that follow the collection of Dickinson's poems on pages 332–340. Dickinson is thought to have been somewhat of a recluse, a woman isolated in her home and in her room, writing her life away in solitude and silence.

Waniek's poem presents a Dickinson that is radically different; this Dickinson is a tough woman, earthy and bold. Ask students to provide specific examples from the poem that redefine Dickinson in this light. Responses might include references to

Dickinson being "dressed for action" (7), smelling human (12), and being a "two-fisted woman" (25). In this way Waniek's poem effectively revises (or at least plays with) the image of Dickinson we've become accustomed to, imagining that underneath her reclusive exterior and "gray old lady / clothes" (5–6) there was a wilder and more adventuresome woman — an idea that is borne out in Dickinson's poetry.

The title of Waniek's poem functions in several ways, and it may be interesting to ask students to discuss or write briefly about the title. *Defunct* means extinct, or no longer living. Having died in 1886, Emily Dickinson is of course literally defunct. But the title may also suggest that the Emily Dickinson we've known in the past is defunct, for a revised image of the New England poet is being suggested by the poem.

After studying the poem, you may wish to ask students to read some Dickinson poems in order to identify connections between Dickinson's poems and the allusions contained in Waniek's poem.

POSSIBLE CONNECTIONS TO OTHER SELECTIONS

E. E. Cummings, "Buffalo Bill 's" (text p. 595; question 1, following)

Emily Dickinson, "I heard a Fly buzz — when I died —" (text p. 324; question 1, following)

CONNECTION QUESTION IN TEXT (p. 276) WITH ANSWER

1. Waniek alludes to at least two other poems in "Emily Dickinson's Defunct." The title refers to E. E. Cummings's "Buffalo Bill 's" (p. 595) and the final lines (27–30) refer to Dickinson's "I heard a Fly buzz — when I died —" (p. 324). Read those poems and write an essay discussing how they affect your reading of Waniek's poem.

   All three poems take on the topic of death, and on the surface all three seem to equate being dead with being "defunct," as the titles of Waniek's and Cummings's poems indicate and as the final line of Dickinson's poem emphasizes: "I could not see to see —." Yet there is the sense that death is not final, that it does not render us "defunct." Waniek's and Cummings's poems celebrate the vitality of their subjects after their deaths, and Dickinson's poem posits a life after death, even after the speaker loses her sight in the final line. Death is staved off through the lack of decisive end punctuation in Cummings's and Dickinson's poems, and the buzzing of the flies in Waniek's poem suggests an ongoing celebration of the life of this poet.

JEFFREY HARRISON, *Horseshoe Contest* (p. 277)

This narrative poem paints a portrait of a Fourth of July observance, complete with all the requisite images of a small-town celebration. The "parade / of tractors and fire trucks" (lines 1–2) and the "cakewalk and hayrides" (6) place the reader at the scene to watch, with Harrison, the "old guys" (19), high stakes, and graceful movements of the contest of the title. The tournament is important to the players because their skill in this field defines them as "their whole idea / of who they are" (25–26). The tournament also enables them to reclaim the glory the participants experienced during their youth while competing in high school athletics.

The speaker stays to the sidelines during the development of this comfortable scene. It is only at the end that the first person "I" is used, a development that establishes a totally new tone for the whole of the poem. The importance of the grace these "heroes, / becoming young again" (54–55) exhibit is not fully realized until the speaker admits that this expertise, in any field or endeavor, is worth "almost anything" (68).

Students may be struck by the prosiness of this narrative. This might be a good time to work together on defining, as a class, what makes something poetry. Who gets to determine what's poetry and what isn't? Are Harrison's line breaks and imagery sufficient to make this a poem, rather than a story broken into lines? Is this a poem because Harrison says so? Is Bruce Springsteen's "You're Missing" (text p. 46) a poem? Is Robert Hass's "A Story about the Body" (text p. 278) a poem? Is something a poem because it appears in a poetry textbook? Opening class discussion so students can define poetry for themselves may help make poetry less threatening and more enjoyable.

A. E. Housman, "To an Athlete Dying Young" (text p. 606)
Yusef Komunyakaa, "Slam, Dunk, & Hook" (text p. 611)

ROBERT HASS, *A Story about the Body* (p. 278)

This prose poem turns on a relationship that fails before it starts. A young man, a composer, decides not to act on his interest in an older woman, a painter, when he discovers that both her breasts have been removed. The conclusion of this poem provides a powerful metaphor: a bowl of dead bees covered with rose petals. It's a rich symbol, mingling the potential of bee stings, the impotence of dead bees, and the delicate beauty of rose petals.

Students may disagree on what this bowl symbolizes: the painter's unseen physical flaws? the superficial nature of the composer's attraction to the painter? Discussing the possibilities could create some interesting tension in your class. Students are likely to see one reading immediately. To initiate discussion, you might want to ask them to write down what they think the petal-covered bowl of bees describes, and then ask them to compare their answers for an enlightening discussion of the power of metaphor.

POSSIBLE CONNECTIONS TO OTHER SELECTIONS

Julio Marzán, "The Translator at the Reception for Latin American Writers" (text p. 280)
John Frederick Nims, "Love Poem" (text p. 44; question 1, following)
Walt Whitman, From "I Sing the Body Electric" (text p. 268)

CONNECTION QUESTION IN TEXT (p. 279) **WITH ANSWER**

1. Discuss the treatments of love in this poem and John Frederick Nims's "Love Poem" (p. 44).

    The love in Hass's poem is troubled from its first mention. In writing that the man "thought he was in love," Hass suggests from the beginning that the idea of love may not correspond with its reality. Indeed, in the next sentence, we learn that the love is actually directed at "her work," which bears a resemblance to her and yet is necessarily separate. With this confused notion of love, the man can't get beyond the woman's revelation that she has lost her breasts to disease. Nims's poem, on the other hand, is more assured about its ability to locate love. While Hass's poem struggles to arrive at a definition of love, this one barely mentions it except in the explicit title. The man in "A Story about the Body" shies away at the potential lover's imperfection, but the speaker in "Love Poem" sees the faults of his "clumsiest dear" (line 1) as the best reasons for loving her.

SHARON OLDS, *Rite of Passage* (p. 279)

Olds's work is often focused on gender distinctions and characteristics. In "Rite of Passage" Olds emphasizes the highly masculine qualities inherent in males of any age.

The title refers not only to the birthday party — a ritual by which we celebrate milestones in the maturation process — but also the boys' transition from child to adult behavior. Even six- and seven-year-olds demonstrate adult male characteristics: "Hands in pockets, they stand around / jostling, jockeying for place, small fights / breaking out and calming" (lines 5-7). They also emulate adult male behavior by comparing themselves to each other and by valuing power, force, assertiveness: "They eye each other, seeing themselves / tiny in the other's pupils. They clear their / throats a lot, a room of small bankers, / they fold their arms and frown" (9-12). The final lines, in which "they clear their throats / like Generals, they relax and get down to / playing war" (24-26), provide an overt context for much of the preceding covert activity. Socializing is akin to war: At this party, even the cake — "round and heavy as a / turret" (14-15) — is evocative of combat.

Play a recording of Sharon Olds reading "Rite of Passage" on Literature Aloud.

The power in Olds's poem lies in her insistence in the final lines, where the birthday boy assures his guests, *We could easily kill a two-year-old* (22), that this transition occurs much earlier than we might commonly expect. The "clear voice" of this child contrasts sharply with the thoughts he expresses, indicating dissonance between the image of a child and the reality of that image. Ultimately, the "rite of passage" refers less to the son's celebrating a birthday than to our own recognition that these children contain and manifest even at this early age the energy and the desire for brutality.

POSSIBLE CONNECTIONS TO OTHER SELECTIONS

Wilfred Owen, "Dulce et Decorum Est" (text p. 122; question 1, following)
Gary Soto, "Behind Grandma's House" (text p. 181)

CONNECTION QUESTION IN TEXT (p. 280) WITH ANSWER

1. Discuss the use of irony in "Rite of Passage" and Owen's "Dulce et Decorum Est" (p. 122). Which do you think is a more effective antiwar poem? Explain why.

   In both cases young boys participate in warfare, somewhat unwillingly at first. The images of actual warfare and death in Owen's poem are likely to make it the popular choice for a more effective antiwar poem. Students are likely to see Olds's poem as nothing more than a birthday party, which is its central irony. The boys at the birthday party might turn into bankers rather than soldiers, so the critique of war is somewhat dispersed.

AUDIOVISUAL RESOURCES (manual p. 379)

JULIO MARZÁN, *The Translator at the Reception for Latin American Writers* (p. 280)

This poem examines the sudden end of a conversation: Once the origins of the speaker are known, the new acquaintance loses interest. The imaginative center of the poem is the comparison of the acquaintance to a director. The speaker imagines the man is disappointed in the "lurid script" (line 19) he sees as the only possible potential for "Puerto Rico and the Bronx" (5). Marzán assumes that readers will recognize the separation between the mundane nature of domestic issues — "dreary streets" (21), "pathetic human interest" (22) — summoned by mention of "Puerto Rico and the Bronx" (1) and the exotic "Mayan pyramid grandeur" (14) associated with other Latin American locales.

The setting helps establish this tension: the reception is "high culture" (23), while "Puerto Rico and the Bronx" (5) represent areas with few economic advantages. This friction sees its result in the abrupt ending of the conversation as the acquaintance seeks other company. The speaker's tone remains amused and detached, however, demonstrating the real separation: Readers would likely choose the company of the speaker over the rude, unimaginative man who prefers cheese.

Mark Halliday, "Graded Paper" (text p. 507)

Tato Laviera, "AmeRícan" (text p. 284)

CAROLINA HOSPITAL, *The Hyphenated Man* (p. 281)

Hospital finds concrete expressions for hyphenated identity in her pairings of American and Cuban elements, such as "a bagel / with café con leche" (lines 2–3), "Cuban bread / at Publix" (10–11), and "Two-Stepping / to salsa beat" (17–18). You might want to point out to your students how often she uses line breaks to separate the two cultures. While these conflations might look confusing to some, the poet revels in duality "without explanations or alienations" (35). She gives directions for how to "get off the see-saw" (39) and "get on the hyphen" (46).

The hyphen is Hospital's linguistic figure for multiple cultural identifications, and it reveals how much of our identity exists in the way we talk about it. "Spanglish" (32) is important to the poem because it is a language that can accommodate both the narrator's American experience and her Cuban heritage. For this reason, it is the chosen language of "Hyphens Anonymous" (28). It helps the hyphenated man to embrace his rich contradictions.

POSSIBLE CONNECTIONS TO OTHER SELECTIONS

Tato Laviera, "AmeRícan" (text p. 284)

John Mitchum and Howard Barnes, "The Hyphen" (text p. 486; question 1, following)

CONNECTION QUESTION IN TEXT (p. 282) WITH ANSWER

1. Compare the theme of Hospital's poem with that of John Mitchum and Howard Barnes's "The Hyphen" (p. 486).

    Mitchum and Barnes's poem also focuses on the hyphen as a figure for being a "divided American" (line 6). However, where Hospital sees having a complicated identity as positive, Mitchum and Barnes think the hyphen can "be a bridge or be a wall" (26). When used maliciously it separates the supposedly "real" Americans from the "others." They would prefer that, regardless of heritage, everyone should be united under the word "Americans" (48).

ROBERT MORGAN, *Overalls* (p. 282)

Morgan's description of the overalls obviously sets up the comparison of work with war, which he makes explicit in the final line. The overalls are decorated with "medals, badges" (line 8), a "sheath" (10) as if for a sword, and "holsters" (20) like those for guns. But he also uses geographic metaphors, describing the patches as "mesas" (16) in a "cloth topography" (18). Beyond the military comparison, what about the laborer can we infer from Morgan's figures? The geography of the overalls suggest age, and their levels of patches indicate that the wearer has little money for new clothes. This begins to look like the portrait of a downtrodden worker. Yet the final line also points back to the childlike quality described at the beginning of the poem. Though this is war, it is a "playful" one (23).

Robert Hayden, "Those Winter Sundays" (text p. 23)

Seamus Heaney, "The Forge" (text p. 245)

ANONYMOUS, *The Frog* (p. 283)

Although a number of violations of grammatical rules appear in this poem — such as lack of agreement between subject and verb in "bird . . . are" (line 1), or "he hop" (3), and double negatives in "He ain't got no" (4) — there is a certain structure to its content. Following the odd assertion that the frog is "a wonderful bird" (1), the poet catalogs the frog's characteristics and follows them up with a list of what the frog lacks. The final line is a sort of culmination of both approaches: "When he sit, he sit on what he ain't got almost" (6). And although the literal meaning of the poem and its ungrammatical sentences might seem confusing, the poet provides a clear image of the frog, almost in spite of the language. The repetition of words such as *almost* and *hardly* and the reliance on many one-syllable words contribute to the overall rhythmic pattern of the work. You might ask students what the effect of comparing a frog to a bird is in this poem.

POSSIBLE CONNECTIONS TO OTHER SELECTIONS

Emily Dickinson, "A Bird came down the Walk —" (text p. 187)

Katharyn Howd Machan, "Hazel Tells LaVerne" (text p. 77)

William Carlos Williams, "The Red Wheelbarrow" (text p. 273)

TATO LAVIERA, *AmeRícan* (p. 284)

"AmeRícan" relies on a complex structure and innovative use of language for its power. Encourage students to examine the components and the physical layout of each section of this ever-changing, ever-moving poem. Each of the first three stanzas begins with the phrase "we gave birth to a new generation." The new generation is composed of those AmeRícans who will gather the elements of their culture and move into the mainstream American culture represented by New York. The seventh stanza (lines 21–24) highlights the poem's narrative development and the poet's creative use of language. Marking the transition between native and American culture, the poet embodies the literal movement, the disorientation, and the character of the new environment through the rearrangement and repetition of *across, forth,* and *back.* Appropriately, residence in New York (an island connected by bridges) is indicated by the line "our trips are walking bridges" (24). What other meaning is indicated by this line?

The eighth stanza breaks from the form established by the preceding stanzas. Ask students why it is appropriate to omit the beginning word "AmeRícan" here. In what way is this physical detail a response to the "marginality that gobbled us up abruptly!" (31)? In what other ways do the content and tone of this stanza contrast with the rest of the poem?

The poem is infused with the poet's sense of both Puerto Rican and American cultures. Encourage students to note the comparisons between the first and second halves of this poem, in which the poet touches on the music, spirit, and language of each culture. Also, students might notice instances (particularly toward the end of this poem) in which the cultures seem fused — for example, in words such as *spanglish* (41).

What is the tone of the final two stanzas? Literally, there is a celebration of the myth of America — "home of the brave, the land of the free." The penultimate stanza alludes to the understanding fostered by our Puritan forefathers that America is God's chosen country, "a city on a hill" that should be an example to all nations. The lines in which the poet refers to "our energies / collectively invested to find other civil- / izations" (52–54) also touch on our history of Manifest Destiny. The final stanza conveys the joy experienced by an assimilated AmeRícan, yet there is also considerable loss of identity in the speaker's "dream to take the accent from / the altercation, and be proud to call / myself american" (57–59).

POSSIBLE CONNECTIONS TO OTHER SELECTIONS

Chitra Banerjee Divakaruni, "Indian Movie, New Jersey" (text p. 544)

Julio Marzán, "The Translator at the Reception for Latin American Writers" (text p. 280)

PETER MEINKE, *The ABC of Aerobics* (p. 285)

Born in Brooklyn, Peter Meinke often experiments with form, preferring to let the poem dictate its own form. Works whose titles begin "The ABC of . . ." usually are primers designed to teach the basic elements of a subject. You might start discussion of this poem by asking whether it fulfills the expectations its title sets up. In a kind of playful, semisatiric thumbing of the nose at cholesterol-level and heart-rate calculators, the poem at least acknowledges the obligations of its title. The speaker, apparently, has tried to ward off the effects of aging by jogging, but he expends all this effort with a despairing sense of his past sins and the dark forebodings of his genetic history manifested in the portrait of Uncle George. Small wonder, then, that his thoughts turn to Shirley Clark, and the poem concludes with the speaker "breathing hard" and gasping for his lost flame at his own "maximal heart rate."

At least two aspects of this poem merit some consideration. One is the carefully controlled use of consonance and alliteration, often for humorous effect. Notice, for example, the alternating *l* and *b* sounds in line 12 followed by the nasal hiss of "my / medical history a noxious marsh." Later, in a spoofing of health and fitness fads, Meinke shows the direction of his true inclinations by exchanging "zen and zucchini" for "drinking and dreaming."

The second aspect of this poem that students should feel comfortable enough to enjoy is the humor, which derives in part from the poem's dip into the vernacular. "Probably I shall keel off the john like / queer Uncle George" Meinke unabashedly tells us in line 16, while he describes the lucky lover who married the fabled Shirley as a "turkey" who lacks all aesthetic appreciation for her wondrous earlobes. We are inclined to like the speaker in this poem, and both his personality and the radiated humor act as rhetorical devices, helping us to feel the way he feels about "The ABC of Aerobics," which, by the way, takes us to the end of the alphabet with "zen and zucchini."

Critical studies of Meinke's work include Philip Jason's "Speaking to Us All" in *Poet Lore* (Washington, D.C.: Heldref Publications, 1982) and Eric Nelson's "Trying to Surprise God" in *Mickle Street Review* (Camden: Walt Whitman House Association, 1983).

POSSIBLE CONNECTIONS TO OTHER SELECTIONS

Galway Kinnell, "After Making Love We Hear Footsteps" (text p. 271; question 2, following)

James Merrill, "Casual Wear" (text p. 175)

Sharon Olds, "Sex without Love" (text p. 93; question 1, following)

CONNECTIONS QUESTIONS IN TEXT (p. 286) WITH ANSWERS

1. Write an essay comparing the way Sharon Olds connects sex and exercise in "Sex without Love" (p. 93) with Meinke's treatment here.

Olds's subject is really not exercise and its obsessions but sex. Her analogy to exercise explores the absence of mutual experience or feeling in sex without love. Meinke's concern *is* exercise. Like Olds, he sees exercise as a desperate attempt to fight off the inevitable process of aging. The difference in the poems' attitudes toward exercise is a matter of diction and theme. Whereas Olds thinks that exercise involves a competition with oneself, Meinke reveals that it is really a struggle against "death and fatty tissue." Meinke's images of exercise are darker and more colloquial.

2.   Compare the voice in this poem with that in Galway Kinnell's "After Making Love We Hear Footsteps" (p. 271). Which do you find more appealing? Why?

Kinnell's poem celebrates a child as a sign of life and love, whereas Meinke's criticizes our culture's inability to accept death. Kinnell's poem will probably appeal to your more optimistic students; the more cynical will be comfortable with Meinke's view.

FOUND POEM

DONALD JUSTICE, *Order in the Streets* (p. 287)

The poem outlines a process, with each step in a separate stanza. As we read the poem we observe the process with the speaker. The word *jeep,* without an article, is repeated at the beginnings of three stanzas, lending an air of impersonality to its actions, as if there were no driver. The poem is itself impersonal, reducing "Order in the Streets" to a series of mechanized steps, devoid of human presence.

POSSIBLE CONNECTION TO ANOTHER SELECTION

Sharon Olds, "Rite of Passage" (text p. 279)

AUDIOVISUAL RESOURCES (manual p. 377)

11

Combining the Elements of Poetry: A Writing Process

Once students have grasped some of the individual elements of a poem, there remains the task of combining these separate insights into a coherent whole. Class discussion in introductory courses often takes up this challenge. While students make specific observations about a poem, the instructor attempts to connect the observations, in order to give students a bigger picture. But this isn't always easy. The Asking Questions about the Elements in Chapter 11 (page 291 of the text) may help students who need to add more component elements to their understanding of the poem or those who have a grasp of the components but still need a way of integrating them in discussion or in written assignments. The questions may also help more advanced students. Even if these students have a good understanding of a poem's structure, the questions could suggest ways of structuring their own papers on the poem.

You might also want to use these questions to facilitate class discussion. After determining which questions are particularly useful for a given poem, have separate groups of students explore separate questions. Then have the groups report to the class as a whole. Ask them to support their responses with citations from the poem. In the discussion following, try to engage the groups in dialogue with one another. How do their insights overlap? How might they combine their observations in a paper? This type of exercise should be valuable because it enacts the very task of the chapter.

Web Ask students to research John Donne at **bedfordstmartins.com/ meyerpoetry**.

Chapter 11 includes a sample student paper explicating John Donne's "Death Be Not Proud." Have your students read Donne's poem and then discuss how they might approach the assignment given to the student writer. You might want to ask them how they would write a similar paper but with a different combination of elements. How would they write such a paper about a different poem? What can they learn about combining elements from this sample paper? You might even ask them to critique the paper and suggest revisions.

APPROACHES
TO POETRY

12

A Study of Emily Dickinson

There are several difficulties in teaching Dickinson. One lies in having students unlearn previous assumptions about her — assumptions dealt with wonderfully in Marilyn Nelson Waniek's "Emily Dickinson's Defunct" (p. 276). Emily Dickinson was, in fact, a real person and did, from time to time, get out of the house. Dickinson can be read as a poet of passion and exuberance as well as irony and playfulness. The popular image of her as an agoraphobic introvert has done a disservice to such readings. Emphasizing that she was an actual human being can help students find a juncture between the erotic Dickinson, the death-obsessed Dickinson, the religious Dickinson, the playful Dickinson, and so on.

In addition, students may find many of her poems to be extremely challenging, though some may seem deceptively simple. When you ask students to "get their hands dirty" with these poems, they may find that they can dig much deeper than they initially thought. The challenging poems are often difficult because of Dickinson's use of occasionally unfamiliar vocabulary, wordplay, understatement, and gaps in her poetry. You may find it useful to encourage students to bring to bear all of the skills they have developed in previous chapters, including reading the poems aloud and writing about them.

EMILY DICKINSON

If I can stop one Heart from breaking (p. 308) **and** *If I shouldn't be alive* (p. 309)

You might wish to impress on your class the difference in quality between these two poems by means of a prereading experiment. Before your students have read the introductory text for this section, show them copies of the two poems with key words removed, and have them attempt to fill in the blanks. They will probably have no trouble with phrases like "in vain," "Robin," or "his Nest again" in the first poem, but do any of them anticipate "Granite lip" in the second?

Ask students to explore contexts for Emily Dickinson on *LiterActive*.

You might begin discussion of "If I can stop" by asking students to consider the comments on sentimentality and the greeting-card tradition in the text (pp. 43–44). Dickinson's relation to such popular occasional verse is, after all, not so far-fetched, as she is reputed to have honored birthdays and other social occasions by composing poems. Ask students to speculate on why this poem was so popularly successful and then to explore its limitations. The poem's simplicity and the extent to which it recounts what we *think* it should are among its popular virtues. If students have trouble seeing the poem's limitations, ask them if it is possible to live life with only one rule of conduct. Would they consider their entire lives successful if they saved one robin? You might also speculate with students on why the least common denominator of a poet's work is so often what the popular mind accepts. Recall as a parallel Walt Whitman's poem on Lincoln, "O Captain! My Captain!" — a rhymed lyric that has found its way into many high-school anthologies and may be even more popular since its use in the film *Dead Poets Society*.

"If I shouldn't be alive" is much more in keeping with Dickinson's usual ironic mode. In what ways is this poem similar to the previous one? What emotions are evoked by the use of the robin in each poem? Where does "If I shouldn't be alive" break away from the world of sentimentality evoked by "If I can stop one Heart . . ."? What does the speaker's concern that she might be thought ungrateful, suggested by the second stanza, say about her? How do the speakers of these two poems differ?

As a way of enabling students to appreciate the master stroke of the "Granite lip" in the last line, you might have them rewrite the line so that it steers the poem back toward a more conventional expression.

POSSIBLE CONNECTIONS TO OTHER SELECTIONS ("If I shouldn't be alive")

Emily Dickinson, "Because I could not stop for Death —" (text p. 326)
Helen Farries, "Magic of Love" (text p. 44)

The Thought beneath so slight a film — (p. 310)

Just as laces and mists (both light, partial coverings) reveal the wearer or the mountain range, so a veiled expression reveals the inner thought or opinion. Dickinson is here implying that the delicate covering makes the eye work harder to see the form behind the veil; therefore, misted objects appear in sharper outline.

Ask students to suggest other metaphors Dickinson might have used to describe the distinctness of things that are partially hidden. Depending on your class, you might be able to discuss one of the more obvious examples: whether or not seminudity is more erotic than complete nakedness. Why does Dickinson use such totally different metaphors — women's clothing and a mountain range — to make her point here? Is there any connection between the two? Do your students agree with Dickinson's premise? Are things more distinct, or simply more intriguing, when the imagination must become involved? Does one see another person's thoughts more clearly when a "film" necessitates working harder to understand, or is it just as likely that the "understanding" that results is a hybrid of two persons' thoughts?

POSSIBLE CONNECTIONS TO OTHER SELECTIONS

Emily Dickinson, "Portraits are to daily faces" (text p. 315)
——, "Tell all the Truth but tell it slant —" (text p. 329)

To make a prairie it takes a clover and one bee (p. 311)

"To make a prairie" reads like a recipe — add this to that and you will get the desired result. But it could just as well be a call for props in a theater production: take these items and add a little reflective imagination and the result will be a prairie, itself a symbol of open-endedness and freedom of spirit.

To enable students to understand the poem more clearly, you might ask them to explore the idea of essential ingredients by writing their own "recipe" poem: How do you make a family? a term paper? a painting? What happens to each of these entities as various ingredients are removed? What cannot be removed without destroying the entity or changing its character completely?

POSSIBLE CONNECTIONS TO OTHER SELECTIONS

Emily Dickinson, "I felt a Cleaving in my Mind —" (text p. 327)
Robert Frost, "Mending Wall" (text p. 359)

Success is counted sweetest (p. 312)

The power of this poem, to some degree, is its intangibility. We puzzle over how desire enables those who will never succeed to know success better than those who actually achieve it. Ask students to talk about the comparison of success to "a nectar" (line 3). It is odd that the verb *comprehend* should be paired with nectar; what does it mean to comprehend? When your students begin to talk about the pairing of understanding and physical images, ask them to think about "need" (4) as both a physical and an intellectual desire for success.

You might also have students discuss the word *burst* in the final line. Are the failures the true achievers? If so, what is it they achieve?

POSSIBLE CONNECTIONS TO OTHER SELECTIONS

Emily Dickinson, "I like a look of Agony," (text p. 317)
———, "Water, is taught by thirst" (text p. 313)
John Keats, "Ode on a Grecian Urn" (text p. 96; question 1, following)

CONNECTION QUESTION IN TEXT (p. 312) WITH ANSWER

1. In an essay compare the themes of this poem with those of John Keats's "Ode on a Grecian Urn" (p. 96).

   The themes of both "Success is counted sweetest" and "Ode on a Grecian Urn" have to do with wanting. Dickinson holds that success, or as she later calls it, "victory" (line 8), is "counted sweetest / by those who ne'er succeed" (1–2). In other words, the want of success makes success itself seem better. To use a cliché, the grass is always greener.... Similarly, Keats's image of the lovers forever chasing one another recalls the agony of the unsuccessful listener in Dickinson's poem. Yet the agony is not entirely negative. Consider how sweetly the success in Keats's poem is counted.

These are the days when Birds come back— (p. 312)

This poem examines Indian summer through images that evoke summer and autumn simultaneously. The coexistence of "a Bird or two" (line 2) and "blue and gold" (6) June-like skies with seeds and "a timid leaf" (12) suggest Indian summer. The former, unauthorized title could help students to identify the paradox of summery conditions when summer has past.

The "fraud" (7) being perpetrated by these aspects of summer is in the suggestion of true summer they establish, when winter is on the way. Still, the "plausibility" (8) of these summer signs makes the speaker long to pledge allegiance to the perception, to place her faith in the "sacred emblems" (16) of the season. The symbolic death of nature in late fall recalls the death of Christ in the line "Oh Last Communion" (14).

It may help students to consider the "sacred emblems" of other seasons. Are winter, spring, and autumn as deserving of the belief the speaker claims? What would the emblems of those seasons look like? Writing imitations of Dickinson's work could help students focus on her technique while considering these questions for themselves.

POSSIBLE CONNECTIONS TO OTHER SELECTIONS

Emily Dickinson, "Some keep the Sabbath going to Church —" (text p. 315)

Jane Hirshfield, "August Day" (text p. 560)

Water, is taught by thirst (p. 313)

Thematically, this poem reiterates the contention in previous Dickinson poems, such as "Success is counted sweetest" (text p. 312) and "The Thought beneath so slight a film —" (text p. 310), that the inability to grasp something physically brings its essential qualities into sharper focus. It might be interesting to have students suggest what Dickinson's pattern is in this poem. The first four lines appear to work by oppositions: water is defined by its lack, land by the oceans surrounding it, transport (ecstasy) by agony, and peace by war. But how is "Memorial Mold" related to love (line 5), and how can a bird be defined in relation to snow? The poem's images seem to move from the concrete to the abstract (although the last line seems to subvert this reading). Perhaps the reader is meant to consider the more abstract connotations of the words in the last line. What are some of the ideas or feelings that birds and snow call to mind? Are any of these ideas opposites?

POSSIBLE CONNECTIONS TO OTHER SELECTIONS

Emily Dickinson, " 'Heaven' — is what I cannot reach!" (text p. 316)

——, "I like a look of Agony," (text p. 317)

——, "Success is counted sweetest" (text p. 312; question 1, following)

CONNECTION QUESTION IN TEXT (p. 313) WITH ANSWER

1. What does this poem have in common with "Success is counted sweetest" (p. 312)? Which poem do you think is more effective? Explain why.

    Both poems argue that we learn through deprivation. We gain not just through necessity but through experiencing desperate circumstances. Students are likely to argue that this poem is more effective because it emphasizes its theme through repetition and variation. But "Success is counted sweetest" is at once more specific and broader in scope. It might be interesting to revisit this question after you have covered more of Dickinson's poetry or to have students try to isolate what they believe her most effective (or affecting) poem is.

Safe in their Alabaster Chambers — (1859 version) (p. 314) and *Safe in their Alabaster Chambers* — (1861 version) (p. 314)

Probably the most physically obvious change Dickinson made in revising this poem was the combining of the last two lines in the first stanza into one line. The latter poem seems more regular because its line and rhyme schemes are the same in both stanzas. The change also has the effect of de-emphasizing the more pleasant image of the original last two lines — the satin rafters — and emphasizing the colder, harder image of the stone. The emphasis becomes even more pronounced with the addition of the strong punctuation at the end of line 5 in the 1861 version.

The physical changes in the first stanza, coupled with a complete change of imagery for the second stanza, result in a different tone for the two versions of the poem. In the 1859 version the dead are lamented but life goes on around their tombs in anticipation of their eventual resurrection at the end of the world (note that in line 4 they only "sleep"). In the 1861 version the dead "lie" in their graves, and the larger universe continues in its course as though human deaths are of little importance. The second poem's mention of "Diadems" and "Doges" (9) serves to emphasize that even the fall of the earth's most powerful people has little impact on the universe. The human relationship to nature here is more like that in Stephen Crane's "A Man Said to the Universe" (text p. 164).

You might have students note at this point Dickinson's emphasis on white, translucent things in her imagery. Have students recall such images from earlier poems. They might mention film, lace, mountain mists, or snow. Note the contrast between Dickinson's conviction that we comprehend life more clearly through the mists and Emerson's idea, for example, that we should ideally become like a "transparent eyeball" in order to know Nature.

POSSIBLE CONNECTION TO ANOTHER SELECTION (1859 version)

Emily Dickinson, "Apparently with no surprise" (text p. 344)

POSSIBLE CONNECTIONS TO OTHER SELECTIONS (1861 version)

Emily Dickinson, "Apparently with no surprise" (text p. 344)
Robert Frost, "Design" (text p. 373; question 1, following)

CONNECTION QUESTION IN TEXT (p. 314) **WITH ANSWER**

1. Compare the theme in the 1861 version with the theme of Robert Frost's "Design" (p. 373).

   Both poems have to do with perspective and proportion, focusing first on something small and then pulling back to examine how those smaller things fit into a larger scheme. Frost's spider and moth retain their significance despite the ironic final line, "If design govern in a thing so small." Dickinson's "meek members of the Resurrection" (line 4), by contrast, are rendered insignificant by the entire second stanza. They are faceless and unimportant; the poet does not bother to pause and observe them, unlike Frost's speaker who concentrates on the spider, moth, and flower in detail before dismissing them.

Portraits are to daily faces (p. 315)

Before asking students to discuss the analogy presented in "Portraits," you might want to remind them of the analogy sections on their SATs or ACTs. They probably were at some point taught the strategy of making a connection between one pair of words and trying to apply it to a second pair. What happens when your students try to apply this strategy to Dickinson's poem? One difficulty lies in determining whether the comparison in the first line is meant to be taken in a positive or a negative manner. Is a portrait a daily face that is perfected and idealized, captured so that it never grows old? Or is it a static, posed rendering of something that was meant to be alive and constantly changing? The word *pedantic* in line 3 suggests a negative connotation for the second term in each analogy. The sunshine is ostentatious in its glory — in its "satin Vest." Do your students object to the characterization of bright sun as "pedantic"? After all, there is nothing inherently inferior about sunshine — or about living human faces, for that matter.

POSSIBLE CONNECTIONS TO OTHER SELECTIONS

Emily Dickinson, " 'Faith' is a fine invention" (text p. 343)
——, "Tell all the Truth but tell it slant —" (text p. 329)
——, "The Thought beneath so slight a film —" (text p. 310; question 3, following)

Robert Francis, "Catch" (text p. 28; question 1, following)
Robert Frost, "Birches" (text p. 365)
———, "Mending Wall" (text p. 359)

CONNECTION QUESTIONS IN TEXT (p. 315) WITH ANSWERS

1. Compare Dickinson's view of poetry in this poem with Robert Francis's perspective in "Catch" (p. 28). What important similarities and differences do you find?

   In both poems the reader must work hard to understand the meaning. Dickinson's poem embodies this circumstance, whereas Francis's illustrates it. But we have the impression that Francis believes in authorial intention, that there is a single "point" that the reader can "get," even if that point is obscure. Dickinson's poem (and her poetry in general) presents wide gaps between the reader and poet; we are not sure if we are meant to understand exactly what one of her poems means or if that meaning can remain stable over multiple readings.

3. How is the theme of this poem related to the central idea in "The Thought beneath so slight a film —" (p. 310)?

   Portraits are held to be superior to daily faces presumably because they allow the viewer to interpret them and to regard them with a sense of wonder. The thought beneath a slight film also allows for interpretation and awe. In both cases, art is preferred to quotidian existence.

Some keep the Sabbath going to Church — (p. 315)

One way to help students grasp more concretely the ideas Dickinson posits here is to have them draw up a chart comparing the practices of the "I" and the "Some" in this poem. How does the level of comparison shift between the first two stanzas and the third? The most important comparisons come in the last stanza; like the Puritans, the speaker claims that his or her religious practices result in a direct relationship to God, with no middleman. While the earlier lines may suggest a "to each his own" approach to religion, stanza 3 leaves little room for doubting which experience the speaker considers to be "real" religion. Discuss the distinction made in the last two lines between focusing on the goal one is journeying toward and focusing on the journey itself. Which attitude do your students feel reflects their own outlook?

POSSIBLE CONNECTIONS TO OTHER SELECTIONS

Gerard Manley Hopkins, "Pied Beauty" (text p. 604)
Walt Whitman, "When I Heard the Learn'd Astronomer" (text p. 629; question 1, following)

CONNECTION QUESTION IN TEXT (p. 316) WITH ANSWER

1. Write an essay that discusses nature in this poem and in Walt Whitman's "When I Heard the Learn'd Astronomer" (p. 629).

   For both poets, nature is sacred and should be approached through direct experience rather than through the filter of other human perspectives. Although both speakers value their direct experience of nature, they contextualize it differently: For Whitman's speaker it is an alternative to science, and for Dickinson's speaker it is an alternative to religion. These contexts give very different meanings to "nature." Science, especially astronomy, is a way of explaining natural phenomena, but religion is a way of providing moral instruction, a human phenomenon. Both speakers demonstrate the same impulse, but their quests differ in specific ways.

"Heaven" — is what I cannot reach! (p. 316)

You might begin discussion of this poem by having students recall other stories they have encountered that deal with the attraction of "forbidden fruit." The first stanza may allude to the story of Adam and Eve or to the myth of Tantalus, who was punished for trying to deceive and humiliate the gods by being placed in a pool in Hades, where the water at his feet receded every time he tried to take a drink and the luscious fruits growing above his head moved away whenever he tried to pluck them to assuage his hunger. Can your students think of other tales that emphasize the same idea? Does this affirm or contradict their own experiences? Why does this speaker consider the unattainable to represent heaven? What does this say about him or her?

Besides the apple that is out of reach, what other images of the unattainable does Dickinson use in this poem? The last stanza is particularly difficult in its syntax as well as its diction. How, for example, can "afternoons" (line 9) be a "decoy" (10)?

As a further topic for discussion, or as a writing assignment, students could be asked to consider other Dickinson poems that posit a thesis similar to or different from this one.

POSSIBLE CONNECTIONS TO OTHER SELECTIONS

Emily Dickinson, "I like a look of Agony," (text p. 317)
——, "Water, is taught by thirst" (text p. 313; question 1, following)
Sharon Olds, "Last Night" (text p. 85; question 2, following)

CONNECTIONS QUESTIONS IN TEXT (p. 316) WITH ANSWERS

1. Write an essay that discusses desire in this poem and in "Water, is taught by thirst" (p. 313).

   In " 'Heaven' —is what I cannot reach! ," desire seems to be created by unavailability, not just heightened by it. There is almost a perverseness in wanting only what is beyond reach, and Dickinson signals this awareness in her ironic quotes around "Heaven" (line 4). In "Water, is taught by thirst," desire is formed not just by absence but also by passing through the opposite of the desired thing. Dickinson implies that gratitude develops through this deprivation.

2. Discuss the speakers' attitudes toward pleasure in this poem and in Sharon Olds's "Last Night" (p. 85).

   For the speaker of this poem, pleasure is always just out of reach. She can presumably *see* the objects of her pleasure, but the experience is frustrating nonetheless, as the allusion to Tantalus makes clear. Whereas Dickinson's speaker cannot reach the apple on the tree, Olds's speaker is fully able to grab her moment of passion, to experience her sexual tryst, and to relive it through memory. Hers is a much less inhibited attitude toward pleasure; she can and does experience it. Dickinson's speaker can neither experience nor enjoy the things she desires.

"Hope" is the thing with feathers — (p. 317)

Dickinson makes her ruling conceit clear in the first line of this poem, but there are some aspects of this metaphor that you might want to have your students tease out in discussion. What might the tune without words stand in for? What crumb might hope ask in return (even though it doesn't)? Is this "thing with feathers" like any birds the students have encountered? If they've read several of the poems from this chapter, they may be aware that Dickinson associates birds with summer and with the figurative implications of summer. How can the qualities that birds usually embody coexist with "the chillest land" (9) and "the strangest Sea" (10)? As a religious statement, what does this poem say about the state of human existence? Does life seem like a frightening storm in Dickinson's other poems?

POSSIBLE CONNECTIONS TO OTHER SELECTIONS

Emily Dickinson, " 'Faith' is a fine invention" (text p. 343; question 1, following)
——, " 'Heaven' — is what I cannot reach!" (text p. 316; question 2, following)
Gerard Manley Hopkins, "The Windhover" (text p. 605)

CONNECTIONS QUESTIONS IN TEXT (p. 317) **WITH ANSWERS**

1. Compare the tone of this definition of *hope* with that of " 'Faith' is a fine invention" (p. 343). How is "Extremity" handled differently than the "Emergency" in the latter poem?

    In this poem, hope sings regardless of the state of the soul. When the speaker is in "Extremity," or in despair, she has the most need for hope and is most drawn to its song. In " 'Faith' is a fine invention," on the other hand, "Emergency" is experienced as a failure of faith, or at least as an instance in which faith cannot help with human affairs.

2. Compare the strategies used to define *hope* in this poem and *heaven* in the preceding poem, " 'Heaven' — is what I cannot reach!" Which poem, in your opinion, creates a more successful definition? In an essay explain why.

    While in this poem Dickinson chooses one figure to elaborate, in " 'Heaven' — is what I cannot reach! ," she runs through a number of comparisons. *Heaven* isn't exactly the thing being defined there. Rather, it's another way of naming the true subject of the poem: the feeling of longing for something unattainable. "Hope" focuses on an emotional state, trying to hold it still with an extended metaphor. "Heaven" demonstrates the difficulty of even formulating an idea of desire.

I like a look of Agony, (p. 317)

You might want to ask your class whether the speaker in this poem has an outlook similar to or different from those of the speakers in other Dickinson poems they have read. Whereas many of the previous speakers have professed a love of things half-seen, this one seems obsessed with certainty. Ask students to point out words that have to do with truth or falsehood; they will be able to find several in this short verse. Is death the only certainty for human beings? Are there any other times when it is possible to be certain that the image a person projects is an accurate one? Note also the words *I like* in line 1 and the characterization of Anguish as "homely" in the last line. Does this speaker actually find pleasure in people's death throes?

Flannery O'Connor once wrote, in justifying her use of violent encounters in her fiction, that "it is the extreme situation that best reveals what we are essentially." What would the speaker of this poem say to such a statement?

POSSIBLE CONNECTIONS TO OTHER SELECTIONS

Emily Dickinson, "The Bustle in a House" (text p. 328)
——, " 'Heaven' — is what I cannot reach!" (text p. 316; question 1, following)
——, "Success is counted sweetest" (text p. 312; question 1, following)
——, "Water, is taught by thirst" (text p. 313)

1. Write an essay on Dickinson's attitudes toward pain and deprivation, using this poem and " 'Heaven' — is what I cannot reach!" (p. 316).

   According to these poems, it would seem that Dickinson is something of an ascetic, if not a masochist. Each poem describes a blissful state that the speaker cannot achieve. Yet each poem also describes a yearning; that is, in each poem the speaker is not content with her state of deprivation and pain so much as she uses that state to gauge her emotions. In this poem the desired condition is not necessarily death but rather honest purity. The same could be said for the other poem as well: on the surface, the speaker inclines toward death, but unadulterated honesty — so rare in our daily lives — is at the heart of her quest.

Wild Nights — Wild Nights! (p. 318)

A class discussion of this poem could focus on a few well-chosen words. Researching the etymology of *luxury* (line 4) will leave no room for doubt as to the intended eroticism of the poem; it comes from the Latin *luxuria,* which was used to express lust as well as extravagant pleasures of a more general sort, which the term has now come to mean. You might also discuss the use of natural imagery in the second and third stanzas. The heart in stanza 2 has no more need of compass or chart. Ask your students what these images mean to them. They seem to imply attention to order, rules, and laws. These images are set aside in the third stanza in favor of Eden and the sea.

A study of "Wild Nights" provides an excellent opportunity to discuss the possibility of disparity between the author of a work and the created narrator who speaks within the work. Students may wish to dismiss the eroticism of this poem if they have stereotyped Dickinson as a pure spinster in a white dress. However, the speaker of this poem cannot be specifically identified as Dickinson. Indeed, it is debatable whether the speaker is male or female.

POSSIBLE CONNECTIONS TO OTHER SELECTIONS

Margaret Atwood, "you fit into me" (text p. 135; question 1, following)
Edna St. Vincent Millay, "Recuerdo" (text p. 494)

CONNECTION QUESTION IN TEXT (p. 318) WITH ANSWER

1. Write an essay that compares the voice, figures of speech, and theme of this poem with those of Margaret Atwood's "you fit into me" (p. 135).

   Atwood's poem is characterized by sarcasm and irony, as though the speaker is trying to flatter her addressee only to deflate him with a wry insult. The speaker of Dickinson's poem is much more sincere, desiring sexual union without anticipating the pain that Atwood's speaker focuses on. The imagery of this poem suggests security, whereas Atwood's imagery upends such security and replaces it with a disturbing image of pain: a fish hook in a human eye.

I reason, Earth is short — (p. 319)

Dickinson does not often use a repeated line as she does in this poem, so it might be fruitful to start there. Does ending each stanza with the same question make this poem static, or does the speaker progress toward some greater understanding in the poem? The dismissive "But, what of that?" takes on different meanings as it is attached to the three different formulations of pain and loss. Dickinson first discusses earthly pain, which leaves some room for hope. In the Christian conception of life, our actions in the world are only preparation for heaven, so the answer to her question would be that this pain is transitory. The next stanza is a little harsher, as most Christians would argue that the soul is a human's "Vitality" (line 6) and that it will exist after death. Yet Dickinson is focused on a quality of vitality in life, which will inevitably end. In the final stanza, Dickinson admits to believing in a heaven, but her "Somehow" contains some doubts about its workings. More devastatingly, she refuses to be consoled by the idea of heaven, still holding onto "But, what of that?" Do your students read this final line as a note of despair? Why wouldn't Dickinson be comforted by heaven? Does "absolute" (2) anguish prevent consolation?

POSSIBLE CONNECTIONS TO OTHER SELECTIONS

Edmund Conti, "Pragmatist" (text p. 139)

John Keats, "When I have fears that I may cease to be" (text p. 610)

What Soft — Cherubic Creatures — (p. 319)

A brief discussion of societal expectations for women in the mid–nineteenth century may help students to appreciate Dickinson's satirical intent in this poem. A woman was expected to be "the Angel in the House" who exerted a spiritual influence on those around her and made family life harmonious. In her book *Dimity Convictions: The American Woman in the Nineteenth Century* (Athens: Ohio UP, 1976), which draws its title from this poem, Barbara Welter notes that "religion or piety was the core of woman's virtue, the source of her strength," and that "religion belonged to woman by divine right, a gift of God and nature." Further, woman was to use her "purifying passionless love [to bring] erring man back to Christ." Among other evidence from mid–nineteenth-century women's magazines, Welter cites a poem that appeared in an 1847 issue of *Ladies' Companion*. The title alone — "The Triumph of the Spiritual over the Sensual" (*Dimity Convictions* 21–22) — is enough to convey the sense of disembodied spirituality Dickinson attacks in the poem.

Play recordings of Julie Harris and Robert Pinsky reading "What soft — Cherubic Creatures —" on *Literature Aloud*.

Ask students to notice the particular adjectives the poet uses to describe the "Gentlewomen." They are "Soft," "Cherubic" (line 1), and "refined" (6), but by the end of the poem they are "Brittle" (11). The crucial lines 7–8, which divide the positive from the negative attributes, are especially important. Not only are the women disconnected from both the human and the divine, but their attitudes would seem, by extension, to dissociate them from the central tenet of Christianity, that God became man. The last two lines make it clear that the first stanza is intended to be read satirically. How might the comparisons to "Plush" (3) and to a "Star" (4) be construed negatively? Notice the two uses of the word *ashamed,* in lines 8 and 12. Who is ashamed in each case? What is the effect of the repetition of this word?

POSSIBLE CONNECTIONS TO OTHER SELECTIONS

Emily Dickinson, " 'Faith' is a fine invention" (text p. 343; question 1, following)

Christina Georgina Rossetti, "Some Ladies Dress in Muslin Full and White" (text p. 618)

CONNECTION QUESTION IN TEXT (p. 321) WITH ANSWER

1. How are the "Gentlewomen" in this poem similar to the "Gentlemen" in " 'Faith' is a fine invention" (p. 343)?

   Dickinson attacks the false faith of "gentlemen" and "gentlewomen" in these poems. Both groups pretend to be pious, but Dickinson characterizes them as hypocritical and superficial, with no clear sense of redemption and no knowledge of their souls.

The Soul selects her own Society — (p. 321)

You might begin a discussion of this poem by asking students to consider whether the image projected here matches the image of a female who spends her life in near solitude. They are likely to notice that one stereotypically assumes that a woman remains alone because she has no other choice (more so when this poem was written than today), whereas the "Soul" described here operates from a position of power. The verbs associated with the soul are all active: She "selects" (line 1), "shuts" (2), chooses (10), and closes off her attention (11), unmoved by chariots (5) or even emperors (7).

How does the meter in lines 10 and 12 reinforce what is happening in the poem at this point? What seems to be the purpose of the soul's restrictions on her society? You might have students discuss both the limitations and the benefits of such exclusiveness. Do they think the advantages outweigh the disadvantages or vice versa? What does the poem's speaker think? How do you know?

POSSIBLE CONNECTIONS TO OTHER SELECTIONS

Emily Dickinson, "I dwell in Possibility —" (text p. 322)

——, "Much Madness is divinest Sense —" (following)

Much Madness is divinest Sense — (p. 321)

This poem could be the epigram of the radical or the artist. For all its endorsement of "madness," however, its structure is extremely controlled — from the mirror-imaged paradoxes that open the poem to the balancing of "Assent" and "Demur" and the consonance of "Demur" and "dangerous." Try to explore with the class some applications of the paradoxes. One might think, for example, of the "divine sense" shown by the Shakespearean fool.

POSSIBLE CONNECTIONS TO OTHER SELECTIONS

Emily Dickinson, "The Soul selects her own Society —" (text p. 321; question 1, following)

William Butler Yeats, "Crazy Jane Talks with the Bishop" (text p. 639)

CONNECTION QUESTION IN TEXT (p. 322) WITH ANSWER

1. Discuss the theme of self-reliance in this poem and "The Soul selects her own Society —" (p. 321).

    In this poem Dickinson scorns conformity, specifically in terms of the often wrong-headed attempt to separate sense from insanity. The theme is that we must try to see beyond the notion that consensus necessarily equals what is right. (You might highlight the fact that the poem was written in 1862, at the start of the Civil War; before this period, slavery was accepted in America because it reflected a majority opinion.) Dickinson focuses on the individual in "The Soul selects her own Society —," turning the focus away from the majority and to the individual who decides for oneself what is right, good, or just by aligning oneself only with others who share the same beliefs, even if those others represent a minority.

I dwell in Possibility — (p. 322)

In the first two lines of the poem the speaker sets up the general premise that poetry is superior to prose. The imagery used in the next ten lines specifies the reason that the speaker values poetry. One possible strategy for teaching the poem is to explore the metaphor of the house and then return to the original premise and ask students whether they find it convincing.

The imagery in this poem moves outward from man-made, earthly examples to examples from nature to a final image of the supernatural. In lines 3 and 4 the speaker compares poetry to prose as though they were both houses. Why is it important that the comparison focuses specifically on the windows and doors of the house? The second stanza draws the metaphor outward to compare the rooms and roof of the house of poetry to entities in nature. The chambers in the house are likened to cedar trees (line 5), trees known for the durability of their wood and for their longevity. The cedars of Lebanon are also a familiar biblical allusion. According to the first book of Kings, the house of Solomon was built "of the forest of Lebanon ... upon four rows of cedar pillars, with cedar beams upon the pillars" (2:2); the lover in the Song of Solomon sings, "The beams of our house are cedar" (1:17). The roof of the house of poetry is compared to the sky (7–8), but again the speaker adds a qualifier — the word *everlasting* (7) — to raise this roof to an even higher level. The final word of the poem — *paradise* — ends the comparison at the farthest possible reaches of expansiveness.

Returning to the comparison made in the opening lines, students will probably see that the speaker considers poetry to be the "fairer House" on the basis of its capacity to expand, to open up to ever wider capacities. A fruitful discussion might result from the question of whether or not students agree with the speaker of this poem. Can they think of examples of prose that are expansive, or poetry that is narrow? How does the example of Dickinson's own prose — her letter to Higginson (text p. 332) — fit into this argument?

POSSIBLE CONNECTIONS TO OTHER SELECTIONS

Emily Dickinson, "The Soul selects her own Society —" (text p. 321)

T. E. Hulme, "On the Differences between Poetry and Prose" (text p. 131; question 1, following)

CONNECTION QUESTION IN TEXT (p. 322) WITH ANSWER

1. Compare what this poem says about poetry and prose with T. E. Hulme's comments in "On the Differences between Poetry and Prose" (p. 131).

    Hulme contrasts the symbolic nature of prose with the metaphorical and imagistic properties of poetry. For him, poetry uses a "visual concrete" language. Dickinson argues that poetry is less confined than prose, which is a different point altogether. For her, poetic language is about the endless possibilities for signification in poetry. Her version of poetry is ethereal, taking us through the "Everlasting Roof" of "The Gambrels of the Sky" (lines 7–8), whereas Hulme sees poetry as "a pedestrian taking you over the ground." Of course, for him prose is no more ethereal but simply more direct, like "a train which delivers you at a destination." Prose for Dickinson is simply more constrained than poetry — a house with fewer windows, inferior doors, and an actual roof.

This was a Poet — It is That (p. 323)

In this poem the speaker defines poetry by contrasting it to ordinary experience and perception. The poet distills extraordinary perfumes from ordinary flowers and discloses a picture that we had not seen before. The speaker endows the poet with "a Fortune — / Exterior — to Time" (lines 15–16) and depicts the rest of the world as living in "ceaseless Poverty" (12).

This poem is complicated by its first line, which sounds like a eulogy: "This was a poet." Why does the speaker use the past tense here? The tense never stays still for long

— ironic given that the poem's final gesture is to declare the poet's "Fortune — / Exterior — to Time" (15–16). Is the speaker's intent to define the role of a poet or to make some philosophical statement about art and time? You can deepen this discussion even further by pointing out that "Attar" (4), in addition to being a perfume derived from flowers, is also the name of a thirteenth-century Persian poet. The timeless fortune of a poet also contrasts nicely with "the familiar species / That perished by the Door" (5–6), which can signify something ordinary that simply lives and dies, unlike the poet, who is extraordinary and who lives on through verse.

POSSIBLE CONNECTIONS TO OTHER SELECTIONS

Emily Dickinson, "A Bird came down the Walk —" (text p. 187; question 2, following)

———, "I dwell in Possibility —" (text p. 322; question 1, following)

John Keats, "When I have fears that I may cease to be" (text p. 610)

William Shakespeare, "Not marble, nor the gilded monuments" (text p. 491)

CONNECTION QUESTIONS IN TEXT (p. 323) WITH ANSWER

1. Write an essay about a life lived in imagination as depicted in this poem and in "I dwell in Possibility —" (p. 322).

   The first line of this poem again presents difficulty. The poet does not truly seem "exterior to time" if he or she is dead. "I dwell in Possibility —" seems much more eternal, with its final gesture of gathering paradise.

2. Discuss "A Bird came down the Walk —" (p. 187) as an example of a poem that "Distills amazing sense / From ordinary Meanings —" (lines 2–3).

   The contrast between the first and last stanzas of "A Bird came down the Walk —" demonstrates this definition well. The sense of a mundane occurrence is expanded through the poet's transformation. A bird hopping and eating becomes the source of wonder at the vast mysteries of nature and a metaphor of humanity's humble relationship to the universe.

After great pain, a formal feeling comes — (p. 323)

In an interesting inversion of her often-used technique of employing metaphors from life to explore the territory of death and beyond, Dickinson in this poem uses a metaphor of death — the ceremony of a funeral — to evoke an image of one who has dealt with great pain in life. It is interesting that psychologists consider the funeral ritual to be generally more valuable for the survivors than for the deceased, because this poem is about survivors and how they are able eventually to get past their pain. In addition to the controlling image of a funeral, the poet uses two other strategies to convey the idea of a place that is past pain. Dickinson's word choices here abound in objects and adjectives that permeate the poem with a sense of numbed feelings. If you ask your students to point out some of these words, they might mention "formal" (line 1), "tombs" (2), "stiff" (3), "mechanical" (5), "wooden" (7), "Quartz" and "stone" (9), "Lead" (10), and "Snow" (12), among others.

The entire poem deals with life after the initial sharp pain of loss has subsided. Lines 12–13 concern the movement from palpable discomfort to apathetic stupor to true release. Ask your students if their own experiences with pain confirm or repudiate this scenario. Does the speaker hedge a bit in line 11? Are there other human rituals besides funerals by which we formally let go of pain?

POSSIBLE CONNECTIONS TO OTHER SELECTIONS

Emily Dickinson, "The Bustle in a House" (text p. 328; question 1, following)

Robert Frost, "Home Burial" (text p. 361)

CONNECTION QUESTION IN TEXT (p. 324) WITH ANSWER

1. How might this poem be read as a kind of sequel to "The Bustle in a House" (p. 328)?

   The poems might be looked at as stages one goes through when coping with loss. "The Bustle in a House" describes an immediate return to daily routine following death, almost a denial about the gravity of the situation even though this bustle is the "solemnest of industries / Enacted upon Earth" (lines 3–4). This poem describes the emotions that might follow the immediate need to return to the relative order of everyday life, the gradual process that allows us to let go of our grief.

I heard a Fly buzz — when I died — (p. 324)

This poem is typical of Dickinson's work as a willed act of imagination fathoming life after death and realizing the dark void and limitation of mortal knowledge. David Porter in *Dickinson: The Modern Idiom* (Cambridge: Harvard UP, 1981) observes:

> At a stroke, Dickinson brilliantly extracted the apt metonymical emblem of the essential modern condition: her intrusive housefly. . . . The fly takes the place of the savior; irreverence and doubt have taken the place of revelation. Her fly, then, "With Blue — uncertain stumbling Buzz" is uncomprehension, derangement itself. It is noise breaking the silence, not the world's true speech but, externalized, the buzz of ceaseless consciousness. (239)

You might introduce this idea and then, either in discussion or in a writing assignment, ask the class to explore the tone of this poem and its accordance with Porter's comment.

POSSIBLE CONNECTIONS TO OTHER SELECTIONS

Marilyn Nelson Waniek, "Emily Dickinson's Defunct" (text p. 276)

Walt Whitman, "A Noiseless Patient Spider" (text p. 149; question 1, following)

CONNECTION QUESTION IN TEXT (p. 325) WITH ANSWER

1. Contrast the symbolic significance of the fly with the spider in Walt Whitman's "A Noiseless Patient Spider" (p. 149).

   The fly in Dickinson's poem is a kind of otherworldly messenger that fills up the space between death and life. Still, there is no connection between the fly and the speaker; nor does the fly seem to belong to the other world, unlike Whitman's spider, whose job is to connect the soul with the world of the living.

One need not be a Chamber — to be Haunted — (p. 325)

This poem, in gothic fashion, describes the psychological terrors of the brain and how it can be haunted by partially repressed, horrifying memories more frightening than real horrors. The first stanza devalues external horrors in comparison to internal ones and explains that "The Brain has Corridors" (line 3) that have the potential to be far scarier than corridors in any haunted house.

You might begin discussion of this poem by asking students to explain Dickinson's comparisons between external and internal "hauntings." What words or lines most effectively characterize the speaker's fear of himself or herself? Ask your class to consider how each stanza is divided into an examination of both external and internal terrors. Each stanza concludes that the inner horrors are much harder to face than the outer ones. For example, the fourth stanza asserts that it is easier to protect oneself from an external "Assassin" (15) than it is to close the door on one's memory. You might ask your class to discuss why one's own personal "hauntings" might be scarier than facing any "External Ghost" (6).

You might also ask your students to consider the tone of this poem. Could it be read as a sort of warning? To whom and from whom? Consider also the poem as an eerie message from an insane mind. Still another vantage point would be to read the poem as a relatively objective discussion of psychological terror. Ask students what words and phrases contribute to their perception of the poem's tone.

Possible Connections to Other Selections

Edgar Allan Poe, "The Haunted Palace" (text p. 159; question 1, following)

Jim Stevens, "Schizophrenia" (text p. 148; question 1, following)

Connection Question in Text (p. 325) with Answer

1. Compare and contrast this poem with Edgar Allan Poe's "The Haunted Palace" (p. 159) and Jim Stevens's "Schizophrenia" (p. 148). In an essay explain which poem you find the most frightening.

   All three poems advance the idea that minds are more likely to be haunted than structures are. All three poems also use haunted structures as metaphors for some sort of mental disorder, yet they do so in different ways. Dickinson's poem is the most direct in terms of this metaphor because it explicitly links the mind and a haunted chamber in the first stanza. Stevens's poem only intimates the connection between mind and building in the title, and Poe never explicitly makes the connection, although it is apparent to the careful reader.

Because I could not stop for Death — (p. 326)

Here is one Dickinson poem in which the speaker manages to go beyond the moment of death. The tone changes in the exact center of the poem, from the carefree attitude of a person on a day's leisurely ride through town and out into the country, to the chill of the realization that he or she is heading for the grave. The final images, however, are not those of horror but of interest in the passage from time to eternity and the ramifications thereof.

The first line makes the reader aware of the speaker's lack of control over the situation; Death is clearly in charge. Still, as Death is described as kind (line 2) and civil (8), and as Immortality is along for the ride, the situation is not immediately threatening. In the third stanza the carriage takes the speaker metaphorically through three stages of life: youth, represented by the schoolchildren; maturity, represented by the fields of grain; and old age, pictured as the setting sun.

Lines 13 and 14, which describe the chill felt as the sun goes down, constitute the turning point of the poem. Both the figurative language and the rhythm pattern signal a change. Dickinson abruptly reverses the alternating four-foot, three-foot metrical pattern of the first twelve lines so that line 13 contains the same number of feet as the line that immediately precedes it. The caesura after "Or rather" serves to emphasize the speaker's double take. You might wish to discuss the speaker's tone as the poem concludes.

Emily Dickinson, "Apparently with no surprise" (text p. 344; question 1, following)

——, "If I shouldn't be alive" (text p. 309)

CONNECTION QUESTION IN TEXT (p. 326) WITH ANSWER

1. Compare the tone of this poem with that of Dickinson's "Apparently with no surprise" (p. 344).

    Both poems cast the process of death as something methodical and mannerly. Yet this poem sounds more philosophical than "Apparently with no surprise," perhaps because its subject is human death as opposed to the cycles of nature. There are also a multitude of dashes in this poem, whereas the other one ends with a period, making it sound more like a clever observation than a deep meditation.

I felt a Cleaving in my Mind — (p. 327)

This poem describes an experience of mental disintegration or serious psychological strain. The speaker relates the feeling that his or her "Brain had split" (line 2), and that as a result the speaker's thoughts become increasingly disjointed. Eventually they seem to unravel, like balls of yarn rolling across the floor. You might discuss with your students this likening of the unraveling balls of yarn (7–8) to a mental breakdown. Ask them what is so effective about connecting the homely, domestic image of yarn with the anguish of psychological decay.

Structured in perfect iambic pentameter and incorporating full rhymes, this Dickinson poem is unusual in its regularity. Much of the power of "I felt a Cleaving" lies in its sharp contrast between form and content. Discuss with your students the disparity between its smooth patterns of rhythm and rhyme and its disturbing theme. Point out that the first stanza reads almost like a jingle — how do the poem's soothing musical qualities increase the horror of the experience? Poetically, the speaker's thoughts are joined together seamlessly, in perfect sequence. Yet this is precisely what the speaker claims is impossible for him or her to do. Ask your students to speculate why Dickinson would write such a smooth poem to describe such a jarring experience.

You might also consider asking your students to investigate the dictionary meanings of several words in this poem. Interestingly, *cleave* is defined as both "to separate" and "to adhere," and *ravel*, which is actually a synonym for *unravel*, means both "to entangle" and "to disentangle." You might ask your students to consider some of the possible implications of these double meanings.

Emily Dickinson, "To make a prairie it takes a clover and one bee" (text p. 311; question 1, following)

John Keats, "Ode to a Nightingale" (text p. 209)

CONNECTION QUESTION IN TEXT (p. 327) WITH ANSWER

1. Compare the power of the speaker's mind described here with the power of imagination described in "To make a prairie it takes a clover and one bee" (p. 311).

    The speaker in this poem is relatively powerless. The cleaving of her mind is beyond her control, and she is not able to mend it, as when one wakes from a dream and tries to fall asleep again to see how it will turn out. In "To make a prairie" the mind has the power to create even without the things of the earth, but it is unclear whether the mind has the power to consciously create in itself a state of reverie.

A Light exists in Spring (p. 327)

In this poem, Dickinson opposes science with nature and commerce with the sacred. The verbs she attributes to "Science" (line 7) and "Trade" (19) — "overtake" (7) and "encroached" (19) — show that they do not just contrast with nature and religion but also actively undermine them. When this special period of light and color ends, where does it leave "Human Nature" (8)? What course does Dickinson imagine people are on? The springtime ends without the "Formula of sound" (15). You might have your students discuss how Dickinson is using this phrase. Does she associate formula with science, or does it have a more metaphysical meaning?

Since this poem was written during the Civil War, it is interesting to consider how Dickinson's personal "quality of loss" (17) might be informed by the larger losses of the nation. Though this is not an overt war poem, the "stand[ing] abroad / On Solitary Fields" (5-6) and the "Horizons step / Or Noons report away" (13-14) seem to echo military movements. How does this historical perspective affect your students' reading of the final encroachment on "Sacrament" (20)?

POSSIBLE CONNECTIONS TO OTHER SELECTIONS

Emily Dickinson, "There's a Certain Slant of light" (text p. 696; question 1, following)
William Carlos Williams, "Spring and All" (text p. 631)

CONNECTION QUESTION IN TEXT (p. 328) WITH ANSWER

1. Compare Dickinson's thematic use of light in this poem and in "There's a certain Slant of light" (p. 696).

    In "A Light exists in Spring," the quality of light is hopeful, and as it fades, it signals dissolution. The "certain Slant of light" in the other poem is a source of despair. However, there's something holy about the "affliction" (line 11) of "Winter Afternoons" (2) because it produces a change in the speaker "Where the Meanings, are" (8).

Oh Sumptuous moment (p. 328)

This poem begs a long-awaited, delightful moment to go by more slowly, to allow the speaker to savor it. However, the poem itself moves away from the specific glories of the "Sumptuous moment" (line 1) to anticipate how much more difficult moments after this one will be. The future, aware of pleasures like those at hand but bereft of them, is compared to someone led to "the Gallows" (8) while it is morning, knowing that the full day will unfold in his absence.

The sounds of the first stanza create an even rhythm and rhyme that makes the reading move more slowly, just as the speaker bets the moment to stay. Reading this poem aloud will likely increase your students' pleasure in it. Consider asking your students to freewrite, imagining what might qualify as a "Sumptuous moment" worthy of this comparison. Considering what students have learned about Dickinson's life, they may be able to anticipate what kind of rarity she's celebrating here.

POSSIBLE CONNECTIONS TO OTHER SELECTIONS

Emily Dickinson, " 'Heaven' — is what I cannot reach!" (text p. 316; question 1, following)
——, "Water, is taught by thirst" (text p. 313; question 1, following)
——, "Wild Nights — Wild Nights!" (text p. 318)

1. Compare and contrast the themes of this poem, "Water, is taught by thirst" (p. 313), and " 'Heaven' — is what I cannot reach!" (p. 316).

   All three poems define something positive in terms of its absence: A thing is more valuable if it is difficult to do without. "Oh Sumptuous moment" skips over the sumptuous moment itself to stress the agony of living without it, in the knowledge of its possibility. "Water, is taught by thirst" demonstrates how we learn to understand and love something only when we are forced to do without it. " 'Heaven' — is what I cannot reach!" demonstrates that the very notion of "Heaven" is predicated on the impossibility of reaching it in this life; therefore, for the speaker, everything out of reach takes on the sheen of paradise.

The Bustle in a House (p. 328)

The images in this poem suggest that getting on with mundane, everyday activities helps us to move beyond the pain of death. In contrast, the use of the funeral metaphor in "After great pain" (text p. 323) promotes the idea that a formal ritual helps us to accomplish this purpose. You might ask students which method strikes them as being more effective. Look closely at the diction in line 7. The phrase "We shall not want" echoes the Twenty-third Psalm, a hymn of comfort and confidence in God's support at the time of death. But does the expression also imply that even though we don't want to deal with any thought other than being reunited with the loved one in eternity, the reality may not be so simple?

In *Literary Women* (Garden City: Doubleday, 1976), Ellen Moers claims that "Emily Dickinson was self-consciously female in poetic voice, and more boldly so than is often recognized" (61). Does the imagery in this poem confirm or repudiate Moers's assertion? Ask your students to consider the many speakers they have encountered in Dickinson's poems. Is her poetic voice generally identifiable as female? If so, how? If not, how would you characterize her poetic voice(s)?

POSSIBLE CONNECTIONS TO OTHER SELECTIONS

Emily Dickinson, "After great pain, a formal feeling comes —" (text p. 323; question 1, following)

——, "I like a look of Agony," (text p. 317; question 2, following)

CONNECTIONS QUESTIONS IN TEXT (p. 329) WITH ANSWERS

1. Compare this poem with "After great pain, a formal feeling comes —" (p. 323). Which poem is, for you, a more powerful treatment of mourning?

   The poems advance two opposing ideas about how people mourn. "The Bustle in a House" describes a flurry of little tasks that distract the grieving person. "After great pain" discusses a shutting down of functions as the mourner contemplates loss in total stillness. They seem to contradict one another, and your students might find that one or the other is more true to their experiences. However, they may also both be true, describing different types of mourning or different stages of the complicated process of dealing with death.

2. How does this poem qualify "I like a look of Agony," (p. 317)? Does it contradict the latter poem? Explain why or why not.

   The focus of the two poems is slightly different because there is no "I" in this poem. "I like a look of Agony," raises questions about the speaker, whereas this poem states a more objective truth. Yet both poems treat the subject of death and its effects, and in that respect there is a slight contradiction between them because this one ends with the notion of eternity, whereas "I like a look of Agony," concentrates on the physical death of a person without alluding to the state of the soul afterward.

Tell all the Truth but tell it slant — (p. 329)

You might open consideration of "Tell all the Truth" by having students discuss how the speaker characterizes "Truth." The imagery used here centers on the idea of light; in only eight lines, the poet uses "slant" (line 1), "bright" (3), "Lightning" (5), "dazzle" (7), and "blind" (8), besides the punning reference in the word *delight* (3). The speaker considers direct truth to be a light so powerful that it is capable of blinding. Students may suggest other contexts in which they have seen this idea expressed. Biblical stories often recount appearances of God as a light too blinding to be looked at directly. What is it about Truth, which after all only allows us to see things as they really are, that is potentially so destructive?

Don't let your students miss the exquisite word choices in lines 3 and 4 as Dickinson contrasts human fallibility — "our infirm Delight" (De-light?) — with the perfection of "Truth's superb surprise."

How does poetry in general affirm this poem's thesis? Would you expect a writer who believed this premise to prefer writing poetry to writing prose?

POSSIBLE CONNECTIONS TO OTHER SELECTIONS

Emily Dickinson, "I know that He exists" (text p. 344; question 1, following)
——, "Portraits are to daily faces" (text p. 315)
——, "The Thought beneath so slight a film —" (text p. 310)

CONNECTION QUESTION IN TEXT (p. 329) WITH ANSWER

1. How does the first stanza of "I know that He exists" (p. 344) suggest an idea similar to this poem's? Why do you think the last eight lines of the former aren't similar in theme to this poem?

   Both poems argue that the truth is not necessarily obvious or that the deepest truths are cloaked in mystery. The difference in theme between the two poems has to do with the difference of the subjects: The implications of "Truth" are not as grave as the implications of God's existence.

A Word dropped careless on a Page (p. 330)

Dickinson depends in this poem on the shades of meaning in the word "careless" (line 1). In the first stanza, the word seems synonymous with thoughtless or even carefree. The consequence of the careless act — stimulation — sounds positive, though the writer who puts down a word so artlessly is "Wrinkled" (4) and imperfect.

After the stanza break however, the consequences get dire very quickly, as the next line begins with "Infection." The stanza only gets worse from here as the contagion "breeds" (5), causes "Despair" (6), and finally ends in "Malaria" (8). Though your students probably have enough distance from malaria that this threat might not have much impact on them, the disease used to be just as destructive in the southern United States as it is still today in many parts of the world. This deadly serious ending reflects back on the opening line, and "careless" takes on a sense of negligence and disregard for others. You might ask your students if they're surprised to see such consequences attached to the act of writing. How often do they drop a careless word?

POSSIBLE CONNECTIONS TO OTHER SELECTIONS

Elizabeth Barrett Browning, "My letters! All dead paper, mute and white!" (text p. 588)

Langston Hughes, "Theme for English B" (text p. 502)

There is no Frigate like a Book (p. 330)

Dickinson had great faith in the transformative power of reading. This poem encapsulates her belief, imagining books and poetry as forms of transportation. Her comparisons suggest reading acts with tremendous speed. You might remind your students to look up "Frigate" (line 1) and "Coursers" (3) to clarify their understanding of these terms. A frigate is a war vessel, but its archaic meaning is a light, quick ship. A courser is a swift horse, often one used in battle. What do your students make of the military connotations of these words? Notice how the adjective "prancing" (4) goes beyond comparison to directly identify poetry with the powerful horse.

Dickinson also uses economic diction, revealing her concerns about the democratic nature of reading. Reading helps the poor to escape the "oppress of Toll" (6). Ask your students what kind of relationship she sets up by rhyming "Toll" (6) with "soul" (8). In this poem it seems that monetary concerns could hinder the development of higher faculties.

POSSIBLE CONNECTIONS TO OTHER SELECTIONS

Anne Bradstreet, "The Author to Her Book" (text p. 137)

Emily Dickinson, "A Word dropped careless on a Page" (text p. 330; question 1, following)

CONNECTION QUESTION IN TEXT (p. 330) WITH ANSWER

1. Compare the tone of this poem with that of the preceding, "A Word dropped careless on a Page" (p. 330).

    Both poems express Dickinson's belief in the serious consequences of reading. "There is no Frigate like a Book" describes the benefits of poetry, even to those who are disadvantaged. "A Word dropped careless on a Page" suggests that the power of reading can be destructive as well as beneficial if the writer does not choose his or her words responsibly.

I took one Draught of Life — (p. 331)

Dickinson uses economic language again in "I took one Draught of Life —," and here it serves to point out the irony of trying to gauge the worth of existence. Her life is valued at "The market price" (line 4) but that price is based on ephemera — "Dust by Dust" (5) and "Film with Film" (6). How these can add up to anything measurable is a mystery.

Dickinson's decision to begin with a "Draught of Life" (1) and end with a "Dram of Heaven" (8) hints at the Puritan idea that this life is only a preparation for the next one. However, notice that a dram is smaller than a draught. Does this diminishment suggest a critique of the doctrine? Dickinson's reading of Emerson, and her interest in transcendental ideas, gave her some freedom to depart from strict Puritan theology and to question the value of trading life for heaven.

POSSIBLE CONNECTIONS TO OTHER SELECTIONS

Emily Dickinson, " 'Heaven' — is what I cannot reach!" (text p. 316; question 1, following)

John Milton, "When I consider how my light is spent" (text p. 615)

CONNECTION QUESTION IN TEXT (p. 331) WITH ANSWER

1. Discuss the meaning of heaven in this poem and in " 'Heaven' — is what I cannot reach!" (p. 316).

    In this poem, heaven is the ultimate measure of the speaker's existence. After being weighed, she finds that her life equals only "A single Dram" (8). In " 'Heaven' — is what I cannot reach!," heaven is a figure for whatever on earth is out of reach. In both cases, Dickinson's view of heaven is somewhat ironic as it seems always unattainable to ordinary people.

PERSPECTIVES ON EMILY DICKINSON

EMILY DICKINSON, *A Description of Herself* (p. 331)

Probably the most immediately evident characteristic of Dickinson's personal correspondence is that, as in her poetry, the language comes in spurts interspersed with an abundance of dashes. Also, as in her poetry, she uses numerous metaphors. Have your students explore some of these metaphors, such as Dickinson's reference to criticism of her poetry as "surgery" (paragraph 2) and her discussion of "undressed thought" (3). Do such metaphors hide or clarify her meaning?

Dickinson's comment that she had written only "one or two" poems before that winter, when in fact she had written nearly three hundred, could lead to a discussion of the constructed self that appears even in personal correspondence. Have your students consider how they might write about last weekend's party in a letter to their parents as opposed to a letter to their best friend from high school. Without necessarily being dishonest, we generally shape any presentation of self depending on how we wish to appear to a particular audience. How do you suppose Dickinson appeared to Higginson when he first read this letter?

THOMAS WENTWORTH HIGGINSON, *On Meeting Dickinson for the First Time* (p. 332)

The first part of Higginson's letter to his wife reports his encounter with Emily Dickinson at her home in Amherst in a fairly straightforward fashion. If your students have read the poet's letter describing herself to Higginson, you might ask them to consider how closely the poet's description of herself matches his observations. Although Higginson refers to the poet's manner and appearance as "childlike" three times in a short space, he is also struck by her wisdom when she begins to speak to him.

Dickinson's definition of poetry would be an interesting topic for class discussion. Students might be encouraged to talk about the aptness or limitations of her definition. Should all poetry produce the violent reaction in a reader that she describes? Would Dickinson's own works qualify as poetry according to her definition? The last comments of Dickinson that Higginson records, concerning her relation to the outside world, also merit consideration. Why would she have such an extreme reaction to the thought of mixing in society? Which of her comments might Mrs. Higginson have considered foolish?

MABEL LOOMIS TODD, *The* **Character** *of Amherst* (p. 333)

While Todd refers to Emily Dickinson both as a character and as a myth, her examples in this letter tend to cast Dickinson more as a ghost; several times she notes that no one ever sees the poet. None of her characterizations of Dickinson is particularly positive. Referring to someone as a "character" usually denotes unusual, even amusing behavior, and portraying that person as a ghost suggests that that person has no substance. Todd does not even use the term *myth* in its powerful, archetypal sense, but more to connote something unreal or not to be believed. The comments in this letter would seem to negate Dickinson's thesis, often stated in her poetry, that things seen half-veiled are more clearly seen than things in plain view. You might ask students what Todd's observations about Dickinson reveal about Todd herself and about the way Dickinson may have been perceived by her Amherst neighbors. As a topic for writing or for class discussion, you may wish to have your students piece together information from this letter and the previous two in order to produce a composite "portrait" of Emily Dickinson. What may emerge from these pieces, however, is the enigmatic quality of her character.

RICHARD WILBUR, *On Dickinson's Sense of Privation* (p. 334)

According to Wilbur, Dickinson's fascination with the concept of want, both human and personal, emerges in her poetry in two ways. Her apprehension of God as a distant, unresponsive deity compels her to write satirical poetry protesting this situation on behalf of other human beings. However, the poet who rages against an uncaring creator on behalf of her fellow creatures also tolerates such privations and emulates such aloofness on a personal level. For Dickinson, "less is more" is merely another Christian paradox to be savored, such as the paradoxes of dying to live or freeing oneself by becoming a slave. In fact, depriving herself of everything possible, especially human companionship, seems to have been Dickinson's technique for achieving that appreciation for and knowledge of what she and other humans were missing that inspired her poetry. You may wish to have your students discuss this second premise more thoroughly; it may be a difficult concept for those not accustomed to dealing with paradox. Do they see any parallels in their own lives or in the culture at large to the idea that, as Wilbur says, "privation is more plentiful than plenty"? Can they think of times when deprivation has produced positive results, or do they feel that Dickinson uses this highly contradictory premise as a rationalization for her own eccentricities?

SANDRA M. GILBERT AND SUSAN GUBAR, *On Dickinson's White Dress* (p. 335)

You might wish to preface your discussion of this piece with a freewriting exercise in which your students explore their own associations with whiteness. Do their connotations mostly involve positive qualities, negative qualities, or nothingness? Gilbert and Gubar contrast William Sherwood's assertion that Dickinson's white dress was a sign of her commitment to the Christian mystery of death and resurrection with Melville's suggestion that whiteness may be the "all-color of atheism." They go on to suggest that whiteness may have been, for Dickinson, the perfect expression of a fascination with paradox and irony, that she was drawn to the color precisely because it was capable of representing opposite ends of any spectrum. You might ask your students whether they find any of the above theories convincing before having them propose their own theories as to why Dickinson wore only white (see question 3 in the text, p. 336).

You might caution your students that Gilbert and Gubar's characterization of the dress on display at the Dickinson homestead as "larger than most readers would have expected" is not shared by all who have seen it. Given the feminist perspective of Gilbert and Gubar's work, why might they emphasize the size of Dickinson's dress in this manner?

CYNTHIA GRIFFIN WOLFF, *On the Many Voices in Dickinson's Poetry* (p. 336)

Wolff acknowledges the multiplicity of voices represented by the speakers in Dickinson's poems, from child to housewife to passionate woman to New England Puritan. She insists, however, that the presence of these different voices affirms cohesion rather than indicates a fragmentation of the poet's psyche. According to Wolff, what the voices have in common is a concern with specific human problems, particularly those problems that threaten "the coherence of the self." Thus the many voices become not a difficulty to be overcome but a tool by which the poet seeks to overcome difficulties. Wolff is especially adamant in her assertion that the voice selected for any particular poem does not represent the poet's particular mood of the moment but is a "calculated tactic," a part of her artistic technique, an aspect of an individual poem that is as carefully chosen as any of the poem's words might be.

In discussing this passage, you might ask your students to consider whether they have different "voices" for different occasions and what determines how they speak at any given time. Do they get a sense of unity in reading Dickinson's poetry? If it is true that Dickinson again and again returns to the idea of encounters that threaten "the coherence of the self," what are some of these encounters, and in what ways are they threatening?

PAULA BENNETT, *On "I heard a Fly buzz — when I died —"* (p. 337)

According to Bennett, the fly in Dickinson's poem represents humankind's ignorance of what awaits us after death. This ignorance is dramatically emphasized in Dickinson's poem by the dying speaker, who, anticipating a divine experience at her death, is shocked when she is assailed by the buzzing of a fly instead. Ask students if they agree with Bennett's assertion that Dickinson's conclusion about death and the afterlife in this poem is that "we don't know much." Are there other ways to interpret Dickinson's depiction of the dying moment? Is Dickinson's poem necessarily, as Bennett puts it, a "grim joke" about the fate of human corpses — to be devoured by flies?

MARTHA NELL SMITH, *On "Because I could not stop for Death —"* (p. 338)

Smith's central interpretation of Dickinson's most famous poem about death is that it is ultimately a joke. This will undoubtedly be hard for many of your students to swallow. How can a poem about death be comic? It may be useful to have your students discuss how they define "jokes" and what they think makes something funny. Smith notes that Dickinson struggled with the faith that her neighbors reveled in, often finding herself believing that they would be disappointed with any revelations they may have on their deaths. With this in mind, do your students find Dickinson's sense of humor (if they see humor at all) to be morbid, or is there something more cruel or self-serving to it?

RONALD WALLACE, *Miss Goff* (p. 339)

As a critic, Wallace is considered an authority on the uses of humor in poetry. His book *God Be with the Clown: Humor in American Poetry* (1984) explores the comic aspects of the poetry of such literary giants as Dickinson, Walt Whitman, Robert Frost, Wallace Stevens, and John Berryman. His interest in humor and Emily Dickinson works to good effect in "Miss Goff." (It may interest your students to know that the *OED* states that in the 1860s a "goff" was a clown or a fool.) In this poem a student's tasteless practical joke seems to defeat a "tired" (line 3) old-maid teacher, who passes out in "horror" (4) at the cruelty, but it also inadvertently introduces another student to the wonders of Dickinson's poetry.

Encourage your students to explore the parallels between the characters of Miss Goff and Emily Dickinson. Like Dickinson, Goff is unmarried and socially unskilled. When faced with difficulty, the teacher, like the poet, turns to poetry for solace. And, like Dickinson, Goff transfixes, even if she is unaware of the effect she has on at least one member of her audience (the poem's speaker). Encourage students, also, to discuss the implications of Miss Goff's faint.

The form of Wallace's paean to Dickinson offers another promising avenue for discussion. "Miss Goff" is a sonnet. What's interesting about Wallace's use of the form is that although he does adhere primarily to the iambic pentameter that is usual in sonnets, he strays from it to emphasize elements of the teacher's and the student's personalities. Note, for example, that an extra unstressed syllable at the end of nearly every line (except 6) of the first stanza gives them feminine endings to poetically evoke the femininity of Miss Goff. Anapests in lines 4 ("hór|rŏr, thĕ héart|lĕss"), 5 ("cŭstó|dĭăn slӯ|lӯ"), and 8 ("Ém|ĭlӯ Díck|ĭnsŏn mím|ĕŏs thére") draw attention to the classroom's heartlessness, the custodian's participation in the students' joke, and Dickinson's poems. The lines of the second stanza, on the other hand, end with masculine stresses. The anapests here draw attention to "ŏn thĕ cóld" (10) and "ŏf oŭr heáds" (14); both phrases introduce allusions to Dickinson's definition of poetry — "My business is circumference" and "If I feel physically as if the top of my head were taken off, I know that is poetry."

POSSIBLE CONNECTIONS TO OTHER SELECTIONS

Thomas Wentworth Higginson, "On Meeting Dickinson for the First Time" (text p. 332)
Cathy Song, "A Poet in the House" (text p. 567)
Mabel Loomis Todd, "The *Character* of Amherst" (text p. 333)
Marilyn Nelson Waniek, "Emily Dickinson's Defunct" (text p. 276)

TWO COMPLEMENTARY CRITICAL READINGS

CHARLES R. ANDERSON, *Eroticism in "Wild Nights — Wild Nights!"* (p. 340)

Anderson finds, in the declaration "Wild Nights should be / Our luxury" (lines 3–4), the image that contains all of the other images in Dickinson's poem. According to Anderson, Dickinson's theme is that love is intense but temporal. He discusses the poem's other images, such as those of Eden and storms, in terms of how they emphasize these qualities of love. Each figure the poet uses, from Anderson's perspective, contains a double reference to ecstasy and brevity, and the phrase "Wild Nights" refers to the tumult outside and inside the lovers' paradise. Anderson's argument is consistent and brings all the poem's major figurative language together in support of a common theme. What he does not deal with in depth is the poem's "frank eroticism" that he mentions at the beginning of his discussion. You might ask your students how erotic they find the poem to be. Is it truly sensual, or does it just upset our expectations of this particular poet? Another possible topic for discussion is the relationship of this poem to themes found in Dickinson's other work. Is her frequent emphasis on how the narrowness of an experience intensifies our response to it connected with the qualities of love she foregrounds here?

DAVID S. REYNOLDS, *Popular Literature and "Wild Nights — Wild Nights!"* (p. 341)

Reynolds contrasts the rhetoric of Dickinson's poem with that of the sensational literature of her day to support his thesis that the greatness of Dickinson's "Wild Nights" lies in its being erotic and distinct from the lesser literature of the genre. He argues that in the first stanza, the yoking of the sensational adjective "wild" to the natural image of the "night" serves to "purify" sexual desire (note that Reynolds ignores Dickinson's use of the word *luxury*, which Anderson focused on in the previous piece in order to highlight the poem's eroticism). In the next stanza the more abstract natural images of sea and harbor further distance the passion expressed in the poem from crude sensationalism. The reference to "Eden," in the last stanza, adds a religious quality to the images that precede it. The cumulative effect, according to Reynolds, is the expression of intense but unconsummated sexual longing without the accompanying connotations of prurience. One question for students to consider, assuming they find Reynolds's argument convincing, is whether or not sexual passion abstracted in this way remains erotic.

ADDITIONAL DICKINSON POEMS ACCOMPANYING QUESTIONS FOR WRITING ABOUT AN AUTHOR IN DEPTH

"Faith" is a fine invention (p. 343)

This poem highlights a witty, even satirical side of Dickinson. Have students note the words that define each of the alternative ways of seeing. "Faith" is an "invention" (line 1), and microscopes are "prudent" (3). When examining Dickinson's diction, it is helpful to note the variety of possible definitions for ordinary words used in an unusual manner. *Invention* not only means a created or fabricated thing; it also carries the more archaic sense of an unusual discovery or a find. Likewise, while *prudence* has a rather stilted, utilitarian ring to it in the twentieth century, it once meant having the capacity to see divine truth. You might want to ask your class whether they feel the speaker favors religion or science. Because both faith and microscopes are meant to help people perceive directly rather than through a mist, is it possible that the poet favors neither side in this argument?

Ask your students what they think of Charles R. Anderson's comment on this poem in *Emily Dickinson's Poetry* (New York: Holt, 1960): "This is a word game, not a poem" (35).

POSSIBLE CONNECTIONS TO OTHER SELECTIONS

Emily Dickinson, "Portraits are to daily faces" (text p. 315)
——, "What Soft — Cherubic Creatures —" (text p. 319)

I know that He exists (p. 344)

Dickinson here seems to be at the cutting edge of modern sensibility and its dare-seeking fascination with death. The poem begins as a testimony of faith in the existence of a God who is clearly an Old Testament figure. If you ask students how the poem's speaker characterizes this deity, they may note the attributes of refinement, hiddenness, and removal from the gross affairs of earthly life. With this in mind, the tone of the next stanza, in which God seems to be the orchestrator of a cosmic game of hide-and-seek between Himself and whichever of His creatures will play, and in which the reward is "Bliss" (line 7), may be puzzling to students. The word *fond* in line 6 begins to sow a seed of doubt about the rules of this game. Does it mean "affectionate," or is it being used in its older sense of "foolish"?

In the third stanza the speaker more fully comprehends the meaning of the game: Finding God can mean finding oneself in God at the moment of death. Instead of death being a discovery that begins a condition of everlasting bliss, one may be confronted with an abrupt and everlasting ending. "Death's — stiff — stare" (12) caps three lines of halting verse, further emphasized by the hardness of the alliteration (you may wish to read these lines aloud so that students will appreciate their impact). By the third stanza, the ironic barb pierces through the texture of ordinary language. Instead of saying that the joke has gone too far, the speaker substitutes the verb *crawled,* which summons up the image of the serpent in the Garden of Eden in addition to bringing the lofty language of the first stanza down to earth.

This poem receives a brief but adequate discussion in Karl Keller's *The Only Kangaroo among the Beauty* (Baltimore: Johns Hopkins UP, 1979, p. 63). Keller observes that the "tone of voice moves from mouthed platitude to personal complaint." Ask your students if they agree with this assessment.

POSSIBLE CONNECTIONS TO OTHER SELECTIONS

Emily Dickinson, "Tell all the Truth but tell it slant —" (text p. 329)

Robert Frost, "Design" (text p. 372)

I never saw a Moor — (p. 344)

This straightforward profession of faith follows a pattern of expansion of imagery from the natural to the supernatural. Despite its simplicity, the poem reflects sound theology; one of the basic theological proofs of the existence of God is the existence of the universe. Ask your students if the poem would be as effective if the first stanza relied on images of man-made things such as the pyramids. Why or why not? How would it change the impact of the poem if the stanzas were reversed?

POSSIBLE CONNECTION TO ANOTHER SELECTION

Emily Dickinson, " 'Heaven' — is what I cannot reach!" (text p. 316)

Apparently with no surprise (p. 344)

While a first reading of "Apparently with no surprise" seems to present the reader with a picture of death in an uncaring, mechanistic universe overseen by a callous God, a closer look reveals a more ambiguous attitude on the part of the speaker. Most of the poem deals with an ordinary natural process, an early morning frost that kills a flower. Framing this event is the viewpoint of the speaker, who acknowledges by means of the word *apparently* that his or her perspective may not be correct. According to the speaker, God is not involved in the event, other than to observe and to approve, as the speaker apparently does not. An examination of the adjectives and adverbs used in the poem reinforces the uncertainty of tone for which we have been prepared by the opening word. "No surprise" (line 1), "accidental power" (4), and the sun proceeding "unmoved" (6) suggest a vision of nature as devoid of feeling. However, how can anything proceed and at the same time be *un*moved? How can power be used forcefully, as "beheads" (3) and "Assassin" (5) imply, and yet be accidental? The description of the frost as a "blond Assassin" in line 5 is particularly worth class discussion. Does the noun *Assassin* suggest that the frost is consciously evil? What about the adjective *blond*? You may wish to have your students recall other images of whiteness in Dickinson's poetry. Can they come to any conclusions as to the connotations this color has for her?

POSSIBLE CONNECTIONS TO OTHER SELECTIONS

Emily Dickinson, "Because I could not stop for Death —" (text p. 326)

——, "Safe in their Alabaster Chambers —" (1859 version) (text p. 314)

ADDITIONAL RESOURCES FOR TEACHING DICKINSON

SELECTED BIBLIOGRAPHY

Anderson, Charles R. *Emily Dickinson's Poetry.* New York: Holt, 1960.

Bennett, Paula. *Emily Dickinson: Woman Poet.* Iowa City: U of Iowa P, 1990.

Bloom, Harold, ed. *Emily Dickinson.* New York: Chelsea, 1985.

Chase, Richard. *Emily Dickinson.* New York: William Sloane Assocs., 1951.

Dickinson, Emily. *The Complete Poems of Emily Dickinson.* Ed. Thomas H. Johnson. Boston: Little, 1955.

———. *The Letters of Emily Dickinson.* Ed. Thomas H. Johnson and Theodora Ward. Cambridge: Belknap Press of Harvard UP, 1958.

———. *The Master Letters of Emily Dickinson.* Ed. Ralph W. Franklin. Amherst: Amherst College P, 1986.

Diehl, Joanne Feit. *Dickinson and the Romantic Imagination.* Princeton: Princeton UP, 1981.

Farr, Judith. *The Passion of Emily Dickinson.* Cambridge: Harvard UP, 1992.

Ferlazzo, Paul J., ed. *Critical Essays on Emily Dickinson.* Boston: Hall, 1984.

Johnson, Thomas H. *Emily Dickinson: An Interpretive Biography.* New York: Atheneum, 1955.

Juhasz, Suzanne, ed. *Feminist Critics Read Emily Dickinson.* Bloomington: Indiana UP, 1983.

Leyda, Jay. *The Years and Hours of Emily Dickinson.* New Haven: Yale UP, 1960.

Martin, Wendy. *The Cambridge Companion to Emily Dickinson.* New York: Cambridge UP, 2002.

Orzeck, Martin, and Robert Weisbuch, eds. *Dickinson and Audience.* Ann Arbor: U of Michigan P, 1996.

Patterson, Rebecca. *Emily Dickinson's Imagery.* Amherst: U of Massachusetts P, 1979.

Porter, David. *Dickinson, the Modern Idiom.* Cambridge: Harvard UP, 1981.

Smith, Martha Nell. *Rowing in Eden: Rereading Emily Dickinson.* Austin: U of Texas P, 1992.

Stocks, Kenneth. *Emily Dickinson and the Modern Consciousness: A Poet of Our Time.* New York: St. Martin's, 1988.

Stonum, Gary Lee. *The Dickinson Sublime.* Madison: U of Wisconsin P, 1990.

Wardrop, Daneen. *Emily Dickinson's Gothic: Goblin with a Gauge.* Iowa City: U of Iowa P, 1996.

AUDIOVISUAL RESOURCES (manual p. 374)

TIP FROM THE FIELD

I have my students become "experts" on one of the poets treated in depth in the anthology. The students then work in pairs and "team-teach" their poet to two other students who are experts on another poet.

— KARLA WALTERS, *University of New Mexico*

13

A Study of Robert Frost

Like Dickinson, Frost may have a somewhat sanitized image in the minds of some students. The introduction addresses this point, but if students remain unconvinced, "Home Burial" and " 'Out, Out —' " should provide ample evidence of the dark side of Frost.

Many of Frost's poems change on a second or third close reading — the text offers "The Road Not Taken" as an example of this. "Mending Wall" and "Nothing Gold Can Stay" also exhibit this tendency. Frost can provide a good opportunity for students to pay attention to their own reading habits. You might assign short writings that ask students to not only interpret the poems, but also to notice how their interpretations might change between readings.

ROBERT FROST

The Road Not Taken (p. 354)

This poem has traditionally been read as the poet's embracing of the "less traveled" road of Emersonian self-reliance, but the middle two stanzas complicate such a reading. Ask students to read the first and last stanzas alone and then to notice that in the middle two stanzas the speaker actually seems to equivocate as to whether or not the roads were actually different. After reading those two stanzas, do students trust the assertion that "I took the one less traveled by" (line 19)? In "On the Figure a Poem Makes" (text p. 377) Frost states that a poem can provide "a momentary stay against confusion." Against what kind of "confusion" is the poet working? How do the uses of rhyme, meter, and stanza form work against confusion? Is there a "clarification of life" (another of Frost's claims for poetry) in this poem?

Ask students to explore contexts for Robert Frost on *LiterActive*.

At least three times in this poem (2, 4, and 15) the word *I* disrupts the iambic rhythm. Why would the poet do this? What is the effect of the dash at the end of line 18?

Richard Poirier, in *Robert Frost: The Work of Knowing* (New York: Oxford UP, 1977), claims that Frost's poems are often about the making of poetry. Is there any sense in which this poem could refer to writing poetry? For instance, do a poet's choices of rhyme, meter, or metaphor at the beginning of a poem dictate how the rest of the poem will proceed? Do poets try to choose roads not taken by their predecessors in order to be original? Are they sometimes unable to return to standard forms later, once they have launched out on a new poetic path?

As a writing assignment, you might ask your students to discuss or write about decisions they have made that closed off other choices for them.

Blanche Farley, "The Lover Not Taken" (text p. 382)
George Herbert, "The Collar" (text p. 602)

The Pasture (p. 356)

Ask students to suggest reasons that Frost chose to place "The Pasture" at the beginning of several volumes of his poetry. What might readers of this poem infer about the poems that followed? Could the references to raking the leaves away and watching the water clear in lines 2 and 3 suggest something more than the performance of spring chores?

Notice that the speaker twice informs the reader that "I shan't be gone long" (lines 4 and 8). The need to return to stable ground after going out and making discoveries is a recurring theme in Frost's poetry, as is evident in "Birches" and "Stopping by Woods on a Snowy Evening." Poems wherein the return is not assured — "Acquainted with the Night," for example — tend to be much more negative in tone. They often foreground what Lionel Trilling called the "terrifying" side of Frost. How does Frost's practice of using a fixed form, such as blank verse or sonnet, yet altering the form by varying the meter or rhyme schemes (something he frequently does through the use of dialogue) demonstrate a similar desire to return to stable ground? Does this put the poet's often-quoted comment that writing free verse is like "playing tennis with the net down" in a different light? Is writing free verse, for Frost, more like casting loose from all one's moorings without an anchor?

Robert Frost, "After Apple-Picking" (text p. 364)
Walt Whitman, "One's-Self I Sing" (text p. 629)

Mowing (p. 357)

This poem offers an amiable meditation on "the sweetest dream that labour knows" (line 13). The "long scythe" (2), so often a symbol of time or death, here establishes the power and pleasure of work. That symbolic resonance combines with references to fairy tales to establish the edge of a forest as a mysterious place where one might receive "the gift of idle hours, / or easy gold at the hand of fay or elf" (7–8). But the speaker discounts these ephemeral notions: "Anything more than the truth would have seemed too weak" (9). These allusions are secondary to the productive and happy relationship between the speaker and the right tool for the job.

The narrative is more clearly conveyed when the poem is read aloud: The first six lines examine the "whispering" (2) voice of the scythe; the last eight resist the tradition of fairy tales that prefer "idle hours" (7) or "easy gold" to the satisfactions of work well done. The speaker is alone, in "the heat of the sun" (4), but these circumstances are not presented in a negative light; the laboring speaker does not complain but revels in his work.

Robert Frost, "The Pasture" (text p. 356)
Jeffrey Harrison, "Horseshoe Contest" (text p. 277)

My November Guest (p. 358)

Frost writes "My November Guest" largely in end-stopped lines. The lack of enjambment tends to slow down the reading of the poem, bringing its pacing into line with the more deliberate movements of winter. What kind of rhetorical shape does this decision give to the poem? Do the strong rhymes make the poem seem more forceful or convincing?

Since most of the images in this poem are the kind of dreary scenes we normally associate with November, your students will probably notice the silvery "clinging mist" (line 10) that the November guest is pleased to see replace plain greyness. This one image allows the reader to see some of the "beauties she so truly sees" (13). You might ask your class why they think Frost refrains from this kind of description in the rest of the poem. What does he gain from the general bareness of his images?

POSSIBLE CONNECTIONS TO OTHER SELECTIONS

Margaret Atwood, "February" (text p. 143; question 1, following)
John Keats, "To Autumn" (text p. 127)

CONNECTION QUESTION IN TEXT (p. 358) WITH ANSWER

1. Compare Frost's treatment of November with Margaret Atwood's evocation of "February" (p. 143). Explain why you prefer one poem over the other.

   Frost sees November as a mournful, though beautiful, time. He looks mostly to the outside world, describing the "withered" (line 4) and "sodden" (5) late fall landscape. In contrast, Atwood's "February" is more internal. She begins with some cozy images of hibernation — eating fat, sleeping — but later we see that those behaviors are destructive, as "pollution pours / out from our chimneys to keep us warm" (lines 23–24). The territorial behavior of a neighborhood cat introduces questions of instinct and desire. His drive to reproduce reminds the speaker of the rebirth to come as winter ends, and she closes her poem by urging her own domesticated cat to overcome his complacency and "Make it be spring" (34). Thus, Frost and Atwood choose different points in time from which to view winter. In November, Frost is witnessing the end of fall and contemplating the long months to come. Atwood, at the end of winter, thinks about how spring will emerge from the cold.

Storm Fear (p. 359)

Frost's pattern of rhymes in this poem is irregular enough that your students may be unconscious of it, except in the strong last couplet, so you might have them start by plotting the rhymes. Ask them what the repeated sounds add to the reading of "Storm Fear." Do they heighten the feeling the speaker relates? And what is the feeling? Try having your class paraphrase the emotion in the poem. It seems like a mixture of anxiety, resignation, and defiance. As they try to describe the feeling of the poem, have them point out words that convey these tones, such as "subdued" (line 3), "comforting" (7), and "unaided" (10).

POSSIBLE CONNECTIONS TO OTHER SELECTIONS

Emily Dickinson, "Presentiment — is that long Shadow — on the lawn" (text p. 136; question 1, following)
Robert Hayden, "Those Winter Sundays" (text p. 23)
Wisława Szymborska, "Nothing's a Gift" (text p. 583)

CONNECTION QUESTION IN TEXT (p. 359) WITH ANSWER

1. Compare the perspectives on nature in "Storm Fear" and in Emily Dickinson's "Presentiment — is that long Shadow — on the lawn" (p. 136). How are they both poems about fear?

In "Storm Fear," nature is a malicious force, one against which humans have to stand "unaided" (line 10). Frost personifies the harsh winter as a "beast" (15) that calls to the family indoors, urging them to " 'Come out.' " (16) and be enveloped by the snow. This speaker's moment of fear occurs during the onslaught of the storm, increasing as the storm obscures the familiar "Dooryard and road" (6) and "comforting barn" (7). Ultimately, he fears the storm less than he fears himself because he acknowledges the temptation to give up his struggle with nature.

The fear in Dickinson's poem is of what is about to happen. Her "Presentiment" of darkness taking over the landscape is frightening because we sense it is inevitable. "Suns go down" (line 2) because it is in their nature to do so. All we can do is take "notice" (3) and prepare for the arrival of darkness.

Mending Wall (p. 359)

Students may already be familiar with this work from their high school reading. Although the poem is often considered an indictment of walls and barriers of any sort, Frost probably did not have such a liberal point of view in mind. After all, the speaker initiates the mending, and he repeats the line "Something there is that doesn't love a wall." For him, mending the wall is a spring ritual — a kind of counteraction to spirits or elves or the nameless "Something" that tears down walls over the winter. It is gesture, ritual, and a reestablishment of old lines, this business of mending walls. The speaker teases his neighbor with the idea that the apple trees won't invade the pines, but to some measure he grants his conservative neighbor his due.

Play a recording of Robert Frost reading "Mending Wall" on *Literature Aloud*.

POSSIBLE CONNECTIONS TO OTHER SELECTIONS

Emily Dickinson, "Portraits are to daily faces" (text p. 315)

———, "To make a prairie it takes a clover and one bee" (text p. 311; question 1, following)

Robert Frost, "Neither Out Far nor In Deep" (text p. 373; question 2, following)

CONNECTIONS QUESTIONS IN TEXT (p. 361) WITH ANSWERS

1. How do you think the neighbor in this poem would respond to Dickinson's idea of imagination in "To make a prairie it takes a clover and one bee" (p. 311)?

    The neighbor in "Mending Wall" might accuse the speaker in Dickinson's poem of being foolish and impractical. Dickinson's speaker does not seem to think that boundaries make people happier, but the neighbor's experience has proved to him that "Good fences make good neighbors." The speaker in Frost's poem, more open to the kind of imagination Dickinson celebrates, wants his neighbor to imagine that elves have brought the wall down — but the neighbor probably won't.

2. What similarities and differences does the neighbor have with the people Frost describes in "Neither Out Far nor In Deep" (p. 373)?

    In both poems Frost presents people who seem to be content with a single point of view, resisting new or even alternative views of the world. The neighbor, "like an old-stone savage armed," appears to be part of some primeval mystery that fascinates the speaker in "Mending Wall." In contrast, the people in "Neither Out Far nor In Deep" are the ones transfixed by a mystery — that of the vast ocean.

Home Burial (p. 361)

"Home Burial" is a dialogue in blank verse between a husband and wife who have recently lost their child and who have different ways of coping with loss. One way to begin discussion is to consider the form of the poem: Does it seem more like a poem or a miniature play? How does the rhythm of the poem affect its theme? The haunting repetition of the word "don't" in line 32, for example, is realistic dialogue when we consider the tension behind the situation, but it also serves to mark a turning point in the poem. At what other points in the poem do similar repetitions occur, and do they also mark turning points in the dramatic situation, or do they reveal something about the psychological state of the characters?

Biographical criticism is beginning to come back into fashion, and you might remind the class of some of the introductory notes on Frost in this chapter before discussing the poem. Clearly the speaker is more matter-of-fact than his wife, and there is decidedly a communication problem between them. Note how Frost splits their dialogue in the interrupted iambic lines. But doesn't the husband deserve some special commendation for possessing the courage and integrity to initiate a confrontation with his wife? Discussion of the poem might also consider the value that ancients and moderns alike ascribe to a catharsis of emotions.

You might, if the class seems at all responsive, examine the speaker's claim that "a man must partly give up being a man / With women-folk" (lines 52–53). What does this statement mean? Has feminism done anything to challenge what are uniquely man's and uniquely woman's provinces of concern?

POSSIBLE CONNECTIONS TO OTHER SELECTIONS

Emily Dickinson, "After great pain, a formal feeling comes —" (text p. 323)
Robert Frost, " 'Out, Out —' " (text p. 368)
Jane Kenyon, "The Blue Bowl" (text p. 125)

After Apple-Picking (p. 364)

The sense of things undone and the approach of "winter sleep" seem to betoken a symbolic use of apple picking in this poem. Moreover, the speaker has already had an experience this day — seeing the world through a skim of ice — that predisposes him to view things strangely or aslant. At any rate, he dreams, appropriately enough, of apple harvesting. Apples take on connotations of golden opportunity and inspire fear lest one should fall. As harvest, they represent a rich, fruitful life, but as the speaker admits, "I am overtired / Of the great harvest I myself desired" (lines 28–29).

Apples are symbolically rich, suggesting everything from temptation in the garden of Eden, with overtones of knowledge and desire, to the idea of a prize difficult to attain, as in the golden apples of Hesperides that Hercules had to obtain as his eleventh labor. Here they can be read as representing the fruit of experience.

POSSIBLE CONNECTIONS TO OTHER SELECTIONS

Robert Frost, "Unharvested" (text p. 371)
John Keats, "To Autumn" (text p. 127)

Birches (p. 365)

This poem is a meditative recollection of being a boyhood swinger of birches. In the last third of the poem, the speaker thinks about reliving that experience as a way of escaping from his life, which sometimes seems "weary of considerations." Swinging on birches represents a limber freedom, the elation of conquest, and the physical pleasure of the free-fall swish groundward. Note, in contrast, Frost's description of what ice storms do to birches. Images like "shattering and avalanching on the snow-crust"

Play a recording of Robert Frost reading "Birches" on *Literature Aloud*.

suggest a harsh brittleness. The speaker in the end opts for Earth over Heaven because he (like Keats, to some extent) has learned that "Earth's the right place for love."

Frost's blank verse lends a conversational ease to this piece, with its digressions for observation or for memory. A more rigid form, such as rhymed couplets, would work against this ease.

In a writing assignment, students might analyze the different forms of knowing in "Birches," contrasting truth's matter-of-factness (lines 21–22) and the pull of life's "considerations" (43) with boyhood assurance and the continuing powers of dream and imagination.

POSSIBLE CONNECTION TO ANOTHER SELECTION

Emily Dickinson, "Portraits are to daily faces" (text p. 315)

A Girl's Garden (p. 367)

Through the retelling of a neighbor's childhood story, this poem provides Frost's perspective on his neighbor, on childhood, on the stories we choose to tell of our lives, and on the lessons gardening can teach us. This poem can serve many disparate readings: it works as a parable about how everything works out regardless of our intent or ability, a pleasant story from childhood without much larger significance, proof of the long-lasting effects of our thoughtless "childlike" activities, or an acknowledgment of the sublime results of simple activities. Examining each reading and discussing the ways in which they can coexist can help students see the rich potential of poetry.

The central comparison in this poem will provide different readings depending on what students think Frost intends when he refers to "village things" (line 42). It may be a good idea to spend some time at the beginning of class reading the poem aloud — very helpful in demonstrating the subtle effect of the enjambed rhymes — and then making a list of possibilities. The levels of comparison are many and complex; asking students to look carefully at the actions of the little girl in the narrative for clues about the nature of "village things" could help focus the discussion.

POSSIBLE CONNECTIONS TO OTHER SELECTIONS

Robert Frost, "Mending Wall" (text p. 359; question 2, following)

——, "Stopping by Woods on a Snowy Evening" (text p. 370; question 1, following)

CONNECTIONS QUESTIONS IN TEXT (p. 368) WITH ANSWERS

1. Compare the narrator in this poem to the narrator in "Stopping by Woods on a Snowy Evening" (p. 370). How, in each poem, do simple activities reveal something about the narrator?

    Both the narrative from the neighbor's childhood and the episode described in "Stopping by Woods" demonstrate an appreciation of the ordinary moments in life. The narrator has considered the events described by the neighbor and noticed that the story is repeated when "it seems to come in right" (line 43). The act of noticing connections and beauty invests these simple activities and observations with the larger meaning.

2. Discuss the narrator's treatment of the neighbor in this poem and in "Mending Wall" (p. 359).

    The speaker's implication of his neighbor in "Mending Wall" is a little more forceful than it is in "A Girl's Garden." The quiet nudges the speaker provides to demonstrate his thoughts on the neighbor's fond use of the story seem more like a smirk than the impatient characterizations of the neighbor as "old-stone savage armed" (line 40) or moving "in darkness" (41).

"Out, Out —" (p. 368)

Often when disaster strikes, we tend to notice the timing of events. Frost implies here that "they" might have given the boy an extra half-hour and thereby averted the disaster. This perspective, coupled with the final line, in which the family seems to go on with life and ordinary tasks, can appear callous. But compare the wife's chastisement of her husband in "Home Burial" (text p. 361). Is the attitude callousness, or is it, rather, the impulse of an earth-rooted sensibility that refuses pain its custom of breaking the routine of life-sustaining chores and rituals? Very little in this poem seems to be a criticism of the survivors; rather, like *Macbeth* and the famous speech that proclaims life's shadowy nature (text p. 134), it seems to acknowledge the tenuous hold we have on life.

Possible Connections to Other Selections

Stephen Crane, "A Man Said to the Universe" (text p. 164; question 3, following)

Robert Frost, "Home Burial" (text p. 361; question 2, following)

——, "Nothing Gold Can Stay" (text p. 371; question 1, following)

Connections Questions in Text (p. 369) with Answers

1. What are the similarities and differences in theme between this poem and Frost's "Nothing Gold Can Stay" (p. 371)?

    In this poem the speaker presents a tragic experience involving human beings or property and then sets it in the larger context of the natural world. In "Nothing Gold Can Stay," the focus is on the natural world and the feeling of an Edenic spring.

2. Write an essay comparing how grief is handled by the boy's family in this poem and by the couple in "Home Burial" (p. 361).

    Grief separates the couple in "Home Burial," as the wife accuses the husband of being unfeeling when the husband suggests that they must go on living despite their child's death. Miscommunication lingers in the split lines as well as in the situation of the couple, separated by the length of a staircase. In " 'Out, Out —' " the bereaved "turned to their affairs," choosing the response of the man in "Home Burial." Death unites them in that it reaffirms their commitment to the duty of living.

3. Compare the tone and theme of " 'Out, Out —' " with those of Stephen Crane's "A Man Said to the Universe" (p. 164).

    " 'Out, Out —' " and Crane's poem share a moral view that there is little ground on which humanity and the universe might meet. Crane's tone is slightly humorous, whereas Frost's approach is more poignant, but both rely heavily on dialogue to make their opinions known. Frost's borrowing from *Macbeth*, as well as the subject of the dead boy, gives his poem a more tragic quality than is present in Crane's sobering message.

Fire and Ice (p. 369)

With a kind of diabolic irony, the theories for the way the world might end grow as our knowledge and technology increase. Students can probably supply a number of earth-ending disaster theories: overheating of the earth because we are moving sunward; the greenhouse effect with the chemical destruction of the ozone layer; war, apocalypse, or "nuclear winter"; a change in the earth's orbit away from the sun; the return of the ice age; and so on. Frost here also speaks of the metaphoric powers of hatred (ice) and desire (fire) as destroyers of the earth. To say that ice would "suffice" to end the world is a prime example of understatement.

POSSIBLE CONNECTIONS TO OTHER SELECTIONS

H. D. [Hilda Doolittle], "Heat" (text p. 118)
William Butler Yeats, "The Second Coming" (text p. 636)

Stopping by Woods on a Snowy Evening (p. 370)

With very few words, Frost here creates a sense of brooding mystery as the speaker stops his horse in a desolate landscape between wood and frozen lake. The attraction of the woods is their darkness, the intimation they offer of losing oneself in them. The speaker gazes into them with a kind of wishfulness, while his horse shakes his bells, a reminder to get on with the business of living. The repetition in the last lines denotes a literal recognition that the speaker must move on and connotes that there is much to be done before life ends.

You might use the final question in the text as a brief writing assignment to show how rhyme relates and interlocks the stanzas and offers in the final stanza (*dddd*) a strong sense of closure.

POSSIBLE CONNECTIONS TO OTHER SELECTIONS

Henry Wadsworth Longfellow, "Snow-Flakes" (text p. 613)
Thylias Moss, "Interpretation of a Poem by Frost" (text p. 151; question 1, following)

CONNECTION QUESTION IN TEXT (p. 370) WITH ANSWER

1. What do you think Frost might have to say about Thylias Moss's version of this poem, "Interpretation of a Poem by Frost" (p. 151)?

   Frost might have been interested to see how Moss places within a new context some of the more subtle themes of his poem. First, she reinterprets the tension in "Stopping by Woods" between the obligations of the social world (the "promises to keep" of line 14) and the beauty of the natural world. In Moss's version, the sense of obligation is even stronger, carrying the force of the law, which operates even in the dark woods. Also, Moss rethinks Frost's intimations of death to question the implications of giving birth to a new generation under the oppressive Jim Crow laws.

Nothing Gold Can Stay (p. 371)

Students often misread the first image in this poem as the brilliant golds of fall fading into winter. Caution them to read carefully; the poem describes the early days of *spring,* when the leaf buds (in New England at least) emerge in a brief burst of yellowish-green before turning their deeper summer green. The other images in the poem — dawn losing its colors and becoming the brighter but less colorful day and the ideal of Eden becoming the reality of life after the Fall — reinforce the sense of loss. You might ask your students to consider the ambiguous nature of the images used in this poem. The speaker certainly takes a negative viewpoint: The leaf "subsides," Eden "sank," and the dawn "goes down." But isn't it true that what early spring gives way to is the glory of summer, and dawn to the fullness of the day? Also, the loss of Eden is often referred to as a "fortunate fall." Why do you suppose there is no indication of the other side of these images? Why would Frost use such ambiguous images, when the gold of autumn fading into winter would fit so much better with the tone of the poem? Do your students agree with the speaker's negative appraisal of the passing of time?

POSSIBLE CONNECTIONS TO OTHER SELECTIONS

Robert Frost, " 'Out, Out —' " (text p. 368)

Robert Herrick, "To the Virgins, to Make Much of Time" (text p. 79; question 1, following)

CONNECTION QUESTION IN TEXT (p. 371) **WITH ANSWER**

1. Write an essay comparing the tone and theme of "Nothing Gold Can Stay" with Robert Herrick's "To the Virgins, to Make Much of Time" (p. 79).

    Both poems have as their basis the idea that youth is ephemeral and that life passes quickly and inevitably. Herrick's poem offers advice regarding this condition, whereas Frost's presents it as a universal truth. The tone of Herrick's poem is somewhat lighter (without explicit reference, for instance, to "grief") as it keeps its young audience in mind. Herrick's purpose is ultimately rhetorical; Frost's is philosophical.

Unharvested (p. 371)

Frost liked to use the sonnet form, and he frequently varied it in expressive ways. Though this sonnet ends with a couplet, Frost does not adhere in the beginning to the traditional Shakespearean rhyme scheme, which might serve to separate the poem into discrete quatrains. Instead, his interlocking rhymes continue the description of the scene until the turn, which occurs here after the tenth, rather than the twelfth, line. At this moment he changes gears from description of the scene to comment on it. However, notice how Frost connects the two sections with a couplet that crosses the break between them.

You might also have your class discuss how Frost mixes poetic diction and syntax, such as "of all but its trivial foliage free" (line 6) and "May something go always unharvested!" (11), with more colloquial phrases. What kind of speaker does Frost create by making him say things like "come to leave" (2) and "sure enough" (4)?

POSSIBLE CONNECTIONS TO OTHER SELECTIONS

Robert Frost, "After Apple-Picking" (text p. 364; question 2, following)

Pablo Neruda, "The United Fruit Co." (text p. 57)

CONNECTION QUESTION IN TEXT (p. 372) **WITH ANSWER**

2. Compare the themes in this poem and in "After Apple-Picking" (p. 364).

    In this poem, Frost revels in a crop that has not been gathered up by man, and through his vision of the tree with all its apples fallen to the ground, he glorifies nature beyond its utility to people. In "After Apple-Picking," the speaker discovers his inadequacy to take in all of the products of nature, in spite of "the great harvest [he himself] desired" (29). Though the subjects of the two poems seem to be opposite, their themes are similar. Both deal with the inevitable separateness of the natural world from human involvement.

Neither Out Far nor In Deep (p. 373)

This poem, particularly in its last stanza, comments on humanity's limitations in comprehending the infinite, the unknown, the inhuman and vast. Again, Randall

Jarrell's comment is useful. He writes, "It would be hard to find anything more unpleasant to say about people than that last stanza; but Frost doesn't say it unpleasantly — he says it with flat ease" (*Poetry and the Age* 42-43). You might organize a writing assignment around the tone of this poem.

POSSIBLE CONNECTIONS TO OTHER SELECTIONS

Robert Frost, "Mending Wall" (text p. 359)
Robert Morgan, "Fever Wit" (text p. 565)

Design (p. 373)

The opening octave of this sonnet is highly descriptive and imagistic in its presentation of spider, flower, and moth, all white. The sestet asks the question of design: Who assembled all these elements in just such a way as to ensure that the moth would end up where the spider was — inside a "heal-all" (ironic name for this flower), its "dead wings carried like a paper kite"? Frost has in mind the old argument of design to prove the existence of God. There must be a prime mover and creator; otherwise, the world would not be as magnificent as it is. But what of the existence of evil in this design, Frost asks. The final two lines posit choices: Either there is a malevolent mover (the "design of darkness to appall") or, on this small scale of moth and spider, evil occurs merely by chance ("If design govern . . ."). The rhyme scheme is *abba, abba, acaa, cc,* and its control provides a tight interlocking of ideas and the strong closure of the couplet.

Randall Jarrell's remarks on the imagery and ideas here are superb; he appreciates this poem with a poet's admiration (see his *Poetry and the Age* [New York: Farrar, 1953, 1972], pp. 45-49). He notes, for example, the babylike qualities of "dimpled . . . fat and white" (not pink) as applied to the spider. Note, too, how appropriate the word *appall* is because it indicates both the terror and the funereal darkness in this malevolently white trinity of images.

A comparison with the original version of this poem, "In White" (text p. 376), should prove that "Design" is much stronger. The title of the revised version, the closing two lines, and several changes in image and diction make for a more effective and thematically focused poem.

As a writing assignment, you might ask students either to compare this poem with its original version or to analyze the use of whiteness in "Design" and show how the associations with the idea of whiteness contrast with the usual suggestions of innocence and purity.

POSSIBLE CONNECTIONS TO OTHER SELECTIONS

Emily Dickinson, "I know that He exists" (text p. 344; question 2, following)
——, "Safe in their Alabaster Chambers —" (1861 version, text p. 314)
Robert Frost, "In White" (text p. 376)
William Hathaway, "Oh, Oh" (text p. 26; question 1, following)
Edna St. Vincent Millay, "I will put Chaos into fourteen lines" (text p. 244)

CONNECTIONS QUESTIONS IN TEXT (p. 374) WITH ANSWERS

1. Compare the ironic tone of "Design" with the tone of William Hathaway's "Oh, Oh" (p. 26). What would you have to change in Hathaway's poem to make it more like Frost's?

    Hathaway's "Oh, Oh" has a far less serious tone than Frost's poem, as the poet plays a joke on his audience, beginning the poem in a slaphappy, conversational tone, only to change it to a note of impending doom. To be more like Frost's poem, "Oh, Oh" would have to make its audience aware of the entire situation from the beginning.

2. In an essay discuss Frost's view of God in this poem and Dickinson's perspective in "I know that He exists" (p. 344).

   In "Design" the speaker questions the existence of God by suggesting that only a malevolent deity could preside over the relentless mechanisms of nature, whereby one species destroys another to survive. In "I know that He exists" Dickinson's speaker speculates not on the nature of God but just on the hiddenness — the absence against which she must assert her belief. Frost is less comfortable with a God who must be malevolent than with no God at all. God's absence is what troubles Dickinson.

The Silken Tent (p. 374)

This Shakespearean sonnet uses an extended conceit to compare one woman's equipoise to the silken tent that remains erect on a summer's day. The center-positioned cedar pole, we are told, points "heavenward," and this detail, as well as the silken substance of the tent, suggests the person's spiritual centeredness. She seems serenely balanced but not aloof from human affairs, as the ties that connect her soul to their groundward stakes are those of "love and thought." Only by slight changes ("the capriciousness of summer air") is she made to feel these ties, which are more connection than bondage. Over all, the tone of the poem, enhanced by the sounds of the words, suggests serenity.

Because the poem is a Shakespearean sonnet, you can begin discussion by considering that form: Does the poem's final couplet change the meaning of the three quatrains before it? Do the quatrains suggest a development of the argument in three distinct points? To what end does Frost use other poetic devices in the poem, such as alliteration? The sonnet was originally titled "In Praise of Your Poise" and was written for Frost's secretary, Kay Morrison.

POSSIBLE CONNECTIONS TO OTHER SELECTIONS

Robert Herrick, "Delight in Disorder" (text p. 226)
William Shakespeare, "Shall I compare thee to a summer's day?" (text p. 243)

The Most of It (p. 375)

Whereas in some of his poems, particularly his early ones, Frost personifies nature, in "The Most of It," he exposes what John Ruskin called the pathetic fallacy. The human tendency to project onto nature the changing weather of his own thoughts and emotions leads the subject of this poem to think "he kept the universe alone" (line 1). The echo of his own voice only serves to reinforce his feeling that the world is there to reflect him.

You might have your students discuss Frost's conception of "original response" (8). If we can't expect it from the universe, can we create it for ourselves? Does Frost's poetry enact a "counter-love" (8) to the world he views? How does the vision of the buck at the end of the poem express a spiritual state, and what does it mean that it disappears into the underbrush?

POSSIBLE CONNECTIONS TO OTHER SELECTIONS

Robert Frost, "Neither Out Far nor In Deep" (text p. 373; question 1, following)
Charles Simic, "To the One Upstairs" (text p. 123)

1. Compare the tone of this poem with "Neither Out Far nor In Deep" (p. 373) as third-person narratives.

   One fundamental difference between the two narratives is that "Neither Out Far nor In Deep" concerns a number of people while "The Most of It" observes a single man. The former poem stays mainly with the watchers' observable actions, while the latter narrative is close enough to the subject's perspective to relate his thoughts. Both poems concern human limitation, but they see this limitation demonstrated in different ways, based on their perspectives.

PERSPECTIVES ON ROBERT FROST

ROBERT FROST, *"In White": An Early Version of "Design"* (p. 376)

Many of the alterations Frost made to "In White" to arrive at "Design" have the effect of shifting the poem's focus from an individual occurrence to a more generalized one, from the questioning of a single death to the questioning of the force that caused, or allowed, the death to occur.

Students could begin by noting as many differences as they can find between the two poems. Probably the most obvious is the change in title. Whereas the title of the earlier poem announces a concern with the color white, which seems to represent death, the later title suggests a larger concern: the question of order (or the lack thereof) in the universe.

Frost retained the sonnet form when he revised, but the rhyme scheme for the sestet changes from six lines with the same rhyme to the much more complex *abaabb*. This throws a sharper emphasis on the last two lines of "Design," the lines in which the poet suggests that events are shaped either by forces of evil or not at all.

Ask students to discuss how changes in individual word choices affect the poem. Some of the most striking of these are the change from "dented" to "dimpled" in line 1 and from "lifeless" to "rigid" in line 3 (i.e., even more dead, as though rigor mortis has set in). Another interesting change is that whereas the poem once *began* with a general observation and *ended* with the very personal "I," it now *begins* with "I" and moves outward to *end* with a general statement. Also note the use of the word *if* in the last line of the final version of "Design." This is one of Frost's favorite ways of injecting ambivalence and uncertainty into his poems.

POSSIBLE CONNECTION TO ANOTHER SELECTION

Robert Frost, "Design" (text p. 373)

ROBERT FROST, *On the Living Part of a Poem* (p. 376)

Intonation in musicians' parlance refers to pitch and the idea of playing in tune. Does Frost use the word in that sense here? If not, what does he mean later on by the "accent of sense" and how the word *come* can appear in different passages as a third, fourth, fifth, and sixth note?

In introducing this prose passage, you might point out that poets construct poetry out of fairly near-at-hand vocabularies — words we have already tasted on our tongues. One of the appeals of poetry is the physical way we intone its sounds, even when we read silently, so that we become in a sense a resonating chamber for the poem. It might be well to recall, too, that poetry originally was a spoken, not a written medium, and those things that were regarded as important enough to be remembered were put in verse.

Frost makes several unqualified statements here. Students by and large receive as part of their first-year college training the advice to be chary of the committed word. You might devote some of the class discussion to exploring when and where rhetoric must be unequivocating.

AMY LOWELL, *On Frost's Realistic Technique* (p. 377)

Elsewhere in her review, Lowell describes Frost's vision as "grimly ironic." She goes on: "Mr. Frost's book reveals a disease which is eating into the vitals of our New England life, at least in its rural communities." In discussing the characters in Frost's poems she calls them "the leftovers of old stock, morbid, pursued by phantoms, slowly sinking to insanity." You might ask students to find evidence for Lowell's observations in the Frost poems in this chapter. Are there opposite tendencies in these characters that save them from what Lowell describes as a "disease eating into the vitals"?

ROBERT FROST, *On the Figure a Poem Makes* (p. 377)

In this introduction to his *Collected Poems,* Frost calls the sounds of a poem "the gold in the ore." Perhaps the best way to discuss Frost's assertion is to put it to the test. How do Frost's own poems stand up? How does he use sound? His more conversational poems, such as "Home Burial," provide insight into individual characters through an imitation of their speech patterns. The contemplative poem, exemplified by "Birches" or "After Apple-Picking," can be analyzed both for the speaker's character as it is revealed in his diction and for the way sounds both reaffirm and undermine the speaker's point.

Poems are, according to Frost, spontaneous in that they are derived from the poet's imagination as it interacts with his surroundings. But the imagination is not groundless because poets take many of their ideas from what they've read, often unconsciously: "They stick to nothing deliberately, but let what will stick to them like burrs where they walk in the fields." Frost's belief in the predestination of poetry involves the idea that the poem is an act of belief, of faith: "It must be a revelation, or a series of revelations, as much for the poet as for the reader." Not entirely the product of either spontaneity or predestination, the poem takes on a life of its own: "Like a piece of ice on a hot stove the poem must ride on its own melting."

In giving up claims to democracy and political freedom, Frost resists the process of naming something that supposedly is without limitation. Once defined as "free," whatever we call free ceases to be just that. Frost uses as an example our "free" school system, which forces students to remain in it until a certain age; it is, therefore, not free. Resisting confining labels, Frost as an artist is more able to reach a world audience; once he states a political bias, his art is one of exclusion. You might ask students to examine Frost's statements in the context of the more political poems in Chapter 23, "An Album of World Literature."

ROBERT FROST, *On the Way to Read a Poem* (p. 380)

Experience with one or two poems by an author often eases the way for reading other poems by him or her. But will reading "Birches," for example, prepare the way for understanding "Fire and Ice"? Not necessarily. Beyond our literary experience, some of our "life learning" enters into the reading of poems as well.

The image of reader as "revolving dog" also seems a little discomforting, no matter what one's feelings about dogs. Poetry reading requires a certain point of stability, like the cedar pole in "The Silken Tent." Without it, one might be at a loss to distinguish sentiment from the sentimental, the power of the image from the fascination of the ornament.

You might ask students to try Frost's advice with two or three of his poems. They can read one in the light of another and then write about the experience.

HERBERT R. COURSEN JR., *A Parodic Interpretation of "Stopping by Woods on a Snowy Evening"* (p. 380)

This critical spoof offers a fine opportunity to articulate just what we seek from literary criticism and why we accept one writer's word and reject another's. One important factor in the Frost poem that is not considered here is tone and the speaker's own fascination with the woods, which are "lovely, dark, and deep."

If we were to isolate factors that mark good literary criticism, we might speak of (1) completeness (Are there any significant details omitted?), (2) coherence (Coursen advertises the simplicity of his theory but then talks at length about veiled allusions and obfuscation), and (3) fidelity to experience (No, Virginia, a horse is never a reindeer, not even on Christmas Eve). Good criticism avoids the overly ingenious.

This spoof also lends itself to a review of principles of good writing, which students have probably already acquired in a composition course. You might ask, too, what it was that inspired Coursen to write this essay. What, in other words, is he objecting to in the practice of literary criticism?

BLANCHE FARLEY, *The Lover Not Taken* (p. 382)

The fun of parodies derives in part from recognition of their sources — in this instance "The Road Not Taken." In Farley's parody, we see again the distressed speaker who wants to have it both ways. As is usually the case with Frost's deliberators, the woman in this poem seems to have many hours to devote to "mulling." Farley mimics Frost's faint archaisms with the line (present in both poems) "Somewhere ages and ages hence." She also plays with and lightly satirizes the rigors of Frost's blank-verse line. Notice, for example, how she carries over the key word that would round out the sense of the line between lines 8 and 9, only to accommodate the pentameter scansion. At the close of her poem, Farley plays down the need for choosing and asserts that there was no difference between the lovers. Appropriately for this parody, she closes with a heroic couplet.

PETER D. POLAND, *On "Neither Out Far nor In Deep"* (p. 382)

In this passage from a longer essay, Poland focuses on a single image in Frost's poem to draw conclusions about the poem as a whole. Ask your students whether they think the details of the poem support Poland's interpretation. The critic himself notes that the comparison he dwells on is "never directly stated." Is it, then, a reasonable comparison to use as the foundation for his analysis of the poem? Why or why not?

For a possible writing assignment, have your students pick another single image from "Neither Our Far nor In Deep" and write an analysis of the poem centered on that image, using Poland's essay as a model.

DEREK WALCOTT, *The Road Taken* (p. 384)

Pay careful attention to Walcott's definition of an uncle as students respond to his description of Frost as "avuncular" rather than "paternal." Students may tend to read their impressions of their *own* uncles into Frost's character. This might not be a bad thing, in terms of extending Walcott's analogy — in what *other* ways can Frost be said to be avuncular? — but Walcott qualifies his analogy in specific ways. Also, note that Walcott seems to answer his own rhetorical question in the second paragraph, but the answer may not satisfy. What is it about the American character that craves an uncle?

"Because uncles are wiser than fathers" seems ironic in its simplicity, and students may want to offer other responses.

If students select a poem demonstrating that Frost is a "master ironist," they have a number to select from, but what about those students who don't think that Frost is a master ironist? Can they find opposite evidence? Much depends on a careful definition of "mastery" rather than of irony; for instance, if mastery denotes subtlety, " 'Out, Out —' " could be used to illustrate that Frost is decidedly *not* a master ironist.

If you are working with either of the other three poets that the anthology covers in depth — Dickinson, Hughes, or Alvarez — you might want to try to apply Walcott's terms *democratic* and *autocratic* to these other poets as a way of comparing them with Frost. Do these terms mean as much when applied to the other writers, or are the terms only useful insofar as they compare Whitman and Frost? This anthology contains many examples of Whitman's poetry, which students can use to test Walcott's observations.

TWO COMPLEMENTARY CRITICAL READINGS

RICHARD POIRIER, *On Emotional Suffocation in "Home Burial"* (p. 385)

You could begin class discussion of this perspective by asking students to find particular moments in Frost's poem that suggest that the couple's home has become, as Poirier suggests, a "mental hospital." What is it about this couple that reveals both their profound suffering and their perceived inability to escape their circumstances? You might ask your students to compare and contrast the anguish of the husband and the wife. In what ways are both emotionally suffocating in the house and in their relationship?

Poirier argues that "Home Burial" suggests "alienation, secretiveness, [and] male intimidation" (paragraph 3); where in the poem do your students find examples of these qualities? Do they agree with Poirier's interpretation? Does your class wholly identify with one character rather than the other? If not, you might explore the reasons that class sympathy is divided between the husband and wife. Why might one elicit more sympathy from the reader than the other?

KATHERINE KEARNS, *On the Symbolic Setting of "Home Burial"* (p. 386)

Kearns asserts that "the woman can 'see' through the window and into the grave in a way her husband cannot." You might open class discussion by asking students to describe these different ways of "seeing." Why do they see differently, and what does each of them see? Kearns also states that the husband and wife in "Home Burial" are "in profound imbalance." Ask your students to explain how they might be considered imbalanced. Responses might include not only the physical but the emotional reactions of the two to their young son's death and the fact that their marriage is in great danger of being permanently "unbalanced" by the woman's escape. Class discussion might also encompass Kearns's idea that this poem is caught up not only in the issues surrounding the death of a child but also in those surrounding the institution of marriage itself and the "rights and privileges" that are associated with marriage. You might ask your students which issue they believe to be the primary one, and why.

ADDITIONAL RESOURCES FOR TEACHING FROST

SELECTED BIBLIOGRAPHY

Bagby, George F. *Frost and the Book of Nature*. Knoxville: U of Tennessee P, 1993.
Bloom, Harold, ed. *Robert Frost*. New York: Chelsea, 1986.
Brodsky, Joseph. *Homage to Robert Frost*. New York: Farrar, Straus & Giroux, 1996.

Cox, James Melville, ed. *Robert Frost: A Collection of Critical Essays*. Englewood Cliffs: Prentice, 1962.

Faggen, Robert, ed. *The Cambridge Companion to Robert Frost*. New York: Cambridge UP, 2001.

Frost, Robert. *Interviews with Robert Frost*. Ed. Edward Connery Lathem. New York: Holt, 1966.

———. *The Poetry of Robert Frost*. Ed. Edward Connery Lathem. New York: Holt, 1979.

———. *Robert Frost: A Time to Talk*. Ed. Robert Francis. Amherst: U of Massachusetts P, 1972.

———. *Robert Frost on Writing*. Ed. Elaine Barry. New Brunswick: Rutgers UP, 1973.

———. *Selected Letters*. Ed. Lawrance Thompson. New York: Holt, 1964.

———. *Selected Prose*. Ed. Hyde Cox and Edward Connery Lathem. New York: Holt, 1966.

Gerber, Philip L. *Critical Essays on Robert Frost*. Boston: Hall, 1982.

Kearns, Katherine. *Robert Frost and a Poetics of Appetite*. Cambridge, Eng.: Cambridge UP, 1994.

Marcus, Mordecai. *The Poems of Robert Frost: An Explication*. Boston: Hall, 1991.

Meyers, Jeffrey, ed. *Early Frost: The First Three Books*. Hopewell: Ecco Press, 1996.

Monteiro, George. *Robert Frost and the New England Renaissance*. Lexington: UP of Kentucky, 1988.

Oster, Judith. *Toward Robert Frost: The Reader and the Poet*. Athens: U of Georgia P, 1992.

Parini, Jay. *Robert Frost: A Life*. New York: Henry Holt, 199.

Poirier, Richard. *Robert Frost: The Work of Knowing*. New York: Oxford UP, 1977.

Pritchard, William H. *Frost: A Literary Life Reconsidered*. New York: Oxford UP, 1984.

Squires, James Radcliffe. *The Major Themes of Robert Frost*. Ann Arbor: U of Michigan P, 1969.

Thompson, Lawrance. *Fire and Ice: The Art and Thought of Robert Frost*. New York: Russell, 1970.

———. *Robert Frost: The Early Years, 1874–1915*. New York: Holt, 1966.

———. *Robert Frost: The Years of Triumph, 1915–1938*. New York: Holt, 1970.

Thompson, Lawrance, and R. H. Winnick. *Robert Frost: The Later Years, 1938–1963*. New York: Holt, 1982.

Audiovisual Resources (manual p. 375)

14

A Study of Langston Hughes

Of the four poets covered in depth, Hughes perhaps demands most to be read aloud: His use of blues and jazz in the structuring of his poems rewards such reading. Additionally, this section may be enriched by the inclusion of audiovisual material dealing with the Harlem Renaissance and jazz. Hughes self-consciously puts himself at the juncture of popular culture and the intellectual and political questions of his time, and you might find it useful to provide some of Ask students to explore contexts for Langston Hughes on *LiterActive*. this background for students, or to have students do their own research and presentations on it. These presentations might be done singly or as group projects, focusing on such topics as jazz and blues music, the situation of African Americans and the struggle for civil rights during Hughes's lifetime, the history of the Harlem Renaissance, labor and radicalism in the 1930s, and so forth. Such presentations have the advantage of making a great deal of information available to the class with relatively little work on the part of any individual and encouraging students to be active contributors of knowledge.

Students' attitudes about race will be inescapable in this section. Nearly every poem in this section could be the focal point of a controversial discussion in class. You might want to foreground these issues early in the discussion, asking students to write about whether or not Hughes has any relevance to current racial issues. This will help them articulate their own assumptions about race in a space that is not directly confrontational.

LANGSTON HUGHES

The Negro Speaks of Rivers (p. 393)

Because rivers are clearly the central image in this poem, you might begin discussion of "The Negro Speaks of Rivers" by asking students what ideas they commonly associate with rivers. How do associations such as fertility, life, timelessness, and exploration add to the poem's meaning? Also note  Play a recording of Langston Hughes reading "The Negro Speaks of Rivers" on *Literature Aloud*. that the Euphrates River is one of the legendary rivers that bordered the Garden of Eden. How does this association with the Christian myth of creation add to the poem's meaning? It may be helpful for your students to recognize the geographic locations of these rivers and the fact that they flow in different directions. The Nile and the Congo are African rivers, the Euphrates flows through Turkey and Iraq, and the Mississippi splits the United States. You might ask your students what these diverse locations and directions suggest about the speaker's history.

Another important dimension of this poem is Hughes's use of time. Notice how the speaker stands outside of historical time; the narrative "I" has experienced these times and places over the course of human existence. You might ask students to explore the connection between the timeless narrator and the endurance and timelessness of rivers.

Consider the serious tone of this poem. Ask your students if they think this poem can be interpreted as a celebration. If so, what is the speaker celebrating, and what details contribute to this interpretation? Ask students to consider how the speaker has taken an active role in the history described in the poem ("I bathed ..." [line 5], "I built my hut near the Congo ..." [6], "I looked upon the Nile and raised the pyramids ..." [7], and so on). What do these actions suggest about the history of the "Negro" in the title?

POSSIBLE CONNECTIONS TO OTHER SELECTIONS

Langston Hughes, "Negro" (text p. 398)
Phillis Wheatley, "On Being Brought from Africa to America" (text p. 537)

I, Too (p. 396)

This poem reveals the speaker's optimism about the future of race relations in America despite the overwhelming discrimination that he must endure daily. The speaker's acknowledgment that "I am the darker brother" (line 2) indicates the brotherhood between blacks and whites that he feels. In the final line the speaker asserts, "I, too, am America" (18), demonstrating his unwavering belief in his rightful national identity and equal standing in society.

In class discussion, consider how this poem incorporates images of racial injustice yet still manages to suggest a hopeful outlook for the future. Ask students to examine the image of the "darker brother" (2) sent to the kitchen to eat. Segregation was still firmly in place when this poem was written; how does the image of eating in the kitchen expose the racial injustices the speaker is forced to endure? You might ask your students to examine the reaction of the speaker to his "banishment" to the kitchen (5–7). What do they think this reaction to discrimination reveals about the speaker?

Ask students to discuss or write about the attitude of the speaker toward his current situation and toward America. Is his optimistic vision of the future clouded by his present predicament? The speaker's pride and confidence in the future are evident in his declaration that "Tomorrow / I'll be at the table / When company comes" (8–10). Discuss how this conviction helps him sustain his vision of a racially unified nation. You might raise the issue of why the speaker longs for acceptance in America, a country that has denied him his freedom for so long. Examine the speaker's prediction that race relations will improve owing to both the strength of black Americans and the shame of white Americans. How has this prophecy of 1925 been realized or not realized?

POSSIBLE CONNECTIONS TO OTHER SELECTIONS

Langston Hughes, "Dinner Guest: Me" (text p. 415)
Walt Whitman, From *Song of Myself* (text p. 180)

Negro (p. 398)

This poem chronicles the history of exploitation that black people have endured through the ages. The speaker acknowledges the broad history of the black experience, including slavery, the unappreciated role that blacks have had in the building of civilizations, the positive contributions blacks have made as artists, and the extent to which blacks have been victimized around the world.

Play a recording of Langston Hughes reading "Negro" on *Literature Aloud*.

Notice that the speaker's role shifts throughout the poem; the speaker has been a slave, a worker, a singer, and a victim. Yet the self-definition of the speaker does not vary; the poem begins and ends with the line "I am a Negro" (lines 1, 17). Ask students to consider how this change in verb tense (from the present to the past and then back to the present) contributes to the speaker's personal and collective sense of identity. You might ask students to consider why the speaker, presumably an American "Negro," nevertheless identifies so closely with "my Africa" (3, 19).

Ask students to discuss, in terms of space and time, the scope of the racial exploitation this poem addresses. In the second stanza, the speaker offers two examples of his enslavement: to Caesar and to Washington (5–6). Ask your students how this image adds to their historical understanding of Caesar. Ask them also to consider the contrasting images of Washington as a revolutionary freedom fighter and as a colonial slave owner. Students might discuss or write about how this poem forces the reader to reconsider and reevaluate particular details of history.

The repetition of the first and last stanza brings this poem full circle; what words or phrases suggest the speaker's ability to endure hardships and victimization? You may want to ask students if they can see other ways in which the experiences of the speaker may be considered "cyclical." Do your students think that this poetic "cycle" suggests that the speaker recognizes no improvement in the living conditions of blacks in America?

POSSIBLE CONNECTIONS TO OTHER SELECTIONS

William Blake, "The Chimney Sweeper" (text p. 179; question 2, following)

Langston Hughes, "Dream Variations" (text p. 401)

——, "The Negro Speaks of Rivers" (text p. 393)

CONNECTION QUESTION IN TEXT (p. 399) WITH ANSWER

2. Write an essay comparing the treatment of oppression in "Negro" with that in William Blake's "The Chimney Sweeper" (p. 179).

    Both Blake and Hughes point to specific rather than general oppression. Blake speaks of the experience of the two chimney sweepers (while incidentally mentioning the other "thousands of sweepers") and indicate, by association, the system that forces them into the job. Hughes's speaker, on the other hand, reaches further, assuming the archetypal personality of Negro "slaves" (line 4), "workers" (7), "singers" (10), and "victims" (14) throughout history. Whereas (ironically, or not) Blake's characters have a chance, through death, of redemption, Hughes seems to indicate, in the first and last stanzas, some redemption in being "black like the depths of [his] Africa."

Danse Africaine (p. 399)

This poetic rendition of an African dance relies heavily on the sound value of the repetition of words like *low, slow, beat,* and *tom-toms.* The effect of these sounds is that the music "Stirs your blood" (lines 5, 15). In attempting to link the sounds with meaning students may respond that the poem has no meaning, that it is "simply" designed to create a mood. If they respond this way, you may have to back up a bit and talk about poetic meaning: who creates it, for whom does it exist, and so on. The "meaning" of this poem might lie in the relationship between the speaker and the addressee, if not the poet and the reader. Why the startling command to "Dance!" in line 6? What is the effect of the repeated line "Stirs your blood"? What is the meaning of that phrase? It connotes some kind of passion, or the exercise of vitality; what might be the manifestations of that stirring?

POSSIBLE CONNECTIONS TO OTHER SELECTIONS

Martín Espada, "Latin Night at the Pawnshop" (text p. 78)

Langston Hughes, "Formula" (text p. 403; question 1, following)
Edgar Allan Poe, "The Bells" (text p. 197)

CONNECTION QUESTION IN TEXT (p. 399) WITH ANSWER

1. CREATIVE RESPONSE. Try rewriting this poem based on the prescription for poetry in Hughes's "Formula" (p. 403).

   Students may have different responses to this question; on one hand, "Danse Africaine" does not "treat / Of lofty things" (lines 1–2) in the sense that it is about something human and primal rather than about something ethereal. At the same time, this poem describes a beautiful moment of a girl whirling softly in a circle of light, but it does not account for the "earthly pain [which] / Is everywhere" (12–13). "Formula" describes not only the content of poetry but also the method that should be used in treating this content. Is it possible to argue that this poem doesn't need to be rewritten in order to conform to the definition of poetry in "Formula"?

Mother to Son (p. 399)

This poem uses dialect and a matter-of-fact tone to establish a mother's voice. The description of the difficulties she has suffered, through the metaphor of a "crystal stair" (line 2), provides encouragement to a troubled son. This central metaphor is lavishly established, providing an ample basis for new metaphors for different difficulties. The speaker's path has been rough, with "tacks in it, / And splinters" (3–4); sometimes it's been difficult to see the way clearly, when "there ain't been no light" (13).

The overly luxurious notion of a crystal stair makes it clear that the mother would frown on the son giving up simply because it's "kinder hard" (16). Carpeted stairs would not be sufficiently grand to draw the son's attention to the difficulties the mother has experienced. Her use of the metaphor allows her to address her son without resorting to lecturing. The tone is not angry or resentful, but tender; the speaker calls her son "honey" (18) and remains focused on encouragement rather than accusation.

Students might enjoy continuing with this metaphor or establishing a new one to describe their own lives: What kind of stairways have their lives been? What kind of roads or rivers?

POSSIBLE CONNECTIONS TO OTHER SELECTIONS

Katharyn Howd Machan, "Hazel Tells LaVerne" (text p. 77)
Lisa Parker, "Snapping Beans" (text p. 51)

Jazzonia (p. 400)

This poem creates both a visual and an aural effect, something like viewing a modernist painting while listening to jazz. On one level the poem serves as a vivid description of a Harlem nightclub in which "Six long-headed jazzers play" (lines 4, 17), but the sense of the poem extends outward with allusions to Eve and Cleopatra and with glimpses of "rivers of the soul" (2, 8, 15).

The repeated and varied lines about the tree ("silver" in line 1, "singing" in line 7, "shining" in line 14) and the lines about the rivers of the soul that follow them are a good way into the poem. What is the relationship between this tree and the rivers of the soul? How do students interpret the tree? What kind of mind might describe a tree as either silver, singing, or shining? The variations within these and other lines in the poem make sense when we consider the title; if you have access to a jazz recording from the 1920s, especially a live recording in which performers allow themselves a good deal of improvisation and variations on a theme, it would be helpful to play it when discussing Hughes's poetry, and especially appropriate when discussing this poem.

The fourth stanza is likely to provide some difficulties, especially when taken along with the rest of the poem. It stands apart — first because of its odd number of lines but also because its words seem unconnected to the rest of the poem. Point out that these musings about Eve and Cleopatra are initiated in lines 5 and 6 when the speaker describes a dancing girl. Students may be baffled as to why he would choose such archetypal female figures to describe this dancing girl, but he has, after all, been describing the soul in terms of rivers and trees. Does this poem address universal themes, or is it limited by its setting in a Harlem cabaret?

POSSIBLE CONNECTIONS TO OTHER SELECTIONS

Langston Hughes, "Danse Africaine" (text p. 399; question 1, following)

——, "Rent-Party Shout: For a Lady Dancer" (text p. 406)

CONNECTION QUESTION IN TEXT (p. 401) WITH ANSWER

1. Compare in an essay the rhythms of "Jazzonia" and "Danse Africaine" (p. 399).

   The rhythms of "Jazzonia" are more even than those in "Danse Africaine," in which the expected rhythms shift because of lines like "Dance!" (line 6). Despite the repetition of lines and phrases, "Danse Africaine" uses an irregular scheme; "Jazzonia" is smoother. Each is consistent with the types of music it describes.

Dream Variations (p. 401)

The dreamlike qualities of this poem seem to surface more easily when read aloud; you may wish to ask one or more students to read this poem to the class. Notice how the natural rhythms of the lines speed up or slow down to reflect the natural rhythms of daytime or nighttime.

Have your students consider the "dream" in this poem as a description of an idyllic experience without boundaries or inhibitions. How do vibrant, energetic words like "whirl" (line 3), "dance" (3), and "fling" (10) suggest the speaker's desire to transcend conventional restrictions? Ask students to connect this abstract dream of freedom with the social and political climate of the 1920s, in which African Americans could not generally enjoy uninhibited freedom. Over all, how does this dream motif reflect the black experience in America?

Ask your students to consider the way in which active images and words (such as "To fling my arms wide" [1] and "To whirl and to dance" [3]) are associated with the "white day" (4) and calmer, more subdued words (such as "cool" [5], "gently" [7], and "tenderly" [16]) are linked to the nighttime. Compare the speaker's vision of day and night. Ask your students how they can be different and yet both be incorporated into the "dream." You might also point out that there are an equal number of lines describing day and night. Yet the speaker directly identifies with the nighttime ("Dark like me" [8], "Black like me" [17]). Ask your class how these details influence the reader's understanding of the speaker.

POSSIBLE CONNECTIONS TO OTHER SELECTIONS

Langston Hughes, "Dream Boogie" (text p. 410; question 2, following)

——, "Negro" (text p. 398)

William Stafford, "Travelling through the Dark" (text p. 169; question 1, following)

CONNECTIONS QUESTIONS IN TEXT (p. 401) **WITH ANSWERS**

1. In an essay compare and contrast the meanings of darkness and the night in this poem and in William Stafford's "Traveling through the Dark" (p. 169).

   In "Dream Variations," the light and the dark seem to balance one another, each exerting a positive force. The "quick day" (line 13) is a time of action and excitement, while the dark night is a time of rest. While in some poems, the coming night is menacing, here the night "comes on gently" (7) and "tenderly" (16). The only hint of uneasiness comes in the description of the "white day" (4), but in this poem, whiteness seems to be offset by the narrator's "Black like me" (17), so that both elements have a place in the cycle Hughes describes.

   In Stafford's poem, the dark symbolizes what we don't know, and maybe don't want to know, about human experience. As the car travels through the night, its headlights illuminate the road in front of it, and its taillights turn what is behind it red. When Stafford gets out of the car to move a deer out of the road, he has to venture away from the car, his moving piece of civilization, and into the darkness. It is here that he has to make his choice to "swerve," to allow his pity for the fawn to overwhelm him, or else to go back toward the headlights and move on.

2. Discuss the significance of the dream in this poem and in "Dream Boogie" (p. 410).

   The dream in this poem connotes an American dream, a hope for a better future; but this dream is also like a literal dream with surreal imagery. As the title indicates, there are slight variations between the two stanzas: the "white day" (line 4) becomes the "quick day" (13), for instance, and "Dark like me" (8) becomes "Black like me" (17). The dream in "Dream Boogie" is the "dream deferred" that is a recognizable hallmark of Hughes's poetry. It is not dreamlike in a literal sense, but rather the dream of a future of equality. The dream is deferred in this poem to the point that it is forgotten.

The Weary Blues (p. 401)

The rhythmical, rhyming lines of "The Weary Blues" suggest that this poem is like the lyrics to a blues song. Singing the blues is depicted as an emotional release — an outlet that is necessary in order to survive one's painful, lonely life. The blues are intensely personal, "Coming from a black man's soul" (line 15). The "drowsy syncopated tune" (1), the "melancholy tone" (17) of the singer's voice, and the "lazy sway" (6) of his body all combine to reveal that the subject of his song may be the weariness of both body and soul. To begin class discussion ask students what the theme of this poem might be and what details in "The Weary Blues" make the theme evident.

Play a recording of Langston Hughes reading "The Weary Blues" on **Literature Aloud**.

The turbulent emotions of the singer are reflected in the lyrics of his song; first he resolves to put aside his troubles and live on (20–21), but then he feels like giving up and wishes that he were dead (27–30). Yet despite the admission that "I ain't happy no mo' / And I wish that I had died" (29–30), "The Weary Blues" may be interpreted as a life-affirming experience. Through the melancholy song, the singer is purged of his personal pain long enough to sleep deeply and enjoy at least a temporary respite from his troubles. Thus the blues may be seen as cathartic, changing pain into peace. You might ask your students to discuss which elements of the poem contribute to this catharsis and what the relationship might be between the singer and the speaker. Has the speaker undergone any sort of catharsis as well?

Ask students to think about certain details of this scene, such as the "old gas light" (5) and the "rickety stool" (12). How do these details and others contribute to the overall effect of the poem? This poem contains many sensual images; ask students to consider which details the poet uses to make the reader "see" or "feel" this scene.

POSSIBLE CONNECTIONS TO OTHER SELECTIONS

Langston Hughes, "The Negro Speaks of Rivers" (text p. 393)

———, "Lenox Avenue: Midnight" (text p. 404; question 1, following)

CONNECTION QUESTION IN TEXT (p. 402) WITH ANSWER

1. Discuss "The Weary Blues" and "Lenox Avenue: Midnight" (p. 404) as vignettes of urban life in America. Do you think that these poems, though written more than seventy years ago, are still credible descriptions of city life? Explain why or why not.

   Some details of urban life have changed since Hughes's time. In these poems specifically, urban life is characterized by jazz and blues rhythms, gas lights, and the rumble of streetcars. The new urban rhythms belong to rap and hip-hop; gas lights seem romantic and quaint compared with today's streetlights, and the rumble of streetcars is also obsolete and, most likely, less deafening than the street noises of today. Students might argue that the weariness that weighs on these two poems has been replaced by a frenetic vitality and the danger that goes along with it. Rage has replaced feelings of weariness and pain. It might be interesting to have students write a contemporary update of Hughes's poems with these changes in mind.

Cross (p. 403)

This brief poem, using stark and simple language, deals with the complicated and often painful issue of biracial identity. There is also the hint of a slave-master relationship between the speaker's father and mother, based on the father's dying in a "fine big house" (line 9) and the mother dying "in a shack" (10). In this poem Hughes suggests some of the implications of miscegenation, including the emotional stress and insecurity of children born of forced interracial relationships. Ask your students to discuss some of the difficulties they may recognize as inherent in trying to forge a biracial identity in America, both when Hughes was writing and today.

Ask your students how the title of the poem, "Cross," may be interpreted on several levels. Possible responses might include the facts that the speaker's identity is a "cross" between races, that the cross is a Christian symbol of suffering and persecution, and that "cross" may refer to the anger the speaker feels toward his or her parents for making the speaker "neither white nor black" (12). You might ask your students which interpretation of the title seems to add the most meaning to the poem.

Because the speaker's parents are both dead, the speaker no longer has anyone to curse for his or her racial in-betweenness. The speaker must now begin a personal journey toward some sense of racial identity. Interestingly, the speaker's preoccupation seems to be not where to live but where to die. Ask your students why this is so and how the speaker's insecurity about where he or she will die adds meaning to the issue of acceptance into a society that devalues biracial people.

POSSIBLE CONNECTIONS TO OTHER SELECTIONS

Robert Francis, "On 'Hard' Poetry" (text p. 48; question 1, following)

Langston Hughes, "Red Silk Stockings" (text p. 406)

1. Read the perspective by Robert Francis, "On 'Hard' Poetry" (p. 48), and write an essay explaining why you would characterize "Cross" as "hard" or "soft" poetry.

   This poem is neither soft in form, as it follows a strict scheme of rhyme and meter, nor soft in thought and feeling, as it addresses its tough subject head-on. There is no excess verbiage, nothing to "water down" the ideas, imagery, or direct language. It would be difficult to argue that this poem is anything but "hard," according to Francis's perspective. In the second half of his perspective, he implies that there are degrees of hardness, and students may debate the relative hardness of this poem. As a way of addressing this point even further, it might help to have students compare this poem to another poem by Hughes that they believe is softer than this one, and to yet another poem that they consider harder.

Formula (p. 403)

"Formula" parodies romantic misunderstandings about poetry that suggest that good poems have only idyllic, extravagantly elegant subjects. The speaker mocks this attitude, particularly in his repeated suggestion that poetry ought to be about "birds with wings" (lines 4, 16). This poem itself does not adhere to its own "formula." While it ostensibly suggests that poetry should be restricted to "lofty things" (2, 14), "Formula" is clearly not a poem about such idealized images.

By denying that poetry should be "dirty," the speaker actually manages to establish the facts "That roses / In manure grow" (7–8) and "That earthly pain / Is everywhere" (11–12). You may want to ask your students how the poem seems to contradict itself and what effect these apparent contradictions might have on the reader.

You may wish to explain to students that "The Muse of Poetry" (5, 9) is a mythical goddess who was called on by ancient poets for inspiration. Ask your students how the Muse is treated in this poem. Can certain information be withheld from the Muse of Poetry?

Langston Hughes's poetry, in general, deals with the "earthly pain" (11) of life; clearly he as a poet does not subscribe to the ideas put forth in this poem. You may wish to open class discussion by asking students why they think Hughes wrote such a mocking poem about lofty, idealistic poetry. What could he have been trying to accomplish? Possible responses might include the idea that through satirizing "lofty" poetry, Hughes may be suggesting that one cannot separate the pain of life from one's art, or that poetry that ignores earthly pain cannot be very real or valuable.

POSSIBLE CONNECTIONS TO OTHER SELECTIONS

Emily Dickinson, "If I can stop one Heart from breaking" (text p. 308)
Helen Farries, "Magic of Love" (text p. 44; question 2, following)

2. Write an essay that explains how Helen Farries's "Magic of Love" (p. 44) conforms to the ideas about poetry presented in "Formula."

   This question should give students plenty of room to explore the parodic intent of Hughes's poem. There is no trace of earthly pain or of the manure that fertilizes roses in Farries's greeting-card verse. Her poem attempts to emphasize that it is lofty and soaring by ending each stanza with an exclamation point. Moreover, it is formulaic verse, which aligns it with the title of Hughes's poem. It might be fun to have students rewrite "Magic of Love" with an awareness of earthly pain or of the manure in which roses grow. Is it possible to do so while maintaining the poem's tone or theme?

Esthete in Harlem (p. 404)

All of the lines in "Esthete in Harlem" contain four beats except for the first two. Hughes separates "Strange" (line 1) from the next line in order to give that word special emphasis and to heighten his satire of the Esthete who is so wrapped up in his pursuit of beauty that he misses Life until it is "stepping on [his] feet" (7). The couplet rhymes, which come more frequently than those in Hughes's more common ballad stanza or his looser schemes, serve to underline the rigidity of the speaker's esthetic views as well as the surprise that greets him in Harlem.

POSSIBLE CONNECTIONS TO OTHER SELECTIONS

John Keats, "To one who has been long in city pent" (text p. 609)
Phillis Wheatley, "On Being Brought from Africa to America" (text p. 537)

Lenox Avenue: Midnight (p. 404)

You might begin discussion of this poem by closely examining the first two lines: "The rhythm of life / Is a jazz rhythm." Ask students why jazz and life are so closely connected. Possible responses might include the ideas that jazz, like life, includes solos, improvisations, varied tempos, and melodies that can range from the joyful to the melancholy. Jazz (and life) is unpredictable and often unrehearsed; therein lies much of its beauty and appeal. Ask students to think also about how the word "Honey" (lines 3, 12) in the poem functions in several different ways. For example, "Honey" could be the person the speaker is addressing, or "Honey" could be the sweet heaviness that characterizes both jazz rhythms and life.

You might continue the discussion by asking students why the poet believes that "The gods are laughing at us" (4, 14). The poet seems to be describing the vast distance between human and godly experience; gods are so far away, or perhaps are so cruel, that they laugh instead of weep for the pain they see on Lenox Avenue.

Ask students to consider how the setting of this poem — midnight on Lenox Avenue in Harlem — contributes to its meaning. Lenox Avenue is the backdrop for the speaker's (and Hughes's) life — it is the place where his life is "located." Our own Lenox Avenues are the places where we see our own lives, where we see ourselves reflected in our surroundings. You might ask students to explore, in discussion or in a writing assignment, the places that best characterize their own life experiences.

POSSIBLE CONNECTIONS TO OTHER SELECTIONS

Stephen Crane, "A Man Said to the Universe" (text p. 164)
Emily Dickinson, "I know that He exists" (text p. 344; question 1, following)
Thomas Hardy, "Hap" (text p. 599; question 2, following)
Langston Hughes, "Jazzonia" (text p. 400)
Octavio Paz, "The Street" (text p. 579)

CONNECTIONS QUESTIONS IN TEXT (p. 405) WITH ANSWERS

1. In an essay compare the theme of this poem with that of Emily Dickinson's "I know that He exists" (p. 344).

   The supreme being in each poem, whether it be God or gods, is distant from humanity and playful at our expense. Hughes's poem implies that the gods are laughing at the way we live our lives. The poem is vital, beginning with "the rhythm of life." Dickinson's poem meditates on the relationship between death and life. For her, the game that God plays with us has a deadly serious element that has to do with the relationship between life and the afterlife, a relationship that Hughes does not address specifically.

2. Compare and contrast the speaker's tone in this poem with that of the speaker in Thomas Hardy's "Hap" (p. 599).

   Hardy's speaker, like Hughes's, imagines gods that are laughing at him, but they are laughing because they take pleasure in his pain and suffering. He realizes that this scenario is not accurate, that the pain we must suffer is a product of chance or fate, the wills only of Time or Casualty. The gods in Hughes's poem do not depress the speaker in the same way that they depress Hardy's speaker. He does not seem to change his behavior as a result of the laughter of the gods but rather to describe the scene as he sees it. He is in this sense more detached than Hardy's speaker is.

Song for a Dark Girl (p. 405)

This poem mourns in the voice of a girl whose "black young lover" (line 3) has been lynched. The bitterly ironic references to "Way Down South in Dixie" (1, 5, 9) allude to the Confederate anthem that swears allegiance to the South, pledging "to live and die in Dixie." The culture that made lynching possible also made seeking justice for those murdered impossible: The "white Lord Jesus" (7) is a symbol of the helplessness the speaker feels in a culture dominated by hatred and racial injustice.

The contrast of this cultural hatred and the speaker's mournful love provides tension and weight to this poem. The impossibility of love in such a place is highlighted by the final sentence: In Dixie, "Love is a naked shadow / On a gnarled and naked tree" (11-12). The vulnerability of that love is apparent in the death of the beloved and in the repetition of "naked" (11, 12).

If students are not familiar with the historical fact of lynchings in the American South, perhaps a small group could be assigned to present some information to the class. Web sites that could prove helpful include **www.journale.org/withoutsanctuary/main.html**, which provides photographs from souvenir postcards of lynchings. A book of these same photographs, *Without Sanctuary: Lynching Photography in America*, by Hilton Als and James Allen, is available from Twin Palms Publishers. While the post office outlawed these postcards in 1908, the most recent image in the book is from 1961. Another Web site, **http://ccharity.com/lynchlist.php**, provides a partial listing of the names of individuals lynched since 1859 and links to other sites.

POSSIBLE CONNECTIONS TO OTHER SELECTIONS

Emily Dickinson, "If I can stop one Heart from breaking" (text p. 308; question 1, following)
Patricia Smith, "What It's Like to Be a Black Girl (for Those of You Who Aren't)" (text p. 123)

CONNECTION QUESTION IN TEXT (p. 406) WITH ANSWER

1. Compare the speakers' sensibilities in this poem and in Emily Dickinson's "If I can stop one Heart from breaking" (p. 308). What kinds of cultural assumptions are implicit in each speaker's voice?

   The plucky sentimentalism of "If I can stop one Heart from breaking" is not unusual for its time, relying on a Christian ethic of cheerful helpfulness to propel its speaker. The speaker in Hughes's poem would be less familiar a figure to contemporary readers. The broken heart of the speaker in "Song for a Dark Girl" addresses an injustice not yet universally condemned when Hughes wrote his poem and indicts the southern Christian culture that permitted lynchings to continue.

Red Silk Stockings (p. 406)

The speaker of this poem urges his addressee, a black woman, to wear red silk stockings so that "de white boys" (line 3) will admire her. The speaker implies that the white boys will do more than admire her, though, because he predicts that "tomorrow's chile'll / Be a high yaller" (8–9): that is, a mixed-race child. The speaker is contemptuous toward the addressee, who evidently thinks that she's "too pretty" (7) for him and for the rest of the black boys. His advice to her is motivated by his scorn rather than by his concern for her best interests.

Students might jump to the conclusion that Hughes is the speaker. You can contrast this poem with almost any other by him to point out the difference between the language this speaker uses and Hughes's typical poetic voice. ("Rent-Party Shout" may be the exception.) Do they feel that Hughes is making a broad statement about race relations, or is he just allowing a voice he has heard to speak in his poetry? Like many of Hughes's other poems, this one relies on repetition for emphasis, but the meter of the lines and the length of the three stanzas are irregular. What is the effect of repeating the last two lines from the first stanza as the third stanza? How would the poem read differently if the third stanza were omitted? In general, why is repetition such a prevalent device in Hughes's poetry?

POSSIBLE CONNECTIONS TO OTHER SELECTIONS

Gwendolyn Brooks, "We Real Cool" (text p. 98)

M. Carl Holman, "Mr. Z" (text p. 524)

Langston Hughes, "Dinner Guest: Me" (text p. 415; question 1, following)

——, "Rent-Party Shout: For a Lady Dancer" (text p. 406; following)

CONNECTION QUESTION IN TEXT (p. 406) WITH ANSWER

1. Write an essay that compares relations between whites and blacks in this poem and in "Dinner Guest: Me" (p. 415).

   The connection to "Dinner Guest: Me" must take into consideration the publication dates of the poem ("Red Silk Stockings" was published nearly forty years earlier). If students feel that Hughes's depiction of race relations has changed based on these two poems, can they account for that change in terms of history?

Rent-Party Shout: For a Lady Dancer (p. 406)

This poem sounds as much like a song lyric as it does a poem; the short lines make the tempo fast and sharp, like the words themselves. You may wish to ask students to consider this "shout" as a story; ask them to describe the speaker's situation and her feelings toward her "man." Ask your students if they see any humor in this "shout." Responses might include the speaker's declaration that "I knows I can find him / When he's in de ground —" (15–16) — her jealousy is taken to a bitingly satirical extreme.

Ask students to describe the setting of this poem. Point out that the backdrop to this piece is desperate poverty, where friends and neighbors have to help raise a person's rent money. So the music played at such a party would need to be energetic, entertaining, and cathartic enough to distract the partyers from their own personal troubles. In this way, "Rent-Party Shout" can be interpreted simultaneously as a threat to the wayward man and as a necessary release for the singer herself. Ask students to discuss what might be considered "therapeutic" about this woman's singing about her troubles.

You might also consider asking your students, in discussion or in writing, to draw comparisons between "Rent-Party Shout" and other poems in which Hughes incorporates song lyrics, such as "The Weary Blues" (text p. 401). Ask them to describe how the lyrics contribute to the poem's meanings.

POSSIBLE CONNECTIONS TO OTHER SELECTIONS

Langston Hughes, "Dream Boogie" (text p. 410)
——, "The Weary Blues" (text p. 401)

Drum (p. 407)

Hughes uses short lines in "Drum" to give the poem a chant quality. Your students might be interested to discuss the role of the talking drums in African culture. The Yoruba people of West Africa used drums to imitate speech sounds and therefore were able to use drumming as a means of communication. Hughes was deeply interested in the relationships between rhythm and communication. In 1963, he edited a collection of poetry by African writers entitled *Talking Drums and New Cadences*. The poem takes the form of an instruction, a kind of memento mori, but rather than using images to convey the immanence of death, Hughes uses the insistent two-stress rhythm which breaks down in the end with a final, and ominous, single beat.

POSSIBLE CONNECTIONS TO OTHER SELECTIONS

Robert Herrick, "To the Virgins, to Make Much of Time" (text p. 79)
Alfred, Lord Tennyson, "Crossing the Bar" (text p. 55)

Park Bench (p. 408)

Hughes uses the parallel between "park bench" (line 1) and "Park Avenue" (2) to interrogate the difference between the poor and the privileged. You might start by having your class talk about how far apart the two really are. In the first stanza, the speaker sees a "Hell of a distance" (3) between himself and his addressee, but at the end he suggests that a move might not be impossible. How does Hughes intend for us to read this final stanza? Is it a sad joke to think that the homeless speaker could end up in a ritzy neighborhood in just "a year or two" (10)? Is it a real possibility? It might help your students to know that Hughes, like many artists of his time, was interested in communist ideas, which imply a particular way of dealing with the disparity.

POSSIBLE CONNECTIONS TO OTHER SELECTIONS

Langston Hughes, "Ballad of the Landlord" (text p. 408; question 1, following)
Louis Simpson, "In the Suburbs" (text p. 100)

CONNECTION QUESTION IN TEXT (p. 408) WITH ANSWER

1. Discuss the politics embedded in this poem and in the next one, "Ballad of the Landlord" (p. 408).

   As noted above, in the 1930s, Hughes was associated with the Communist Party in America. Communism takes social disparities like the one described in "Park Bench," as both inherently unfair and remediable through revolution. "Ballad of the Landlord" dramatizes a similarly unequal relationship between two people, but in this case the verbal threat is swiftly punished with jail time. The reaction of the authorities in this poem demonstrates the suspicion of communist sympathizers in the United States. The threatened assault on the landlord is interpreted as an attempt to "ruin the government / And overturn the land." (lines 23–24).

Ballad of the Landlord (p. 408)

In his poetry Hughes was often concerned with incorporating the rhythms and feeling of blues and jazz. It's not difficult to imagine "Ballad of the Landlord" as a slow blues. Whereas the results of the protagonist's rebellion are anything but unfamiliar, his willingness to fight for what little is his — and the verve with which he speaks of that struggle — affords him a certain nobility even though the landlord undeniably "wins." The poem also shows in derisive terms the idiocy of the landlord's and authorities' overreaction to reasonable and modest concerns about safety (even the landlord's) and comfort.

Ask your students how this poem might be interpreted as political and social commentary. You might point out to them that the tenant is not jailed for his legitimate complaints about the condition of his home but because the landlord unfairly accuses him of being a political radical. As a background for this poem, you might discuss with your students the influence of Senator Joseph McCarthy's anticommunist initiatives in 1950s America and how this poem reflects the rampant political paranoia of that era. Students might also consider manifestations today of a social system that tends to victimize the powerless and defend the privileged.

Possible Connections to Other Selections

Mahmoud Darwish, "Identity Card" (text p. 574)

Wole Soyinka, "Telephone Conversation" (text p. 538; question 1, following)

Connection Question in Text (p. 409) with Answer

1. Write an essay on landlords based on this poem and Wole Soyinka's "Telephone Conversation" (p. 538).

   Landlords are either indifferent toward their tenants, discriminatory, or both based on these two poems. Both landlords seem complicit in a larger pattern of societal discrimination. It could be argued that they are more than complicit in this pattern, that they represent the worst aspects of the societal divisions fostered by modern capitalist society.

Morning After (p. 409)

The repetitions in "Morning After" are guided by the blues form. Traditionally, a blues singer would improvise lyrics, so after singing the initial line of a verse, he or she would repeat while thinking of a rhyming line. Hughes follows this form, and he also uses the technique of subtly varying the line when it is repeated, so "Had a dream last night I" (line 7) becomes "I drempt last night I" (9). This capacity for both structured repetition and expressive interpretive changes made the blues a supple medium for singers, and one that appealed to many writers. Here Hughes begins with a tale that could become frightening, but he turns his story to comic effect as the vision of hell gives way to the snoring mouth of his lover.

Possible Connections to Other Selections

Keith Casto, "She Don't Bop" (text p. 254)

Langston Hughes, "The Weary Blues" (text p. 401)

Dream Boogie (p. 410)

This poem, like many of Hughes's others, relies heavily on musical influences. You might ask your students what makes this poem so closely resemble a song. Responses might include the fast-paced rhymes of the first stanza and the final four lines, which sound more like lyrics than the conclusion of a poem.

You might also ask your students about the voices in this poem, which seem to interrupt each other. The voice in line 7 is interrupted by a new voice that poses the question: *"You think / It's a happy beat?"* (lines 8–9). This question seems to refer back to "The boogie-woogie rumble / Of a dream deferred" (3–4) in the first stanza. Ask students to examine the meaning of this "rumble" — to what or to whom is the speaker referring? Students might mention that the "rumble" could allude to the lives of those black Americans who cannot achieve their dreams in this country, and that the beat, or rhythm, of their lives is not necessarily a happy one. Students might connect this poem to blues music, which can appear to be uplifting but in fact may be deeply melancholy and troubled.

Play a recording of Langston Hughes reading "Dream Boogie" on **Literature Aloud***.*

Ask students to comment on the final four lines of this poem. Have them speculate on why Hughes ended his poem this way. Who might this poem be specifically addressing? You might also ask your students to discuss "The boogie-woogie rumble / Of a dream deferred" (3–4) in the context of another Hughes poem in this collection: "Harlem" (text p. 411).

POSSIBLE CONNECTIONS TO OTHER SELECTIONS

Langston Hughes, "Dream Variations" (text p. 401; question 2, following)
——, "Harlem" (text p. 411; question 1, following)

CONNECTION QUESTIONS IN TEXT (p. 411) WITH ANSWERS

1. In an essay compare and contrast the thematic tensions in this poem and in "Harlem" (p. 411).

   The tension in "Dream Boogie" comes from the contrast between the exuberance of African American music and the social and political unrest in the African American community. Hughes again treats the theme of frustration in "Harlem." In this poem, the questions he ventures about the nature of a "dream deferred" (line 1) are in tension with the one statement he makes. "Maybe it just sags / like a heavy load" (9–10) is less forceful than the grotesque images that precede it and the violent one that follows it. Thus the tension of "Harlem" is rhetorical, as Hughes seems most certain of his brief but portentous final question.

2. How are the "dreams" different in "Dream Boogie" and "Dream Variations" (p. 401)?

   Both dreams connote hope for the future, but the dream in this poem does not seem to connote a literal dream as well, as it does in "Dream Variations." In other words, this poem's sensibility is wide awake. "Dream Variations" has an impressionistic quality, making its dream both literal and figurative.

125th Street (p. 411)

In this celebration of blackness, Hughes sets up three similes to describe the beauty of the people he sees on 125th street. You might ask your students if the similes at first seem silly: a "chocolate bar" (line 1), a "jack-o'-lantern" (3), and a "slice of melon" (5) may not be entirely flattering comparisons for a human face. In each couplet, however, Hughes turns the quotidian object into a lovely figure, suggesting sweetness, incandescence, and joy. His descriptions of fellow Harlemites don't just capture their physical beauty; they imply a spiritual understanding as well.

POSSIBLE CONNECTIONS TO OTHER SELECTIONS

Lucille Clifton, "this morning (for the girls of eastern high school)" (text p. 591)
Langston Hughes, "Esthete in Harlem" (text p. 404)

Harlem (p. 411)

Discussion of this poem might be couched in a discussion of how your students define "the American Dream." You might ask your class to discuss or to compile a list of their associations with the American Dream. Their responses might include education, financial security, hopeful prospects for their children, social status, respect, justice, and so on. You might then ask your students how people might be affected if they found their "dreams" to be unattainable for social, political, economic, or racial reasons. This discussion leads into a discussion of the poetic similes that Hughes uses to describe the results of the dreams themselves, when they are "deferred" (line 1).

Play a recording of Langston Hughes reading "Harlem" on *Literature Aloud*.

Ask your students to consider the words that Hughes uses to describe the possible results of "a dream deferred." Words such as "dry up" (2), "fester" (4), "stink" (6), "crust and sugar over" (7), and "sag" (9) offer very diverse images of decay and deterioration. Ask them if they recognize any sort of progression in these images — from the raisin that dries up fairly harmlessly to a sore that causes pain to an individual to rotten meat and sweets gone bad, which can poison several individuals, to a heavy load that can burden many. The final alternative that Hughes offers is that a deferred dream might "explode" (11). Ask students how this final possibility is different from the previous ones and how this violent image of explosion might be related to the social and political realities in the United States at the time Hughes wrote this poem. Although this poem predates the civil rights movement, the 1950s were a time of great social upheaval and tense race relations in America. You might ask your students to discuss whether or not this poem may be interpreted as a threat to white Americans who contribute to "deferring" the dreams of minority Americans.

POSSIBLE CONNECTIONS TO OTHER SELECTIONS

Langston Hughes, "Dream Boogie" (text p. 410)
——, "Frederick Douglass: 1817–1895" (text p. 416)
James Merrill, "Casual Wear" (text p. 175; question 1, following)

CONNECTION QUESTION IN TEXT (p. 412) WITH ANSWER

1. Write an essay on the themes of "Harlem" and James Merrill's "Casual Wear" (p. 175).

   The theme of "Casual Wear" is that the lives of strangers can meet randomly and result in tragedy. The theme of "Harlem" also ends in tragedy, but it is not so specific or individualized. It is the direct result of a "dream deferred," whereas the terrorist in Merrill's poem is not necessarily a disillusioned dreamer, although he may be disillusioned in general.

Un-American Investigators (p. 412)

To appreciate this poem, it is important for your students to have some understanding of the political climate of the 1950s and the operations of the congressional Special Committee on Un-American Activities. You might begin class discussion by asking students what they know about McCarthyism and the influence of the Special Committee. This background information may assist students in recognizing that the members of this committee are, according to the tone of the poem and the vision of the speaker, as "un-American" as the activities they are supposedly investigating.

You might ask your students to examine carefully the words the poet uses to describe the investigators on this committee. The "fat" (line 1) and "smug" (2) investigators are sharply contrasted with the "brave" (7) victims of their interrogation. Furthermore, the repeated fact that the "committee shivers / With delight in / Its manure" (21–23) clearly condemns their actions for being arbitrary, intrusive, and corrupt.

Given the radical political background of Langston Hughes and the communist sympathies he held for many years, you might ask students to discuss the risks the poet might have been taking in satirizing this very powerful committee in 1953. In discussion or in a writing assignment, you might ask students to compare and contrast this poem with some of Hughes's earlier, more hopeful poems about America such as "I, Too" (p. 396). You might also ask your class how the "victim" in this poem differs from the "victims" in other poems by Hughes. In this case, the person summoned before the Committee is named Lipshitz, a Jewish name. Students might recognize that there are no specific racial issues addressed in this poem; the speaker is attacking a committee that scapegoats unfortunate individuals from many different backgrounds.

POSSIBLE CONNECTIONS TO OTHER SELECTIONS

E. E. Cummings, "next to of course god america i" (text p. 163; question 1, following)
Langston Hughes, "I, Too" (text p. 396)

CONNECTION QUESTION IN TEXT (p. 412) WITH ANSWER

1. Write an essay that connects the committee described in this poem with the speaker in E. E. Cummings's "next to of course god america i" (p. 163). What do they have in common?

   The committee in this poem and the speaker in Cummings's are both smug and filled with empty patriotism and a false sense of religion. Both try to manipulate and influence others while preserving their own polished self-image.

Old Walt (p. 413)

This poem has been interpreted as a celebration of the poetry of Walt Whitman (1819–1892). To begin class discussion, you might ask your students what they already know about Whitman. Important details might include the fact that Whitman considered himself to be a poet of the people and that he tried to include the common man in his poetry by using common language. Given this fact, you might ask your students to make some comparisons between Hughes and Whitman. How might the two poets be considered "poets of the people"? Ask your students to give examples of Hughes's poems that are particularly directed toward the "common man." You might also mention to your students that Whitman's poetry has been noted for its long lists of people or details, intended to include many different kinds of people and situations.

It might also be useful to have students characterize the tone of this poem. The speaker refers to Whitman as "Old Walt" (lines 1, 10); ask your students what this familiarity reveals about the speaker's attitude toward Whitman. What other details do they believe might contribute to the poem's tone?

POSSIBLE CONNECTIONS TO OTHER SELECTIONS

Langston Hughes, "Frederick Douglass: 1817–1895" (text p. 416; question 1, following)
Walt Whitman, "One's-Self I Sing" (text p. 629)

1. How does Hughes's tribute to Whitman compare with his tribute to Frederick Douglass (p. 416)?

   Hughes's respect for Douglass as a person is more evident than his respect for Whitman. He admires what Whitman did — his endless pleasure in seeking and finding truth through his poetry — but he admires Douglass both for what he did and for who he was. Even the titles of the poems indicate the difference in tone between them: Hughes's respect for "Old Walt" is fondness, as opposed to the unmitigated admiration and formal tribute he shows Douglass.

doorknobs (p. 414)

You might begin discussion of this poem by offering some historical context to your students. Ask them what they know about the social and political climate of the early 1960s in America. The civil rights movement was gaining momentum when this poem was published, and the nation was facing an important turning point. In this context, ask your students what the "doorknob on a door / that turns to let in life" (lines 2–3) might represent. Ask them to explain what might be so terrifying about a metaphorical doorknob turning and opening the door to "life."

Students might also consider the uncertainty and fear that the speaker feels toward whoever might be behind that door, waiting to enter. Ask them to examine the implications of the description that the "life / on two feet standing" (3–4) may be male or female, drunk or sober, happy or terrified. Ask your students to characterize the speaker in this poem. What details contribute to the readers' understanding of the speaker's persona?

Stylistically, this poem is very different from the other Hughes poems in this collection. One unusual detail is that "doorknobs" is one long sentence that may be read both literally and symbolically. You might ask students to examine the final three lines. Why might the "yesterday" (24) that is "not of our own doing" (25) be so terrifying to the speaker?

POSSIBLE CONNECTION TO ANOTHER SELECTION

Jim Stevens, "Schizophrenia" (text p. 148; question 1, following)

CONNECTION QUESTION IN TEXT (p. 415) WITH ANSWER

1. Write an essay comparing the theme of this poem with that of Stevens's "Schizophrenia" (p. 148).

   Both poems play with the psychological tension between physical places and the people who inhabit them. Both imply that the terror associated with doorknobs or other elements of houses symbolizes the terror of the people who are shut up in those houses. Yet the two poems differ subtly in their treatment of the subject: Stevens's poem uses his house as a metaphor for a troubled mind, whereas Hughes's doorknob is symbolic.

Dinner Guest: Me (p. 415)

It is important for students to know that "the Negro Problem" was at one time a common term used by whites to refer to the complicated issues of civil rights and the social treatment of blacks in America. The speaker's immediate announcement that "I know I am / The Negro Problem" (lines 1–2) reveals both the speaker's understanding of this term and his keen sense of the irony of his situation, in which white guests at an elegant dinner party inquire of their single black companion the details of the black American experience. This scenario ridicules the white "quasi-liberalism" of the 1960s.

Ask your students to consider the white diners' statement, "I'm so ashamed of being white" (14), in the context of this luxurious lobster dinner on Park Avenue. Do they see humor in this remark? Empathy? Sarcasm? You might ask your students to discuss the speaker's impression of the white diners. Do they believe the speaker when he says "To be a Problem on / Park Avenue at eight / Is not so bad" (19–21)? What does it cost the speaker to partake of this lavish dinner?

You might also ask your students to consider the way Hughes uses setting in his poems, particularly his tendency to name actual streets in New York in order to set the scene for his readers. Ask your class to compare Hughes's mention of Park Avenue (20) in this poem with his reference to Lenox Avenue — in "The Weary Blues" (text p. 401) and "Lenox Avenue: Midnight" (text p. 404). You might ask your students how Hughes incorporates these specific streets into his poetry so that even someone who has never been to New York understands these points of reference.

POSSIBLE CONNECTIONS TO OTHER SELECTIONS

M. Carl Holman, "Mr. Z" (text p. 524)

Maxine Hong Kingston, "Restaurant" (text p. 206; question 1, following)

CONNECTION QUESTION IN TEXT (p. 415) WITH ANSWER

1. Write an essay on the speaker's treatment of the diners in this poem and in Kingston's "Restaurant" (p. 206).

   The diners in both poems are complacent about their country's problems. In Kingston's poem, though, the diners seem oblivious to the problems. There is no connection between the speaker and the diners once the former has prepared dinner for the latter. The speaker in Hughes's poem is aware of the problems; he even describes himself as "the Problem" in lines 19 and 22. His complacency stems not from ignorance but from the fact that he has been wooed by the white diners who seek solace from him, if not solutions.

Frederick Douglass: 1817–1895 (p. 416)

You might begin class discussion by asking your students to share what they already know about Frederick Douglass. Important points that may arise might include the facts that Douglass was born a slave, escaped from his master, and became a well-known and well-respected abolitionist, writer, orator, and freedom fighter for all oppressed people in America. In this poem, Hughes seems to be celebrating Douglass's personal courage, spirit, and dedication to his beliefs. Douglass overcame seemingly insurmountable odds to become the mouthpiece for all those Americans who were not free and could not speak for themselves.

You might ask your students to consider the second stanza: *"Who would be free / Themselves must strike / The first blow,* he said" (lines 18–20). Hughes attributes these lines to Douglass addressing the slaves. Ask your students how those words might have been interpreted more broadly in 1966 and if this poem can be interpreted as an incitement to violence. You might further this idea by asking your class to debate whether or not using violence to gain freedom is justifiable.

You might ask your students, in discussion or in writing, to examine the seemingly contradictory final two lines of this poem: "He died in 1895. / *He is not dead*" (21–22). Ask your students to explain in what sense Douglass is not dead. If his spirit lives on, in what form does it endure?

POSSIBLE CONNECTION TO ANOTHER SELECTION

Langston Hughes, "Harlem" (text p. 411; question 1, following)

CONNECTION QUESTION IN TEXT (p. 416) WITH ANSWER

1. How is the speaker's attitude toward violence in this poem similar to that of the speaker in Hughes's "Harlem" (p. 411)?

    Violence is not construed as negative in either poem. In this poem it is necessary for Douglass to use violence in order to realize his life's goal. In "Harlem" violence is an inevitable outcome, or at least a possibility. It is not necessarily positive, but given the choice of other possibilities Hughes presents for a dream deferred, it is the best option.

PERSPECTIVES ON LANGSTON HUGHES

LANGSTON HUGHES, *On Harlem Rent Parties* (p. 417)

Hughes describes rent parties in a deeply nostalgic tone; ask your students what details in this excerpt suggest that he longs to reexperience these evenings of "dancing and singing and impromptu entertaining." You might also open discussion about this piece by asking your students to identify details of these rent parties that Hughes does not include in this description. For instance, Hughes makes no mention of the impoverished, desperate conditions that forced people to throw rent parties in the first place. He eliminates any mention of human suffering in his celebration of the warm, compassionate community spirit that these social gatherings fostered.

You might ask your students to look closely at the invitation card. Have them consider the language used. Nowadays would they consider these cards to be offensive in any way? This might lead into a class discussion about the nature of "labels" to define people in terms of their color; ask students to articulate some of the reasons the term "yellow girls" might not be as acceptable now as it was in the 1930s.

DONALD B. GIBSON, *The Essential Optimism of Hughes and Whitman* (p. 418)

One way to open discussion about this excerpt is to ask your students how many agree with Gibson's description of Hughes and how many do not. Using evidence from Hughes's poetry, ask your class to debate whether or not Hughes had any genuine sense of racial injustice as evil. They might pay particular attention to the ways in which Hughes's poetry changed and developed over the years. You could ask them, in discussion or in writing, to compare Hughes's social vision of America in the 1920s with his vision in the 1960s.

Gibson maintains that Hughes could not have written "The Negro Speaks of Rivers" or "I, Too" in the 1960s; ask your students if they agree with this statement. In the 1920s, Hughes was a young man full of hope for his country; in the 1960s, he was an adult who had witnessed the disintegration of the civil rights movement and had perceived little actual improvement in race relations in America. You might ask your students to discuss whether or not they think Hughes might have developed a more threatening, real sense of evil over the years.

JAMES A. EMANUEL, *Hughes's Attitudes toward Religion* (p. 419)

In this excerpt, Emanuel cites Hughes's comment that he (Hughes) is against "the misuse of religion." Ask your students to reread some of Hughes's poems, looking for religious images and symbols. If they can identify the influence of religion in one or more poems, have them discuss whether Hughes "misuses" Christianity, as he was accused of doing. If he seems to dismiss or embrace Christianity, is he also dismissing or embracing Christians?

You might also ask your students to comment on Hughes's statement that "we live in a world . . . of solid earth and vegetables and a need for jobs and a need for housing." How and where do they recognize Hughes's practical understanding of worldly needs in his poetry? You might also discuss with your students Hughes's acknowledgment that his formative religious experiences related more to music than to preaching. How does this musical influence surface in his poetry?

RICHARD K. BARKSDALE, *On Censoring "Ballad of the Landlord"* (p. 419)

You might approach this excerpt by asking students to discuss current social tensions between the "haves" and "have-nots" in our society or between whites and blacks. Would a poem or story written today about social inequality and oppression have the same incendiary potential that it did in the 1960s? Ask them to articulate why they do or do not think so. You might help students to understand the social climate at the time of the poem's censoring by reminding your class about the Rodney King beating and subsequent riots in Los Angeles in 1992. Ask them to consider how a poem about police brutality written in the 1970s might take on "new meanings reflecting the times" in the 1990s. Ask students to think of other examples of texts acquiring new meanings as time passes.

Hughes's "Ballad of the Landlord" was censored ostensibly to avoid exacerbating racial tensions between whites and blacks. This plan obviously backfired, resulting in a great deal of unanticipated attention to this particular poem. This might lead into a class discussion about the nature of censorship and whether or not censoring inflammatory literature can be a useful way of soothing social tensions.

KAREN JACKSON FORD, *Hughes's Aesthetics of Simplicity* (p. 420)

Ford argues for a reevaluation of Langston Hughes by rejecting the notion that complexity is the most important marker of poetic merit. She proposes that Hughes draws his "aesthetics of simplicity" from the materials of African American folk art. After your students have read this excerpt, you might have them discuss where exactly they see "simplicity" in the preceding poems by Hughes. Is it in the structure of the poems, the diction, or the themes? If a critic says a poem is simple, does that mean that it is missing something? If so, what might be missing in Hughes's work? For a comparison, you could bring in poems like William Blake's "The Lamb" and "The Tyger," which might also be described using the derogatory adjectives Ford lists.

DAVID CHINITZ, *The Romanticization of Africa in the 1920s* (p. 421)

Students may find this passage tough going, but it is worthwhile to spend some time reading it closely. Part of the difficulty may come from the discourse (words like *atavism*), part from their potential lack of understanding of the historical context for such a discussion. It is important that students understand not only the tenets of primitivism but also Chinitz's take on this development (he refers to "clichés" at one point, indicating that he thinks this primitivist strain is a little hokey). Is there any such romanticization of African culture today? If not, do students find post–World War I dis-illusionment to be a valid explanation of why this romanticization took place in the 1920s?

Many of Hughes's poems from the 1920s can be productively examined through Chinitz's lens. As far as some later poems that show Hughes rejecting this mind-set, "Harlem" and "Dinner Guest: Me" work well.

TWO COMPLEMENTARY CRITICAL READINGS

ARNOLD RAMPERSAD, *On The Persona in "The Negro Speaks of Rivers"* (p. 422)

This excerpt from Rampersad's essay is a good reminder that the person speaking in the poem is not necessarily identical to the poet. It is easy to assume that "I" is the writer, but as Rampersad points out, the voice in "The Negro Speaks of Rivers" encom-passes more than the personal experiences of one person. Rather, it represents a histor-ical consciousness of generations of American slaves and their descendents. Hughes's story about the creation of the poem sheds an interesting light on this composite voice. Once they've read over the anecdote, have your students look more deeply into its details: Why might it be significant that Hughes was traveling to meet his father and had been thinking about him? How might the story be different if Hughes had seen the river at sunrise rather than sunset? These may seem like small points, but they may also help in examining how, as Rampersad argues, the poem turns from "personal memory . . . toward a rendezvous with modern history."

ADRIAN OKTENBERG, *Memory in "The Negro Speaks of Rivers"* (p. 423)

Like Rampersad, Oktenberg focuses on how Hughes speaks in this poem not just for himself but for a collective history. Rather than contextualizing the creation of the poem, Oktenberg closely examines the sounds and the imagery of the poem to explain this effect. Students who are used to reading more for content may object to Oktenberg's analysis of the sound patterns as far-fetched. To focus a discussion of this claim, it might be helpful to compare "The Negro Speaks of Rivers" with one of Hughes's other persona poems, one that clearly represents individual speech, such as "Mother to Son" or "Ballad of the Landlord." Oktenberg also explicates the historical progression that underlies the scenes of different rivers Hughes represents. This analysis shows how carefully chosen images can both engage the imagination on a sensory level and also appeal to an intel-lectual understanding of the theme.

ADDITIONAL RESOURCES FOR TEACHING HUGHES

SELECTED BIBLIOGRAPHY

Bloom, Harold. *Langston Hughes*. New York: Chelsea, 1988.

Bonner, Pat E. *Sassy Jazz and Slo' Draggin' Blues: Music in the Poetry of Langston Hughes*. New York: Lang, 1992.

Emanuel, James A. *Langston Hughes*. New York: Twayne, 1967.

Gates, Henry Louis, Jr., ed. *Langston Hughes: Critical Perspectives Past and Present*. New York: Penguin USA, 1993.

Hughes, Langston. *The Collected Poetry of Langston Hughes*. Ed. Arnold Rampersad. New York: Knopf, 1994.

Jemie, Onwuchekwa. *Langston Hughes: An Introduction to the Poetry*. New York: Columbia UP, 1976.

Miller, R. Baxter. *The Art and Imagination of Langston Hughes*. Lexington: UP of Kentucky, 1989.

Mullen, Edward J., ed. *Critical Essays on Langston Hughes*. Boston: Hall, 1986.

O'Daniel, Therman B., ed. *Langston Hughes, Black Genius: A Critical Evaluation*. New York: Morrow, 1971.

Rampersad, Arnold. *The Life of Langston Hughes*. 2 vols. New York: Oxford UP, 1986–88.

Tracy, Steven C. *Langston Hughes and the Blues*. Urbana: U of Illinois P, 1988.

AUDIOVISUAL RESOURCES (manual p. 376)

15

A Study of Julia Alvarez:
Five Poems

This chapter invites a number of approaches — biographical, feminist, and post-colonial readings, analysis of cultural materials and the material products of writing — all in addition to basic close reading. Though academics often treat these as separate endeavors, for the poet they are all part of the one enterprise of making art. This will be especially salient to your students in Chapter 15 because they can hear Alvarez's voice in the text as well as in the poems, interview, and essay. For students who have been taught that a poem is simply a riddle to unlock, this multiplicity of approaches — each illuminating the work in a different way — may seem liberating.

JULIA ALVAREZ

Queens, 1963 (p. 432)

Alvarez's work has such a conversational tone, one that seems to take the reader into confidence; students may pass over some of her subtle wordplay without noticing it. You might point out to them how the description of how the speaker's family "blended into the block" (line 6) and, later, "melted / into the United States of America" (63–64) calls up the idea of America as a melting pot. Have them discuss the extent to which the melting pot is working to incorporate the many different families in the neighborhood. In some cases it seems to work remarkably well. Not only does the speaker's family become acclimated to the new environment, but even the Jewish counselor and a German family coexist peacefully. However, the African American family remains very much unmelted into the common life of the neighborhood.

Another issue that Alvarez points to in this poem is the hypocrisy of America's prejudice given its status as a former colony. The appearance of the "mock Tudor house" (7) at the beginning of the poem is a reminder of America's relationship to Britain. At the end, as the speaker imagines "the houses / sinking into their lawns, / the grass gown wild and tall" (75–77), she has a vision of pre-colonial America before the "first foreigners" (79), the ancestors of those who discriminate against her neighbors, arrived in the country.

POSSIBLE CONNECTIONS TO OTHER SELECTIONS

John Ciardi, "Suburban" (text p. 518; question 1, following)

Chitra Banerjee Divakaruni, "Indian Movie, New Jersey" (text p. 544; question 2, following)

Tato Laviera, "AmeRícan" (text p. 284; question 3, following)

CONNECTIONS QUESTIONS IN TEXT (p. 434) WITH ANSWERS

1. Compare the use of irony in "Queens, 1963" with that in John Ciardi's "Suburban" (p. 518). How does irony contribute to each poem?

Both Alvarez's and Ciardi's sense of irony comes from the contrast between the idealistic and the realistic. In "Queens, 1963," the traditional images of "Americanness" contrast with the diversity of families in the neighborhood. The sprinkler on the lawn is one of the suburban markers that allow the speaker's family to feel like a part of the neighborhood. However, on the lawn of the new African American family, the sprinkler is confused with a "burning cross" (15), a mistake that shows how open such symbols of belonging are to interpretation. For Ciardi, the irony resides in the divorce of domesticated plants like the neighbor's "'petunias'" (line 5) from the reality of excrement, that "organic gold" (11). There is also an irony in the speaker's statements to the neighbor. We read these conciliatory moves with the knowledge that he actually thinks her complaint is ridiculous.

2. Discuss the problems immigrants encounter in this poem and in Chitra Banerjee Divakaruni's "Indian Movie, New Jersey" (p. 544).

    The problems of immigrants in "Queens, 1963" have to do with fitting into the community. Through the names of the families in the neighborhood, Alvarez reveals how immigrants from various parts of the world have been stigmatized and then accepted in the course of American history. When most of the inhabitants of America were English (represented by Mrs. Scott in this poem), they discriminated against southern Europeans (like the Castelluccis). As time went on, those families were more accepted as a new group of immigrants (like the speaker's Dominican family) came along. These facts suggest how tensions can arise not just between immigrants and the majority but also among ethnic groups.

    The moviegoers in Divakaruni's poem have similar concerns about fitting in. They worry that their language will fall "like lead pellets into foreign ears" (line 19). Moreover, they have to worry about overt discrimination and even persecution, such as "motel raids, canceled permits, stones / thrown through glass windows" (34–35). This poem also considers the older generation's worry that their children will become too assimilated, that they will "want Mohawks and refuse to run / the family store" (22–23). The movie theater presents an opportunity to temporarily forget these concerns and to imagine living in an America like what it was "supposed to be" (51).

3. Write an essay comparing and contrasting the tone and theme in "Queens, 1963" and in Tato Laviera's "AmeRícan" (p. 284).

    The tone of "AmeRícan" is exuberant and musical. The poem works as a kind of manifesto for people who identify as AmeRícan, celebrating their heritage and advocating a stronger stand against "marginality" (line 31). Alvarez's tone is more measured and wry. Rather than proclaiming a new way of living, she focuses on memory and on her observations of how people of different ethnicities interact in the world.

MARNY REQUA, *From an Interview with Julia Alvarez* (p. 435)

One of the most interesting statements Alvarez makes in this interview is that books form a "portable homeland." Have your students talk about how this might fit into Alvarez's feeling that she didn't quite belong either in her adopted country of America or in her country of origin, the Dominican Republic. Does escaping to the homeland of books help a writer to maintain independence from any particular nation? The political implications of this idea are important; taken to an extreme it might exempt a writer from political responsibilities to a country or a region. The "escape" into the imaginary world of books could lead readers away from the problems of the real world. However, Alvarez doesn't seem to be a proponent of art purely for its own sake.

The "portable homeland" has allowed her to present a more complicated notion of identity that reflects the values of both of her countries.

Housekeeping Cages (p. 437)

In this essay, Alvarez is ahead of the curve in promoting activities traditionally seen as part of the "women's sphere." In fact, the recent craze for knitting and other needlecrafts, has been led by feminists who want to reclaim the domestic arts as a worthwhile form of expression. Alvarez's interest in the forms that art takes is at the heart of this essay. She wants to affirm both the traditionally female forms that became stigmatized at the beginning of the feminist era and to claim her right to enter the traditionally male forms that have often been barred to women. For some artists, adopting forms that have been used by oppressive cultures indicates a conservative point of view, but Alvarez argues that this is a false understanding of art. The artist is free to use whatever form she wants and in fact, by remaking the form, can change its history. For example, the sonnet form began as a way for men to praise their lovers — function that is flattering but empty, taking away women's voices. Alvarez conveys the problem of the sonnet form beautifully in her phrases "golden cages of beloved" and "perfumed gas chambers," (para. 6) which juxtapose beauty and malice. Once these patterns have been broken though, the form is "totally different . . . from the one [Alvarez] learned in school" (para. 7). The tradition changes not just for the individual poet but for all of her followers as well.

"Housekeeping Cages" also calls into question the ownership of language. Since English is not her first language, Alvarez sometimes worries that she is writing in someone else's voice. However, she points out that Spanish, too, was the language of a colonizing power (para. 3). What matters is not the origin of a language, but how the people that speak and write in it are able to inhabit it and make it their own. Alvarez doesn't just preach this idea as gospel; she practices it as well. Though the tone of the essay is casual, she's working hard with the language, and she occasionally has to manipulate it in order to make her point as she does by turning the nouns muse and housekeeping into the verbs "musing" (para. 5) and "housekeep" (para. 8). These changes reveal Alvarez's emphasis on the active power of the writer and her attempts to wrest the control of the language away from its traditional guardians.

Dusting (p. 440)

The writing that happens in this poem is a kind that can be easily erased. In fact, the writer's mother cleans it away immediately with her "crumpled-up flannel" (line 8). It seems that the speaker is doomed to become, like the mother, "anonymous" (18). However, she refuses this fate. In "Dusting," "fingerprints" (9) are synonymous with "alphabets" (12). In other words, writing is a central aspect of the young woman's identity. At this point, she is only "practising signatures like scales" (5), but this warming up suggests that she is getting ready to make real art.

The attitude of the mother in this poem is ambiguous. Erasing her daughter's work is a destructive act, but it could also be a protective one, meant to shield her from a world unsympathetic to women's art. In fact, the mother seems like a repressed artist herself. She doesn't just clean, but makes her home "jeweled" (14) and "luminous" (16). Her name has been "swallowed in the towel" (13) along with her daughter's.

Possible Connections to Other Selections

Marge Piercy, "For the Young Who Want To" (text p. 616; question 2, following)
Cathy Song, "The Youngest Daughter" (text p. 94; question 1, following)
Natasha Trethewey, "Domestic Work, 1937" (text p. 274)

1. Discuss the mother-daughter relationship in "Dusting" and in Cathy Song's "The Youngest Daughter" (p. 94).

   Both "Dusting" and "The Youngest Daughter" involve some tension between the mothers' needs and expectations and the daughters' desires for their own lives. In Alvarez's poem, the mother's dusting suggests her need to thwart her child's larger ambition to be a writer. Though this act aligns her with traditional ideas about what women's work should be, it also has a protective quality, as she tries to keep her daughter from taking the risk of entering a profession that hasn't always been open to women. However, the young girl will not be erased and seems determined to keep up with her writing. "The Youngest Daughter" presents a picture of a woman who has been playing along with her mother's expectations and has begun to resent the role. The relationship seems even more strained than that in "Dusting" because the mother knows her daughter is "not to be trusted" (line 44), and that she wants nothing more than to escape from those suffocating expectations.

2. Compare the attitudes toward writing in "Dusting" and in Marge Piercy's "For the Young Who Want To" (p. 616).

   The writers in both of these poems face resistance from the more realistically minded. In Piercy's poem, the writer is shamed for not doing the usual things like getting a job or having a baby; in Alvarez's, writing becomes a frivolous hobby that gets in the way of necessary chores. However, both seem determined to go on in spite of resistance. Piercy finally arrives at the definition of a writer as someone who "really writes" (line 32). She would probably see a writer in the young narrator of "Dusting," whose habit seems incorrigible.

Ironing Their Clothes (p. 441)

In this poem, as the empty clothes of the speaker's family members become stand-ins for the loved ones themselves, they retain some of the owners' preoccupations and so give us an evocative picture of the family. The father's shirt, "cramped / and worried with work" (lines 2–3), tells the reader that he carries a large burden for the family. The mother, too, has so much work to do that she has *"no time for love!"* (14), but the speaker can "lay [her] dreaming iron on her lap" (20), imagining a time when there would be enough leisure to indulge her affections. Even the sister puts practical considerations first, like keeping her "fresh blouses, starched jumpers, and smocks" (28) neat.

You might have the students discuss which of the characters in the poem they find sympathetic. The love that the speaker lavishes on the clothes certainly makes us feel her sensitivity and affection. Do they feel that the other family members are callous? Or do their many cares make them sympathetic figures, too? You might point out to your class that the speaker has a particular gift in being able to perform these acts of love through the mundane chore of ironing. She is not without duties, but she can find redeeming qualities in them.

POSSIBLE CONNECTIONS TO OTHER SELECTIONS

Robert Hayden, "Those Winter Sundays" (text p. 23)
Natasha Trethewey, "Domestic Work, 1937" (text p. 274; question 2, following)

CONNECTION QUESTION IN TEXT (p. 442) WITH ANSWER

2. Discuss the perspective provided on housework in "Ironing Their Clothes" and in Natasha Trethewey's "Domestic Work, 1937" (p. 274).

While housework is often seen as an oppressive chore, both of these poems offer ways that it can be pleasant and even creative. In "Ironing Their Clothes," the speaker turns the mundane task of ironing into a way of expressing her love for her family. Rather than just going through the motions of ironing, she imagines it as a form of caress toward her absent parents and sister. Similarly, in "Domestic Work, 1937," chores become a loving expression, but here they are a celebration and praise for god. It is important in Trethewey's poem that housework only takes on this function on the weekends, when the professional housekeeper has a break from other people's cleaning and can work in her own home.

Sometimes the Words Are So Close (p. 443)

The fact that several lines in this sonnet end with forms of *be* or *become* indicates how central to this poem are ideas about the existence of the self. The clothing metaphor that Alvarez comes to in lines 5 and 6, saying she is "unbuttoned" and "undressed," suggests that one way she wants to arrive at an understanding of self is to try some different ones on first. However, the most comfortable self is the one "down on paper" (line 2). Here the speaker is more herself than "anywhere else" (3), an interesting choice of words since it indicates that the space of the poem is somehow parallel to the space of a home or city. Though this poem space is comfortable to occupy, it is hard to get to. The finished poem is clear enough that "a child could understand" (8), but she asks, "Why do I get so confused living it through?" (9). Through the drafting process, the many versions of the self, which can't be pinned down in regular time, become the poem-self which is "essentially" (13) right, expressing the essence of the writer.

Possible Connections to Other Selections

Emily Dickinson, "This was a Poet — It is That" (text p. 323; question 1, following)
Walt Whitman, From "I Sing the Body Electric" (text p. 268; question 2, following)
——, "One's-Self I Sing" (text p. 629; question 2, following)
——, From *Song of Myself* (text p. 180; question 2, following)

Connections Questions in Text (p. 446) with Answers

1. Compare the transformative power of poetry in this poem and in Emily Dickinson's "This was a Poet — It is That" (p. 323).

   The ability of poetry to "[Distill] amazing sense / From ordinary Meanings —" (lines 2–3) seems like one possible restatement of the theme of Alvarez's poem, as well as Dickinson's. In "Sometimes the Words Are So Close," the poem has the ability to take the many fragmented versions of the self that exist in time and turn it into a single, whole self. The transformation in Dickinson's poem retains even more mystery than Alvarez's; the difficulty of sorting out her syntax makes this poem a puzzle to the reader. However, the idea of poetry as "Poverty" (12) that can't feel "Robbing" (14) suggests that its timeless values are radically different from those of the world inside of time.

2. The poem's final line alludes to Walt Whitman's poem "So Long" in which he addresses the reader: "Camerado, / This is no book, / Who touches this touches a man." Alvarez has said that Whitman is one of her favorite poets. Read the selections by Whitman in this anthology (check the index for titles) along with "So Long" (readily available online) and propose an explanation about why you think she admires his poetry.

   Whitman's poetry is expansive, and he is interested in encompassing the broad variety of American life in his unique voice. Though Alvarez's poems tend to be formally tighter than Whitman's, with shorter lines and more traditional shapes, the two poets share an interest in how personal experience intersects with communal life.

First Muse (p. 448)

The invocation of the Muse, the goddess of the arts, goes back to Greek poetry. Poets would call on the Muse for help in creating art. In "First Muse," the young poet doesn't know to appeal to a Muse, but is surprised to discover one, who restores to her the power to write. Her feelings about poetry had been suddenly complicated when she heard a famous poet "pronounce" (line 1) against writing poetry in a second language. Alvarez's choice of verbs here is important, as it suggests not just the famous writer's assertiveness but also brings up questions of what is a "proper" accent for pronouncing English. Suddenly the speaker recognizes boundaries that she didn't know existed before. It is as if a "literary border guard" (19) was keeping her from writing more.

Luckily, the Muse comes with a "lilting accent so full of feeling" (26) to contradict the famous poet's "pronouncement." The Chiquita Banana offers a positive picture of the blending of cultures. You might want to remind your students that when Alvarez was growing up, she would have seen few representations of Latinas in the media. Though there is humor in naming Chiquita as the muse, the discovery is also poignant.

POSSIBLE CONNECTIONS TO OTHER SELECTIONS

Judy Page Heitzman, "The Schoolroom on the Second Floor of the Knitting Mill" (text p. 508; question 3, following)

Julio Marzán, "Ethnic Poetry" (text p. 173; question 2, following)

CONNECTIONS QUESTIONS IN TEXT (p. 449) WITH ANSWERS

1. Discuss the speaker's passion for language as it is revealed in "First Muse," "Sometimes the Words Are So Close" (p. 443), and "Dusting" (p. 440).

    In both "Sometimes the Words Are So Close" and "Dusting," language is intricately connected with the formation of the self. Writing her name over and over, the speaker asserts her individuality through language. Similarly the sonnet allows the writer to move through the "many drafts" (line 12) of her personality to exist "briefly, essentially" (13) in the poem. In "First Muse," language is important not just in asserting the self, but also in understanding its relationship to others. For the young writer in this poem, language is a way of negotiating her allegiances to multiple cultures — her Spanish-speaking homeland and her new life in America. The proclamation of the "famous poet" (line 1) wants to confine the writer to a single identity, but the cheerful image of the Chiquita Banana makes the counterassertion that she doesn't have to simplify her understanding of herself.

2. Compare the themes concerning writing and ethnicity in "First Muse" and in Julio Marzán's "Ethnic Poetry" (p. 173).

    Each of the poets in Marzán's poem relates a different way of understanding the universe and humans' place in it. Marzán sees this questioning of existence as a crucial function of poetry. His description of the audiences' reactions, though, reveals more about his perspective on how poetry is received. Each of the first four responses involves some ethnic marker, which seems to suggest that the work would have an appeal only to the particular "ethnic audience." However, when we get to the famous Robert Frost line in the final stanza, the audience's reaction changes. This ironic last line is a comment on the assumptions about white culture — not only is it perceived as the "norm," but it also often pretends to have a monopoly on "deeply understood humanity" (line 20).

While Marzán is interested in how the ethnicity of the poet affects the audience, Alvarez is more concerned with how the poet herself can be limited by ethnic identifications. The speaker in "First Muse" resists being policed by "a literary border guard" (19). Rather than dividing her native Spanish from the English of people born in America, she wants to speak the new language with her own accent, "the way the heart would speak English / if it could speak" (27–28).

3. Consider the speakers' reactions in "First Muse" and in Judy Page Heitzman's "The Schoolroom on the Second Floor of the Knitting Mill" (p. 508) to the authoritative voice each hears. What effects do these powerful voices have on the speakers' lives?

The voice that cows Heitzman's narrator is one of the first authorities that we encounter after our parents: the teacher. When she humiliates the child for not keeping the line in check, it leaves such a deep impression that the speaker hears her voice again "every time [she fails]" (line 23). The authority of the "famous poet" (line 1) in Alvarez's poem comes not so much from her power over the child's life as from the societal endorsement that calls artists great. Though the famous poet does not speak directly about the young writer, the words are equally devastating. In this case they produce not just a lasting impression but also actually prevent the speaker from writing for months and make her consider burning her "notebooks filled with bogus poems" (6). Luckily, in "First Muse," another voice comes along to contradict the idea troubling the speaker. It is funny that this enabling voice would come from a commercial, but the Chiquita Banana is able to break the spell cast by the older poet. Later the speaker is able to look back on the event not as an instance of failure but as one of triumph.

KELLI LYON JOHNSON, *Mapping an Identity* (p. 451)

The geographic metaphor Johnson employs in this essay is an illuminating way of looking at Alvarez's poems. The mapping of identity, rather than of rivers or states, suggests that this is an imaginative geography. Indeed, the idea of "'mapping a country that's not on the map'" (para. 1) relates to Alvarez's attraction to the "portable homeland" that books provide (see her interview with Marny Requa, text p. 435). Alvarez's maps avoid the restrictive boundaries of countries but instead provide a view of the creating self through the lenses of multiple cultures. She breaks up the elements of "linguistic, national, and cultural identity" (para. 2) and recombines them in whatever ways are most hospitable to her work as a poet. As Johnson notes, by doing this she also broadens the sense of the word *America*, lessening the hegemonic power of United States culture and applying the term again "across continents and seas" (para. 3) to indicate all of the "New World."

16

A Critical Case Study: T. S. Eliot's "The Love Song of J. Alfred Prufrock"

One of the problems you may encounter with this chapter is that the presence of material by professional critics may intimidate students into silence about their own readings. You may find it appropriate to have students articulate their own approaches to the poem before they turn to critical sources. On the other hand, critical sources can help in students' understandings of a poem, particularly one as complex as this. If students seem to be having trouble with the poem, you might direct them to one or more of the critical selections.

Another difficulty students may have with this chapter lies in their ability to deal with competing critical attitudes toward the same poem. Students tend to fall into an easy relativism, claiming that each approach highlights a different aspect of the poem and that each is equally valid. While this is true, it would be fair to put a bit of pressure on this attitude. The critical perspectives provided here are incommensurable in many ways. You might recognize this in class and assign an informal writing or hold a class discussion centered on the question "Which of these readings are better and why?" This discussion should lead into considerations of evidence and argumentation, as well as situation or context: why certain readings are better for certain purposes or more interesting to certain audiences. This will help students when it comes time for them to write using outside sources, as it will give them valuable experience with thinking critically about other positions.

T. S. ELIOT, *The Love Song of J. Alfred Prufrock* (p. 456)

This dramatic monologue is difficult but well worth the time spent analyzing the speaker, imagery, tone, and setting. Begin with the title — is the poem actually a love song? Is Eliot undercutting the promise of a love song with the name J. Alfred Prufrock? Names carry connotations and images; what does this name project?

Ask students to explore contexts for T. S. Eliot on *LiterActive*.

The epigraph from Dante seems to ensure both the culpability and the sincerity of the speaker. After reading the poem, are we, too, to be counted among those who will never reveal what we know?

The organization of this monologue is easy enough to describe. Up until line 83, Prufrock tries to ask the overwhelming question. In lines 84–86, we learn that he has been afraid to ask it. From line 87 to the end, Prufrock tries to explain his failure by citing the likelihood that he would be misunderstood or by making the disclaimer that he is a minor character, certainly no Prince Hamlet. Notice how the idea of "dare" charts Prufrock's growing submissiveness in the poem from "Do I dare / Disturb the universe?" to "Have I the strength to force the moment to its crisis?" (which rhymes lamely with "tea and cakes and ices") and, finally, "Do I dare to eat a peach?"

You might ask students to select images they enjoy. Consider, for example, Prufrock's assertion that he has measured out his life in the shallowness of the ladies

Prufrock associates with: "In the room the women come and go / Talking of Michelangelo" (lines 13–14). The poem offers many opportunities to explore the nuances of language and the suggestive power of image as a means of drawing a character portrait and suggesting something about a particular social milieu at a particular time in modern history.

Grover Smith, in his *T. S. Eliot's Poetry and Plays* (Chicago: U of Chicago P, 1960), provides extensive background and critical comment on this poem.

As a writing assignment, you might ask the class to explore a pattern of images in the poem — those of crustaceans near the end, for example — and how that pattern adds to the theme. You might also ask the class to give a close reading of a particular passage — the final three lines come to mind — for explication.

POSSIBLE CONNECTIONS TO OTHER SELECTIONS

John Keats, "La Belle Dame sans Merci" (text p. 610)
Alberto Ríos, "Seniors" (text p. 53)
Wallace Stevens, "The Emperor of Ice-Cream" (text p. 624)
Walt Whitman, "One's-Self I Sing" (text p. 629; question 1, following)

CONNECTION QUESTION IN TEXT (p. 460) WITH ANSWER

1. Write an essay comparing Prufrock's sense of himself as an individual with that of Walt Whitman's speaker in "One's-Self I Sing" (p. 629).

    These two songs have very different melodies as well as harmonies. Eliot's "love song" is really a dirge for an individual whose isolation from society far outweighs his connection to it. Prufrock never manages to connect himself with any other figure in his poem, except for the "eternal Footman" who snickers at him. His tone is morbid, self-pitying at best, as opposed to Whitman's speaker, who celebrates all aspects of both the individual and of the society he or she belongs to. The "Life immense in passion, pulse, and power" (6) that he celebrates has drained out of Prufrock "like a patient etherized upon a table" (3). Whitman's speaker is eternally awakening to life, Eliot's is eternally dying.

AUDIOVISUAL RESOURCES (manual p. 375)

ELISABETH SCHNEIDER, *Hints of Eliot in Prufrock* (p. 460)

Schneider acknowledges that literal details of Eliot's life do not match those of Prufrock yet asserts that "Prufrock was Eliot, though Eliot was much more than Prufrock." Her essay suggests that readers look at the internal workings of Prufrock's mind rather than the details of his life for links to the poet who created him. What kind of "character profile" of Eliot could students create by using Prufrock's personality as a model? What does Schneider mean by her statement that "Eliot was much more than Prufrock"? Does Schneider's comment that "friends who knew the young Eliot almost all describe him, *retrospectively* but convincingly, in Prufrockian terms" (emphasis added) strengthen or weaken her argument? Does the fact that Eliot was in his early twenties when he wrote the poem (around 1910–11) argue for or against a biographical interpretation?

BARBARA EVERETT, *The Problem of Tone in Prufrock* (p. 461)

Everett asserts that it is difficult to describe tone in Eliot's poetry because the voice in his poems "seems disinterested in what opinions it may happen to be expressing." That is, the distance that Eliot establishes between the speaker and the scene is so great that the tone of the voice becomes unrecognizable and, to some extent, undefinable. You might ask students to locate particular moments in the poem when this detachment becomes especially noticeable. What might this suggest about Prufrock's character? Everett quotes from the poem: "I have known them all already, known them all." You might ask your class to discuss how this retrospective moment in the poem complements Everett's argument for the speaker's detachment from the action.

MICHAEL L. BAUMANN, *The "Overwhelming Question" for Prufrock* (p. 462)

Baumann's formalist approach cites specific passages in the text of "Prufrock" to argue that the "overwhelming question" facing Eliot's character is whether or not to commit suicide. In particular, he mentions the allusion to John the Baptist (lines 81–83) and the references to drowning in the poem's closing lines to substantiate his thesis. You might ask your students why he does not also use the reference to Lazarus. Are there other passages regarding death that Baumann does not choose to discuss? In concentrating on a few examples and developing them thoroughly in order to make his point, does he ignore details that would weaken his theory? Do your students agree with Baumann that the "overwhelming question" concerns suicide? What else might it be?

FREDERIK L. RUSCH, *Society and Character in "The Love Song of J. Alfred Prufrock"* (p. 464)

Rusch uses the socio-psychological theories of Erich Fromm to pose yet another possible interpretation of Prufrock's "overwhelming question." Fromm contends that because human beings are separated by their self-consciousness from nature, they turn to human society for a sense of belonging. Prufrock's dilemma is that he is alienated by the depersonalizing structure of modern life. Rusch argues that Prufrock understands his alienation but does not know what to do about it. He concludes that Prufrock's solution is an imaginary return to the animal state, suggested by the image of the "ragged claws" in the sea at the end of the poem. The significance of water as an archetypal symbol of the unconscious or of rebirth lends further credence to Rusch's conclusion. The essay ties in nicely with Baumann's argument by supporting the depiction of Prufrock as a hopelessly depressed man, although its conclusion differs.

It might be interesting to discuss with your students whether Fromm's work and Rusch's analysis of Prufrock's dilemma are gender based. That is, do women, who historically have grown up knowing they are separate from the power structures of society, suffer the same shock of alienation Fromm describes? Do women feel the same disconnectedness from other human beings that men do?

ROBERT SWARD, *A Personal Analysis of "The Love Song of J. Alfred Prufrock"* (p. 467)

If students do not think that this dialogue approach to criticism is serious, point out that it has been used since Plato, if not before, and revived by modern critics such as Oscar Wilde. This dialogue between a sailor and a ranking officer is highly stylized, although it seems to rely on earthy sailor talk (like how the T. S. of Eliot's name stands for "Tough Shit"), it seems like a fictionalized portrait, if not a fictional one. You might ask students to select passages of the essay that indicate that Sward's narrative couldn't really have happened that way; is the essay truly "personal"? Why is this setting, on a ship en route to Korea with sailors drinking rum out of coffee cups, crucial to this particular reading of the poem? Although it seems radically different from the other critical selections in terms of tone, point out that this reading has many elements in common with the other readings, such as the need to sort through Eliot's biography, the analysis both of Prufrock's character and Eliot's method in conjunction with one another, and the will to construct Prufrock as a kind of "everyman" at the end of the essay. If students attempt to analyze another poem using Sward's method, do they embellish their account at all by relying on some device like a dialogue? If not, will the reading suffer, or will it be that much fresher for its honesty?

17

A Cultural Case Study:
Louise Erdrich's "Dear John Wayne"

This chapter presents Louise Erdrich's "Dear John Wayne" along with various materials that will aid students in understanding the poem's historical and cultural context. This may seem a great departure to students if the class has previously taken a more formalist approach, or even to students who have dealt with the poems more thematically, as it grounds the discussion in a consideration of a specific historical moment. While the poem could stand on its own despite the limited knowledge that most students have of recent history, the other materials, however, can show students what can be added to the understanding of a poem by a careful investigation of its cultural context.

"Dear John Wayne" addresses the portrayal of Native Americans as the "enemy" in Hollywood movies. It is followed by an excerpt from an interview with Erdrich. The interview presents Erdrich's views on writing, particularly about Native Americans. Her poems often break down stereotypes, offering a complex and endearing look at the Native American culture, though she has never felt pressure to make a political statement. She says her writing is influenced by "inside and not outside pressure."

The other resources deal more with public views of Native Americans and how they fit in with notions of manifest destiny. The idea of European settlers being destined to colonize the West justified the unfair treatment of Native Americans, creating a distorted public view of the people and their culture.

In stark contrast to the ideas in "Dear John Wayne," the painting of English settlers creates a positive and tranquil view on westward expansion. Paintings like this, as well as books and movies that glorified westward expansion, created a distorted public view of Native Americans, making it more difficult for the Native Americans to overcome their oppression.

As an interesting exercise for this unit, you might have students create either a cultural case study for one of the other poems in the text or a cultural portfolio of a place familiar to them, such as their hometown or their college campus. You may find that it is easier on students if you make this an assignment for small groups, which will enable them to cover more ground with less work.

LOUISE ERDRICH, *Dear John Wayne* (p. 473)

This poem addresses Hollywood's distorted portrayal of Native Americans and the public's reaction. It contains an interesting meditation on Native Americans, their difficulties assimilating into American culture, and racism.

The speaker, a young Native American girl, watches a John Wayne movie with her family at a drive-in. She recounts what she sees on the screen — the western hero ridding the world of a so-called enemy — which brings cheers from the audience. But the Ask students to explore contexts for Louise Erdrich on *LiterActive*.

217

speaker sees through the Hollywood drama, viewing John Wayne's face as "a thick cloud of vengeance, pitted like the land that was once flesh." When the film ends, the speaker and her family feel small and insignificant, much like the people who have been victimized in the movie. She leaves, however, with the understanding — which she considers a "disease" — that things have been taken from her people and that the movie has wrongly glorified the event.

The Hollywood view of Native Americans in contrast to the speaker's point of view makes this a fascinating poem. You might ask your students if they think the media affect public opinion as much as is suggested in the poem. If the media can influence fashion and trends, can they also influence ideas on race and culture?

This poem can be read as an indictment of American culture on many levels. When facilitating a class discussion, you might want to take into account that students may find such an indictment unsettling. You can use the analyses of the later cultural materials to present the ideas in the poem in a less threatening manner, one that will enable productive discussion and agreement.

If you have been following the previous chapters and dealing with formal issues in the course, you may find it interesting to have students apply their skills in these areas to this poem, particularly noting the use of significant detail and irony.

PERSPECTIVES

KATIE BACON, *From an Interview with Louise Erdrich* (p. 477)

The interview deals with several themes that are important to the consideration of the poem: cultural oppression, racism, identity, stereotypes. Erdrich speaks of the view of Native Americans as "casino-rich Indians," when in truth, most work hard and live modestly. She also speaks of the individuality of different native tribes, each having a specific "tradition, history, religion, and worldview." Yet Westerners view Native Americans as one culture. You might have students write an essay on their view of Native American culture, asking them to separate fact from fiction and stereotypes.

Painting: JOHN GAST, *American Progress* (p. 479)

Gast's famous depiction of the idea of manifest destiny can give insight into how English settlers viewed the West: as a vast and promising land waiting to be taken. The woman, portrayed as a benevolent angel, looks west with a look of peace and satisfaction, and the horse, carriage, wagon, and locomotives all move in that direction. The settlers are located in the center of the image under a wash of light while the displaced inhabitants scurry off at the edges under a haze of darkness. The title itself is unambiguous: As Gast sees it, the settling of the American West is a positive development, an indication of "progress." You might ask students what they see as the painting's message. What response might the artist try to elicit from the viewer? Could the painting also be considered propaganda? How are Native Americans portrayed in the picture? You might also ask students to imagine the speaker of Erdrich's poem viewing this painting. What reaction might she have?

TERRY WILSON, *On Hollywood Indians* (p. 480)

This article discusses Ronald Reagan's remarks on Native Americans as having a "primitive lifestyle." Reagan's opinions are used as an example of the nature of relations between Native Americans and Euro-Americans. Wilson explains that like much of the country, Reagan "regarded the Native presence in America as scant or of relative insignificance." These attitudes were continually expressed in movies and even in history books, portraying Native Americans as "an obstacle, to be overcome and tamed." You might ask students to write an essay on what they know of Native American culture, taking into consideration where they obtained this information. How many of their ideas are based on misinformation or stereotypes? Where do these things originate? Reagan's views could be used as an example of why Erdrich felt the need to write the poem "Dear John Wayne."

RICHARD WARREN LEWIS, *From an Interview with John Wayne* (p. 482)

This interview sheds light on a popular opinion toward Native Americans. John Wayne's "survival of the fittest" attitude justifies western expansion and the mistreatment of Native Americans. You might have students compare this interview with Erdrich's poem " Dear John Wayne." What specific issues does Erdrich address in the poem? Why does she use John Wayne to help get her point across?

Photograph: *John Wayne as Cavalry Officer* (p. 485)

The photograph shows John Wayne looking out across the vast plains, searching for the Native American enemy. The fence and sword represent a need for settlers to protect themselves form the unseen Native Americans, a dangerous and mysterious element. Wayne's profile against the beautiful landscape creates the feeling of a soldier prepared to fight a noble battle. Much like the *American Progress* painting, this photograph is subtly persuasive. You might ask students to write about their initial reaction to the photo, then discuss how the picture could be considered propaganda. What makes a photo manipulative?

John Wayne and Hyphenated Americans (p 485) and JOHN MITCHUM AND HOWARD BARNES, *The Hyphen* (p. 486)

Mitchum and Barnes's poem begins with the dictionary definition of the hyphen as something that divides. They argue that by identifying with particular ethnic or national backgrounds, Americans create divisions among themselves. Their examples of evil, however, come from outside of American borders. Erdrich's poem prompts readers to examine the ruthless and destructive conflicts that have occurred within the United States. For her, John Wayne represents a force as brutal as Mitchum and Barnes's Nazis and Communists. Behind the pieties of equality and freedom, America has a history of cruelty to people not considered "true Americans." Does "The Hyphen" offer a sufficient response to this history? You might have students discuss how John Wayne's screen persona would affect the reception of the poem. Does his position as a model of American manhood give him authority, or does it complicate his message?

CHIEF LUTHER STANDING BEAR, *An Indian Perspective on the Great Plains* (p. 487)

This perspective gives a relatively unheard point of view toward the western settlers. Here, Euro-Americans are viewed not as brave adventurers, but as savage people who used brutality to take land from Native Americans. You might ask students to compare this perspective with Ronald Reagan's ideas of the western settler. How might Reagan have responded to this opinion?

18

A Thematic Case Study:
Love and Longing

Students of poetry are usually good at brainstorming. When they get past whatever initial fear of poetry they've had, they often excel at making observations about the poem and connections between those observations. But once they've done this, they need to use their observations and connections to address the poem's central theme. The questions in Chapters 18–21, which follow the poems in the four thematic case studies, encourage students to focus on theme and to back up their statements about theme with specific evidence. These questions should be useful to students who need to make the jump from analyzing specifics to understanding the whole. The questions, however, might also have a reverse application. Sometimes, when discussing themes, students can get a little too abstract. These questions encourage students to ground their abstractions in specifics.

You might decide to use the questions during class time. Try having students spend a few minutes jotting down their responses to the questions about a given poem. Then have them read their responses to the class. In the discussion that follows, try isolating their thematic observations from the more formal observations. Then try integrating the two in a way that would suggest the kind of movement between abstractions and specifics that you'd like to see in a cogent paper. You could even ask students to write their own creative response to the issues of the poem (see question 3 for "The Passionate Shepherd to His Love"). By sparking their interest in the theme, this exercise should get students to relate the poem to the world they inhabit.

The questions should also help students prepare to write essays on a given poem. You might want to choose specific questions for a paper assignment. Or you might ask students to write a paper that addresses two questions of their choosing. Try making connections between the way you've discussed theme in class and the way you'd like to see your students do it in a paper. Class discussion can be a good primer for essay writing.

[Web] Ask students to research the poets in this chapter at **bedfordstmartins.com/ meyerpoetry**.

CHRISTOPHER MARLOWE, *The Passionate Shepherd to His Love* (p. 490)

Marlowe was the first English dramatist to use blank verse in his plays. He completed a master of arts at Cambridge in 1587 and was stabbed to death six years later, having lived an eventful, though somewhat mysterious, life.

Anyone with an ounce of romance will respond favorably to this pastoral lyric, whose speaker pledges to do the impossible (yet how inviting to entertain the vision of "a thousand fragrant posies" on demand!) if only his beloved will be his love. What lovers have not believed, for a time at least, that they could "all the pleasures prove," that all the pleasure the world offered was there for the taking?

It's significant, of course, that his song is sung in May, the month when spring takes firm hold (in England, at least) and when the end of winter was (and still is) celebrated with great exuberance.

POSSIBLE CONNECTIONS TO OTHER SELECTIONS

Sir Walter Raleigh, "The Nymph's Reply to the Shepherd" (text p. 617; question 1, following)

William Shakespeare, "Not marble, nor the gilded monuments" (text p. 491)

CONNECTION QUESTION IN TEXT (p. 491) WITH ANSWER

1. Read Sir Walter Raleigh's "The Nymph's Reply to the Shepherd" (p. 617). How does the nymph's response compare with your imagined reply?

   Students will likely enjoy writing their own more contemporary versions of this love poem: The pastoral lyric used in a more modern setting is likely to produce humorous results. Raleigh's response presents a pragmatic nymph with very real concerns: "rocks grow cold" (line 6). The idealized world Marlowe evokes is lovely in May, but winters as a shepherd's wife are unlikely to hold "a thousand fragrant posies" (10).

AUDIOVISUAL RESOURCES (manual p. 378)

WILLIAM SHAKESPEARE, *Not marble, nor the gilded monuments* (p. 491)

The central point of this poem, that poetry, more than any monument, possesses the power to immortalize its subject, was a common one in the Petrarchan love sonnets of Shakespeare's day. This same conceit appears in Shakespeare's "Shall I compare thee to a summer's day?" (text p. 243). Have students find conventional images of permanence in the poem. With what destructive forces are these images juxtaposed? Even marble, the most durable of building materials, becomes "unswept stone" when it is "besmeared with sluttish time" (line 4), the most destructive force of all. Yet according to the poet, his lover will live until judgment day in "this powerful rhyme" (2). How do your students respond to this conceit? Can a poem immortalize a person? Do poems last forever? Can students suggest other things that might last longer, other ways of achieving immortality?

Ask students to explore contexts for William Shakespeare on LiterActive.

POSSIBLE CONNECTIONS TO OTHER SELECTIONS

Emily Dickinson, "This was a Poet — It is That" (text p. 323)

Christopher Marlowe, "The Passionate Shepherd to His Love" (text p. 490; question 2, following)

Andrew Marvell, "To His Coy Mistress" (text p. 81; question 1, following)

CONNECTION QUESTIONS IN TEXT (p. 492) WITH ANWERS

1. Compare the theme of this poem with that of Andrew Marvell's "To His Coy Mistress" (p. 81), paying particular attention to the speakers' beliefs about how time affects love.

   While both poets acknowledge the eternal worth of the beloved, Marvell uses "Deserts of vast eternity" (line 24) to convince her to "sport us while we may" (37). Shakespeare's pledges do not have such obvious ulterior motives.

2. Discuss whether you find this love poem more or less appealing than Christopher Marlowe's "The Passionate Shepherd to His Love" (p. 490). As you make this comparison, consider what the criteria for an appealing love poem should be.

Students will have to choose between the lush detail of Marlowe's shepherd's ephemeral "ivy buds" (line 17) or Shakespeare's speaker's confident pledge that the beloved shall be praised "in the eyes of all posterity" (11). Both have their charms.

ANNE BRADSTREET, *To My Dear and Loving Husband* (p. 492)

Anne Bradstreet, Anglo-America's first female poet, is noted for her Puritan devotion, her belief that all worldly delights are meaningless when placed in the context of the afterlife. Yet there is an ambiguous strain within her poetry that complicates this position; she is human, and thus drawn to worldly things. Note how she describes not only love but heaven in terms of material wealth. With this ambiguity in mind, ask students to assess whether Bradstreet's devotion is directed more toward her husband here on earth or toward the eternal rewards of heaven. The final two lines are themselves ambiguous; she does indicate that she believes in eternal life, but she also declares that at some point she and her husband will "live no more" (line 12). You might also point out that the final two lines comprise the only part of the poem not written in heroic couplets (they are eleven syllables each), a fact that adds to their ambiguity. Students might also enjoy discussing the tone of the poem as a dedication to one's husband: Does the speaker seem warm? Rational? Self-absorbed or self-effacing?

POSSIBLE CONNECTIONS TO OTHER SELECTIONS

Anne Bradstreet, "Before the Birth of One of Her Children" (text p. 588; question 1, following)

Sharon Olds, "Last Night" (text p. 85)

CONNECTION QUESTION IN TEXT (p. 493) WITH ANSWER

1. How does the theme of this poem compare with that of Bradstreet's "Before the Birth of One of Her Children" (p. 588)? Explain why you find the poems consistent or contradictory.

    "To My Dear and Loving Husband" closes with the hope that "we may live ever" (line 12); "Before the Birth of One of Her Children" concedes, in the first line, "All things within this fading world hath end" (1). Students may find the fear of death contradictory to the faith in eternal life, or they may see both as different facets of a very human and vivid love.

ELIZABETH BARRETT BROWNING, *How Do I Love Thee? Let Me Count the Ways* (p. 493)

The wide scope and specific reach of this poem's depiction of love remains, for many readers, timeless. The extremes of the speaker's devotion, the confident tone established by the simple declarative sentences, and the employment of human nature and the speaker's own "childhood's faith" (line 10) and "lost saints" (12) establish a familiar fulfillment. While the poem acknowledges God's power, it establishes a hierarchy in which love retains the superlative position until the penultimate line, when God is invoked only to permit the love to extend "after death" (14).

POSSIBLE CONNECTIONS TO OTHER SELECTIONS

Christina Georgina Rossetti, "Promises like Pie-Crust" (text p. 619; question 1, following)

William Shakespeare, "Not marble, nor the gilded monuments" (text p. 491)

CONNECTION QUESTION IN TEXT (p. 494) WITH ANSWER

1. Compare and contrast the images, tone, and theme of this poem with those of Christina Rossetti's "Promises Like Pie-Crust" (p. 619). Explain why you find one poem more promising than the other.

   Students will have different preferences here: Rossetti's poem provides an open-eyed account of the possibilities of love's disappointment that will strike some readers as honest and accurate, while Browning's presents a heartfelt, earnest declaration of undying love that may be convincing for others. Browning's speaker focuses on the thorough penetration of the "breath, / Smiles, tears" (lines 12–13) attained by the beloved, using an earnest tone and a wide array of comparisons. Rossetti uses a matter-of-fact tone, while she acknowledges previous relationships, scrutinizes her current love and its possibilities, and then chooses "frugal fare" (23). Browning declares her love with the extravagance of "all my life" (13) and proposes to continue "after death" (14).

AUDIOVISUAL RESOURCES (manual p. 373)

EDNA ST. VINCENT MILLAY, *Recuerdo* (p. 494)

"Recuerdo" celebrates the joys of youthful romance. The lilting rhythm of its thrice-repeated couplet ("We were very tired, we were very merry — / We had gone back and forth all night on the ferry") establishes and reinforces the couple's childish glee at the silliness and pointlessness of their evening's entertainment. After a night of riding the boat (presumably the Staten Island Ferry) and living in the moment far away from the cares of the city, the exhausted youth consider returning to reality but reject the idea, buying a newspaper but not reading it. Their idyllic escape from the city ends with a potentially sobering encounter with a street woman, but in their exhilaration and exhaustion they either fail or refuse to let the reality of her situation bring them down: They simply give her their food and money and go on their way.

The adventure narrated in "Recuerdo" will almost certainly resonate with your students. Most every high school student has experienced a long night of pointless (even bohemian) entertainment similar in spirit to Millay's, although probably not with the sense of beauty and transcendence that she records. Encourage your students to share stories of their own adventures; as a writing assignment, you might ask them to attempt to describe them in Millay's style.

POSSIBLE CONNECTIONS TO OTHER SELECTIONS

E. E. Cummings, "since feeling is first" (text p. 495; question 1, following)
Emily Dickinson, "Wild Nights — Wild Nights!" (text p. 318)
Richard Wilbur, "A Late Aubade" (text p. 84)

CONNECTION QUESTION IN TEXT (p. 495) WITH ANSWER

1. Discuss how the couple in this poem essentially follows the advice provided in the next selection, E. E. Cummings's "since feeling is first" (p. 495).

   Cummings encourages his readers to ignore the rules of the head in favor of the joys of the heart, arguing that "kisses are a better fate / than wisdom" (lines 8–9) and appealing to his lover to "laugh, leaning back in my arms" (14). The couple in Millay's "Recuerdo" share this sentiment of carpe diem and take it to extremes, enjoying themselves immensely and finding pleasure in the mundane — even in the face of others' hardship.

AUDIOVISUAL RESOURCES (manual p. 378)

E. E. CUMMINGS, *since feeling is first* (p. 495)

Once again in the head-heart debate, the heart comes out the winner in this poem. The eliding of the syntax supports the value of feeling over rational thought. Students will probably enjoy the syntactical turn of line 3, which can either complete line 2 or be the subject of line 4. Considering the mention of death and its prominent position in the poem, you might explore with the class — or use as a writing assignment — a defense of this as a carpe diem poem.

Ask students to explore contexts for E. E. Cummings on *LiterActive*.

POSSIBLE CONNECTIONS TO OTHER SELECTIONS

John Donne, "The Flea" (text p. 597)

Christopher Marlowe, "The Passionate Shepherd to his Love" (text p. 490; question 1, following)

Molly Peacock, "Desire" (text p. 245; question 2, following)

CONNECTIONS QUESTIONS IN TEXT (p. 495) WITH ANSWERS

1. Contrast the theme of this poem with that of Marlowe's "The Passionate Shepherd to His Love" (p. 490). How do you account for the differences, in both style and content, between the two love poems?

   While Marlowe's theme revolves around convincing the beloved by means of physical offerings — "beds of roses" (line 9), "A gown made of the finest wool" (13) — Cummings's poem focuses on the primacy of the intangible: "feeling" (1), "Spring" (6), "kisses" (8), and "your eyelids' flutter" (12). The style of Marlowe's poem, with its formal accomplishments, concise stanzas, and clean rhymes, makes sense of his love in the same concrete fashion as his gifts. Cummings, on the other hand, uses loose stanzas, absent punctuation, and lowercase letters to defy the conventions that drive more traditional verse and more traditional notions of love.

2. Discuss attitudes toward "feeling" in this poem and in Molly Peacock's "Desire" (p. 245).

   Cummings presents "feeling" as an entity unfettered by syntax and rules, briefly glimpsed in images of eyelids, "blood" (line 7), and laughter. Although these images serve to shape the primacy of feeling, their reach is beyond even images, untouchable, immune to rules and description. Peacock's speaker also stresses the importance of "the drive to feel" (14), but she is not bothered by the difficulty of trying to capture it in language. Instead, she constructs a series of images, metaphors, and definitions to provide boundaries for understanding desire: it "doesn't speak and it isn't schooled" (1), it has "wettened fur" (2), "smells and touches" (7), like "a paw" (9) or "a pet" (10). These descriptions conjure up a strange creature, but it dwells in a much more concrete place than that evoked by Cummings.

JANE KENYON, *The Shirt* (p. 496)

The sly, sensual wit of this poem provides a rapid departure from the chaste visions offered by the title in only six lines. The last words of each line — "neck" (line 1), "back" (2), "sides" (3), "belt" (4), "pants" (5), and "shirt" (6) — do little to demonstrate how Kenyon moves from a description of a garment on a man to an expression of desire. An obvious title like "Below His Belt" would prepare readers too quickly and thoroughly for the poem's ultimate direction.

Anne Bradstreet, "To My Dear and Loving Husband" (text p. 492; question 1, following)

Elizabeth Barrett Browning, "How Do I Love Thee? Let Me Count the Ways" (text p. 493; question 1, following)

CONNECTION QUESTION IN TEXT (p. 496) WITH ANSWER

1. What does a comparison of "The Shirt" with Bradstreet's "To My Dear and Loving Husband" (p. 492) and Browning's "How Do I Love Thee? Let Me Count the Ways" (p. 493) suggest to you about the history of women writing love poems?

    Bradstreet's poem, published in 1678, directs the powerful love she feels for her husband toward a religious devotion: "Thy love is such I can no way repay, / The heavens reward thee manifold, I pray" (lines 9–10). Browning's 1850 poem also incorporates the spiritual, but only to request of a higher power an extension, a place in the afterlife so her speaker can "love thee better after death" (14). Kenyon's poem does not concern itself with an afterlife at all, nor does it focus on declarations of love. While Bradstreet propels her poem through love toward faith, and Browning uses faith to expand the reach of her love, Kenyon keeps her rhetoric subtle, just remarking obliquely on the body of the beloved.

W. S. MERWIN, *When You Go Away* (p. 496)

Unfortunately, most of your students will associate Dido with the British pop star rather than the figure of Greek mythology, which is bound to cause at least some of them embarrassing confusion. Before they read the poem you may want to either assign them to research the story of Dido or tell it to them yourself. Edith Hamilton's *Mythology* (Little, Brown, 1942) and Bulfinch's *Mythology* (1855, available online at **http://www .greekmythology.com/Books/Bulfinch/bulfinch.html**) are excellent sources of the tale. The founder and queen of the African city of Carthage, Dido was the sister of Pygmalion, whose murder of her first husband had forced her to flee Tyre. Through interference of the gods, she fell deeply in love with the Trojan war hero Aeneas and lavished gifts and affection on him with no expectation that he would return her favors. But Aeneas — again at the instigation of the gods — betrayed her and left her to resume his voyage of conquest to Italy. Devastated and humiliated, Dido killed herself on a funeral pyre.

As the dedication to Dido suggests, "When You Go Away" simultaneously explores the pain of loss and the guilt of hurting a loved one. The story of the Carthaginian queen's betrayal by Aeneas and her subsequent suicide serve as a metaphor for the speaker's own sense of shame. We might imagine that the "You" he speaks to has killed herself and that he is "the reason" (line 10), but the present tense of the poem's title and first line, as well as the poem's references to continuous cycles of day and night, render it possible that the speaker's lover leaves him and comes back with some regularity, or that he relives her death in his mind.

Merwin's final image — of acceptance of guilt being as useless as the sleeve for a missing arm — makes a startling departure from the poem's primary metaphor. What sense do your students make of the shift?

POSSIBLE CONNECTIONS TO OTHER SELECTIONS

Luisa Lopez, "Junior Year Abroad" (text p. 57)

Sappho (trans. Thomas Wentworth Higginson), "Beautiful-throned, immortal Aphrodite" (text p. 103)

William Shakespeare, "Not marble, nor the gilded monuments" (text p. 491; question 1, following)

CONNECTION QUESTION IN TEXT (p. 497) WITH ANSWER

1. Compare the treatment of time in this poem and Shakespeare's "Notmarble, nor the gilded monuments" (p. 491).

   Shakespeare presents time as a "sluttish" enemy that destroys ephemeral things, and confidently argues that his poetry can overpower the ravages of time and immortalize his beloved better than any other memorial. Merwin's poem, on the other hand, sees time as something cyclical: The same dread event occurs over and over again. In the face of this relentlessness of time, he concludes that his poetry is impotent and useless.

MARK DOTY, *The Embrace* (p. 497)

In Doty's poem, the lover's return in a dream is a kind of wish fulfillment, a chance to "see [him] / once more, plainly" (lines 21–22). However, the speaker doesn't try to block out thoughts of death; even in the dream, he recognizes that the lover is gone. Given the realistic nature of the dream Doty recalls, you might have your students start by discussing why the image of the lover's face is so jarring that the speaker is "shocked out of narrative" (12). Is his experience of having difficulty remembering faces, even those of intimates, familiar to them? What might Doty be saying about relationships?

Why does his dream settle on this particular moment? Rather than remembering his partner in perfect health, Doty recalls a time when he wasn't "well or really ill yet either" (1), when he would have been conscious of death, but not yet physically deteriorating. The moving scene, with its sense of transition and "disarray" (11), contributes to an understanding of why Doty would have chosen this moment of their life together. Illness, too, is a transition, that makes the speaker more fully aware of his love.

POSSIBLE CONNECTIONS TO OTHER SELECTIONS

E. E. Cummings, "since feeling is first" (text p. 495)
John Frederick Nims, "Love Poem" (text p. 44)

JOAN MURRAY, *Play-by-Play* (p. 498)

This series of hypothetical questions makes us consider the effect of older women gazing at and admiring the bodies of young men. One way to begin discussion is to try to answer each of the questions, read exactly as it is written, as a way to determine the speaker's intent in raising the questions. That is, are there implicit answers to the questions? It is a very different thing to ask "I wonder how men would react if they knew that women occasionally scrutinized their bodies" than it is to phrase the questions as the speaker of this poem does, in careful detail with a definite setting. Consider the word "caress" (line 16). If discussion strays too far into general questions of the effect of the female gaze, you might need to bring students back to the specific nature of this poem. It is all about perception, as the final lines make clear. One possible assignment is to have students write a poem from the perspective of these young men — either how they see themselves or how they see the women who are gazing at them. Try to encourage students to recognize the fine line between appreciation of beauty and sexual desire in this poem; how might the poem be different if the poem did not take place at an artists' colony with "marble Naiads" (21) as part of the background?

Robert Herrick, "To the Virgins, to Make Much of Time" (text p. 79)

Molly Peacock, "Desire" (text p. 245; question 1, following)

CONNECTION QUESTION IN TEXT (p. 499) WITH ANSWER

1. Write an essay on the nature of desire in this poem and in Molly Peacock's "Desire" (p. 245).

    Peacock locates the most intense desire in infancy, when people have not been socialized to moderate or obscure their wants. Murray, on the other hand, sees desire surviving through all the stages of life. As the older women admire the bodies of the baseball players, Murray wonders if the young men would guess that desire lasts beyond what we think of as the sexual prime. She seems not only to observe the women's reactions but also to celebrate them for looking beyond the staid beauty of the Naiad statues that "pose and yawn" (line 22) in the garden to the dynamic "beauty that would otherwise / go unnoticed" (26–27) in the baseball players. Murray's is an aesthetic concept of desire, dependent on the attraction to what is beautiful. Peacock understands desire more in terms of "the drive for what is real" (line 13) or "the drive to feel" (14). For her desire is less appreciation than a wild grasping. It is "more raw / and blinder and younger and more divine, too" (11–12).

BILLIE BOLTON, *Memorandum* (p. 499)

Bolton's poem uses a form very different from the ones described in Chapter 9. You could start by having your students discuss how Bolton's appropriation of the business-world form of the memo contributes to the tone of the poem. They will probably appreciate the contrast between the more formal aspects of business writing and the very personal and detailed gripes Bolton lists about her boyfriend. The terseness of her statements — this poem doesn't contain any full sentences — also contributes to the humor.

This poem might be a good opportunity to try a creative response with your class, since the form lends itself to imitation. Have them create their own memo to a significant other, parent, roommate, or someone else who inspires their irritation. Emphasize that what makes Bolton's "Memorandum" fun to read is not her pure ire but rather her clever, indirect characterization of the boyfriend. In their imitations, the students should try to use colorful adjectives and sound patterning like alliteration and repetition to enhance their list of complaints.

POSSIBLE CONNECTIONS TO OTHER SELECTIONS

Michelle Boisseau, "Self-Pity's Closet" (text p. 555; question 1, below)

William Shakespeare, "My mistress' eyes are nothing like the sun" (text p. 243)

CONNECTION QUESTION IN TEXT (p. 500) WITH ANSWER

1. Compare the use of descriptive detail to create tone in "Memorandum" and in Michelle Boisseau's "Self-Pity's Closet" (p. 555).

    Bolton uses pop-culture details, including the names of movie stars and discount stores, to create a portrait of the "Boyfriend from Hell." She also incorporates some of his own language into her indictment, which further reveals what kind of character he is. The references to women as "dames" whom he "balled," as well as the comments on the "deep psychological need" of his son and his "long-suffering" mother, portray the boyfriend as someone who depends on stock phrases and has very little original thought.

The critique in Boisseau's poem is self-directed, as she attempts to describe an extreme and somewhat self-involved state of despair. Here the details come from the natural world and the domestic sphere, rather than from observations of people. Boisseau moves from the outdoor images of the "empty bird call" (line 6) and the "dog barking" (7) to the indoor scene of "wet upholstery" (14) and "newspapers eaten slowly / in the bathtub" (20–21) as her pain turns increasingly inward.

19

A Thematic Case Study:
Teaching and Learning

Students will certainly want to relate their experiences with bad teachers to the experiences in many of these poems, but they might also find it illuminating to describe what they gather the poets in this section value about education. Do they look for the same things from their teachers that your students do? What do the poets seem to have learned, either from good teaching or from bad examples? This thematic discussion can then lead into the more formal matters of the poems, as students try to make connections between the language and rhythms of the poems and the lessons they reinforce.

LANGSTON HUGHES, *Theme for English B* (p. 502)

This poem reads like a personal narrative, and indeed it does embody certain elements of Hughes's life. For example, "the college on the hill above Harlem" (line 9) is a reference to Columbia University, where Hughes was (briefly) a student. Therefore, asking a student to read this narrative to the class might make the speaker's story appear more poignant than if it were read in silence. You might ask students to pay particular attention to lines 21–26. The speaker defines himself in terms of the things he likes, which are nearly universal in their appeal, and recognizes that "being colored doesn't make [him] *not* like / the same things other folks like who are other races" (25–26). Ask students how this observation complicates the speaker's understanding of his relationship with the white college instructor and with whites in general.

Ask students to explore contexts for Langston Hughes on *LiterActive*.

You might also ask students how the double meaning of "theme" — adds to the meaning of the poem. The speaker's assignment is to write a one-page "theme" — that is, a brief composition. But the subject, or "theme," of that "theme" is far broader and more complicated: race relations and personal experiences. You might ask students if they noticed any other words with more than one interpretation in the context of this poem. One example might be the word *colored*, which means both that the writer is black and that he has been "colored" — that is, affected, by the racial conditions into which he was born.

Ask your class to consider, in discussion or in a brief writing assignment, the importance of lines 31–33. How does the speaker understand himself and the white instructor to be part of each other? Why does he consider this to be particularly "American" (33)? You might also ask your students to think about this poem in the context of other poems in which Hughes attempts to define what is "American," such as "I, Too" (text p. 396). How would your students describe Hughes's vision of America?

POSSIBLE CONNECTION TO ANOTHER SELECTION

Mark Halliday, "Graded Paper" (text p. 507)

ROBERT BLY, *Gratitude to Old Teachers* (p. 503)

Bly brings new life to the idea that ideas are built on the backs of previous ideas by creating a landscape that correlates with this feeling of indebtedness. The coldness and "stillness" (line 8) of the scene suggest both the reverential attitude toward the old teachers and the loneliness of going ahead without them. The attitude of the speaker toward this situation is somewhat ambiguous. The verbs in the first line, "stride or stroll," suggest a confidence and nonchalance to the action, but in the third line, the speaker admits to being "uneasy" with the dependence on former teachers. "Uneasy" echoes "unwalked" earlier in the line, emphasizing the anxiety that comes with the move into unknown territory. The fact that the ice stretches on "ahead of us for a mile" (7) shows that there is much farther to go on the "unwalked" path.

POSSIBLE CONNECTIONS TO OTHER SELECTIONS

Emily Dickinson, "Water, is taught by thirst" (text p. 313)

Jane Kenyon, "Trouble with Math in a One-Room Country School" (text p. 506)

LINDA PASTAN, *Pass/Fail* (p. 504)

As the passage from *Time* magazine suggests, dreams of taking a test for which one is unprepared are almost universal. According to Sigmund Freud, however, these dreams seem to start only after a student has received his or her degree. You may want to begin class discussion by asking students to share examples of their own test-related anxiety dreams. At least one or two students should have stories to relate; if they don't, you might want to tell them about one of your own examination dreams.

What's interesting about Pastan's poem is not so much the universality of the dreams she explores, but her interpretation of their meaning. Freud, in *The Interpretation of Dreams* (1900), argues that we have these dreams "whenever we fear that we may be punished by some unpleasant result because we have done something carelessly or wrongly, because we have not been as thorough as we might have been — in short, whenever we feel the burden of responsibility." In other words, Freud interprets the examination dream as a fear of punishment. But Pastan takes a slightly different tack. In her evaluation, examination dreams reflect anxiety about being judged by oneself and failing in *one's own* estimation, "No matter how / you succeed awake" (lines 4–5). (Freud picks up on this aspect of the dream as well, noting that sleepers never seem to dream about tests they've actually flunked in their waking lives — the dream seems to concern only those tests that the dreamer has already taken successfully.) Dreams, like poems, invite interpretation but resist easy answers. Ask your students which interpretation seems more valid to them.

POSSIBLE CONNECTIONS TO OTHER SELECTIONS

Mark Halliday, "Graded Paper" (text p. 507)

Linda Pastan, "Marks" (text p. 151; question 1, below)

CONNECTION QUESTION IN TEXT (p. 505) WITH ANSWER

1. Discuss the significance of being graded in this poem and in Pastan's "Marks" (p. 151).

   In both poems, grading is a form of judgment that both the assessor and the assessed take personally. The female speaker of "Marks" resents being graded and decides not to subject herself to it anymore, she announces she is "dropping out" (line 12) of the family that judges her. The gender of the speaker in "Pass/Fail" is deliberately neutral because the subject matter of the poem is the universality of a particular kind of anxiety dream. The person doing the grading in this poem is the dreamer him- or herself: Judgment, in "Pass/Fail," comes from within and cannot be escaped. Note, also, the repeated use of the phrase "Pass/Fail" in both poems. Although it's the least judgmental of grading systems, it nonetheless gives the subject a degree of anxiety, especially because the stakes are so high personally. To fail a test becomes synonymous with failing as a person.

AUDIOVISUAL RESOURCES (manual p. 379)

PAUL ZIMMER, *Zimmer's Head Thudding against the Blackboard* (p. 505)

Although the situation recounted in this poem seems tragic, its overall effect is comic. The title suggests humor from the beginning: the sounds of the name "Zimmer" and the word "Thudding" are funnier than the scene they describe might suggest. Deliberate mechanical errors reinforce this sense of humor. Although the speaker "had missed / Five number problems in a row" (lines 1–2), he claims he was punished for his "six mistakes" (6). (If your students insist that this number is correct, point out to them that he was *about* to foul a sixth" [3], but the nun didn't give him the chance.) The run-on sentence in line 8 suggests that the student is not much better with words than he was with math.

The central theme of this poem isn't math or poetry so much as it is a student's reaction to abuse of authority. His response to punishment is a vow of revenge, but the "curse" (10) he eventually flings at his teacher is ineffectual at best; by immortalizing his teacher in poetry and citing her unwitting influence in his becoming a writer, the speaker may even be doing her a favor.

If any of your students attended a Catholic grade school or high school, you may want to ask if they have ever heard of or witnessed a corporal punishment as severe as the one described in this poem. Chances are, they haven't: the nun's reaction seems severe and, perhaps, apocryphal. How does the implausibility of the scene described affect students' reading of this poem?

POSSIBLE CONNECTIONS TO OTHER SELECTIONS

Jeffrey Harrison, "Fork" (text p. 512)

Jane Kenyon, "Trouble with Math in a One-Room Country School" (text p. 506; question 1, following)

Peter Meinke, "(Untitled)" (text p. 91)

Ronald Wallace, "Miss Goff" (text p. 339)

CONNECTION QUESTION IN TEXT (p. 505) WITH ANSWER

1. Compare the themes of Zimmer's poem with those of Jane Kenyon's "Trouble with Math in a One-Room Country School" (p. 506).

   Both poems look back to a time when punishment for schoolchildren was often much harsher than it is today. While Zimmer's punishment is physical, and Kenyon's lies in being humiliatingly separated from the class, both have a similar effect: an internal revolt against the teacher. While shut in the closet, Kenyon "hardened [her] heart against authority" (line 22) and when she emerges, she has been "changed" (25). Her faith in the fairness of powerful figures has been shaken. Similarly, Zimmer's punishment results in a plot against authority. In his case, it takes the form of poetic ambition which will allow him to "curse [the nun's] yellow teeth" (line 10).

RICHARD HAGUE, *Directions for Resisting the SAT* (p. 505)

Hague's poem undercuts itself when it insists that the reader "follow no directions" (line 14). Once your students have identified the immediate reasons for Hague's revolt — having to spend a "Saturday morning with pencils" (2), the constrictive "rules of gravity, / commas, history" (3–4) — you might have them discuss how his poem works as a direction against directions. Would he encourage the reader to ignore his rules as well?

You might also ask your class to talk about the alternative Hague proposes, living "whole / like an oyster or snail" (12–13). Does that sound like a rewarding existence? What would its benefits be? And how does the image of the snail inform a reading of the last line? Besides the marks that aren't supposed to go outside the SAT bubbles, Hague may also be thinking of the purposeless trails that animals make.

POSSIBLE CONNECTIONS TO OTHER SELECTIONS

Linda Pastan, "Pass/Fail" (text p. 504; question 1, following)
Marge Piercy, "The Secretary Chant" (text p. 22)

CONNECTION QUESTION IN TEXT (p. 506) WITH ANSWER

1. Compare the treatment of tests in this poem and in Linda Pastan's "Pass/Fail" (p. 504).

   Hague is clearly scornful of tests and wants to undermine them in any way possible. His critique moves from skepticism, from not believing in the SAT, to outright subversion, through lying and refusal to obey the rules. Pastan's poem, on the other hand, describes an anxiety about tests that implies an acceptance of their authority. The irrational fear, which comes out in dreams, doesn't just apply to actual tests, but extends to courses she hasn't taken and languages she doesn't know. This sense of the absolute power of the test may be a precursor to Hague's attitude of resistance.

JANE KENYON, *Trouble with Math in a One-Room Country School* (p. 506)

This narrative poem describes a transforming moment in the speaker's life. A young girl, presumably middle class (suggested by her knowledge of Haydn from piano lessons), asks a classmate for help with a math problem. For reasons that the reader can only guess, the teacher finds the speaker's actions reprehensible and punishes her with a severity usually reserved for older boys. Ashamed and angry, the girl responds by rejecting authority. By the time she is returned to the classroom, she is "blinking / and changed" (lines 24–25).

Ask your students whether they think this poem simply tells a story or if they can find more to it. Some may be puzzled about the detail regarding Ann's bookmark, with its gruesome image of the sacred heart. Why does Kenyon include this detail? With a little prodding, students familiar with the Christian tradition should be able to recognize the similarities between the speaker's transformation and the crucifixion and resurrection of Jesus Christ: Note the unreasonable and public punishment, the "burial" in a dark, gloomy space, and the speaker's return from it after somebody else opens the door. The detail about Haydn, too, should help students with a musical background see the religious overtones of this poem. The eighteenth-century composer is known for his great masses and religious music. If you have access to any of his symphonies or masses, you might want to bring one in to play to the class.

POSSIBLE CONNECTIONS TO OTHER SELECTIONS

Judy Page Heitzman, "The Schoolroom on the Second Floor of the Knitting Mill" (text p. 508; question 1, following)

Paul Zimmer, "Zimmer's Head Thudding against the Blackboard" (text p. 505)

CONNECTION QUESTION IN TEXT (p. 507) WITH ANSWER

1. Discuss the tone and theme of Kenyon's poem and Judy Page Heitzman's "The Schoolroom on the Second Floor of the Knitting Mill" (p. 508).

    Both poems relate a schoolroom incident that probably meant nothing to the teacher but had a profound effect on the student. The speakers' responses, however, are quite different. Kenyon's speaker reacts to a harsh punishment by rejecting authority, which gives her a quiet sense of strength. Heitzman's speaker, on the other hand, is haunted by the painful memory of her teacher's thoughtless remark.

AUDIOVISUAL RESOURCES (manual p. 377)

MARK HALLIDAY, *Graded Paper* (p. 507)

This poem takes the theme of a professor's written comments on a paper and examines them for poetic content. Using humor and taking advantage of the diction used in academic contexts, the poem establishes a connection between professor and student, examining the ways in which the graded paper serves as a communiqué between generations, a kind of love note shuffled back and forth. In its conclusion, the speaker acknowledges that, despite the student's difficulty with semicolons, the real problem is that "You are not / me, finally" (lines 34–35). The "delightful provocation" (38) this presents is the crux of the poem.

The grader of the paper is characterized as intelligent and familiar with academic culture but ultimately willing to allow room for honesty in the teacher-student relationship, opening the way for examination of a larger possibility. The final lines, beginning with "And yet" (29), offer an excuse for the fine grade awarded: Anyone who is having trouble with semicolons, opaque thinking, and confused syntax shouldn't be getting an A-, but the "impressive, . . . cheeky" (33) confidence of the student overrides the professor's initial "cranky" reaction.

POSSIBLE CONNECTIONS TO OTHER SELECTIONS

Robert Browning, "My Last Duchess" (text p. 177; question 1, following)

Linda Pastan, "Marks" (text p. 151)

CONNECTION QUESTION IN TEXT (p. 508) WITH ANSWER

1. Compare the ways in which Halliday reveals the speaker's character in this poem with the strategies used by Robert Browning in "My Last Duchess" (p. 177).

    Halliday and Browning both use formal speech in the first lines of their poems and then settle into a more honest, revealing informality. Halliday moves from "your thinking becomes, for me, alarmingly opaque" (lines 7–8) to "you are so young, so young" (37) over the course of his poem; Browning moves from the formal niceties of a host — "Will't please you sit and look at her?" (5) — to a vivid description of jealousy and the implication, in "I gave commands" (45), of murder.

JUDY PAGE HEITZMAN, *The Schoolroom on the Second Floor of the Knitting Mill* (p. 508)

This small, quiet poem demonstrates the impact the words of adults can have on the young; the speaker, an adult, is still haunted by a teacher's judgment. In the first stanza the reader is led to believe that the speaker holds Mrs. Lawrence tenderly in her memory; seeing the cardinals makes the speaker miss her. However, the details given in the first stanza include only Mrs. Lawrence's classroom manicure and a blueprint of the building that housed her classroom. The image of the teacher as she "carved and cleaned her nails" (line 2) can be read most immediately as an indictment of her teaching technique, but it can also be seen as an implied metaphor that foreshadows the harm Mrs. Lawrence can do. The nails can be read as claws, the cleaning and carving the daily maintenance of her weapons.

Play a record-ing of Judy Page Heitzman reading "The Schoolroom on the Second Floor of the Knitting Mill" on Literature Aloud.

Another image that conveys a sense of the teacher's physical and pedagogical characteristics is the simile at the conclusion of the poem: "Her arms hang down like sausages" (22). Here Mrs. Lawrence is a figure to be pitied, a tired, defeated person who is totally oblivious to the effects of her words. The carving and cleaning of nails, the hanging arms, the quiet statement about Judy's poor leadership — all are mundane images. Harm is present all the time, ready to inflict lasting damage at any moment. You might want to ask your students to consider other insidious sources of quiet but serious harm: Students are likely to have their own stories of how quickly words can hurt, regardless of the speaker's awareness or intent.

Possible Connections to Other Selections

Jeffrey Harrison, "Fork" (text p. 512)

Jane Kenyon, "Trouble with Math in a One-Room Country School" (text p. 506)

Paul Zimmer, "Zimmer's Head Thudding against the Blackboard" (text p. 505; question 1, following)

Connection Questions in Text (p. 509) with Answers

1. Compare the representations and meanings of being a schoolchild in this poem with those in "Zimmer's Head Thudding against the Blackboard" (p. 505).

   In both poems, schoolchildren are relatively powerless against the harsh punishments inflicted by a pathetic authority figure. However a student fails, he or she is subject to arbitrary punishment that seems to have no real relation to his or her behavior and is publicly humiliating to boot; both poets intimate that the teacher is so powerless in her own life that she takes out her frustrations on children who have no recourse against her. In Zimmer's poem, the child is able to exert a quiet, inward revenge against deliberate and physical cruelty by resolving to become a poet. In Heitzman's narrative, however, the student is irrevocably harmed by a teacher's thoughtlessly cruel words. In both cases, the teacher's actions have lasting psychological consequences of which they are unaware.

RICHARD WAKEFIELD, *In a Poetry Workshop* (p. 509)

This poem provides a kind of in-joke for people who are familiar with "the basics of modern verse" (line 1), prosody, the structure of a poetry class, Marx, Plato, and Wordsworth. Students may need a little guidance to understand the humor here; while they are likely to pick up on the tone, they may not see what's going on. You may want to ask what students know about poetry workshops and the concept of bringing poems to read with a group, reading them aloud, and working on them together. The rhyme and meter, in a poem that warns against both, provide tension between the poem's form and content. This tension renders the tone less than serious.

Wakefield's verse provides a good beginning for students' study of poems. One quick lesson learned is the distinction between poet and speaker: Wakefield's speaker may take his or her position as leader of a poetry workshop seriously, but Wakefield himself does not take his speaker's advice. This poem gives students a chance to articulate what they value in a poem. Are meter and rhyme important to them? Do they want to learn about the historical perspective of a piece, how it fits into larger artistic movements? Do they want to understand how Wordsworth and others have affected modern verse? Through humor, this poem provides a productive introduction to these issues.

TOM WAYMAN, *Did I Miss Anything?* (p. 510)

The structure of Wayman's poem — alternating between nothing and everything — both emphasizes the importance of learning and undercuts standard formulations of its importance. Your students will easily understand that the "Nothing" sections don't really mean what they say; they expose the solipsism behind the title question. However, the "Everything" sections don't present a perfect opposite because they, too, are tongue-in-cheek. The "Everything" of education can't be accounted for in grades, the subject of the second strophe. Wayman subtly undermines the importance of grading by weighting his quiz more than his test. Because students know that quizzes are usually more casual, shorter, and therefore worth fewer points, they might notice that the points handed out in this section seem arbitrary, which probably reflects on the practice of grading in general.

The fourth strophe challenges common ideas about education in another way. Here Wayman goes over the top with his description of its benefits: "a shaft of light suddenly descended and an angel / or other heavenly being appeared" (lines 16–17). Even those who value learning don't expect this kind of result. These two strophes suggest that the question is inadequate not just in its self-centeredness but also in its assumption that the effects of education are immediately apparent and easily measurable. Wayman's final answer is the one that reflects the most realistic view of learning. He sees the classroom as an opportunity for the student to "query and examine and ponder" (28). This isn't the only place they can come to learn but "it was one place" (30), and once the opportunity is gone it can't be reclaimed.

POSSIBLE CONNECTIONS TO OTHER SELECTIONS

Robert Bly, "Gratitude to Old Teachers" (text p. 503)
Jane Kenyon, "Trouble with Math in a One-Room Country School" (text p. 506)
Paul Zimmer, "Zimmer's Head Thudding against the Blackboard" (text p. 505)

CONNECTION QUESTION IN TEXT (p. 511) WITH ANSWER

1. Compare the portrait of this teacher with that of any other teacher that appears in a poem of your choice from this chapter. Explain why you prefer one to the other.

   In Bly's "Gratitude to Old Teachers," the teachers are only present in that they've allowed the speaker to reach the point he has. Submerged under the ice, they're no longer a dynamic part of his learning. Zimmer's, Kenyon's, and Heitzman's teachers are all punitive, though in different ways. Their poems tap into a common experience of early shame and resentment toward cruel or just insensitive teachers. Halliday's and Wayman's poems begin from the teacher's point of view and speak to the occasional difficulty of communicating with students who are, as Halliday notes, ultimately, "not / me" (lines 34–35). The most positive view of teachers in this chapter is probably Anderson's "The Thing You Must Remember" (p. 511). Like some of the other poems, it describes the emotional perils of early schooling, but here the teacher is a reassuring presence, "holding on" (line 16) as the child confronts uncertainty.

MAGGIE ANDERSON, *The Thing You Must Remember* (p. 511)

In this comment on the nature of creative work, Anderson provides consolation for the inevitable failure to reach the desired outcome. Even as a child, the artist has a form in mind — "the imagined dog's fur, the shape of his ears" (line 5) — toward which the creative act reaches. If the materials are "dangerous" (6), it is mostly because they are inherently flawed in comparison to the ideal. The clay is made more dangerous by the fact that the child has not yet developed many means of expression. Her "limited words" (8) prevent her from recreating the "imagined" dog in writing; they also foreshadow the increasing mastery that allows the adult to produce this poem.

The child's intense dedication to her "single vision" (12) eventually becomes counterproductive. When the labored sculpture cracks in the kiln, she learns "how the beautiful / suffers from too much attention" (10–11). The consolation in the poem comes in the form of the teacher, whose reassuring presence steadies the child and supports her through disappointment.

POSSIBLE CONNECTIONS TO OTHER SELECTIONS

Robert Bly, "Gratitude to Old Teachers" (text p. 503; question 2, following)

Judy Page Heitzman, "The Schoolroom on the Second Floor of the Knitting Mill" (p. 508; question 1, following)

CONNECTIONS QUESTIONS IN TEXT (p. 512) WITH ANSWERS

1. Discuss the sense of direction provided by the teacher in Anderson's poem and in Judy Page Heitzman's "The Schoolroom on the Second Floor of the Knitting Mill" (p. 508).

   The teacher in "The Thing You Must Remember" encourages the speaker in the pursuit of her "single vision" (line 12), which can feel "dangerous" (6). The "capable / hands" (14–15) reassure the child after the initial failure of her creation. The narrator in Heitzman's poem is also faced with a "dangerous" task (line 14). However, when she fails to keep the children in line behind her from crossing the threshold, the teacher's response is judgmental rather than supportive. Her disapproval makes such an impact that the speaker thinks of the teacher whenever she confronts failure.

2. What do you think is learned by the "you" of "The Thing You Must Remember" and the "we" of "Gratitude to Old Teachers" by Robert Bly (p. 503)? To what extent does the shift in pronouns indicate a shift or difference in attitudes about the learning that is described?

   The lesson learned in "The Thing You Must Remember" seems to be an ethical lesson while "Gratitude to Old Teachers" is concerned more with the knowledge that allows people to build new ideas. Anderson's poem, addressed to "you," has the feeling of self-address. The narrator reminds herself of this incident in order to set up an emotional response to later failure. Bly's poem includes the reader in the pronoun "we," suggesting that the pattern is one that informs not just the poet's life but also the life of anyone who has been educated. It outlines a way of thinking about the knowledge we have gained from others and assumes an obligation to carry on with their work.

JEFFREY HARRISON, *Fork* (p. 512)

Students are sure to enjoy the humor of this poem. A writing student is so hostile to his teacher that he steals a family heirloom (a silver fork) and takes it with him to Europe, sending photos of it in different locations back to the teacher as a taunt. The prank is a popular one and has reached almost urban-legend status. Some students may be familiar with a variation on the theme from the popular French film *Amelie*, in which the title character steals her father's garden gnome and recruits friends to bring it around the world and send back photos. A book by Willy Puchner shows a pair of ceramic penguins staged and photographed in world-famous locations. An enormous collection of photos is cataloged at **http://dir.yahoo.com/Recreation/Travel/Photos/ Travel Buddies and Props/**. Countless other examples exist.

Ask your students if they've heard stories or seen photographs of similar pranks. What do they think of them? Is the theft cruel, amusing, harmless, wrong? What do they think is the speaker's real motivation? He says it was a "perverse inspiration" (line 24) — certainly his obsession with the fork, as well as the time and energy he spends on a teacher he professes to hate, is perverse — but what else is going on in his head? Why does he need to torment his teacher? What effect does it have on him as a writer? as a person? Considering how derivative his prank is, was his teacher perhaps justified in maligning his creative ability? Perhaps more telling is the long-term influence "the worst teacher [he] ever had" (61) managed to exert over the speaker. Is Harrison suggesting, perhaps, that intense hostility can be an effective teaching tool?

POSSIBLE CONNECTIONS TO OTHER SELECTIONS

Billy Collins, "Introduction to Poetry" (text p. 42)

Mark Halliday, "Graded Paper" (text p. 507; question 1, following)

Richard Wakefield, "In a Poetry Workshop" (text p. 509; question 1, following)

CONNECTION QUESTION IN TEXT (p. 514) WITH ANSWER

1. Consider the treatment of the writing teacher in this poem, Halliday's "Graded Paper" (p. 507), and Wakefield's "In a Poetry Workshop" (p. 509). What do these portraits of teachers have in common? What significant differences do you find?

   All three writing teachers presume to judge their students, ostensibly the writers of the poems. Each poem depends on a certain amount of irony: Although the teachers dismiss their students' abilities and offer poor writing advice, the poems penned by the speakers reveal their talent. And as each poem suggests, the nature of creative writing makes it unteachable in a classroom setting: each poet reveals the futility of trying to give somebody rules for writing poetry. At the same time, however, the teachers in these three poems are portrayed very differently. The "red-lipsticked and silk-scarved" (line 35) professor of Harrison's poem is a famous writer, a diva who disdains her students and cares for nothing but her own work. The teacher of Halliday's "Graded Paper" is more conflicted: After going through a list of faults in his student's poem he reconsiders the nature of the relationship between teacher and student and grants an A-. The teacher of Wakefield's "In a Poetry Workshop" recognizes the unteachability of poetry writing more directly: he (or she) rattles off a list of rules for writing "modern" poetry — no meter, no rhymes, no "Alliteration / and assonance" (6-7), no traditional subjects — while breaking every one of them. Note the different approaches to humor in these three poems as well: Halliday's is a gentle humor that depends on the reader identifying with the teacher's dilemma; Harrison's relies on a childish prank; Wakefield's is an in-joke.

JEFFREY HARRISON, *On "Fork" as a Work of Fiction* (p. 514)

Anticipating a question that probably occurred to many of your students, Harrison insists that the hated teacher (a famous female poet) in "Fork" doesn't really exist. Asking your students whether they believe him or not (and why) can lead to a productive conversation about a poet's voice and intention, as well as the expectations that readers bring to poetry.

20

A Thematic Case Study: Humor and Satire

Students often expect poems to express love or to recall childhood experiences, but they may be less used to the idea of poems using humor. If they do have the misconception that all poems are serious all of the time, they may miss the poet's humor or even suspect that they're misreading when they do encounter something funny. Grouping these poems together calls students' attention to the fact that amusing the reader is one technique among the poet's many means of communicating. These poems cover a wider range of themes than those in the previous two chapters, and they use humor in a number of different ways — from the setup/punch-line structure to an extended series of puns. What brings them all together is a willingness to question orthodoxies and to see the ridiculous in ordinary situations.

FLEUR ADCOCK, *The Video* (p. 517)

Adcock sets up the two main players in the first line of her poem: Ceri and her new baby sister, Laura. Though their parents and aunt and the midwife figure into the poem, the real drama occurs between the two children. Adcock reserves the humor in this poem until the last line, in which technology makes it possible to do what many children have wanted to do with their new siblings, make them "go back in" (line 12). The simplicity of this pretend disappearance underlines the real difficulty of sibling relationships. It also mimics the child's understanding of the world, in which things happen quickly and causes are unknown. If she could suddenly have a little sister, and her mother could suddenly go back to her pre-pregnancy body, then why couldn't the new baby be taken away just as easily?

POSSIBLE CONNECTIONS TO OTHER SELECTIONS

William Blake, "Infant Sorrow" (text p. 587)
Mary Jo Salter, "Home Movies: A Sort of Ode" (text p. 260; question 1, following)

CONNECTION QUESTION IN TEXT (p. 518) WITH ANSWER

1. Compare the treatment of family life and the purpose of home videos in "The Video" and in Mary Jo Salter's "Home Movies: A Sort of Ode" (p. 260).

   In "The Video" the home movie is used in a common way, to capture an important event in the life of the family. In this case, the video documents the birth of a new baby. Though the older sister, Ceri, wishes the baby hadn't come along to disrupt her life, the video does bring the members of the family together in their shared history. Rewinding it can't remove the memory of Laura's birth. The videos in Salter's poem don't serve the same documentary purpose. Her father begins by recording "Christmases, the three-layer cakes / ablaze with birthday candles, the blizzard / Billy took a shovel to" (lines 3–5), but then he turns to abstract subjects that appear separate from family life. These videos are more "artistic or universal" (14), but they don't reflect the particular experiences of the family members.

JOHN CIARDI, *Suburban* (p. 518)

In "Suburban," Ciardi satirizes the artificial behavior of those who live in the suburbs. Note that Mrs. Friar seems unable to look at or refer to by name the object that incites her to phone the poet — the word *turd* does not occur until the final stanza, when the poet is returning to his own property. Ask students to compare Ciardi's perception of the turd — "organic gold" (line 11) — to Mrs. Friar's — "a large repulsive object" (5). What does the difference indicate about their contrasting worldviews?

How do the poet's tone and behavior alter when he crosses the property line? His attitude when Mrs. Friar first asks him to come over and remove the offending object — a humorous observation that his dog is in another state — is contrasted with his behavior in Mrs. Friar's yard, as he scoops and bows (16). How would Mrs. Friar have responded if Ciardi had shared his vision of what his dog, his son, and his son's girlfriend were doing in Vermont? How would she have responded if he had refused to come over? If Ciardi lacks any respect for the pseudodelicate sensibilities of his suburban neighbors, why does he humor them and conform to their accepted behavior in this instance?

Suburban neighborhoods are noted for being well organized and highly developed; like them, the first four stanzas of the poem conform to a single pattern (note the perfect, standard indentation of the second and fourth lines in each). Yet the final line of the poem stands alone, beyond the conformity of the preceding stanzas. As Ciardi seems to be alone in his ability to accept the "turd" as an aspect of "real life," so this final line presents a different aspect of the suburbs. Ask students to assess the tonal shift and meaning of this final, isolated line, which provides a key to much of the preceding material.

POSSIBLE CONNECTIONS TO OTHER SELECTIONS

Louis Simpson, "In the Suburbs" (text p. 100)
John Updike, "Dog's Death" (text p. 24; question 1, following)

CONNECTION QUESTION IN TEXT (p. 518) WITH ANSWER

1. Compare the speakers' voices in "Suburban" and in Updike's "Dog's Death" (p. 24).

   The speaker of Ciardi's poem is much more satirical than Updike's speaker, which is consistent with the subject matter of each. There is something raw and honest about the way Updike's speaker approaches his topic, but Ciardi's speaker has his tongue in his cheek throughout the poem, emphasizing the "I said" and "she said" of his story to comic effect. The settings of the poems are similar, but the comic presence of Mrs. Friar in this poem and the tragic death of the dog in Updike's poem alter the tones of each considerably.

AUDIOVISUAL RESOURCES (manual p. 373)

DAISY FRIED, *Wit's End* (p. 519)

You might begin by discussing the double meaning of Fried's title. It has the colloquial sense of being fed up, as the father in the poem is with his daughter's new make-up habits. It also suggests that the vanity implied in the bathroom rituals is in some way the opposite of or beyond wit. How do your students read the relationship of physical beauty and intellect in this poem? The narrator's "mooning," "sighing" (line 26) and "singing stupid / love songs" (27–28) seem to suggest that preoccupation with looks makes her act silly. Furthermore, the father's use of the word "civilization" (2) implies that the young girl has traded better pursuits for "mirrors and sinks" (2).

As the narrator observes, however, what really bothers the father is "makeup's pre-monition / of sex" (8–9). The daughter's maturing body becomes a barrier between the father and the "used-to-be-lovable 12-year-old / formerly his" (16–17). The mask of make-up, the profusion of bras, and finally, his daughter's shaved leg, hold him at a distance.

Possible Connections to Other Selections

Rachel Hadas, "The Compact" (text p. 177)
Li Ho, "A Beautiful Girl Combs Her Hair" (text p. 56; question 1, following)
Sylvia Plath, "Mirror" (text p. 145; question 2, following)
Cathy Song, "Sunworshippers" (text p. 146)

Connections Questions in Text (p. 520) with Answers

1. Compare the tone and theme of "Wit's End" with that of Li Ho's "A Beautiful Girl Combs Her Hair" (p. 56).

   Both of these poems express a sense of loss that comes with a child's maturing into adulthood. They both focus on vanity as evidence that the girls are no longer children. However, Li Ho writes from the perspective of an observer. Like the father in "Wit's End," he is frustrated by the elaborate beauty ritual he witnesses, and he is shut off at the end from knowing where the girl is going. Fried's poem is written from the girl's point of view, and the narrator is the one who actively shuts the door on her father's obtrusive comments. Fried's tone though is somewhat cynical since she is reflecting on a younger version of herself. She seems both to defend her vanity and to understand her father's criticism. The tone of Li Ho's poem is much more celebratory. Although the girl's "slovenly beauty upsets" (24) him, the careful description of that beauty suggests that he appreciates it as well.

2. How might the daughter in "Wit's End" be considered a youthful version of the speaker in Sylvia Plath's "Mirror" (p. 145)?

   The young girl's preoccupation with making herself attractive foreshadows the self-criticism Plath illustrates in "Mirror." Plath also suggests that the young girl will be consumed by the mirror as the older version of her emerges. In Plath's poem the mirror's absolute objectivity, "unmisted by love or dislike" (line 3), relates to the daughter's rejection of her father's assessment in "Wit's End." The father's love prevents him from seeing his daughter clearly, so she has to look to the mirror to see, as Plath says, "what she really is" (11). Though Fried's poem is largely lighthearted, the more grave implications of "Mirror" shadow words like "pained" (4), "snarls" (11), and "welts" (18).

RONALD WALLACE, *In a Rut* (p. 520)

Wallace uses his series of folk expressions to describe an exchange between a man and woman, but in the play of finding new animal metaphors to continue the description, the actual events of the poem become secondary. Wallace reveals the commonness of the scene but also the natural human tendency to describe our experiences in terms of what we see in the natural world. By watching each of these animals, people have observed traits that remind them of human behavior, and the comparisons have been so useful in talking about humans that they have taken on the status of clichés. "In a Rut" shows how people can embody all of these traits, even in the space of a few minutes. The move toward generalization in the last line, where the woman insists that the narrator is "a real animal" (line 45), emphasizes the figurative work of all these common sayings.

Billie Bolton, "Memorandum" (text p. 499)

E. E. Cummings, "next to of course god america i" (text p. 163; question 1, following)

Anthony Hecht, "The Dover Bitch" (text p. 529)

CONNECTION QUESTION IN TEXT (p. 521) WITH ANSWER

1. Compare Wallace's organizing strategy in this poem and E. E. Cummings technique in "next to of course god america i" (p. 163).

    Wallace's poem proceeds through his series of animal metaphors that have become common speech. Nearly every line contains some comparison in it. Wallace also groups the animals, so that saying "I give her something to crow about" (line 37) leads him to other bird metaphors like "*lovey-dove*" (38), "odd ducks" (39), and "swan- / song" (40–41). Cummings organizes "next to of course god america i" in a similar way, by incorporating language from patriotic songs and sayings. As in Wallace's poem, each phrase seems to remind Cummings of another, but here they occur so quickly that they begin to bleed into one another. In the course of a few lines (2–4), Cummings echoes "Let Freedom Ring," "The Star-Spangled Banner," and "My Country 'Tis of Thee." Rather than reinvigorating these clichés, Cummings emphasizes their emptiness.

HOWARD NEMEROV, *Walking the Dog* (p. 521)

Partly a paean to his dog and partly a rumination on the nature of power, this poem compares "two universes" (line 1): the human and the canine. Some of the details suggest that the human world is the more evolved of the two: man puts the dog on a leash (2), man looks heavenward while the dog inspects the ground (3–4), and of course man "write[s] the poem" (24). But other instances in the poem imply that the dog is actually the master: it determines the pace of the walk, forcing "patience" (10) from the man; it has a "secret knowledge" (5); it is the one who teaches (13); it has a "keener sense" (14). Most significant, the dog causes the man to question whether he really is the "master" (24), whereas the animal presumably has no doubts about the nature of the relationship.

You might want to start class discussion by asking students whether or not dog waste is an appropriate subject for a poem. Some, undoubtedly, will find the subject tasteless and unworthy of any kind of literary attention; others may read deeper meanings into it, perhaps even interpreting the poem itself as the author's own output of shit, as the last line implies. Is shit a metaphor for something else? The first two stanzas of the poem, with their emphasis on "universes" (1) and the relationship between two "symbionts" (11) — or separate entities that are interdependent — privilege a heady interpretation. But the second two stanzas focus on physical, indeed, repugnant — elements of life.

Another possibility for approaching the poem is to explore its comparisons of human civilization and the natural world. Do humans control nature, or does it control them? Which has more to teach, according to the poem, and which has more to learn?

POSSIBLE CONNECTIONS TO OTHER SELECTIONS

John Ciardi, "Suburban" (text p. 518; question 1, following)

Ronald Wallace, "Building an Outhouse" (text p. 152; question 2, following)

CONNECTIONS QUESTIONS IN TEXT (p. 522) WITH ANSWERS

1. Discuss the speakers' attitudes toward the dogs in "Walking the Dog" and in John Ciardi's "Suburban" (p. 518). How does humor inform those attitudes?

The attitude toward the dog in "Suburban" is made apparent in contrast with the stuffy neighbor. While she claims "'I have always loved dogs'" (line 15) she acts repulsed by them. The speaker ironically restates her position when he says "The animal of it" (16). In fact, the speaker values the animal nature of the dog including the "organic gold" (11) it provides his garden. In this poem, Ciardi suggests that there is something unnatural, or even antinatural, in suburban life. The problems of suburbaintes can largely be attributed to their humorless rejection of anything that doesn't fit their rigid conceptions of order.

2. Consider the subject matter of this poem and Ronald Wallace's "Building an Outhouse" (text p. 152). Some readers might argue that the subject matter is taste-less and not suitable for poetic treatment. What do you think?

These poems may be blunter than some in the way they deal with excrement, but they both address a broad theme that many poems address: the idea that we can celebrate beauty but can't thereby ignore the rest of life. Wallace's first line, which breaks after the word "pure," seems to suggest some pious ideas about what is poetic. He reveals, though, that poetry isn't at all as easy as the "mathematics of shape; the music of hammer" (line 2). The artist has to struggle though setbacks in order to produce the final, "Functional" (12) object. In Nemerov's poem, the speaker becomes the one who is impatient, while the dog has the kind of curiosity we expect in poets. His incessant sniffing provides him "a secret knowledge" (line 5), and he has taught his owner to take an "interest in shit" (14). In the last line, Nemerov draws a parallel between the dog's excretion, which is his response to the world, and the poetic act of creation.

LINDA PASTAN, *Jump Cabling* (p. 522)

In this poem, Pastan uses form to humorous effect, shaping her lines to mimic the activity of jump-starting a car. The two columns represent the two vehicles, which are, at the end, joined by the current through the jumper cables. They also represent the figu-rative connection that brings the two people to "ride the rest of the way together" (line 8). The sexual suggestion in the poem is reinforced by the language used to describe the cars, the "intimate workings   underneath" (3) and the "pulse of pure   energy" (5). In this way, Pastan exploits a common association of cars with sex, elaborating on the general idea to find a more specific figure for the initial attraction between strangers.

POSSIBLE CONNECTIONS TO OTHER SELECTIONS

E. E. Cummings, "she being Brand" (text p. 73; question 1, following)
Jane Kenyon, "The Shirt" (text p. 496)
Sonia Sanchez, "c'mon man hold me" (text p. 255)

CONNECTION QUESTION IN TEXT (p. 523) WITH ANSWER

1. Compare the style and theme of Pastan's poem with that of E. E. Cummings's "she being Brand" (p. 73).

Both Pastan and Cummings use typography to express the hesitations and acceler-ations of the beginning of a romance. Cummings uses punctuation to break up lines like "again slo-wly;bare,ly nudg. ing" (line 15), suggesting a tentativeness before the poem speeds up. Pastan inserts extra space in her lines to mirror the dis-tance between the strangers which will be bridged at the end of the poem. In Cummings's, however, only one of the figures is compared to a car, which creates a power differential. The female is controlled throughout the poem by the male fig-ure of the driver. In "Jump Cabling," both figures are compared to cars, and the cru-cial element becomes the cables that carry the current between them.

PETER SCHMITT, *Friends with Numbers* (p. 523)

Schmitt's imagining of the actions and personalities of numbers seems to begin as an exercise, but toward the end, it becomes a meditation on the difficulty of finding love. He begins by saying the numbers are "not hard to get to know" (line 1), but it becomes clear that two is, in fact, hard, not only to find but to maintain, as it "seems on the verge, / yet, of always coming apart" (24–25). You might call your students' attention to the fact that Schmitt refers to the numbers as "he" until he gets to two, which he characterizes as female. His wry last line suggests that though he has "friends in numbers" (line 29) he lacks the only one that matters.

POSSIBLE CONNECTION TO ANOTHER SELECTION

Kate Clanchy, "Spell" (text p. 128; question 1, following)

CONNECTION QUESTION IN TEXT (p. 524) WITH ANSWER

1. Discuss the originality — the fresh and unusual approach to their respective subject matter — in Schmitt's poem and in Kate Clanchy's "Spell" (p. 128). What makes these poems so interesting?

    Both "Friends with Numbers" and "Spell" deal with subject matter common to poetry — love and loneliness. However, both writers use figurative language not usually associated with these subjects to cast them in a new light. In lamenting his solitary condition, Schmitt imagines a cast of characters to keep him company. His personification of the numbers is funny and surprising, but when he gets to the numbers 1 and 2, we realize that his clever observations have been ways of talking around loneliness. By the last line, he's given new meaning to the phrase "in numbers." In a similar way, Clanchy goes beyond standard formulations that say we can read someone "like a book" or have a life "like an open book." In "Spell," both she and her lover aren't just like books, they actually take on some of their physical attributes. She also complicates our notions of storybook romance as these two people become conflated in the acts of reading and being read about. In both cases, the surprise of the poem comes from the new way of describing a familiar sentiment.

MARTÍN ESPADA, *The Community College Revises Its Curriculum in Response to Changing Demographics* (p. 524)

Espada uses administrative language and the conventions of college course listings to make this satirical comment on perceptions of Spanish speakers. The straightforward beginning of his poem takes a turn when the course aligns itself with the needs of the police. We tend to think of higher education providing pure knowledge, unaffected by ideology, but here Espada reminds us that colleges can't remain completely apart from politics. The "matters of interest" (line 7) to those in power can infiltrate educational institutions as well.

POSSIBLE CONNECTIONS TO OTHER SELECTIONS

Langston Hughes, "Theme for English B" (text p. 502)
Donald Justice, "Order in the Streets" (text p. 287; question 1, following)
Gary Soto, "Mexicans Begin Jogging" (text p. 525)

CONNECTION QUESTION IN TEXT (p. 524) WITH ANSWER

1. Compare the themes in Espada's poem and in Donald Justice's "Order in the Streets" (p. 287).

The neutral title Espada chooses for this poem belies, but also underscores, its pointed political commentary. The language of both title and poem mimics that of college catalogs and brochures. It sounds purely informational but actually contains significant clues about the values and biases of the curriculum planners. Here, those values include police-enforced order at the expense of fairness to all citizens. The suggestion of the course description is that any matters conducted in Spanish would be of interest to the police.

Like Espada, Justice uses a form of public language in his poem. As we see in the epigraph, these statements are from the instructions to a child's toy. Like a course catalog, they reveal much more about the society that produced them than might first be apparent. Also, as in Espada's poem, there is little human agency in "Order in the Streets." All of the enforcing work in this poem is attributed to the Jeep, which is controlled not by a driver but by "mystery action" (line 8). The return to headquarters at the end of the poem suggests a larger power directing military action, but this power is removed from the mechanistic actions of "putting down riot" (14).

M. CARL HOLMAN, *Mr. Z* (p. 524)

Students will readily perceive the irony of this poem: The man who lived so that his racial identity was all but obliterated earned as his summary obituary the reductive, faint, and defaming praise "One of the most distinguished members of his race." His loss is a double loss, to be sure; not only did he fail finally to be judged according to white standards (those he aspired to) but in the process of living up to those standards he "flourish[ed] without [the] roots" of his own racial identity. Review the poem for its ironic phrases. You may have to explain that racial, religious, and ethnic differences were often suppressed in favor of assimilation and that the celebration of and return to these differences is a relatively recent tendency.

POSSIBLE CONNECTIONS TO OTHER SELECTIONS

Langston Hughes, "Cross" (text p. 403)
——, "Dinner Guest: Me" (text p. 415; question 1, following)
Janice Mirikitani, "Recipe" (text p. 547; question 2, following)
Pat Mora, "Legal Alien" (text p. 540)

CONNECTIONS QUESTIONS IN TEXT (p. 525) WITH ANSWERS

1. Compare the satirical treatment of race in "Mr. Z" and in Langston Hughes's "Dinner Guest: Me" (p. 415).

   In Holman's poem, the title character is the focus of the satire. Though Holman seems sympathetic to Mr. Z's choices, the poem demonstrates that attempting to become "raceless" (line 5) is futile. In spite of Mr. Z's careful avoidance of any markers of African American identity, he is still identified after his death by his race. The irony of this ending is that what the obituary writers frame as a compliment actually perpetuates the destructive racial categorization Mr. Z tried to avoid.

   In Hughes's poem, the "Me" of the title is entirely aware of this irony of African American life, as we see in his sarcastic phrase "darkness U.S.A." (line 9). Unlike Mr. Z, he is happy to accept the hospitality of people who see him as exotic, but he has no illusions about how they will respond to the "Problem" of African American identity.

2. Discuss the preference for "Anglo-Saxonized" (line 8) appearances in "Mr. Z" and in Janice Mirikitani's "Recipe" (p. 547).

Mr. Z's desire to cling to "Anglo-Saxonized" views is an issue of propriety and social conduct. Though he's been taught that "his mother's skin was the sign of error" (line 1), he's less concerned with physical appearances than with manners. In response to social pressures, he looks to the "best schools" (3) and the "right addresses" (17), which he thinks will give him the status he desires. In Mirikitani's poem we see the strictures of white American culture as they apply specifically to ideas about beauty. The young woman in "Recipe" goes through an involved and painful process in order to create "Round Eyes" (line 1). Though the prescriptive norms about physical appearance have also affected men, they have usually been most destructive for women. It's telling that in "Mr. Z," physical traits come more directly into play with his wife, who "lost her Jewishness, / But kept her blue eyes" (14–15).

GARY SOTO, *Mexicans Begin Jogging* (p. 525)

Born in America but mistaken for a Mexican, the speaker of this poem is encouraged by his factory boss to run out the back door and across the Mexican border when the border patrol arrives. Rather than protest, the speaker runs along with a number of Mexicans, yelling *vivas* to the land of "baseball, milkshakes, and those sociologists" (line 18) who are apparently keeping track of demographics.

It is noteworthy that the speaker doesn't protest his boss's orders but joins the throng of jogging Mexicans because he is "on [the boss's] time" (11). Why wouldn't he simply stand his ground and show proof that he is a U.S. citizen? The key may lie in the word "wag" (12), which describes a comic person or wit in addition to its familiar associations with movement: to move from side to side (as in "tail") or even to depart. The speaker's parting gesture, after all, is "a great silly grin" (21). The joke is on the boss, or the border patrol, or on America in general with its paranoid sociologists. Although the tone is somewhat comic, the subject is serious, whether students take it to be the exploitation of workers from developing nations, or prejudice based on appearance (i.e., the speaker is taken to be Mexican because he looks like he is). What effect does the tone have on a consideration of these subjects? Is there a "point" to his irony?

Ask students to explore contexts for Gary Soto on *LiterActive*.

Possible Connections to Other Selections

Julio Marzán, "The Translator at the Reception for Latin American Writers" (text p. 280)
Peter Meinke, "The ABC of Aerobics" (text p. 285; question 1, following)

Connection to Another Selection (p. 526) with Answer

1. Compare the speakers' ironic attitudes toward exercise in this poem and in Peter Meinke's "The ABC of Aerobics" (p. 285).

   Whereas each poem uses running as a vehicle for meditation, Gary Soto's speaker runs to avoid the border patrol, and the speaker of "The ABC of Aerobics" exercises for exercise's sake. For each speaker, exercise is somewhat futile: Soto's speaker doesn't really need to be running, as he is an American, and Meinke's speaker comes to realize that if he had love, it would replace the exercise. (Meinke's speaker spends lines 1–16 discussing how, regardless of exercise, the city's air is still filthy, and how it does him little good anyway because of "tobacco, lard and bourbon" [12].)

BOB HICOK, *Spam leaves an aftertaste* (p. 526)

Prompted by receiving an impersonal and disembodied e-mail regarding the most personal part of his body, the speaker of this poem finds himself questioning modern life and human isolation. In the end, he longs for human contact and, ironically, sends an impersonal and disembodied plea for interpersonal connection into the "digital ether."

In addition to irony, this poem relies heavily on symbolism. On a larger scale, the Internet serves as a symbol of the modern world; unsolicited e-mails ("spam") as a symbol of disconnectedness and lack of communication. There are smaller symbols as well: the small penis of inadequate manhood (lines 2 and 35), for example, and the cosmic "ether" that dulls physical sensation (10), as well as federally subsidized trains that kill romance (13–15) and distant "stars" of an impersonal universe (28).

The poem's subject matter is sure to engage your students, who are quite familiar with the Internet and spamlike messages. Many of your computer-savvy students are likely to question why the poem's speaker doesn't use a filter to eliminate unwanted messages (almost all e-mail programs offer this feature); others may raise the idea of instant messaging as an example of disembodied communication that allows for interpersonal connection. Take advantage of the solutions they offer for the speaker's situation to explore how poets choose their details. Why doesn't Hicok recognize the availability of filters, for example? Perhaps the speaker is so desperate for human contact that he doesn't want to eliminate any of it. Encourage your students to identify other details (those included and those left out) that help Hicok zero in on the theme of his poem.

Possible Connections to Other Selections

T. S. Eliot, "The Love Song of J. Alfred Prufrock" (text p. 456; question 1, following)

Robert Frost, "Mending Wall" (text p. 359)

Tony Hoagland, "America" (text p. 561; question 2, following)

William Wordsworth, "The World Is Too Much with Us" (text p. 242)

Connections Questions in Text (p. 527) with Answers

1. How might Hicok's poem be considered a latter-day version of T. S. Eliot's "The Love Song of J. Alfred Prufrock" (p. 456)?

   Like "Prufrock," Hicok's poem documents anxiety about the self among the comings and goings of modern life. Hicock translates this bustling to the new world of e-mail which is constantly confronting him with new impressions of himself. The suggestion of physical inadequacies in the e-mail "offer of a larger penis" (line 2) echoes Prufrock's concerns about aging. Another e-mail offers to tell the speaker of "Spam leaves an aftertaste," "anything about anyone" (12), which prompts questions about his own existence and reason for being. Significantly, both poems end with the speakers being caught up in communication with other people. However, in "Prufrock," the "human voices" (131) recall the speaker from his dream state to drown in reality. In Hicok's poem, on the other hand, he wants to retain communication, but can't as the voices become unintelligible, "making the sounds once known / as conversation" (38–40).

2. Discuss the perspective on American contemporary life implicit in "Spam leaves an aftertaste" with respect to the view offered in Tony Hoagland's "America" (p. 561).

   Hicok's poem leaves us feeling that contemporary life is shallow and meaningless. Much of the humor of the poem comes from the absurdity of responding to spam with questions like "who am I, why am I here" (line 13), but this irony also points out the widening gap between popular culture and any sense of spirituality. "America" also concerns the way that media glosses over the deeper questions people have about life. In this poem, a student advances the view that American culture is all surface, and at first the speaker is suspicious that he is just repeating commonplaces about the oppressive quality of material culture. However, through recalling a dream, he comes to see some truth in the student's view. Unlike Hicok, who tries to challenge the dominant culture, Hoagland implicates himself in its callous materialism. At the end, he responds to to the cries of those displaced by American culture by "[turning] the volume higher" (36).

THOMAS LUX, *Commercial Leech Farming Today* (p. 528)

The irony of Lux's statement that there is "a living / in leeches" (lines 3–4) summarizes the appeal the topic has for him. The resurrection of a practice once considered barbaric in order to further the image-obsessed ends of plastic surgery is a fascinating reversal. You might have your students analyze how Lux uses the language of the medical profession and of the industry that supports it in his poem. His use of abbreviations such as "wrinkle erad" (11) and "temp control" (23) suggests that the poet is very comfortable within the world of medical terminology. However, the ease of his language and his delight in the science of the leech cover his ambivalence about the procedures for which the leeches are used and the "capitalist / spirit" (13–14) that can profit even from what seems repulsive.

POSSIBLE CONNECTIONS TO OTHER SELECTIONS

Emily Dickinson, "'Faith' is a fine invention" (text p. 343)

Alice Jones, "The Foot" (text p. 222; question 1, following)

Pablo Neruda, "The United Fruit Co." (text p. 577)

CONNECTION QUESTION IN TEXT (p. 529) WITH ANSWER

1. Discuss the perspectives on human vanity offered in Lux's poem and in Alice Jones's "The Foot" (p. 222).

> In both poems, the body is described in scientific terms that hold off aesthetic judgment of the subject. Jones focuses first on the bone structure of the foot and then describes in precise but grotesque detail the fat, skin, and hair that cover it. She departs from anatomical description only to emphasize that the foot is "humble" (line 9) as it keeps us grounded to the earth and to recall that the foot once supported a functional claw. Similarly unsentimental, Lux discusses the farming of leeches in terms of the processes used to raise them and the chemistry behind their work. The image of the leeches in his poem also emphasizes the contrast between beauty and the sometimes repulsive ways that we obtain it. Both of these writers use scientific language to cut through the typical views of the body that vanity inspires.

ANTHONY HECHT, *The Dover Bitch* (p. 529)

The subtitle of this poem is "A Criticism of Life," and Hecht indirectly makes his criticism by having as a backdrop Matthew Arnold's "Dover Beach" (text p. 115). That poem, too, was a criticism of society, of declining religious values and the disappearance of a moral center. The tone of this poem is initially amusing; the young woman is not going to be treated "as a sort of mournful cosmic last resort." She desires a relationship more carnal than platonic. The speaker obliges her, and now, in what seems to be a continuing casual relationship, he occasionally brings her perfume, called *Nuit d'Amour*. At the edges of this poem we still hear the sound of Arnold's armies of the night, a reminiscence that doesn't make the current times seem so much worse but does make our moral comprehension of them so much more slight and haphazard.

Matthew Arnold, "Dover Beach" (text p. 115; question 1, following)

Peter De Vries, "To His Importunate Mistress" (text p. 262)

CONNECTION QUESTION IN TEXT (p. 530) WITH ANSWER

1. What does a comparison of the speakers' diction in "The Dover Bitch" and in "Dover Beach" (p. 115) reveal about the tone of each poem?

   The diction in "Dover Beach" stays close to what most people would expect from a poem. Arnold describes the landscape with an elegiac quality, and the emotions of the poem are heightened as he moves toward the despairing ending. By contrast, Hecht's diction in "The Dover Bitch" is casual and speechlike. It contributes to his deflating of the drama of Arnold's poem and gives life to the other character, the woman Arnold speaks to, who we never hear in "Dover Beach." Phrases like "really felt sad" (line 13) and "really tough on a girl" (19) sound as much like her talking as the speaker, and suggest that while the distraught lover of "Dover Beach" sees the world as a tragedy, his "love" (line 29) has a more moderate view.

CATHERINE WING, *Paradise-Un* (p. 530)

Working from Milton's alternate title, Wing rewrites the story of the expulsion from Paradise through the insistent use of the prefix un-. Not only does she find an un- word for each line of the poem, but she also frequently uses rhyme or slant rhyme to bring out the thematic relationships between concepts: "unfastened" (line 7) and "unhastened" (9), "unwound" (4) and "unbound" (12), "unappled" (17) and "unabled" (18). At first the uns emphasize the newness of the world and the lack of pain or self-consciousness. However, with the appearance of the serpent and the turn of the poem, the uns describe the fall of Adam and Eve and the beginning of their life outside of Eden.

POSSIBLE CONNECTION TO OTHER SELECTIONS

Anna Akhmatova, "Lot's Wife" (text p. 570)

May Swenson, "A Nosty Fright" (text p. 186; question 1, following)

CONNECTION QUESTION IN TEXT (p. 531) WITH ANSWER

1. Consider the ways in which "Paradise-Un" and "A Nosty Fright" by May Swenson (text p. 186) demonstrate a kind of wild delight in language and its sounds.

   Both Wing's and Swenson's poems play freely with language to create effects that straight prose would not accommodate. The fun of coming up with un-words leads Wing to new ways of understanding the story of the Fall. Some of these words are standard English, such as "unaccompanied" (line 1) and "unashamed" (15). Others, like "unfallen" (10) and "unparadized" (22), are her coinages. The mixture of familiar and unfamiliar forms forces the reader to question all of the un- words and emphasizes how the negations they contain can characterize the story of Adam and Eve's expulsion from Eden. Swenson's poem also makes the reader reflect on how he or she receives language. At first glance, "A Nosty Fright" looks like nonsense, but after a few lines, we quickly learn to read through Swenson's transpositions. Although many of the words in the poem are meaningless, the reader can still fashion a narrative. In addition to being fun to read out loud, Swenson's poem makes the reader think about how meaning is communicated.

ANN LAUINGER, *Marvell Noir* (p. 531)

In this poem, Lauinger transports Marvell's carpe diem into the crime-filled world of film noir. Instead of feeling rushed by impending death, the speaker in "Marvell Noir" feels the pressure of the police who will come to take away his "Sweetheart" (line 1). By recounting the woman's story in broad outline, Lauinger calls on some of the typical aspects of the crime movie, especially the character of the femme fatale. As the female poet takes on a male voice, she can more effectively satirize Marvell's original plea to his lover. At the same time, she critiques how women are portrayed in noir movies as both tragic "angel face[s]" (19) and dangerous sexual predators. You might have your class discuss where their sympathies lie after they've read the poem. The woman is clearly a perpetrator, but is the speaker innocent? What does the language he uses suggest about him?

POSSIBLE CONNECTIONS TO OTHER SELECTIONS

Peter DeVries, "To His Importunate Mistress" (text p. 262; question 1, following)
Anthony Hecht, "The Dover Bitch" (text p. 529)
Andrew Marvell, "To His Coy Mistress" (text p. 81; question 1, following)

CONNECTION QUESTION IN TEXT (p. 532) **WITH ANSWER**

1. Compare the speaker's voice in this poem with the respective speakers in Marvell's "To His Coy Mistress" (p. 81) and Peter DeVries's "To His Importunate Mistress" (p. 262). Explain which parody you prefer — Lauinger's or DeVries's.

   Though some of Marvell's language is unfamiliar to modern readers, the voice in his poem is not rarified. While his mistress remains standoffish, his plea has to be direct and immediate. Even when he talks about abstract concepts like eternity, he invents metaphors to give them a physical presence, as he does in the last lines: "Thus, though we cannot make our sun / Stand still, yet we will make him run" (lines 45–46). Lauinger's parody of the poem attempts to retain this down-to-earth voice, but translate it into the modern idiom of film noir. The voice in her poem is worldly, slangy, and straightforward. The sentences are short and declarative, largely avoiding figurative language. As in "To His Coy Mistress" they suggest a speaker who sees beyond romanticized ideas about love. De Vries takes a different approach in his parody. Rather than updating Marvell's language, he keeps much of it to give his poem a courtly feeling, emphasizing his deference to the mistress. In a contemporary poem, this comes off as formal, but the speaker's voice here is ironic. The mistress is the one who's actually making the demands, and the speaker is aware that he can't meet them.

CHARLES BUKOWSKI, *poetry readings* (p. 532)

Bukowski's poetry appeals to many students because of his stature as an iconoclast. They will find the challenge to authority here as they realize that Bukowski uses his poem to critique the workings of the poetry world. One way to approach his view of the reading would be to discuss the people he endorses at the end. What unites plumbers, waitresses, and drunks as a contrast to the poets?

You might have students discuss how Bukowski's decision not to capitalize at the beginning of this poem and his idiosyncratic punctuation contribute to his depiction of the poetry reading. How does the mood change when he reaches the three capital *I*s in lines 29–31? Does Bukowski's assertion of selfhood provide an alternative to the poetry reading scene he describes?

This would also be an interesting poem to discuss after your students had attended a real poetry reading. Do their observations of the crowd reinforce Bukowski's, or would they argue that he's being too harsh?

Possible Connections to Other Selections

Emily Dickinson, "This was a Poet — It is That" (text p. 323)
Bob Hicok, "Making it in poetry" (text p. 165)
Richard Wakefield, "In a Poetry Workshop" (text p. 509; question 1, following)

Connection Question in Text (p. 533) with Answer

1. Describe how poets and poems are represented in "poetry readings" and in Richard Wakefield's "In a Poetry Workshop" (p. 509). What do the two poems have in common in terms of their perspective on the contemporary poetry scene?

   Bukowski is skeptical, and even derisive, about the poetry world, which he sees as entirely insular and out of touch with reality. He prefers the straightforward work of plumbers and waitresses to the work of poetry, which seems to have no purpose. Wakefield is not quite so cynical about contemporary poetry, but he does chafe at the restrictive rules that some people want to place on it, which are in fact antirules. They say that poems shouldn't be too poetic in their sound patterns or their subjects. Wakefield believes that in rejecting the practices of earlier generations, contemporary poets have gotten to a point where only pretense structures their work. However, he has the last word by writing this poem in rhyme.

21

A Thematic Case Study: Border Crossings

The poems in this section deal in varied ways with the divisions that determine identity, both geographically marked and socially constructed. The photographs and drawings that accompany them provide several opportunities to discuss with your students the differences between reading a poem and "reading" an image. With any of the pairings in this chapter, you could call attention to the ways that visual information is communicated. Poems often rely heavily on visual imagery, but that imagery is mediated by words instead of being represented directly. You might ask your students to describe the different experiences they get from reading a poem and looking at a photograph or painting. Which do they think is better at creating an impression? How does poetry engage the senses other than sight? These questions might lead into a discussion of the themes of the chapter. How much of what determines borders is purely visual? What other factors are involved?

Web Ask students to research the poets in this unit at **bedfordstmartins.com/ meyerpoetry**.

TRANSCENDENCE AND BORDERS

PHILLIS WHEATLEY, *On Being Brought from Africa to America* (p. 537)

Diagram: **An Eighteenth-Century Slave Ship** (p. 536)

Advertisement: **A 1784 Slave Auction Poster** (p. 537)

Phillis Wheatley was born in West Africa, kidnapped in 1761, and brought to Boston as a slave. Her owners, John and Susannah Wheatley, were impressed with Phillis's intelligence and taught her along with their own children how to read and write in English, Latin, and Greek. Her only book, *Poems on Various Subjects*, received international acclaim. Though she died in poverty, her poems held significance for members of the abolition movement as well as aspiring African American writers.

You might want to begin classroom discussion by asking students what they know about the slave trade and the Atlantic passage. Once they've discussed the treatment of slaves in early America, confront them with what for Wheatley's poem is a big question: Why would an intelligent, articulate slave woman writing about racism say so little about the horrors of slavery itself?

Students might also wonder about Wheatley's accommodating tone. Certainly, she refers to her native Africa as "pagan" and to her "benighted" race as an unrefined one. Remind students of the time in which Wheatley wrote and the restrictions imposed on her as a woman writer of color. After a close reading, it becomes clear that Wheatley's poem is an open indictment of racism as well as a request for understanding. Indeed, the poem offers a revealing look at early American attitudes — the necessity of faith and redemption, the inherent "evil" of dark skin, and the importance of the Cain and Abel story as an argument for the enslavement of African men, women, and children. Point

252

students toward Wheatley's ambivalent stance — though she is challenging white attitudes, she is also embracing their religion, language, and literary style. By so fully aligning herself with American ideals, Wheatley effectively disproves contemporary arguments that black slaves were less than human and incapable of existing on an intellectual or emotional par with whites, indeed, that they were unable even to take care of themselves and needed white oversight to ensure their physical survival. Late eighteenth-century assumptions that Africans were subhuman creatures are painfully illustrated in the way they were packed into ships' cargo holds as well as by advertisements that described them as though they were farm animals.

POSSIBLE CONNECTION TO ANOTHER SELECTION

Frances E. W. Harper, "Learning to Read" (text p. 601)

RACE AND BORDERS

WOLE SOYINKA, *Telephone Conversation* (p. 538)

Poster: **COLUMBIA PICTURES,** *Guess Who's Coming to Dinner?* (p. 539)

"Telephone Conversation" is a narrative poem that takes a satiric look at the emotionally charged issue of racism. One way to begin discussion of racism (and race in general) is to have your students paraphrase the poem. Student paraphrases will undoubtedly focus on the racial dimensions of the conversation and the racial theme of the poem. In comparing their work to the language of the poem, students may notice several things about the poet's style that are lost in a paraphrase: the short sentences and sentence fragments, the unusual syntax of many lines, the terse language, and the fast pace. After identifying some of these characteristics, you may wish to ask students about their effects on the tone of the poem.

You may want to ask students to do a Marxist reading of this poem. In addition to race, they should consider issues of class, power, and social injustice in Soyinka's poem. Although the poet's deft handling of the account leaves little doubt as to who got in the last word, given the inevitable outcome of the exchange, who seems to have "won," and how?

It may also be interesting to talk about the effect the poet achieves by printing the words of the landlady in capital letters. What are the political implications of this shift? By the end of the poem, what do readers know about the speakers based solely on the words that have passed between them? They may notice, for example, that in asking about degrees of color, the landlady seems to consider herself progressive: the implication is that she would be willing to rent to a light-skinned black — but not to a dark-skinned one. Soyinka exposes her purported liberalism as outright racism, however, much as the liberalism of the parents in *Guess Who's Coming to Dinner?* is questioned when they are confronted with the possibility of their daughter's interracial marriage. If any of your students have seen the movie, ask them how they would connect its themes with those of the poem. Encourage your class, also, to examine closely the imagery of the movie poster. They should be able to determine that like the speaker of Soyinka's poem, Sidney Poitier's character is middle-class. Ask your students how class figures in the story.

POSSIBLE CONNECTIONS TO OTHER SELECTIONS

Langston Hughes, "Ballad of the Landlord" (text p. 408)
Gary Soto, "Mexicans Begin Jogging" (text p. 525)

IDENTITY AND BORDERS

PAT MORA, *Legal Alien* (p. 540)

Image: JACALYN LÓPEZ GARCÍA, *I Just Wanted to Be Me* (p. 541)

Both the artist who created "I Just Wanted to Be Me" and the speaker of Mora's poem consider the liminality of their identities as neither fully Mexican nor fully American (nor fully white). Even the official status of Mora's speaker — legal alien — highlights a lack of belonging to either culture fully. His poem fluctuates between two identities, naming the benefits of biculturalism in the first seven lines, then turning to the personal turmoil occasioned by it in the last fourteen — but always stressing the comparison. Given the percentage of lines given to the speaker's "discomfort" (line 20), the poem's emphasis is clearly on the difficulty the speaker experiences as being partly of both worlds but wholly of neither. Note, too, that the benefits of Americanness outweigh those of Mexicanness: the former gives economic security; the latter merely allows the speaker to say "They are driving me crazy" and to order food in Spanish.

Like Mora, García is conflicted about her bicultural identity — and like his poem, her image fluctuates between two competing perceptions. García juxtaposes her mother's reasons for wanting to raise her children as Americans with her own desires: the daughter "never wanted to be 'white'" suggesting that the mother's hopes of making her child's life simpler only succeeded in complicating it. Ask your students what they think the mother means by "privileges." How do they compare to the advantages described in Mora's poem? What is the daughter's attitude about her mother's desires? About her Mexican heritage?

"Legal Alien" and "I Just Wanted to Be Me" offer a good opportunity to discuss what makes a person American. Consider starting class with a five-minute freewriting assignment that asks students to list the necessary qualities; you may be surprised by their responses, especially if the class is multinational. Segue from the assignment to a debate about whether the speakers of the poem and of the multimedia exhibit are truly American. Is nationalistic pride a prerequisite? What about language? Color? Self-definition? Do the speakers of these pieces identify as American or not?

POSSIBLE CONNECTIONS TO OTHER SELECTIONS

Jimmy Santiago Baca, "Green Chile" (text p. 117)

Chitra Banerjee Divakaruni, "Indian Movie, New Jersey" (text p. 544)

Langston Hughes, "I, Too" (text p. 396)

Julio Marzán, "The Translator at the Reception for Latin American Writers" (text p. 280)

Gary Soto, "Mexicans Begin Jogging" (text p. 525)

IMMIGRATION AND BORDERS

SANDRA M. GILBERT, *Mafioso* (p. 542)

Photograph: **(PHOTOGRAPHER UNKNOWN),** *Baggage Examined Here* (p. 543)

Gilbert's poem focuses on stereotypes of Italian American men to examine the Italian ethnic heritage and finds that those images leave her needing more information. The stereotypes of Italians are conveyed primarily through violence and food. The "half dozen Puritan millionaires" (line 23), who arrived ahead of the Italians and wait onshore to judge the newcomers' fitness as potential Americans, are contrasted with the public images of the "bad uncles" (9) who are represented by the violent and imprisoned gangsters.

The conclusion of the poem contains multiple meanings in the readiness of the Puritans to "grind the organs out of you" (26); brainstorm with your students what some of those meanings might be. Gilbert invokes stereotypical images of Italians to protest the legacy they have left for her speaker. It is, presumably, the "Puritan millionaires" who had already established control over the country who stood ready to stereotype the Italians. Gilbert's imagined relationship between those millionaires and the new immigrants is compellingly portrayed in the photograph "Baggage Examined Here." In it, an Ellis Island official examines a young immigrant boy who has no choice but to submit; the physical examinations conducted at Ellis Island not only could be painful (the worst test involved turning a person's eyelid inside out with a button hook to check for redness) but they also resulted in the deportation of about one of every fifty immigrants who came to the United States by way of New York. Be sure to point out to your students the words on the chalkboard and the boys sitting below them. Does the photographer imply that the young Italians are "baggage," or is the photograph a comment about attitudes toward poor immigrants? How do these children compare to the "mafiosi" Gilbert describes? Ask your students whether they think Gilbert had Italians like them in mind when she wrote her poem.

POSSIBLE CONNECTIONS TO OTHER SELECTIONS

Jimmy Santiago Baca, "Green Chile" (text p. 117; question 1, following)
S. Pearl Sharp, "It's the Law: A Rap Poem" (text p. 47)

CONNECTION QUESTION IN TEXT (p. 544) WITH ANSWER

1. Discuss the ways in which ethnicity is used to create meaning in "Mafioso" and in Jimmy Santiago Baca's "Green Chile" (p. 117).

   The bitterness of Gilbert's borrowed stereotypes of mafia members as "bad uncles" (line 9) is in contrast with the deliberate examination of an actual grandmother in Baca's poem. The fondness Baca's speaker conveys for his grandmother and the "old, beautiful ritual" (45) is viewed tenderly from firsthand experience. In contrast, Gilbert is unable to locate an authentic image of her Italian ancestors and regards with bitterness the "Puritan millionaires" (23) who were ready to destroy the Italian immigrants she imagines arriving at Ellis Island. Ethnicity is a borrowed construct of externally established, insufficient stereotypes in Gilbert's poem; it shapes a home in Baca's.

EXPECTATIONS AND BORDERS

CHITRA BANERJEE DIVAKARUNI, *Indian Movie, New Jersey* (p. 544)

Soundtrack cover: RAWAL FILMS, *Ladki Pasand Hai (I Like This Girl)* (p. 546)

The speaker in "Indian Movie, New Jersey" contrasts the safety and hope of the world inside the movie theater with the threats and disappointments of the world outside. Aside from the threat of physical violence, the speaker's overwhelming experience of America is exclusion: accents betray the Indians' outsider status (lines 18–19), children embrace Americanism and reject their parents in the process (21–24), and neighbors shun them. One irony of the poem is that the theater itself underscores the thwarted possibilities and expectations that America represents — "the America that was supposed to be" (51). Another irony is that the Indians' "American Dream" has been displaced by a dream to "retire / in India, a yellow two-storied house / with wrought iron gates, our own / Ambassador car" (42–45).

You might begin a discussion of this poem by asking students to identify and describe a "world" of their own that disappointed their expectations. What did they think it would be like, and how were they wrong? How did they respond to the surprise of reality? Once they're thinking along these lines, turn them back to the poem to explore how the speaker responds to her own disappointment. Ask them to identify elements of the poem that suggest that the speaker is bound to be disappointed all over again.

Another way to explore the poem is to have your students think about the escapist functions of moviegoing. Divakaruni's poem emphasizes the fantasies played out in the Indian movie theater and contrasts them to the problems in the audience's real lives. The movie still from the Bollywood musical *Ladki Pasano Hai* should help your students better comprehend the flavor of the stories Divakaruni describes. Ask them what emotions the image conveys, as well as what emotions it might evoke. Why do the theatergoers find the experience so satisfying? What, according to the poem, are the possible positive and negative effects of turning to a movie like this for solace and a sense of community?

POSSIBLE CONNECTIONS TO OTHER SELECTIONS

Langston Hughes, "Theme for English B" (text p. 502)

Tato Laviera, "AmeRícan" (text p. 284)

Florence Cassen Mayers, "All-American Sestina" (text p. 250; question 1, following)

CONNECTION QUESTION IN TEXT (p. 547) WITH ANSWER

1. Explain how the speaker's idea of "the America that was supposed to be" (line 51) compares with the nation described in Florence Cassen Mayers's "All-American Sestina" (p. 250).

    Divakaruni's poem doesn't explicitly describe what constitutes the "America that was supposed to be," but the last stanza does offer some hints that the speaker expected to find franchises, easy millions, maybe a "rich white suburb" (46). A close reader will find in the speaker's new dreams an idea of what else America meant to her before she arrived: she wanted a continuation of Indian cultural traditions, a sense of belonging, and a sense of security. Mayers's America, with its emphasis on consumer goods and money, echoes the more materialistic aspects of the Indians' idea of America but doesn't seem to have the same preoccupation with community.

BEAUTY AND BORDERS

JANICE MIRIKITANI, *Recipe* (p. 547)

Photograph: CHIAKI TSUKUMO, *Girl with Licca Doll* (p. 548)

Before discussing "Recipe," be sure students understand the literal message of the poem. This is a recipe for "Round Eyes" (that is, Caucasian eyes) written by a Japanese American poet. The poem is fairly straightforward, outlining the necessary equipment and the step-by-step process involved in making almond-shaped eyes round. However, a close examination shows that the poem is loaded with double meanings. For instance, examine the final instruction of the recipe: "Do not cry" (line 16). Ask your students to consider the tone and stance of the speaker in this line. What do the round eyes represent, and why does this speaker imply that round eyes might be desirable? Discuss what the poem and the photograph imply about the cultural standards of beauty and the price individuals — particularly women — are required to pay to meet these standards.

Chiaki Tsukumo's photograph of a Japanese girl with a round-eyed doll might also seem unremarkable at first — students might insist that it's merely a publicity shot — but the image rewards closer scrutiny. Tsukumo took this photograph at the toymaker's celebration of the doll's thirty-fifth anniversary, a happy occasion. It's a little unsettling, then, that the photo's subject appears so unexcited. At the same time, she doesn't look at her doll or the poster (which celebrates the sale of more than fifty million dolls) but stares directly at the photographer: by making eye contact with the viewer the girl seems to be issuing some kind of challenge. Ask your students to consider what kind of argument the photographer might be making. Do they think this little girl would be interested in following Mirikitani's recipe?

POSSIBLE CONNECTIONS TO OTHER SELECTIONS

Michelle Boisseau, "Self-Pity's Closet" (text p. 555; question 1, following)
Martín Espada, "Bully" (text p. 166)
Kenneth Fearing, "AD" (text p. 162)

CONNECTION QUESTION IN TEXT (p. 548) WITH ANSWER

1. How might the speaker in Michelle Boisseau's "Self-Pity's Closet" (p. 555) be read as a version of the speaker in "Recipe"?

   Both speakers have allowed outside influences to damage their self-esteem, although both are aware at some level that their own conciliations are at least partly to blame for their pain. Both have internalized what they believe others expect of them and inflict abuse on themselves (physical in the case of Mirikitani's speaker and emotional in Boisseau's case). An important difference between the two speakers can be found in their actions: Mirikitani's actively attempts to alter her appearance in a futile effort to fit in with her surroundings; Boisseau's does nothing but wallow in her misery. Neither seems prepared, however, to fight the pressures they feel: Mirikitani's speaker cajoles herself not to cry (line 16); Boisseau's wishes everything to "go away" (24).

FREEDOM AND BORDERS

THOMAS LYNCH, *Liberty* (p. 549)

Photograph: ALEX MacLEAN, *Somerville, Massachusetts* (p. 550)

Lynch's poem resists the limitations that suburban life places on man's wild nature by claiming one small holdover from the romantic "fierce bloodline" (line 6) of the past: the freedom to "piss on the front lawn" (1). The speaker defines not "liberty" but what he seeks liberty from: "porcelain and plumbing and the Great Beyond" (3). The speaker uses a humorous tone and claims his own silliness as well as his own right to "do it anywhere" (14). The presence of the ex-wife serves to allow the reader to take sides. Is the reader suffering from the "gentility of envy" (13) that plagued the wife, or is the reader aligned with the speaker, tied genetically to "the hedgerow of whitethorn" (19) and the "vast firmament" (30)? "Crowns," "crappers," and "ex-wives" (32), representing figures of authority and the suffocating nature of domestic life, are what Lynch's speaker seeks to escape.

Students may find the poem foolish and trifling, or they may enjoy its humorous perspective. The photograph of a typical suburb of Boston should help them appreciate the serious complaint behind Lynch's humor: crowded and impersonal, the neighborhood makes privacy nearly impossible and is almost devoid of the signs of nature (such as the trees and "hedgerows") so important to Lynch's speaker's sense of his heritage and identity. For classroom discussion or a writing assignment, have your students compare and contrast Lynch's descriptions of Ireland's "West Clare" (17) with what they see in the photograph of Somerville, Massachusetts. Would they add any other points of difference?

POSSIBLE CONNECTIONS TO OTHER SELECTIONS

John Ciardi, "Suburban" (text p. 518; question 1, following)

Robert Frost, "Acquainted with the Night" (text p. 157)

Ronald Wallace, "Building an Outhouse" (text p. 152)

CONNECTION QUESTION IN TEXT (p. 551) **WITH ANSWER**

1. Discuss Lynch's treatment of suburban life and compare it with John Ciardi's in "Suburban" (p. 518). What similarities are there in the themes and metaphoric strategies of these two poems?

   Both speakers use humor to portray themselves as separate from the suburban culture they hope to subvert. Ciardi's feigned indictment of the mystery dog's act — "The animal of it" (line 16) — parallels the speaker in "Liberty," who at times refuses to "pee / in concert with the most of humankind / who do their business tidily indoors" (10–12). The "animal" in Ciardi's poem is connected to the "fierce bloodline" in line 6 of Lynch's in a refusal to be tamed or fenced in by the stultifying surroundings of the suburbs.

AN ANTHOLOGY
OF POEMS

22

An Album of Contemporary Poems

Both the difficulties and the rewards of contemporary poetry derive from the same characteristics; namely, there are no set principles for the construction of contemporary poetry or the range of its style. It can be structured in stanzas or in open free-verse paragraphs or even as an uninterrupted block of prose. Contemporary poetry is as likely to be rhymed as unrhymed. The level of diction can be lofty and elegant or it can be spiced with slang, as in Peter Meinke's "The ABC of Aerobics" (text p. 285). In short, the idea of decorum, if it exists at all in contemporary poetry, is open ended.

Thematically, the field for discovering material for poems is also more extensive than ever before. Some of the poems here take as their motive an area of public concern relevant not only to the country of the poet but also to an area other than or far more inclusive than a specific nation. We are living in an age that has given new meaning to the word *global*, and North American poetry especially seems to reflect this broadened interest. Other poems, such as Michelle Boisseau's "Self-Pity's Closet," embody a more private concern and voice the particular anxieties and observations of the individual. One point, though, that students should grasp is that our age does not dictate either an introspective poetry bound to extol and explore nature and the human mind or a public poetry pitched for a celebration of reason, country, and the famous. We can, and do, address both public and private issues, and certain poems manage to merge the dialectic of *polis* and *poesis*.

Without question, contemporary poets write about the age-old issues of love and death and the pain of growing up, but these themes, seemingly so essential and enduring, are changed by recent history, technology, and our systems of belief and values. Knowledge of the casualness of death and one's consequent vulnerability, as well as the prospect of mass extinction, also influences the way poets today think and write about death. The world of the contemporary poet is violent and nonsensical, but it is also diverse and exotic.

(Web) Ask students to research the poets in this chapter at **bedfordstmartins.com/ meyerpoetry**.

The poetry included here exhibits a wide range of techniques and levels of diction. The tools for reading poetry learned in earlier chapters will find their fullest application here. On the whole, though, the poems are highly accessible and offer a fine occasion for you and your students to observe the events, vocabulary, and concerns of the day worked into a poetic context. Perhaps that context will enable all of us to articulate more clearly what we desire, value, and wish to protect in this world.

MICHELLE BOISSEAU, *Self-Pity's Closet* (p. 555)

Even if some won't admit it, every student in your class has at one point or another experienced the kind of self-inflicted agony described so painstakingly in this poem. Ironically, most readers will find it difficult to stay focused on the speaker's endless list of metaphors for pain that she focuses on so relentlessly. Their self-conscious identification with the speaker may even cause some of your students to express frustration with her wallowing: they may want to scream "Get over it!" at her. "Make it all go away" (line 24) indeed.

Try asking your students which of the poem's metaphors resonate most for them. Are some more effective than others? Why? Some may notice that the poem's images vacillate between exterior and interior and between self and others: the speaker seems to want to reach beyond her "closet" and to reconnect with others but repeatedly retreats back inside and within. Draw their attention, also, to the unclear antecedent of "your vast and painful declarations" (12) that seems to generate a shift in the poem's tone. Who is "you"? Is it the speaker, or somebody who has hurt her with his or her declarations?

POSSIBLE CONNECTIONS TO OTHER SELECTIONS

Emily Dickinson, "One need not be a Chamber — to be Haunted —" (text p. 325)
——, "The Soul selects her own Society —" (text p. 321)
Stephen Dobyns, "Do They Have a Reason?" (text p. 559; question 1, following)
Edgar Allan Poe, "The Haunted Palace" (text p. 159; question 2, following)

CONNECTIONS QUESTIONS IN TEXT (p. 556) WITH ANSWERS

1. Compare the pain experienced by the speaker in this poem with the speaker's pain in Stephen Dobyns's "Do They Have a Reason?" (p. 559). How do the images in each poem reveal the speaker's state of mind?

    In "Do They Have a Reason?" Dobyns looks back to childhood to understand the painful aspects of his life. His images are drawn from a child's world and reflect what is important in it: "loll[ing] about the riverbank" (line 17) with friends, going after school for "a Coke and a hot pretzel" (30), the fear of being bullied by older children. By returning to these earlier scenes, Dobyns gets closer to the feeling of being let down by life. The simple pleasures the young boys experience and their optimism about the future are interrupted by a force that is impersonal and inexplicable. Like Dobyns, Boisseau uses images from the natural world before turning to indoor scenes as the speaker's self-pity intensifies. However, many of Boisseau's images are extremely personal, relating the physical sensations that attend the speaker's mental state: "the skin sticky, / the crotch itchy, the tongue stinking" (7–8). While "Do They Have a Reason?" suggests that the young boy's disillusionment is a universal experience, common to the all of the friends who encourage one another's imagined futures, "Self-Pity's Closet" is interested in the solitary experience of depression, and Boisseau chooses images that remain closely tied to the speaker's consciousness.

2. Discuss the themes you find in this poem and in Edgar Allan Poe's "The Haunted Palace" (p. 159). Explain whether or not you think the differences between these two poems are greater than their similarities.

    Poe's "Haunted Palace" is an allegory of a mind that has succumbed to the kind of "evil" thoughts that plague the speaker of Boisseau's "Self-Pity's Closet." Both poems explore the destructiveness of negative thinking, but whereas Boisseau's speaker is the cause of her own suffering, it's not clear whether the suffering mind of Poe's poem brought on its own demise or if it was influenced from without. Both poems, as well, use house metaphors to describe the subjects' state of mind. The question of whether the poems are more alike than similar will depend on individual students' perspectives and the details they choose to focus on.

BILLY COLLINS, *Marginalia* (p. 556)

At one time or another, everyone has found the margins of a borrowed paperback or textbook filled with handwritten observations and responses. Collins's meditation elevates this common occurrence to a transformative experience. In Collins's eyes, the scribbles are attempts to participate in and possess the text, to seize "the white perimeter as our own" (line 34). While *marginalia* refers to the handwritten comments one would find in the margins of a book, it can also refer to the seemingly peripheral concerns of life. Play a recording of Billy Collins reading "Marginalia" on *Literature Aloud*. Collins's poem is deceptively humorous and informal as he comments on the many kinds of marginalia he has enjoyed. Notice how the speaker compares the marginalia to various locations — a battlefield, a shore, a football field. In doing so, he suggests that the page is the site of conquest, reflection, or enthusiasm, depending on whatever the reader brings with him or her. The speaker's realization at the end of the poem is heartbreaking as well as affirmative: some marginalia carry the most urgent of messages — in this case, the loneliness of a girl in love. When the speaker recounts this story, we realize the revelatory power of a few scribbled notes.

POSSIBLE CONNECTIONS TO OTHER SELECTIONS

Bob Hicok, "Spam leaves an aftertaste" (text p. 526)

Philip Larkin, "A Study of Reading Habits" (text p. 34)

STEPHEN DOBYNS, *Do They Have a Reason?* (p. 559)

With deceptive simplicity, Dobyns explores how young children lose their innocent enthusiasm for life and discover that the world is cruel. Trying to pinpoint the cause of disillusion is pointless, he argues: the world is what it is, and we all eventually discover the unpleasant truth sooner or later.

On first reading, it seems that the poem follows a clear progression from childhood innocence to the pain of discovery. But press your students to look for clues — as early as line 3 — that the poem's children have at least some subconscious knowledge that the world isn't as safe and nurturing as they pretend it is. Is the speaker of this poem one of the kids who "get it right away" (line 25), or does he count himself among the "not so quick" (25)? You might want to ask your students to talk about their own moments of discovery — they might be surprised to learn that most people cannot identify with any certainty the day they lost their faith that everything would always be OK.

POSSIBLE CONNECTIONS TO OTHER SELECTIONS

William Blake, "Infant Sorrow" (text p. 587)

Andrew Hudgins, "Seventeen" (text p. 170; question 1, following)

Sharon Olds, "Rite of Passage" (text p. 279; question 2, following)

Linda Pastan, "Pass/Fail" (text p. 504)

CONNECTIONS QUESTIONS IN TEXT (p. 560) WITH ANSWERS

1. Discuss the speaker's sense of undergoing a shift in sensibility in this poem with the speaker in Andrew Hudgins's "Seventeen" (p. 170).

    Although most people couldn't pinpoint when their sense of the world changed, both of these poems identify a moment when the speakers lost their youthful idealism. Dobyns writes of "the moment when you at last catch on" (line 24) as a realization that good intentions have little bearing on cold reality. Hudgins locates the shift in the choice the young man makes: he goes through with the painful act of killing the dog in order to spare it further pain. Both poems offer some early hints that foreshadow the disillusionment at the end. The specificity of the line "No failures here, no one sent to prison" (3) in "Do They Have a Reason?" suggests that these will, in fact, be some of the boys' fate. And Hudgins's speaker's angry reactions to the driver's carelessness make it inevitable that he will get emotionally involved in the accident.

2. How might Sharon Olds's "Rite of Passage" (p. 279) be read as a means of providing the "reason" for what happens in Dobyns's poem?

Olds's poem implies that children, boys especially, are taught aggression from an early age. Although the Romantic poets (like Wordsworth) may have embraced the notion of inherently innocent childhood, both Olds and Dobyns suggest that children are quite aware of the evils that surround them and that they adjust their expectations and attitudes accordingly.

JANE HIRSHFIELD, *August Day* (p. 560)

Though Hirshfield's poem is made up of simple elements, it touches on some large questions about existence. The first line suggests a view of human life that is shaped by outside forces, or "given." This knowledge leads the speaker to look at the world in a detached manner. Giving up human willfulness, which would attempt to change what is given, she becomes like an unself-conscious animal: "A bear would be equally happy, this August day" (line 9).

In an interview for the San Diego *Reader*, Hirshfield addressed the subject of attention and how it relates to her poetry. She said, "Whatever is going on for us, if we can experience it fully, without reservation — that is not only information, but a kind of happiness." (You can read the rest of the interview at **http://www.poems.com/hirinter.htm**.) In her poems, Hirshfield's close attention to everyday objects and natural scenes leads her to larger revelations about life. Here the ripening summer fruits and vegetables are not figures for "love nor love's muster of losses" (6). By simply contemplating them in and of themselves, the speaker becomes more aware of her place in the "kingdom" of nature (15).

POSSIBLE CONNECTIONS TO OTHER SELECTIONS

Margaret Atwood, "February" (text p. 143; question 1, following)
A. E. Housman, "Loveliest of trees, the cherry now" (text p. 238)
Mary Oliver, "Mindful" (text p. 50; question 2, following)

CONNECTIONS QUESTIONS IN TEXT (pp. 560–561) WITH ANSWERS

1. Discuss the moods created in "August Day" and in Margaret Atwood's "February" (p. 143). To what extent do you think each poem is successful in capturing the essence of the title's subject?

The mood of "August Day" is tranquil and accepting. Through the images of the maturing plants, the speaker's "lazy" (line 12) attitude, and her feeling of being "drunk" (15) on the pleasures of the day, Hirshfield conveys the still and heavy feeling of late summer. "February" also has a lazy feeling, but Atwood is interested in the sluggishness of winter's hibernation. While Hirshfield's poem is set in the open air, Atwood's is closed in and "musty" (10). By describing the cocoon of warmth we create in the winter, Atwood also anticipates the fresh air of spring.

2. Compare the attitudes expressed toward nature in "August Day" and in Mary Oliver's "Mindful" (p. 50).

   Both of these poems value paying intense attention to the external world, especially to, as Oliver writes, "the common, the very drab" (line 24). Both attempt to relate the intense personal experiences that such attention can produce. However, the emotion in the two poems is somewhat different. Hirshfield records a feeling of calm elation while Oliver seems to be struck more violently by the beauty of the world.

TONY HOAGLAND, *America* (p. 561)

This poem records a change in attitude on the part of the speaker. The view of America as a country whose culture is one of empty materialism, first expressed by his student, is so extreme that he reacts with cynicism. To perceive America as a "maximum-security prison / Whose walls are made of RadioShacks and Burger Kings, and MTV episodes" (lines 2–3) sounds like a parody of the now-familiar criticisms of popular culture. However, his response to the student is interrupted by the memory of a dream that incorporated a similar kind of capitalist symbolism. In the dream his father's heart is burdened by the weight of "bright green hundred-dollar bills" (15). The speaker remembers Marx's wish that he had spent more time "'listening to the cries of the future'" (28), which suggests not only a concern for the speaker's future but also for that of the student whose attitudes represent a younger generation. You might have your students discuss their own sense of contemporary American culture. Do they feel the emphasis on material goods is a "nightmare" (30), or do they relate more to the speaker's first cynical reaction?

POSSIBLE CONNECTIONS TO OTHER SELECTIONS

Michelle Boisseau, "Self-Pity's Closet" (text p. 555; question 1, following)
Barbara Hamby, "Ode to American English" (text p. 87; question 2, following)
Tato Laviera, "AmeRícan" (text p. 284)
Florence Cassen Mayers, "All-American Sestina" (p. 250)

CONNECTIONS QUESTIONS IN TEXT (p. 562) WITH ANSWERS

1. Discuss the treatment of self-pity in "America" and in Michelle Boisseau's "Self-Pity's Closet" (p. 555).

   Boisseau writes from the inside of the "closet," giving the reader a litany of complaints from the point of view of a self-pitying speaker. The emotional reactions in the poem are so extreme that at times it is hard for the reader to sympathize. Hoagland experiences similar difficulties sympathizing with the student in "America." His sense of being downtrodden by popular culture also comes across as disproportionate. After initially dismissing the student, Hoagland does come to identify with his feeling of alienation. He does not, however, give in to self-pity. At the end of the poem, the speaker implicates himself in the callousness of contemporary culture.

2. Explain how "America" and Barbara Hamby's "Ode to American English" (p. 87) offer contrasting visions of American life and culture.

   Hamby revels in American consumer culture, celebrating media-driven words and phrases like "Dick Tracy" (line 7), *"Suffering Succotash"* (31), and "Cheetoes" [sic] (29). She sees the broad vocabulary of American English as evidence of its liveliness and democratic nature. In "America," on the other hand, the language of marketing, especially brand names like "MTV" (line 3) and "Isuzu" (6) are central to Hoagland's critique of the culture. He views much of American English as "spin doctoring" (12), a kind of superficial speech that never approaches the truth.

RACHEL LODEN, *Locked Ward: Newtown, Connecticut* (p. 563)

Because of the circumstances of the parent-child relationship in this poem, the usual roles are reversed, with the daughter taking on the responsibility of taking care of her mother and the guilt of feeling that she has failed. Her desire to "wrap you up and carry you away" (line 16) is made impossible by the mother's condition. At the beginning of "Locked Ward," before we know this is the speaker's mother whom she's visiting, she describes the addressee as being "like a whipped child" (6). We learn that they are related when the speaker mentions the things she brought "from home" (12). However, it is only at the end that the relationship is named, as the speaker grieves over her inability to help: "there is no end to the lament / of daughters" (26–27). The line break in this phrase reinforces the surprise the reader gets from knowing the relationship and shows how painful it is for the daughter to assume the role of guardian.

POSSIBLE CONNECTIONS TO OTHER SELECTIONS

Judith Ortiz Cofer, "The Game" (text p. 592)

Emily Dickinson, "One need not be a Chamber — to be Haunted —" (text p. 325; question 2, following)

Ben Jonson, "On My First Son" (text p. 607)

Cathy Song, "The Youngest Daughter" (text p. 94, question 1, following)

CONNECTIONS QUESTIONS IN TEXT (p. 563) WITH ANSWERS

1. Discuss the parent-daughter relationship as it is revealed by the images in Loden's poem and in Cathy Song's "The Youngest Daughter" (p. 94).

    Loden uses images of blank whiteness to convey the mystery of her mother's condition, which puts her beyond the reach of understanding. The trailing "moon" (line 2) and the "white page" (21) suggest that the speaker doesn't know how to respond to her mother's condition. Contrasting these images are the "foul winds" (22) and the "stains that cannot be removed / by any washing of the hands" (23–24), which convey the speaker's guilt. Loden also takes the received language, "sharp objects," out of its original context, which we see in line 7, and turns it into "the sharp objects in the heart" (28), a figure for the daughter's pain at seeing her mother in the locked ward.

    In "The Youngest Daughter," Song's domestic images serve to separate mother and daughter. The speaker of this poem is repulsed by her mother's body, and so she detaches herself from her own body, imagining it not as flesh, but as "rice paper" (line 4) or "aspirin-colored" (12). Her "white body" (42) contrasts with her mother's bruised, aging skin. The final image of the poem, the cranes taking off in flight, moves the language of the poem out of the domestic space and prefigures the speaker's escape from the home.

2. Compare the themes in Loden's poem and in Emily Dickinson's "One need not be a Chamber — to be Haunted —" (p. 325).

    Both of these poems take physical structures as representations of the complexities of the mind. For Dickinson, the internal space of a room, which might seem like a figure for security, represents the dangers of individual perception. Meeting ghosts or assassins isn't nearly as frightening as meeting one's self "In lonesome Place —" (line 12). In Loden's poem, the speaker — who enters the locked ward from the outside — sees the enclosed space as an outward representation of her mother's mind, which is closed off to the daughter. In both poems, the rooms emphasize the essentially solitary nature of consciousness.

SUSAN MINOT, *My Husband's Back* (p. 564)

The details Minot chooses to describe domestic life in "My Husband's Back" characterize "Breakdown hour" (line 2) with deft economy. The "pot of burnt rice" (3), "baby flushed with the flu" (6), and firewood "caked / with ice" (9–10) and the kind of small mishaps that can add up to a disaster. These irritations are mirrored in Minot's figures: she describes the setting sun as a "light bulb gone out" (4) and compares the feeling of sitting down to her spine "collid[ing] with all its bones" (12). All of these elements make up a world that feels like it is spinning out of control. At this moment, the sight of her husband's back grounds her and gives her something stable to hold on to. You might have your students discuss why someone's back would cause this reaction. What is it about seeing him with his face turned away from her that makes the speaker realize he is "the one point in the world" (30) she has been searching for?

POSSIBLE CONNECTIONS TO OTHER SELECTIONS

Anne Bradstreet, "To My Dear and Loving Husband" (text p. 492; question 1, following)
Jane Kenyon, "The Shirt" (text p. 496; question 2, following)
Richard Wilbur, "Love Calls Us to the Things of This World" (text p. 630)

CONNECTIONS QUESTIONS IN TEXT (p. 565) WITH ANSWERS

1. Compare Minot's "My Husband's Back" and Anne Bradstreet's "To My Dear and Loving Husband" (p. 492) as love poems.

   Bradstreet's poem is a direct address to her husband with a brief aside to compare her love favorably to that of other women. It is full of superlatives and grand comparisons. Gold mines and great wealth can't compare to love, and it "is such that rivers cannot quench" (line 7). Bradstreet claims the love she receives is so strong that only heaven can repay her husband for it. Beside "To My Dear and Loving Husband," Minot's poem is very down-to-earth. The images she uses are located within the household and the emotions of the poem are tied to its daily activities. Minot's poem does not speak directly to her husband, and so is more a meditation than a profession of love. Rather than describing her feelings to him, it leads her to a self-revelation.

2. Discuss the speakers' tones in Minot's poem and in Jane Kenyon's "The Shirt" (p. 496).

   The speaker's frustration comes through in the beginning of Minot's poem through her use of short sentences and fragments. The frequent breaks in her list of irritations give the opening a staccato feeling. However, as the speaker takes comfort from looking at her husband, she relaxes into longer sentences, and the tone becomes lyrical and even humorous. "The Shirt," on the other hand, has a more overt humor and a suggestive tone. While the shirt in "My Husband's Back" signifies warmth and dependability, Kenyon envies the shirt for its proximity to her lover's body.

ROBERT MORGAN, *Fever Wit* (p. 565)

It seems a truism in our society that children possess a deeper knowledge and better capacity for truth than adults do. Our culture's obsession with last words suggests, furthermore, that we also expect the dying to shed the mantles of social propriety and reveal profound truths for the benefit of the living. This poem adds an interesting twist to these clichés, speculating on why adults seem to flock around desperately sick children. The speaker is not charitable in his descriptions: He portrays the healthy adults crowded around a child's sickbed as selfish and callously indifferent to the sufferings of the person they hope will produce revelation.

Ask your students if they find any evidence in the poem that its sick children are a metaphor for the poet and their delirious mutterings a metaphor for the act of writing. Does Morgan resent his readers' demand that poetry reveal some kind of deeper truth? If so, how would students respond to him? As an interesting creative writing assignment, consider having your students write a poem, using Morgan's as a model, from the point of view of the "neighbors and kin" that surround the dying child of "Fever Wit."

POSSIBLE CONNECTIONS TO OTHER SELECTIONS

Billy Collins, "Introduction to Poetry" (text p. 42)

Emily Dickinson, "Tell all the Truth but tell it slant —" (text p. 329; question 1, following)

Robert Frost, "Neither Out Far nor In Deep" (text p. 373)

Ben Jonson, "On My First Son" (text p. 607)

CONNECTION QUESTION IN TEXT (p. 566) WITH ANSWER

1. Compare the theme of this poem with that of Emily Dickinson's "Tell all the Truth but tell it slant —" (p. 329).

    Dickinson's poem suggests that real truths are too much to bear for ordinary people and so must be told indirectly. She sees the poet's role as one of providing revelation without "blinding" her readers. Morgan seems to reject the notion that it's the job of the poet to reveal truths that people might otherwise miss, portraying readers as parasitical seekers of truth that must be wrought from others' (presumably his own) suffering.

ALBERTO RÍOS, *The Gathering Evening* (p. 566)

The controlling metaphor of "The Gathering Evening" is that of shadows as the unconscious. The metaphor is difficult, and you'll have to struggle to get your students to think through Ríos's surrealism. To accomplish this, start by asking why shadows are personified in this poem. What defines a shadow? Some students will undoubtedly point out that shadows are dark, others that they are created when something obstructs light, still others may note that *shadow* is a synonym of *ghost*. Pursue your inquiry by asking what else shares these characteristics. Why does Ríos associate their greatest power with sleep? It is hoped that at least one student will make the connection between sleep and dreams, but if nobody does you might want to do it for them. You may also want to give them a hint by telling them that Ríos is revered as a master of magical surrealism, which celebrates the power of the unconscious and rejects linear thinking.

POSSIBLE CONNECTIONS TO OTHER SELECTIONS

Emily Dickinson, "Presentiment — is that long shadow — on the lawn —" (text p. 136; question 1, following)

Robert Frost, "Acquainted with the Night" (text p. 157; question 2, following)

1. Compare the treatment of shadows in this poem and in Emily Dickinson's "Presentiment — is that long shadow — on the lawn —" (p. 136).

    Dickinson uses shadow to evoke a feeling of fearful anticipation, the definition of "presentiment." Your students may remember the text's suggestion that Dickinson links darkness with death, which explains the uneasiness that attends the coming of night. Ríos also gives shadows a foreboding quality, suggesting that they are patiently waiting to overtake us. Where Dickinson uses shadow as a metaphor for death, Ríos uses it as a metaphor for the thoughts and understandings that linger below our consciousness. In both cases, however, shadows are threatening and a justifiable source of fear.

2. Discuss the significance of the night in this poem and in Robert Frost's "Acquainted with the Night" (p. 157).

    Both Ríos and Frost intimate that the night is a dangerous time. It is a source of nightmares, of uneasiness, and of unrecognized threats. The fact that most people sleep through it intensifies its power. For Ríos, it is the time when our unconscious minds take over; for Frost, it is equated with dark alleys and unsavory characters. Neither poet provides enough clues to definitively identify what the night is a metaphor of, but in both cases its traditional associations with death and danger lend powerful resonance to unseen enemies.

CATHY SONG, *A Poet in the House* (p. 567)

Probably the first thing your students will notice about this poem is Song's use of dashes — a conscious attempt to incorporate Dickinson's famous style into her own. Take advantage of this to ask your students what else about Song's poem mirrors Dickinson's work. Among the stylistic elements they might identify are elision, surprising turns of phrase, unconventional imagery, ambiguity, and paradox. Some may recognize allusions to Dickinson poems, including "I felt a Cleaving in my Mind —" (line 19: "the pressure seized upon her mind —"); "Success is counted sweetest" (line 11: "the noises she heard"); and "Oh Sumptuous moment" (line 3: "she vanished daily into paper, famished"). But there are significant diversions from Dickinson's style as well: Song's poem is relatively long, there is no mid-sentence capitalization, and there is a clear narrative progression — all of which highlights Song's reverence of Dickinson as a source of inspiration whose originality has encouraged later poets to develop their own voices.

You might want to ask your students about voice in this poem. Who is the speaker? Cathy Song or Emily Dickinson's sister Lavinia (or both at once)? Be sure to press your students for evidence for their positions. You could also ask them what difference it makes, if any, who is speaking.

POSSIBLE CONNECTIONS TO OTHER SELECTIONS

Howard Nemerov, "Walking the Dog" (text p. 521; question 1, following)
William Trowbridge, "Poets' Corner" (text p. 568; question 1, following)
Ronald Wallace, "Miss Goff" (text p. 339; question 2, following)
Marilyn Nelson Waniek, "Emily Dickinson's Defunct" (text p. 276)

1. Compare Song's assessment of the life of a poet with the view expressed in Howard Nemerov's "Walking the Dog" (p. 521) or William Trowbridge's "Poets' Corner" (p. 568).

From Song's perspective, the poet's "job [is] to think." The other members of the household recognize the importance of the poet's struggles to make sense of the world and accord it the same value as their own labors. "A Poet in the House" suggests that it is a poet's lot to suffer from the strain of writing, but that her work is "divine" (12). Howard Nemerov takes a more grounded approach, comparing the process of writing with the bodily function of excrescence — something both necessary and not a little unpleasant. For him, writing poetry is an effort, sometimes futile, to prove human superiority over other species. Trowbridge suggests — in defiance of the assumption that poets are "sissy" — that writing is its own kind of sport, something that a bored or idle mind can't help but turn to.

2. Discuss the perspective on Dickinson in this poem and in Ronald Wallace's "Miss Goff" (p. 339).

In both poems Emily Dickinson serves as an inspiring figure but in different ways. Song portrays her as muse and a medium for divine revelation. Wallace suggests that her poetry serves as an oasis for outcasts and a balm for the afflicted. Both poets are clearly grateful for Dickinson's legacy and influence. Although they recognize her quirks and acknowledge her hermitlike reluctance to interact with others, they treat her with the kind of extreme admiration reserved for heroes and deities.

WILLIAM TROWBRIDGE, *Poets' Corner* (p. 568)

Students might enjoy debating the question of cause and effect as it is presented in this poem. Is the speaker placed in right field because of his poetic sensibilities, or does the isolation and calm of right field inspire a poetic note in the boy? There are sure to be baseball fans in your class, so you might ask them why baseball is so often described as a poetic sport; encourage them to find descriptions in the poem that support their explanation.

The description of "Coach Bob Zambisi" (line 29) that concludes the poem is both amusing and somewhat tragic. Adult coaches of children's teams have long been accused of trying to relive their youth or overcome their own sense of inadequacy vicariously through their charges. Cases of parents and coaches erupting in inappropriate violence at children's games have been making the news in recent years. You might want to question whether your students think Trowbridge is sympathetic to the coach or if he condemns him, and why. What do they imagine is the speaker's response to his coach's haranguing?

POSSIBLE CONNECTIONS TO OTHER SELECTIONS

Gary Gildner, "First Practice" (text p. 275; question 2, following).
Robert Francis, "Catch" (text p. 28)
——, "The Pitcher" (text p. 208)

CONNECTIONS QUESTIONS IN TEXT (p. 569) WITH ANSWERS

1. Explain the coach's allusion to "Percy Bitch Shelby."

The coach means to refer to Percy Bysshe Shelley, whose "Ozymandias" and "Ode to the West Wind" are included in the text. The reference both suggests the coach's ignorance — he can't get the last name right — and highlights the association of poetry with effeminacy. For an American boy in the twentieth century, to read or write poetry would be to risk looking like a "Bitch" (line 41).

2. Compare the treatment of the coaches in this poem and in Gary Gildner's "First Practice" (p. 275).

In "First Practice" Gildner examines a football coach's misuse of the power he holds over a group of boys. The speaker does not respect this coach, and Gildner offers subtle hints that the coach is not worthy of the boys' respect; the poem implies that he is trying to relive his glory through the boys. Trowbridge approaches the coach of "Poets' Corner" with a detached amusement and sense of pity: He quotes the coach's malapropism of Shelley's name — "Percy Bitch Shelby" — both to highlight his nonunderstanding of poetry and to suggest that his hypermasculine stance toward the boys on his team stems from a fear of being considered effeminate.

23

An Album of World Literature

The poems in this section give students an opportunity to experience more than fifty years of world literature written from often contradictory perspectives. The poems range from general comments on modern sensibility to more specific pleas for relief from the political upheaval that has torn apart many of the countries represented. Although it is hardly necessary to teach them chronologically, the poems do present some of the major historic events of the twentieth century, including World War II and the revolutions that have racked Central and South American countries in the latter part of that century.

Students will read these poems not only for historical and geographical information but for new perspectives on their own lives as well. Your class will have to reassess the reading they have done in English courses throughout their scholastic careers. How many readings from cultures other than their own have they encountered? What might be the effect of this very limited education?

Web Ask students to research the poets in this chapter at **bedfordstmartins.com/ meyerpoetry**.

Questioning their own biases will lead students to open up the poems to the extent that they realize that world literature is not simply about some "Other"; it is about all of us, living in an ever-contracting world where we must think as much about our labels and notions of "the Other" as we do about ourselves.

ANNA AKHMATOVA, *Lot's Wife* (p. 570)

Students are likely to be familiar with the story of Lot's wife. You may want to ask a student to bring in the biblical text for comparison (the story can be found in Genesis 19:15–26). Akhmatova imagines the "wild grief" (line 3) felt by Lot's wife in much greater detail than is provided in the original text. While the moral of the story is generally understood to be that Lot's wife should not have looked back, Akhmatova reexamines the act and sees it as a kind of courage. The familiar story, then, is given a new and unexpected conclusion: In the speaker's heart "she will not be forgot / Who, for a single glance, gave up her life" (15–16). Students may see this as an opportunity for a creative writing exercise, in which they flesh out the inner life of another famous person.

Possible Connections to Other Selections

Margaret Atwood, "you fit into me" (text p. 135)
Bruce Springsteen, "You're Missing" (text p. 46)

Audiovisual Resources (manual p. 371)

CLARIBEL ALEGRÍA, *I Am Mirror* (p. 571)

Born in Estelí, Nicaragua, Alegría moved to El Salvador six months later; she therefore considers herself more Salvadoran than Nicaraguan. She attended George

Washington University, graduating in 1948, and is married to the American writer Darwin J. Flakoll. She received the Casa de las Americas prize of Cuba in 1978 for her book *Sobrevivo*. Alegría and her husband have lived in many countries; they now divide their time between Majorca, Spain, and Managua, Nicaragua.

The speaker in this poem describes her attempts to feel again after she has been numbed by violence. She looks for her identity in the mirror, only to see herself as another person; note her use of third-person pronouns to refer to herself: "she also pricks herself" (line 11). In an ironic twist of Descartes's *Cogito ergo sum*, the speaker feels her arm, saying, "I hurt / therefore I exist" (32–33). Her attention continually turns to the horror around her as she alternates between scenes of violence and an attempt to keep her identity amid the turmoil. In a series of negations that begins in line 44, the speaker denies the violence, losing herself in the process. She cannot sustain an identity and survive, so she becomes an object: "I am a blank mirror" (48).

In a writing assignment, you might ask students to trace the poem's two strands of images: the images the speaker uses to describe herself and the images of violence. Students might construct an argument explaining the relationship between the two, discussing the effect of the images on the poem's tone and theme.

POSSIBLE CONNECTIONS TO OTHER SELECTIONS

William Blake, "London" (text p. 121)

Sylvia Plath, "Mirror" (text p. 145; question 1, following)

CONNECTION QUESTION IN TEXT (p. 573) WITH ANSWER

1. Compare the ways in which Alegría uses mirror images to reflect life in El Salvador with Sylvia Plath's concerns in "Mirror" (p. 145).

   Plath's speaker is first mirror, then lake. In a reversal of Alegría's technique, in which the speaker becomes the mirror, Plath shows how the mirror absorbs the woman looking into it. Both poets play with the notion of women as objects, but Alegría does so to reflect the turmoil in war-torn El Salvador, whereas Plath considers the woman's aging process and approaching death.

AUDIOVISUAL RESOURCES (manual p. 371)

YEHUDA AMICHAI, *Jerusalem, 1985* (p. 573)

This brief poem contrasts the "bits of crumpled, wadded paper" (line 3) that represent wishes made or granted at the Wailing Wall with the failed journey of one that only made it as far as the "old iron gate" "across the way" (4). The spare language and mysterious source of the last two lines could make for some inventive discussion: Do students think the note is addressed to God or to someone else? What might have prevented the writer from reaching the Wailing Wall?

POSSIBLE CONNECTIONS TO OTHER SELECTIONS

Emily Dickinson, "I know that He exists" (text p. 344)

William Wordsworth, "London, 1802" (text p. 148)

MAHMOUD DARWISH, *Identity Card* (p. 574)

Darwish's poem dramatizes the tension between identity in the sense of allegiance to one's culture and identity as a means of political control. His repeated "I am an Arab" is a statement of his heritage, but it is also a label placed on him by the issuers of his "identity card." You might have your students discuss their notions of national or ethnic identity. Who gets to give a name to a group of people — insiders or outsiders? What differences would it make?

The other repeated line in the poem, "What's there to be angry about?" (lines 6, 16, 46), goes through some subtle shifts as the poem progresses. We read it first as a response to the stereotype of the angry Muslim man, but the question becomes increasingly ironic as we are told more of the hardships of the speaker's life. That question is reinforced by the characterization of the speaker's country as a "whirlpool of anger" (21). Although the pervasive anger in the atmosphere makes the question seem even more sarcastic, the speaker continues to combat the stereotype, claiming "I don't hate people, / I trespass on no one's property" (58–59). However, the "And yet" in line 60 marks a turning point in the poem, signaling the place where the speaker has been pushed enough to strike back. In spite of the repeated denials, he now warns the listener to "beware of my hunger / And of my anger!" (62–63).

POSSIBLE CONNECTIONS TO OTHER SELECTIONS

Sherman Alexie, "On the Amtrak from Boston to New York City" (text p. 174)

Langston Hughes, "Harlem" (text p. 411; question 1, following)

Pablo Neruda, "The United Fruit Co." (text p. 577)

Norman Stock, "What I Said" (text p. 234; question 2, following)

CONNECTION QUESTIONS IN TEXT (p. 575) WITH ANSWERS

1. Discuss the relation between anger and political history in "Identity Card" and in Langston Hughes's "Harlem" (p. 411).

   In both of these poems, the anger of a politically oppressed group boils under a surface that must remain somewhat conciliatory. For Darwish, the loss of a Palestinian homeland provokes an angry response: "You stole my forefathers' vineyards . . . And you left us and all my grandchildren / Nothing but these rocks" (lines 49–53). His speaker's anger remains dormant, but he warns if he "were to become hungry" (60) then it would emerge violently. As in "Identity Card," much of "Harlem" is occupied with describing a controlled but festering anger. Hughes's poem also suggests that a suppressed anger will eventually "explode" (11) in a violent response. Though he does not mention anger outright, Hughes's question about the dream deferred reminds readers of the historical barriers that have kept African Americans from realizing their hopes.

2. Consider "Identity Card" and Norman Stock's "What I Said" (p. 234) as two halves of a dialogue that voice personal responses to public, political events. In what sense do the two poems speak to each other?

   As a reflection on the September 11, 2001, attacks, Stock's poem describes the series of emotions a particular individual goes through in his response to the event. It follows his mind from sadness through bewilderment to rage. Before he comes to the frightening conclusion with "let's kill them" (line 13), Stock tries but fails to understand "how could / anyone do such a thing to us" (6–7). Darwish's poem might be read as an answer to this question, an explanation of the circumstances that have led some Muslims to become radically anti-Western. Next to Stock's "how can we expect to go on after this" (11), Darwish's description of the difficulty of providing for his children shows how others have had to "go on" through tragic circumstances.

TASLIMA NASRIN, *At the Back of Progress* . . . (p. 576)

The images of "progress" in this poem recall the kind of middle-class security some people in the United States take for granted: "the air-conditioned office" (line 1), "the cocktail party" (4), the "movie tickets" (25). However, these symbols of prosperity only cover a social dynamic in which women are still treated as house servants or sex objects. The "fellow" Nasrin describes "beats his wife" for trivial matters (9). For him a wife is an object to be used for labor. Similarly, he sees other women as objects to be used for sex. He has raped women and cheats on his wife to "[try] out his different tastes / in sex acts" (7–8).

However, the boss, who "gives out character references for people," (19) is not alone in his attitudes toward women. His employee also goes home and beats his wife "over a bar of soap or / the baby's pneumonia" (32–33). Even the "bearer who brings the tea" (34) has discarded a number of wives who haven't provided him an heir or brought some economic benefit. Through the structure of this poem, which moves from one man to another down the social ladder, Nasrin shows how the patriarchal oppression crosses all classes.

POSSIBLE CONNECTIONS TO OTHER SELECTIONS

Daisy Fried, "Wit's End" (text p. 519; question 2, following)

Eliza Griswold, "Occupation" (text p. 202; question 1, following)

Marge Piercy, "The Secretary Chant" (text p. 22)

CONNECTIONS QUESTIONS IN TEXT (p. 577) WITH ANSWERS

1. Discuss the status of women in Nasrin's poem and in Eliza Griswold's "Occupation" (p. 202). Which poem, in your opinion, presents women in a more desperate situation? Explain your response.

   Both of these poems describe political situations in which women are oppressed. It is clear how the cruel details of women's lives in "At the Back of Progress . . ." could be the outcome of a patriarchal system that values women, as Griswold says, as "worth [their] weight in tin" (line 7). The rhythms and diction of Griswold's poem feel more lighthearted than do Nasrin's, but they set the desperate situation of the women into stark relief. Her poem at least gives the women some agency in their struggle. The defeated feeling of Nasrin's comes in part from the fact that her women seem to have no ability to act at all, only to be acted upon by men.

2. Compare the treatment of men in Nasrin's poem and in Daisy Fried's "Wit's End" (p. 519). How do the cultural differences depicted in the poems result in divergent tones?

   Nasrin and Fried both deal with anxieties about women's sexuality, but the relative freedom of the young girl in "Wit's End" allows her to reject her father's desire to keep her as a little girl. Though the world of *"Sassy, Seventeen, Glamour"* (line 14) doesn't seem like the height of liberation, the speaker is moving toward autonomy as an adult woman, which is not possible for the women in Nasrin's poem. The men in her society are real barriers to freedom, keeping control through physical violence and economic strictures. While the father in "Wit's End" is still "loving" (15), the men in "At the Back of Progress . . ." don't seem to have any redeeming affection for their wives.

PABLO NERUDA, *The United Fruit Co.* (p. 577)

In an essay on "impure poetry," Chilean-born Pablo Neruda defended the impor-tance of the poet's craft of not-so-nice images and words. Neruda criticized American poets for ignoring politics to pursue their own, "loftier" pleasures. Art was life for Neruda; he believed that poetry must be kept near the bone, where it originates, and not elevated to irrelevancy. "The United Fruit Co." illustrates this point with visceral descrip-tions of the blood-cost of the foods we take for granted, which contrasts with the dull-ness of more abstract poetry. The speaker defends the poor, the politically oppressed, the mundane, and the earthly as the truly valuable subjects for poetry.

As is the case with most politically informed poetry, your students will benefit from a little historical background of the United Fruit Company. Consider assigning a stu-dent to research it and present his or her findings to the class. Historian Juan Gonzalez has noted that "more than any other U.S. company, United Fruit became the twentieth-century symbol of U.S. imperialism." Established by a merger in 1899, the United Fruit Company owned in excess of 1.5 million Latin American acres and nearly 1,500 miles of railroad — its budget was larger than the budget of any of the *countries* in the region. The United States' deep financial investment in Central America, particularly Guatemala, led to frequent military and political intervention; throughout the 1950s the Guatemalan president Jorge Ubico supported American business interests to the point of confiscat-ing property and forcing landless Guatemalans to work for the large U.S. companies. American intervention helped contribute to a long and bloody civil war in Guatemala, the most violent in Central American history.

This poem locates the production of fruit and coffee in its violent political context. Neruda argues that the Boston-based United Fruit Company, which effected what some historians have called a "bloodless" takeover of Central American farmlands in the 1890s, earned its financial and imperialistic success at the expense of native lives and autonomy. In Neruda's poem, we see that seemingly harmless foods exact a human toll: The consumers of wealthier countries are literally stealing food from the mouths of the poor. Even fruit flies take on a sinister aspect, forming a "dictatorship" (line 20) and being "bloodthirsty" (29).

Neruda's poetry has been discussed in Manuel Duran and Margery Safir's *Earth Tones* (Bloomington: Indiana UP, 1980); Rene de Costa's *The Poetry of Pablo Neruda* (Cambridge: Harvard UP, 1979); and "Pablo Neruda, 1904–1973," *Modern Poetry Studies* 5.1 (1974).

POSSIBLE CONNECTIONS TO OTHER SELECTIONS

Louise Erdrich, "Dear John Wayne" (text p. 473)

Galway Kinnell, "Blackberry Eating" (text p. 189; question 2, following)

Julio Marzán, "The Translator at the Reception for Latin American Writers" (text p. 280; question 1, following)

CONNECTIONS QUESTIONS IN TEXT (p. 578) WITH ANSWERS

1. Discuss the political perspective in this poem and in Julio Marzán's "The Translator at the Reception for Latin American Writers" (p. 280). What significant similarities are there between the two poems?

    Both poets criticize American commodification of Latin American culture. Neruda is the more damning of the two, making direct connections between American imperialism and Central American bloodshed. The Mayans, in "The United Fruit Co.," are murdered by American interests, their bodies "a cluster of dead fruit /

thrown down on the dump" (41–42). Marzán is more ironic in his approach, accusing the translator at a party of romanticizing the culture from which he makes a living. In this poem the Mayans "inspire a glorious epic / of revolution across a continent" (17–18), but the epic ignores the brutality of the warfare. Both poems take an interesting stance on American food consumption as well: the fruits and coffee provided by the United Fruit Company are portrayed as the spoils of war, and cheese serves as an escape route for a translator disappointed that the person he's talking to isn't exotic as he had imagined.

2. Contrast the treatment of fruit in this poem and in Galway Kinnell's "Blackberry Eating" (p. 189).

Kinnell's poem is a sensous celebration of the act of eating fresh blackberries plucked straight from the vine. There is no political agenda in his poem, which is concerned solely with pleasure. Neruda, on the other hand, uses fruit to make a political statement, ignoring its pleasures and focusing on the flies that attend to its decay and the bloodshed that makes it available to distant consumers.

OCTAVIO PAZ, *The Street* (p. 579)

A Mexican poet of metamorphic surrealism, Octavio Paz has influenced many writers, including William Carlos Williams, Denise Levertov, and Muriel Rukeyser, each of whom has translated him. He has served the Mexican diplomatic service in Paris, New Delhi, and New York.

Students may let this poem too easily defeat them or too easily collapse into platitudes: "OK, a guy becomes his own shadow or he can't tell whether he's real or not." The poem's simple diction, pleasing (and very frequent) rhymes, and skillful alliteration work in opposition to its mournful tone and shadowy imagery, a tension that mirrors the speaker's situation: The everyday world of streets, leaves, stones, and people is not at all everyday. Nothing has definition on "The Street" (note the references to night, blindness, and awkwardness and to the unstated reasons for the pursuit), yet the urgent certainty of the "narrative" is almost palpable.

You might ask students to change all of the verbs in the poem to the past tense and comment on the resulting differences in tone. Other questions that would yield productive discussion or writing include: How would the poem's effect be altered if it ended with line 11? How does the speaker know the street is "long" if he walks "in blackness"? How can stones be anything but "silent"? To what extent could the poem's logic be considered dream logic?

Possible Connections to Other Selections

Robert Frost, "Acquainted with the Night" (text p. 157; question 1, following)
Langston Hughes, "Lenox Avenue: Midnight" (text p. 404; question 2, following)

Connections Questions in Text (p. 579) with Answers

1. How does the speaker's anxiety in this poem compare with that in Robert Frost's "Acquainted with the Night" (p. 157)?

Frost's speaker in "Acquainted with the Night" vacillates between himself and the outside world, alternating between images of light and darkness, good and evil. Paz's speaker begins and ends in darkness, in the solipsistic prison of his own mind. Whereas Frost's speaker seems indecisive and brooding, Paz's is forever fixed in darkness, without hope. Frost's speaker feels alone in a realistic night setting where he sees "one luminary clock against the sky." His poem conveys loneliness rather than anxiety. Paz's scene, in contrast, is the landscape of persecution and nightmare.

2.   Write an essay comparing the tone of this poem and that of Langston Hughes's "Lenox Avenue: Midnight" (p. 404).

Both Paz and Hughes set their poems on particular streets, and the setting affects the tone of the poems. The tone of Hughes's poem is one of melancholy, shaped by the jazz "rhythm of life" (line 1). The image of the gods laughing at the "weary heart of pain" (6) is oppressive and hopeless. Likewise, Paz's speaker does not leave any room for hope or escape from his own consciousness; thus the tone of both poems is dismal.

AUDIOVISUAL RESOURCES (manual p. 379)

YOUSIF AL-SA'IGH, *An Iraqi Evening* (p. 579)

By showing "clips" of the family at home and mentioning the "Clips" from the battlefield, al-Sa'igh gives this poem a cinematic point of view. The isolated moments from domestic life mirror those scenes of war that the family sees from their "peaceable" (line 3) but threatened home. When the news comes on, those two realms come together in "the smell of war / and the smell of just baked bread" (13–14). Al-Sa'igh reveals the importance of this moment in the way that the family becomes pure sense receptor — all ears and eyes. His use of "clips" also carries a critique of the way war is reported on television, which is always inadequate to the suffering of the mother who "raises her eyes to a photo on the wall / whispering / — May God protect you" (15–17). That they are "carefully selected for hope" (22) suggests the situation is much more frightening than the news report admits.

POSSIBLE CONNECTIONS TO OTHER SELECTIONS

John Milton, "On the Late Massacre in Piedmont" (text p. 614)

Shu Ting, "O Motherland, Dear Motherland" (text p. 581)

Alfred, Lord Tennyson, "The Charge of the Light Brigade" (text p. 231; question 1, following)

Dylan Thomas, "The Hand That Signed the Paper" (text p. 140; question 2, following)

CONNECTIONS QUESTIONS IN TEXT (p. 580) WITH ANSWERS

1.   Compare the attitudes expressed toward war in "An Iraqi Evening" and in Alfred, Lord Tennyson's "The Charge of the Light Brigade" (p. 231).

The sympathies of al-Sa'igh's poem are with the individual families who are affected by the war and not with its larger causes. He is also suspicious of the way the war is conducted, both by the military and by the journalists who report it to the families at home. Tennyson, on the other hand, takes a much broader view of war. Rather than bringing the focus to individual people, he follows the movements of "the six hundred" (line 8) soldiers that make up the brigade, and he sees the war as honorable and "Noble" (55). Though he notes that some of the six hundred died in the charge, his poem affirms the cause for which they died.

2.   Discuss how the images in "An Iraqi Evening" and in Dylan Thomas's "The Hand That Signed the Paper" (p. 140) create the respective tone for each poem.

By reducing the leaders he indicts in this poem to their hands, Thomas emphasizes how faceless and impersonal decisions can lead to great suffering. The hand is a symbol for action in "The Hand That Signed the Paper"; it is pure agency without reflection or remorse and thus has "no tears to flow" (line 16). The tone of this poem is cold and critical. By contrast, the images in "An Iraqi Evening" present the family members as pure receptors. They cannot act to change the war; they can only passively hear, see, and smell it. There is much more pathos in al-Sa'igh's poem because it asks us to empathize with the family members in their position of helplessness.

LÉOPOLD SÉDAR SENGHOR, *Totem* (p. 580)

For Senghor, race is not just a matter of pigment, but of the blood "down in [his] deepest veins" (line 1). He describes his blood as "loyal" (6) but there is an implication that he has in some ways failed its demand for loyalty in return. The two figures that Senghor uses for this heritage form an interesting contrast. The capitalized Ancestor (2) suggests the speaker's respectful and even worshipful appreciation of the tradition of his predecessors. On the other hand, Senghor says "He is the guardian animal" (4). In the ancestor figure, Senghor brings together the animal and the human, the wild and the rational. He is both the source of pride and the protection from pride.

POSSIBLE CONNECTIONS TO OTHER SELECTIONS

M. Carl Holman, "Mr. Z" (text p. 524; question 2, following)
Langston Hughes, "I, Too" (text p. 396)
———, "Theme for English B" (text p. 502)
Alden Nowlan, "The Bull Moose" (text p. 171; question 1, following)

CONNECTIONS QUESTIONS IN TEXT (p. 581) WITH ANSWERS

1. Discuss the significance of the symbols in "Totem" and in Alden Nowlan's "The Bull Moose" (p. 171). Despite their differing subject matter, how can the poems' themes be related to one another?

    Animals play a central symbolic function in both of these poems, as both use them to contrast with more "civilized" surroundings. In "Totem," the unspecified animal represents the restless force threatening to "burst the dam of scandal" (line 5). In Nowlan's poem the moose, among the herd of cows, appears even wilder than it would in its natural setting; it is "like the ritual mask of a blood god" (9). The description of "a gelded moose yoked with an ox for plowing" (17) seems to summarize both poems' concern with the coexistence of the wild and the domesticated in human life. The end of "The Bull Moose" also suggests the cruelty of humans toward that which they identify as wild.

2. Consider what race means to the speakers in "Totem" and M. Carl Holman's "Mr. Z" (p. 524).

    Holman's Mr. Z seems to think that race is a matter of habits. In trying to distance himself from "his mother's skin" (line 1), he adopts the views and tastes that are either "raceless" (5) or "Anglo-Saxonized" (8). He disavows those habits that would mark him as African American, such as an appreciation for "jazz and spirituals" (4) or a desire for "pork in its profane forms" (10). Race has a deeper meaning for the speaker in Senghor's "Totem" because it resides deep in his body, not just in his skin. Like Mr. Z, he must "hide" (line 1) his race, but rather than a matter of political views and table manners, for Senghor race is a matter of "lightning and thunder" (3) and of "naked pride" (7).

SHU TING, *O Motherland, Dear Motherland* (p. 581)

Like the relationship between a daughter and a mother, the relationship between this poem's speaker and her country is complex and full of contradiction — it is simultaneously frought with resentment and a source of joy. Rather than dwell on Chinese history (which is too long and complicated to cover adequately in one class period), encourage your students instead to consider the parallels between family and country, especially as they are suggested by Shu's poem. Is it possible, for example, to love and hate at the same time? Almost every one of your students will be able to provide an example from his or her own life. After they've discussed the dynamics of family for a short time (maybe ten minutes), your students will have a better grasp on the speaker's conflicting emotions about her "motherland."

Ask them whether Shu's tone is ultimately positive or negative, or a little bit of both. To help them with this, draw their attention to the poem's symbols and metaphors and try to unpack as many of them as time allows. What, for example, do your students make of the image of a "barge mired in a silt shoal / As the tow rope cuts deeply into your shoulder" (lines 6–8)? Some students will quickly recognize the idea that the speaker is stuck in her identity and is trying to extract herself. But do they notice that the effort to release herself inflicts damage on her country, and that she is sorry for it? Almost every image in the poem contains this kind of paradox, which frustrates any definitive reading but promises rich and lively discussion.

POSSIBLE CONNECTIONS TO OTHER SELECTIONS

Mahmoud Darwish, "Identity Card" (text p. 574; question 1, following)

Tato Laviera, "AmeRícan" (text p. 284)

Li Ho, "A Beautiful Girl Combs Her Hair" (text p. 56)

Florence Cassen Mayers, "All-American Sestina" (text p. 250; question 2, following)

CONNECTIONS QUESTIONS IN TEXT (p. 582) WITH ANSWERS

1. Compare the speaker's tone in this poem and in Mahmoud Darwish's "Identity Card" (p. 574).

    In both "Identity Card" and "O Motherland, Dear Motherland," the speakers take on the voice of an entire nation of people. The statement "I am" establishes a personal identity but also has larger implications for national identity. However, in Shu's poem, the tone of these statements is celebratory. Though she relates some of the hardships of life in China — "I am poverty, / I'm sorrow, / I'm the bitterly painful hope / Of your generations" (lines 10–13) — her ultimate goal is to glorify her country. The tone of Darwish's poem, on the other hand, is frustrated and confrontational. This tone is largely a function of Darwish's audience — not citizens of his own country, but those outside of it.

    Also, both poets use a repeated line to structure their poems, but in "Identity Card" that line falls at the beginning of the stanza, while in "O Motherland, Dear Motherland" it is placed at the end. For Darwish, all of the details of the poem flow out of perceptions of Arab identity. For Shu, the details together add up to a complete picture of China.

2. Discuss the view of China in this poem and the perspective on the United States in Florence Cassen Mayers's "All-American Sestina" (p. 250).

    "All-American Sestina" paints a one-dimensional portrait of the United States, implying through its list of consumer goods that America is overly dependent on capitalism and is bereft of deeper meaning for its citizens. Shu's perspective is more nuanced, exploring both positive and negative associations of China; her refusal to reconcile them can be seen as an extension of the complexity of Chinese culture.

WISŁAWA SZYMBORSKA, *Nothing's a Gift* (p. 583)

"Nothing's a Gift" follows the long poetic tradition of contrasting body and soul, sacred and profane. Unlike most of her predecessors, however, Szymborska uses humor and puns to convey her message that the body is temporary but the soul is eternal. Students should enjoy the double entendre of lines such as "I'm drowning in debts up to my ears" (line 2) and "I'll be fleeced, / or, more precisely, flayed" (12–13), although you may have to press to get them to see the multiple meanings. The poem's extended metaphor of debt adds an interesting twist to the tradition as well, implying that earthly emphases on money and commerce exact a toll on the body, which itself must be paid for. It also allows Szymborska to comment on the inequities of class, ironically observing that "Some are saddled with the burden / of paying off their wings. / Others must, willy-nilly, account for every leaf" (16–19). In this context, the soul's immortality promises recompense for those who are oppressed by capitalism.

POSSIBLE CONNECTIONS TO OTHER SELECTIONS

John Donne, "A Valediction: Forbidding Mourning" (text p. 150)

John Milton, "When I consider how my light is spent" (text p. 615)

Walt Whitman, From "I Sing the Body Electric" (text p. 268; question 1, following)

CONNECTION QUESTION IN TEXT (p. 583) WITH ANSWER

1. Compare attitudes toward the body in this poem and Walt Whitman's "I Sing the Body Electric" (p. 268).

   Asserting that the body is temporary and profane, "Nothing's a Gift" gives preference to the soul, which is "the protest against" (line 32) the tyranny of the body and the only thing that can't be taken away from us. Whitman clearly disagrees. "I Sing the Body Electric" celebrates the minutest details of the human body and argues that they "are not the parts and poems of the body only, but of the soul, / O I say now these are the soul!" (35–36). Whereas Szymborska, then, delineates the difference between body and soul, Whitman insists that they are one and the same.

TOMAS TRANSTRÖMER, *April and Silence* (p. 584)

Students may find their traditional romantic notions about the connotations of spring challenged by Tranströmer's poem, in which "Spring lies desolate" (line 1). However, "April and Silence" is part of a tradition in which poets have expounded on the negative qualities of spring. For example, Tranströmer's opening line recalls that of Eliot's *The Wasteland*: the cruelest month. The speaker's depression manifests itself throughout the poem. He focuses almost solely on what he lacks, on what he cannot achieve, and on his own inability to gain control. As he notes, "I am carried in my shadow / like a violin / in its black box" (7–9). Perhaps because of the limitations of translation, the poem may seem flat to some readers — some students may argue that the speaker is merely suffering from light deprivation. You might ask students whether they are inspired to empathize with the speaker of the poem. Why or why not?

POSSIBLE CONNECTION TO ANOTHER SELECTION

William Carlos Williams, "Spring and All" (text p. 631; question 1, following)

CONNECTION QUESTION IN TEXT (p. 584) WITH ANSWER

1. Discuss the description of spring in this poem and in William Carlos Williams's "Spring and All" (p. 631).

By the time April rolls around, we are so desperate for warmth and new growth that if the weather remains wintry, our souls contract and we become pessimists. If spring comes early, we are somehow more optimistic. Tranströmer's "April and Silence" is reminiscent of our thoughts while enduring a late spring, when all we can recognize is what we are unable to achieve. Williams's "Spring and All," in contrast, reminds us of the moment when winter turns to spring and the dormant plants awaken.

AUDIOVISUAL RESOURCES (manual p. 382)

24

A Collection of Poems

ANONYMOUS, *Bonny Barbara Allan* (p. 585)

Ballads can provide a good introduction to poetry, for they demonstrate many devices of other poetic forms — such as rhyme, meter, and image — within a narrative framework. Ballads, however, often begin abruptly, and the reader must infer the details that preceded their action. They use simple language, tell their story through narrated events and dialogue, and often use refrains. The folk ballad was at its height in England and Scotland in the sixteenth and seventeenth centuries. These ballads were not written down but were passed along through an oral tradition, with the original author remaining anonymous. Literary ballads are derivatives of the folk ballad tradition. Keats's "La Belle Dame sans Merci" (text p. 610) is an example.

Notice how often this ballad refers to a broken love relationship. What can you infer about the relationships of the people in this ballad? Is it always one sex or the other who suffers? Is there a relationship between this ballad and modern-day popular songs? "Scarborough Fair" (text p. 184) might provide the basis for a discussion of the romantic situations presented in this ballad and the durability of such old "songs." Despite the list of impossible tasks that the speaker presents to his former lover as the price of reconciliation, the refrain names garden herbs associated with female power. Thyme traditionally is thought to enhance courage, sage wisdom, and rosemary memory, and parsley was used to decorate tombs — but both sage and rosemary had the additional connotations of growing in gardens where women ruled the households. You might wish to have your students speculate on how such "mixed messages" might have been incorporated into this ballad. Also, "Scarborough Fair" was the basis for an anti-war song by the folk-rock duo Simon and Garfunkel in the 1960s. Your students might be interested in hearing how this old folk song was adapted for twentieth-century purposes.

Web Ask students to research the poets in this chapter at **bedfordstmartins.com/ meyerpoetry**.

Despite their ostensible narrative directness, ballads can be highly suggestive (rather than straightforward) in their presentation. Psychological motivation is often implied rather than spelled out. To explore this point, you might request, for example, that students in a two- to three-page essay examine the reasons for and effects of the vengeful acts of Barbara Allan.

These ballads contain central characters whose awareness (and hence voice) comes into full power near the moment of their death. Again, this observation seems to support the psychological realism and suggestive truth that ballads can convey.

TIP FROM THE FIELD

When teaching "Bonny Barbara Allan" and other ballads, I begin by reading the selection aloud or playing a recording of it, followed by a recording of early blues music from Mississippi (e.g., songs by Robert Johnson or Howlin' Wolf). In conjunction, I distribute the lyrics from the blues songs to the class. I then ask my students to compare these two oral-based forms.

– TIMOTHY PETERS, *Boston University*

WILLIAM BLAKE, *The Garden of Love* (p. 586)

This brief lyric poses in customary Blakean fashion the natural, free-flowing, and childlike expression of love against the restrictive and repressive adult structures of organized religion. The dialogue between the two is effectively demonstrated in the closing two lines, with their internal rhyme patterns, in particular the rhyming of "briars" (of the priests) and "desires" (of the young boy). The process of growing into adulthood is costly, according to Blake; it requires the exchange of simple pleasures for conventional morality.

Ask students to explore contexts for William Blake on *LiterActive*.

POSSIBLE CONNECTIONS TO OTHER SELECTIONS

Emily Dickinson, "Some keep the Sabbath going to Church" (text p. 315)

Robert Frost, "Birches" (text p. 365)

WILLIAM BLAKE, *Infant Sorrow* (p. 587)

This brief poem uses the voice of an infant to demonstrate distrust of "the dangerous world" (line 2). Arriving "Helpless naked" (3) and "Struggling" (5), the baby is soon "Bound and weary" (7) and has little hope. The parental response is not encouraging: the pain and fear of childbirth preclude a proper greeting. Blake's speaker seems to have been aware of the dangers of the world before his arrival, knowing that the world into which he "leapt" (2) was "dangerous" (2). His first contact does not seem to dissuade him from this bias.

POSSIBLE CONNECTIONS TO OTHER SELECTIONS

Anne Bradstreet, "Before the Birth of One of Her Children" (text p. 588)

Sharon Olds, "Rite of Passage" (text p. 279)

ROBERT BLY, *Snowfall in the Afternoon* (p. 587)

In these four three-line stanzas the speaker of this poem describes an almost hallucinatory winter scene. By the end of the poem the distant barn has been fully transformed into a ship, emphasizing the speaker's transforming perception, influenced by the hypnotic falling snow. You might begin discussion by talking about the structure of this poem. Bly very deliberately separates the stanzas by giving them numbers, and you might ask students to consider how the poem might read differently if the stanzas were merely separated by space. Do the numbers provide a sense of progression or differentiation between the various stanzas? Ask students to consider also whether the structure of the poem reflects the poem's content.

Examine in class the contrasts that Bly sets up in the poem — between the images of snow and darkness in the first two stanzas and the images of moving away and moving toward in the third and fourth stanzas. Ask students to consider these images and describe how they affect the mood of the poem.

Have students examine the final line of the poem: "All the sailors on deck have been blind for many years" (line 12). Who are the sailors on deck, and why might they be blind?

Gregory Djanikian, "When I First Saw Snow" (text p. 595)

Henry Wadsworth Longfellow, "Snow-Flakes" (text p. 613)

ANNE BRADSTREET, *Before the Birth of One of Her Children* (p. 588)

Until Anne Bradstreet's brother-in-law took a collection of her poems to London and had it published in 1650, no resident of the New World had published a book of poetry. Bradstreet's work enjoyed popularity in England and America. She was born and grew up on the estate of the earl of Lincoln, whose affairs her father managed. Bradstreet's father was eager to provide his daughter with the best possible education. When she was seventeen she and her new husband, Simon Bradstreet, sailed for Massachusetts, where she lived the rest of her life.

As a child Bradstreet contracted rheumatic fever, and its lifelong effects compounded the dangers attending seventeenth-century childbirth. What may seem at first an overdramatized farewell to a loved one can be viewed in this context as a sober reflection on life's capriciousness and an understandable wish to maintain some influence on the living. Perhaps the most striking moment in the poem occurs in line 16, when the only inexact end rhyme ("grave") coincides with a crucial change in tone and purpose. What had been a summary of Puritan attitudes (deeply felt, to be sure) toward life and death and a gently serious offering of "best wishes" to the speaker's husband becomes, with that crack in the voice, a plea to be remembered well.

You might discuss the appropriateness of the poet's choosing heroic couplets for this subject: How does the symmetry of the lines affect our understanding of the subject? You might also consider the way the speaker constructs her audience, like someone writing a diary. Is this truly private verse? Or does the speaker sense that people other than her children will read the poem?

Anne Bradstreet, "The Author to Her Book" (text p. 137)

John Donne, "A Valediction: Forbidding Mourning" (text p. 150)

ELIZABETH BARRETT BROWNING, *My letters! all dead paper, mute and white!* (p. 588)

This sonnet is part of Browning's *Sonnets from the Portuguese,* written during her courtship with Robert Browning. Their relationship started as an epistolary one — and the ongoing letters between Elizabeth and Robert are famous for their romance and beauty — so it should be no surprise to students that Browning would cherish her love letters so much. This poem describes a woman (presumably Browning herself) reading through old love letters (presumably from Robert) with joy.

If you're having trouble getting your students to read poems imaginatively, try the mystery of the last two lines to get their curiosity going. What does the last letter say? Why doesn't she dare to repeat it? If your students have trouble with the poem's erotic implications, ask them about the progression of letters: How does their content change?

Anne Bradstreet, "To My Dear and Loving Husband" (text p. 492)

Elizabeth Barrett Browning, "How Do I Love Thee? Let Me Count the Ways" (text p. 493)

Emily Dickinson, "Wild Nights — Wild Nights!" (text p. 318)

Helen Farries, "Magic of Love" (text p. 44)

ROBERT BROWNING, *Meeting at Night* and *Parting at Morning* (p. 589)

The titles of these two lyrics ask that they be taught together. Have students summarize in a writing assignment the poems' themes and suggest their complementarity. Here are portrayed the coexisting desires in human beings for the bonds of love and the freedom of adventure. Discuss with the class the use of natural imagery in each poem and the relative displacement of the sense of a speaker.

You might also ask students if we can still read these poems with the unhesitating acceptance of the divisions that Browning seems to take for granted — namely, that Eros and the night world are linked in the acceptance of the feminine but that the day world of action and adventure is the exclusive realm of man.

POSSIBLE CONNECTION TO ANOTHER SELECTION

Richard Wilbur, "A Late Aubade" (text p. 84)

WILLIAM CULLEN BRYANT, *To a Waterfowl* (p. 589)

The action of this poem takes place all in a moment, as the speaker sees a waterfowl, contemplates its relation to the "Power" (line 13) of the world, and then watches it disappear. In this short period of time, however, Bryant uses his meditation on the bird to address some larger issues of human existence. Bryant begins the poem with two questions, wondering where the bird has come from and where it is going, and he introduces an imagined threat in the form of the fowler. The beginning of the fourth stanza marks a turning point, however, as the speaker moves from questioning and speculation to the confident assertion, "There is a Power" (13). This power makes intelligible the difference between wandering and being lost (16). This suggests that the bird is not just aimlessly flying but that there is in nature a path which it can follow or lose. Bryant connects this "Power" that guides the bird's actions with the Christian God who establishes a path for people to follow. As the waterfowl disappears on his journey, the speaker expresses faith in "He, who . . . Will lead my steps aright" (29–32).

POSSIBLE CONNECTIONS TO OTHER SELECTIONS

Elizabeth Bishop, "The Fish" (text p. 32)

Sheila Wingfield, "A Bird" (text p. 119)

ROBERT BURNS, *A Red, Red Rose* (p. 590)

Some of Burns's metaphors have become so familiar that we could hardly imagine poetry without them. Linking love with a red rose has even become a poetry cliché. However, some of his figures are still striking and vivid. The drying up of the seas and the melting of rocks present an apocalyptic scene that belies the poem's gentle beginning. Like many older poems, this one also has a close relation to song. The effects of meter and rhyme are musical, as are the repetitions of phrases like "Till a' the seas gang dry" (lines 8, 9) and "fare thee weel" (13, 14). It might be fun to have your students compare this poem to a contemporary love song. In what ways are the two alike? Besides the obvious dialect differences, how is this poem foreign to the tradition they are used to? Which one seems more original?

POSSIBLE CONNECTIONS TO OTHER SELECTIONS

Anonymous, "Scarborough Fair" (text p. 184)

William Shakespeare, "My mistress' eyes are nothing like the sun" (text p. 243)

GEORGE GORDON, LORD BYRON, *She Walks in Beauty* (p. 591)

In the nineteenth century, George Gordon, Lord Byron, was commonly considered the greatest of the Romantic poets. He spent his childhood with his mother in Aberdeen, Scotland, in deprived circumstances despite an aristocratic heritage. In *Childe Harold, Don Juan,* and much of his other work, Byron chronicled the adventures of one or another example of what came to be known as the "Byronic hero," a gloomy, lusty, guilt-ridden individualist. The poet died of fever while participating in the Greek fight for independence from Turkey.

The title and first line of "She Walks in Beauty" can be an excellent entrance to the poem's explication. Students might puzzle over what it means to walk *in* beauty: is the beauty like a wrap or a cloud? The simile "like the night" hinges on that image. You might ask students if the speaker makes nature subservient to the woman, or the reverse. You might point out "gaudy" (line 6), a strange adjective for describing the day, to draw attention to the speaker's attitude toward nature.

Note the mood of timeless adoration in the second stanza. There is really no movement, only an exclamation of wonder. The exclamation is even more direct in the final stanza, where the woman's visage becomes a reflection of her spotless character. Students might explore the images in all three stanzas, looking for shifts from natural to social. How does the speaker move from "like the night" (1) to "a mind" (17) and "a heart" (18)? Why would he want to describe a woman in these terms? What effect does this description have on our idea of her? Do we really know her by the end of the poem?

For discussion of Byron's poetry, consult *Byron: Wrath and Rhyme,* edited by Alan Bold (London: Vision, 1983); Frederick Garber's *Self, Text, and Romantic Irony: The Example of Byron* (Princeton: Princeton UP, 1988); and Peter Mannings's *Byron and His Fictions* (Detroit: Wayne State U, 1978).

POSSIBLE CONNECTION TO ANOTHER SELECTION

William Wordsworth, "The Solitary Reaper" (text p. 634)

AUDIOVISUAL RESOURCES (manual p. 373)

LUCILLE CLIFTON, *this morning (for the girls of eastern high school)* (p. 591)

In this joyous poem of self-affirmation a teenage girl announces to the classmates who have taunted her that she knows who she is — and she likes herself. The speaker of this poem has clearly been tormented by the other girls (presumably white) in her school for her difference. But she takes their derogatory descriptions of black girls — "jungle girl" (line 6), "shining" (7), "snake" (8), and "tall/tree girl" — and embraces them as positive attributes that give her a feeling of power and superiority over the others.

High school students, especially girls, are notorious for their casual cruelty to each other. Ask your students if the ostracism implied in this poem sounds familiar to them. Can they think of any girls who might have felt the way the speaker does? How does this poem affect their feelings about her?

Another way to approach this poem is to talk about school desegregation in the 1950s. Clifton was born in 1936; she was eighteen years old when *Brown v. Board of Education* ordered that black students be integrated into white schools. If you can get a copy of it, consider bringing in Norman Rockwell's famous painting *The Problem We All Live With,* which shows a young black girl being escorted to school by federal marshals. How does this image complicate or deepen students' understanding of the speaker's feelings of defiance?

Langston Hughes, "Theme for English B" (text p. 502)

Patricia Smith, "What It's Like to Be a Black Girl (for Those of You Who Aren't)" (text p. 123)

JUDITH ORTIZ COFER, *The Game* (p. 592)

Your students might find it useful to begin with a comparison of the differing reactions of adults and children in "The Game." The adults respond to the girl's birth defect by asking questions. The interpretation of her curved spine as a "question mark, / the eternal *why*" (lines 9–10) is aligned with her mother's point of view. That unanswered why is directed at God, and with the mention of the "cross Christ bore / to Calvary" (13–14), it echoes Christ's completion of the question: why have you forsaken me? The speaker's mother, too, sees the girl as God's work. Her view of the affliction as one of His "small mysteries" (29) suggests that she, too, wonders about the explanation.

The speaker and Cruz herself react not by questioning but by imagining. During playtime, they can forget that she is different and she can pretend to be a normal member of a family. As the title implies, this play is only a game, and the real world won't ignore Cruz's curved spine. However, the children's play is compared in a puzzling way with God's work: Cruz is made "like a child's first attempt / at cutting and pasting a paper doll" (21–22). In this figure, Ortiz Cofer takes away some of the awesome power that the adults attribute to God, imagining that Cruz might not be "humpbacked" (1) for some reason, but by mistake.

POSSIBLE CONNECTIONS TO OTHER SELECTIONS

Robert Hass, "A Story about the Body" (text p. 278)

Cathy Song, "The Youngest Daughter" (text p. 94)

SAMUEL TAYLOR COLERIDGE, *Kubla Khan: or, a Vision in a Dream* (p. 593)

Samuel Taylor Coleridge was born in Ottery St. Mary, Devonshire, but was sent to school in London, where he impressed his teachers and classmates (among whom was Charles Lamb) as an extremely precocious child. He attended Cambridge without taking a degree, enlisted for a short tour of duty in the Light Dragoons (a cavalry unit), planned a utopian community in America with Robert Southey, and married Southey's sister-in-law. He met William Wordsworth in 1795 and published *Lyrical Ballads* with him three years later. Coleridge became an opium addict in 1800–1801 because of the heavy doses of laudanum he'd taken to relieve the pain of several ailments, principally rheumatism. For the last eighteen years of his life, he was under the care (and under the roof) of Dr. James Gillman, writing steadily but never able to sustain the concentration needed to complete the large projects he kept planning.

Reputedly, "Kubla Khan" came to Coleridge "as in a vision" after he took a prescribed anodyne and fell into a deep sleep. What Coleridge was able to write down on waking is only a fragment of what he dreamed. Figures such as the "pleasure-dome" and "the sacred river" take on an allegorical cast and suggest the power that inspires the writing of poetry. Although phrases such as "sunless sea" and "lifeless ocean" appear gloomy, they could also suggest mystery and the atmosphere conducive to bringing forth poems.

For a reading of this poem, consult Humphrey House's "Kubla Khan, Christabel, and Dejection," in *Coleridge* (London: Hart-Davis, 1953), reprinted in *Romanticism and Consciousness,* edited by Harold Bloom (New York: Norton, 1970). Another good essay to turn to is "The Daemonic in 'Kubla Khan': Toward Interpretation" by Charles I.

Patterson Jr., in *PMLA* 89 (October 1974): 1033–42. Patterson points out, for example, that the river in the poem is "sacred" because it seems to be possessed by a god who infuses in the poet a vision of beauty. Likewise, he identifies the "deep delight" mentioned in line 44 as "a daemonic inspiration." In a writing assignment you might ask students to explore imagery and sound patterns in order to demonstrate how Coleridge uses words to embody and suggest the idea that poetry is truly a "pleasure-dome," visionary and demonically inspired.

You could initiate discussion by asking students to locate and discuss the way Coleridge uses unusual language to describe the scene and to shape our perceptions of it. What is the effect, for instance, of alliteration in line 25 ("Five miles meandering with a mazy motion")?

POSSIBLE CONNECTIONS TO OTHER SELECTIONS

John Keats, "Ode to a Nightingale" (text p. 209)

William Butler Yeats, "Sailing to Byzantium" (text p. 637)

AUDIOVISUAL RESOURCES (manual p. 373)

RICHARD CRASHAW, *An Epitaph upon a Young Married Couple, Dead and Buried Together* (p. 594)

In this "Epitaph," Crashaw takes a tragic subject — the untimely deaths of a young couple — and turns it into a celebration of love that survives beyond death. Because Crashaw knows this is an upsetting subject, he directly reassures us: "Peace, good reader. Do not weep" (line 7). He takes a common euphemism for death and transforms it into an allegory for the resurrection of the soul. To say someone is "asleep" (8) is a polite and comforting way to talk about death. Here though, the sleep is only temporary until "th' eternal morrow dawn" (17). After their period of rest, the couple will wake into a light more constant than that of the physical world. The "stormy night" (16) of existence will be followed by lasting sunshine.

POSSIBLE CONNECTIONS TO OTHER SELECTIONS

Anne Bradstreet, "To My Dear and Loving Husband" (text p. 492)

John Donne, "Death Be Not Proud" (text p. 290)

E. E. CUMMINGS, *Buffalo Bill 's* (p. 595)

An interesting few moments of class discussion could address whether Cummings is singing the praises of Buffalo Bill in this poem. How does the word *defunct* strike our ears, especially in the second line of the poem? What is the speaker's tone as he asks the concluding question? Is he sincere or contemptuous? 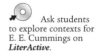 Ask students to explore contexts for E. E. Cummings on *LiterActive*.

POSSIBLE CONNECTIONS TO OTHER SELECTIONS

Louise Erdrich, "Dear John Wayne" (text p. 473)

Marilyn Nelson Waniek, "Emily Dickinson's Defunct" (text p. 276)

GREGORY DJANIKIAN, *When I First Saw Snow* (p. 595)

This is a poem of transformation — a moment that is much larger and more significant in the poet's life than the simple event it describes. Ask students to point to specific lines in the poem that describe in detail the feel of this moment. Students are likely to point out the red bows (line 13), the dusting of snow on the gray planks of the porch (17), the smell of the pine tree (6), the feel of the sticky sap on his fingers (5), and, most particularly, the sounds (the music, the sound of the Monopoly game in progress, his boot buckles, and the imagined whistling of the train).

These images are woven together to effectively re-create the speaker's first experience of snow, but they take on larger relevance within the context of the beginning and ending of the poem. After reading the poem in class, you may wish to ask students about the beginning and the end — what do they make of the "papers" the family is waiting for (3)? How does an understanding of that phrase affect an understanding of the final two lines of the poem?

POSSIBLE CONNECTION TO ANOTHER SELECTION

John Keats, "On First Looking into Chapman's Homer" (text p. 241)

JOHN DONNE, *The Apparition* (p. 596)

Donne's poem carries the Renaissance conceit of the lover, pining away at the mercy of a cruel and scornful mistress, one step further; after the lover has died from his mistress's neglect, he takes his revenge by coming back to haunt her. Ask students to notice the various means by which the speaker seeks to characterize his former love. He calls her a "murderess" in the very first line. How else does he attempt to cast her in a bad light? Students may need to be informed that quicksilver (line 12) — mercury — was a common treatment for venereal disease in Donne's day. Do your students trust the speaker's description of his former love? What are the implications of the fact that there are actually *two* ghosts — the speaker (4) and the woman (13) — in this poem? Notice that Donne uses three different metrical lengths in the first four lines. What is the effect of this constant change of rhythm and of the rhyme between "dead" and "bed" in these lines?

POSSIBLE CONNECTIONS TO OTHER SELECTIONS

Margaret Atwood, "you fit into me" (text p. 135)
John Donne, "The Flea" (text p. 597)

JOHN DONNE, *Batter My Heart* (p. 596)

Christian and Romantic traditions come together in this sonnet. Employing Christian tradition, Donne here portrays the soul as a maiden with Christ as her bridegroom. Borrowing from Petrarchan materials, Donne images the reluctant woman as a castle and her lover as the invading army. Without alluding to any particular tradition, we can also observe in this poem two modes of male aggression — namely, the waging of war and the pursuit of romantic conquest, again blended into a strong and brilliantly rendered metaphysical conceit. Donne is imploring his "three-personed" God to take strong measures against the enemy, Satan. In a typical metaphysical paradox, Donne moreover asks God to save him from Satan by imprisoning him within God's grace.

Rhythm and sound work remarkably in this sonnet to enforce its meaning. Review the heavy-stressed opening line, which sounds like the pounding of a relentless fist and is followed by the strong reiterated plosives of "break, blow, burn."

POSSIBLE CONNECTION TO ANOTHER SELECTION

Mark Jarman, "Unholy Sonnet" (text p. 246)

JOHN DONNE, *The Flea* (p. 597)

An interesting discussion or writing topic could be organized around the tradition of the carpe diem poem and how this poem both accommodates and alters that tradition.

The wit here is ingenious, and after the individual sections of the poem are explained, more time might be needed to review the parts and give the class a sense of the total effect of the poem's operations.

The reason the speaker even bothers to comment on the flea stems from his belief that a commingling of blood during intercourse (here, admittedly, by the agency of the flea) may result in conception. Hence his belief that the lovers must be "yea more than" united and that the flea's body has become a kind of "marriage temple." For the woman to crush the flea (which she does) is a multiple crime because in so doing she commits murder, suicide, and sacrilege (of the temple) and figuratively destroys the possible progeny. The flea in its death, though, also stands as logical emblem for why this courtship should be consummated. The reasoning is that little if any innocence or honor is spent in killing the flea, then, likewise, neither of those commodities would be spent "when thou yield'st to me."

Play a recording of Richard Burton reading "The Flea" on Literature Aloud.

One way to begin discussion is to consider the poem as an exercise in the making of meaning: What does the flea represent to the speaker, and how does its meaning change as the poem progresses? What, in effect, is the relation between the flea and the poem?

POSSIBLE CONNECTIONS TO OTHER SELECTIONS

Sally Croft, "Home-Baked Bread" (text p. 126)

John Donne, "Song" (text p. 203)

GEORGE ELIOT [MARY ANN EVANS], *In a London Drawingroom* (p. 598)

This poem could more accurately be titled "*From* a London Drawingroom," as the speaker's gaze seems to be directed entirely outward, through a window that makes London (or even the world) seem like a prison. The colors are drab, the people are lifeless, the architecture monotonous. Despite the monotony of the landscape, everyone is in constant motion, which is part of the problem; "No figure lingering / Pauses to feed the hunger of the eye / Or rest a little on the lap of life" (lines 10–12). Ask students to unpack these lines; what do they imply about these people and their surroundings, or about the relationship between this speaker and the rest of the world? What is meant by the phrase "multiplied identity" (16)? And in the last two lines, what do students suppose "men" are being punished for? By whom? The relationship between humankind and nature is also worth pursuing; we have presumably created the "smoke" of the first line and the "solid fog" of the fourth line, yet the punishment seems to come from elsewhere. This poem is a good example of how an outward-looking description really reflects inward psychology.

POSSIBLE CONNECTIONS TO OTHER SELECTIONS

Matthew Arnold, "Dover Beach" (text p. 115)

T. S. Eliot, "The Love Song of J. Alfred Prufrock" (text p. 456)

CHARLOTTE PERKINS GILMAN, *Whatever Is* (p. 598)

In "Whatever Is," Gilman criticizes the habits of mind that keep us from acknowledging anything beyond what we want to believe. These habits are so strong that it takes violence to overcome them: "we simply have to go / And choke each fiction old and dear" (lines 11–12) before we can replace it with the truth. When she begins the poem, Gilman seems to include herself in the "we" that is reluctant to see a "staring fact" (3). However, at one point in the poem, she implicates a "they" in this kind of thinking (8). If any of your students have read Gilman's "The Yellow Wallpaper," they might have ideas about the kind of facts that she would want people to recognize. How do they understand the "we" in the poem? Does Gilman really suspect herself of ignoring "Whatever is"? And what verbs would they oppose to "is"? *Seems? Pleases?*

Possible Connections to Other Selections

Fleur Adcock, "The Video" (text p. 517)
Richard Hague, "Directions for Resisting the SAT" (text p. 505)

SAM HAMILL, *Sheepherder Coffee* (p. 599)

In Hamill's poem, the peaceful scene of the riverbank with its redwood trees contrasts sharply with the images of destruction and loss: "Palestinians huddled in their ruins / the Afghani shepherd with his bleating goats, / the widow weeping, sending off her sons, / the Tibetan monk who can't go home" (lines 15–18). The act of drinking coffee, though, seems to bring all of the people in these scenes together, establishing an experience even more universal than love. Part of the reason there are fewer names for coffee is that it is a product that spread around the world from the Middle East, taking its name with it. Love, on the other hand, is indigenous and the words for it vary.

This poem also brings up questions of authenticity. You might have your students discuss why the speaker "used to" like coffee prepared in this particular way. Does the introduction of the other people in the poem cast a different light on the pleasant "hardships" of his austere life?

Possible Connection to Another Selection

Eliza Griswold, "Occupation" (text p. 202)

THOMAS HARDY, *Hap* (p. 599)

Bad luck, pain, and sorrow seem so happenstance, Hardy says in this sonnet. Does the attitude of the speaker ring true? He claims that it would be easier to bear ill chance if some vengeful god would openly proclaim his malevolent designs. Discuss with the class why even the machinations of some divinity appear preferable to the silent, indeterminate (and inhuman) operations of caprice.

Possible Connections to Other Selections

Michelle Boisseau, "Self-Pity's Closet" (text p. 555)
Langston Hughes, "Lenox Avenue: Midnight" (text p. 404)

THOMAS HARDY, *In Time of "The Breaking of Nations"* (p. 600)

This poem, published shortly after the beginning of World War I, demonstrates the speaker's belief in the timelessness of domestic life. Nations may break into pieces and kingdoms may be destroyed, as the footnote to this poem suggests, but life and love in the countryside "will go onward the same / Though Dynasties pass" (lines 7–8).

Students may see this as a naive view of international politics, or they may find it comforting. A discussion of this poem could center on what they've learned in history classes: How has the history they've studied been ordered? How do they imagine the speaker of this poem would choose to organize a history of the world?

Possible Connection to Another Selection

Dylan Thomas, "The Hand That Signed the Paper" (text p. 140)

JOY HARJO, *The Path to the Milky Way Leads through Los Angeles* (p. 600)

The title of Harjo's poem reveals her interest in bringing the celestial together with the terrestrial. Right away in "The Path to the Milky Way," she defies our normal sense of space, describing the "strangers above me, below me and all around me" (line 1). In a city so packed with anonymous faces, people have to struggle to remain individuals. When they "turn toward the changing of the sun and say [their] names" (9), they use the names as a way of asserting selfhood.

In addition to these questions of identity, Harjo is also concerned in this poem with the conflicts between commerce and nature. In some ways, the development of Los Angeles has made it more beautiful: the "shimmer of the gods" (6) in the sky is probably the result of pollution, which makes sunsets look more spectacular. However, civilization has also effaced nature, including the sight of the Milky Way. The speaker "can't easily see that starry road from the perspective of the crossing of / boulevards, can't hear it in the whine of civilization or taste the minerals of / planets in hamburgers" (13–15). The real stars have been replaced by the figurative "stars" in the movies, and even the elements have been reduced to commodities. In Los Angeles you can purchase "several brands of water or a hiss of oxygen" (17). Finding herself in this environment, the speaker turns to Native American culture for a model and finds Crow, who teaches her to sort through the busy city life and "collect the shine of anything beautiful" (28).

POSSIBLE CONNECTIONS TO OTHER SELECTIONS

Tony Hoagland, "America" (text p. 561)
John Keats, "To One Who Has Been Long in City Pent" (text p. 609)

FRANCES E. W. HARPER, *Learning to Read* (p. 601)

This sonnet, written shortly after the end of the Civil War, eloquently praises the efforts of Yankees from the North who traveled to the South after the war to help teach slaves to read. Harper also recalls her own passion for learning how to read, despite the fact that she "was rising sixty" (line 35). Harper chooses not to characterize any one Yankee or "Reb," but rather focuses on people such as Uncle Caldwell and Chloe to personalize the poem. This technique shows the struggle to be free through the experiences of not only Harper but also those around her.

Students should be reminded of the relationship between the poet and the poem: Harper is writing about adjusting to life as a free woman, and about learning how to read; this poem is a product of that endeavor. It represents a switch from spoken language to written. Expand on this point with students, for the poem takes on more depth as this is fleshed out. Also alert students to what ultimately drove Harper to learn to read: her desire to read the Bible. Although she was "rising sixty," she "got a pair of glasses" (37) and "never stopped till [she] could read The hymns and Testament" (39–40). The Bible, and the ability to read it, becomes symbolic of Harper's freedom from slavery.

POSSIBLE CONNECTIONS TO OTHER SELECTIONS

Langston Hughes, "Theme for English B" (text p. 502)
Philip Larkin, "A Study of Reading Habits" (text p. 34)

GEORGE HERBERT, *The Collar* (p. 602)

Herbert's poems were published after his death. Many of them deal with the hesitancy of commitment he felt before becoming an Anglican priest.

The title "The Collar" echoes *choler* (anger) and suggests the work collar that binds horses in their traces as well as the clerical collar. Explore with the class how the speaker's situation, the stress he feels, and his particular argument gradually emerge. In his meditation, he tries to argue himself out of his position of submission. His life is free; he deserves more than thorns. He would like to have some of the world's secular awards. The speaker then admonishes himself to forget the feeble restrictions — his "rope of sands." But when all is said and done, he capitulates. You might observe how this poem demonstrates a strong measure of psychological insight.

As a writing assignment, you might ask the class to explore in a two- to three-page paper how rhythm reinforces the meaning in this poem.

POSSIBLE CONNECTION TO ANOTHER SELECTION

Sir Philip Sidney, "Loving in Truth, and Fain in Verse My Love to Show" (text p. 622)

AUDIOVISUAL RESOURCES (manual p. 376)

CONRAD HILBERRY, *The Calvinist* (p. 603)

Though your students will probably have learned about Calvinism at some point, they might benefit from a discussion of the ideas relevant to this poem. The most important is the idea of predestination — that all people are either "elect" or not prior to their birth and neither good works nor faith can change one's status in the afterlife. Hilberry makes the connection between this religious doctrine and the use of language in that he questions whether words have a given referent, whether they are predestined to indicate a certain thing, or whether their meanings are fluid. Hilberry "like[s] to think" (line 1) the latter is true, but he also has a tendency to believe in set meanings, a tendency he imagines as a Calvinist who resides "in the chamber just behind / my tongue" (4–5). The non-Calvinist part of him sees beauty in the blankness of words, which fly "white / against the sky" (12–13). Yet the Calvinist brings the words "home" (20) to their given meaning. Hilberry does hint at some middle ground at the end of this poem. Though the return home represents the burdens of meaning, it is also a comforting image, and the "ragged line" (19) the words take suggests that they retain some freedom in their movement.

POSSIBLE CONNECTIONS TO OTHER SELECTIONS

Anne Bradstreet, "The Author to Her Book" (text p. 137)

Thomas Lux, "Onomatopoeia" (text p. 196)

Gary Snyder, "How Poetry Comes to Me" (text p. 143)

GERARD MANLEY HOPKINS, *Hurrahing in Harvest* (p. 604)

This Italian, or Petrarchan, sonnet begins with a vivid description of the glories of early autumn. The repetition of "these things" (line 11) creates an insistence that shifts the intent of the poem outside its boundaries. The "beholder" (11) of all this beauty realizes that it was here all along; it's the act of seeing that has been absent. The response of the speaker to this beauty, then, is transcendent, powerful, joyous: "The heart rears wings bold and bolder / And hurls for him, O half hurls for him off under his feet" (13–14).

The poem provides many examples of Hopkins's signature sound innovations. The pleasure of these phrases infiltrates the whole of the poem, establishing sound that is as rich as the harvest time discussed. The intense language mimics the scene that Hopkins's speaker paints for his reader: the description of "stooks" (1), "clouds" (3), and "azurous hung hills" (9) establishes a relationship between speaker and reader as the sight of them unites the speaker and "our Saviour" (6). The speaker characterizes "all that glory in the heavens" (6) as "a / Rapturous love's greeting" (8), again sharing the roles of natural grandeur and carefully crafted language.

Hopkins's work provides good opportunities for the study of sound and meter; asking students to identify alliteration in the poem could help them see its effectiveness, and helping them to scan the poem could make its detailed pleasures more accessible. To clarify the basic optimism of this poem, you might want to try comparing it to William Blake's "Infant Sorrow" (p. 587). Blake's speaker's natural pessimism contrasts nicely with the sublime joy that Hopkins's speaker details.

POSSIBLE CONNECTIONS TO OTHER SELECTIONS

William Blake, "Infant Sorrow" (text p. 587)

Anne Bradstreet, "To My Dear and Loving Husband" (text p. 492)

GERARD MANLEY HOPKINS, *Pied Beauty* (p. 604)

It seems appropriate for Hopkins to have used so many innovations in style, structure, and diction in a poem that glorifies God — the only entity "whose beauty is past change" (line 10) — by observing the great variety present in the earth and sky. Ask students to point out examples of poetic innovation in this poem and to suggest their effects on the poem.

In form, "Pied Beauty" is what Hopkins termed a "curtal [that is, shortened] sonnet." Not only is it shortened, but it is shortened to exactly three-fourths of a traditional sonnet: the "octet" is six lines, the "sestet" four and a half. Having compressed the sonnet structure to ten and a half lines, Hopkins must make careful word choices to convey meaning in fewer words. Note the hyphenated words, which are his own creations; is it possible to understand the meanings of these made-up compounds? Compare Hopkins's practice of creating new words to that of Lewis Carroll in "Jabberwocky" (text p. 200).

Students will need to know what *pied* means (patchy in color; splotched). How do the many synonyms for *pied* in the first few lines emphasize the theme of the poem? How does the repetition of the *le* sound (dappled, couple, stipple, tackle, fickle, freckled, adazzle) add a sense of rhythm and unity to this poem's untraditional metrics?

POSSIBLE CONNECTION TO ANOTHER SELECTION

E. E. Cummings, "in Just-" (text p. 267)

GERARD MANLEY HOPKINS, *The Windhover* (p. 605)

At the midpoint of his poetic career, Hopkins considered this poem "the best thing I ever wrote" (*The Letters of Gerard Manley Hopkins to Robert Bridges*, edited by C. C. Abbott, rev. 1955 [New York: Oxford UP], 85). Regardless of the poem's quality, students should be forewarned that this is a difficult work by a difficult poet. It may help them to know that even literary specialists have had a difficult time agreeing on the poem's exact meaning. In fact, Tom Dunne's Hopkins bibliography (1976) lists nearly one hundred different readings of the poem before 1970. With this in mind, you might ask students to discuss the overall feeling conveyed by this lyric, rather than expecting them to be able to explicate it line by line. In general, the poem begins with the speaker's observation of a kestrel hawk in flight. The speaker is drawn from passive observation into passionate feeling for the "ecstasy" (line 5) of the bird's soaring freedom: "My heart in hiding / Stirred for a bird, — the achieve of, the mastery of the thing!" (7–8). It then occurs to the speaker that the bird's creator is "a billion / Times told lovelier, more dangerous" (10–11) than the creature, and his awe expands to consider an even greater power.

Have students note that the poem is addressed "To Christ our Lord." The speaker directly speaks to Christ as "my chevalier" in line 11. Realizing that the poem is addressed to Christ leads to an interpretation of the final lines as references to Christ's suffering and death. Despite Christ's earthly humility (the "blue-bleak embers" of line 13), his true glory — "gold-vermilion" (14) — is revealed when he falls, galls, and gashes himself (14).

One might approach "The Windhover" structurally by comparing it to the less complex poem that precedes it in the text. In "The Windhover," as in "Pied Beauty," Hopkins alters the sonnet form to suit his purposes. Discuss how "The Windhover" conforms to and deviates from traditional sonnet form. In particular, note its division into thirteen lines and the indication of the "turn" not at the beginning of the sestet but with the poet's emphasis on the word *and* in line 10. How do these deviations from the traditional sonnet form affect the poem's meaning?

Also worth discussing are the striking use of alliteration in the first long line and the poet's choices of unusual words, as seen in previous poems. Note that to the poet, a Jesuit priest, the "billion" in line 10 is not hyperbole; if anything, it is an understatement.

Fortunately, a number of glosses and extended critical interpretations of the works of this difficult poet are available. Among these are Graham Storey's *A Preface to Hopkins* (London and New York: Longman, 1981); Paul Mariani's *A Commentary on the Complete Poems of Gerard Manley Hopkins* (Ithaca: Cornell UP, 1969); *Hopkins: A Collection of Critical Essays,* edited by Geoffrey Hartman (Englewood Cliffs: Twentieth-Century Views/ Prentice-Hall, 1966); and J. Hillis Miller's *The Disappearance of God* (Cambridge: Harvard UP, 1963).

POSSIBLE CONNECTION TO ANOTHER SELECTION

Gerard Manley Hopkins, "God's Grandeur" (text p. 194)

A. E. HOUSMAN, *Is my team ploughing* (p. 605)

This poem is in ballad form, with a typical question-response exchange between the Shropshire lad who has died and a supposedly impersonal voice that answers his queries. The surprise comes, of course, with the introduction of the second "I," who has a decidedly vested interest in the earthly life of the deceased.

You might ask students to trace the development of the worldly objects the speaker is interested in: What is the effect of his beginning with his team of horses and ending with questions about his girl and his friend? Does the development say anything about his sense of priority, or is the effect meant only to heighten the poem's final irony?

POSSIBLE CONNECTIONS TO OTHER SELECTIONS

Stephen Crane, "A Man Said to the Universe" (text p. 164)
Emily Dickinson, "Because I could not stop for Death —" (text p. 326)

A. E. HOUSMAN, *To an Athlete Dying Young* (p. 606)

You might discuss this poem in relation to the carpe diem tradition. Is it perverse to imagine such a connection in a poem that treats youth and death? Many students will have read this poem in high school. They might enjoy picking out recurrent words and themes — such as "shoulder-high" in stanzas 1 and 2, "shady" in stanza 4, and "shade" in stanza 6; the various thresholds and sills or doorways in the poem; and the image of both the laurel and the rose as evanescent tokens of glory and youth — and exploring their function in the poem.

Gary Gildner, "First Practice" (text p. 275)

Theodore Roethke, "Elegy for Jane" (text p. 255)

JULIA WARD HOWE, *Battle-Hymn of the Republic* (p. 607)

You might consider using this poem as a way of talking about the relationship between poetry and politics. Poems have been used as political tools in many ways. They have glorified governments and criticized them, and their effects haven't been limited to the realms of literature. In oppressive dictatorships, poets and other artists are particularly feared and persecuted. In this "Battle-Hymn," Howe supports the Union and the abolitionist cause, whose members will "die to make men free" (line 19), aligning their sacrifice with that of Christ.

Howe first sets the apocalyptic scene of the Civil War. The losses were so large and so close to home that the war must have felt like the end of time. However, Howe thinks the Union will be on the righteous side at the time of judgment. She compares the army encampments to altars. Although the fighting is violent, the cause is holy, so the army's actions are a form of praise. Through military force, the Union will "crush the serpent with [its] heel" (11), defeating that which brings sin into men's lives. The trumpet call near the end of the poem signals the triumphant judgment day and the resurrection of the country after the trials of war.

Possible Connections to Other Selections

Yousif al-Sa'igh, "An Iraqi Evening" (text p. 579)

Alfred, Lord Tennyson, "The Charge of the Light Brigade" (text p. 231)

BEN JONSON, *On My First Son* (p. 607)

A father's deep grief for his lost child as expressed in this beautiful epitaph needs little explication. However, the poem contains several ideas worthy of class discussion. Why does the poet think that we should envy those who die at an early age? Do your students agree? Do they think the poet believes it himself? How can a child be considered a "best piece of poetry" (line 10)? Have students suggest paraphrases for the last two lines, which are confusing because of the convoluted grammatical construction. Do these lines mean that the poet has learned a lesson about not caring too much for earthly joys, a reading that the use of the word *lent* in line 3 supports? Is he proposing that his great attachment to the child had something to do with his death?

Possible Connections to Other Selections

Anne Bradstreet, "Before the Birth of One of Her Children" (text p. 588)

Peter Meinke, "(Untitled)" (text p. 91)

BEN JONSON, *To Celia* (p. 608)

This poem is a laudatory devotion to a lover in which the speaker moves through conceits of drinking in the first stanza and conceits of the tribute of a rose in the second. This poem is in fact a good opportunity to examine a Petrarchan conceit, or rather, two conceits. After students have worked through each stanza, you might ask them if there is a definite relationship between them. Does the poem read like two poems, or do the two stanzas depend on each other in a fundamental way?

You may also want to discuss whether the poem seems to be a bit *too* devotional; students may find the speaker's praise for his lover to be a bit too much, a bit unbelievable.

You may want to discuss how poetic conventions change over time. Jonson's Celia is an exaggerated lover (her name connotes heaven), but that type of love or devotion was the subject of poetry in seventeenth-century England. An interesting writing assignment might be to have students trace the way in which such devotion changes over time by selecting representative love poems from the seventeenth century through the present.

POSSIBLE CONNECTIONS TO OTHER SELECTIONS

Robert Herrick, "Upon Julia's Clothes" (text p. 239)

Christopher Marlowe, "The Passionate Shepherd to His Love" (text p. 490)

William Shakespeare, "Not marble, nor the gilded monuments" (text p. 491)

JUNE JORDAN, *The Reception* (p. 608)

You might start the discussion of this poem by having your students talk about the connotations of the title. "Reception" refers immediately to the party that the characters attend, but the poem is also interested in the community's "reception" of Dorothea. Sexuality makes her a controversial figure, garnering attention both wanted and unwanted, from both men and women. For Dorothea, sex is contrasted with employment. She works all day in a servant position, but at night flirting and wearing sexy clothes gives her a release and a feeling of power. During the day she cleans "the rich white downtown dirt" (line 7), but at the party she takes on a creative agency. She "work[s] / the crowded room like clay like molding men / from dust" (17–19). Though recognizing that the relationship between sex and commerce is scandalous, it allows Dorothea to own her sexuality in a way that the other women can't.

POSSIBLE CONNECTIONS TO OTHER SELECTIONS

Edna St. Vincent Millay, "I, Being Born a Woman, and Distressed" (text p. 614)

Marge Piercy, "The Secretary Chant" (text p. 22)

Natasha Trethewey, "Domestic Work, 1937" (text p. 274)

JOHN KEATS, *To one who has been long in city pent* (p. 609)

This Petrarchan sonnet is a kind of love poem to the countryside. The speaker moves quickly away from the trap the city represents in the first line to focus instead on the pleasures of escaping it. The "blue firmament" (line 4), "wavy grass" (7), "notes of Philomel" (10), and "sailing cloudlet's bright career" (11) paint a portrait of a pastoral experience that the city dweller longs for, one that slips by as quickly as "an angel's tear" (13). The absence of the city is a presence in the poem, and the vivid description of what the city lacks combines with the first line to depict it as a prison.

Ask students to explore contexts for John Keats on LiterActive.

Discussion might center on how the speaker's pleasures reflect on the city. Students might enjoy doing a little freewrite from the perspective of one who has been long in classroom pent; what pleasant presences are absent from the classroom?

POSSIBLE CONNECTIONS TO OTHER SELECTIONS

John Ciardi, "Suburban" (text p. 518)

Christopher Marlowe, "The Passionate Shepherd to His Love" (text p. 490)

JOHN KEATS, *The Human Seasons* (p. 609)

In this poem, Keats gives new life to the figurative connection of the seasons with the stages of human life. The limited "measure" (line 1) of the seasons' progress parallels the limits of our existence. Keats's description of the early stages of life, the spring and summer, has an erotic undertone in words like "lusty" (3) and "luxuriously" (5). The chewing of the "honied cud of fair spring thoughts" (6) in summer suggests the digestion of spring. The experiences of youth are *incorporated* into the body. The hunger of summer recedes, though, as autumn brings the desire for rest. At this stage, man is no longer acquisitive. While spring "Takes in all beauty" (4), autumn lets it "Pass by unheeded" (12). With the final lines, Keats turns to winter and the reminder of our "mortal nature" (14). The structure of the sonnet, with spring, summer, and autumn each occupying a quatrain, adds finality to the winter with the couplet rhyme.

POSSIBLE CONNECTIONS TO OTHER SELECTIONS

Robert Herrick, "To the Virgins, to Make Much of Time" (text p. 79)

John Keats, "To Autumn" (text p. 127)

William Shakespeare, "When forty winters shall beseige thy brow" (text p. 620)

JOHN KEATS, *When I have fears that I may cease to be* (p. 610)

The fears described in this sonnet are increasingly human, mortal, and intimate. Keats fears first that death may cut short the writing of his imagined "high-piled books"; then that he may never trace the "shadows" of "huge cloudy symbols of a high romance"; and, finally, that he might not see his beloved again. In the couplet, love and fame sink to nothingness, but Keats confronts his fear and is deepened by the experience.

There is a subtle order to the presentation of Keats's objects of regret. In a writing assignment, you might ask the class to comment on how one item seems to lead to the next and how their arrangement lends form and substance to this sonnet.

POSSIBLE CONNECTIONS TO OTHER SELECTIONS

Emily Dickinson, "This was a Poet — It is That" (text p. 323)

William Shakespeare, "Not marble, nor the gilded monuments" (text p. 491)

JOHN KEATS, *La Belle Dame sans Merci* (p. 610)

You might read this ballad in connection with other ballads in this book. How is it that ballads have stood the test of time and have continued to appeal to many generations of listeners and readers? Is this ballad any different from medieval ballads? Is it more suggestive, perhaps, of a state of mind?

The opening three stanzas hold a descriptive value for the reader, for they present the knight as pale, ill, possibly aging and dying. The stanzas possess a rhetorical value as well, for they whet our curiosity. Just why is the knight trapped in this withered landscape? Play a recording of Sir Ralph Richardson reading "La Belle Dame sans Merci" on *Literature Aloud*.

The femme fatale figure goes back at least to Homeric legend and the wiles of Circe. Note how the "belle dame" appeals here to several senses — with her appearance, her voice, the foods she offers, the physical comforts of sleep. Above all else, though, she seems otherworldly, and Keats here seems to insist on her elfin qualities, her wild eyes, and her strange language.

Words change meaning and grow in and out of popularity over generations (even decades). Contrast the way we might use *enthrall* today (with what subjects) and what Keats intends by "La Belle Dame sans Merci / Hath thee in Thrall!" (lines 39–40). Note how the shortened line of each quatrain gives both a sense of closure and the chill of an inescapable doom.

In his well-known essay on the poem, Earl R. Wasserman begins by remarking, "It would be difficult in any reading of Keats's ballad not to be enthralled by the haunting power of its rhythm, by its delicate intermingling of the fragile and the grotesque, the tender and the weird, and by the perfect economy with which these effects are achieved" (from "La Belle Dame sans Merci," in his *The Finer Tone: Keats's Major Poems* [Baltimore: Johns Hopkins UP, 1953, 1967], 65–83, and reprinted in *English Romantic Poets: Modern Essays in Criticism,* edited by M. H. Abrams [New York: Oxford UP, 1960], 365–380). In a writing assignment you might ask students to select any one of these elements and discuss it with several examples to show how it shapes the poem's tone and mood.

Other studies of this poem include Jane Cohen's "Keats's Humor in 'La Belle Dame sans Merci,'" *Keats-Shelley Journal* 17 (1968): 10–13, and Bernice Slote's "The Climate of Keats's 'La Belle Dame sans Merci,'" *Modern Language Quarterly* 21 (1960): 195–207.

POSSIBLE CONNECTIONS TO OTHER SELECTIONS

Anonymous, "Bonny Barbara Allan" (text p. 585)
Emily Dickinson, "Because I could not stop for Death —" (text p. 326)

YUSEF KOMUNYAKAA, *Slam, Dunk, & Hook* (p. 611)

On its surface this poem is a narrative of how a young basketball player used extreme physical exertion and the game of basketball to cope with his mother's death. You may want to start classroom discussion by asking students about coping mechanisms: What other ways do people, especially boys, react to the loss of a loved one? Do they think it's normal or appropriate for "Sonny Boy" to respond by playing basketball?

Once your students have explored their emotional reactions to the poem's theme, try to get them to grapple with the poem's mythological allusions. (Consider having them read the book's section on mythological criticism, pages 660–662, before discussing the poem in class.) Your students may need help understanding the references. Mercury (line 1) is the Roman messenger of the gods, as well as a symbol of mercantilism (*mercury* shares the same root as *merchant*), best known for inventing the lyre (note the connection between this and the "swish of strings like silk" of line 5) and for his speed, symbolized by his winged sandals (probably the insignia on the boy's sneakers); he was also responsible for leading the dead into the underworld. "Bad angels" (4) is probably a reference to the Furies, three spirits responsible for avenging the dead. The "storybook sea monsters" (10) allude to Poseidon's attendants; they also suggest the fearsome creatures used to illustrate the seas in antique maps. The presence of these mythological characters, combined with the statement that "we were metaphysical" (18), strongly suggests that Komunyakaa is using the sport of basketball as a metaphor for the cosmic order.

POSSIBLE CONNECTIONS TO OTHER SELECTIONS

Robert Frost, "'Out, Out —'" (text p. 368)
W. S. Merwin, "When You Go Away" (text p. 496)

TED KOOSER, *A Death at the Office* (p. 612)

In "A Death at the Office," Kooser meditates on how the modern world has removed some of the humanness of even so significant an event as death. While in previous generations, people would have used funeral rituals to deal with loss, in the impersonal atmosphere of the workplace, the rite is translated into the office ritual of passing around a memo. The remembrances at work are presided over by the faceless authority of the "management," which has come early to remove the deceased's personal possessions. You might have your students discuss the implications of their actions. Does "bury[ing] her nameplate / deep in her desk" (lines 6–7) honor her as the burial of the body does? Or is it, and the removal of her "Midol and Lip-Ice" (8), a way of erasure? For whose benefit do they perform these tasks? At the end, as the rest of the employees reclaim what is left in her office, her presence in the office seems to be completely effaced.

Emily Dickinson, "The Bustle in a House" (text p. 328)
A. E. Housman, "To an Athlete Dying Young" (text p. 606)

EMMA LAZARUS, *The New Colossus* (p. 613)

Students are likely to recognize at least part of the concluding five lines of this poem, which are – of course – inscribed on the Statue of Liberty's pedestal. They're probably so familiar with it, in fact, that you may have trouble getting them to take a close look at the poem as a whole or to move beyond what they think they know about it. You might try a number of different approaches to accomplish this.

For example, consider focusing on the poem's form. "The New Colossus" is a sonnet. Although it mostly conforms to the usual iambic pentameter associated with the form, it also strays from it at signficant moments. You may want to work through a scansion of the poem in class, then ask students to comment on the effects of the poet's departure from tradition. The most notable variation is probably the trochee that opens line 6, where the word *mother* receives the poem's strongest emphasis. Consider also the anapest in "with conquering limbs" (line 2) and the spondee in the first two words of "keep, ancient lands" (9). What do these diversions from iambic pentameter contribute to your students' understanding of the poem's intent?

Another way to approach the poem is to consider its historical context. "The New Colossus" was written as part of an effort to raise money to pay for the statue's pedestal. What's interesting is that "The New Colossus" had a strong effect on how Americans think about the Statue of Liberty. The sculptor, Frédéric Auguste Bartholdi, conceived of the statue as a bit of propaganda for France, meant to symbolize the friendship between France and the United States. America, at the time, was experiencing unprecedented waves of immigration from poorer European countries, particularly Ireland and Italy; the resulting overcrowding and visible poverty in large cities like New York and Boston strained resources and led many Americans to feel animosity toward its newest residents. But thanks to the cultural influence of Lazarus's poem, we tend to think of the statue as a welcome to beleaguered immigrants. Ask your students if they can think of any other examples of poems (or any works of literature) that had such a profound effect on American cultural perspectives.

A mythological approach to the poem could also lead to an interesting discussion. As the title suggests, Lazarus compares the Statue of Liberty to the famous Colossus of Rhodes, an enormous bronze statue of Apollo, the Roman god of the sun as well as the arts. At the time it was built, the colossus was one of the seven wonders of the world. As the oracle of Delphi, Apollo was able to cure social ills and prevent plagues. Specifically, he used his ministrations and purification rituals to bring an end to long cycles of vengeance, thereby promoting peace in a war-torn region. Ask your students what political and cultural hopes the poet expresses by making this association between the Statue of Liberty and this tradition.

Thomas Lynch, "Liberty" (text p. 549)
Shu Ting, "O Motherland, Dear Motherland" (text p. 581)

HENRY WADSWORTH LONGFELLOW, *Snow-Flakes* (p. 613)

The snow, generally described in terms of emotions and falterings of the human spirit, is taken in this poem to reveal something about "the troubled sky" (line 11) and "our cloudy fancies" (7) at the same time. The air is personified; the speaker insists that the snow is this poem which reveals "the secret of despair, / Long in its cloudy bosom hoarded" (15–16).

A good place to begin discussion is with the question of the speaker, who removes himself from the scene as much as possible. The only time he alludes to himself at all is with the plural pronoun "our" in line 7. What type of person must he be? Do we assume that he is feeling troubled, that he is full of grief and despair? What is his relationship to the scene that he is witnessing?

POSSIBLE CONNECTIONS TO OTHER SELECTIONS

Robert Frost, "Stopping by Woods on a Snowy Evening" (text p. 370)

Percy Bysshe Shelley, "Ode to the West Wind" (text p. 257)

EDNA ST. VINCENT MILLAY, *I, Being Born a Woman and Distressed* (p. 614)

The humor of this poem is present in the contrast between tone and content; the formal tone belies the harsh sentiments it conveys. The speaker admits that she desires "your person" (line 4) but wants to make clear that this physical desire is "the poor treason / of my stout blood against my staggering brain" (9–10). The "treason" will be overridden once the body has its desires met; the sexual "frenzy" (13) initiated by "needs and notions" (2) and the "propinquity" (3) of "you" does not signify the beginning of a romance. On the contrary, the speaker wants to "make it plain" (12) that she doesn't plan to speak to the object of her desires once those desires have been met.

Students may initially resist the stuffy tone here, especially if they need to turn to the dictionary to look up "propinquity" (3). However, salacious detail can often encourage even reluctant readers to scan a page more thoroughly. Focusing on the cool and cutting remarks hidden in the heightened language of this poem could help students with more challenging work.

POSSIBLE CONNECTIONS TO OTHER SELECTIONS

Robert Hass, "A Story about the Body" (text p. 278)

Sharon Olds, "Sex without Love" (text p. 93)

AUDIOVISUAL RESOURCES (manual p. 378)

JOHN MILTON, *On the Late Massacre in Piedmont* (p. 614)

Born in London, Milton began writing poetry at the age of fifteen. He had a remarkable aptitude for languages, mastering Latin, Greek, Hebrew, and most modern European languages before he completed his education in 1637. After earning his master's degree from Christ's College, Cambridge University, in 1632, he disappointed expectations that he would become a minister and embarked instead on a six-year period of carefully self-designed study in which he read everything he could. (The eyestrain caused by his voracious study eventually led to his blindness in 1651.)

Milton dedicated his literary talent to the causes of religious and civil freedom from 1640 to 1660, writing Puritan propaganda and numerous political and social tracts. He argued vociferously on many issues: "Of Reformation Touching Church Discipline in England" (1641) denounced the episcopacy; his troubled relationship with seventeen-year-old Mary Powell, who left him after one month of marriage, inspired him to support the legalization of divorce in "Doctrine and Discipline of Divorce" (1643);

"Areopagitica," (1644), one of his most famous polemics, argued the necessity of a free press; and his defense of the murder of King Charles I in "The Tenure of Kings and Magistrates" (1649), although contributing to his appointment as the secretary for foreign languages in Cromwell's government, nearly got him executed when the monarchy was restored in 1660.

He was arrested, but friends and colleagues intervened on his behalf, and he was eventually released. Blind and unemployed, he returned to his poetry and a quiet life with his third wife, Elizabeth Minshull. It was during these last years of his life that Milton produced (by dictating to relatives, friends, and paid assistants) his most famous and substantial works: the epic poems *Paradise Lost* (1667) and *Paradise Regained* (1671) and the verse drama *Samson Agonistes* (1671).

"On the Late Massacre in Piedmont" is a sonnet of accountability — in an almost bookkeeper sense of the term. The basic premise is contractual. The Waldenses have preserved piety and faith in God over four centuries; now God should avenge their massacre. *Even,* as the first word of line 3, is an imperative verb form, as in *Even the score.* Scorekeeping, in fact, matters in this sonnet, and students might find it a good exercise in reading to identify and analyze the numerical images. Nature, moreover, is shown as sympathetic to the Waldenses, for it redoubles the sound of their lamentations. The passage ends with the elliptical phrase "and they / To heaven." Syntax again provides the verb *redoubled* and says, in effect, that the hills echoed the moans to heaven. Milton expresses the wish that future generations of Waldenses will augment their number "a hundredfold" to offset the Pope's power.

You might ask students to write an analytical and persuasive essay proving that this is either a plea for vengeance or the expression of a hope that the Waldenses will receive God's protection and strength throughout history.

POSSIBLE CONNECTIONS TO OTHER SELECTIONS

Wilfred Owen, "Dulce et Decorum Est" (text p. 122)
Alfred, Lord Tennyson, "The Charge of the Light Brigade" (text p. 231)

AUDIOVISUAL RESOURCES (manual p. 378)

JOHN MILTON, *When I consider how my light is spent* (p. 615)

This sonnet is sometimes mistakenly titled "On His Blindness." You might begin by asking just what the topic of Milton's meditation is. He seems to be at midlife, neither old nor young. If Milton's blindness comes to mind as the subject, does that idea accommodate itself to the description "And that one talent which is death to hide / Lodged with me useless"? It would take some ingenuity to make blindness the equivalent of "talent" here. Far better to let "talent" stand in its old (biblical) and new senses and refer to Milton's poetic capability. At any rate, a discussion of this sonnet should prove useful in developing students' ability to select or discard extraliterary details in connection with a poem.

Play a recording of Robert Speaight reading "When I consider how my light is spent" on *Literature Aloud*.

POSSIBLE CONNECTIONS TO OTHER SELECTIONS

Anne Bradstreet, "To My Dear and Loving Husband" (text p. 492)
Ben Jonson, "On My First Son" (text p. 607)
John Keats, "When I have fears that I may cease to be" (text p. 610)

N. SCOTT MOMADAY, *Crows in a Winter Composition* (p. 615)

The speaker of this poem paints a portrait of a cold world in which "the hard nature of crows" (line 17) presents a vague threat. The "soft distances" (2) beyond the trees and "the several silences, / Imposed on one another" (7) are "unintelligible" (8). In this context, in which a Zen-like "Nothing appeared" (5), the crows provide an unwelcome "definite, composed" (15) certainty.

Students might enjoy drawing some of the contrasts between the disdain felt for crows in this poem and the awe developed in Gerard Manley Hopkins's "The Windhover" (p. 605). While both poems turn their attention to birds, their tones and conclusions provide satisfying contrasts.

POSSIBLE CONNECTIONS TO OTHER SELECTIONS

Gregory Djanikian, "When I First Saw Snow" (text p. 595)
Robert Frost, "Stopping by Woods on a Snowy Evening" (text p. 370)
Gerard Manley Hopkins, "The Windhover" (text p. 605)

SARAH MORGAN BRYAN PIATT, *A New Thanksgiving* (p. 616)

Though Sarah Morgan Bryan Piatt was a prolific poet, her work is not widely studied today. Her style might seem archaic to students at first, but there is much that they can learn from this poem. Remind students that poets often respond to traditional poems or prayers — in this case the traditional Thanksgiving prayer. Ask students to determine the rhythm and rhyme scheme of the poem (iambic pentameter with quatrains rhymed in an *abab* pattern). Does the poem's form contribute to or detract from its powerful message? Have them consider the poet's first-person plural perspective. Is it too presumptuous? Or do all of us secretly pray for horrible things that will serve our own ends? Ask students to examine Piatt's melodramatic personification of the ocean in line 5. How does it compare with the tone in other parts of the poem?

POSSIBLE CONNECTION TO ANOTHER SELECTION

Charles Simic, "To the One Upstairs" (text p. 123)

MARGE PIERCY, *For the Young Who Want To* (p. 616)

In "For the Young Who Want To," Piercy plays with some contrasting notions of what it means to be a poet. On one hand, writers in America are generally not highly valued for their contribution to society. As Piercy notes, writers are treated as lazy or delusional by more "productive" peers. On the other hand, writers who do manage to achieve some success are seen as not only talented but also as geniuses. The kind of reverential treatment we give to the best authors suggests that poetry is a kind of priesthood. Yet another contradiction arises in the fact that creative writing programs, which adopt a "workshop" style of instruction, are increasingly popular training for writers. They take the approach that writing is *not* a matter of genius but rather of craft, which can be perfected and even licensed. Poetry workshops credential MFAs in the same manner veterinary schools credential vets to practice.

Piercy wants to distance herself from all of these perspectives. For one thing, the MFA degree does not guarantee skill at writing just as "you may be a clumsy sadist / whose fillings fall into the stew / but you're still certified a dentist" (lines 28–30). Also, extreme positions on genius are unrealistic: "Talent / is an invention like phlogiston / after the fact of fire" (32–34). She finally takes a commonsense stance on the matter, suggesting that "The real writer is one / who really writes" (31–32). The writer has to give up external definitions and rely on his or her own habits to define the work. In fact, being a writer is so solitary an occupation that "You have to / like it better than being loved" (35–36).

Bob Hicok, "Making it in poetry" (text p. 165)

Louis Jenkins, "The Prose Poem" (text p. 271)

SIR WALTER RALEIGH, *The Nymph's Reply to the Shepherd* (p. 617)

This poem's speaker makes a reply to the shepherd in Christopher Marlowe's well-known poem, "The Passionate Shepherd to His Love" (p. 490). Raleigh's imagined nymph responds with a pragmatic realism, in contrast to Marlowe's shepherd's romantic idealism. The "pretty pleasures" (line 3) the shepherd offers to entice his beloved — "gowns," "shoes," and "beds of roses" (13) — can't compete with the truth: Youth does not last, and love may not "still breed" (21) in its absence.

Discussion and assignments could examine this pragmatism closely: Consider assigning a fictitious journal entry from the nymph as she ponders what to say. Her reply doesn't focus on her feelings for the shepherd. Does she love him? Are her stated concerns merely the means by which she avoids telling him she doesn't feel romantic toward him? What kind of future might she imagine for herself in contrast to the one the shepherd offers?

POSSIBLE CONNECTIONS TO OTHER SELECTIONS

Christopher Marlowe, "The Passionate Shepherd to His Love" (text p. 490)

Patricia Smith, "What It's Like to Be a Black Girl (for Those of You Who Aren't)" (text p. 123)

CHRISTINA GEORGINA ROSSETTI, *Some Ladies Dress in Muslin Full and White* (p. 618)

The speaker of this poem transforms herself from a rather benign observer of fashion into a misanthrope who would selectively eliminate men and women based on what they are wearing. You might ask students to locate the precise moments where her attitude seems to shift: Does anything cause it? You might first ask students what they think the poet's tone or intention is. Which words indicate that light humor is the intended tone, and which words make the poem seem a biting satire? The poem may allow you to discuss the aggressive nature of humor, the very fine line between comedy and tragedy. Do students know anyone, or can they think of examples of professional comedians, whose brand of humor reveals antisocial tendencies? What motivates these humorists? Would they put Rossetti's speaker in the same camp?

POSSIBLE CONNECTION TO ANOTHER SELECTION

Emily Dickinson, "The Soul selects her own Society —" (text p. 321)

CHRISTINA GEORGINA ROSSETTI, *In Progress* (p. 618)

This Petrarchan sonnet describes a woman who has mellowed with age and reveals the speaker's ambivalence about the changes in her personality: Although the woman has become "calm" (line 2), "slow-speaking" (5), "silent" (6), eager to please (7), and "patient" (10) — all considered desirable feminine characteristics in the mid-nineteenth century — the speaker seems to prefer her former spark, hoping "that we may one day see / Her head shoot forth seven stars from where they lurk / And her eyes lightnings and her shoulders wings" (12–14). The woman, possibly the speaker's mother, seems to be close to death. You might ask your students whether the poet is hoping the woman will regain her vitality or if she is wishing for her death. If the latter, is her "fancy" (12) selfish or caring?

If you like to take a cultural or historical approach to literature, you may want to tell your students about the seeming epidemic of illness and frailty in middle-class women of the second half of the nineteenth century. (For a full explanation, refer to Ann Douglas Wood's 1973 essay "'The Fashionable Diseases': Women's Complaints and Their Treatment in Nineteenth-Century America," *Journal of Interdisciplinary History,* 4.) As the title of Wood's essay suggests, female sickness was "fashionable" in many circles, and thousands of otherwise healthy women complained of weakness and nerves and took to bed for months at a time. Some — including other women, doctors, and middle-class men — saw the epidemic as a reaction to the stultifying effects of society's expectation that middle-class women would contain their lives within the home and not pursue any intellectual or worldly activities. While most believed that the women's illnesses were real, others accused sick women of using claims of sickness to shirk their domestic duties. Rossetti's poem suggests an awareness of these competing arguments: How does knowing the cultural context of the poem affect your students' interpretation of it?

POSSIBLE CONNECTIONS TO OTHER SELECTIONS

Emily Dickinson, "What Soft — Cherubic Creatures" (text p. 319)

Cathy Song, "The Youngest Daughter" (text p. 94)

Dylan Thomas, "Do Not Go Gentle into That Good Night" (text p. 247)

CHRISTINA GEORGINA ROSSETTI, *The World* (p. 619)

Rossetti's sonnet imagines the world as a temptress by day and a monster by night. By combining the allure of the world and its dangers, Rossetti aligns herself with a traditional Christian view, which values heaven and sees worldly life as brutal and sinful in comparison. Rossetti's religious assumptions inform the imagery of the sonnet as well. The "subtle serpents gliding" (line 4) in the hair of the world at night remind the reader of the serpent that tempted Eve in the Garden of Eden. The "sweet flowers" (6) of the earth in daytime also suggest the paradise scene, and the "Ripe fruits" (6) foreshadow Eve's eating from the tree of knowledge and the expulsion from the Garden. By the end, the temptations of the world have ruined the innocence of the speaker who has given all her "life and youth" (13). The "cloven" (14) feet of the final line indicate the fall into sin, which mirrors the fall of the devil from his original position as one of God's angels.

POSSIBLE CONNECTIONS TO OTHER SELECTIONS

Joy Harjo, "The Path to the Milky Way Leads through Los Angeles" (text p. 600)

Sharon Olds, "Last Night" (text p. 85)

Richard Wilbur, "Love Calls Us to the Things of This World" (text p. 630)

CHRISTINA GEORGINA ROSSETTI, *Promises Like Pie-Crust* (p. 619)

This poem's speaker offers a straightforward, no-nonsense response to romantic possibility. Some students may find the crisp tone a pleasure, while others may find her cynicism unwarranted. Do students agree with the speaker's assessment of the risks of relationships? What might the speaker and her addressee be missing if they maintain their relationship as "the friends we were / Nothing more but nothing less" (lines 21–22)? You may find it productive to focus on that "more" and "less"; what do we have to gain in romantic relationships? What do we stand to lose? Asking students to write a journal entry to consider their own feelings on the matter may help make discussion more productive. An essay assignment could establish correlations between students' own beliefs about love and the pessimistic or optimistic views of romantic relationships found in poems in this collection. Some possibilities for comparison follow.

POSSIBLE CONNECTIONS TO OTHER SELECTIONS

Helen Farries, "Magic of Love" (text p. 44)

Christopher Marlowe, "The Passionate Shepherd to His Love" (text p. 490)

Edna St. Vincent Millay, "I, Being Born a Woman and Distressed" (text p. 614)

Sharon Olds, "Sex without Love" (text p. 93)

Sir Walter Raleigh, "The Nymph's Reply to the Shepherd" (text p. 617)

WILLIAM SHAKESPEARE

Shakespeare's sonnets have been widely discussed. Useful studies of them include *A Casebook of Shakespeare's Sonnets*, edited by Gerald Willen and Victor B. Reed; Edward Hubler's *The Sense of Shakespeare's Sonnets* (Westport: Greenwood, 1976); and *Shakespeare's Sonnets*, edited with commentary by Stephen Booth (New Haven: Yale UP, 1977). The two songs given in this section, "Spring" and "Winter," are discussed by Bertrand Bronson in *Modern Language Notes* 63 (1948) and by C. L. Barber in *Shakespeare's Festive Comedy* (Princeton: Princeton UP, 1972).

Ask students to explore contexts for William Shakespeare on *LiterActive*.

WILLIAM SHAKESPEARE, *That time of year thou mayst in me behold* (p. 620)

Images of death and decay predominate in this sonnet. Ask students to identify the different metaphors for death that are presented in the poem's three quatrains. The first quatrain evokes the approach of winter as dying leaves drift to the ground; the image of "bare ruined choirs" in line 4 would probably have reminded Shakespeare's contemporaries of the many monastery churches that had gone to ruin in the wake of Henry VIII's dissolution of the English monasteries in the 1530s. The second quatrain evokes images of falling night and the third of a dying fire whose embers are being extinguished by its own ashes.

The tone of the poem's concluding couplet could be a topic for class debate. Do students find the grimness of the first three quatrains to be mitigated by the poem's last two lines? The speaker seems to be suggesting to his friend or lover that the inevitability of death should sharpen his or her appreciation of the speaker's affections. Ask students to compare the portrayal of love as an anodyne against the inevitability of death in this poem with that idea as expressed in Matthew Arnold's "Dover Beach" (text p. 115).

POSSIBLE CONNECTIONS TO OTHER SELECTIONS

Matthew Arnold, "Dover Beach" (text p. 115)

Anne Bradstreet, "To My Dear and Loving Husband" (text p. 492)

Richard Wilbur, "A Late Aubade" (text p. 84)

WILLIAM SHAKESPEARE, *When forty winters shall besiege thy brow* (p. 620)

"When forty winters shall besiege thy brow" provides another excellent example of the form of an English, or Shakespearean, sonnet. The poem's central concept is expressed through three complementary quatrains, and the rhyme scheme — *abab cdcd efef gg* — adheres to the traditional Shakespearean sonnet form. Students unfamiliar with sonnet form should be referred to Chapter 9, "Poetic Forms," for a fuller explanation of the genre. They should then be encouraged to consider how form and content comple-ment each other in this sonnet.

It may be useful to suggest that the sonnet is a well-organized argument. Generally, Shakespeare marshals his rhetoric to convince his audience — both the per-son addressed in the sonnet and the poem's readers — of a specific truth. Here the poet warns the poem's youthful subject that age, like winter, offers no true sustenance, and that the best antidote to old age is children. The poet's powers of persuasion rest primarily on threats: In the first quatrain he depicts the physical effects of "forty win-ters" (line 1) and predicts that "Thy youth's proud livery, so gazed on now / Will be a tattered weed" (3–4). The second quatrain extends this rhetorical approach: the beau-ty of youth and "the treasure of thy lusty days" (6) are reduced merely to "deep-sunken eyes" (7) and "all-eating shame and thriftless praise" (8). In the final quatrain Shakespeare offers an alternative to what he has depicted as a wasteful life: instead of having nothing to show for youth, the addressee might instead say, "This fair child of mine / Shall sum my count and make my old excuse" (10–11). In addition, the beauty of the parent's youth will live on in the next generation. The couplet emphasizes the advantages of the alternative described by the third quatrain: "This were to be new made when thou art old, / And see thy blood warm when thou feel'st it cold" (13–14). The final line smoothly blends with the opening line, touching on the harsher aspects of "forty winters" and yet contrasting the potential emptiness with the warmth offered by the poet's suggested alternative.

POSSIBLE CONNECTIONS TO OTHER SELECTIONS

Anne Bradstreet, "Before the Birth of One of Her Children" (text p. 588)

Judith Ortiz Cofer, "Common Ground" (text p. 75)

WILLIAM SHAKESPEARE, *When, in disgrace with Fortune and men's eyes* (p. 621)

This sonnet posits a future scenario in which the speaker will be outcast because of his fortune. He claims that he will be comforted by remembering his idyllic time with his lover, which presumably occurs in the present. A good starting point for analysis of this poem is its diction, as it contains several words — *bootless, featured, scope* — whose meanings have changed. Another interesting point for discussion is the religious allu-sion in line 12. Students might be invited to entertain the possibility that the "thee" in line 10 and "thy" in line 13 refer not to the conventional Petrarchan lover but to God.

The sonnet's structure also merits attention. Ask students to compare the arrange-ment of the quatrains and concluding couplet in this poem with that of the other Shakespearean sonnets in the text. In which of the poems is there a sharp logical break between the quatrains and the couplet, and in which does this break occur after the octave? Is there any obvious relation between structure and content?

POSSIBLE CONNECTIONS TO OTHER SELECTIONS

John Donne, "A Valediction: Forbidding Mourning" (text p. 150)

William Shakespeare, "That time of year thou mayst in me behold" (text p. 620)

PERCY BYSSHE SHELLEY, *Ozymandias* (p. 621)

Many students will have read this Petrarchan sonnet in high school. You might begin by asking whether in an unintentionally ironic way Ozymandias may have been right; although he is far from outdistancing the rest of humanity in possessions and power, his statue is a reminder that all things are subject to decay and is thus a source of despair. The sonnet, despite its familiarity, still surprises by the quality of its versification. Observe in line 6 the delayed placement of "well," which underscores the closing cautionary note. The final lines, moreover, with the alliterated "boundless and bare" and "lone and level," do suggest the infinite reaches of both the desert and time.

POSSIBLE CONNECTIONS TO OTHER SELECTIONS

John Keats, "Ode on a Grecian Urn" (text p. 96)

William Butler Yeats, "Sailing to Byzantium" (text p. 637)

SIR PHILIP SIDNEY, *Loving in Truth, and Fain in Verse My Love to Show* (p. 622)

This sonnet's irregular meter matches its speaker's labored attempt to write it. Ask students to scan its lines, looking for irregularities. For example, the trochees at the beginnings of lines 1, 3, 4, 13, and so on illustrate the forced style that the speaker is trying to avert, while the irregular meter in line 9 aptly illustrates "words . . . halting forth."

Ask students to think about the images the speaker uses to describe his struggle to find the perfect writing style. His "sunburnt brain" (8) and the pregnancy metaphor ("great with child to speak" [12]) evoke an overfull, overcooked speaker who has worked too hard and gained little. How does the final line affirm our suspicions that there may be an easier way to write? Of course, Sidney has constructed his poem to make us feel this affirmation in the end.

Studies of this sonnet are included in the following discussions of *Astrophel and Stella* ("Loving in Truth" is the first sonnet in that sequence): David Kalsone's *Sidney's Poetry* (New York: Norton, 1970); Richard Lanham's "Pure and Impure Persuasion," and Collin Williamson's "Structure and Syntax in *Astrophel and Stella*" (both in *Essential Articles for the Study of Sir Philip Sidney*, edited by Arthur Kinney [Hamden: Archon, 1986]).

POSSIBLE CONNECTION TO ANOTHER SELECTION

E. E. Cummings, "since feeling is first" (text p. 495)

LYDIA HUNTLEY SIGOURNEY, *Indian Names* (p. 622)

Sigourney's "Indian Names" points out the hypocrisy in the representation of Native Americans. The "Ye" she addresses herself to talks about them as a "noble race and brave" (line 2). However, it is easy to romanticize a group of people you have removed from the land. As Sigourney points out, Native Americans can only be idealized this way after European Americans have "Crushed [them] like the noteless worm amid / The regions of their power" (43–44). These violent acts of removal are downplayed by the descendants of settlers who "say their cone-like cabins . . . Have fled away like withered leaves" (17–19), but they required much more force than an "autumn gale" (20).

In spite of this desire to efface the presence of Native Americans, their language is written into the landscape of the country because so many of the names for geographical places in America — including Massachusetts, Kentucky, and Missouri — come from native words. Though the physical presence of Native Americans has been confined, "their name is on your waters, / Ye may not wash it out" (7–8). They give names to the elemental powers — rivers and mountains — and their mark on Western consciousness endures.

POSSIBLE CONNECTIONS TO OTHER SELECTIONS

Sherman Alexie, "On the Amtrak from Boston to New York City" (text p. 174)

Barbara Hamby, "Ode to American English" (text p. 87)

DAVID R. SLAVITT, *Height* (p. 624)

Masking a sense of unanticipated despair with humor, the narrator of this poem contemplates the implications of discovering that he has grown shorter in his old age. Realizing that he had been "proud" of something he'd "done nothing to earn" (line 11), he questions whether other sources of pleasure in his life — talent, grace, and love, specifically — are equally tenuous.

The epigram that opens the poem is a quote from Robert Frost's "Oven Bird." In that poem Frost questions the assumed superiority of summer over spring: the "diminished thing" is mid-summer, which has been tarnished by a comparison with the fresh beauty and promise of spring. Like the listener of Frost's poem, the speaker of "Height" discovers that something taken for granted has been lost. Unfortunately "Oven Bird" is not included in this edition of *Poetry*, so you may want to obtain and distribute a copy of it in class.

Probably the best way to approach the poem in class is to draw students' attention to the epigram and ask what the speaker has made "of a diminished thing" and whether his response is reasonable. Is it only his height that has been diminished, or something else — perhaps his sense of self-worth? How does he resolve his dilemma?

POSSIBLE CONNECTIONS TO OTHER SELECTIONS

Robert Frost, "Nothing Gold Can Stay" (text p. 371)

William Shakespeare, "That time of year thou mayst in me behold" (text p. 620)

WALLACE STEVENS, *The Emperor of Ice-Cream* (p. 624)

Even more than a parting word to the old woman about to be buried, this poem is a celebration of her mourners, who could still touch imagination's fire despite their impoverished surroundings. By covering the woman in her own embroidered winding sheet ("fantails" here are fantail pigeons), transforming the cigar roller into ice-cream creator, and gathering together like extras in a film extravaganza, they celebrate and affirm the gaudy, bawdy vitality of their lives, together with their creative power to "Let be be finale of seem." As a note, "deal" is furniture made of cheap wood, lacquered over to look more expensive.

You may want to ask students why the emperor of ice-cream is an emperor. Is this an indication that he knows how to move people through the pleasure principle, perhaps?

POSSIBLE CONNECTIONS TO OTHER SELECTIONS

E. E. Cummings, "Buffalo Bill 's" (text p. 595)

T. S. Eliot, "The Love Song of J. Alfred Prufrock" (text p. 456)

AUDIOVISUAL RESOURCES (manual p. 381)

ALFRED, LORD TENNYSON, *Ulysses* (p. 625)

Tennyson was only twenty-four when he wrote this monologue, magnificently creating the thoughts that must have plagued this hero who had striven with the gods. The poem is written in blank verse and preserves a certain conversational eloquence through its use of parallelism. Consider the infinitives in "How dull it is to pause, to make an end, / To rust unburnished, not to shine in use!" (lines 22–23). Ulysses seems to be passing on his power and authority to his son Telemachus, who will, apparently, have a gentler, less warlike (though no less important) kind of work to do. You might ask the class what they suppose Ulysses has in mind when he says in the final stanza, "Some work of noble note, may yet be done." Could this poem bear some autobiographical reflection on the life of a poet? This question could prompt a brief research paper.

Emily Dickinson, "This was a Poet — It is That" (text p. 323)
William Butler Yeats, "Sailing to Byzantium" (text p. 637)

ALFRED, LORD TENNYSON, *Tears, Idle Tears* (p. 627)

The nostalgic tone of this poem is immediately apparent in the first stanza. Although the speaker claims to "know not what [his tears] mean" (line 1), he is able to link them to "the days that are no more" (5). Paradoxes and ambivalence are present throughout the poem: Tears "Rise in the heart" (3) while the speaker gazes on "happy Autumn-fields" (4); the bygone days are described as "fresh" (10); dawn rises, witnessed by "dying ears" and "dying eyes" (13).

This final paradox is also present in Emily Dickinson's "Oh Sumptuous moment" (p. 354). Students may benefit from a close reading of these poems in tandem, examining in detail this notion of the value of a moment. While Tennyson's poem looks back on "the days that are no more" (5, 10, 15, 20), Dickinson's poem looks forward to imagine how her speaker's present happiness will be remembered. Both offer a paradox that is centered on the idea of memory. How do they compare?

POSSIBLE CONNECTIONS TO OTHER SELECTIONS

Emily Dickinson, "Oh Sumptuous moment" (text p. 328)
———, "Water, is taught by thirst" (text p. 313)
Robert Frost, "Nothing Gold Can Stay" (text p. 371)

DYLAN THOMAS, *Fern Hill* (p. 627)

"Fern Hill" starts in the middle of things, the "Now" giving the reader a sense of immediacy that belongs to the consciousness of the child subject. At the beginning of this poem, Thomas presents an idyllic view of his boyhood on the farm and conveys the youthful sense that he is at the center of the world. Since he is the "prince of the apple towns" (line 6), everything obeys his command: "the calves / Sang to my horn, the foxes on the hills barked clear and cold" (15–16). When he goes to sleep, the rest of the world disappears, borne away by owls (24). The greenness of the landscape mirrors the youth and promise of the young boy. As the poem progresses, however, Thomas introduces the idea of aging and mortality, which will lead children "out of grace" (45) and into the world of sin and worry. The green of the beginning becomes "green and dying" (53). Thomas's famous final line, "Though I sang in my chains like the sea" (54), suggests both the joys of childhood and the adult narrator's consciousness of the bonds of time.

"Fern Hill" was finished in 1945, so it may be interesting to discuss the poem with your students in the context of the world war. The appeal of a younger and more innocent stage of his life may have been particularly appealing to Thomas during this period of horrors.

POSSIBLE CONNECTIONS TO OTHER SELECTIONS

William Blake, "The Garden of Love" (text p. 586)
Gerard Manley Hopkins, "Hurrahing in Harvest" (text p. 604)

WALT WHITMAN, *I Heard You Solemn-Sweet Pipes of the Organ* (p. 629)

The combination of solemn and sweet encapsulates the tone of Whitman's poem. The sound of the organs that begins his reflection is both a call to worship and a sign of mourning; it encompasses both joy and sorrow. The poem takes place in autumn, which is a time of mingled feelings. The abundance of the harvest is contrasted with the awareness of coming winter. Art, too, takes on a bittersweet quality for Whitman, as perfection in music is set off by its impermanence. However, the most important of the solemn-sweet sensations in this poem is love. Even the speaker's love must eventually end, and Whitman emphasizes this fact by making love a bodily response. The lover's pulse turns into the sound of "ringing little bells" (line 5), but the joy of hearing this sound is tempered by the knowledge of mortality.

POSSIBLE CONNECTIONS TO OTHER SELECTIONS

Emily Dickinson, "Some keep the Sabbath going to Church—" (text p. 315)
William Wordsworth, "I Wandered Lonely as a Cloud" (text p. 633)

WALT WHITMAN, *When I Heard the Learn'd Astronomer* (p. 629)

Whitman's poem sets forth in verse the often-debated argument over the relative values of art and science; true to the traditions of American romanticism, art is the winner in Whitman's view. You might ask your students to recall other instances in which they have seen this issue debated. Which side seemed to have the stronger argument in each case? Is this necessarily an either/or debate? That is, are art and science ever interconnected? What about stanzaic and metrical patterns, in which art depends on numbers? (You might ask students why a poet like Whitman might not be impressed with this particular example.) Can your students think of any poet whose use of imagery or structures depends on scientific principles? Does science owe anything to the power of the artist's imagination?

POSSIBLE CONNECTION TO ANOTHER SELECTION

Emily Dickinson, "Some keep the Sabbath going to Church —" (text p. 315)

WALT WHITMAN, *One's-Self I Sing* (p. 629)

This poem opens *Leaves of Grass* and is a kind of bugle announcement of several of Whitman's fondly held themes: the individual as both separate and a member of the democratic community; the equality of the sexes; the importance of both body and soul; and the "divinity" of modern humanity, which is not subject to kingly law. Some students will probably hear echoes of the opening lines of a traditional epic poem. Whitman is inverting epic convention somewhat by not singing of arms and men with the requisite bowings to the gods, but hailing the individual self.

Ask students to explore contexts for Walt Whitman on *LiterActive*.

As a writing assignment, you might ask the class to describe how and why this brief poem is a good opening for a book of poems. You might also ask students to say what seems particularly American about the poem.

POSSIBLE CONNECTIONS TO OTHER SELECTIONS

Joy Harjo, "The Path to the Milky Way Leads through Los Angeles" (text p. 600)
John Keats, "To one who has been long in city pent" (text p. 609)

RICHARD WILBUR, *Love Calls Us to the Things of This World* (p. 630)

You might begin a discussion of this poem by talking about how a poet controls and convinces us of the truth of metaphors. Wilbur spends some time describing the motions of the wind-tossed laundry in order for us to see the laundry as "angels," and thus offer his prayer (lines 21–23) for a heaven on Earth.

Play a recording of Richard Wilbur reading "Love Calls Us to the Things of This World" on *Literature Aloud*.

To live as soul in a mock heaven would be incomplete, to say the least. The soul, like someone trying to sleep a while longer, resists the "punctual rape" of the day, which calls the soul back into the world of business and reality. Only when the sun rises does the soul out of "bitter love" join with the waking body and take down the laundry, an image for heaven. As it dismantles heaven, it clothes this daily world, without moral consideration for who wears the laundry — itself an act of graciousness and love. The nuns "keeping their difficult balance" suggest both the literal act of walking and the spiritual act of mediating between things of this world and things of the next.

You might review in class discussion phrases such as "punctual rape" (19), "every blessed day" (19), and "bitter love" (26).

POSSIBLE CONNECTION TO ANOTHER SELECTION

Gerard Manley Hopkins, "God's Grandeur" (text p. 194)

MILLER WILLIAMS, *Thinking about Bill, Dead of AIDS* (p. 631)

Williams's poem is about the experience of watching a friend with AIDS deal with the world around him as he succumbs to the disease. In the first stanza the speaker admits ignorance of the processes by which the body turns on itself. Ask students to point out the metaphors of battle or war that the speaker uses to describe the onslaught of AIDS: "blood surrenders" (line 2), "rescinding all its normal orders" (4), "defenders of flesh" (5), "betraying the head" (5), and "pulling its guards back from all its borders" (6).

The second stanza moves from describing what is happening in Bill's body to describing the responses of others to his disease. Students may find line 9 particularly evocative — "your eyes drained of any reprimand." In the last three stanzas the speaker explains the response of the "we" of the poem. Ask students to consider who the "we" represents. You may wish to pay special attention to lines like "partly to persuade / both you and us . . . that we were loving and were not afraid" (10–12), "stopping, though, to set our smiles at the door" (15), and "we didn't know what look would hurt you least" (18). What emotion is the speaker intending to convey? Ask students to identify the conflict that occurs in this part of the poem. Who experiences this tension? Discuss whether this underlying conflict is ever resolved.

POSSIBLE CONNECTIONS TO OTHER SELECTIONS

John Donne, "A Valediction: Forbidding Mourning" (text p. 150)

Robert Hayden, "Those Winter Sundays" (text p. 23)

Andrew Hudgins, "Elegy for My Father, Who Is Not Dead" (text p. 256)

AUDIOVISUAL RESOURCES (manual p. 383)

WILLIAM CARLOS WILLIAMS, *Spring and All* (p. 631)

All sounds a good deal like *fall*, and indeed there is something autumnal about Williams's chill spring, with its "reddish/purplish" bushes and "dead, brown leaves." But these tokens of death actually bespeak a quickening life of the season that connotes rebirth. The images of human birth are not far from Williams's mind in this poem, as he talks about the nameless "They" who come into the world naked. Syntactically "They" (line 16) stands for the vegetation of grass, wild carrot leaf, and the rest (all), but we do not know this until after the pronoun appears. Williams can thus have it both ways and point to both a human and a nonhuman world.

Williams's spring, like so many of his subjects, is earth-rooted, literally. No surface change here; this profound "change" is " rooted" far down, so that life springs forth from its depths.

You might ask the class whether there is any significance in the setting of the poem — by the road to the contagious hospital.

POSSIBLE CONNECTION TO ANOTHER SELECTION

Margaret Atwood, "February" (text p. 143)

WILLIAM CARLOS WILLIAMS, *This Is Just to Say* (p. 632)

Three possible writing assignments can be organized around this poem: (1) an essay talking about line breaks, necessary brevity, and careful word choice that validates this seemingly conversational statement as poetry; (2) a found poem, using a scrap of conversation or some lines from a short story, to make a poem about the length of this one; (3) a parody of this poem.

POSSIBLE CONNECTIONS TO OTHER SELECTIONS

Helen Chasin, "The Word *Plum*" (text p. 209)

Donald Justice, "Order in the Streets" (text p. 287)

Ezra Pound, "In a Station of the Metro" (text p. 129)

WILLIAM WORDSWORTH, *A Slumber Did My Spirit Seal* (p. 632)

This is one of Wordsworth's "Lucy poems," and the "she" in line 3 alludes to Lucy. Apparently, this poem marks a loss for which the poet was unprepared. He was asleep to the possibilities of aging and death, and Lucy now seems well beyond the province of earthly years and more the spirit of eternal time. Is there a paradox in this poem? Probably so. The speaker's dream, which he had had in a more pleasant period, when he felt that they were both beyond the effects of time, turns out to be for Lucy ironically accurate, for like the rocks and stones and trees, she is now unaffected by the passage of time.

POSSIBLE CONNECTIONS TO OTHER SELECTIONS

John Keats, "When I have fears that I may cease to be" (text p. 610)

Percy Bysshe Shelley, "Ozymandias" (text p. 621)

WILLIAM WORDSWORTH, *I Wandered Lonely as a Cloud* (p. 633)

The speaker of this poem finds comfort for his loneliness in nature. His connection to daffodils comforts him even in memory. In his preface to *Lyrical Ballads,* Wordsworth describes poetry as "the spontaneous overflow of powerful feelings: it takes its origin from emotion recollected in tranquillity." To some extent, this quotation explains the "wealth" that Wordsworth alludes to in line 18, for while reclining on his couch he can recall the heightened sense of pleasure the daffodils first brought him. From his mood of loneliness, he moves to a state of gladness. What else characterizes how the daffodils appear to him? Seemingly, they are a token of cosmic splendor in their extensiveness and golden sparkle.

POSSIBLE CONNECTION TO ANOTHER SELECTION

Emily Dickinson, "A Bird came down the Walk —" (text p. 187)

WILLIAM WORDSWORTH, *It Is a Beauteous Evening, Calm and Free* (p. 633)

Wordsworth wrote this Petrarchan sonnet after a trip to France with his young daughter. Romantic ideals of nature, childhood, and pantheistic divinity (in which God is found in nature and within the individual) inform the poem. The first octet describes the divine beauty of nature, finding evidence of "the mighty Being" (6) in the sunset and the sound of breaking waves. The sextet that follows it shifts the poet's focus to his daughter, whose innocence is evidence of the divinity to be found in every individual. Paradox is central to the meaning of this poem: Although the title suggests "calm," note that the hour is "breathless" (implying excitement). And although the poem asserts that "the holy time is quiet as a nun" (line 2), "a sound like thunder" (8) fills the air. Similarly, the poem suggests the paradox of God and nature: Not only did the "mighty Being" create nature, but it *is* nature. Paradox affects the child as well: She is both unaware of religion and infused with it.

It may help your students to know that Romantic ideas about internal divinity, or "the Temple's inner shrine" (13), were not widely accepted in the early nineteenth century. Publishing a poem that argues the presence of God in nature and children would have occasioned controversy and censure for the author. This poem, then, is not simply a beautiful and romantic image of the seashore and the presence of God; it is in many ways a daring political statement.

POSSIBLE CONNECTIONS TO OTHER SELECTIONS

Emily Dickinson, "Some keep the Sabbath going to Church —" (text p. 315)
Gerard Manley Hopkins, "God's Grandeur" (text p. 194)
Mark Jarman, "Unholy Sonnet" (text p. 246)

WILLIAM WORDSWORTH, *The Solitary Reaper* (p. 634)

This poem seems to spill beyond its limits as fit lyric to become a spontaneous overflow of powerful feeling. Ask the class to note how many boundaries are exceeded here. In stanza 1, for example, the song overflows the vales. In the final stanza the song seems without end, and the listener hears it long after he leaves the singer behind. Implied, too, in the second and third stanzas is the song's ability to transcend place and history. As with other poetic figures of Wordsworth, this solitary reaper and her song provide a way into perceiving an order of existence beneath the surface. You might ask the class if it matters at all that the singer is female.

POSSIBLE CONNECTIONS TO OTHER SELECTIONS

William Blake, "The Chimney Sweeper" (text p. 179)
Langston Hughes, "The Weary Blues" (text p. 401)

WILLIAM WORDSWORTH, *Mutability* (p. 635)

This poem examines the inevitability of change and the ability to see it clearly. The "unimaginable touch of time" (line 14) proves everything to be temporary, even the "outward forms" of "Truth" (7). Truth itself "fails not" (7), but the awesome changes in our lives may have some of us fooled; those "who meddle not with crime / Nor avarice, nor over-anxious care" (5–6) can see change as it is, a nonthreatening part of life.

Among the examples Wordsworth offers are nature and political order; these provide comparisons to the "outward forms" of truth. Frost melts, and "the tower sublime / Of yesterday" (10–11) is no longer so impressive today.

Students are likely to be unfamiliar with the terms of this linguistically dense poem. Reading it aloud and working together on a line-by-line analysis of its meaning may prove helpful. Students may glean much of the meaning through an exercise that includes rewriting or restating the poem in more contemporary terms.

William Shakespeare, "Not marble, nor the gilded monuments" (text p. 491)

MITSUYE YAMADA, *A Bedtime Story* (p. 635)

Irony is this poem's most striking feature. A father tells his child an ancient story from his culture (we presume), and his daughter, the speaker, is unable to understand the story's message. To figure out the speaker's inability to grasp this message, we must look into the way the story is framed. At the beginning of the poem, the time is non-specific; the father begins his story as many stories begin: "Once upon a time" (line 1). At the end of the story, the speaker describes where the story is told, "In the comfort of our / hilltop home in Seattle / overlooking the valley" (41–43). This tension between the timeless and the present indicate a gap between father and daughter that goes beyond a typical generation gap. The daughter cannot grasp the moral of her father's story because she is safe and comfortable and, presumably, privileged. The irony is that she cannot identify with the woman in the story who is turned away from houses in town, identifying instead with the townspeople who turn the old woman away. The speaker can no more see the message of the story than the people in that town can see the beauty of the moon. As readers of the poem, we are put in a similar position: what are we to take away from the story, frame-tale and all? Do students identify with the daughter (who wants a fuller story with a more exciting plot), with the father (who wants to pass on a piece of his culture), with both, with neither, or with the woman in the story? One way to enter such a discussion is to ask students how they read the poem's tone; is it meant to be humorous or instructive? Compare the poem's tone with that of the legend recounted.

POSSIBLE CONNECTIONS TO OTHER SELECTIONS

Margaret Atwood, "Bored" (text p. 86)

Jimmy Santiago Baca, "Green Chile" (text p. 117)

WILLIAM BUTLER YEATS, *The Second Coming* (p. 636)

The pattern here of the falcon circling around the falconer indicates the pattern of the gyre, now tracing its widest circle and thus least subject to the control of the falconer. "Mere anarchy" is loosed on a world troubled by recent wars (World War I and the Russian Revolution). Yeats later claimed he was describing the rise of fascism in Europe. What kind of order will assume its place over the next two thousand years, if the nature of that world is imaged by a description of the annunciating beast as blank, pitiless, and rough?

Ask students to explore contexts for William Butler Yeats on *LiterActive*.

POSSIBLE CONNECTIONS TO OTHER SELECTIONS

Robert Frost, "Fire and Ice" (text p. 369)

William Butler Yeats, "Leda and the Swan" (text p. 637)

WILLIAM BUTLER YEATS, *Leda and the Swan* (p. 637)

Some references in this poem might require clarification: The offspring of Leda and Zeus (as swan) was Helen, the most beautiful of women, who married Menelaus but was later awarded to Paris. Paris took her to Troy with him, thus occasioning the Trojan War and the death of Agamemnon, the leader of the Greeks. Agamemnon was married to Clytemnestra, Helen's sister.

According to Yeats's view, this rape marks a turning point in history and the downward spiraling of the gyres. The moment is dark and fraught with the onset of much tragedy that Leda cannot possibly know, yet she does seem to take on a measure of Zeus's power and come closer to assuming a consciousness of the divine than is ordinarily possible. One point to consider in class discussion is Yeats's use of the rhetorical question in this poem. Does the poem suggest any answers to these questions? What do they do to the poem's tone?

POSSIBLE CONNECTION TO ANOTHER SELECTION

Anna Akhmatova, "Lot's Wife" (text p. 570)

WILLIAM BUTLER YEATS, *Sailing to Byzantium* (p. 637)

Byzantium, in historical terms, was the capital of the Eastern Roman Empire and the holy city of Greek Orthodoxy. Explore with the class what Byzantium symbolizes, especially in terms of Yeats's career as a poet. In a note to the poem, Yeats commented, "I have read somewhere that in the Emperor's Palace at Byzantium was a tree made of gold and silver and artificial birds that sang" (*The Collected Poems of William Butler Yeats* [New York: Macmillan, 1972], 453). Increasingly in his later poems, Yeats turned to art rather than nature as a means of transcending time.

POSSIBLE CONNECTIONS TO OTHER SELECTIONS

John Keats, "Ode on a Grecian Urn" (text p. 96)
William Shakespeare, "Not marble, nor the gilded monuments" (text p. 491)

WILLIAM BUTLER YEATS, *Crazy Jane Talks with the Bishop* (p. 639)

Tradition has it that the fool is the purveyor of truth, and Crazy Jane, whose retort to the bishop is that "fair needs foul," is no exception. The paradoxical mutualities that Crazy Jane endorses find other correspondences in the last stanza, where the romantic ideal of love, we are told, pitches its mansion in "the place of excrement." Puns on *sole* and *whole* also invite a commingling of the platonic with the blatantly physical. According to John Unterecker, the bishop in the poem was a divinity student turned down by Jane for Jack the Journeyman. The bishop banished Jack, but Jane remained true to him (*A Reader's Guide to William Butler Yeats* [New York: Noonday, 1959]).

POSSIBLE CONNECTION TO ANOTHER SELECTION

Emily Dickinson, "Much Madness is divinest Sense —" (text p. 321)

APPENDICES

Thematic Units for
Discussion and Writing

In addition to the Thematic Contents included in the student edition of *Poetry: An Introduction*, we offer the following thematic units as options for your teaching. These selections are organized around a particular subject or theme and can be used to generate topics for discussion and writing. Students' own perceptions of how the works are linked may prove to be particularly revealing.

HOME AND FAMILY

Margaret Atwood, *Bored,* 86
Margaret Atwood, *February,* 143
Emily Dickinson, *The Bustle in a House,* 328
Robert Frost, *Home Burial,* 361
Rachel Hadas, *The Red Hat,* 225
Robert Hayden, *Those Winter Sundays,* 23
Andrew Hudgins, *Elegy for My Father, Who Is Not Dead,* 256
Colette Inez, *Back When All Was Continuous Chuckles,* 76
Galway Kinnell, *After Making Love We Hear Footsteps,* 271
Sharon Olds, *Rite of Passage,* 279
Theodore Roethke, *My Papa's Waltz,* 233
Mary Jo Salter, *Home Movies: A Sort of Ode,* 260
Cathy Song, *Sunworshippers,* 146

QUESTIONS FOR DISCUSSION AND WRITING

1. Choose any five works and discuss the treatment of children in them. To what extent are children at the center of the conflicts in the works?

2. Discuss the importance of family grief in Hudgins's "Elegy for My Father, Who Is Not Dead," Dickinson's "The Bustle in a House," and Frost's "Home Burial." How does grief reveal character in these works?

3. Compare the views of the young boys in Olds's "Rite of Passage" to any three fathers included in the list. How does Olds's assessment of the boys' futures square with their adult counterparts?

4. Compare the themes of Kinnell's "After Making Love We Hear Footsteps" and Hayden's "Those Winter Sundays." What accounts for the tone of these poems? Explain whether or not you think either one can be charged with being sentimental.

5. Compare the speakers' attitudes toward their parents in Song's "Sunworshippers" and Roethke's "My Papa's Waltz." What role does a sense of awe play in each poem?

6. How do the speakers of Hudgins's "Elegy for My Father Who Is Not Dead" and Atwood's "Bored" invoke a sense of family? How does loss affect each speaker?

7. Compare the diction of Atwood's "February" and Hayden's "Those Winter Sundays." How do the sounds of the words contribute to each poem's sense of home?

8. How does point of view affect the tone of Inez's "Back When All Was Continuous Chuckles" and Salter's "Home Movies: A Sort of Ode"?

LOVE AND ITS COMPLICATIONS

QUESTIONS FOR DISCUSSION AND WRITING

1. Using Marvell's "To His Coy Mistress" and Browning's "My letters! all dead paper, mute and white," explore how men and women agree and differ in their expectations about love.

2. Discuss Cummings's "since feeling is first," Herrick's "To the Virgins, to Make Much of Time," and Wilbur's "A Late Aubade" as carpe diem poems. (This type of poem is defined on p. 79 of the text.) Pay particular attention to the speakers' tones in the poems. What do they have in common?

3. How might Keats's "La Belle Dame sans Merci" be used as a commentary on Olds's "Sex without Love"?

4. Explain why love fails in Eliot's "The Love Song of J. Alfred Prufrock" and in Olds's "Sex without Love."

5. Compare the humorous tone of Shakespeare's "My mistress' eyes are nothing like the sun" with that of Atwood's "you fit into me."

6. Compare the sensuousness and sensuality in Croft's "Home-Baked Bread" and Song's "The White Porch." What is the effect of the implicit — rather than the explicit — nature of the sexuality in each poem?

7. Consider Dickinson's "Wild Nights — Wild Nights!" and Olds's "Sex without Love" as commenting on each other. What do these works suggest to you about sexuality and love?

8. Compare the speakers' attitudes toward their loved ones in Cummings's "since feeling is first" and Shakespeare's "My mistress' eyes are nothing like the sun." How does each speaker portray positive images through negatives?

9. Choose several works and discuss how and why you feel they provide useful perspectives on love.

THE NATURAL WORLD

QUESTIONS FOR DISCUSSION AND WRITING

1. Choose a poem from among Bishop's "The Fish," and Blake's "The Tyger," and discuss the effectiveness of their imagery. To what extent do the poems' meanings go beyond the subjects they describe?

2. Compare Dickinson's "A narrow Fellow in the Grass" with Blake's "The Tyger." How does the speaker's attitude toward the animal in each poem develop and grow complicated? How does your own response to snakes and tigers affect your reading of these poems?

3. Compare the imagery and themes of Keats's "To Autumn" and Williams's "Spring and All." Which poem appeals to you more? Explain why.

4. Discuss Hopkins's attitude toward nature in "Pied Beauty" and Frost's in "Design." What connections does each poem make between nature and God?

5. Contrast the individual's relations to nature in Stafford's "Traveling through the Dark" and Bishop's "The Fish." What attitudes about society are implicitly expressed in each poem?

6. How is nature discussed in Nowlan's "The Bull Moose" and Frost's "Unharvested"?

7. How do the speakers of Stafford's "Traveling through the Dark" and Frost's "Design" define themselves in terms of the wildlife in their poems?

8. What do Blake's "The Tyger" and Nowlan's "The Bull Moose" have in common, in the speakers' assessments?

OTHER CULTURES

QUESTIONS FOR DISCUSSION AND WRITING

1. Choose a work from the list and explain how it causes you to adjust or reassess your own cultural assumptions in order to understand and appreciate the perspective offered in the work.

2. Compare Espada's treatment of American food with Baca's look at his native "Green Chile." How do these two treatments reflect the speakers' attitudes toward their own cultures and American culture?

3. Discuss Baca's and Divakaruni's respective attitudes toward their own cultures in "Green Chile" and "Indian Movie, New Jersey."

4. How do Marzán's "Ethnic Poetry" and Divakaruni's "Indian Movie, New Jersey" comment on American culture while seeking to avoid it?

5. How do generational differences account for the speakers' attitudes toward their cultures in Yamada's "A Bedtime Story" and Divakaruni's "Indian Movie, New Jersey"?

6. How does point of view affect the portrayal of Native American culture in Alexie's "On the Amtrak from Boston to New York City" and Sigourney's "Indian Names"?

WORK AND BUSINESS

QUESTIONS FOR DISCUSSION AND WRITING

1. Consider attitudes toward success in Dickinson's "Success is counted sweetest" and Robinson's "Richard Cory." How is true success defined and measured in these works?

2. How is humor used to characterize the world of work in Machan's "Hazel Tells LaVerne" and Piercy's "The Secretary Chant"? What serious points are made about work through the use of humor in these selections?

3. Choose three works that, in your opinion, present the most severe judgment on business as a dehumanizing process.

4. Discuss the significance of the images used in Piercy's "The Secretary Chant" and Blake's "The Chimney Sweeper." What attitudes toward work emerge from these images?

5. How are advertisements and commercialism used as a means to comment on societal values in Fearing's "AD"?

6. Compare the use of symbolism in Piercy's "The Secretary Chant" and Frost's "After Apple-Picking." How and for what purpose is work symbolized in each poem?

7. Compare the tones of Machan's "Hazel Tells LaVerne" and Dickinson's "Success is counted sweetest." How does each poet use diction to illuminate the speaker's attitudes toward the work presented?

Supplementing the Anthology with Bedford/St. Martin's Literary Reprints

Instructors who wish to supplement *Poetry: An Introduction* with longer works may be interested in volumes from Bedford/St. Martin's literary reprints, now available with the fifth edition at a special price. Following the list of titles below are descriptions of each series — Bedford Cultural Editions, The Bedford Series in History and Culture, The Bedford Shakespeare Series, Case Studies in Contemporary Criticism, and Case Studies in Cultural Controversy.

Jane Addams, ***Twenty Years at Hull House*** (1910), The Bedford Series in History and Culture, ed. Victoria Bissell Brown

Joseph Addison and Richard Steele, ***The Commerce of Everyday Life: Selections from* The Tatler *and* The Spectator** (1709-1714), Bedford Cultural Editions, ed. Erin Mackie

Louisa May Alcott, ***Hospital Sketches*** (1863), The Bedford Series in History and Culture, ed. Alice Fahs

Jane Austen, ***Emma*** (1816), Case Studies in Contemporary Criticism, ed. Alistair M. Duckworth

Aphra Behn, ***Oroonoko*** (1688), Bedford Cultural Editions, ed. Catherine Gallagher

Edward Bellamy, ***Looking Backward: 2000–1887*** (1888), The Bedford Series in History and Culture, ed. Daniel H. Borus

Charlotte Brontë, ***Jane Eyre*** (1847), Case Studies in Contemporary Criticism, ed. Beth Newman

Emily Brontë, ***Wuthering Heights*** (1847), Case Studies in Contemporary Criticism, ed. Linda H. Peterson

Bill Brown, ed., ***Reading the West: An Anthology of Dime Westerns*** (1860-1890), Bedford Cultural Editions

William Wells Brown, ***Clotel*** (1853), Bedford Cultural Editions, ed. Robert Levine

Frances Burney, ***Evelina*** (1778), Bedford Cultural Editions, ed. Kristina Straub

Geoffrey Chaucer, ***The Wife of Bath*** (c. 1387), Case Studies in Contemporary Criticism, ed. Peter G. Beidler

Charles W. Chesnutt, ***The Marrow of Tradition*** (1910), Bedford Cultural Editions, ed. Nancy Bentley and Sandra Gunning

Kate Chopin, ***The Awakening*** (1899), Case Studies in Contemporary Criticism, ed. Nancy A. Walker

Samuel Taylor Coleridge, ***The Rime of the Ancient Mariner*** (1798-1817), Case Studies in Contemporary Criticism, ed. Paul H. Fry

Joseph Conrad, ***Heart of Darkness*** (1902), Case Studies in Contemporary Criticism, ed. Ross Murfin

Joseph Conrad, ***The Secret Sharer*** (1912), Case Studies in Contemporary Criticism, ed. Daniel R. Schwarz

Stephen Crane, ***Maggie*** (1893), Bedford Cultural Editions, ed. Kevin J. Hayes

Rebecca Harding Davis, ***Life in the Iron Mills*** (1861), Bedford Cultural Editions, ed. Cecelia Tichi

Charles Dickens, *Great Expectations* (1860), Case Studies in Contemporary Criticism, ed. Janice Carlisle

Frederick Douglass, *Narrative of the Life of Frederick Douglass*, 2e (1845), The Bedford Series in History and Culture, ed. David W. Blight

Arthur Conan Doyle, *Sherlock Holmes: The Major Stories* (1887–1904), Case Studies in Contemporary Criticism, ed. John A. Hodgson

W. E. B. Du Bois, *The Souls of Black Folk* (1903), The Bedford Series in History and Culture, ed. David W. Blight and Robert Gooding-Williams

Olaudah Equiano, *The Interesting Narrative of the Life of Olaudah Equiano* (1791), The Bedford Series in History and Culture, ed. Robert J. Allison

E. M. Forster, *Howards End* (1910), Case Studies in Contemporary Criticism, ed. Alistair M. Duckworth

Benjamin Franklin, *The Autobiography of Benjamin Franklin* 2e (1793), The Bedford Series in History and Culture, ed. Louis P. Masur

Charlotte Perkins Gilman, *The Yellow Wallpaper* (1892), Bedford Cultural Editions, ed. Dale M. Bauer

Elliott J. Gorn, ed., *The McGuffey Readers: Selections from the 1879 Edition*, The Bedford Series in History and Culture

Thomas Hardy, *Tess of the d'Urbervilles* (1891), Case Studies in Contemporary Criticism, ed. John Paul Riquelme

Nathaniel Hawthorne, *The Blithedale Romance* (1852), Bedford Cultural Editions, ed. William E. Cain

Nathaniel Hawthorne, *The Scarlet Letter* (1850), Case Studies in Contemporary Criticism, ed. Ross Murfin

William Dean Howells, *A Traveler from Altruria* (1894), The Bedford Series in History and Culture, ed. David W. Levy

Henry James, *The Turn of the Screw* (1898), Case Studies in Contemporary Criticism, ed. Peter G. Beidler

James Joyce, *The Dead* (1914), Case Studies in Contemporary Criticism, ed. Daniel R. Schwarz

James Joyce, *A Portrait of the Artist as a Young Man* (1915), Case Studies in Contemporary Criticism, ed. R. B. Kershner

Eve Kornfeld, ed., *Margaret Fuller: A Brief Biography with Documents*, The Bedford Series in History and Culture

Gotthold Ephraim Lessing, *Nathan the Wise* (1779), The Bedford Series in History and Culture, ed. Ronald Schecter

Thomas Mann, *Death in Venice* (1912), Case Studies in Contemporary Criticism, ed. Naomi Ritter

Russ McDonald, ed., *The Bedford Companion to Shakespeare: An Introduction*, The Bedford Shakespeare Series

Sir Thomas More, *Utopia* (1516), The Bedford Series in History and Culture, ed. David Harris Sacks

Margot Norris, ed., *A Companion to James Joyce's* Ulysses (1922), Case Studies in Contemporary Criticism

Alexander Pope, *The Rape of the Lock* (1714), Bedford Cultural Editions, ed. Cynthia Wall

Jacob Riis, *How the Other Half Lives* (1890), The Bedford Series in History and Culture, ed. David Leviatin

Mary Rowlandson, *The Sovereignty and Goodness of God* (1675), The Bedford Series in History and Culture, ed. Neal Salisbury

William Shakespeare, *The First Part of King Henry the Fourth* (1596), The Bedford Shakespeare Series, ed. Barbara Hodgdon

William Shakespeare, *Hamlet* (1599), Case Studies in Contemporary Criticism, ed. Susanne L. Wofford

William Shakespeare, *Macbeth* (1606), The Bedford Shakespeare Series, ed. William C. Carroll

William Shakespeare, *Measure for Measure* (1623), The Bedford Shakespeare Series, ed. Ivo Kamps and Karen Reber

William Shakespeare, *The Merchant of Venice* (1596), The Bedford Shakespeare Series, ed. Lindsay M. Kaplan

William Shakespeare, *A Midsummer Night's Dream* (1594), The Bedford Shakespeare Series, ed. Gail Kern Paster and Skiles Howard

William Shakespeare, *The Taming of the Shrew* (1592), The Bedford Shakespeare Series, ed. Frances E. Dolan

William Shakespeare, *The Tempest: A Case Study* (1611), Case Studies in Critical Controversy, ed. Gerald Graff and James Phelan

William Shakespeare, *Twelfth Night* (1600), The Bedford Shakespeare Series, ed. Bruce R. Smith

Mary Shelley, *Frankenstein* (1831), Case Studies in Critical Controversy, ed. Johanna M. Smith

Bram Stoker, *Dracula* (1897), Case Studies in Contemporary Criticism, ed. John Paul Riquelme

Eric Sundquist, ed., *Cultural Contexts for Ralph Ellison's* **Invisible Man** (1952)

Jonathan Swift, *Gulliver's Travels* (1726), Case Studies in Contemporary Criticism, ed. Christopher B. Fox

Nat Turner, *The Confessions of Nat Turner* (1831), The Bedford Series in History and Culture, ed. Kenneth S. Greenberg

Mark Twain, *Adventures of Huckleberry Finn* (1884), Case Studies in Critical Controversy, ed. Gerald Graff and James Phelan

Voltaire, *Candide* (1759), The Bedford Series in History and Culture, ed. Daniel Gordon

Booker T. Washington, *Up from Slavery* (1901), The Bedford Series in History and Culture, ed. W. Fitzhugh Brundage

Ida B. Wells, *Southern Horrors and Other Writings* (1892–1900), The Bedford Series in History and Culture, ed. Jacqueline Jones Royster

Edith Wharton, *The House of Mirth* (1905), Case Studies in Contemporary Criticism, ed. Shari Benstock

BEDFORD CULTURAL EDITIONS

Series Editors: J. Paul Hunter, University of Chicago; William E. Cain, Wellesley College

Particularly appropriate for courses that emphasize a new historicist or cultural studies approach, **Bedford Cultural Editions** reprint authoritative editions of British and American literary works with an abundance of thematically arranged historical and cultural documents. The documents — relevant excerpts from such sources as diaries, letters, periodicals, conduct books, legal documents, and literary works that parallel the themes of the main text — are carefully selected to give students a rich sense of a work's historical and cultural contexts. Each volume also provides a full complement of useful pedagogical aids: a historical and critical introduction to the work, a chronology, an introduction to each thematic unit of documents, headnotes for the documents, appropriate text annotations, illustrations and maps, and an extensive bibliography.

THE BEDFORD SERIES IN HISTORY AND CULTURE

Series Editors: Natalie Zemon Davis, Princeton University; Ernest R. May, Harvard University; David Blight, Amherst College; Lynn Hunt, University of California, Los Angeles

Introduced in 1993 to meet the need for well-crafted, brief, and inexpensive supplements, **The Bedford Series in History and Culture** has won the high regard of instructors everywhere. Focusing on a specific topic or period, each book uniquely combines first-rate scholarship, historical narrative, and important primary documents. Each volume also offers a full complement of useful pedagogical aids, including text annotations, chronologies, questions for consideration, bibliographies, and indexes.

THE BEDFORD SHAKESPEARE SERIES

Series Editor: Jean E. Howard, Columbia University
Designed to give students firsthand knowledge of the cultural and historical contexts from which Shakespeare's work emerges, **The Bedford Shakespeare Series** facilitates a variety of approaches to Shakespeare. Each volume provides an authoritative edition of a widely taught play accompanied by an intriguing collection of thematically arranged historical and cultural documents such as homilies, polemical literature, emblem books, excerpts from conduct books, court records, medical tracts, chronicle histories, popular ballads, playhouse records, and facsimiles of early modern documents, including play texts, maps, and woodcut prints. Each volume also includes a general introduction, glosses for the play, an introduction to each thematic unit, a headnote and annotations for each document, a bibliography, and a topical index.

CASE STUDIES IN CRITICAL CONTROVERSIES

Series Editors: Gerald Graff, University of Illinois at Chicago; James Phelan, Ohio State University
Each volume in the **Case Studies in Critical Controversy** series reprints an authoritative text of a classic literary work, along with documents and critical essays that have been selected and organized to introduce students to the major critical debates and cultural conflicts concerning the work.

CASE STUDIES IN CONTEMPORARY CRITICISM

Series Editor: Ross C Murfin, Southern Methodist University
Adopted at more than one thousand colleges and universities, Bedford/St. Martin's innovative **Case Studies in Contemporary Criticism** series has introduced more than a quarter of a million students to literary theory and earned enthusiastic praise nationwide. Along with an authoritative text of a major literary work, each volume presents critical essays, selected or prepared especially for students, that approach the work from several contemporary critical perspectives, such as gender criticism and cultural studies. Each essay is accompanied by an introduction (with bibliography) to the history, principles, and practice of its critical perspective. Every volume also surveys the biographical, historical, and critical contexts of the literary work and concludes with a glossary of critical terms. New editions reprint cultural documents that contextualize the literary works and feature essays that show how critical perspectives can be combined.

These volumes provide a useful supplement for instructors who want to cover the different schools of literary theory in more depth than is provided in Chapter 25, Critical Strategies for Reading, in *Poetry: An Introduction*, Fifth Edition. The critical essays in each **Case Studies** volume can serve as models for helping students understand how to apply a particular approach to works in the anthology.

To obtain complimentary copies of any of these titles, please call the Bedford/St. Martin's College Desk at 1-800-446-8923 or contact your local Bedford/ St. Martin's sales representative at bedfordstmartins.com.

Table of Contents for the
LiterActive Multimedia CD-ROM

LiterActive, an innovative new CD-ROM — available free with student copies of the book — offers groundbreaking interactive tools that help students read, understand, and respond to literature. To order the book and CD-ROM for your course, use package **ISBN: 0–312–46110–0**. *LiterActive*'s resources are divided into three main categories:

- **VirtuaLit Interactive Tutorials** for Fiction, Poetry, and Drama guide students step-by-step as they explore the literary elements, critical perspectives, and cultural contexts of eleven featured works, helping them become more engaged readers.

- **A Multimedia and Document Library** provides hundreds of images, audio clips, video clips, and contextual documents supporting thirty-three authors, enriching students' experience and comprehension of literature.

- **A Research and Documentation Guide** gives students concrete advice for working with sources — how to find, evaluate, summarize, interpret, and document them. Advice for avoiding plagiarism and scorable exercises help students evaluate and improve their research and documentation practices.

Following is a complete table of contents for *LiterActive*.

I. VIRTUALIT INTERACTIVE TUTORIALS

VirtuaLit Interactive Fiction Tutorial

Kate Chopin, "The Story of an Hour"
Biography for Kate Chopin
Audio Clip for "The Story of an Hour"
Elements of Fiction in "The Story of an Hour"
Character in "The Story of an Hour"
Symbolism, Allegory, and Image in "The Story of an Hour"
Plot in "The Story of an Hour"

Nathaniel Hawthorne, "Young Goodman Brown"
Biography for Nathaniel Hawthorne
Audio Clip for "Young Goodman Brown"
Elements of Fiction in "Young Goodman Brown"
Plot in "Young Goodman Brown"
Setting in "Young Goodman Brown"
Theme in "Young Goodman Brown"
Symbolism, Allegory, and Image in "Young Goodman Brown"

Jamaica Kincaid, "Girl"
Biography for Jamaica Kincaid
Audio Clip for "Girl"

Critical Approaches for Drama

Wilfred Owen

Wilfred as a Soldier [image]
Harold Owen, "Wilfred Was a Poet" [document]
The Landscape of War [image]
Wilfred Owen, "Letters Home" [document]
"Dulce et Decorum Est" facsimile [image]
Robert Graves, "Two Letters" [document]

Sylvia Plath

Sylvia with Her Children [image]
Facsimile of Original Draft of "Stings" [image]
Sylvia Plath, "Journal Entry July 14th, 1953" [document]
Sylvia Plath, "Journal Entry, February 26th, 1956" [document]
Otto Plath [image]
Ted Hughes, "Observations of a Husband" [letter and interview]
A. Alvarez, "A Memoir" [document]

Edgar Allan Poe

Flavius J. Fisher, Portrait of Poe [image]
Thomas Gibson, "Poe the Prankster" [document]
Fall of the House of Usher [image]
"3 Reviews of Poe" [documents]
Facsimile of "The Bells" [image]
Susan Ingram, "Reminiscences of Poe" [document]

William Shakespeare

A Likeness of the Bard on a Collected Edition of His Plays (1623) [image]
Map of Stratford-upon-Avon (c. 1768) [image]
George Puttenham, "Poetry in Shakespeare's Time" (1589) [document]
Francis Meres, "An Evaluation of England's Literary Scene" (1598) [document]
Facsimile of a flawed version of "To be or not to be" (1603) [image]
John Ward, "A Diary Entry" (1662–63) [document]
Laurence Olivier as Henry V (1944) [image]
Audio Clip of William Shakespeare, "My mistress' eyes are nothing like the sun"
    (read by Sir John Gielgud)
[See also all contexts for *Hamlet*]

Gary Soto

Carolyn Soto, "Gary Soto" [image]
Postcard from Fresno (1939) [image]
Harold Bloom, "Bloom and Doom" [document]
Gary Soto, "Who Is Your Reader?" [document]
Gary Soto, "The Grandfather" [document]
Postcard of Fieldworkers Drying Raisin Grapes [image]
Audio Clip of Gary Soto, "Mexicans Begin Jogging" (read by Gary Soto)
Audio Clip of Gary Soto, Interview with Gary Soto (Gary Soto in conversation
    with Joseph Parisi)

Amy Tan

Michael Ferguson, Photograph of Amy Tan [image]

Table of Contents for the
Literature Aloud Audio CD

Literature Aloud is a two-CD set of audio recordings featuring celebrated writers and actors reading poems from *Poetry: An Introduction,* as well as stories and selected dramatic scenes. (To order *Literature Aloud,* use **ISBN: 0–312–46140–2**.) Following is a list of the selections offered on the CD.

LITERATURE ALOUD

Disc 1

FICTION

1. **James Joyce,** *Eveline* (read by Gabriel Byrne) 11:22

2. **Jamaica Kincaid,** *Girl* (read by Jamaica Kincaid) 3:50

3. **E. Annie Proulx,** *55 Miles to the Gas Pump* (read by Campbell Scott and Frances Fisher) 0:47

4. **John Updike,** *A & P* (read by John Updike) 16:52

POETRY

5. **Regina Barreca,** *Nighttime Fires* (read by Regina Barreca) 1:57

6. **Elizabeth Bishop,** *The Fish* (read by Randall Jarrell) 3:36

7. **William Blake,** *The Lamb* (read by Brian Murray) 0:52

8. **William Blake,** *The Tyger* (read by Brian Murray) 1:12

9. **Gwendolyn Brooks,** *We Real Cool* (read by Gwendolyn Brooks) 2:02

10. **Robert Browning,** *My Last Duchess* (read by Richard Howard) 3:22

11. **Kelly Cherry,** *Alzheimer's* (read by Kelly Cherry) 1:42

12. **Billy Collins,** *Marginalia* (read by Billy Collins) 3:12

13. **E. E. Cummings,** *next to of course god america i* (read by E. E. Cummings) 0:57

14. **Emily Dickinson,** *I heard a Fly buzz — when I died —* (read by Glenda Jackson) 0:52

15. **Emily Dickinson,** *I heard a Fly buzz — when I died —* (read by Robert Pinsky) 0:45

16. **Emily Dickinson,** *There's a certain Slant of light* (read by Julie Harris) 0:53

17. **Emily Dickinson,** *What Soft — Cherubic Creatures —* (read by Robert Pinsky) 0:29

18. **Emily Dickinson,** *What Soft — Cherubic Creatures —* (read by Julie Harris) 0:34

The *VirtuaLit Interactive Poetry Tutorial* — a free resource available at **bedford stmartins.com/virtualit/poetry** — is a multimedia tutorial designed to help students learn interactively about the elements of poetry, cultural contexts informing the composition of poetry, and critical approaches to literary analysis. Its aim is to help students gain insight into the craft of poetry.

Because students learn best by doing, *VirtuaLit* is structured so that students can work directly with the activities, tools, and information presented. *VirtuaLit's* electronic medium is ideal for this interaction — students can read a poem, listen to it read aloud, start writing about it, and access cultural material and definitions of key literary terms and approaches to help them as they analyze the poem, all within the same interface.

In the following pages you'll find sample activities to assign to your students, directions for using the tutorial and the *VirtuaLit* Notebook, and downloadable handouts for you to share with your students. This guide is organized according to the approaches to and contexts of poetry purely for ease of differentiation; you can easily explore what we offer by focusing on the poems themselves. The materials are organized as follows:

INTRODUCTION: USING *VIRTUALIT* TO TEACH POETRY

Why should I use the VirtuaLit Interactive Poetry Tutorial?

Helping students learn how to read poetry critically is very difficult; often they have no idea how to even describe the effect of a poem, let alone explain how a poem creates its message. Students do get better at understanding poems with enough practice and when the approach of close-reading a poem is modeled for them. The *VirtuaLit Interactive Poetry Tutorial* does both: It models for students the process of close-reading a poem, and it gives them practice working with the elements of poetry, cultural contexts, and critical approaches to poetry.

When you explore *VirtuaLit* you'll probably notice immediately that the tutorial divides "Poems in Depth" from "Approaches and Contexts." This division is largely superficial; every part of the tutorial intersects with hyperlinked cross-references. For example, if a student first reads a poem, then looks at the explanations of metaphor in the poem, and then wants to refer to a definition of metaphor, he or she will have moved from the "Poems in Depth" section to the "Approaches and Contexts" section that easily.

How is the VirtuaLit Interactive Poetry Tutorial structured? What kind of approaches to teaching literature does it support?

The *VirtuaLit Interactive Poetry Tutorial* is divided into two primary parts. One part focuses on three poems in depth, and one part focuses on approaches to analyzing poetry. The "Poems in Depth" part helps students to first look at a poem and then to respond to it and apply critical tools to it. The "Approaches and Contexts" part helps students understand the basic definitions and theories that inform the critical analysis of literature and then see poems as examples of a literary device or critical position. The division between "Poems in Depth" and "Approaches and Contexts" is largely a question of how you want to begin your study of literature; these two parts of *VirtuaLit* intersect, interact with, and illustrate each other.

Click on the green tab or on any of the poem titles to access the "Poems in Depth" section.

"**POEMS IN DEPTH**" *VirtuaLit* helps students explore three poems in depth. They are "The Fish" by Elizabeth Bishop, "To His Coy Mistress" by Andrew Marvell, and "My Papa's Waltz" by Theodore Roethke. Each poem is augmented with a suite of resources: a biography of the author, an audio rendition of the poem, and three approach modules. The approach modules include (1) an exploration of the *Elements of Poetry* found in the poem, (2) information about the *Cultural Contexts* that influenced the poem's content and the poet's strategies in crafting the poem, and (3) *Critical Approaches* that can be used for analyzing the poem. In the *Elements of Poetry* and *Critical Approaches* modules, highlighted portions of the poem and pop-up explanations and questions lead students through an analysis of the literary elements and critical approaches at play in each poem. Connection links to the "Approaches and Contexts" units allow students to access definitions, exercises, and sample essays that fill in more information about literary devices and theories as needed. The *Cultural Contexts* module presents cultural materials and questions students can respond to, encouraging them to think critically about the history and culture shaping the poem and contextualizing both within the framework of the poem.

"**APPROACHES AND CONTEXTS**" *VirtuaLit* also helps students explore critical tools and methods of inquiry available to guide their efforts at literary analysis. The *Elements of Poetry* unit in "Approaches and Contexts" includes general definitions, examples, and exercises on alliteration, assonance, denotation and connotation, diction, imagery, irony, metaphor, meter, rhyme, simile, symbol, tone, and word order. The *Cultural Contexts* unit includes document collections that feature images relating to and information about historical and cultural events and ideas for the times and places surrounding each poem. The *Critical Approaches* unit offers definitions of and sample essays for Deconstruction Theory, Feminist Criticism, Formalism, Marxist Criticism, New Criticism, New Historicism, Postcolonial Criticism, Psychoanalytic Criticism, Reader-Response, and Structuralism. Connection links to the "Poems in Depth" unit allow students to access examples in the featured poems of various literary devices and help students apply the approaches and theories they learn.

Why are there only three poems featured in the VirtuaLit Interactive Poetry Tutorial?

"The Fish," "To His Coy Mistress," and "My Papa's Waltz" are used to teach three different methods of close-reading poetry. These are a formalist approach, through the poems' poetic elements; a cultural critical approach, through the historical and cultural events and ideas that permeated the periods in which the poems were composed; and a literary critical approach, through the various theories serving as lenses in an examination of these poems. Thus the goal of the *VirtuaLit Interactive Poetry Tutorial* is not necessarily to teach students about these particular poems, though the site serves well in this function; rather, by using three poems that are well anthologized and widely taught, the *VirtuaLit Interactive Poetry Tutorial* challenges students to read, think, and write critically about poetry using these three poems as a backdrop for those important activities.

What form do students' responses to the exercises and questions take?

As you will notice, sprinkled throughout *VirtuaLit* are interactive exercises and writing prompts aimed at guiding students to think critically. Students can complete each exercise or type their responses to questions into the text boxes provided. Once finished, students can save their work to their "Notebook," an electronic archive of their work. Sending their Notebook allows them to e-mail their responses to you and to themselves.

TEACHING THE ELEMENTS OF POETRY WITH *VIRTUALIT*

Getting Started

In the "Approaches and Contexts" part of the *VirtuaLit Interactive Poetry Tutorial*, there is a section called "Elements of Poetry." This section offers definitions and interactive exercises on several elements of poetry.

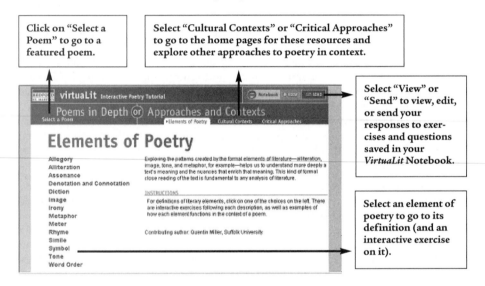

Click on "Select a Poem" to go to a featured poem.

Select "Cultural Contexts" or "Critical Approaches" to go to the home pages for these resources and explore other approaches to poetry in context.

Select "View" or "Send" to view, edit, or send your responses to exercises and questions saved in your *VirtuaLit* Notebook.

Select an element of poetry to go to its definition (and an interactive exercise on it).

If, however, if you want to work with elements of poetry in the context of a poem, you should look for the "Elements of Poetry" tab on the pale green tabbed box for any of the featured poems in *VirtuaLit.*

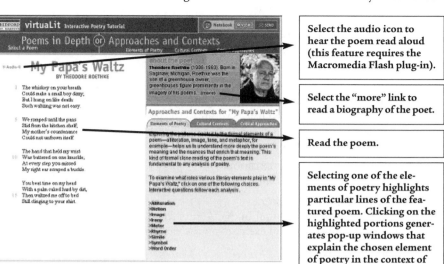

Select the audio icon to hear the poem read aloud (this feature requires the Macromedia Flash plug-in).

Select the "more" link to read a biography of the poet.

Read the poem.

Selecting one of the elements of poetry highlights particular lines of the featured poem. Clicking on the highlighted portions generates pop-up windows that explain the chosen element of poetry in the context of the highlighted portions of the poem.

VirtuaLit walks students through explanations of how various elements of poetry function in the featured poem.

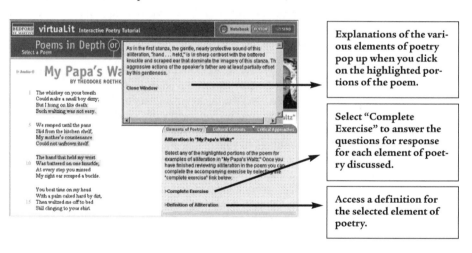

Explanations of the various elements of poetry pop up when you click on the highlighted portions of the poem.

Select "Complete Exercise" to answer the questions for response for each element of poetry discussed.

Access a definition for the selected element of poetry.

Activities

The activities in this section of the *Resources for Teaching Poetry* may be grouped under the heading "Teaching the Elements of Poetry," but they in fact focus on the featured poems in *VirtuaLit* and how the elements of poetry function in each. Cross-references in some of the activities to your textbook and to *VirtuaLit* suggest useful supporting material.

VirtuaLit *Activity: Analyzing Meaning in Elizabeth Bishop's "The Fish" through the Elements of Poetry*

TO THINK ABOUT:

Often, when you first read a poem, it evokes feelings and thoughts and you're not immediately aware of why. Poetry can be complex and the language so concentrated that it's difficult to unpack. Articulating what you feel about a poem and describing what in the poem generates those feelings helps you to understand more deeply a text's meaning and the nuances that enrich that meaning. The elements of poetry — *alliteration, image, tone,* and *metaphor,* for example — help give us a language through which to express the ways in which a poem creates meaning.

Elizabeth Bishop's "The Fish" is a surprising poem. In many ways deceptively simple, the poem seems to be about fishing and letting a caught fish go. Is there more to the poem than that? What do you feel as you read the poem, especially when you get to the end and the lines, "— until everything / was rainbow, rainbow, rainbow!" How would you describe how you feel about the fish? About the speaker?

HELPFUL MATERIAL IN YOUR TEXTBOOK:
- The discussion of the elements of poetry, particularly Chapter 1, "Reading Poetry"

HELPFUL MATERIAL IN *VIRTUALIT*:
- The "Elements of Poetry" unit in the "Approaches and Contexts" part of *VirtuaLit* contains definitions of and exercises on the elements of poetry.

STEPS IN THE ACTIVITY
1. Go to the *VirtuaLit Interactive Poetry Tutorial* and read Elizabeth Bishop's "The Fish." This poem is on page 32 of the text.
2. Think about your initial response to the poem. What thoughts and feelings does it evoke? Keep these in mind as you progress through the next steps in the activity.
3. Go through each discussion of the elements of poetry in "The Fish," clicking on the highlighted portions of the poem and reading the explanations for each (assonance, denotation and connotation, diction, image, irony, simile, symbol, and tone). Think about how each element contributes to creating meaning in the poem.
4. Decide which element of poetry seems to contribute the most to generating the thoughts and feelings you had when you first read the poem.
5. Complete the exercise for that element in the poem, responding to the questions in the text boxes provided. Save your responses to your Notebook by selecting the "Add to Notebook" link at the bottom of the screen.
6. E-mail your Notebook responses to yourself by clicking on the "Send" Notebook tool at the top of the screen and entering the appropriate e-mail address.
7. Using your copy of your e-mailed notebook, write a one- to two-page paper that fleshes out your *VirtuaLit* Notebook responses and describes fully how the element of poetry you selected creates meaning in the poem. Also explain how the effect of the element in "The Fish" induces the reaction you had to the poem.
8. Attach a copy of your e-mailed Notebook to your final paper and turn in all work.

GENERAL DIRECTIONS FOR THE ESSAY
Think of this essay as a description of your experience reading a poem and the knowledge you gained about the relationship between meaning and the elements of poetry.

You will need to provide your reader with a statement that briefly explains what the essay is about, and then, following good compositional practice, you will need to organize your ideas into paragraphs of related ideas. Keep in mind that one to two pages is a very short paper, so you will need to write concisely. As in all literary essays, be sure to follow MLA style for titling and formatting.

VirtuaLit *Activity: Explicating the Fish's Beauty in Elizabeth Bishop's "The Fish"*
TO THINK ABOUT:
There are many tools available to assist our efforts to understand poetry. Before addressing historical context or other extratextual elements, however, it's often worth-

while to look very closely at the poem itself, delving into the language to figure out how the poem achieves its effect. Articulating the poem's effect and describing what in the poem's language generates its meaning helps you to understand more deeply the nuances that enrich its message. The elements of poetry — *alliteration, image, tone,* and *metaphor,* for example — help give us a vocabulary through which to express the ways in which a poem creates meaning. *Explication,* a detailed exploration of the text — line by line and word by word — addresses all of the various elements of poetry as they play off of one another and as they affect the overall meaning of the text.

A rich poem to unpack, there are many parts of Elizabeth Bishop's "The Fish" that merit explication. Ostensibly about fishing and letting go a caught fish, the poem also describes a transformation in the speaker. In the first lines, the speaker describes the fish as "battered" and "a grunting weight" — not very attractive. By the end of the poem, however, everything becomes "rainbow, rainbow, rainbow!" as the speaker stares at the fish. What beauty does the speaker see? What causes this transformation?

HELPFUL MATERIAL IN YOUR TEXTBOOK:
• The discussion of the elements of poetry, particularly Chapter 1, "Reading Poetry"

HELPFUL MATERIAL IN *VIRTUALIT*:
• The "Elements of Poetry" unit in the "Approaches and Contexts" part of *VirtuaLit* contains definitions of and exercises on the elements of poetry.
• *VirtuaLit's* sample essay pulling together analyses of the elements of poetry in "The Fish"

STEPS IN THE ACTIVITY
1. Go to the *VirtuaLit Interactive Poetry Tutorial* and read Elizabeth Bishop's "The Fish." This poem is also on page 32 of the text. Think about the beauty that the speaker learns to see by the end of the poem. What do you think is the source of the beauty? What causes the speaker's transformation?
2. Go through each discussion of the elements of poetry in "The Fish," clicking on the highlighted portions of the poem and reading the explanations for each (assonance, denotation and connotation, diction, image, irony, simile, symbol, and tone).
3. Choose a portion of the poem of around fifteen lines to focus on an explication of the source of the fish's beauty and how the speaker comes to appreciate it.
4. Write a one- to two-page paper explicating the fifteen lines of the poem you selected, unpacking the language and accounting for the fish's beauty and the speaker's transformation in appreciating it. You may use *VirtuaLit's* analyses of the elements of poetry in "The Fish" as a model, but keep in mind that an explication uses all of the elements of poetry in its scrutiny of the text.
5. Turn in all work.

GENERAL DIRECTIONS FOR THE ESSAY
Think of this essay as a description of your experience reading a poem and the knowledge you gained about the relationship between meaning and the elements of poetry.

You will need to provide your reader with a statement that briefly explains what the essay is about, and then, following good compositional practice, you will need to organize your ideas into paragraphs of related ideas. Keep in mind that one to two pages is a very short paper, so you will need to write concisely. As in all literary essays, be sure to follow MLA style for titling and formatting.

VirtuaLit *Activity: Understanding Poetic Form in Andrew Marvell's "To His Coy Mistress"*
TO THINK ABOUT:
Understanding the relationship between a poem's form and the themes embedded in the poem makes us aware of the art and craft required in writing poetry. The *form* of

a poem (its overall structure and shape) is generally described as being *open* or *closed* (also referred to as *fixed form*). Poems that use patterns in their meter, rhyme, lines, and stanzas have a *closed* or *fixed form*. Some examples of *closed* or *fixed* poetic forms are the *sonnet, villanelle, sestina, limerick,* and *ode*. Poems that do not exhibit established patterns in their lines, stanzas, rhyme, and meter have an *open form* and are often called *free verse*.

Andrew Marvell's "To His Coy Mistress" is an example of a *fixed-form* poem. The poem is constructed as a three-part logical argument (the three parts of the argument are represented by the three stanzas of the poem). The poem has a very regular meter, and it never deviates from a pattern of rhyming couplets. As such, in terms of poetic form, "To His Coy Mistress" is very formal and conservative. The subject matter of the poem is, however, much more racy. The speaker is trying to get a young woman to sleep with him. Try to imagine how the subject matter would be affected if Marvell had chosen another poetic form, particularly an open form. What does the poem's fixed form contribute to the speaker's seduction? How successful would the speaker be in convincing his mistress to sleep with him if he did not rhyme and use a specific meter? Do you think the combination of high style (the fixed form of the poem) with low subject matter (an argument for having sex) is effective? Consider the historical context of the poem: Would this combination be as effective today? What kind of changes would you have to make to the poem's form to make it relevant for a contemporary audience? Why?

HELPFUL MATERIAL IN YOUR TEXTBOOK:
- Peter De Vries's parody of Marvell's poem, "To His Importunate Mistress," on page 262
- The discussions of poetic form and open form on pages 237 and 267

HELPFUL MATERIAL IN *VIRTUALIT*:
- The "Cultural Context" document collection on female sexuality in the "Approaches and Contexts" part of *VirtuaLit*

STEPS IN THE ACTIVITY
1. Go to the *VirtuaLit Interactive Poetry Tutorial* and read Andrew Marvell's "To His Coy Mistress." This poem is also on page 81 of the text.
2. Write your own poem with a similar theme and using a fixed form.
3. Choose another poetic form (either open or another fixed form) and rewrite your poem using it.
4. Write a short essay (one to two pages) explaining the following:
   a) the choices you had to make in creating the first poem
   b) the choices you had to make in creating the second poem
   c) the reasons Marvell's choices were successful for his time period
   d) potential problems you had to resolve when writing in the period of history in which you live
5. Attach your two poems to the back of the essay and turn all work in.

GENERAL DIRECTIONS FOR THE ESSAY
Think of this essay as a description of your experience writing and translating poetry from one form into another and the knowledge you gained about the relationship between meaning and poetic form.

You will need to provide your reader with a statement that briefly explains what the essay is about, and then, following good compositional practice, you will need to organize your ideas into paragraphs of related ideas. Keep in mind that one to two pages is a very short paper, so you will need to write concisely. Using the issues listed above to frame your ideas may help to focus your writing. As in all literary essays, be sure to follow MLA style for titling and formatting.

VirtuaLit *Activity: Understanding Meter in Andrew Marvell's "To His Coy Mistress"*
To think about:
The *rhythm* of a poem, or its *meter,* is determined by the pattern of accented and unaccented syllables in the words that make up the poem. Each word with more than one syllable has at least one *strong accent* or *stressed* syllable. The *stressed* syllable is the part of the word that we tend to emphasize when we speak the word aloud. For example, in the word "mistress," the *accent* is on "mis," making it the *stressed* syllable in the word. The "tress" part of "mistress" is unaccented, making it the *unstressed* syllable in the word. Marking the stressed and unstressed syllables in a poem and analyzing any resulting pattern is called *scansion.* Stressed syllables are marked with a small accent (ʹ) and unstressed syllables are marked with a breve (˘).

Andrew Marvell's "To His Coy Mistress" uses a fairly regular metrical pattern — eight syllables per line consisting of four *iambs,* or *feet* (that is, an unstressed syllable followed by a stressed syllable). If you read the poem aloud (or listen to it read aloud in *VirtuaLit*), you'll hear the rhythm of stressed and unstressed syllables.

While doing the following activity, think about the way the poem's rhythm works in relation to its theme and the ideas expressed by the poet. What does the meter contribute to the poem's meaning?

Helpful material in your textbook:
• The discussion of rhythm and meter on page 215

Helpful material in *VirtuaLit:*
• The definition for and exercise on meter in the "Elements of Poetry" part of *VirtuaLit,* which provides directions for scansion.

Steps in the Activity
1. Go to the *VirtuaLit Interactive Poetry Tutorial* and read Andrew Marvell's "To His Coy Mistress." This poem is also on page 81 of the text.
2. Select "meter" from the elements of poetry treated with reference to the poem. Click through the highlighted portions of the poem and read the analyses of meter.
3. Go to the accompanying exercise on meter in "To His Coy Mistress" and answer the questions in the text boxes provided. Save your responses to your Notebook by selecting the "Add to Notebook" link at the bottom of the screen.
4. E-mail your notebook responses to yourself and to me by clicking on the "Send" Notebook tool at the top of the screen and entering the appropriate e-mail addresses.
5. Using what you have learned about meter in "To His Coy Mistress," scan the following poem by Robert Herrick (1591–1674), "Delight in Disorder":

> A sweet disorder in the dress
> Kindles in clothes a wantonness
> A lawn° about the shoulders thrown   *linen scarf*
> Into a fine distraction;
> An erring lace, which here and there
> Enthralls the crimson stomacher,
> A cuff neglectful, and thereby
> Ribbons to flow confusedly;
> A winning wave, deserving note,
> In the tempestuous petticoat;
> A careless shoestring, in whose tie
> I see a wild civility;
> Do more bewitch me than when art
> Is too precise in every part.

6. Ask yourself the following questions:
   a) How does the rhythm of "To His Coy Mistress" work in relation to its theme and the ideas expressed by the poet?
   b) How does the rhythm of "Delight in Disorder" work in relation to its theme? Is it "precise in every part"?
   c) How does the meter of each poem forward its theme and the ideas expressed by the poet? What new insights can you gain about each poem from studying its rhythm and meter?
7. Describe your insights about the relationship between the meter of a poem and the poem's meaning in a two- to three-minute oral presentation.
8. Turn in your scanned copy of "Delight in Disorder."

VirtuaLit *Activity: Understanding Rhyme in Theodore Roethke's "My Papa's Waltz"*
TO THINK ABOUT:
Rhyme is a way of creating sound patterns. Poets make use of rhyme so that the sounds of lines of poetry contribute to their meaning. Rhyming two words can also connect the ideas they represent, helping to form the general effect of a poem. *Exact rhymes* share the same stressed vowel sound as well as any sounds that follow the vowel. *Near (slant) rhymes* have almost identical sounds. *Masculine rhymes* are single-syllable words that rhyme; *feminine rhymes* have a rhymed strong (stressed) syllable followed by one or more rhymed weak (unstressed) syllables.

Unlike many poets in the early twentieth century, Theodore Roethke did not move away from regular rhyme schemes and often used it in his poetry. The rhyme scheme of "My Papa's Waltz" is very simple: *abab cdcd efef ghgh*. This simple rhyme scheme matches the swinging action of the waltz described in the poem, and it also preserves the lack of sophistication of the speaker's perspective (he is a small boy, after all).

While doing the following activity, think about the effects of rhyme in "My Papa's Waltz." The poem is dominated by end rhyme, but of what type? Exact rhymes or near rhymes? Masculine or feminine rhymes? What do the rhymes in the poem contribute to the poem's meaning?

HELPFUL MATERIAL IN YOUR TEXTBOOK:
- The section on "Rhyme" on pages 190–193

HELPFUL MATERIAL IN *VIRTUALIT*:
- The definition of and exercise on rhyme in the "Elements of Poetry" part of *VirtuaLit*

STEPS IN THE ACTIVITY
1. Go to the *VirtuaLit Interactive Poetry Tutorial* and read Theodore Roethke's "My Papa's Waltz." This poem is also on page 233 of the text.
2. Select the "Elements of Poetry" tab on the green "Approaches and Contexts" box on the "My Papa's Waltz" poem page.
3. Select "rhyme" from the elements of poetry treated with reference to the poem. Click through the highlighted portions of the poem and read the analyses of the rhyme.
4. Go to the accompanying exercise on rhyme in "My Papa's Waltz" and answer the questions in the text boxes provided. Save your responses to your Notebook by selecting the "Add to Notebook" link at the bottom of the screen.
5. E-mail your Notebook responses to yourself by clicking on the "Send" Notebook tool at the top of the screen and entering your e-mail address.
6. Using your copy of your e-mailed notebook, write a one- to two-page paper on the effect of rhyme in "My Papa's Waltz." Discuss the masculine and feminine rhymes in the poem. What effect do they have? The poem's transition from near rhyme to exact rhyme may sharpen the poem's focus and thus create some tension, but

the exact rhymes also suggest a greater sense of control by the end of the poem. What does this contribute to the overall effect of the poem?

7. Attach a copy of your e-mailed Notebook to your essay and turn in all work.

GENERAL DIRECTIONS FOR THE ESSAY

Think of this essay as a description of your experience reading "My Papa's Waltz," examining rhyme in the poem and analyzing what it contributes to the overall effect of the poem.

You will need to provide your reader with a statement that briefly explains what the essay is about, and then, following good compositional practice, you will need to organize your ideas into paragraphs of related ideas. As for all literary essays, be sure to follow MLA style for titling and formatting.

VirtuaLit *Activity: Understanding Imagery in Theodore Roethke's "My Papa's Waltz"*

TO THINK ABOUT:

Images are a powerful poetic device; they capture readers' imaginations and add dimension to the language in a poem. Imagery can be literal or figurative, and it can appeal to other senses besides the visual. A reference to a "thick, plush, wool blanket" evokes more than an image of a blanket; it suggests the blanket's weight, the soft texture of the wool, and the warmth it provides.

The organizing image in Theodore Roethke's "My Papa's Waltz" is of a waltz: the speaker, a small boy, describes how he and his "papa" romp together. On the surface, this image is playful and endearing. Why, then, is the mother unable to stop from frowning in the poem? What details in the poem's imagery suggest that the waltz is not just a carefree diversion between father and son?

While doing the following activity, think about the details of the waltz described by the speaker in "My Papa's Waltz." How do these details complicate the image of the father and son waltzing?

HELPFUL MATERIAL IN YOUR TEXTBOOK:

• The section on "Poetry's Appeal to the Senses" on pages 109–118

HELPFUL MATERIAL IN *VIRTUALIT*:

• The definition of and exercise on image in the "Elements of Poetry" part of *VirtuaLit*

STEPS IN THE ACTIVITY

1. Go to the *VirtuaLit Interactive Poetry Tutorial* and read Theodore Roethke's "My Papa's Waltz." This poem is also on page 233 of the text.
2. Select the "Elements of Poetry" tab on the green "Approaches and Contexts" box on the "My Papa's Waltz" poem page.
3. Select "image" from the elements of poetry treated with reference to the poem. Click through the highlighted portions of the poem and read the analyses of the imagery.
4. Go to the accompanying exercise on images in "My Papa's Waltz" and answer the questions in the text boxes provided. Save your responses to your Notebook by selecting the "Add to Notebook" link at the bottom of the screen.
5. E-mail your notebook responses to yourself by clicking on the "Send" Notebook tool at the top of the screen and entering your e-mail address.
6. Using your copy of your e-mailed Notebook, write a one- to two-page paper describing the effects of imagery in "My Papa's Waltz." In your essay address the following questions:
   a) What do the visual details in the poem imply about the father? about the boy? about their relationship?

b) How does the imagery affect the poem's meaning?

7. Attach a copy of your e-mailed Notebook to your essay and turn in all work.

GENERAL DIRECTIONS FOR THE ESSAY

Think of this essay as a description of your experience reading "My Papa's Waltz," examining details in the poem's use of imagery and analyzing what consequences they have for the poem's meaning.

You will need to provide your reader with a statement that briefly explains what the essay is about, and then, following good compositional practice, you will need to organize your ideas into paragraphs of related ideas. As for all literary essays, be sure to follow MLA style for titling and formatting.

The VirtuaLit Interactive Poetry Tutorial *Handout: Definitions of Analysis and Explication*

An **analysis** examines a single element — such as rhyme, symbol, tone, or irony — and relates it to the entire work. An analysis separates the work into parts and focuses on a specific one; however, the element focused on must be related to the work as a whole or it will appear irrelevant. For example, it is not enough to point out that there are many death images in Andrew Marvell's "To His Coy Mistress"; the images must somehow be connected to the poem's overall effect.

An **explication** is a detailed explanation of a passage of poetry or prose. Because explication is an intensive examination of a text line by line, it is mostly used to interpret a short poem in its entirety or a brief passage from a long poem, short story, or play. An explication pays careful attention to language — the connotations of words, allusions, figurative language, irony, symbol, rhythm, sound, and so on.

The VirtuaLit Interactive Poetry Tutorial *Handout: Quick Reference for Metrical Conventions*

Foot: one unit of the rhythmic pattern that makes up a poem's meter, conventionally marked by the symbol "|" (Hickory, | dickory |, dock,)

Iamb: a foot composed of one weak syllable followed by a strong syllable ($\smile$ ')

Iambic meter: a rhythmic pattern composed of iambs

Trochee: a foot composed of one strong syllable followed by a weak syllable (' $\smile$)

Trochaic meter: a rhythmic pattern composed of trochees

Anapest: a foot composed of two weak syllables followed by a strong syllable ($\smile\smile$ ')

Anapestic meter: a rhythmic pattern composed of anapests

Dactyl: a foot composed of a strong syllable followed by two weak syllables (' $\smile\smile$)

Dactylic meter: a rhythmic pattern composed of dactyls

Monometer: a line (of a poem) of one foot

Dimeter: a line (of a poem) of two feet

Trimeter: a line (of a poem) of three feet

Tetrameter: a line (of a poem) of four feet

Pentameter: a line (of a poem) of five feet

Hexameter: a line (of a poem) of six feet

Heptameter: a line (of a poem) of seven feet

Octameter: a line (of a poem) of eight feet

Caesura: a break in the meter, conventionally marked by the symbol "| |"

End-stopped line: a line that has a pause at its end

Run-on line: a line that ends without a pause and continues into the next line for its meaning; also referred to as **enjambment**

Spondee: two strong (accented) syllables together (′′)

Pyrrhus: two weak (unaccented) syllables together (◡◡)

Rising meter: term used to refer to the two feet that begin with a weak syllable, iambic and anapestic

Falling meter: term used to refer to the two feet that begin with a strong syllable, trochaic and dactylic

The **VirtuaLit Interactive Poetry Tutorial** *Handout: Quick Reference for Rhyme Conventions*
Rhyme: two or more words or phrases that repeat the same sounds. Rhyme words often have similar spellings, but that is not a requirement of rhyme; what matters is that the words sound alike (*vain* rhymes with *reign*). Moreover, words may look alike but not rhyme at all. In *eye rhyme* the word spellings are similar but the pronunciations are not, as in *through* and *cough*.

End rhyme: the rhyming words come at the ends of lines of poetry

Internal rhyme: at least one of the rhymed words is within the line of poetry

Masculine rhyme: the rhyming of single syllable words, as in *glade* and *shade*

Feminine rhyme: a rhymed strong (stressed) syllable followed by one or more rhymed weak (unstressed) syllables, as in *butter, clutter; gratitude, attitude; quivering, shivering*

Exact rhyme: rhyming words that share the same stressed vowel sound as well as any sounds that follow the vowel

Near rhyme (off rhyme, slant rhyme, approximate rhyme): rhyming words for which the sounds are almost but not exactly alike. Consonance occurs when the words have an identical consonant sound preceded by different vowel sounds, as in *home, same; worth, breath.* Assonance occurs when the words have an identical vowel sound but the surrounding consonant sounds are different, as in *tune, food; kill, wit.*

The **VirtuaLit Interactive Poetry Tutorial** *Handout: Questions to Ask Yourself While Reading Poetry*
- What is your response to the poem on first reading?

- Who is the speaker? What does the poem reveal about the speaker's character? In some poems, the speaker may be nothing more than a voice meditating on a theme, while in others the speaker takes on a specific personality.

- Is the speaker addressing a particular person? If so, who is that person, and why is the speaker interested in him or her?

- Does the poem have a setting? Is the poem occasioned by a particular event?

- Is the theme of the poem stated directly or indirectly?

- From what perspective (or point of view) is the speaker describing specific events? Is the speaker recounting events of the past or events that are occurring in the present? If past events are being recalled, what present meaning do they have for the speaker?

- Does a close examination of the symbolism, imagery, possible allegorical meanings, use of metaphors and/or similes in the poem reveal any patterns?

- What is the structure of the poem?
- What do sound and meter contribute to the poem?

TEACHING CULTURAL CONTEXTS FOR POETRY WITH *VIRTUALIT*

Getting Started

For each poem featured in the *VirtuaLit Interactive Poetry Tutorial*, there is a "Cultural Contexts" tab in the pale green tabbed box. This tabbed section offers document collections that provide cultural, biographical, and historical context for the poems featured in *VirtuaLit*. You can also access these document collections through the "Cultural Contexts" section of the general "Approaches and Contexts" part of *VirtuaLit*.

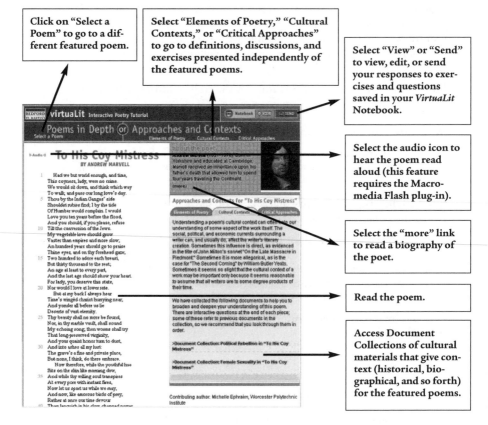

Click on "Select a Poem" to go to a different featured poem.

Select "Elements of Poetry," "Cultural Contexts," or "Critical Approaches" to go to definitions, discussions, and exercises presented independently of the featured poems.

Select "View" or "Send" to view, edit, or send your responses to exercises and questions saved in your *VirtuaLit* Notebook.

Select the audio icon to hear the poem read aloud (this feature requires the Macromedia Flash plug-in).

Select the "more" link to read a biography of the poet.

Read the poem.

Access Document Collections of cultural materials that give context (historical, biographical, and so forth) for the featured poems.

Each document collection features paintings, photographs, interviews, and other texts that give context to the featured poems.

Activities

The activities in this section of the *Resources for Teaching Poetry* focus on the featured poems in *VirtuaLit* and how understanding the cultural context of a literary text enriches our sense of the text's meaning. Cross-references in some of the activities to your textbook and to *VirtuaLit* suggest useful supporting material.

VirtuaLit Activity: Elizabeth Bishop as Painter and Poet

TO THINK ABOUT:

Elizabeth Bishop gained fame for her writing, yet many of her readers were unaware that she was an avid visual artist as well. Her passion for painting, mainly in watercolors, continued throughout her adult life: She recorded the banal landmarks of her childhood as well as scenes from her years in Brazil. Such visual diaries, sometimes cynical and humorously quirky, often give us a window into Bishop's darker emotional life, which was plagued by alcoholism and family trauma. The paintings also continue a central theme in Bishop's poetry; as in her written work, Bishop's sketches are intended to evoke questions about the function of art itself.

While doing the following activity, think about similarities in Bishop's approach to painting and her approach to poetry.

STEPS IN THE ACTIVITY

1. Go to the *VirtuaLit Interactive Poetry Tutorial* and read Elizabeth Bishop's "The Fish." This poem is also on page 32 of the text.
2. Select the "Cultural Contexts" tab on the green "Approaches and Contexts" box on the "The Fish" poem page.
3. Select the Document Collection *Elizabeth Bishop as Painter* from the "Cultural Contexts" green tab.
4. Read William Benton's "Introduction to *Exchanging Hats.*"
5. Return to the directory of documents in the Document Collection *Elizabeth Bishop as Painter.*
6. Register to view the Bishop paintings. In order to register, click on the "register here" link. Enter your e-mail address and your first and last name, create a password for yourself, and fill in the other form fields as required. Click on "Submit."
7. Return to the *Elizabeth Bishop as Painter* Document Collection in the *VirtuaLit Interactive Poetry Tutorial.*
8. Look at the *Sha-Sha* painting by Elizabeth Bishop.
9. Look at the *County Courthouse* painting, responding to the question accompanying the painting in the text box provided. Save your response to your Notebook by selecting the "Add to Notebook" link at the bottom of the screen. (DO NOT send your Notebook until you have completed the next two steps of this activity.)
10. Look at the *Interior with Extension Cord* painting.
11. Look at the *Red Stove and Flowers* painting, responding to the questions that accompany the painting in the text boxes provided. Save your responses to your Notebook by selecting the "Add to Notebook" link at the bottom of the screen.
12. E-mail your Notebook responses to yourself by clicking on the "Send" Notebook tool at the top of the screen and entering your e-mail address.
13. Using your copy of your e-mailed Notebook (especially your response to the first question accompanying *Red Stove and Flowers,* make an illustration that depicts the events narrated in Bishop's "The Fish." Try to copy Bishop's own style as a painter. What details would she emphasize if she were painting the scene described in her poem?
14. Write a paragraph or two describing the choices you made in representing "The Fish" visually. What elements of Bishop's artistic style did you imitate?
15. Attach a copy of your e-mailed Notebook to your paragraph(s) and turn in both with your illustration of "The Fish."

VirtuaLit *Activity: Elizabeth Bishop and the Craft of Poetry*
TO THINK ABOUT:

Accounts of Elizabeth Bishop teaching students about writing poetry indicate that Bishop was a very deliberate poet, exceedingly careful in her craft, and she expects the same of her students. She exclaims at one point in her University of Washington class, "If you students want so badly to *express* yourselves, why don't you bother to learn even the simplest things about your own language?"

The actual events that take place in Bishop's "The Fish" are not that remarkable: Someone goes out fishing on a boat, catches a large fish with old hooks in its mouth, and throws it back into the water. Yet Bishop's description does a lot more than just narrate these events. What effects does Bishop's language have? What are sources of power in "The Fish"?

While doing the following activity, think about the function of art, the choices Bishop makes in her description of a fishing experience, and what "The Fish" conveys about the power of language and poetry.

HELPFUL MATERIAL IN YOUR TEXTBOOK:
• The section on "The Pleasure of Words" on pages 24–29

STEPS IN THE ACTIVITY
1. Go to the *VirtuaLit Interactive Poetry Tutorial* and read Elizabeth Bishop's "The Fish." This poem is also on page 32 of the text.
2. Select the "Cultural Contexts" tab on the green "Approaches and Contexts" box on the "The Fish" poem page.
3. Select the Document Collection *Elizabeth Bishop as Painter* from the "Cultural Contexts" green tab.
4. Read the "Conversations and Class Notes" document by Bishop and Wesley Wehr, responding to the questions accompanying the selection in the text boxes provided. Save your responses to your Notebook by selecting the "Add to Notebook" link at the bottom of the screen. (DO NOT send your Notebook until you have completed the next step of this activity.)
5. Read the "Studying with Miss Bishop" document by Dana Gioia, responding to the second and third questions accompanying the selection in the text boxes provided. Save your responses to your Notebook by selecting the "Add to Notebook" link at the bottom of the screen.
6. E-mail your Notebook responses to yourself by clicking on the "Send" Notebook tool at the top of the screen and entering your e-mail address.
7. In "Conversations and Class Notes," Bishop tells Wehr that "if my students would concentrate more on all the difficulties of writing a good poem, all the complexities of language and form, I think that they would find that the truth will come through quite by itself." What do you think the "truth" is in Bishop's "The Fish"? Using your copy of your e-mailed Notebook (especially your response to the last question accompanying the Wehr interview), write a one- to two-page paper that fleshes out what you think "The Fish" reveals about Bishop's craft as a poet and the function of poetry for Bishop.
8. Attach a copy of your e-mailed Notebook to your essay and turn in all work.

GENERAL DIRECTIONS FOR THE ESSAY
Think of this essay as a description of your experience reading "The Fish," examining Bishop's approach to writing poetry and making connections between Bishop's theory and her practice.

You will need to provide your reader with a statement that briefly explains what the essay is about, and then, following good compositional practice, you will need to organize your ideas into paragraphs of related ideas. It may help to organize your paper around a discussion of Bishop's approach to poetry followed by a discussion of "The Fish," concluding with an explanation of how the two relate. As for all literary essays, be sure to follow MLA style for titling and formatting.

VirtuaLit *Activity: Issues of Sexuality in Andrew Marvell's "To His Coy Mistress"*
TO THINK ABOUT:
Understanding the cultural context of a poem can often help our understanding of some aspect of the poem itself. The social, political, and economic currents surrounding

a writer can, and usually do, affect the writer's literary creation. Sometimes this influence is direct, as evidenced in the title of John Milton's sonnet "On the Late Massacre in Piedmont." Sometimes it is more allegorical, as is the case for "The Second Coming" by William Butler Yeats. Sometimes it seems so slight that the cultural context of a work may be important only because it seems reasonable to assume that all writers are to some degree products of their time. However, we can only appreciate if and how a poem is responding to society when we explore the poem's cultural context.

Andrew Marvell's "To His Coy Mistress" was published in 1681. With the Protestant Reformation of the early sixteenth century, there was a shift away from the medieval church's embrace of celibacy to an emphasis on "holy matrimony": after the Reformation, clergy were allowed to marry. Yet seventeenth-century preachers still emphasized the importance of female chastity and warned also of the moral and spiritual repercussions of lust.

While doing the following activity, think about the moral and spiritual choices confronting the mistress in Marvell's poem. How were lust, sex, and marriage viewed in seventeenth-century Britain?

HELPFUL MATERIAL IN YOUR TEXTBOOK:

- The excerpt from Bernard Duyfhuizen's article " 'To His Coy Mistress': On How a Female Might Respond" on page 82

STEPS IN THE ACTIVITY

1. Go to the *VirtuaLit Interactive Poetry Tutorial* and read Andrew Marvell's "To His Coy Mistress." This poem is also on page 81 of the text.
2. Select the Document Collection *Female Sexuality in "To His Coy Mistress"* from the "Cultural Contexts" green tab on the "To His Coy Mistress" poem page.
3. Read John Chrysostom's "On Virginity," responding to the questions at the end of the selection in the text boxes provided. Save your responses to your Notebook by selecting the "Add to Notebook" link at the bottom of the screen. (DO NOT send your Notebook until you have completed the next two steps of this activity.)
4. Read Henry Bullinger's "Fifty Godly and Learned Sermons," responding to the questions at the end of the selection in the text boxes provided. Save your responses to your Notebook by selecting the "Add to Notebook" link at the bottom of the screen. (DO NOT send your Notebook until you have completed the next step of this activity.)
5. Read William Perkins's "Christian Oeconomy," responding to the questions at the end of the selection in the text boxes provided. Save your responses to your Notebook by selecting the "Add to Notebook" link at the bottom of the screen.
6. E-mail your Notebook responses to yourself by clicking on the "Send" Notebook tool at the top of the screen and entering your e-mail address.
7. Think about how the three documents have added to your assessment of the role of the mistress in Marvell's poem. What are possible implications for the mistress of the speaker's successful seduction? If he is unsuccessful? Does it seem likely that the speaker is interested in marrying the mistress?
8. Using your copy of your e-mailed Notebook, write a one- to two-page paper that integrates some of your *VirtuaLit* Notebook responses with an explanation of how your view of "To His Coy Mistress" has changed as a result of reading the pieces by Chrysostom, Bullinger, and Perkins.
9. Attach a copy of your e-mailed Notebook to your final paper and turn in all work.

GENERAL DIRECTIONS FOR THE ESSAY

Think of this essay as a description of your experience working with primary source material about female sexuality and views on marriage in Britain during the seventeenth century and the contextual knowledge you gained about the significance of the speaker's attempted seduction in Marvell's "To His Coy Mistress."

You will need to provide your reader with a statement that briefly explains what the essay is about, and then, following good compositional practice, you will need to organize your ideas into paragraphs of related ideas. Keep in mind that one to two pages is a very short paper, so you will need to write concisely. It may help to organize your paper around the questions posed in Step 7 of the activity. As in all literary essays, be sure to follow MLA style for titling and formatting.

VirtuaLit *Activity: Issues of Political Rebellion in Andrew Marvell's "To His Coy Mistress"*

TO THINK ABOUT:

Understanding the cultural context of a poem can often help our understanding of some aspect of the poem itself. The social, political, and economic currents surrounding a writer can, and usually do, affect the writer's literary creation. Sometimes this influence is direct, as evidenced in the title of John Milton's sonnet "On the Late Massacre in Piedmont." Sometimes it is more allegorical, as is the case for "The Second Coming" by William Butler Yeats. Sometimes it seems so slight that the cultural context of a work may be important only because it seems reasonable to assume that all writers are to some degree products of their time. However, we can only appreciate if and how a poem is responding to society when we explore the poem's cultural context.

Andrew Marvell's "To His Coy Mistress" was published in 1681, just two decades after the Restoration that gave Charles II the British throne, breathing new life into the doctrine of *divine right* (that a monarch is not empowered by the people but by the divine ordinance of his birthright). Marvell had served as a tutor to Oliver Cromwell's family and had supported the anti-royalists during the interregnum government that followed the execution of Charles I. With the return of the king to the throne, Marvell's political position became much more precarious.

While doing the following activity, think about the possible political ramifications of "To His Coy Mistress." The speaker of the poem issues a call to arms against time, an insurrection against natural order, and a rebellion against the sun (a popular pun for the son of the monarch). What political significance does this carpe diem (seize the day) position have?

HELPFUL MATERIAL IN *VIRTUALIT*:
- "Andrew Marvell's 'To His Coy Mistress': A New Historicist Reading"

STEPS IN THE ACTIVITY

1. Go to the *VirtuaLit Interactive Poetry Tutorial* and read Andrew Marvell's "To His Coy Mistress." This poem is also on page 81 of the text.
2. Select the Document Collection *Political Rebellion in "To His Coy Mistress"* from the "Cultural Contexts" green tab on the "To His Coy Mistress" poem page.
3. Look at *Eikon Basilike*, responding to the accompanying questions at the end of the selection in the text boxes provided. Save your responses to your Notebook by selecting the "Add to Notebook" link at the bottom of the screen. (DO NOT send your Notebook until you have completed the next two steps of this activity.)
4. Look at John Nalson's "An Allegory of 1649," responding to the accompanying questions in the text boxes provided. Save your responses to your Notebook by selecting the "Add to Notebook" link at the bottom of the screen. (DO NOT send your Notebook until you have completed the next step of this activity.)
5. Read John Milton's "The Tenure of Kings and Magistrates," responding to the questions at the end of the selection in the text boxes provided. Save your responses to your Notebook by selecting the "Add to Notebook" link at the bottom of the screen.

6. E-mail your Notebook responses to yourself by clicking on the "Send" Notebook tool at the top of the screen and entering your e-mail address.

7. Think about how the two images and the document have added to your understanding of Marvell's poem. What are possible political implications for rebelling against natural order and the sun? Both Milton and Marvell use rhetoric that applauds freedom and agency. Are there any other similarities between Milton's argument and the speaker's argument in Marvell's poem? Do either *Eikon Basilike* or Nalson's "An Allegory of 1649" seem at all emblematic of the political implications of "To His Coy Mistress"?

8. Keeping the questions in Step 7 in mind, draw a picture that illustrates the political message you read in Marvell's "To His Coy Mistress."

9. Attach a copy of your e-mailed Notebook to your illustration and turn in all work.

VirtuaLit *Activity: The Evolving Composition of Theodore Roethke's "My Papa's Waltz"*

To think about:

Currently housed in the Theodore Roethke Manuscripts Collection at the University of Washington in Seattle, the early drafts of "My Papa's Waltz" show us Roethke's important revisions of the poem. Roethke's variations begin with the title itself, which shifts between "Dance with Papa," "The Dance," "Papa's Dance," "Dance with Father," and finally "My Papa's Waltz." But the most striking alteration in the drafts is the change from "girl" to "boy" in the poem's first stanza. Perhaps with a female narrator in mind, Roethke revises "At every step you missed / My forehead scraped a buckle" as "At every step you missed / My right ear scraped a buckle" so as to temper the potential sexual implications of the dance.

While doing the following activity, think about the poetic choices Roethke made as he composed "My Papa's Waltz" — how does the meaning of the poem change with his revisions?

Steps in the Activity

1. Go to the *VirtuaLit Interactive Poetry Tutorial* and read Theodore Roethke's "My Papa's Waltz." This poem is also on page 233 of the text.

2. Select the "Cultural Contexts" tab on the green "Approaches and Contexts" box on the "My Papa's Waltz" poem page.

3. Select the Document Collection *Draft Versions of "My Papa's Waltz"* from the "Cultural Contexts" green tab.

4. View side 1 and side 2 of Draft 1 of "My Papa's Waltz."

5. Return to the menu of drafts by clicking on the "Draft Versions" link on the left-hand portion of the screen. View side 1 and side 2 of Draft 2 of "My Papa's Waltz."

6. Return to the menu of links for either draft and answer the accompanying questions in the text boxes provided. Save your responses to your Notebook by selecting the "Add to Notebook" link at the bottom of the screen.

7. E-mail your notebook responses to yourself by clicking on the "Send" Notebook tool at the top of the screen and entering your e-mail address.

8. Using your copy of your e-mailed Notebook, write a one- to two-page paper about the poem's evolution. What parts of the poem were revised the most heavily? What parts remained consistent from the poem's first draft to its final form? What consequences do the choices Roethke made have on the overall effect of the poem? How does the poem's message evolve?

9. Attach a copy of your e-mailed Notebook to your essay and turn in all work.

General Directions for the Essay

Think of this essay as a description of your experience reading "My Papa's Waltz," examining draft versions of the poem and analyzing how the poem's message evolved with Roethke's revisions.

You will need to provide your reader with a statement that briefly explains what the essay is about, and then, following good compositional practice, you will need to organize your ideas into paragraphs of related ideas. As for all literary essays, be sure to follow MLA style for titling and formatting.

VirtuaLit *Activity: Autobiographical Contexts for Theodore Roethke's "My Papa's Waltz"*

TO THINK ABOUT:

Theodore Roethke's biographer and close friend Allan Seager identifies "Papa" as a story Roethke penned in high school shortly after his father's death. Roethke's father, Otto, worked in the family greenhouse business as the Roethkes had done in their native Germany (hence the father's hands "caked with dirt" in "My Papa's Waltz"). In this story Roethke's father appears tyrannical and cruel. "John," representing Roethke himself, knows that his father favors his nephew "Bud," Roethke's cousin, yet he still defends his father when "Bud" refers to his uncle as "nothin' but a watchman and coaldriver." Despite his father's antagonism in this story, Roethke depicts himself as an intensely loyal son. The waltz in the story becomes a symbol of an idealized — and elusive — relationship between father and son; it is unclear whether Roethke understands this bond as an impossibility because of his father's belligerence or because of his death when the poet was still a teenager. Regardless, as Roethke suggests, in the story he imagines his father with his grandfather's maid not as evidence of adultery (it is unclear whether the story is true) but as a means through which to protect himself from the emotional devastation of his father's death. "He wouldn't have to worry any more," he concludes at the end of the essay, "[h]e hated papa."

STEPS IN THE ACTIVITY

1. Go to the *VirtuaLit Interactive Poetry Tutorial* and read Theodore Roethke's "My Papa's Waltz." This poem is also on page 233 of the text.
2. Select the "Cultural Contexts" tab on the green "Approaches and Contexts" box on the "My Papa's Waltz" poem page.
3. Select the Document Collection *"My Papa's Waltz" as Autobiography* from the "Cultural Contexts" green tab.
4. Read "Papa" by Theodore Roethke and answer the accompanying questions in the text boxes provided. Save your responses to your Notebook by selecting the "Add to Notebook" link at the bottom of the screen.
5. E-mail your Notebook responses to yourself by clicking on the "Send" Notebook tool at the top of the screen and entering your e-mail address.
6. Using your copy of your e-mailed Notebook (especially your response to the second question), write a one- to two-page paper comparing "My Papa's Waltz" to "Papa." How similar is the relationship between John and Papa in "Papa" to that between the speaker and Papa in "My Papa's Waltz"? "Papa" concludes with John's successful emotional distancing from his father. Is there an analogous moment in "My Papa's Waltz"? What effect does this omission have on the poem's meaning?
7. Attach a copy of your e-mailed Notebook to your essay and turn in all work.

GENERAL DIRECTIONS FOR THE ESSAY

Think of this essay as a description of your experience reading "My Papa's Waltz" and comparing it with "Papa."

You will need to provide your reader with a statement that briefly explains what the essay is about, and then, following good compositional practice, you will need to organize your ideas into paragraphs of related ideas. As for all literary essays, be sure to follow MLA style for titling and formatting.

TEACHING CRITICAL APPROACHES TO POETRY WITH *VIRTUALIT*

Getting Started

The "Approaches and Contexts" part of the *VirtuaLit Interactive Poetry Tutorial* contains a section called "Critical Approaches." This section offers definitions of several critical approaches as well as sample essays incorporating each approach in analyzing *VirtuaLit*'s featured poems.

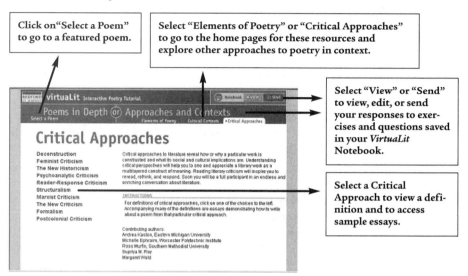

Click on "Select a Poem" to go to a featured poem.

Select "Elements of Poetry" or "Critical Approaches" to go to the home pages for these resources and explore other approaches to poetry in context.

Select "View" or "Send" to view, edit, or send your responses to exercises and questions saved in your *VirtuaLit* Notebook.

Select a Critical Approach to view a definition and to access sample essays.

If you want to work with critical approaches in the context of a poem, you should look for the "Critical Approaches" tab on the pale green tabbed box for any of the featured poems in *VirtuaLit*.

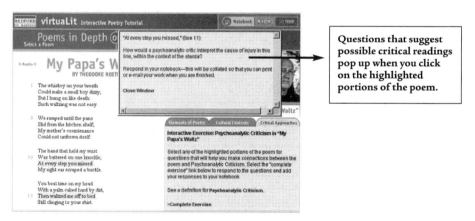

Questions that suggest possible critical readings pop up when you click on the highlighted portions of the poem.

This section of *VirtuaLit* highlights portions of each poem that lend themselves to particular critical approaches. The exercises help students make connections between the various critical approaches and the featured poems.

Activities

The activities in this section of the *Resources for Teaching Poetry* focus on the featured poems in *VirtuaLit* and how to analyze portions of each poem using the analytical tools supplied by the critical approaches to literature. Cross-references in some of the activities to *VirtuaLit* suggest useful supporting material.

VirtuaLit *Activity: Deconstructing Paradoxes in Andrew Marvell's "To His Coy Mistress"*
   To think about:
   Critical approaches to literature reveal how or why a particular work is constructed and what its social and cultural implications are. Understanding critical perspectives will help you to see and appreciate a literary work as a multilayered construct of meaning. Reading literary criticism will inspire you to reread, rethink, and respond.

   One source of irony in Andrew Marvell's "To His Coy Mistress" is that the speaker attempts to seduce his mistress by describing the unpleasant death of her "quaint honor." Of course, should the speaker succeed in his seduction, the mistress will still experience the death of her "quaint honor," literally and figuratively. Taken literally, her "quaint honor" will meet its end (death). Figuratively, death was commonly used as an analogy for sexual climax among seventeenth-century poets, and, should the mistress give in to the speaker's appeal, she will experience this kind of death, too. "To His Coy Mistress" is full of these kinds of paradoxes. How do they complicate the meaning of the poem?

   While doing the following activity, think about the paradoxes in "To His Coy Mistress" and how the critical methods of deconstruction can help clarify the tensions in the poem. In what ways does the poem defy resolution?

   Helpful material in *VirtuaLit*:
   • Definition of *Deconstruction*
   • "Andrew Marvell's 'To His Coy Mistress': A Feminist Reading"
   • "Theodore Roethke's 'My Papa's Waltz': A Deconstructionist Reading"

   Steps in the Activity
   1. Go to the *VirtuaLit Interactive Poetry Tutorial* and read Andrew Marvell's "To His Coy Mistress." This poem is also on page 81 of the text.
   2. Select the "Critical Approaches" green tab on the "To His Coy Mistress" poem page. Select the "Deconstruction" option in the green tabbed box.
   3. Click through the highlighted portions of the poem, reading the explanations for each.
   4. Read the definition of *deconstruction*.
   5. Select the "Complete Exercise" link in the "Critical Approaches" tab of the "To His Coy Mistress" poem page.
   6. Answer the questions for response in the text boxes provided. Save your responses to your Notebook by selecting the "Add to Notebook" link at the bottom of the screen.
   7. E-mail your Notebook responses to yourself by clicking on the "Send" Notebook tool at the top of the screen and entering your e-mail address.
   8. Think about the rhetorical paradoxes in "To His Coy Mistress." The speaker would spend a hundred years to praise "thine eyes and on thy forehead gaze," but he only devotes two lines to this activity. The speaker suggests that, in order to counteract their ephemeral state, he and his mistress will make the sun run, but that will have the effect of hastening their deaths (as the sun dries the "morning dew" that is the mistress's youth). The speaker describes his love's power as having epic proportions — "I would / Love you ten years before the Flood, / And you should, if you please, refuse / Till the conversion of the Jews" (7–10) — and yet his love is impotent in confronting "Time's wingèd chariot" (22). Examine the poem closely. Can you find other paradoxes? How do the critical methods of deconstruction help you to clarify tensions in the poem?

9. Use your responses to the *VirtuaLit* questions as the foundation for a one- to two-page essay on the paradoxes in "To His Coy Mistress" and how they complicate the poem's meaning.
10. Attach a copy of your e-mailed Notebook to your essay and turn in all work.

GENERAL DIRECTIONS FOR THE ESSAY

Think of this essay as a description of your experience reading a poem and the knowledge you gained about using a critical approach as a lens through which to analyze its meaning.

You will need to provide your reader with a statement that briefly explains what the essay is about, and then, following good compositional practice, you will need to organize your ideas into paragraphs of related ideas. You may find it useful to organize your paper around the questions posed in Step 7 of the activity. Keep in mind that one to two pages is a very short paper, so you will need to write concisely. As for all literary essays, be sure to follow MLA style for titling and formatting.

VirtuaLit *Activity: Father and Son in Theodore Roethke's "My Papa's Waltz"*

TO THINK ABOUT:

Critical approaches to literature reveal how or why a particular work is constructed and what its social and cultural implications are. Understanding critical perspectives will help you to see and appreciate a literary work as a multilayered construct of meaning. Reading literary criticism will inspire you to reread, rethink, and respond.

Theodore Roethke's poem "My Papa's Waltz" describes a waltz between a father and his small son — a romp, as it is described in the fifth line. Yet many of the poem's details imply that the waltz is not carefree and fun for the son, who must hang on "like death" (3) and who scrapes his ear against his father's belt buckle. What kind of relationship do the boy and his father have?

While doing the following activity, think about control in "My Papa's Waltz," how the critical methods of psychoanalytic criticism can help clarify the relationship between the father and the son, and how the waltz represents both literally and figuratively their interaction.

HELPFUL MATERIAL IN *VIRTUALIT*:

- Definition of *psychoanalytic criticism*
- "Elizabeth Bishop's 'The Fish': A Psychoanalytic Reading"
- "Theodore Roethke's 'My Papa's Waltz': A Deconstructionist Reading"

STEPS IN THE ACTIVITY

1. Go to the *VirtuaLit Interactive Poetry Tutorial* and read Theodore Roethke's "My Papa's Waltz." This poem is also on page 233 of the text.
2. Select the "Critical Approaches" tab on the green "Approaches and Contexts" box on the "My Papa's Waltz" poem page.
3. Select the "Psychoanalytic Criticism" interactive exercise from the "Critical Approaches" green tab.
4. Click through the highlighted portions of the poem, reading the questions that pop up for each and thinking about possible responses within the context of the poem.
5. Read the definition of *psychoanalytic criticism*.
6. Select the "Complete Exercise" link in the "Critical Approaches" tab of the "My Papa's Waltz" poem page.
7. Answer the questions for response in the text boxes provided. Save your responses to your Notebook by selecting the "Add to Notebook" link at the bottom of the screen.
8. E-mail your Notebook responses to yourself by clicking on the "Send" Notebook tool at the top of the screen and entering your e-mail address.

9. Think about the father's control over the boy in "My Papa's Waltz." The father roughly handles his son, who, because of his lack of control over the situation and his youth, is unable to prevent his ear from scraping against his father's belt. The boy characterizes his physical connection to his father as requiring him to "hang on like death" (3), and at the poem's end the son is "still clinging" (16) to the father's shirt. Why does the son cling to the father's shirt? How does the waltz represent their relationship? How do the critical methods of psychoanalytic criticism help you to analyze the son's unconscious reaction to his father and the significance of the poem's ending?

10. Keeping the questions in Step 9 in mind and using your copy of your e-mailed Notebook, write a one- to two-page paper analyzing the relationship between the father and the son in "My Papa's Waltz."

11. Attach a copy of your e-mailed Notebook to your essay and turn in all work.

GENERAL DIRECTIONS FOR THE ESSAY

Think of this essay as a description of your experience reading "My Papa's Waltz" and the knowledge you gained about using a critical approach as a lens through which to analyze its meaning.

You will need to provide your reader with a statement that briefly explains what the essay is about, and then, following good compositional practice, you will need to organize your ideas into paragraphs of related ideas. Keep in mind that one to two pages is a very short paper, so you will need to write concisely. As for all literary essays, be sure to follow MLA style for titling and formatting.

Film, Video, and Audio Resources

The following list organizes resources alphabetically by author. Resources include films and videos, tapes of poets reading their work, interviews with poets, and films and videos that provide biographical information on a poet or general information on a particular period. This list is not intended to be exhaustive; rather, it is meant to provide a number of exciting possibilities for supplementing and provoking class discussion.

Many of the films and videos in this list will be most readily available from a local retailer. If not, you may contact the distributor by using the addresses, phone numbers, and Web sites provided at the end of the list. The films and videos marked with an asterisk (*) are available for rental from member institutions of the Consortium of College and University Media Centers. For further information, consult *The Educational Film & Video Locater*, published by R. R. Bowker.

Anna Akhmatova

Akhmatova Reads Akhmatova [*recording*]
1 cassette (60 min.).
Akhmatova reads her poems in Russian. Includes transcript.
Distributed by Interlingua VA.

The Anna Akhmatova File
65 min., color, 1989.
VHS.
Documentary of the Russian poet. Russian with English subtitles.
Distributed by Facets Multimedia, Inc.

Fear and the Muse: The Story of Anna Akhmatova [*video*]
Color, VHS (60 min.), 1995.
With voices of Claire Bloom and Christopher Reeve.
Available at libraries.

Claribel Alegría

Claribel Alegría: Who Raised Up This Prison's Bars? [*recording*]
1 cassette (58 min.), 1988.
Alegría reads her poems in Spanish, with translations by Carolyn Forché.
Distributed by The Writer's Center.

Claribel Alegría [*recording*]
1 cassette (29 min.), 1991.
The Salvadoran poet and writer talks about her autobiographical novel *Luisa in Reality Land*.
Distributed by New Letters on the Air.

Claribel Alegría [*recording*]
1 cassette, 1996
Alegría reads from her collection *Fugues*. She talks about the political involvement that forced her and her late husband into exile from her native El Salvador.
Distributed by New Letters on the Air.

A. R. Ammons

A. R. Ammons [*recording*]
1 cassette (29 min.), 1984.
Distributed by New Letters on the Air.

Matthew Arnold

Matthew Arnold
See **"Literature: The Synthesis of Poetry"** on manual p. 385.

Margaret Atwood

Margaret Atwood Reads [*recording*]
1 cassette (36 min.).
Available at libraries.

371

The Poetry and Voice of Margaret Atwood
[recording]
1 cassette (59 min.), 1977, reprint 1992.
Available at libraries.

Jimmy Santiago Baca

Jimmy Santiago Baca [recording]
1 cassette (29 min.), 1991.
Distributed by New Letters on the Air.

William Blake

*Essay on William Blake
52 min., color, 1969.
3/4" U-matic cassette, 16-mm film, special
order formats.
A profile of the poet.
Distributed by Indiana University Instructional Support Services.

Poetry of William Blake [recording]
1 cassette.
Available at libraries.

*William Blake
26 min., color, 1973.
16-mm film.
Hosted by Kenneth Clark. Focuses on Blake's
drawings and engravings.
Distributed by Pyramid Media.

*William Blake: Poems [recording]
1 cassette (80 min.).
Distributed by HighBridge.

William Blake: Selected Poems
[recording]
2 cassettes (180 min.), 1992.
Includes "Tyger! Tyger!" and "A Poison Tree."
Distributed by Blackstone Audio Books.

William Blake: The Book of Thel
[recording]
1 cassette.
Distributed by Audio-Forum.

William Blake
See also **"Introduction to English Poetry"**
on manual p. 385.

Robert Bly

The Poetry of Robert Bly [recording]
1 cassette (38 min.), 1966.
Part of the YM-YWHA Poetry Series.
Distributed by Audio-Forum.

*Robert Bly — A Home in the Dark Grass:
Poems & Meditations on Solitudes,
Families, Disciplines [recording]*
2 cassettes (131 min.), 1987.
Distributed by Ally Press.

Robert Bly: A Man Writes to a Part of Himself
57 min., color, 1978.
3/4" U-matic cassette, special order formats.
Poetry and conversation with the writer.
Distributed by the Center for International
Education.

Robert Bly: Booth and Bly, Poets
30 min., color, 1978.
1/2" open reel (EIAJ), 3/4" U-matic cassette.
A four-part series of workshops and readings
by the poets.
Distributed by GPN Educational Media.

*Robert Bly: For the Stomach — Selected Poems,
1974 [recording]*
64 min.
Bly reads his poetry.
Distributed by Ally Press.

Robert Bly I & II [recording]
1 cassette (60 min.), 1979, 1991.
Distributed by New Letters on the Air.

Robert Bly: Poems of Kabir [recording]
1 cassette.
Distributed by Audio Literature.

Robert Bly: Poetry East and West [recording]
140 min., 1983.
Bly gives a poetry lecture, accompanied by
the dulcimer.
Distributed by Big Sur Tapes.

*Robert Bly: Poetry Reading — an Ancient
Tradition [recording]*
2 cassettes (150 min.), 1983.
Bly talks about the oral tradition in poetry.
Distributed by Big Sur Tapes.

Robert Bly: Selected Poems [recording]
2 cassettes (131 min.), 1987.
Distributed by Ally Press.

Robert Bly: The Human Shadow [recording]
2 cassettes.
Distributed by Ally Press.

Robert Bly: The Six Powers of Poetry
[recording]
1 cassette (90 min.), 1983.
A lecture from the San José Poetry Center.
Distributed by Big Sur Tapes.

Robert Bly
See also **"Moyers: The Power of the Word"**
on manual p. 385.

Gwendolyn Brooks

*Gwendolyn Brooks
30 min., b/w, 1966.
3/4" U-matic cassette, 16-mm film, special
order formats.

Brooks talks about her life and poetry.
Distributed by Indiana University Instructional Support Services.

Gwendolyn Brooks I & II [recording]
1 cassette (60 min.), 1984, 1988.
Distributed by New Letters on the Air.

Gwendolyn Brooks Reading Her Poetry [recording]
1 cassette.
Available at libraries.

Elizabeth Barrett Browning

Elizabeth Barrett Browning: Sonnets from the Portuguese [recording]
1 cassette.
Performed by Katherine Cornell and Anthony Quayle.
Available at libraries.

Elizabeth Barrett Browning
See also **"Victorian Poetry"** (film) on manual p. 387.

Robert Browning

*Robert Browning — His Life and Poetry
21 min., color, 1972.
Beta, VHS, 3/4″ U-matic cassette, 16-mm film, special order format.
A dramatization of Browning's life and several of his poems, including "My Last Duchess."
Available at libraries.

Robert Browning: Selected Poems [recording]
4 cassettes (360 min.).
Read by Frederick Davidson.
Distributed by Blackstone Audio Books.

George Gordon, Lord Byron

Lord Byron: Selected Poems [recording]
2 cassettes (180 min.).
Read by Frederick Davidson.
Distributed by Blackstone Audio Books.

Treasury of George Gordon, Lord Byron [recording]
1 cassette.
Available in libraries.

George Gordon, Lord Byron
See also **"English Romantic Poetry"** on manual p. 384 and **"The Younger Romantics"** on manual p. 387.

John Ciardi

As If: Poems Selected and Read by John Ciardi [recording]

1 cassette or CD, 1956.
Distributed by Smithsonian/Folkways Recordings.

Hans Juergensen & John Ciardi: World War II [recording]
1 cassette (29 min.).
Distributed by New Letters on the Air.

John Ciardi [recording]
1 cassette, 1991.
Distributed by Audio-Forum.

John Ciardi, I, II & III [recording]
1 cassette (60 min.), 1983, 1984, 1986.
The author reads poems about war, Italy, and aging.
Distributed by New Letters on the Air.

John Ciardi: Twentieth-Century Poets in English: Recordings of Poets Reading Their Own Poetry, No. 27 [recording]
Distributed by the Library of Congress.

The Poetry of John Ciardi [recording]
1 cassette (56 min.), 1964.
Distributed by Audio-Forum.

Lucille Clifton

Lucille Clifton [recording]
1 cassette (29 min.), 1989.
Distributed by New Letters on the Air.

Lucille Clifton: The Place for Keeping [recording]
1 cassette (45 min.), 1979.
Distributed by The Writer's Center.

Judith Ortiz Cofer

Judith Ortiz Cofer
See **"Birthwrite: Growing Up Hispanic"** on manual p. 384.

Samuel Taylor Coleridge

The Poetry of Coleridge [recording]
1 cassette.
Available in libraries.

Samuel Taylor Coleridge: The Fountain and the Cave
57 min., color, 1974.
VHS.
A biography of the poet, filmed on location. Narrated by Paul Scofield.
Distributed by Pyramid Media.

Samuel Taylor Coleridge
See **"Romantic Pioneers"** on manual p. 386.

E. E. Cummings

E. E. Cummings: A Poetry Collection
[recording]
3 cassettes (210 minutes), 2001.
Cummings reads his lectures and poems.
Distributed by HarperAudio.

E. E. Cummings Reads His Collected Poetry, 1920–1940, & Prose *[recording]*
2 cassettes (79 min.).
Available in libraries.

E. E. Cummings Reads His Collected Poetry, 1943–1958 *[recording]*
2 cassettes.
Available in libraries.

E. E. Cummings: Twentieth-Century Poetry in English: Recordings of Poets Reading Their Own Poetry, No. 5 *[recording]*
Distributed by the Library of Congress.

E. E. Cummings
See also **"Caedmon Poetry Collection," "Inner Ear, Parts 5 and 6,"** and **"Poetry for People Who Hate Poetry"** on manual pp. 384–386.

Emily Dickinson

Emily Dickinson: A Self-Portrait
[recording]
2 cassettes (90 min.), 1968.
Available in libraries.

Emily Dickinson: Poems and Letters *[recording]*
2 cassettes.
Distributed by Recorded Books.

Emily Dickinson: Selected Poems *[recording]*
4 cassettes (360 min.), 1993.
Read by Mary Woods.
Distributed by Blackstone Audio Books.

*Emily Dickinson: The Belle of Amherst
90 min., color, 1980.
VHS.
With Julie Harris.
Available in libraries.

Fifty Poems of Emily Dickinson
[recording]
1 cassette or CD (45 min.).
Distributed by Dove Audio.

Poems and Letters of Emily Dickinson
[recording]
1 cassette.
Available in libraries.

Poems by Emily Dickinson *[recording]*
2 cassettes (236 min.), 1986.
Distributed by Audio Book Contractors.

Emily Dickinson
See also **"Inner Ear, Parts 3 and 4," "Introduction to English Poetry," "Voices and Visions,"** and **"With a Feminine Touch"** on manual pp. 385 and 387.

John Donne

Essential Donne *[recording]*
From the Essential Poets Series.
Distributed by the Listening Library.

John Donne
40 min., color.
VHS.
Discusses the poet's life and works.
Distributed by Insight Media.

John Donne: Love Poems *[recording]*
1 cassette.
Distributed by Recorded Books.

John Donne: Selected Poems *[recording]*
2 cassettes (180 min.), 1992.
Read by Frederick Davidson.
Distributed by Blackstone Audio Books.

The Love Poems of John Donne
[recording]
1 cassette, 1994.
Distributed by HarperAudio.

Treasury of John Donne *[recording]*
1 cassette.
Available in libraries.

John Donne
See also **"Metaphysical and Devotional Poetry"** on manual p. 385.

H. D. [Hilda Doolittle]

H. D. [Hilda Doolittle]: Helen in Egypt
[recording]
1 cassette (39 min.), 1955.
Part of the Archive Series.
Distributed by The Writer's Center.

Paul Laurence Dunbar

*Paul Laurence Dunbar: American Poet
14 min., color, 1966.
Beta, VHS, 3/4″ U-matic cassette, 16-mm film, open-captioned.
A biographical sketch of the poet.
Distributed by Phoenix/BFA Films.

*Portraits in Black
60 min., color, 1973.
Beta, VHS, 3/4″ U-matic cassette.
A biographical tribute to Paul Laurence Dunbar. Directed by Carlton Moss.
Available in libraries.

T. S. Eliot

*****The Mysterious Mr. Eliot**
62 min., color, 1973.
Beta, VHS, 3/4″ U-matic cassette, 16-mm film.
A biographical film about the poet.
Distributed by Insight Media and CRM Films.

T. S. Eliot and George Orwell [recording]
1 cassette (41 min.), 1953.
Read by Stephen Spender.
Available in libraries.

T. S. Eliot Reads "The Love Song of J. Alfred Prufrock" [recording]
1 cassette, 2000.
Distributed by HarperAudio.

T. S. Eliot Reads "The Waste Land," "Four Quartets" & Other Poems
3 cassettes (180 min.), 2000.
Distributed by HarperAudio.

T. S. Eliot: Twentieth-Century Poetry in English: Recordings of Poets Reading Their Own Poetry, No. 3 [recording]
Distributed by the Library of Congress.

T. S. Eliot
See also **"Caedmon Collection of English Poetry," "Caedmon Poetry Collection," "Modern American Poetry,"** and **"Voices and Visions,"** on manual pp. 384–385 and 387.

Robert Frost

Afterglow: A Tribute to Robert Frost
35 min., color, 1989.
VHS.
Starring and directed by Burgess Meredith.
Distributed by Pyramid Media.

Frost and Whitman
30 min., b/w, 1963.
Beta, VHS, 1/2″ open reel (EIAJ), 3/4″ U-matic cassette, 2″ quadraplex open reel.
Will Geer performs excerpts from the two poets' works.
Distributed by New York State Education Department.

An Interview with Robert Frost
30 min., b/w, 1952.
Beta, VHS, 3/4″ U-matic cassette.
Bela Kornitzer interviews Frost, who reads from his poetry.
Distributed by Social Studies School Service.

Robert Frost [recording]
1 cassette, 1981.

Includes "The Pasture" and "Stopping by Woods on a Snowy Evening."
Distributed by the Library of Congress.

*****Robert Frost**
10 min., color, 1972.
Beta, VHS, 3/4″ U-matic cassette, 16-mm film.
A biographical sketch of the poet.
Distributed by AIMS Media Inc.

*****Robert Frost: A Lover's Quarrel with the World**
40 min., b/w, 1970.
Beta, VHS, 3/4″ U-matic cassette, 16-mm film.
A documentary film on Frost's philosophic and artistic ideas.
Distributed by Phoenix/BFA Films.

*****Robert Frost: An American Poet**
25 min., b/w, 1961.
VHS, DVD.
Vintage television broadcast of Frost commenting on his art and his country.
Distributed by Films for the Humanities and Sciences.

Robert Frost Poetry Collection [recording]
2 cassettes (100 min.), 2000.
Frost reads his poems.
Distributed by HarperAudio.

Robert Frost Reads His Poetry [recording]
1 cassette (48 min.).
Distributed by Recorded Books.

*****Robert Frost's New England**
22 min., color, 1976.
Beta, VHS, 3/4″ U-matic cassette, 16-mm film, special order formats. Ancillary materials available.
Explores some of Frost's poetry relating to New England and its seasons.
Distributed by Churchill Media.

Robert Frost: Twentieth-Century Poetry in English: Recordings of Poets Reading Their Own Poetry, No. 6 [recording]
Distributed by the Library of Congress.

Robert Frost
See also **"Caedmon Poetry Collection," "Literature: The Synthesis of Poetry," "Modern American Poetry," "Poetry by Americans,"** and **"Voices and Visions"** on manual pp. 384–387.

Thomas Hardy

Thomas Hardy
See **"Introduction to English Poetry," "Romantics and Realists,"** and **"Victorian Poetry"** (recording) on manual pp. 385–387.

Joy Harjo

Joy Harjo [recording]
1 cassette (29 min.), 1991.
The author plays the saxophone and reads
from her work.
Distributed by New Letters on the Air.

Joy Harjo & Barney Bush [recording]
1 cassette (29 min.), 1983.
Native American poets Harjo and Bush read
from their work.
Distributed by New Letters on the Air.

William Hathaway

William Hathaway [recording]
1 cassette (29 min.), 1984.
Distributed by New Letters on the Air.

Seamus Heaney

Seamus Heaney [recording]
2 cassettes, 1990.
Heaney reads his work and a personal selec-
tion of classic poems by Shakespeare,
Marvell, Hardy, Yeats, Blake, and others.
Available in libraries.

*Seamus Heaney: Poet in Limboland
29 min., color, 1972.
Beta, VHS, 3/4″ U-matic cassette, 16-mm film.
Heaney discusses his poetry and political
problems in Ireland.
Distributed by Films for the Humanities and
Sciences.

Seamus Heaney: Stepping Stones [recording]
1 cassette (72 min.), 1996.
Distributed by Penguin Audiobooks.

Anthony Hecht

Anthony Hecht I & II [recording]
1 cassette (60 min.), 1985, 1988.
Distributed by New Letters on the Air.

George Herbert

George Herbert
See **"Introduction to English Poetry"**
and **"Metaphysical and Devotional
Poetry"** on manual p. 385.

Gerard Manley Hopkins

*The Poetry of Gerard Manley Hopkins
[recording]*
1 cassette.
Available in libraries.

Gerard Manley Hopkins
See also **"Romantics and Realists"** and

"Victorian Poetry" (recording) on
manual pp. 386–387.

A. E. Housman

A. E. Housman
See **"Romantics and Realists"** and
"Victorian Poetry" (recording) on
manual pp. 386–387.

Langston Hughes

*Langston Hughes
24 min., color, 1971.
Beta, VHS, 3/4″ U-matic cassette, 16-mm
film.
A biographical sketch of the poet.
Distributed by Carousel Film & Video.

*Langston Hughes: Dream Keeper and Other
Poems [recording]*
1 cassette or CD, 1955.
Distributed by Smithsonian/Folkways Recordings.

*Langston Hughes: The Dream Keeper
[video]*
Color, VHS (60 min.), 1988.
Distributed by the Annenberg/CPB Collection.

*Langston Hughes: Looking for Langston
[video]*
Color, VHS (45 min.), 1992. Produced by
Isaac Julien.
Distributed by Water Bearer Films.

Langston Hughes Reads [recording]
1 cassette (60 min.), 2000.
Distributed by HarperAudio.

*Langston Hughes Reads and Talks about His
Poems [recording]*
1 cassette (42 min.).
Distributed by Dove Audio.

*Langston Hughes Reads and Talks about His
Poems [recording]*
1 cassette, 1959.
Includes "The Negro Speaks of Rivers" and
"Dream Boogie."
Available in libraries.

*Langston Hughes: The Making of a Poet
[recording]*
1 cassette (30 min.).
Read by the poet.
Distributed by National Public Radio.

*The Voice of Langston Hughes: Selected Poetry
and Prose [recording]*
1 cassette or CD (38 min.), 1994.
Selections from 1925–1932. The author
reads poetry from *"The Dream Keeper"*

and Other Poems and *Simple Speaks His Mind* and narrates his text from *The Story of Jazz, Rhythms of the World,* and *The Glory of Negro History.*
Distributed by Smithsonian/Folkways Recordings.

Langston Hughes
See also **"Anthology of Negro Poets," "Modern American Poetry," "Twentieth-Century Poets Reading Their Work,"** and **"Voices and Visions"** on manual pp. 384–385 and 387.

Randall Jarrell

The Poetry of Randall Jarrell [recording]
1 cassette (67 min.), 1963.
Part of the YM-YWHA Poetry Center Series.
Distributed by Audio-Forum.

Randall Jarrell Reads and Discusses His Poems against War [recording]
1 cassette, 1972.
Available in libraries.

Donald Justice

Donald Justice: "Childhood" & Other Poems [recording]
1 cassette (55 min.), 1985.
Distributed by The Writer's Center.

Donald Justice I & II [recording]
1 cassette (60 min.), 1989.
Distributed by New Letters on the Air.

John Keats
*John Keats — His Life and Death
55 min., color, 1973.
Beta, VHS, 3/4″ U-matic cassette, 16-mm film.
Extended version of **"John Keats — Poet"** (see below). Explores the poet's affair with Fanny Browne and the events surrounding his death. Written by Archibald MacLeish.
Distributed by Britannica Films.

John Keats: Odes [recording]
1 cassette.
Distributed by Audio-Forum.

*John Keats — Poet
31 min., color, 1973.
Beta, VHS, 3/4″ U-matic cassette, 16-mm film.
A biography of the poet, with excerpts from his letters and poems. Written by Archibald MacLeish.
Distributed by Britannica Films.

John Keats: Selected Poems [recording]
2 cassettes (180 min.), 1993.
Read by Frederick Davidson.
Distributed by Blackstone Audio Books.

The Poetry of Keats [recording]
1 cassette, (90 min.), 1996.
Distributed by HarperAudio.

John Keats
See also **"The Younger Romantics"** on manual p. 387.

X. J. Kennedy

X. J. Kennedy: Is Seeing Believing? [recording]
1 cassette (60 min.), 1985.
Distributed by The Writer's Center.

Jane Kenyon

Donald Hall and Jane Kenyon: A Life Together
VHS, DVD (60 min.), color, 1993.
Bill Moyers interviews these husband-and-wife poets at their home in New Hampshire.
Distributed by Films for the Humanities and Sciences.

Jane Kenyon I & II [recording]
1 cassette, 1987, 1995.
Distributed by New Letters on the Air.

Maxine Hong Kingston

Maxine Hong Kingston [recording]
1 cassette, 1986.
Interview.
Distributed by American Audio Prose Library.

The Stories of Maxine Hong Kingston
54 min., color, 1990.
VHS.
Kingston discusses her perspective on the "Great American Melting Pot."
Distributed by University of Washington Educational Media Collection.

Galway Kinnell

Galway Kinnell I & II [recording]
1 cassette (60 min.), 1982, 1991.
Distributed by New Letters on the Air.

The Poetry of Galway Kinnell [recording]
1 cassette (33 min.), 1965.
Part of the YM-YWHA Poetry Center Series.
Distributed by Audio-Forum.

The Poetry & Voice of Galway Kinnell
[recording]
1 cassette (59 min.), 1973.
Distributed by HarperAudio.

Galway Kinnell
See also **"Moyers: The Power of the Word"** on manual p. 385.

Carolyn Kizer

Carolyn Kizer: An Ear to the Earth
[recording]
1 cassette (63 min.), 1977.
Distributed by The Writer's Center.

Carolyn Kizer I, II, III, & IV [recording]
1 cassette (29 min.), 1982, 1985, 1994, 1997.
Distributed by New Letters on the Air.

Carolyn Kizer: Reading Her Poetry
[recording]
1 cassette.
Distributed by Sound Photosynthesis.

Ted Kooser

Ted Kooser [recording]
1 cassette (29 min.), 1984.
Distributed by New Letters on the Air.

Philip Levine

Philip Levine: Hear Me [recording]
1 cassette (62 min.), 1977.
Features selected poems.
Distributed by The Writer's Center.

Philip Levine I & II [recording]
1 cassette (29 min.), 1981, 1986.
Distributed by New Letters on the Air.

The Poetry and Voice of Philip Levine
[recording]
1 cassette (48 min.)
Available in libraries.

Philip Levine
See also **"Spoken Arts Treasury of 100 Modern American Poets Reading Their Poems, Vol. II"** (recording) on manual p. 386.

Christopher Marlowe

Christopher Marlowe
See **"Medieval to Elizabethan Poetry"** on manual p. 385.

Andrew Marvell

Andrew Marvell
See **"Metaphysical and Devotional Poetry"** on manual p. 385.

James Merrill

James Merrill: Reflected Houses [recording]
1 cassette (60 min.), 1988.
Distributed by The Writer's Center.

James Merrill: Voices from Sandover
VHS, DVD (116 min.), color.
A dramatic adaptation of Merrill's "The Changing Light at Sandover" and a summation of the poetic thought of this influential American poet. The cassette concludes with an interview of Merrill by Helen Vendler.
Distributed by Films for the Humanities and Sciences.

James Merrill
See also **"Poets in Person, No. 4"** on manual p. 386.

Edna St. Vincent Millay

Edna St. Vincent Millay: Renascence
VHS, DVD (60 min.), color.
A biography of the poet.
Distributed by Films for the Humanities and Sciences.

Poems of Edna St. Vincent Millay [recording]
1 cassette (60 min.), 1981.
Part of the Poetic Heritage Series.
Distributed by Summer Stream.

Poetry of Edna St. Vincent Millay [recording]
1 cassette.
Available in libraries.

Edna St. Vincent Millay
See also **"With a Feminine Touch"** on manual p. 387.

John Milton

*Milton
VHS, DVD (28 min.), color, 1989.
Looks at Milton's sonnets to his wife, Katherine, and "Paradise Lost."
Distributed by Films for the Humanities and Sciences.

Milton by Himself
VHS (27 min.), color, 1989.
A biography constructed from Milton's autobiographical writings.
Distributed by Films for the Humanities and Sciences.

Milton the Puritan: Portrait of a Mind
[recording]
10 cassettes (900 min.).
Distributed by Books on Tape.

Treasury of John Milton [recording]
1 cassette.
Available in libraries.

John Milton
See also **"Introduction to English Poetry"**
on manual p. 385.

Pablo Neruda

Pablo Neruda: Chile's Master Poet
VHS, DVD (29 min.), color, 1999.
A profile of the poet.
Distributed by Films for the Humanities and
Sciences.

Pablo Neruda: Poet
30 min., b/w, 1972.
Beta, VHS, 3/4″ U-matic cassette.
A profile of the poet.
Distributed by Cinema Guild.

Pablo Neruda: Selected Poems [recording]
1 cassette.
In Spanish.
Distributed by Applause Productions.

John Frederick Nims

John Frederick Nims [recording]
1 cassette (29 min.), 1986.
A reading by the Chicago poet.
Distributed by New Letters on the Air.

Sharon Olds

*Michael O'Brien & Sharon Olds
[recording]*
1 cassette (29 min.), 1985.
Distributed by New Letters on the Air.

Sharon Olds [recording]
1 cassette (29 min.), 1993.
Distributed by New Letters on the Air.

Sharon Olds
See also **"Moyers: The Power of the Word"**
on manual p. 385.

Wilfred Owen

Wilfred Owen: The Pity of War
VHS, DVD (58 min.), color, 1987.
A documentary drawn from Owen's poems,
diaries, and letters.
Distributed by Films for the Humanities and
Sciences.

Wilfred Owen: War Requiem [video]
Color & b/w, VHS (92 min.), 1988.
Written and directed by Derek Jarman,
music by Benjamin Britten.
Distributed by Mystic Fire Video.

Wilfred Owen: War Requiem [recording]
2 compact discs, 1993.
Distributed by Deutsche Grammophone.

Dorothy Parker

*An Informal Hour with Dorothy Parker
[recording]*
1 cassette.
The author reads her short story "Horsie" as
well as twenty-six poems.
Available in libraries.

Dorothy Parker [recording]
2 cassettes.
Read by Mary M. Lewis.
Distributed by Cassette Works.

Dorothy Parker
See also **"Spoken Arts Treasury of American
Jewish Poets Reading Their Poems,
Vol. 1"** (recording) on manual p. 386.

Linda Pastan

Linda Pastan: Mosaic [recording]
1 cassette (51 min.), 1988.
Distributed by The Writer's Center.

Linda Pastan I & II [recording]
1 cassette (29 min.), 1982, 1997.
Distributed by New Letters on the Air.

Octavio Paz

*Mexico's Muse: Octavio Paz
VHS, DVD (28 min.), color, 1999.
The poet talks about the distinctions
between his two careers: poet and polit-
ical activist.
Distributed by Films for the Humanities and
Sciences.

Octavio Paz
See also **"Moyers: The Power of the Word"**
on manual p. 385.

Marge Piercy

*Marge Piercy: At the Core
[recording]*
1 cassette (58 min.), 1977.
Distributed by The Writer's Center.

Sylvia Plath

Sylvia Plath [video]
Color, VHS (1988).
Distributed by Annenberg/CPB Collection
and Mystic Fire.

Sylvia Plath
4 programs (30 min. each), color, 1974.

VHS, 1/2"open reel (EIAJ), 3/4" U-matic cassette, 2" quadraplex open reel.
A biographical examination of the poet and her work.
Distributed by New York State Education Department.

Sylvia Plath *[recording]*
1 cassette (48 min.), 1962.
A historic reading of fifteen poems recorded the month before the poet's suicide.
Distributed by The Writer's Center.

Sylvia Plath, Part I: The Struggle
30 min., color, 1974.
Beta, VHS, 1/2"open reel (EIAJ), 3/4" U-matic cassette, 2" quadraplex open reel.
A dramatization of Plath's poetry by the Royal Shakespeare Company.
Distributed by New York State Education Department.

Sylvia Plath, Part II: Getting There
30 min., color, 1974.
Beta, VHS, 1/2"open reel (EIAJ), 3/4" U-matic cassette, 2" quadraplex open reel.
Plath's poems are set to music by Elizabeth Swados and performed by Michele Collison.
Distributed by New York State Education Department.

Sylvia Plath Reads *[recording]*
1 cassette (50 min.), 2000.
Distributed by HarperAudio.

Sylvia Plath: The Bell Jar
113 min., color, 1979.
Beta, VHS.
Based on Plath's semiautobiographical novel.
See local retailer.

Sylvia Plath
See also **"Voices and Visions"** and **"With a Feminine Touch"** on manual p. 387.

Alexander Pope

Alexander Pope
See **"Restoration and Augustan Poetry"** on manual p. 386.

Ezra Pound

Ezra Pound Reads *[recording]*
2 cassettes (90 min.), 2001.
Distributed by HarperAudio.

Ezra Pound
See also **"Caedmon Poetry Collection,"** **"Modern American Poetry,"** and

"Voices and Visions" on manual pp. 384–385 and 387.

Rainer Maria Rilke

Rainer Maria Rilke: Selected Poems
[recording]
2 cassettes (118 min.), 1988.
From the Spiritual Classics on Cassette Series.
Distributed by Audio Literature.

Alberto Ríos

Alberto A. Ríos: Reading His Poetry *[recording]*
1 cassette.
Distributed by Sound Photosynthesis.

Alberto Ríos
See also **"Birthwrite: Growing Up Hispanic"** on manual p. 384.

Theodore Roethke

The Poetry of Theodore Roethke *[recording]*
1 cassette (36 min.).
Part of the YM-YWHA Poetry Center Series.
Distributed by Audio-Forum.

Theodore Roethke *[recording]*
1 cassette (48 min.), 1972.
A collection of Roethke reading his poetry.
Available in libraries.

Theodore Roethke: Twentieth-Century Poetry in English: Recordings of Poets Reading Their Own Poetry, No. 10 *[recording]*
Distributed by the Library of Congress.

Words for the Wind: Read by Theodore Roethke
[recording]
1 cassette or CD, 1962.
Distributed by Smithsonian/Folkways Recordings.

William Shakespeare

***William Shakespeare: Poetry and Hidden Poetry**
VHS, DVD (53 min.), color, 1984.
A micro-examination of Shakespeare's poetry and its hidden meanings. Produced by the Royal Shakespeare Company.
Distributed by Films for the Humanities and Sciences.

William Shakespeare Sonnets *[recording]*
2 cassettes (120 min.).
Distributed by HarperAudio.

William Shakespeare's Sonnets
VHS, DVD (150 min.), color, 1984.
An in-depth look at fifteen of Shakespeare's

sonnets. With Ben Kingsley, Roger Reese, Claire Bloom, Jane Lapotaire, A. L. Rowse, and Stephen Spender. Distributed by Films for the Humanities and Sciences.

William Shakespeare: The Sonnets [recording]
1 cassette.
Distributed by Recorded Books.

William Shakespeare
See also **"Introduction to English Poetry," "Medieval to Elizabethan Poetry,"** and **"Poetry for People Who Hate Poetry"** on manual pp. 385–386.

Percy Bysshe Shelley

Percy Bysshe Shelley
See **"English Romantic Poetry"** manual p. 384.

Louis Simpson

Louis Simpson [recording]
1 cassette (29 min.), 1983.
Distributed by New Letters on the Air.

Louis Simpson: Physical Universe [recording]
1 cassette (57 min.), 1985.
Distributed by The Writer's Center.

Gary Soto

Gary Soto I & II [recording]
1 cassette (60 min.), 1982, 1992.
The author reads his work and talks about the recent rise of Chicano literature.
Distributed by New Letters on the Air.

Gary Soto
See also **"Poets in Person No. 7"** (recording) on manual p. 386.

Bruce Springsteen

Bruce Springsteen's Greatest Hits [recording]
1 CD.
Distributed by Columbia Records.

The Rising [recording]
1 CD.
Contains Springsteen's song "You're Missing."
Distributed by Sony BMG Music Entertainment, Inc.

William Stafford

William Stafford I & II [recording]
1 cassette (60 min.), 1983, 1984.
The author reads his poetry and discusses politics, poetry, and the writing process.
Distributed by New Letters on the Air.

William Stafford: Troubleshooting [recording]
1 cassette (50 min.), 1984.
Distributed by The Writer's Center.

William Stafford
See also **"Moyers: The Power of the Word"** on manual p. 385.

Wallace Stevens

Wallace Stevens Reads [recording]
1 cassette (47 min.), 1998.
Part of The Poet Anniversary Series.
Distributed by HarperAudio.

Wallace Stevens
See also **"Caedmon Poetry Collection," "Inner Ear, Parts 3 and 4," "Modern American Poetry,"** and **"Voices and Visions"** on manual pp. 384–385 and 387.

May Swenson

The Poetry and Voice of May Swenson [recording]
1 cassette.
Distributed by HarperAudio.

The Poetry of May Swenson [recording]
1 cassette (32 min.), 1963.
Part of the YM-YWHA Poetry Center Series.
Distributed by Audio-Forum.

Alfred, Lord Tennyson

Treasury of Alfred, Lord Tennyson [recording]
1 cassette.
Read by Robert Speaight.
Includes "Ulysses," "The Lotus Eaters," and "The Charge of the Light Brigade."
Available in libraries.

Alfred, Lord Tennyson
See also **"Victorian Poetry"** (film and recording) on manual p. 387.

Dylan Thomas

*The Days of Dylan Thomas
21 min., b/w, 1965.
Beta, VHS, 3/4″ U-matic cassette, 16-mm film.
A biography of the poet.
Distributed by CRM Films.

Dylan Thomas
25 min., color, 1982.
Beta, VHS, 3/4″ U-matic cassette.
A portrait of the poet.
Distributed by Films, Inc.

Dylan Thomas: A Portrait
VHS (26 min.), color, 1989.

A biographical film.
Distributed by Films for the Humanities and
Sciences.

*A Dylan Thomas Memoir
VHS (28 min.), color, 1972.
A character study of the poet.
Distributed by Pyramid Media.

*Dylan Thomas Reading "Quite Early One
Morning" & Other Poems [recording]*
1 cassette.
Available in libraries.

*Dylan Thomas Reading "Over Sir John's Hill"
& Other Poems [recording]*
1 cassette.
Available in libraries.

*Dylan Thomas: The Caedmon Collection
[recording]*
Cassettes or 11 CDs, 2002.
Distributed by HarperAudio.

*Dylan Thomas: Under Milkwood
[recording]*
2 cassettes (90 min.).
Distributed by S & S Audio.

*An Evening with Dylan Thomas
[recording]*
1 cassette.
Available in libraries.

The Wales of Dylan Thomas
VHS, DVD (15 min.), color, 1989.
Images of Wales in Thomas's poetry, prose,
and drama.
Distributed by Films for the Humanities and
Sciences.

Dylan Thomas
See also **"Caedmon Poetry Collection"** on
manual p. 384.

Tomas Tranströmer

*Tomas Tranströmer: The Blue House
[recording]*
1 cassette (58 min.), 1986.
Distributed by The Writer's Center.

John Updike

John Updike, I and II [recording]
2 cassettes (58 min.), 1987.
Distributed by New Letters on the Air.

*The Poetry of John Updike
[recording]*
1 cassette (47 min.), 1967.
Part of the YM-YWHA Poetry Center Series.
Distributed by Audio-Forum.

Walt Whitman

*Selections from Walt Whitman's "Leaves of
Grass" [recording]*
1 cassette or CD, 1957.
Distributed by Smithsonian/Folkways Recordings.

*Treasury of Walt Whitman: "Leaves of Grass,"
I & II [recording]*
2 cassettes (92 min.).
Unabridged edition.
Available in libraries.

*Walt Whitman
10 min., color, 1972.
Beta, VHS, 3/4″ U-matic cassette, 16-mm
film, open captioned.
Readings of Whitman's poems and a discus-
sion of his life. Hosted by Efrem
Zimbalist Jr.
Distributed by AIMS Media Inc.

Walt Whitman
VHS (12 min.), color, 1983.
A brief biography of the poet.
Distributed by Films for the Humanities and
Sciences.

*Walt Whitman: American Poet, 1819–1892
[recording]*
Color, VHS (30 min.), 1994
Distributed by Kultur.

*Walt Whitman: Endlessly Rocking
21 min., color, 1986.
Beta, VHS, 3/4″ U-matic cassette.
Shows a teacher's unsuccessful attempts to
interest her students in Whitman.
Distributed by Centre Communications.

Walt Whitman: Frost and Whitman
30 min., b/w, 1963.
Beta, VHS, 1/2″open reel (EIAJ), 3/4″ U-matic
cassette, 2″ quadraplex open reel.
Will Geer performs excerpts from the two
poets' works.
Distributed by New York State Education
Department.

*Walt Whitman: Galway Kinnell Reads Walt
Whitman [recording]*
1 cassette (59 min.).
Kinnell reads excerpts from *Song of Myself*, "I
Sing the Body Electric," and several
shorter poems.
Distributed by Sound Rx.

*Walt Whitman: Memoranda during the
War: From "Specimen Days" [recording]*
240 min.
Distributed by Recorded Books.

*Walt Whitman: Orson Welles Reads "Song of
   Myself" [recording]*
1 cassette.
Distributed by Audio-Forum.

Walt Whitman: Poet for a New Age
29 min., color, 1972.
Beta, VHS, 3/4″ U-matic cassette, 16-mm
   film.
A study of the poet.
Distributed by Britannica Films.

Walt Whitman: The Living Tradition
20 min., color, 1983.
Beta, VHS, 3/4″ U-matic cassette.
Allen Ginsberg reads Whitman's poetry.
Distributed by Centre Communications.

*Walt Whitman: Twentieth-Century Poetry in
   English, Nos. 13–17 [recording]*
From the Leaves of Grass Centennial Series.
Distributed by the Library of Congress.

Walt Whitman's Civil War
15 min., color, 1988.
Beta, VHS, 3/4″ U-matic cassette.
Discusses Whitman's perspective on the war.
Distributed by Churchill Media.

Walt Whitman
See also **"Poetry by Americans"** and
   "Voices and Visions" on manual
   pp. 385–387.

Richard Wilbur

Poems of Richard Wilbur [recording]
1 cassette.
Available in libraries.

Poetry — Richard Wilbur and Robert Lowell
30 min., b/w, 1966.
3/4″ U-matic cassette, 16-mm film, special
   order formats.
Interviews with the two poets.
Distributed by Indiana University Instructional Support Services.

Richard Wilbur [recording]
1 cassette (29 min.), 1990.
The author reads his poems and talks about
   early influences and censorship.
Distributed by New Letters on the Air.

*Richard Wilbur Reading His Poetry
   [recording]*
1 cassette.
Available in libraries.

Richard Wilbur
See also **"Twentieth-Century Poets Reading
   Their Work"** on manual p. 387.

Miller Williams

Miller Williams [recording]
1 cassette (29 min.), 1985.
Distributed by New Letters on the Air.

William Carlos Williams

*William Carlos Williams: People and the
   Stones: Selected Poems [recording]*
1 cassette (60 min.), 1991.
Distributed by The Writer's Center.

William Carlos Williams Reads [recording]
1 cassette (43 min.), 1993.
Distributed by HarperAudio.

William Carlos Williams
See also **"Caedmon Poetry Collection," "Inner Ear, Part 1,"** and **"Voices and Visions"** on manual pp. 384–385 and 387.

William Wordsworth

William Wordsworth
VHS, DVD (28 min.), color, 1989.
Beta, VHS, 3/4″ U-matic cassette.
An examination of the poet's work set
   against the Lake District, subject for
   many of the poems.
Distributed by Films for the Humanities and
   Sciences.

William Wordsworth and the English Lakes
VHS, DVD (15 min.), color, 1989.
Looks at Wordsworth's use of language.
Distributed by Films for the Humanities and
   Sciences.

*William Wordsworth: Selected Poems
   [recording]*
2 cassettes (180 min.).
Read by Frederick Davidson.
Distributed by Blackstone Audio Books.

William Wordsworth: William and Dorothy
VHS, DVD (52 min.), color, 1989.
Explores Wordsworth's poetry and his trou-
   bled relationship with his sister. Direct-
   ed by Ken Russell.
Distributed by Films for the Humanities and
   Sciences.

William Wordsworth
See also **"Introduction to English Poetry,"
   "Romantic Pioneers,"** and **"The
   Younger Romantics"** on manual
   pp. 385–387.

William Butler Yeats

The Love Poems of William Butler Yeats
30 min., b/w, 1967.

Beta, VHS, 1/2" open reel (EIAJ), 3/4" U-matic cassette, 2" quadraplex open reel.

Selections from the poet's works.

Distributed by New York State Education Department.

Poems by W. B. Yeats and Poems for Several Voices

1 cassette or CD, 1973.

Includes "Sailing to Byzantium" and features poems by Thomas Hardy, Robert Graves, and Gerard Manley Hopkins.

Read by V. C. Clinton-Baddeley, Jill Balcon, and M. Westbury.

Distributed by Smithsonian/Folkways Recordings.

W. B. Yeats [recording]

1 cassette (49 min.), 1953.

Read by Stephen Spender.

Available in libraries.

*Yeats Country

19 min., color, 1965.

VHS, 3/4" U-matic cassette, 16-mm film.

Juxtaposes Yeats's poetry with scenes of the Ireland he wrote about.

Distributed by International Film Bureau.

Yeats Remembered

30 min.

VHS.

Biographical film using period photographs and interviews with the poet and his family.

Distributed by Insight Media.

William Butler Yeats

See also "**Caedmon Collection of English Poetry**," "**Caedmon Poetry Collection**," "**Introduction to English Poetry**," and "**Twentieth-Century Poets Reading Their Work**" on manual pp. 384–385 and 387.

General Resources for Poetry

Anthology of Contemporary American Poetry [recording]

1 cassette or CD, 1961.

Includes poems by John Ciardi, Richard Ebhardt, Theodore Roethke, Howard Nemerov, Galway Kinnell, Donald Justice, May Swenson, Richard Wilbur, Karl Shapiro, and others.

Distributed by Smithsonian/Folkways Recordings.

Anthology of Negro Poets [recording]

1 cassette or CD, 1955.

Includes the poetry of Langston Hughes, Sterling Brown, Claude McKay, Margaret Walter, and Gwendolyn Brooks.

Distributed by Smithsonian/Folkways Recordings.

Archive of Recorded Poetry and Literature

Library of Congress

Birthwrite: Growing Up Hispanic

VHS (59 min.), color, 1989.

Focuses on the achievements of Hispanic American writers. Includes the work of Alberto Ríos and Judith Ortiz Cofer.

Distributed by Cinema Guild.

Caedmon Collection of English Poetry [recording]

2 cassettes, 1998.

Features poetry by William Shakespeare; John Donne; John Milton; William Blake; Robert Burns; William Wordsworth; Samuel Taylor Coleridge; John Keats; Alfred, Lord Tennyson; Robert Browning; Elizabeth Barrett Browning; Gerard Manley Hopkins; Thomas Hardy; D. H. Lawrence; Rudyard Kipling; Wilfred Owen; William Butler Yeats; T. S. Eliot; Dylan Thomas; and Ted Hughes.

Distributed by HarperAudio.

Caedmon Poetry Collection: A Century of Poets Reading Their Work [recording]

2 cassettes (95 min.), 2000.

Includes T. S. Eliot, W. B. Yeats, Edith Sitwell, Dylan Thomas, Robert Graves, Gertrude Stein, E. E. Cummings, Robert Frost, William Carlos Williams, Wallace Stevens, Ezra Pound, and others.

Distributed by HarperAudio.

Conversation Pieces: Short Poems by Thomas, Hardy, Housman, Auden, Keats, and Others

1 cassette or CD, 1964.

Distributed by Smithsonian/Folkways Recordings.

English Romantic Poetry [recording]

2 cassettes (2 hours), 1996.

Authors include William Blake, Robert Burns, Lord Byron, Samuel Taylor Coleridge, John Keats, Percy Bysshe Shelley, and William Wordsworth. Read by Claire Bloom, Anthony Quayle, Ralph Richardson, and Frederick Worlock.

Distributed by HarperAudio.

*Fried Shoes, Cooked Diamonds

55 min., color, 1982.

Beta, VHS, 3/4" U-matic cassette.

Documents a summer at the Jack Kerouac

School of Poetics at the Naropa Institute in Boulder, Colorado. Features such poets from the Beat generation as Allen Ginsberg, Gregory Corso, William S. Burroughs, Peter Orlovsky, and Timothy Leary.
Distributed by Centre Communications, Inc. and Mystic Fire.

Inner Ear, Part 1 [recording]
1 cassette (60 min.).
Includes the poetry of Carl Sandburg and William Carlos Williams.
Distributed by National Public Radio.

Inner Ear, Parts 3 and 4 [recording]
1 cassette (60 min.).
Emily Dickinson, Marianne Moore, and Wallace Stevens.
Distributed by National Public Radio.

Inner Ear, Parts 5 and 6 [recording]
1 cassette (60 min.).
E. E. Cummings and Gary Snyder.
Distributed by National Public Radio.

In Their Own Voices: A Century of Recorded Poetry [recording]
4 compact discs.
Distributed by Rhino Records.

*Introduction to English Poetry
VHS, DVD (28 min.), color, 1989.
Introduces students to English verse, with readings from Chaucer, Shakespeare, Herbert, Milton, Swift, Blake, Wordsworth, Shelley, Emily Brontë, Dickinson, Hardy, Yeats, and Ted Hughes.
Distributed by Films for the Humanities and Sciences.

*Lannan Literary Series [video]
83 cassettes (1 hour each), color, VHS, 1988–2003.
Carolyn Forché, Allen Ginsberg, Louise Glück, Galway Kinnell, W. S. Merwin, Lucille Clifton, Czeslaw Milosz, Octavio Paz, Yehuda Amichai, Joy Harjo, Victor Hernandez Cruz, Kay Boyle, Alice Walker, Ishmael Reed, Richard Wilbur, Carlos Fuentes, Robert Creeley, Larry Heinemann, Sonia Sanchez, Andrei Voznesensky, Ernesto Cardenal, Anne Waldman, Sharon Olds, Amiri Baraka, Gary Snyder, and Gary Soto.
Distributed by The Lannan Foundation.

Literature: The Synthesis of Poetry
30 min.
VHS.
Hosted by Maya Angelou, who reads some of her work as well as the poetry of Robert Frost, Carl Sandburg, and Matthew Arnold.
Distributed by Coast Learning Systems.

Medieval to Elizabethan Poetry
28 min., color, 1989.
VHS, DVD.
Examines trends of the period, focusing on John Skelton, Thomas Wyatt, Tichborne, Nashe, Christopher Marlowe, Michael Drayton, and William Shakespeare.
Distributed by Films for the Humanities and Sciences.

*Metaphysical and Devotional Poetry
28 min., color, 1989.
VHS, DVD.
Looks at the works of John Donne, George Herbert, and Andrew Marvell.
Distributed by Films for the Humanities and Sciences.

Modern American Poetry
VHS (45 min.), 1989.
Hosted by Helen Vendler. Deals with poets from between the wars: Eliot, Pound, Stevens, Hughes, Frost, Moore, and Crane. Focuses on development of an American, as distinct from European, voice.
Available in libraries.

Moyers: The Power of the Word
6 programs (60 min. each), color, 1989.
Beta, VHS, 3/4″ U-matic cassette.
Bill Moyers talks with modern poets: James Autry, Quincy Troupe, Joy Harjo, Mary Tallmountain, Gerald Stern, Li-Young Lee, Stanley Kunitz, Sharon Olds, William Stafford, W. S. Merwin, Galway Kinnell, Robert Bly, and Octavio Paz.
Available in libraries.

Poetic Forms [recording]
5 cassettes (300 min.), 1988.
Includes the list poem, the ode, the prose poem, the sonnet, the haiku, the blues poem, the villanelle, the ballad, the acrostic, and free verse.
Distributed by Teachers & Writers Collaborative.

*Poetry: A Beginner's Guide
26 min., color, 1986.
Beta, VHS, 3/4″ U-matic cassette.
Interviews contemporary poets and examines the tools they use.
Distributed by Coronet/MTI Film & Video.

*Poetry by Americans
4 programs (10 min. each), color, 1988.
Beta, VHS, 3/4″ U-matic cassette, 16-mm film.
Robert Frost, Edgar Allan Poe, James Weldon

Johnson, and Walt Whitman. Narrated by Leonard Nimoy, Lorne Greene, Raymond St. Jacques, and Efrem Zimbalist Jr.
Distributed by AIMS Media Inc.

*Poetry for People Who Hate Poetry
3 programs (15 min. each), color, 1980.
Beta, VHS, 3/4″ U-matic cassette, special order formats.
Roger Steffens makes poetry accessible to students. Three programs: (1) About words; (2) E. E. Cummings; (3) Shakespeare.
Distributed by Churchill Media.

Poetry in Motion
90 min., color, 1982.
Laser optical videodisc.
A performance anthology of twenty-four North American poets, including Ntozake Shange, Amiri Baraka, Anne Waldman, William Burroughs, Ted Berrigan, John Cage, Tom Waits, and others. Performed by Ntozake Shange and Anne Waldman.
Distributed by Voyager Company.

Poets in Person: A Series on American Poets & Their Art [recording]
7 programs (30 min. each), 1991.
Thirteen poets in conversation, reading their poems, discussing their lives, work, and the changing styles in contemporary American poetry: (1) Allen Ginsberg; (2) Karl Shapiro, Maxine Kumin; (3) W. S. Merwin, Gwendolyn Brooks; (4) James Merrill, Adrienne Rich; (5) John Ashbery, Sharon Olds; (6) Charles Wright, Rita Dove; (7) Gary Soto, A. R. Ammons.
Distributed by Modern Poetry.

*Restoration and Augustan Poetry
VHS, DVD (28 min.), color, 1989.
Discusses the age of satire in England, including the Earl of Rochester, John Dryden, Jonathan Swift, and Alexander Pope.
Distributed by Films for the Humanities and Sciences.

*Romantic Pioneers
28 min., color, 1989.
VHS, DVD.
Readings of poems by Christopher Smart, William Blake, William Wordsworth, and Samuel Taylor Coleridge.
Distributed by Films for the Humanities and Sciences.

*Romantics and Realists
28 min., color, 1989.
VHS, DVD.

Discusses Thomas Hardy, Gerard Manley Hopkins, A. E. Housman, and Rudyard Kipling.
Distributed by Films for the Humanities and Sciences.

Serenade: Poets of New York
[recording]
1 cassette or CD, 1957.
Read by Aaron Kramer, Maxwell Maxwell, and Bodenheim.
Distributed by Smithsonian/Folkways Recordings.

Spoken Arts Treasury of American Jewish Poets Reading Their Poems
[recording]
7 cassettes.
Includes the work of Dorothy Parker, Phillip Levine, Anthony Hecht, Denise Levertov, Allen Ginsberg, and John Hollander.
Available in libraries.

Spoken Arts Treasury of 100 Modern American Poets Reading Their Poems
[recording]
1985.
Available in libraries.

A Survey of English and American Poetry
16 programs (28 min. each), color, 1987.
VHS, DVD.
A history and anthology of English-language poetry. Programs include: (1) Introduction to English Poetry; (2) Old English Poetry; (3) Chaucer; (4) Medieval to Elizabethan Poetry; (5) The Maturing Shakespeare; (6) Metaphysical and Devotional Poetry; (7) Milton; (8) Restoration and Augustan Poetry; (9) Romantic Pioneers; (10) William Wordsworth; (11) The Younger Romantics; (12) Victorian Poetry; (13) American Pioneers; (14) Romantics and Realists; (15) The Earlier Twentieth Century; (16) The Later Twentieth Century.
Distributed by Films for the Humanities and Sciences.

Teaching Poetry
30 min., color, 1990.
VHS.
A new approach to teaching poetry. Includes discussion questions and homework assignments.
Distributed by Video Aided Instruction.

Twentieth-Century Poets in English:
 Recordings of Poets Reading Their Own
 Poetry *[recording]*
33 volumes.
Distributed by the Library of Congress.

Twentieth-Century Poets Reading Their Work
 [recording]
6 cassettes.
Includes William Butler Yeats, Stephen Spender, Langston Hughes, Richard Wilbur, and James Dickey.
Available in libraries.

***Victorian Poetry**
VHS, DVD (28 min.), color, 1989.
An examination of works by Alfred, Lord Tennyson, Emily Brontë, Christina Rossetti, Elizabeth Barrett Browning, Matthew Arnold, and Algernon Swinburne.
Distributed by Films for the Humanities and Sciences.

***Voices and Visions**
13 programs (60 min. each), color, 1988.
Beta, VHS, 3/4″ U-matic cassette, CD-ROM.
A series exploring the lives of some of America's best poets. Hosted by Joseph

Brodsky, Mary McCarthy, James Baldwin, and Adrienne Rich. Programs include: (1) Elizabeth Bishop; (2) Hart Crane; (3) Emily Dickinson; (4) T. S. Eliot; (5) Robert Frost; (6) Langston Hughes; (7) Robert Lowell; (8) Marianne Moore; (9) Sylvia Plath; (10) Ezra Pound; (11) Wallace Stevens; (12) Walt Whitman; (13) William Carlos Williams.
Distributed by the Annenberg/CPB Collection.

With a Feminine Touch
45 min., color, 1990.
VHS.
Readings from Emily Dickinson, Anne Brontë, Charlotte Brontë, Emily Brontë, Sylvia Plath, and Edna St. Vincent Millay. Read by Valerie Harper and Claire Bloom.
Distributed by Monterey Home Video.

The Younger Romantics
VHS, DVD (28 min.), color, 1989.
Features the work of John Keats, William Wordsworth, and Lord Byron.
Distributed by Films for the Humanities and Sciences.

DIRECTORY OF DISTRIBUTORS

Academy of American Poets
584 Broadway, Suite 1208
New York, NY 10012-3250
(212) 274-0343
www.poets.org

Acorn Media
801 Roeder Road
Silver Spring, MD 20910
(301) 608-2115, (800) 999-0212
www.acornmedia.com

AIMS Multimedia
9710 DeSoto Avenue
Chatsworth, CA 91311-4409
(818) 773-4300, (800) 367-2467
aimsmultimedia.com

The American Poetry Archive
San Francisco State University
1600 Holloway Avenue
San Francisco, CA 94132
(415) 338-1056

The Annenberg/CPB Collection
P.O. Box 2345
South Burlington, VT 05407-2345
(800)-LEARNER
www.learner.org

Audio Book Contractors
P.O. Box 40115
Washington, DC 20016
(202) 363-3429

Audio Bookshelf
174 Prescott Hill Road
Northport, ME 04849
(800) 234-1713
www.audiobookshelf.com

Audio-Forum see
 Jeffrey Norton Publishers

Audio Literature see
 Publishers Group West

Audio Partners see **Publishers Group West**

Blackstone Audio Books
P.O. Box 969
Ashland, OR 97520
(541) 482-9239, (800) 729-2665
www.blackstoneaudio.com

Books on Tape
P.O. Box 7900
Newport Beach, CA 92658
(714) 548-5525, (800) 626-3333
www.booksontape.com

Caedmon/HarperAudio
P.O. Box 588
Dunmore, PA 18512
(800) 242-7737, (800) 982-4377 (in Pennsylvania)
www.harpercollins.com

Carousel Film & Video
250 Fifth Avenue, Suite 204
New York, NY 10001
(212) 683-1660, (800) 683-1660
www.carouselfilms.com

Centre Communications
1800 30th Street, Suite 207
Boulder, CO 80301
(800) 886-1166

Churchill Media
6901 Woodley Avenue
Van Nuys, CA 91406-4844
(818) 778-1978, (800) 334-7830

Cinema Guild
130 Madison Avenue, Second Floor
New York, NY 10016
(212) 685-6242, (800) 723-5522
www.cinemaguild.com

Columbia Records
550 Madison Avenue
New York, NY 10022-3211
(212) 833-8000
www.sonymusic.com

Crown Publishers see *Random Audiobooks*

Facets Multimedia Inc.
1517 West Fullerton Avenue
Chicago, IL 60614
(773) 281-9075, (800) 331-6197
www.facets.org

Films for the Humanities and Sciences
P.O. Box 2053
Princeton, NJ 08543-2053
(609) 275-1400, (800) 257-5126
www.films.com

First Run Features/Icarus Films
32 Court Street, 21st Floor
Brooklyn, NY 11201
(800) 876-1710
www.frif.com

Indiana University Instructional Support Services
Franklin Hall, Room 0009
601 East Kirkwood
Bloomington, IN 47405-5901
(812) 855-2853
www.indiana.edu/~mediares/

Insight Media
2162 Broadway
New York, NY 10024
(212) 721-6316, (800) 233-9910
www.insight-media.com

Interlingua VA
P.O. 4175
Arlington, VA 22204
(703) 575-7849
www.foreign-audio-books.com

Kultur
195 Highway #36
West Long Branch, NJ 07764
(908) 229-2343, (800) 458-5887
www.kultur.com

Lannan Foundation
313 Reed Street
Santa Fe, NM 86501
(505) 986-8160
www.lannan.org

Library of Congress
Motion Picture, Broadcasting &
Recorded Sound Division
101 Independence Avenue SE
Washington, DC 20540-4690
(202) 707-5840
www.loc.gov

Listening Library
Box 611, 1 Park Avenue
Old Greenwich, CT 06870
(203) 637-3616, (800) 243-4504
www.listeninglib.com

Modern Poetry Association
60 W. Walton Street
Chicago, IL 60610
(312) 255-3703
www.poetrymagazine.org

Monterey Home Video
28038 Dorothy Drive, Suite 1
Agoura Hills, CA 91301
(818) 597-0047, (800) 424-2593
www.montereymedia.com

National Public Radio
Audience Services
635 Massachusetts Avenue NW
Washington, DC 20001
(202) 414-3232, (877) 677-8398
www.npr.org

New Dimensions Radio
P.O. Box 569
Ukiah, CA 95482
(707) 468-5215, (800) 935-8273
www.newdimensions.org

New Letters on the Air
University of Missouri at Kansas City
5101 Rockhill Road, U-House
Kansas City, MO 64110
(816) 235-1159
www.newletters.org/onTheAir.asp

Jeffrey Norton
96 Broad Street
Guilford, CT 06437
(203) 453-9794, (800) 243-1234
www.audioforum.com

PBS Video
1320 Braddock Place
Alexandria, VA 22314-1698
(703) 739-5380, (800) 645-4727
www.shop.pbs.org/education/

Phoenix/BFA Films see *Phoenix Learning
    Group*

Phoenix Learning Group
2349 Chaffee Drive
St. Louis, MO 63146
(800) 221-1274
www.phoenixlearninggroup.com>

Poet's Audio Center
P.O. Box 50145
Washington, DC 20091-0145
(202) 722-9105

Publishers Group West
1700 4th Street
Berkeley, CA 94710
(800) 383-0174
www.pgw.com

Random Audiobooks
400 Hahn Road
Westminster, MD 21157
(800) 733-3000
www.randomhouse.com/audio

Recorded Books
270 Skipjack Road
Prince Frederick, MD 20678
(301) 535-5590, (800) 638-1304
www.recordedbooks.com

Rhino Records
10635 Santa Monica Boulevard
Los Angeles, CA 90025-4900
www.rhino.com

The Roland Collection
22D Hollywood Avenue
Hohokus, NJ 07423
(201) 251-8200, (800) 59-ROLAND
www.roland-collection.com

Smithsonian Folkways Recordings
Office of Folklife Programs
955 L'Enfant Plaza, Suite 2600
Smithsonian Institution
Washington, DC 20560
(202) 287-3262
www.folkways.si.edu

Teachers & Writers Collaborative
5 Union Square West
New York, NY 10003
(212) 691-6590
www.twc.org/pubs/

Time-Life Multimedia
2000 Duke Street
Alexandria, VA 22314
(703) 838-7000
www.timelifeinc.com

*University of California Extension Media
    Center*
2000 Center Street, 4th Floor
Berkeley, CA 94704
(510) 642-0460
ucmedia.berkeley.edu

Index of Authors and Titles